Religion in Contemporary Society

RELIGION
in
CONTEMPORARY
SOCIETY

THIRD EDITION

H. Paul Chalfant

Robert E. Beckley
West Texas A&M University

C. Eddie Palmer
The University of Southwestern Louisiana

F. E. PEACOCK PUBLISHERS, INC. *Itasca, Illinois*

ACKNOWLEDGMENTS

Excerpts from *Extraordinary Groups: An Examination of Unconventional Life Styles* by William Kephart and William W. Zellner. Reprinted with permission of St. Martin's Press, Incorporated.

Table 4.2. Reprinted with permission of Macmillan Publishing Company from *The Scientific Study of Religion*, Milton Uinger, © 1970 by Macmillan Publishing Company.

Excerpt from Miles Richardson, "Anthropologist—The Myth Teller," *American Ethnologist*. *American Anthropoligist* 2:3, August, 1975. Used with permission of the American Anthropological Association.

Excerpt and Table 6.2 from *The Churching of America 1776–1990* by Roger Finke and Rodney Stark, © 1992. Reprinted by permission of Rutgers, The State University.

Table 8.1 from "Cults of America: A Reconnaissance in Space and Time" by Rodney Stark, William Sims Bainbridge, and Daniel P. Doyle, 1979, *Sociological Analysis* 40: 347–59. By permission of the Association for the Sociology of Religion.

"I Sing a Song of the Saints of God." Words by Lesbia Scott. Used by permission of Morehouse Publishing.

"The Nail Scarred Hand" by B. B. McKinney. Used by permission of Boardman Press.

Excerpt from *Steeples and Spires* by John Earle, Dean Knudsen, and Donald Shriver. Used by permission of Dr. Donald Shriver, Jr.

Tables 6.1 and 6.3 from *Yearbook of American and Canadian Churches*. Reprinted with permission of the National Council of Churches.

Tables 12.1 and 12.3 from *Yearbook of American and Canadian Churches*. Reprinted with permission of the National Council of Churches.

Library of Congress Catalog Card No. 93-86173

ISBN 0-87581-382-8

Printed in the United States of America

Printing: 10 9 8 7 6 5 4 3 2 1

Year: 98 97 96 95 94

To my wife and children
Lois, Marsha, and Craig
and to my grandson
Paul Craig
H. P. C.

To my wife and son
Cheryl and Brian
R. E. B.

To my parents and stepparents
Faye Crane and Eddie
Shelby Palmer and Mina
and to my wife
Ann
C. E. P.

A note from the publisher

It is with regret that the publisher announces the death of Professor Chalfant as this book was going to press. Paul was a personal friend as well as esteemed author. I shall miss him.

F. Edward Peacock
May 1994

Contents

Tables

Preface

The publication of a new edition of a familiar text may mean only that references have been updated and minor changes in the text made. Or, it can mean that major revisions have been made to meet the changing field of study. We truly believe that this third edition of *Religion and Contemporary Society* represents the latter option. It has taken us more years than we thought to respond to the drastic way in which religion in the United States, and the rest of the world, has changed since 1987. In the dozen or so years since the first edition, the situation of religion in the United States and the world in general has seen dramatic shifts. For instance, at the time of the first edition in 1981 the dominance of the secularization hypothesis was still evident in most research in the field. Today, while acknowledging the decline in what we refer to as the mainline churches, we take into account the idea that research focuses not on the disappearance of the sacred but also on its relocation, often outside any institutionalized religious organization.

The career of the televangelists has been mixed, at best. Both the televangelists and the New Religious Right were important aspects of the religious scene in the eighties. The televangelists have suffered from the abuse and misdeeds of such as Jim Bakker, Jimmy Swaggert, and Oral Roberts; they no longer hold center stage. And the New Religious Right has lost national power in the election of Bill Clinton and Al Gore (ironically, members of an evangelical denomination) though "religion watchers" are careful to take note of its power in local elections.

Similarly, New Religious Movements (referred to as *cults* or *sects* in the media) have been the object of much attention. They receded before the onslaught of the religious right, only to come again to our attention as postmodern or late modern times have resulted in more individual approaches to the location of the sacred. It is significant that a recent conference concerning New Religions in the New Europe (London School of Economics, March 1993) drew more than two hundred participants from all over the world.

Alongside the new movements, historic religions from outside the Western world are having an impact on religion in the United States. The lowering of restrictions on immigrants from Asia and the influx of those from the Middle East have made Islam and other historic religions of Asia an influence in religious life in America. Today, for example, adherents of Islam comprise the third largest identifiable religious group in the United States.

We have attempted, it is hoped with success, to be attentive to these shifts as we prepared this third edition. In the process of including new research in the text, we have reorganized the book in what we feel are significant ways. Attentive to the emphasis in new research we have combined four of the chapters on the social organization of religion into two. One reflects research on the processes of becoming and being religious. The second combines the organization and leadership of religious groups. While we have not excluded coverage from the first two editions we have downplayed those areas not currently at the center of research.

There is a renewed focus on contemporary trends in religious life in the United States (and the Western world), backed by our general focus on the relation of history to the current situation. Certainly we have included an analysis of the widened profile of religious groups in the United States as well as an emphasis on the importance of both resurgent fundamentalism and the renascence of New Religious Movements as a significant factor in the mosaic of our religious life.

The processes of social stratification continue to be important in the analysis of religion, though perhaps in ways that differ from Reinhold Niebuhr's analysis. Clearly economic, or class, variations can still be viewed as important in an analysis of religion in contemporary society. Equally important in these times are the effects of racial/ethnic and gender stratification. Both of these latter topics are discussed in separate chapters.

This revision has been, as before, a sensitive task. We have continually sought to balance the perspective of the student with the total scope of the field. Although students are familiar with religion as they have known it, they have difficulty looking at it objectively. In addition, since many of the terms and concepts necessary to unfold the sociological perspective were appropriated from theology and philosophy, they are unfamiliar to many students. It is not easy, then, to cover this material in a way that really reaches the student and yet adequately presents the sociological interpretation of religion.

It will be obvious that we have not solved every problem. We do believe that we have taken steps that contribute to overcoming the difficulties of communicating the important contributions that the sociological study of religion can make to our understanding of our religious and social world.

First, we have taken care to present the subject matter clearly as a *sociology* of religion, resisting the temptation to get sidetracked into psychology, anthropology, or theology. We have been especially careful to avoid the pitfalls of either siding with or lining up against institutional religion. Some have used this subdiscipline as a pulpit to promote religion while others have used the same pulpit as a platform from which to denounce "superstition." The sociology of religion, however, is clearly neither of these. It is not an attempt to convince nor discourage personal faith or its lack. Such matters are beyond the scope of our concern, based as they are on that which is not discernable by empirical means.

Second, we have concentrated on religion as it is expressed in the Western world, particularly the United States. Comparative material is used only when it helps us to understand religion in our own society. We have regrets about this. Material on religion in other societies and cultures is interesting and important. But to us it seems best to analyze the familiar in sociological terms as a way of appreciating what that perspective contributes to our understanding of the phenomenon of religion.

In the changes we have made we have been responsive to the comments of colleagues and friends with whom we share the sociological study of religion. We appreciate their comments and hope that this edition is improved because of our response to their contributions.

We are especially thankful for the help, support, and advice of our publisher, Ted Peacock. He has been patient as the project has taken more time than envisioned; he has also been generous with the wisdom that his years in publishing have given him. We are also grateful to the manuscript editor, Robert Cunningham, and the pro-

PART ONE

The Sociological Perspective and Religion

1.

Introduction to the Study of Religion in Society

Religion today, especially in the United States, presents a paradox. It is, at the same time, enjoying an apparent revival of influence and going through a period of crisis and potential decline (Robbins and Anthony, 1990). While "new religious movements" seem to be proliferating wildly, the older mainstream groups in our religious society (e.g., the Presbyterians, Episcopalians, and Methodists) are actually losing ground and struggling to maintain their former position of prestige and power. Meanwhile, the fundamentalists, who many thought had been effectively vanquished in the 1930s, show every sign of a remarkable vitality and have experienced a rapid growth. All the while, members of the Baby Boom generation, now returning to religious life, appear to be "shopping" for a religion that suits them, choosing, as in a supermarket, those items of faith they want and putting them together in an inconsistent mélange that seems not to disturb them in the least.

Once it was possible for North American sociologists (both Canadian and U.S.) to concentrate on a religion or religions we all accept. Particularly in the years just following the Second World War, religion was viewed as an integrating force for society. Religion was seen as a "good" thing, although it was not really viewed as involved in societal strife. It was, in Beckford's phrase, the "wallpaper" which held society together without really intruding on the course of social life (Beckford, 1989). Contrasted with the religious "peace" of the Eisenhower years, when there was more or less general agreement on the goodness of *any* religion, religion is now a "hot" and controversial topic. Different versions of religious belief now seem embroiled in controversy at every turn. As Wuthnow puts it (1988:6):

> Whether it be acrimonious arguments about abortion, lawsuits over religion in the public schools, questions of who is most guilty of mixing religion and politics, or discussion of America's military presence in the world, religion seems to be in the thick of it. Scarcely a statement is uttered by one religious group on these issues without another faction of the religious community taking umbrage.

Almost every edition of a major newspaper or newsmagazine, as well as television news and specials, brings to our attention some aspect of religious life that provokes controversy. For nearly two months in 1993 newspapers, magazines, and broadcast news were filled with the standoff between a small sectarian group, the Branch Davidians, and federal authorities. In late February agents of the Alcohol, Tobacco and Firearms Administration laid siege to the compound occupied by the sect with resulting death and injury on both sides. Six weeks later the standoff remained and:

> Bibles in hand and the U.S. Constitution in mind, an unlikely combination of preachers, civil libertarians and white supremacists has come from across the country to rally behind David Koresh (Jennings and Yearwood, 1993:31a).

Their support was not the result of agreement with the doctrine proclaimed by Koresh (the leader of the group) but from a fear that the federal government was intruding on our First Amendment rights, especially after the Scalia decision in *Smith* v. *Oregon*, which seemed to undercut the right of free expression in denying the legal use of peyote in the ritual of the Native American Church.

In a quieter revolution Baby Boomers returning to religion were doing so in highly unorthodox ways (Ostling 1992; Roof, 1993). Old creeds were dismissed as new generations found the sacred outside the old institutional boundaries. The battles are many: Fundamentalists inveigh against secular humanists, who respond in kind; devotees of new religious movements are faced with the threats of deprogrammers; pro-lifers and pro-choicers square off against one another, both claiming religious validity for their position regarding abortion; traditional Roman Catholics accuse those who would introduce modern changes in liturgy and belief of destroying the fabric of an ancient faith; and within mainline congregations members are divided by issues concerning human sexuality. To add to these controversies, non-Western religions are taking a more prominent place in the religious life of the West, with Muslims now being the third-largest religious group in the United States.

Events in the last decades of the twentieth century seem to demonstrate that there is no longer such a thing as "religion as we know it." Religion in the United States no longer serves to "bring us together." As Bellah (1975) has phrased it, the covenant of a perceived civil religion holding the nation together has been broken. These years have seen liberals and conservatives bitterly divided over the civil rights movement and the Vietnam War, often facing off within the same congregation. Now equally sincere Christians and others disagree on matters ranging from abortion to nuclear disarmament and the environment. Not only is there conflict within the United States; religion is also producing violent action from Northern Ireland to the Middle East. Meanwhile, in the former Yugoslavia Catholic Croats and Orthodox Serbs have fought against each other over disputed territory, and both these groups have attacked their Muslim neighbors in Bosnia in the name of *ethnic cleansing* (Ramet, 1992).

Certainly, the controversies in the Middle East, underscored by the Gulf War of 1991 and the bitter struggles in the former Yugoslavia, remind us that religious concern can no longer be isolated to what is happening in the United States and Canada. It is significant that the ideologies provoking conflict between Shi'ite and other Muslims in Iraq and Iran, as well as the confrontations between Lebanese Christians and a Muslim majority, directly affect our daily lives. Actually, in a sense the controversy between Druze Christians and Muslims, as well as other internal struggles in Islam, may have a greater effect on our lives than do the religious beliefs of our next-door neighbors. We live in a time of a globalization which affects our religious life as well as our secular world.

We were not really prepared for the upheavals of the current religious scene, lulled as we have been by a quiescent, compromising faith. We have been used to an evangelical religion which "knew its place" as a sideline observer of the political scene. Thus, the renascence of fundamentalist belief and its involvement in political strife is a bit jarring. But, on the other hand, neither were we really ready for the totalistic attitude of the liberal end of the religious spectrum. And nothing could have prepared us for the fragmentation of religious belief that for some has meant a very privatized, personally selected doctrinal world.

What we have learned in the past few decades is that *religion* is an extremely broad term, encompassing wide variations in belief, practice, and values. The term is applied to many ideologies. As we examine religion, from the sociological perspective, we must surely realize that religion is a subject that can be viewed from a number of different points of view: comparative, psychological, theological, historical, and sociological, among others. The focus of this book is on one of these, religion as it relates to society. This simple statement establishes our boundaries, defining both the opportunities and limitations of our approach.

Our emphasis in this book is on religion as it affects society in the United States and the Western world since this prevents the distraction of what are to us the "quaint and curious" religious practices of other traditions. For example, Asian religion connects religious ideology more fully with the total culture than does Western religion (Raulin, 1991). While current events demand that we incorporate the incursion of non-Western religious traditions into the life of North American society both within it and as a force in world politics, our sociological understanding of religion is best served by concentrating on the religion we know. Obviously, the strategy of limiting our attention mainly to religion as it finds social expression in the Western world keeps us from a full inquiry into the subject. A complete understanding of religion as a social phenomenon would require looking at the broad horizons of human behavior and beliefs concerning what can be defined as religious. Still for purposes of understanding religion as a social fact, in this book we will rely mainly on the historical and contemporary traditions of the Western world to illustrate and help us understand the social meaning of "being religious," while not completely ignoring the global religious scene so essential to life in the late modern or postmodern world.

This chapter sets forth our frame of reference for a sociological investigation of religion. In the study of religion as a social phenomenon, our attention is concentrated on the "known" aspects of religion so that we will be able to put our study of religion into a sociological perspective, undistracted by what some might consider the quaint beliefs of others. While we will consider, *passim*, religious traditions not familiar to the American scene, our emphasis remains on the religion that you know, ensuring that your attention is focused on what *you* have been familiar with, so that sociological analysis dominates interest in the unusual. The chapter starts with some comments on the relationship between religion and society in general; considers sociology's interest in religion as a social institution, both in the past and now; and lists the problems associated with developing a sociological definition of religion.

RELIGION AND SOCIETY INTERTWINED

From its very beginning, religion has played a significant role in the development of national life in North America. To some extent, those who first journeyed to the New World did so for religious reasons; indeed, nearly all of the first thirteen colonies that now form the United States were formed around particular interpretations of Christian faith. When the colonies were finally united into one nation, religious freedom was a necessary part of the compromises that resulted in the union, and the principle of freedom of religious belief led to the separation of church and state. Somewhat ironically, that doctrine was hammered out by individuals who themselves had only the most philosophical conception of the place of a deity in the conduct of human affairs. Washington, Jefferson, Franklin, and many other early leaders espoused deism, a theological stance that holds that a Divine Creator made the world but no longer has any involvement with it.

Certainly the United States tolerates more interpretations of the Judeo-Christian tradition than does any other nation. According to a thesis advanced by Herberg (1955), participation in one of the three major Judeo-Christian religious communities—Protestant, Catholic, or Jewish—provides us with both self-identification and self-placement in a heterogeneous society. The matter simmers down to the idea that religion is a way of belonging. For Herberg, it is *the* way we answer the question Who am I?

Today, belonging is not as simple as it was when Herberg's assessment was first made. For many in the contemporary United States, the old labels that told who we are no longer provide a primary source of identity. As Roof and McKinney (1987) point out, though the United States was largely settled by people defending a basically Calvinist faith, the most popular forms of faith were heavily loaded with Arminianism.* That is, they relied far more on the individual's ability to work out both worldly and otherworldly success than they did on a destiny predetermined by an all powerful, all knowing deity. In the United States there has been a close relationship between individualism and faith, especially on the frontier (see Chalfant, 1986). Our primary emphasis is on freely given assent to a practical kind of faith. We tend to view religious groups not as God-given institutions but as institutions made by the members themselves (Roof and McKinney, 1987:44).

Arminianism, a theological perspective named for Jacobus Arminius, a Dutch Reformed theologian who argued against a strict Calvinistic view of predestination, stressing the role of human free will in working out individual salvation.

Just after World War II, the faiths accepted by most Americans were closely related to the faith of their forebearers. Despite diversity, there were many common assumptions as to what religion was, beliefs built on centuries of Judeo-Christian tradition (Wuthnow, 1988:15). But as the Eisenhower years ended, so also did much of the cultural and value consensus of the nation's religious life. The 1960s and 1970s presented a much different culture, one in which dissensus was more evident that consensus. Young adults were no longer willing to unthinkingly affirm the materialistic culture, built on the basis of ascetic religious faith, but sought some faith, some identity that would provide new meaning (Roof and McKinney, 1987; Roof, 1993).

Herberg had argued that it was religion which served to give Americans their sense of identity as Catholic, Protestant, or Jew. But others were quick to point out that such identity was by no means uniform (Wuthnow, 1988). Denominations and other groups, as well as sects, each provided different identities based, in large part, on the social class divisions inherent in each.

Actually, the three broad communities of faith encompassed a considerable degree of diversity. When we look at the variations within each of the communities—from the staid Presbyterians to the ecstatic members of the Assembly of God; from the emotional Italian Catholics to the more puritanical Catholics of German descent; from the meticulously orthodox Hasidic Jews to the liberal members of a suburban Reform synagogue—religious expression in our society seems even more diverse. And today this diversity is increased as Muslims as well as Buddhists become a significant part of American religious life.

If religion has lost its centrality in society, it might be assumed that a lack of consensus in matters of faith would have little effect on our national life. Yet religion is, and always has been, a central issue in life in Western society. Whether we support and cherish religion, or would like to see its influence diminish, it still occupies a central place in our life. Yet the diminishing influence of denominational loyalties can mean that the ability of religion to provide individuals with an identity is seriously damaged.

There has been a weakening of denominational (including Catholic) loyalty (Roof and McKinney, 1987). During our years of relative prosperity, religion has undergone considerable restructuring (Wuthnow, 1988). It was able to do so because of the tremendous resources available to religious institutions which enabled them to respond to cultural change. But the changes have had an effect on the symbolic meaning of religion in our lives. New, and unfamiliar, modes of being religious have brought about new patterns of both religious interaction and moral obligations. Ours is a world in which religion has not only been restructured but also fragmented. Changes have broken our national covenant (Bellah, 1975), and we have not yet been able to put the pieces back together.

Some contemporary theorists doubt that they will ever be put back together, as a postmodern society cannot develop a unified social system (see Crook, Pakulski, and Waters, 1992). As viewed by some social theorists, the diversity of social life is so great that no unifying structure, religious or otherwise, can provide an overarching system of norms and values. As Shibley (1990) has pointed out, we no longer experience our world with a sense of unity. Life in general, and religious life in particular, is *fragmented.* Our relationships with one another lack continuity, a situation which previously might have been overcome by common religious ties. But we live in the present and our past religious heritage no longer provides a connection to our past. In short, the world is characterized by discontinuity and, as viewed by postmodern theorists, religion cannot bridge the chasm of reality.

A major concern, then, for religion in contemporary society is the lack of strong allegiances to the traditions of the past. Even the evangelical or fundamentalist view of religion is discontinuous with the past. As Roof and McKinney (1987) note, voluntarism is the benchmark of religion in contemporary society; believers are free to believe those things they wish—and to ignore what they don't like. The Belgian sociologist Karel Dobbelaere (1981, 1984, 1990) likens contemporary faith to a bricolage, that is, a compilation of those items of belief we choose as from a smorgasbord of beliefs. Giddens (1979, 1984, 1990), in his critique of postmodernist theory, remarks that religion in contemporary society is characterized by duality rather than dualism. We can comprehend several seemingly incompatible ideologies without discomfort or even the realization that ambiguity is involved. We can combine orthodox and novel religious ideas without strain. In the modern age, implicit religious beliefs can mix with, and perhaps be more powerful than, the orthodoxies of those who have gone before us.

Religious Values and Secular Values

Clearly, religious values, behaviors, and beliefs are intertwined with numerous other aspects of societal life. The way in which one is religious—whether measured by affiliation, attendance, or strength of religious preference—is usually correlated with views about various issues and problems in society. For example, attitudes toward radical groups, voting behavior, tolerance of communism, views of homosexuality, and even happiness in marriage are significantly associated with religious variables, as are attitudes toward mercy deaths, abortion, and women's rights (National Opinion Research Center, 1992).

It is also true that interaction between religion and other aspects of society is multidirectional. Religion is affected by the dominant patterns of culture: In *The Restructuring of American Religion*, Wuthnow (1988) comments that American religion has been as much molded by its social environment as vice versa. Its organization and theology in a particular place are in some measure shaped by the characteristics of the society in which it is found. Even such a powerful heritage of ecclesiastical authority as that of the Roman Catholic Church has not been immune from the influence of American life. Greeley (1990) argues that much of the defection of Roman Catholics from the church can be attributed to changing attitudes toward sexuality and a rejection of the papacy's authority. In short, the American emphasis on democracy and participation in voluntary associations has drastically affected the character of the Roman Catholic Church in this country by encouraging greater involvement by the laity and diminished confidence in the leadership (Roche, 1968). Similarly, the perceived threat of communism in the United States has influenced a number of religious movements to make opposition to this threat a major part of their ministry.

On the other hand, religion affects most other aspects of society. For instance, the German sociologist Max Weber (1881–1920) proposed that capitalism could not have developed except under the particular religious ethos associated with an ascetic Calvinist version of Protestantism, the so-called Protestant ethic. According to this thesis, a particular religious attitude toward the world and worldly success was essential to such economic development. Indeed, one might trace many current conservative attitudes toward the poor and governmental programs helping them to a somewhat secularized version of this same ethic.

But we need to be aware that simple statements about causation are precarious when dealing with complex historical forces and broad sociological variables. Even with seemingly simple variables the relationships are not clear-cut. To make the point more salient, let us look at several cases where conclusions might be drawn about the influence of religion on sociological variables and vice versa, from data concerning religious preference.

Religious preference varies considerably by regions of the country (Stump 1984a, 1984b; Finke and Stark, 1989). In fact, membership in certain religious denominations is seen as a distinctive mark of various regional cultures in the United States (Newman and Halvorson, 1984). The Episcopal and Presbyterian churches are evenly spread throughout the nation although they are not dominant in any region. Similarly, the Methodists are well represented in most parts of the country without dominating anywhere. The Baptists, especially those belonging to the Southern Baptist Convention, have established dominance in the South, where one can speak of a Baptist empire. The Lutheran churches have their own empire in Iowa, Minnesota, and the Dakotas. Roman Catholics are found predominantly in urban areas, particularly in the Northeast; in fact, they have their own fiefdom in the Northeast, particularly in Massachusetts (Carroll, Johnson, and Marty, 1979).

Chalfant and Heller (1991) also found that the region of residence, as well as rural as opposed to urban living, affect styles of religious behavior. Church attendance, for example, was most frequent for residents of the South and Midwest and lowest for those living in the West. Literal belief is highest in the South. Except for the Northeast, rural residents are more likely to attend church than are their counterparts in other parts of the country. In a study of four regions of the nation, Hammond (1992) demonstrates how the religious climate of an area affects the religiosity of residents, even those who profess no religious affiliation.

Is it appropriate to say that religious preference causes individuals to see certain areas of the country as desirable places to live, or that living in a certain region influences the tendency to prefer particular religious groups, and engage in particular religious behavior or both? Or are other, intervening variables at work in this relationship? In fact, sociohistorical data could be important for a fuller understanding of this phenomenon of regional religion. Episcopalians, Presbyterians, and Congregationalists, the first religious groups in the colonies, spread throughout the United States by capitalizing on their initial strength. Roman Catholics immigrated heavily into the Northeast, leading to dominance there, and the Southern Baptist Church has continued to grow because more of the nation's population is moving into its stronghold, the South and Southwest. The Lutheran church has capitalized on its immigrant following in the upper Midwest and thus is dominant there. All of this suggests that sociohistorical rather than sociological factors account for the regional strength of particular religious groups.

When we examine attitudes toward sexually related issues, such as abortion and pornography, it is easily assumed that there is a direct relationship between certain types of religiosity and negative appraisals. But is the relationship so simple? While research has shown a relationship between religious belief and opposition to both abortion and pornography, it has also shown that the relationship is neither direct nor simple (see, e.g., Jelen, 1986 and 1988; Hertel and Hughes, 1987; Swatos, 1988).

It is certainly well established that religiosity, especially such indicators as conservative belief and regular attendance at worship, is powerfully associated with attitudes toward abortion. However, such attitudes are also strongly related to age, gender, marital status, and education. In their study of residents of an urban center in North Carolina, Woodrum and Davison (1992) found that all these factors were involved in responses to questions about abortion, and that a rather complex constellation of these variables appeared to form individual attitudes toward abortion. For example, religious variables tended to be involved in negative attitudes toward abortion. At the same time, the variables of gender and race were also linked to religiosity as well as attitudes toward abortion. In fact, when level of religiosity was controlled or held constant, the demographic variables were most significant in predicting attitudes about abortion. In this situation, women were seen as more likely to support abortion, as were blacks. On the other hand, both women and blacks tend to support liberal political attitudes, in general, more often than white men. As a result, this tendency must also be taken into account in "explaining" attitudes toward abortion.

The matter is similarly cloudy when we try to explain attitudes toward pornography. Commenting on previous research, Woodrum (1992) notes findings that indicate an unusual "coalition" between religious conservatives and feminists in opposition to pornography. Studies by Jelen (1986) and Swatos (1988) indicate that conservative religious attitudes may be the root of antipornography attitudes for some, while support for women's issues motivates others. Woodrum's findings suggest that sexually restrictive attitudes, frequently found among conservative church members, were critical for antipornography attitudes while feminism was not. But if sexually restrictive attitudes are most significant, from what do these attitudes derive? Are they the result of conservative religious teachings or do those with such restrictive attitudes seek out groups, such as fundamentalist churches, to support previously formed attitudes?

Confusing? Yes it is, for questions about the cause of attitudes are not simple matters. Indeed, issues like these always haunt the social scientist, and make analytical skill necessary to avoid the pitfalls confronting those looking for objective information about religion in society. We hope these questions demonstrate that any attempt to define the complex relationship between society and religion is fraught with problems. Such problems have intrigued, motivated, and baffled scholars for some time, and have taught them to use great caution in evaluating the evidence and accepting conclusions. Still, given enough data, theory, and conceptual ability, sociologists are able to provide very relevant insights concerning this complicated relationship.

THE SOCIOLOGICAL INTEREST IN RELIGION

We have indicated that our perspective in this book is sociological. What, exactly, does that mean? Three characteristics distinguish this angle of vision from others we might use (Demerath and Hammond 1969:4, 5). First, sociology requires empirical observation (direct observation through the physical senses) to support its theories and propositions; this means that since much of what is religious is beyond our gaze, it is also beyond sociological consideration. Thus sociology cannot rule on whether a religious faith is true or false, good or bad. Second, sociology views events, persons, and groups in terms of their relationship to more general social phenomena rather than in and of themselves. It views the Moonies and the Hare Krishnas, for example, with regard to how they relate to the phenomenon of cult behavior rather than in terms of their unique and special meaning. And, finally, sociology is concerned with the relationship of religion, as a social phenomenon, to all other social phenomena; thus, from a sociological perspective, religion cannot be viewed apart from such social institutions as the family, education, politics, and the economy.

We need to stress that our major focus is on religion as one aspect of group behavior. This focus does not imply that the individual response to and expression of religion is unimportant; private aspects of being religious are an important part of the whole. However, sociology views religion as it expresses itself in group behavior. By looking at religion from the perspective of sociology, we can discern aspects—patterns, roles, structures, and behaviors resulting from the activity of the group—that would escape us if we only viewed it from a psychological or individual perspective (see Stark and Bainbridge, 1985). We study the individual's religious experience here only as it can be related to the experience of the group. With this understanding of the sociological perspective in mind, we will now look more closely at characteristics of that perspective as it relates to religion—at the interest in religion demonstrated by early sociologists; at sociology's focus on religion as an institution; and at the limitations of a sociology of religion.

Early Sociological Interest

Religion and its relationship to the rest of society was a major area of interest for sociologists in the early years of the discipline. Pioneer sociologists Emile Durkheim (1858–1917), Georg Simmel (1858–1918), and Max Weber all focused attention on the relationship between religion and society, although as Beckford (1989) points out they all saw religion as fading in importance in the industrial or modern age. Each was concerned with trends in the drastically changing society of their day and interested in the role that religious beliefs, attitudes, and structures were playing in these changes and in the emerging industrial society.

As Beckford (1990) notes, some early sociologists felt that religion had been the key to the stability of the old order and should be the answer to providing a new modern order. Durkheim was almost obsessed with the question of how society was held together, that is, how humans came to accept and obey the dictates of their group. He believed that religion was one of the central factors binding individuals to their society, and wondered what effect the loss of religion might have. In *Suicide* ([1897] 1951), for example, he argued that societies embracing individualistic Protestantism (a religion encouraging only low cohesiveness) had a higher ratio of deaths by suicide than those societies in which Catholicism (a religion encouraging high cohesiveness) was the predominant religion. Durkheim felt that the fragmentation and individualistic thought engendered in Protestantism destroyed the sense of a cohesive community that gave meaning to individuals, thus increasing the probability of anomic, or normless, suicide.

Like Durkheim, sociological pioneer Georg Simmel (1905) saw religion as a model for the integration and stabilization of social life. He contended that we can find in all patterns of social interaction evidence of what can be categorized as religious. Feelings evoked by the state, the political party one belongs to, or the region in which one lives resemble the emotion, commitment, devotion, and loyalty common to strong religious faith. In particular, piety—the quintessential religious element—is the basis of most social relationships, according to Simmel. Through such piety we develop faith in our government, in members of our families and our friends, and, when ill, in the ministrations of the physician. In the manner of Durkheim, Simmel saw the origin of religion in the everyday events of social life. For Simmel, religion is simply the superordinate authority for our human existence.

Beckford (1990) has similarly indicated that other early sociologists thought religion had been important in the formation of the new order but would disappear when new structures were established. Max Weber ([1920] 1958) was primarily concerned with the effects of the increasing rationalization and bureaucratization of society. These developments produced a more efficient organization, but they also dehumanized individuals and alienated them from their work and most aspects of their social lives. He saw these processes as inevitable and forecast that they would be a continuing part of modern life. His studies in religion were related to his feeling that religious life, too, was becoming rationalized, and would eventually be displaced. The concept of the Protestant ethic was, to Weber, an example of this process. As rationalism increased in religion, the modern world would be disenchanted and those living in that world would have lost a significant source of common meaning. This loss would be one more way in which the integration of society would be reduced, Weber felt.

Not all early theorists saw religion as having the positive effects suggested by Durkheim, Simmel, and Weber. For some, religion had been one of the major obstacles to the establishment of the new industrial order (Beckford, 1990). Karl Marx ([1844] 1964:170–71) regarded religion as promoting a dehumanization that was an important factor in the alienation of modern life. He further saw religious institutions as playing a pivotal role in sustaining the vested interests of the dominant capitalist class within society. According to Marxist theory, religion contributes to the exploitation of the non-propertied class, the lower class; religion sustains the dominant class structure and, therefore, aids in perpetuating the unequal distribution of wealth.

The founders of sociology made major contributions to our understanding of religion as a social phenomenon and to our comprehension of society itself, but sociologists' interest in the study of religion waned after the initial period of development. This may have been due, at least partially, to an evolutionary perspective common to most early social scientists that saw religion as dying out as human knowledge increased. Some undoubtedly still hold such a view and downplay the importance of the scientific study of religion. Yet others have come to see the easy disparagement of religion as in itself unscientific. And since the end of World War II, a vital and renewed interest in the study of religion as one of the continuing, important presences in social life has been evident. Glock (1973:1) has observed that religion is receiving more attention from sociologists today than it has since the last century. This renewed interest has brought forth a considerable amount of quality empirical research.

The Focus of Sociological Study: Institutions

If, as we have noted, interest in the sociological study of religion is increasing, and if researchers are taking a more empirical stance, how can we best understand the focus of the sociological study of religious life? Our interest as sociologists is obviously quite different from that of theologians. It is not the value or validity of religious belief systems in general or of any specific system of theological belief that the sociologist seeks to study. Rather, we see religious systems as networks of norms, values, and patterns of action, similar to other social systems existing to solve essential problems of survival in groups. The behavior resulting from these norms, values, and patterns of action provides our sociological data. Included in such data are expressed beliefs, affiliations with particular religious groups, types of religious organizations, as well as material concerning the relation of such standard demographic and sociological variables as social class, age, and sex to religious behavior.

Put in two simple phrases, we as sociologists are interested in social structures and social processes: "[S]tructure means an identifiable pattern in the symbolic expressive dimension of social life" (Wuthnow, 1988:9). That is, our concern is with the means by which human beings structure social life and the processes whereby individuals are channeled into positions in those structures and come to internalize them as the patterns of reality. To paraphrase Berger and Luckmann (1967), we are concerned as sociologists with how social interaction constructs the reality both individuals and the group accept.

Looked at as a pattern of roles and role relationships, religion is what is called in sociology a *social institution*. The norms, roles, and patterns of interaction in an institution become a more or less integrated system; a number of these systems merge to create the fabric of society. Some would argue that in many industrial societies disintegration is more prevalent than many realize, and that traditional patterns are breaking down. Any society that does not find ways of organizing and integrating its various elements to some degree must face the possibility of extinction or radical social change. And even though change is characteristic of human relationships, some semblance of order, stability, and predictability is necessary (at both the concrete and abstract levels) for their continuation. The maintenance of these patterns in social life is due to the fact that persons devise and use particular methods and techniques to meet their basic needs.

If we view the various elements of culture as operating to deal with the basic problem of adaptation to one's environment, we can assume that societies develop the basic institutions—family, government, education, economy, and religion—to solve some of the most basic problems they face. Such institutions are not mutually exclusive; that is, their functions overlap and new institutions may assume tasks traditionally carried out by others.

Institutional arrangements, thus, are not totally static, but fluctuate according to perceived needs and the sociohistorical time period. In general, institutional arrangements are supportive of one another and thus supportive of the culture. For example, Western industrial society's institution for dealing with problems of health and illness leans upon scientific information and techniques; Azande society, a tribal group residing in central Africa in both the Sudan and the Central African Republic, defines the same problems in terms of supernatural forces and thus deals with them with a different institution—witchcraft (Evans-Pritchard, 1972). Each approach fits its particular social system and thus is basically harmonious with other elements in the society. American medicine is based on scientific skill and knowledge, which are highly valued in the United States; Azande healing takes its shape and form from the dominant beliefs of a religious society. Neither way is more "correct" than the other in the sociological sense; each is correct in terms of its larger social context.

In some cases, the various institutional arrangements compete with one another. This may cause change in the functions of an institution without altering its significance in the overall scheme of things. Changes in the function of the family in the United States, for example, have been documented by social scientists and historians for years. Yet, even though radical changes have occurred in some cases, the family has not disappeared from society. We can see not only the flexibility but also the interconnectedness of institutions in the following report by Kephart and Zellner (1991:31–32) of an observation made a number of years ago by William F. Ogburn, a sociologist interested in the study of cultural change, about changes in the American family:

> From the colonial period to the present,…the family has been characterized by a progressive loss of functions. He went on to list the declining functions of education, religion, protection, recreation, and the economic function. Thus, the functions of religion, once centered in the home, had been taken over by the church. Education had become the province of the schools. The economic function had been lost because the family was no longer a producing unit—due largely to the fact that child labor laws and compulsory school laws prohibited children from seeking work.

Similar arguments can be made about the changing functions of organized religion in our society. As we have noted, we currently face the paradox of a revitalization of belief in the sacred coupled with the apparent decline of the influence of institutionalized religion in important decisions about our national life (see, for example, Beckford, 1990). Since at least the sixties, sociologists have been speculating on the role religion plays in contemporary life. Some, like Luckmann (1967), have seen religion as increasingly privatized or relegated to the task of embellishing large public ceremonies (Berger, 1967). In other words, religion may be losing some of its functions of integrating the community and providing a means of social control (Roof and McKinney, 1987; Wuthnow, 1988). At the same time, it has adopted some of the functions of the family, such as the moral education of the young. And, as we will later see, religious participation also serves educational, economic, and political needs.

In our study of religion as a social institution, our subject matter ranges from broad theoretical concerns about the meaning of religion in society to an understanding of how individuals come to internalize a particular religious belief system as their own. Such concerns, of course, are not always easy to discuss and study. A number of problems arise when we attempt a scientific study of religion.

Limits of a Sociology of Religion

In covering the broad area of religion, some difficulties and special problems appear. In one sense the very nature of religion makes scientific approaches difficult. As sociologists, we are limited to studying what we can observe empirically. This means that while we can study attitudes that people express, beliefs they say they hold, ritual behavior such as attendance at worship services, the organization of the religious group, and so forth, we cannot go beyond what can be observed. If we were to claim that such matters comprised all that was important in religion, we would be sadly mistaken. We do not and cannot study everything that relates to the process of being a religious person.

In this limiting characteristic of the sociological approach lie the roots of some of the difficulties of and objections to such an investigation. Many feel that the subject of religion is too varied and rich to be comprehended within the narrow boundaries imposed by sociology. Surely, say these people, only a combination of theology, philosophy, anthropology, history, psychology—and sociology—can even begin to comprehend such complex subject matter. Some would say that the abstractions arrived at by sociology, particularly because they come from outside religious faith, never really embrace the essence of religion. Certainly, in Yinger's (1970) imagery, from the outside we cannot have the same view of the stained glass window of religion as do those who are inside. For the latter, it is the light of faith shining through the window that makes it visible. However, those viewing the window from the outside can also see many things that might be missed by those who never step outside. Just as the view from the inside provides a part of the picture, so does the outside view furnish knowledge important to understanding the whole.

Another problem is that the focus of a sociology of religion has been misunderstood, both by those who confuse it with theology and by those who see it as an attack on religious beliefs and practices. It thus seems important to clarify that a sociological perspective on religion seeks neither to promote nor to discourage religious faith. Neither does it merely compare the great religions of the world, except as such a comparison relates to the basic problems of social structure and social process. In short, sociology of religion is a scientific approach to the institution of religion, viewed in the same way sociologists look at the institutions of the family or medicine.

All this has been summarized by Vernon (1962:16–17). He indicated that it must be made clear that the sociology of religion is not (1) a study of the truth or falsity of religion or religious ideas; (2) a promotion of the correctness of one set of ideas as opposed to another set; (3) an attack upon religion, since the realm of the beyond cannot be attacked by a scientific discipline; (4) an attempt to answer the question of whether or not religion is a good thing; or (5) a program of reform—either of society or of religion. Whether you have deep religious convictions, have rejected such convictions, or fall somewhere in between, keep these points in mind as you read this book so that you can understand statements made and evidence presented in the proper context.

TOWARD A SOCIOLOGICAL DEFINITION OF RELIGION

To consider the sociology of religion in a theoretical framework, we must come to some understanding of what we mean when we speak of religion. One thing in particular is necessary. In developing a sociological definition of religion, we need to be able to differentiate between what is and what is not religion. In a commonsense way of thinking, this does not seem too difficult. Everyone knows that religion is...what? When we begin to think about all of the possibilities involved in separating religion from other phenomena, the number of criteria for making such a distinction can be staggering.

To state that all, or most, societies throughout history have had some kind of religion is almost a truism. But such a commonplace statement implies that an amazing variety of behaviors, practices, and beliefs can be placed under the single umbrella term *religion*. To think for a few moments about this extreme diversity is useful. The term *religion* is applied to such differing practices as the high pageantry of a Roman Catholic mass and a snake-handling ceremony in a crude wooden church in the mountains of West Virginia; religion can be seen as the basis for ritual cannibalism as well as for the absolute silence of a Quaker meeting; it results in the intellectual discourse of a Unitarian-Universalist fellowship as well as in the emotional fervor of an old-fashioned camp meeting that leads some of the revived to roll on the floor and bark at the moon like dogs. It is the reason for the staid services and organization of a middle-class Presbyterian congregation as well as for the superbly choreographed performances of the electronic church that possesses our television screens on Sunday mornings. Some even refer to various political creeds such as communism as a religion, and to a basic belief in the rectitude of the American way of life in a similar manner. With such an assortment of behaviors to consider, it is a small wonder that the student of the sociology of religion is hard put to propose a precise definition of the subject matter.

Basic Elements of a Definition

As we approach the task of definition, then, a number of questions come to mind. Is there any special characteristic that ought to be considered concerning the nature of that which is at the center of this thing we call religion? Can religion be separated from group activity? Are there practices peculiar to religion? What sorts of goals seem particularly appropriate to what we call religious behavior?

These questions relate to some of the basic elements that have been found important in distinguishing religion from nonreligion. While some, like Weber, have suggested that no real definition of religion can be developed until the phenomenon has actually been studied, most would follow Durkheim in suggesting that at least a provisional definition is needed at the outset. A definition given by Durkheim ([1897] 1947:61) has come to be seen as one benchmark for those attempting to develop such a sociological definition. He described religion as "a unified system of beliefs and practices relative to sacred things, that is to say, things set apart and forbidden—beliefs and practices which unite into one single moral community called a Church all those who adhere to them."

This definition tells us three things about what is to be called religion. First, it marks as religious the concern for those things that are considered sacred, by virtue of their being set off from daily activity and seen as somehow foreboding. For the Australian Arunta about whom Durkheim (1947) wrote, the totem object, which symbolized the object of worship, was sacred; the Roman Catholic sees the crucifix as sacred; and the Jew evinces awe for the scroll of the Torah.

Second, a religion involves beliefs and practices directed in some fashion at the sacred. Such beliefs may range from the extremely unsophisticated to the highly philosophical. Primitive religions may center on only a few beliefs while the religions of highly industrialized societies, such as those of the Western world, may result in the complex and highly intellectual reasoning of John Calvin's theory of double predestination, the idea that some people are chosen before their birth for either glory or damnation. Regardless of complexity, each religion develops a set of beliefs and practices defining the sacred and appeasing or relating to it.

Finally, Durkheim's definition insists that religion is a property of the group, not the individual; that is, religion cannot be without a unifying community of some sort built around the phenomenon. While some (like Williams, 1962) make a place for religion as an individual enterprise, the focus of the sociological study of religion is the group and the individual's relationship to the group. In this view, religion is never a completely solitary matter—even when the individual is engaging in behavior of a religious nature and is alone. Religion is a product of the group; the group is central in its formation, formulation, and future.

While Durkheim's definition might be accused of begging the question, leaving much still vague and uncertain, the elements of his definition have been used by many investigators as a starting point in developing other definitions. The points Durkheim made have been elaborated and considered by most of those engaged in the sociological study of religion. Glock and Stark (1965:4) have suggested that all of these elaborations can be summarized in one brief generalization: "Religion, or what societies hold to be sacred, comprises an institutionalized system of symbols, beliefs, values and practices focused on questions of ultimate meaning." The three basic elements found in Durkheim's definition are included in this summary statement, although the focus of beliefs, values, and practices is somewhat differently defined. What is original is the qualification that the kinds of questions that religion is set to address are those concerning ultimate meaning—that is, questions related to matters of the significance of life and the explanation of those things that threaten this significance.

What does life mean? How can we deal with the tragedies that occur in our lives? How can we face the death of a loved one or look forward to our own death?

Gustafson and Swatos (1990:10) incorporate many of these elements in their definition of religion as "a patterning of social relationships around a belief in supernatural powers, creating ethical considerations." This definition differs, however, in the lack of insistence on a unified body of beliefs built around a sacred/secular dichotomy which unites people in the community of the church. They feel that this definition heightens the most important aspects of a sociological definition and avoids some of the problems presented by the Durkheimian definition.

Accepting any of these definitions, certain elements can be considered bedrock for a definition of religion...or can they? As simple as this brief list of criteria seems, the questions that can be raised concerning their appropriateness for a sociological definition of religion are many. For instance, should we confine our definition of religion to those sets of beliefs that deal with supernatural realms in some way, or should it be broadened to include anything seen as providing answers to questions of ultimate meaning? Are we to see religion as specifically referring to the functions associated with a particular set of beliefs, or is there a unifying, universal meaning attached to the concept of religion?

Purposes of a Sociological Definition

As we ponder such questions, we need to understand the purpose of a sociological definition—the reason or reasons that such a definition is formulated. We can, as Yinger (1970:3) has reminded us, create such rigid pigeonholes with our definitions that they cease to represent reality or hide much of reality in the service of the definition. Thus, in looking for an absolute idea of what constitutes religion, we might well consider that the distinction between religion and nonreligion is not a sharp dividing line but rather a flowing continuum in which some things are merely more or less religious than others. But because our concern is with increasing our ability to explain accurately the social fact of religion and to make predictions on the basis of these findings, we need a working, pragmatic definition—one that will aid in research and study. To the extent that a definition does assist this process, it is useful. If it does not help in this task, or if it clutters the concept of religion with contradictions so that no one can identify what it means, or if it seems to mean something different to everyone who uses it, then it no longer serves our purpose (Osborne 1977:2).

What we look for in a definition depends upon the question we are asking. For example, if we are interested in finding out how people give meaning to their lives, we need to decide whether to classify certain political philosophies as religions, because these political philosophies sometimes give meaning to life. If, however, we wish to determine the effects of having no ideology concerning the significance of life, we may not be interested in how quickly we exclude some phenomena from under the religious umbrella. Again, if we want to investigate the way religious norms undergird the traditional ways of society, we are concerned with the broadness of the definition to the extent that we want to differentiate between kinds of norms serving such a function.

Such considerations lead to the suggestion that different definitions and definitional strategies prepare us to receive different information about the social world. We need to evaluate definitions in terms of their usefulness for gathering specific types of information. Different definitions are constructed for different ends. In practice, definitions are adopted most frequently for operational reasons, and we may gain little in attempting to construct a definition to suit all situations and all needs. As Machalek has noted (1977:400), "Definitions must be evaluated in terms of their utility with regard to the intellectual tasks at hand or in terms of the adequacy with which they purportedly represent an empirical phenomenon." Given the tentative nature of many definitions, we should look more fully at what is involved in the choices made and the strategies used in constructing a definition of religion.

Substantive versus Functional Definitions

A major question in deciding what fits under the "sacred canopy" (Berger 1967) of religion is, Should religion be defined in terms of its substance or in terms of its functions? The issue is better understood if we look at examples of the two approaches.

In *The Sacred Canopy* Berger (1967:26) has defined religion in a way that focuses on its substance: He has spoken of religion as "the human enterprise by which a sacred cosmos is established." The emphasis here is on the activity of human beings related to a specific kind of realm—the sacred—that is different in every way from the mundane world. The substance of religion, and its most important defining point, then, is that it is related to something that can be termed *sacred*.

Certainly a substantive definition such as Berger's provides us with a way to distinguish between what is religion and what is not.

Yet the distinctive substance, sacredness, may be so subject to defini-tional bias that it causes us to exclude from consideration things that could meaningfully be referred to as religion. For example, Berger (1967), Herberg (1955), and Bellah (1967) have all described devotion to, and faith in, the American way of life as a set of religious beliefs. Can this fit into something that is defined in terms of sacredness?

Such a consideration leads to the suggestion that religion might best be defined in terms of the functions it performs for both society and the individual. Yinger (1970) has defined religion in such terms: For him, religion is the set of beliefs, practices, and symbols human groups evolve in order to deal with the ultimate problems of ex-istence.

From this perspective, religion functions for human beings as a way of dealing with what O'Dea and Aviada (1983:5) have referred to as "the three brute facts of contingency, powerlessness, and scarcity" in everyday life. This way of looking at religion, and at other social in-stitutions, began within anthropology as a counter to the ethnocentric attitudes of many early students of primitive cultures who equated what was primitive with what was superstitious or false. The func-tional approach sees any social structure as aimed at performing cer-tain functions. It looks at the issue of why religion exists and what difference it makes, rather than at issues of truth or falsity, right or wrong. It is an attempt to see which structures function in various so-cieties to solve certain kinds of problems, a perspective that obviously calls for a different definition of religion than the substantive one.

Sociologists probably do, in fact, define religion very frequently in terms of its functions. Bellah (1964), for example, has defined reli-gion as those symbols, beliefs, and behaviors by which people attempt to relate their lives to some ultimate condition of existence. In many ways, the functional definition is a useful one for the pur-poses of sociological analysis. It clearly allows for shifts in religious style and does not let the content of a particular belief system de-fine whether it qualifies as religion or not. Using such a definition, we can postulate that all societies have some value system common to the group that serves the general functions of religion and can be so defined.

But the conceptualization of religion in terms of functions raises questions. First, as Swatos (1990) points out, the functional definition of religion seems tied to the idea that religion, at least as we have known it, is dying. It will, in an evolutionary process, be replaced by some "functional alternative."

Second, what happens in societies where religion has been sup-pressed or in the case of individuals who have rejected traditional religious interpretations? A functional perspective might suggest that in a society where many members bypass the traditional religions, functional alternatives are found—that is, some set of values, beliefs, and symbols replace the more customary types of religious belief: Faith in the nation, a political ideology, or even belief in the efficacy of science may serve as such an alternative. In some cases such secular ideologies can swallow up and use the religious institution. For example, in one city in the Southwest, a whole congregation became so consumed with anticommunist ideology that this became the raison d'être for the group, and they withdrew from their parent church. In such cases, should we see the functional alternative as different from religion or just another form of it? Another way of asking this question is, How inclusive should our definition of religion be?

Inclusive versus Exclusive Definitions

Inclusive views of religion tend to define it as a force in the life of the individual and the group that may be present in many ways. In such a view, communist ideology, for example, would be a religious faith. We can find a number of concepts in communism that match those of Christianity. The proletariat is the savior that leads the faithful into the battle of Armageddon (the class war) in the struggle to free society and humanity from the evil clutches of the devil (the capitalist bourgeoisie). The classless society, then, is heaven or eternity. Likewise, the belief systems found in a political ideology such as Nazism or the psychiatric model of Freud contain symbols and values that appear to serve the same function religion has traditionally served.

There has been much debate about whether groups such as Alcoholics Anonymous (A.A.) are religions (Rudy and Greil, 1987; Chalfant, 1992). The question revolves around what is meant by belief in a "higher power." An extreme response, from one A.A. member, is that if one so believes, a doorknob can be your higher power. Is this the stuff of which religion is made? In a totally inclusive definition one would assume it would have to be, even though the object of awe seems pedestrian to most of us. Likewise one of the respondents in *Habits of the Heart* (Bellah et al., 1985) who found ultimate meaning in herself would have this individualistic belief considered a religion under this definition. Since her name was Sheila, she called her religion *Sheilaism*!

The exclusive view, on the other hand, would restrict the term *religion* to beliefs and behaviors intentionally directed to the supranatural or transcendent as a way of fulfilling specific functions. Religion is seen from this perspective as serving certain functions, but only with reference to a realm that transcends our physical existence. Using the Gustafson and Swatos (1990) definition, the higher power of A.A., for example, would have to be seen as transcendent and supernatural—the doorknob would not seem to do. However, the phrase frequently used in A.A. groups, "god as we know him," would seem to include this element. Certainly for most of us the idea of a supernatural power, God in most cases, is inherently part of religion.

The problem, as Demerath (1974:6) has reminded us, is that too inclusive a view of religion may lead to defining the term out of meaningful existence. Once we start the process of including any value system related to ultimate meaning or societal integration under the definition of religion, we may lose touch with conventional meanings of the term to the point that our definition becomes muddled and meaningless. Under such a definition, the atheist who subscribes to objectivity in science as a value system would have to be called religious, even though such an appellation runs against common sense.

On the other hand, too exclusive a view of religion may lead us to a definition that is so limiting it causes us to miss meaningful data that could help us understand religion. As Hargrove (1979b:5) has pointed out, "To limit the study of the sociology of religion to the observation of behavior in organized groups labeled as religious and generalized categories of faith, denomination, geographical area, or social class, is to deal with so small a segment of the meaning of religion as to be almost useless." In other words, we should not be too quick to accept one answer or the other to this question of inclusive versus exclusive definitions. The question is complex and important for the way in which we come to understand religion. The definitions we use, by directing where we look when we analyze religion, determine what we see.

For example, using an inclusive definition of religion has led some scholars in the sociology of religion to suggest that today we are faced with nontheological religions. Yinger (1969) has postulated the existence of what he refers to as *nondoctrinal religion*. He suggests that many people at this time may be religious, but in ways that differ from the traditional. According to this view, religion exists wherever individuals are concerned with ultimate problems, the human condition, or have hope for better relations with other human beings.

Luckmann (1967) has similarly formulated the existence of what he calls *invisible religion*. He concludes that the traditional forms of religious belief and expression are less relevant to modern society. Seeing religion as that which provides ultimate meaning to existence, he notes that this term has traditionally been confined to practices and beliefs involving a transcendent realm. Luckmann (1990) has recently modified this statement, suggesting that our sense of the transcendent is shrinking at the same time that our concept of religion is expanding. He contends that other systems of meaning exist that have the same function as traditional religion; he refers to these systems as invisible religion, religion that is not visible to us in terms of the usual practices and structures we associate with it. It is not that people are no longer religious, or are not as frequently religious as before, asserts Luckmann; they are religious in different ways, ways that are not observed because they do not fit the traditional models. Thus Luckmann's definition of religion is both functional and inclusive, and it has important consequences in terms of the conclusions it leads us to form about the institution of religion today.

Are inclusive definitions like Yinger's and Luckmann's realistic? A few sociologists have attempted research to either confirm or reject the notion that nontheological religions exist for segments of the population. Some, like Nelsen, Yokeley, and Madron (1971), have found no support for the ideas expressed by Yinger and Luckmann. However, others have found evidence that such nontheological systems of belief exist and serve traditionally religious functions for individuals in our society. Machalek and Martin (1976), going beyond Yinger's suggestions, have carried such an inclusive definition to what seems its logical extreme. They suggest that Yinger's definition is limited because he insists that religion contains "elements of ritual and shared beliefs as well as organized groups." They contend that we should include under the term anything or anyone except those individuals who specifically never acknowledge the existence of any ultimate problems in life and thus make no attempt to cope with them; only these would be seen as having no religious belief system. In research in Baton Rouge, Louisiana, they found evidence that individuals other than those with traditional religious beliefs have a sense of the ultimate problems of existence. Further, they found that individuals have many mechanisms for coping with such problems, mechanisms that are unrelated to the traditional religious institution. Thus, they conclude that Luckmann's observations about the existence of a privatized religion in modern society are credible, justifying the tendency to use the term *religion* for a broad range of behavior.

Our discussion of these definitional questions cannot really lead us to some final solution. However, it does sensitize us to the various nuances of the term *religion* and the various ways in which the word is used by sociologists. We need to understand that the definition we use may vary in terms of the problem being addressed and that no one definition can be right at all times. McGuire (1992) suggests that substantive definitions are most often used in designing and carrying out research, as they are more easily expressed in concrete terms, while functional definitions are favored by those engaged in theoretical work concerning the sociology of religion.

SUMMARY

Religion is important in our society, as evidenced by its implication in our history and in current events. Religious values, behaviors, and beliefs are strongly correlated with attitudes toward other societal institutions and issues. Just as religion affects other aspects of society, so religion is affected by the dominant patterns of culture. But establishing simple cause-and-effect relationships is difficult and precarious; we need to use great caution in evaluating the evidence and accepting conclusions about the relationship between religion and society.

The existence of a relationship was recognized by early sociologists like Durkheim, Simmel, and Weber. Today sociologists take a vital interest in religion as one of the basic societal institutions. Any analysis of human behavior at the social level would be incomplete without attention being paid to religious beliefs, expressions, and structures. Because religious beliefs are interwoven throughout the social fabric, influencing and being influenced by other institutional arrangements (family, government, education, and the economy), the study of religion and its impact is a necessity for students of society.

The sociological perspective, however, is limited in that it looks for explanations in terms of social forces and processes and does not look to psychology or biology alone to explain the human condition. In addition, as an empirical science, sociology cannot investigate those important aspects of religion that are beyond our gaze. We must realize from the outset what the sociology of religion is not. As sociologists, we are not concerned with the truth or falsity of religious beliefs, nor do we posit the correctness of one set of beliefs over another. Likewise, we are not reformers stating that religion is a good or bad thing for society or individuals. In fact, we consider both the functions and dysfunctions of religion and try to maintain an objective stance toward the operation of belief systems within society. Our task is to explore, not expound; to hypothesize, not proselytize; to theorize, not theologize; and to consider rather than to convert.

To approach the sociology of religion we need to have a definition of religion that is adequate to the sociological purpose. *Religion* can be seen as an umbrella term covering a wide variety of beliefs, attitudes, behaviors, and practices. Because the term covers such a variety of phenomena, definition of it often creates ambiguity and poses special problems for our investigation.

While clear definitions are important to all scientific inquiry, the precise boundaries of the term *religion* depend upon the purpose for which the definition is used. Those who have wrestled with the definitional problem have sensitized us to a major recurring question: Shall we define religion in terms of some special substance such as a sacred realm, or shall we define it in regard to the functions it performs for individuals and society, such as helping us cope with the unknown or with death? In addition, we might ask whether the definition should include all things that might possibly be considered as religion, or some selected subset thereof.

As can readily be seen, numerous questions arise concerning what is to be called religion. In fact, we may not be able to choose one correct definition that will fit all times and purposes. Still, there are four aspects that we think should be considered in any sociological definition: Religion (1) is concerned with what is seen as sacred; (2) has a complex of beliefs and practices directed in some fashion toward this sacred aspect; (3) is concerned with group, rather than solely individual, activity and belief; and (4) deals with what can be termed problems of ultimate meaning.

2.
Theoretical Approaches to the Sociology of Religion

Just as sociology is only one of a number of perspectives that can be used in viewing the phenomenon of religion, sociology itself has developed a number of different theoretical approaches to the study of religion. Sociologists have variously seen religion as a need characterizing an immature phase of human knowledge; as a concrete way to worship society; as a tool used by an elite to maintain power over the masses; as a mirror to let us know who we are and a lens through which to interpret situations; as a way to make sense of the universe; as an integrating force in society; and as a divisive force in society. Some of these views have been virtually discarded; others are of contemporary importance. That such a variety of theoretical interpretations exists gives evidence that no one approach is adequate to explain the complex relationship between religion and society.

Still, each of these various approaches does have explanatory power. In this chapter we will discuss some of the significant sociological approaches, past and present, to the study of religion. We will begin with macro level approaches of functionalism and conflict theory. Then, we will use these theoretical perspectives to approach religious phenomena, showing that religion can function in certain circumstances to assist society in maintaining itself and solving basic problems. At other times it can be dysfunctional to the continuing justification of society and can itself become problematic.

We will then turn our attention to micro level approaches, emphasizing interpretations of religion from the perspectives of symbolic interactionism and phenomenology. Such approaches allow us to see religion on a more personal and emotional level.

THE BACKGROUND OF SOCIAL SCIENTIFIC RESEARCH IN RELIGION

As sociology was taking shape as a unique academic discipline, it was deeply influenced by the intellectual currents of the time. Charles Darwin's theory of the evolution and descent of humanity was adapted to a theory of social evolution. Social norms and organization were seen as developing from those of the earliest, least complex social groups. For example, the French philosopher Auguste Comte (1798–1857), usually considered the founder of sociology, viewed religion as something appropriate to the childhood of humanity. As our rational understanding of the universe gradually increased, according to Comte, religion would be displaced first by philosophy and then by science as we came to a rational understanding of our universe.

This evolutionary theory of religion had obvious significance for later sociological interpretations. However, its most immediate effect was to make it nearly inevitable that the sociological study of religion would begin with a search for its primitive origins from which contemporary forms of religion evolved. In this search, early students were caught in a trap. That is, instead of looking for underlying factors that could explain the persistence of religion in all places and times, they tried to explain the origins of religious expression.

In our examination of theoretical approaches, we will examine those early theories that were based on the search for the primitive origins of religion. We will look first at two evolutionary theories—animism and naturism—and then turn to Durkheim's theory of religion as society worship.

Evolutionary Approaches to Understanding Religion

Given this orientation, early scholars turned to the evidence of primitive societies in order to find the bare essentials of religious life. From their studies two specific theories arose—animism and naturism. Both theories explain religion as a stopgap for inadequate explanations of natural events that the primitives did not understand.

Animism is an explanation of religion that traces the origin of belief in spirits to common experiences that so-called primitive people could not explain. Examples of this are fairly easy to find. We all have dreams in which we seem to move in a different world; awake, we observe a reflection of ourselves in a pond of calm water. The animists proposed that such events or experiences in primitive society required an explanation, and that in an attempt to explain these experiences the primitive individuals posited the existence of a totally separate order of reality. Such an order was peopled with other kinds of beings—spirits. From this the animists drew the conclusion that a spirit lived in the individual and was released during times of sleep and permanently left the body at the time of death. This latter kind of spirit became especially important, because it represented the dead individual. Rituals for the dead and beliefs about life in another existence developed. In some tribal religions, as in the former Belgian Congo, the belief developed that a "God" had created the world but that the world had later been taken over by evil spirits that needed constant appeasement. From these beliefs evolved the idea of groups of spirits, and eventually the concept of gods. The animistic approach, therefore, posits that religion is an irrational response to the rational quest for explanation.

Naturism is similar to, and a variation of, animism. It too explains religion as a result of the primitives' inability to understand what we would see as natural; that is, it too sees the cause of religion as existing in the need for explanation. But in naturism, the origin of religion is not seen as lying in the kinds of events that lead to belief in spirits. Rather, the need for explanation is seen as arising from certain mystifying events of nature—thunderstorms, sunrises, tides, and a variety of other awe-inspiring acts of nature. Primitive groups, being at the mercy of such events, created beliefs in the existence of agents that controlled these forces. So if it poured rain, the primitives believed that someone must be doing the pouring; if a boat was rocked in a storm, the primitives saw the rocking as caused by some agent. Thus, according to the naturistic approach, early peoples developed a belief in the existence of gods or divine agents that had to be worshiped, appeased, or manipulated to ward off evil, to gain advantage, or to secure the safety of the group.

Today neither animism nor naturism is considered a viable explanation for the existence of religion. The evolutionary hypothesis assumes generally that religion is the result of ignorance and that progression up the evolutionary trail will result in a lesser need for religion in society; this hypothesis clearly distorted the thinking of early sociologists of religion, even though they did contribute relevant material to the field. The difficulty with the evolutionary hypothesis, at least as used by earlier sociologists, is in its assumption of inevitable evolutionary progress. One of the fallacies of this perspective, as Demerath and Hammond (1969) have suggested, is that because primitive societies are simple, small in population, limited in geography, uncomplicated by politics and economics, and generally preliterate, drawing conclusions about contemporary religion in complex modern societies on the basis of religion in primitive societies can be misleading. Further, this hypothesis sees religion as withering away; clearly this has not happened, and explanations based upon such assumptions are obviously inadequate.

From these early anthropological explanations the social scientific study of religion moved on to more complex analyses. In the work of Emile Durkheim, sociological analysis moved from an intellectual approach to one emphasizing the functional aspects of religion.

Durkheim's Theory: Religion as Society Worship

The fullest and most productive attempt to explore religion in its most elementary forms was made by Emile Durkheim ([1897] 1947), whose theories we mentioned in Chapter 1. Durkheim went beyond a simple evolutionary hypothesis in his attempt to document themes that were important both to understanding primitive religion and also to understanding *all* religion. Durkheim discarded prior theories concerning religion, including both animism and naturism. He believed that these did not touch the most elementary forms of religious behavior and belief.

According to Durkheim, a sociological approach to understanding religion had to begin with the recognition of the interconnectedness of religion and society. He believed that this relationship would be highlighted in studies of religion in primitive societies since in industrial societies religious groups exhibit an autonomy from traditional culture not found in more primitive societies (Johnson, 1986:189).

As we learned from his definition in Chapter 1, for Durkheim religion has two essential characteristics: (1) it makes a distinction between the sacred and profane, and (2) it is a product of a church or group. Recall that from these elements Durkheim (1947:61) defined religion as "a unified system of belief and practices relative to sacred things, that is to say, things set apart and forbidden—beliefs and practices which unite into one single moral community called a Church all those who adhere to them." This characterization of religion led to a central question for Durkheim. How did it happen that human beings first came to make a distinction between the sacred and the profane and then form groups around such distinctions?

To answer this question, Durkheim studied the form of religion he considered to be the most primitive—totemism. He based his study on reports concerning the Arunta of Australia, a tribe that practiced this ritualistic belief. Totemism occurs in societies composed of clans united by real or fictitious kinship (Hartland, 1951) and is based on a ritual relationship with totems. A *totem* is an object that generally belongs to either the animal or vegetable world and gives its name to the clan. The totem provides more than a name; it is an emblem, a veritable coat of arms. Images of the totem are placed on the walls of houses, on the sides of canoes, on weapons, utensils, and even tombs. These totemic decorations are employed in the course of religious ceremonies as part of the liturgy, indicating the fundamentally religious character of the totem. In all of this Durkheim maintained that individuals were *formed by* society as opposed to the view that individuals *formed* society (Johnson, 1986:169). This latter view was implied in the thought of Herbert Spencer (1820–1903), a British sociologist who likened societal evolution to Darwinian concepts of human evolution.

The totem also serves as the basis for the distinction between the sacred and the profane. Totemic images are not the only things that become sacred because of their relationship to the totem; the species that correspond to the totem and the members of the clan adopting such a totem are also considered sacred. Thus, in totemism three classes of things are considered sacred: (1) the totem, (2) the animal or plant represented by this totem, and (3) members of the totemic clan. Since all of these are sacred, Durkheim found a clue to the real meaning of the sacred and the origin of beliefs in the sacred.

Such beliefs, according to Durkheim, are obviously of a religious nature since they imply the distinction between the sacred and the profane. However, they are also inseparable from the social organization called the *clan,* the simplest form of organization known. The religious character of the things sacred in totemism cannot be due to any special attributes of these things as these play no part in the distinction. It must come from some principle common to the totem, the people of the clan, or the corresponding plant or animal. From this, Durkheim concluded that totemism is a religion not of animals, people, or images, but of the anonymous and impersonal force found in each of these things.

This force or power is not definite or definable; it is power in the absolute sense. This makes clear how thoroughly the idea of an impersonal religious force enters into the meaning and spirit of Australian totemism. The totemic clan is addressed to a power spread through all things. This power is the original matter out of which every sort of being that religion consecrates was created. Thus, what we find at the origins of religious thought are not determined and distinctive objects and beings, but indefinite powers and anonymous forces.

But where do these indefinite powers and anonymous forces originate? The totem seems to be the symbol of *both* the sacred and the society. If so, is it because the sacred and the society are one? For Durkheim, the totemic principle *can be nothing other than the clan itself personified.* By analogy, our sense of patriotism, along with its symbols such as the flag and the American eagle, arouses this sense of power and anonymous forces within us. The energy and fanaticism associated with patriotic rallies and the celebration of national holidays are produced, in part, by embracing and interacting with the symbolic representations of the nation. Thus the fierce battles among Serbs, Croats, and Muslims in the former Yugoslavia are, at least in part, reaffirmation of the power of the totems or icons of their "nationhood." To attack the national totem, whatever it be, is blasphemy and is cause for righteous indignation and the declaration of a holy war against infidels who dare to profane the sacred.

Unquestionably, society has all that is necessary to arouse the sensation of the divine in our minds, because it is the source of authority and dependence for all of us. However, because it also has a nature peculiar to itself, it seems like something outside of us that demands our allegiance. When we yield to its orders, we do so not merely because it is strong enough to triumph, but primarily because we give it our respect.

We are thus brought to an understanding of how the totemic principle, and in general every religious force, comes to be thought of as outside the object in which it resides. It is because the *idea* of it is inspired by the group, projected outside of the consciousness of the individual, and objectified. For Durkheim, the primitives' religion was the expression in symbolic terms of their awareness of the social system upon which they were dependent for both the material and psychic necessities of life. In short, Durkheim indicated that we feel the presence of another world—the world of social forces—and that we give it concrete expression in religion.

Durkheim explained the necessity to objectify social forces by pointing to the needs of the clan; the clan needs a constant reminder of its value, which the totemic religion provides. Social life is made possible and continuous by this symbolism, which finds expression in ritual practices. Durkheim assumed that the unanimous sentiment of so many believers throughout history could not be purely illusory.

This reality, represented in many forms by many mythologies, is the universal and eternal expression of society itself. Thus, in Durkheim's view, religion can be seen as society worship.

Durkheim proclaimed that the more unified the collective beliefs and practices of a society, the more cohesive would be the society. Contrariwise, where collective beliefs are weak the cohesiveness of society will be seriously weak (Haritos and Glassman, 1991). Without this collective consensus the integration of society is seriously interrupted (Johnson, 1986:185ff).

Therefore, religion serves a vital need of every society—the uniting of the people in a common purpose. As Haritos and Glassman (1991) point out, the stronger the collective beliefs, and thus the more ingrained the *sacred*, the more cohesion there will be in the life of the society. Conversely, where the collective beliefs are weak (as Durkheim proposed they were in Protestant countries), societal cohesion will decline.

The Search for Causes and Functions

As evolutionary theories came to be seen as less useful in explaining religion, other students of religion began to use different approaches to religion. Freud envisioned religion as caused by a universal neurotic reaction while Marx saw religion as an attempt by the ruling class to control the masses.

Freud's Theory: Religion as a Universal Neurosis. Although obviously not basically sociological in nature, the theories of the Viennese neurologist Sigmund Freud (1856–1939) concerning the motivation for religious beliefs and behavior present an interesting example of the search for the causes of religion. Freud sought, by looking into the beginnings of human existence, some clue as to what continued to bring out the religious response in individuals and societies. He treated religion in a variety of ways, but basically he saw it as a sort of universal neurosis mainly resulting from the Oedipus complex, for religion seemed to him to be a mixture of love and dependence, respect and fear, and hostility and love. Freud then traced the religious drive to a biological heritage of crime and guilt, positing some great primal crime that took place in the childhood of the human race.

Freud (1930) also contended that the basis of human civilization is found in the individual's denial of instinctual desires. Religion, according to Freud, is a soporific that justifies acts of self-denial and provides meaning for the individual in the face of a demanding society. Although illusory, religion can play a part in protecting the individual, and society, from neuroses (Budd, 1973).

Marx's Theory: Religion as an Opiate.   The German political philosopher Karl Marx (1818–1883) was primarily interested in the dehumanizing effects of industrial capitalism. He was concerned with the process of change in society, feeling that equilibrium theories gave only a superficial analysis of the complexity of society in motion (Mayer, 1991:102). We cannot possibly do his ideas justice here and will attempt only to summarize briefly his main ideas on religion. As we noted in Chapter 1, he saw religion as part of the alienating effects of the capitalist mode of production. In fact, as D. Paul Johnson (1986:130–31) has written:

> The compensating and distorting function of ideology is most evident in Marx's analysis of religion. Marx argued that the traditional religious emphasis on a transcendental nonmaterial realm of hope for life after death in this realm helped divert people's attention from their physical sufferings and material hardship in this life....[R]eligious ideologies typically provide tacit support for the existing social, political and economic arrangements of society....In American society the traditional, widely accepted idea that our society has divine support is a similar source of political legitimacy. More generally, religious support for various norms that underlie the social order legitimate the status quo and motivate individuals to act in accordance with the requirements for maintaining the existing social order.

So Marx's explanation of religion was very much embedded in his complete analysis of industrial, capitalist society. As summarized by Winter (1977:35), the Marxian position is "(1) that God, as conceived by the bourgeoisie, is a metaphoric representation of the basic characteristics of the economic order; and (2) that belief in such a God helps one cope with the distresses or frustrations of life in such a society." So, according to Marx, religion placed a burden on humankind, but it was a burden that would be lifted when human beings were freed from the bonds of the capitalist economic system. Thus, to Marx, religion was dead or dying and deserved little intellectual attention. But as Scharf (1970:27) and Budd (1973:56–57) have pointed out, Marx's follower and colleague Friedrich Engels (1820–1895) spent considerable time and effort on attempts to correlate sectarian movements and radical social and political change.

Engels described early Christianity (sectarian in itself because it broke away from prevalent beliefs) as being like the ancient religions in reflecting the need of the oppressed, exploited, and struggling masses to free themselves from physical and economic bondage. Engels wrote (Marx and Engels, 1957:352–53) of numerous sects that clashed with the ruling classes over economic matters during the Middle Ages, when the poor again had to throw off the shackles of a Christianity turned oppressive. For example, he described how the Waldenses, a sect made up of the lower urban classes in southern France in the late twelfth century, condemned the accumulation of wealth by the Catholic Church and desired a return to early Christianity, how in the fifteenth century the Calixtines and the Taborites formed part of the Hussite Reformation movement in Bohemia and Moravia and called for the abolition of feudal oppression, and how the Lollards, widespread in England in the fourteenth century, followed John Wycliffe's reformist teachings and took part in a peasant insurrection culminating in Wat Tyler's Rebellion of 1381.

Engels also used other examples to point up the drama of the dialectic that takes place between different actors with different audiences at different stages of history. Martin Luther's Reformation, for example, produced a clash between Luther and Thomas Münzer (c. 1489–1525), a radical sectarian who claimed that the Reformation was only a "burgher reformation" because Luther, rather than continue with his early revolutionary zeal against the church, had sold out to the "burghers, the nobility and the princes" (Marx and Engels, 1957:105). Münzer became an "outright political agitator" (Marx and Engels, 1957:111) who called for the establishment of the Kingdom of God, the beginning of the prophesied millennium, and the overthrow of all existing authorities who would not join the effort to establish a classless society. In this case, according to Marx and Engels, Luther the reformer became part of the new establishment, defending it against the more radical Münzer.

For Engels, then, religious changes are prompted by a conflictual impetus lodged within an antagonistic class system. Engels's writings show that the poor are usually the ones most responsive to sectarian movements because the ruling class, and the belief systems of the ruling class, are often unresponsive to the needs of the poor. Thus, Engels's analysis suggests that the nobility attempts to keep the proletariat in place by feeding them the "opiate of the people" (religion). But when the religious opiate loses its potency, or when a new, more exciting, and more palatable drug is introduced, the religious fervor may erupt in a manner not in keeping with the needs of the nobility or the bourgeoisie, prompting the original suppliers to turn to outright oppression in an attempt to keep the users in line. As

Johnson (1986:131) remarks, "[R]eligious support for various norms that underlie the social order legitimate the status quo and motivate individuals to act in accordance with the requirements for maintaining the existing social order."

Neo-Marxism.   Many sociologists in the United States and elsewhere wanted to retain the theoretical principles of Marxism divorced from Soviet politics (Etzkowitz and Glassman, 1991:44). An important aspect of contemporary interpretations of social theory derives from the Frankfurt school, centering on the work of Jürgen Habermas. Now referred to as the *critical theory*, it is a synthesis of the theories of Marx with those of Freud and Weber. Within such a broad terminology, variant views coalesce. In general, these theorists continue the critique of capitalist production and the role which religion plays in it (Etzkowitz and Glassman, 1991).

MACRO THEORETICAL PERSPECTIVES ON RELIGION AND SOCIETY

What early theorists were actually looking for in their search for religion's primitive origins was some idea of what causes religious belief and practice (Yinger 1970:89). As we noted earlier, society today is so different from its beginnings in terms of population, environment, and social, economic, and political structure that it is nearly impossible to draw relevant conclusions about present-day religion on the basis of its primitive origins. Thus, modern theories are necessary to help us better understand the causes of religion in our own place and time. We will begin by exploring the two major theoretical perspectives that take a large-scale macro approach to society, functionalism, and conflict theory. Then we will discuss how religion can be seen as functional to the life of society in some ways while dysfunctional in others.

Functionalism and Conflict Theory

Functionalism and conflict theory seek to describe how religion actually works rather than illuminate its causes. These competing viewpoints are both rooted in earlier theories—functionalism in Durkheim's work and conflict theory in Marx's. We will summarize briefly these two theories and suggest how they apply to the study of religion in society before turning to a discussion of research that seems to support each of these two theories.

Functionalism.   As a theory of society, functionalism arose in anthropological thought to deal with *ethnocentrism,* which refers to the tendency to take for granted the rightness and superiority of one's own subculture or culture, seen in the views of early students who found the ways of traditional peoples incomprehensible and quickly dismissed them as primitive, naive, or simply wrong. Functionalism opened up the notion that in all societies the various features, mores, and ways of doing things are tied together in a functional whole that works toward the solution of society's various problems of adaptation, integration, tension management, and pattern maintenance. As Johnson (1986:385) summarizes it, functionalism is valuable in that it:

> ...draws attention to the needs and requirements of society, as opposed to individual needs. Some...might argue that the overall welfare of society is best served by attending to the welfare of all its citizens. Nevertheless participants in our...discussion would have to transcend individual concerns and problems in order to assess the state of society.

Most simply put, three basic principles underlie the functionalist view. First, any society has problems that must be solved if the society is to maintain itself. One of these problems is finding a way to pass on patterns of doing things to the next generation. Each society, then, must develop ways in which these traditions can be passed on and ways to enforce among the new members the traditional manner of doing things. Second, society is in a state of ongoing equilibrium; that is, society depends upon the somewhat precarious balance of a number of elements, all of which must maintain a degree of consistency lest the society be thrown out of balance. Third, each part of the society, seen as a system, makes a contribution to the solution of the problems; thus, each part is necessary to the maintenance of the equilibrium. In summary, then, functionalism views society as an interdependent and carefully balanced system of parts which are all aimed at the basic problem of societal survival.

Alexander (1991: 268–69) cites six aspects of functionalism in sociological analysis: (1) it provides an overall picture of the complex interrelation of societal elements; (2) it concentrates on the action involved in this interrelation, not only the structures which support it; (3) while concerned with integration, it recognizes deviance and social control as facts connected to this integration; (4) while recognizing the distinctions that remain between the parts of the social structure, it perceives the tension between these parts as inherent in social structure; (5) the theoretical position recognizes differentiation of institutions as a fundamental part of social processes; and (6) such theory implies the independence of other levels of sociological analysis.

Theorists from the functional perspective have summarized the function of religion in society in terms of its integrative aspects. That is, they have seen religion's chief function as its ability to achieve a successful melding of the individual members and groups of the society into a whole that can function effectively to solve basic problems and maintain the society. Thus, the functionalist view of religion emphasizes the way in which religion is used by the society to solve both group and individual problems.

Alexander (1991:270) notes that there has been a reconsideration of this approach which he calls *neofunctionalism*. This approach is a critique of some of the basic propositions of functionalism. While seeking to include elements of that theoretical perspective, it would still put the enlightenments of functional theory into an amalgamation with competing perspectives. Neofunctionalism recognizes the inadequacies of a single perspective.

Conflict Theory.   Conflict theory maintains that societal processes, rather than being in cooperative equilibrium, are dominated by conflictual power struggles. Conflict theorists warn that viewing elements of society (such as class systems) as necessary and inevitable places us in a narrow frame of reference from which to selectively perceive society. In some ways the conflict perspective is complementary to that of functionalism (Chalfant and LaBeff, 1991). From this perspective the reality of social life involves an intense struggle for power among various interest groups in society. Rather than emphasizing the balance of functionalism, this approach emphasizes conflict as a basic dynamic of social life.

Institutionalized procedures can and do collide with one another, as when religious groups prescribe certain behaviors contrary to the law of the land. When such collisions occur, power becomes of paramount importance in handling the conflict. For instance, the Amish, who do not heartily accept frills and modern inventions, have been forced by state law to install headlights and turn signals, powered by under-the-seat batteries, on their horse-drawn buggies (Kephart and Zellner, 1991). Amish parents were also convicted, in Wisconsin, for refusing to send their children to local schools. Even though on appeal the Amish were found to be in the right, they were, nevertheless, originally victimized by state laws that assumed the correctness of a formal, bureaucratic, and standardized educational system. Such antagonism between institutional arrangements and religious beliefs (in this case among religion, education, and government) has provided support for the conflict perspective.

Some theorists (known as *pluralists*) maintain that power, within the United States at least, is of a pluralistic nature—power is spread out among individuals who have a voice regarding the use of it. Others (known as *power theorists*) contend that there exists some sort of an elite—whether conspiratorial or not—that controls most societal operations. Regarding religion, the functionalists would tell us that it serves an integrative function while the power theorists would agree that this is the way religion has been *used*, and at the expense of those not in powerful societal positions. Through some societal con game, the powerful use religious values to keep those without power pacified. Dominant religions are thought to be conservative and even reactionary in emphasizing and maintaining the status quo, particularly the economic and political status quo. Boughey (1978:22–23) has articulated this position as follows:

> Institutionalized religion from this perspective is and always has been a counterrevolutionary force in human society. The demands and the struggles of the masses for concrete benefits, such as economic and social justice and freedom from domination by others, have traditionally been met with offers of "spiritual" rewards instead. You save your soul, and I'll invest my profits, say the elites through their religious spokesmen. Be patient, slave, you'll get justice in heaven. Blessed are the poor. Your sufferings under my heel are the expression of God's will, so take your complaints to the head office. You'll never get justice, so try bliss instead, you'll feel better.

From a conflict perspective, then, people have been co-opted, have allowed themselves to be co-opted by an "opiate of the people" (religion), and have developed a mistaken sense of their value as human beings, pliably accepting and passively experiencing their station in life ("The meek shall inherit the earth"). One must remember that this position is heavily laden with ideological biases and represents a particular theoretical stance. The claim that the proletariat is a passive group or that an elite is conspiratorial and self-seeking has given impetus to numerous arguments. On balance, both the pluralists *and* the power theorists can marshal supporting data and show elements of logical consistency in their arguments.

In summary, then, most scholars recognize that neither functionalism nor conflict theory is adequate as a grand theory of social arrangements nor as an explanation of individual or group behavior. However, both theoretical approaches are conceptually rich and provide basic points of departure for the study of social change and stability and, in our case, for the study of religion in society.

RELIGION'S FUNCTIONS AND DYSFUNCTIONS

Theories are only useful insofar as they help us understand real phenomena in our world. In this section we will focus attention on how theories can help us understand religious phenomena. Specifically, we will examine the functions and dysfunctions of religion, phenomena that can be understood with reference to functionalism and conflict theory. Functionalism leads us to expect that religion can have an integrating function in society; conflict theory leads us to expect that we can also find instances where religion acts as a source of conflict and breakdown, as a cause of dysfunction. We can in fact find instances of both, and we will look at some of these in this part of our description.

Six Basic Functions

O'Dea and Aviada (1983) have cited three specific conditions of life that find some answer in the religious institution: (1) the contingency of life—that is, the very conditional sense in which we live one moment and may be dead the next; (2) powerlessness, our inability to solve many problems; and (3) scarcity, the problem of allocating scarce resources in some fashion that is seen as just to the members of society. In expanding these ideas, O'Dea and Aviada have noted that religion can be seen as having the following six basic functions:

1. *Support, consolation, and reconciliation.* Because religion provides human society with a point of reference (that is, the divine or supernatural) that transcends the everyday world, it also provides individuals and groups with a sense of meaning in life. Thus, we can find support, consolation, and reconciliation for the events of our lives. For example, however lowly one's status might be, one can justify this status and the misery of this existence by reference to some heavenly reward that awaits. And, looking at the other side, those who have spent their lives accumulating goods may find deeper meaning in this as a sign of divine support or approval. Religion may also be used to justify tragedies and sorrowful happenings that befall us by "explaining" them. For example, a seemingly senseless occurrence, such as the death of a very young child, may be given some meaning if that child's parents believe they may see the child in another realm (cf. Palmer and Noble, 1986).
2. *New security and firmer identity.* Again, belief in a transcendent realm can lead to a feeling of security and a sense of worth. O'Dea and Aviada refer to this as the priestly function of religion and note that it

contributes to stability, order, and generally, the maintennace of the status quo. In short, having a reference point beyond the present life can give individuals and groups a sense that an order to life exists beyond what appears to them in the present.

3. *Sacralization of norms and values.* Religion tends to give an added emphasis or importance to the norms and values of society and thus helps to maintain their dominance over the individual or group. That is, social values and norms are given not only a legal sanction but also a divine one. In past times, going to war when required by society has been a social norm for young men. However, it has also taken on, particularly during the Second World War, religious overtones. That war was seen as sacred, one in which we were fighting for "God's will," and so to fail to fight was to "let God down." Thus religion reinforced the societal norm and few openly refused to take up arms against "God's enemies." Today some conservative religious views would support traditional views of the role of women. Citing Scripture, they would contend that feminism and women's liberation defy God's order of creation and should not be recognized.

4. *A prophetic function.* Religion can also perform a function contrary to the preceding one. It can provide standards or values against which existing norms can be critically examined and called into question. Several churches in our day have challenged traditional views. The concept of women as serfs of their husbands, based on Pauline references, has been loudly proclaimed by fundamentalist groups. Yet more liberal bodies have challenged this standard; they proclaim that in Christ there is no distinction between the sexes and that equality should be the prophetic goal of those who call themselves Christian.

5. *Identity functions.* Religion can also be seen as assisting the individual to establish identity. It provides the individual with an answer to the question, Who am I? Frequently the answer that is most meaningful to the individual is in terms of a religious group. One is a Catholic, a Presbyterian, or, even, an agnostic. In any of these cases, the individual is defined in reference to the religious group and finds identity in this relationship. For the Baptist, baptism (at about age twelve) signifies acceptance into the Kingdom; for Presbyterians the rite of infant Baptism bonds parents to their obligation to rear their children in the Christian tradition; for Orthodox Jews the Bar Mitzvah is a symbol of the cementing of the individual to the traditional faith.

6. *Facilitation of growth and maturation.* Finally, religion can be seen as related to the processes of growth and maturation of the individual. As individuals pass through the various age categories constructed by society, religion provides symbols and ceremonies that effectively mark off these new positions in society. Even in religious groups that do not practice infant baptism the dedication of children to the promise of Christ is a significant event.

Other Possible Functions

O'Dea and Aviada's listing does not exhaust all possibilities for the functions performed by religion. In one sense, as Jacobs (1971) has pointed out, we can simply look at religion as providing a general sense of morality and responsibility. He decries the fact that in the more or less secularized society of today much of our lives has a negative character—a defiance of authority, a contagious irresponsibility, a kind of moral delinquency, no longer restrained by religion or ethical faith. He sees these attitudes as threatening personal serenity and public order in many parts of the world. He points to the paradox of an increasingly secular order, particularly within individualized Protestantism, being led by a Christian morality based upon spiritualism. In short, religion may not be fulfilling as many critical functions as it possibly could.

One comfort that may be provided by religious belief and participation is physical comfort. Missions provide food, shelter, and clothing, as do collectivities such as the Salvation Army and other active religious agencies. One movement in our recent history demonstrates that comfort may come in quite physical forms. The Father Divine movement peaked in this country in the 1930s and early 1940s and still maintains a few followers. The movement was led by a charismatic black man who claimed to be God and admonished his followers to abstain from sexual behavior, drinking, smoking, and obscenity. Father Divine (1882–1965) was the leader of a religious movement centered on his personal leadership; he also established an employment network and chains of hotels in the Harlem section of New York City and elsewhere. There he prepared elaborate feasts for "true believers." During the Depression years, for example, a typical "communion banquet" was described as follows (Kephart and Zellner, 1991:185–86):

> And what a banquet it is! A dozen different vegetables, roast beef, fried chicken, baked ham, roast turkey and duck, meat loaf, steak, cold cuts, spare ribs, liver and bacon, four different kinds of bread, mixed salad with a choice of dressing, celery and olives, coffee, tea, and milk, and a variety of desserts, including layer cake, pie, pudding, fresh fruit, and great mounds of ice cream.

The practical comforts, or functions, of religious participation are many times intertwined with other functions. As Kephart and Zellner (1991:202) have pointed out, these are real-life considerations and influence numerous people regarding religious participation.

Things were so bad for black Americans in the 1930s that a feeling of alienation often prevailed.... More than any other leader of his time, it was Father Divine who fought against the spread of alienation, and he was a superb practitioner. He understood the masses. He could talk to them. He could engender feelings of self-respect, and he could play the role of God. Most important, he never lost sight of two basics: food and jobs. These were the bedrock. As long as he was helmsman, his followers would have ample food at little or no cost. And—through his employment service or within his own economic establishment—they would have jobs.

Numerous other studies have provided evidence of the interplay of the social structure, religion, religious institutions, and the individual. Throughout the past fifty years, some religion has been seen as functioning to provide a substitute for the primary ties broken down by increased urbanization and industrialization. As early as 1940, Holt suggested that Holiness sects, which prescribe extremely ascetic norms based loosely on the Book of Leviticus, developed in response to the cultural disorganization produced by the migration of rural southerners to the industrial centers. Such religious movements, he claimed, provided a new form of community for the displaced and disoriented. Likewise, Frazier (1974) has seen such groups as functioning to give rural southern blacks a replacement for their ritual communities, thus providing escape from the anonymity of the city. Flora (1973) studied the relationship of social dislocation and Pentacostalism, a fundamentalist religion characterized by the practice of speaking in tongues and other expressions of the baptism of the Holy Spirit. Noting that social dislocation gives rise to mass movements, she attempted to relate individual histories of social dislocation to adherence to religious movements. Based on data from respondents from Palmira in the Cauca Valley of Colombia, she found that individuals of low socioeconomic status who had experienced personal social dislocation in terms of migration and employment were more likely to be Pentecostals than their fellows without similar experiences.

In another study, Photiadis and Schnabel (1977) examined some of the reasons that religious fundamentalism persists in Appalachia more strongly than in the rest of the United States. Their major hypothesis was that it forms a buffer for rural and low-income residents of Appalachia who feel alienated because of social change that has taken place in that region in the last few decades. Their findings showed that dimensions of religiosity that may reduce anxiety tend to be associated not only with lower socioeconomic status but also with alienation in terms of bewilderment and confusion. The authors contend (1977:40) that religion provides meaning for those of low socioeconomic status and enables them to avoid "the anomie of dislocation and alienation from self."

The attraction of fundamentalism, especially when aligned with Pentacostalism, for disadvantaged segments of the population is reaffirmed in studies of recent Hispanic immigrants to the United States. In what Greeley (1988) calls an unprecedented failure of the Catholic Church in America, Hispanic immigrants are defecting to Protestant sects in large numbers. Unlike their European counterparts of the nineteenth century, the Hispanics are finding various means to overcome the alienation of their immigrant status by turning to the Pentecostal Protestant faiths (Christiano, 1991).

The functions of religion mentioned thus far are basically adaptive and integrative, serving both the needs of the individual and those of the larger social structure. But we must remember that religious beliefs and participation may also have negative consequences for individuals and groups. Put differently, religion is a two-sided coin having both a functional and a dysfunctional side. For each of the integrative or support functions of religion cited in popular theories, it is possible to find corresponding dysfunctions of religious ideology and practice.

Dysfunctions at the Individual Level

All individuals undergo a process of socialization—learning the norms (folkways, mores, laws) of their culture. The socialization process involves conditioning, which may or may not be intentionally carried out by socialization agents (parents, teachers, peers). Conditioning teaches not only sensorimotor behavior (Do not stick your hand in the fire) but also ideas of appropriate and inappropriate conduct toward others (It is not nice to kick Mom's shins). Numerous social and developmental psychologists have immersed themselves in the study of the socialization process and have articulated concepts with which to better understand this phenomenon. Freud spoke of the id, ego, and superego; Charles H. Cooley of the looking-glass self; George H. Mead of the generalized other; and Jean Piaget of various developmental stages.* Implicit in these studies are notions of the internalization of psychological mechanisms that guide individuals' behavior in "appropriate" directions. Pleasure, shame, fear, guilt, and

---

*The theories of Cooley and Mead are discussed later in this chapter in the Symbolic Interaction section.

approval are vehicles for keeping the individual on the "right track" psychologically and socially. Adherence to the norms promotes "healthy" personal development and makes for conformity, which is, of course, necessary for a "healthy" society. Such are the bases of the conservative nature of society.

But does internalizing the proscriptions and prescriptions of society always have beneficial effects? Are there dysfunctional elements to socialization in general, and religious socialization in particular? The answer is, maybe! Psychopathologists have long chronicled the damaging impact of unrelieved guilt and feelings of unworthiness present in the psyches of those who have violated certain religious proscriptions. Religious beliefs may "drive a person crazy" if that person cannot resolve concomitant dilemmas and contradictions. Striking out against what one has been taught may also be dangerous to the individual, especially if it encompasses an emotional trauma in the process.

Religiously induced psychic stress, then, is a possible dysfunction of religion. Chesen (1972), in his book *Religion May Be Hazardous to Your Health,* has addressed the relationship between emotional instability and authoritarian religious practices, and Rokeach (1979:173) has commented that "people with formal religious affiliation are more anxious. Believers, compared with nonbelievers, complain more often of working under great tension, sleeping fitfully, and similar symptoms." Additionally, novels, plays, and movies with the theme of religiously induced psychic stress abound. If "religious toilet training" is not conducted properly, then individuals may develop neuroses and psychoses associated in some way with this socialization.

Dealing with guilt, indecision, and frustration produced by religious doctrine has actually become big business in American society today, as a quick glance through bookstores will attest. Competing alternatives for "curing" oneself abound. The extension of the twelve-steps principle of Alcoholics Anonymous to almost every human condition (with some advocates of "codependency" as illness claiming that 95 percent of the population is "sick") and as a means of recovery bears more similarity to an implicit religion than to a "medical" condition (Chalfant, 1992).

Numerous biographies, autobiographies, and literary classics could be cited as continuing examples of the frustrations and crises of identity provoked by religious beliefs, but the following striking comments by an anthropologist will serve to illustrate our point. Miles Richardson (1975:517–19), in referring (somewhat allegorically) to his association with the Southern Baptists, has written:

You would think that a person with an intense religious upbringing would become someone compatible with that background.… One of my brothers was a preacher, and my sister married one. But it didn't work out that way with me. Actually, that is not too uncommon either. I suspect that for every minister the Southern Baptists have produced, they have turned out five atheists. Pound for pound, the Baptists have probably put more souls in hell than any other religion. And I'm one of them. It was in my early adolescence that I discovered I was evil. Because I was evil, I was going to die.… I tried hard not to be evil. I did not swear, I did not smoke, and certainly I did not drink.… I went to church twice on Sunday plus attending the morning Sunday School and the evening Training Union. I tried to think pure thoughts…and here I was, looking at girls with lust on my mind and even stealing glances at the big-bosomed preacher's wife. How could I be saved?… "Look to Jesus," the preacher said. But Jesus was a Levi-Strauss paradox. Jesus-Christ-God was perfect femininity. He was kind, sweet, and full of love.… Jesus-Christ-God was perfect masculinity.… He was victor over death and his blood was full of power. He taught gentleness and peace; he sent people to burn forever in hell. How could I touch such a figure?… I have never tried anything harder nor wanted anything more. But I did not succeed, and then I knew I hated God.… [Anthropology] was going to free me from the view of man groveling before a God that, on the one hand was sweetly sissy and on the other remotely brutal, from a religion that makes the gentle touching between a man and a woman evil.… My freedom from the things that nearly destroyed me (and that continue to haunt me) would come from studying them, from wrestling with them in order to expose their secret. At that point, just short of stomping on them and destroying them, for some reason my private battle stops. Today, I have no love for the Southern Baptists, but I can almost say "Billy Graham" without sneering.

This narrative only scratches the surface of the ways in which frustration and indecision caused by religious socialization may haunt a person. Richardson himself may not consider his turmoil as totally dysfunctional—such may be the price one pays for intellectual growth—but these problems can result in debilitating consequences for individuals.

On a group level, an extreme, but revealing, example is distress portrayed in the account of the experiences of boys in Texas "confined" to a Baptist home for troubled boys (Draper, 1992). Evidence revealed that boys placed in the mercies of the missionaries were chained to their beds at night and placed in stocks for long periods of time. One boy was handcuffed to a chair with his feet in stocks. And, perhaps worst of all, a tape recorder played (incessantly) the sermons of one of the righteous Baptist ministers.

Indirectly, strict internalization of religious mores may limit the individual's receptivity to new ideas. Religious doctrine may promote hostility to critical, open-minded thought; but, to again indicate the contextual nature of the argument, such intellectual conservatism may also be functional for the individual in that it provides *some* interpretation of reality. Individuals may, nevertheless, find themselves in situations in which their conservatism becomes dysfunctional. Feelings of the superiority (or inferiority) of one's religious self, and the prejudices that result, may place individuals in hostile circumstances that may be psychologically and even physically dangerous. Martyrs may benefit from their deaths in otherworldly salvation and in the foreknowledge of martyrdom, but torture and death can hardly be seen as functional for the individual organism.

Even following religious prescriptions may be harmful to the biological well-being of the individual. Overzealous fasting may have deleterious effects on the body as well as on the mental health of the individual. Religious pilgrimages, if over rough terrain at unfamiliar altitudes, may prove hazardous to life and limb. Gazing into the sun at Medjugore, Yugoslavia, in search of a vision of the Virgin Mary, may produce temporary blindness and/or permanent damage to the retina. Certain beliefs in the inefficacy of modern medicine may allow diseases to spread and wounds to fester and may provide parents with justification for withholding medical attention from their children. And among certain congregations (Gerrard 1968:11, 23), scriptural interpretations propel certain adherents to handle poisonous snakes:

> The serpent-handling ritual was inaugurated between 1900 and 1910, probably by George Went Hensley.... He died in Florida at age 70—of snakebite. To date, the press has reported about 20 such deaths among the serpent-handlers.... For their part, the serpent-handlers say the Lord causes a snake to strike in order to refute scoffers' claims that the snakes' fangs have been pulled. They see each recovery from snakebite as a miracle wrought by the Lord.

While these examples may border on the extreme, they do serve to make our point—in certain circumstances religious beliefs and practices can be dysfunctional to the individual as a biological and psychological organism. These dysfunctions may be more or less group-induced and may be suffered singularly or in conjunction with other group members. In some cases, the group itself, as a sociological entity, may engage in beliefs and practices that are dysfunctional. This brings us to the next level of analysis—the group level.

Dysfunctions at the Group Level

The size of groups we will consider in our discussion here ranges across the continuum from small (dyads, cliques, church groups, congregations) to large (religious bodies, religious organizations, societies); the groups at the large end of the scale might even be considered to be national or international in scope. To further set the stage for our brief discussion of how dysfunctions and conflict may emerge at the group level, let us consider the term *religiocentrism*. This term is related to a common word used in sociological literature, *ethnocentrism*. Similarly, we might refer to feelings of rightness and superiority resulting from religious affiliation as religiocentrism.

Religiocentrism inhibits the ability of a society to achieve adaptation, integration, and goal attainment. For example, concentration on traditional religious interpretations of the role of women can deter the development of a realistic appraisal of women's role in our modern society. This has been particularly true when issues of male dominance, the right to abortion, and general family issues are involved (Conover and Gray, 1983; Huber and Spitze, 1983). As a result, a large portion of the religious community has fought against feminist concerns, particularly the Equal Rights Amendment.

On the community level, numerous instances of religious squabbles, splits, and schisms have had real consequences for participants caught up in the conflict. Bitterness, gossip, and hostility caused by religiocentrism have been known to divide communities. Families, social clubs, and even neighborhood schools have been victimized as a result of religiocentric values.

These conflicts may arise within a basically homogeneous religious group or between different religious groups such as Protestants, Catholics, Jews, or Muslims. Or such conflict may arise from generalizing religious views to political or economic issues. The continuing controversy over prayer in public schools is one example. While the net effect of such conflict may be a merger or synthesis, it is nevertheless at some point social conflict that may impede social adjustment.

Religiocentric views may hamper a group's viability in the world. For instance, some millenarian groups, such as the Jehovah's Witnesses, would have ceased to exist when the world did not end when expected, had they not modified their original religious views (Zygmunt, 1970). Some groups have been so steadfastly religiocentric as to damage their very survival. The United Society of Believers in Christ's Second Appearing—or Shakers—have held to their beliefs, including the prohibition of marriage and sexual relations, until there remained only nine members, seven women and two men at Sabbath-day Lake, Maine (Kephart and Zellner, 1991:154–55). Even though a revival of Shakerdom could possibly occur, the present membership of is a far cry from the all-time high membership of sixty-four thousand (Kephart and Zellner, 1991) claimed for the group. Thus the religiocentric views of the Shakers, involving celibacy, economic communism, and separation from the world, have drastically influenced their viability as a religious group.

Religious groups are sometimes confronted with problems of adaptation that do not immediately threaten their survival but that may eventually require them to change their views or else face decline. For example, even though the system of courtship and marriage practiced by the Amish may continue for some time as successful, Kephart and Zellner (1991:26) have described an interesting facet of the religious proscriptions surrounding an Amish marriage:

> Amish parents forbid their young people to date the "English" (non-Amish). As a matter of fact, the only permissible dating is (a) within the district or (b) between districts that have full fellowship with one another. Endogamy among the Amish, therefore, does serve to limit the number of eligible mates. In outlying districts, this limitation may present some real problems.

One other dysfunction of religion on the group level should be pointed out—that of conflict, bloodshed, and warfare prompted by religiocentrism. Such conflict may occur at both the national and international levels; history is full of examples. Religious persecution and attempts at religious genocide still linger in the memories of many Americans and citizens of other countries. More recently, several hostage situations and international acts of terrorism have been marked by religious motives, and hot spots such as Lebanon, where religious conflict between Christians and Muslims, and among the Sunni, Shi'ite, and Druze Muslim factions is fierce, remind us of the potentially destructive effects of religiocentrism. And in northern India Muslims and Hindus fight against one another from modern barbed wire and sandbagged bunkers (Gargan, 1991).

It is, however, difficult to determine causality in cases of religious violence. As John Fulton (1991:2) notes concerning the situation in Ireland, religion and political loyalties are very mixed with one another:

> [T]he root cause of communal violence in Ireland is the opposition of two groupings each with their own material and spiritual interests and now living in overlapping geographical boundaries of power, the Protestant-

loyalist and the Catholic-nationalist alliance. To be a nationalist in Ireland practically means to be a Catholic or former Catholic, and to be a loyalist means to be an Ulster Protestant. These identities are rooted in two opposing cultures for which religious belief and attitude are incorporated. Churches too are important, though religion plays a role far beyond its church identity.... As a constituent ideology of group dominance, religion underlies the structure of the two state powers in Ireland. It is not the principal, direct contributor to violence in contemporary Ireland, though it was also never quite such in the past. But because it forms a principal, now strong and now weak, constituent of the two antagonistic ideologies, religion enters into the existing antagonisms from which open violence stems. Consequently, religion in the concrete church form it takes on in Ireland bears significant direct responsibility for social division and indirect responsibility for violence.

With such a caveat noted, we can conceptualize religiocentrism as being dysfunctional to the degree that it promotes needless violence, intolerance, and hostility toward others. When religious differences serve as justifications for conflict, they are dysfunctional facets of social life. This, again, must be interpreted in context. Judging holy wars, or other attempts at religious genocide, to be functional or dysfunctional depends upon one's perspective and level of analysis. Still, we hope we have shown that there *are* different perspectives and that religious values and behaviors *can* be interpreted as functional *as well as* dysfunctional.

THE MICRO PERSPECTIVE

We now turn to theories that focus more on small groups, the micro level of analysis. Principally we will look at symbolic interactionism and phenomenology.

Symbolic Interaction

Symbolic interactionism is a major school of sociological thought that arose early in this century based in part on the social psychology of Charles H. Cooley (1864–1929) and George H. Mead (1863–1931). Essentially, these theorists believed that mind and self arise in experience and are constructed in a process of social interaction. They concerned themselves with social interaction at the primary level of intimate personal communication and not at the level of large-scale social structures and social classes, as did Marx and Engels.

As Chalfant and LaBeff (1991:15–16) put it:

Symbolic interactionists delight in observing and accounting for the rich texture of everyday life. They are interested in how fashion, clothes, and hairstyle are used as symbols of communication about the self. They are interested in how close friends keep secrets from one another or in the way a stripper maintains a sense of self-worth in the face of strong social disapproval.

Similarly, they are interested in how people come to define the meaning of religious symbols and gestures and how they interact with one another in this process.

Cooley (1902) advanced the notion of a "looking-glass self" that one develops based on one's reflection in interaction with others. For Cooley, the self-concept does not unfold according to some innate biological pattern, but rather as a result of one's experiences with others and one's imaginings of other's ideas of oneself. Implicit in Cooley's theory is that *significant others* have an impact on our self-concept, and also that our social self has many facets corresponding to the feedback we get from members of our important reference groups. Thus, one implication of this theory is that religion may provide a reference group for us, and we may have a religious self along with a work self, family self, school self, and so on.

Mead (1934) contributed to our understanding of human behavior by developing the concept of the *generalized other*. Mead believed that many of our actions are guided by the awareness we have of others' values and their expectations of us. So based on Mead's theory, we can speculate that religion can be an important part of the generalized other that we form in our minds, and can thus help us to develop a concept of self by applying the teachings of our religion to our actions. We internalize religious beliefs as a result of our interaction with others in our religion, and these beliefs serve as a guide for us in social behavior.

William I. Thomas (1863–1947), a sociologist and a colleague of Mead's, proposed (1937) that the way we define a situation determines how we act in it, and that definitions of situations are learned and passed from one generation to the next. For Thomas, moral codes and religious beliefs are produced by "successive definitions of the situation" (Stryker, 1980:31–32). Additionally, the W. I. Thomas theorem (Thomas and Thomas, 1928) states that if people define situations as real, they are real in their consequences. It follows from this that if a religious group considers its beliefs to be factual, they interpret situations and events on the basis of those beliefs, and thus the beliefs are real in their consequences. The subjective nature of interpretation can also be seen in religious symbolism. We respond to a cross in a certain way because we have learned to define it as a religious symbol and have assigned it meaning based on that definition. As Karp and Yoels (1993:39) have pointed out, "To Christians, a crucifix has meaning because it represents (or better, re-presents) a historical event, the crucifixion of Christ, which they have designated as a divine event. Whether a crucifix is made out of gold, iron, or wood is irrelevant to Christians, who define it as a holy object and respond to it reverently."

Rothman (1991) interprets Blumer's (1969) three basic premises of symbolic interactionism. The first premise deals with the fact that the nature of a thing is embedded in the meaning given to it. Meaning emerges from the group's definition. Second, Blumer sees meanings as the result of social interaction. What an object or symbol means to people is the product of interaction. Finally, we must also understand the ways in which the meanings of things are handled. People do choose between meanings and how to respond to them. The crucifix for Roman Catholics is a continual reminder of the sacrifice of Jesus which brings redemption; for the Southern Baptists it is the empty cross which proclaims Christ's victory over death. To the Orthodox church the icons are true representations which continually remind the faithful of the teachings of the Church (Chalfant, 1992); for the Pentecostalists the *glossolalia* (speaking in tongues) communicates the meaning of the Holy Spirit's continual presence in the world (Zygmunt, 1970).

So, in summary, symbolic interactionism tells us that religion provides a reference group for us that helps us define ourselves, and specifically our religious self; that out of religious and other teachings we form an idea of a generalized other against which we measure our social conduct; and that religious beliefs help us define a situation and thus determine how to interpret it and how to act in it. This theoretical approach can help us understand a number of religious phenomena. For example, it can help us understand Bibby's (1978) finding that church members' interaction with others who share the same beliefs and who socialize their offspring to do likewise are more important in the recent growth of conservative churches than such factors as the church's ability to provide an ultimate answer or the church's seriousness that requires its members to make a personal commitment.

Symbolic interactionism can also help us understand how religious persons come to see adverse circumstances as God's will and as a test of the strength of one's commitment to the church's religious principles. It can help us see prayer as a dialogue between the person and that person's internalized conception of God (similar to Freud's superego). It can help us see the need to belong to a church as a need to be accepted as a member of a reference group whereby one can maintain a positive self-image and gain the acceptance of one's significant others. Symbolic interactionism is also a useful way to understand the diversity of religious belief systems. This diversity occurs because of different definitions of the religious situation, and thus is evidence of the myriad ways in which persons interpret and pass on to others religious doctrine and religious norms. By the same token, it is a useful way to understand how religious in-groups form as a consequence of definitions and how hostility toward those who do not share a group's definition of a situation may occur as another consequence. And it allows for changes in religious belief, as it sees our formation of self as ongoing and based on the changing circumstances of social interaction.

A recent development within symbolic interaction focuses a slightly different light on self-formation and the changing circumstances of social interaction. The recent development of the sociology of emotions (cf. Palmer, 1991) provides a fertile arena for the study of religious behavior. Kemper (1987:265) contends that there are four primary emotions (fear, anger, depression, and satisfaction), and that secondary emotions such as guilt, shame, gratitude, love, and nostalgia are grafted onto the primary emotions through the process of socialization. Hochschild (1979, 1990) sharpened the sociological focus on emotions by her work on *feeling rules*. Feeling rules are those rules, standards, or norms about the appropriateness of certain feelings in particular settings. When one feels, where one feels, and what one feels are often situationally produced according to the changing circumstances of social interaction. Holy days, feast days, fasting days, periods of pilgrimage, religious calendars, and seasonable activities demonstrate that we temporally program certain feelings. The fact that there are holy places and that people report emotional catharses at these places (chapels, shrines, places of miracles, places of religious revival, pilgrimage points, etc.) show that feeling rules are at work.

The fact that emotional states are produced by definitions of the situation weds the study of all emotions, and particularly religious emotions, to the subdiscipline of symbolic interaction. Since all theoretical approaches to the study of religion involve the human being as a common denominator, and since human beings are emotional beings, the sociology of emotions offers much to symbolic interaction. Such a perspective allows symbolic interactionists to refine their abilities to study seemingly bizarre religious expressions and articulate the context of feeling rules, emotion work, and emotional culture

(Gordon, 1990; Kemper, 1990) to the untrained observer in such a way as to make the behavior "make sense." Receiving or being visited by the Holy Spirit, glossolalia, religiously induced trances, baptismal spasms, tears of joy, tears of grief, penitential pain or sorrow, acts of contrition, conversion hysteria (individual and collective), and various feelings of exaltation may be inexplicable to outsiders who are uninitiated in the believer's emotional culture. As we will see in Chapter 3, becoming religious involves emotion work and certain patterns of religious behavior depend upon the "rules" of feeling religious.

The symbolic interactionist contention that interacting persons create their own reality, religious or otherwise, brings us to another modern theoretical approach. In some ways, as we will see, this approach, called *phenomenology*, is similar to symbolic interaction.

Phenomenology

Phenomenology—the study of how human consciousness develops—derives from philosophy (Husserl, 1931) and has been interpreted in a variety of ways by sociologists (Thevenaz, 1962; Heap and Roth, 1978). Basically it posits that humans try to make sense of phenomena and it studies how we do so. This theoretical approach is akin to symbolic interactionism in that it recognizes the importance of introspection, reflectivity, and the interpretation of events—in essence, the bestowal of meanings upon phenomena by humans. It is most interested in studying how humans answer questions such as, Who am I? What is the nature of the universe? and How am I to conceive of and relate to God?

As suggested by Orleans (1991:170) the essence of the phenomenological approach is that:

> ...one might approach the situation as though one were from another culture, or even another world. How could such a person interpret the object we have called a coffee table? Perhaps the table would be viewed as a receptacle for items which lack all apparent use. Perhaps, after bumping into it, it would be viewed as an object dangerous to life and limb, particularly limb.

Peter Berger has articulated the phenomenological approach to religion in *The Sacred Canopy*. Berger (1967:28) calls religion "the audacious attempt to conceive of the entire universe as being humanly significant." According to Berger, through learning language and being socialized, the individual internalizes knowledge that has been generated by society, thus learning to live an ordered and meaningful life by structuring consciousness according to the laws (or *nomos*) of the parent society. Berger (1967:25) points out that "whenever the socially established nomos attains the quality of being taken for granted, there occurs a merging of its meanings with what are considered to be the fundamental meanings inherent in the universe." Thus, the entire universe comes to be seen as meaningful, and from this bestowal of significance, religion—"the human enterprise by which a sacred cosmos is established"—is born. Because separation from the meaning provided by the nomos would cause chaos and loss of a person's "sense of reality and identity," individuals act to shield themselves from the meaninglessness inherent in such a separation by being guided by what Berger (1967:47) calls *plausibility structures.* These are social structures which are "taken for granted and within which successive generations of individuals are socialized in such a way that this world will be *real to them.*" The reality of the Christian world depends upon such a plausibility structure, and "when this plausibility structure loses its intactness or continuity, the Christian world begins to totter and its reality ceases to impose itself as self-evident truth. The firmer the plausibility structure is, the firmer will be the world that is 'based' upon it," writes Berger (1967:47).

As pointed out by Scimecca (1979), both Berger and another phenomenologist, Ernest Becker (1973, 1975), take a position that involves the active, phenomenological *creation* of meaning through dialectical relationships between culture and the individual. So in summary, the phenomenological approach to religion sees it as a social structure for creating meaning in interaction with others and in the face of our fear of anomie and our recognition of the inevitability of death.

SUMMARY

In this chapter we have focused upon theoretical approaches to a sociological study of religion. Early sociological theories of religion were strongly influenced by the popular Darwinian theory of evolution, and thus they tended to try to explain religion by piecing together the primitive origins from which it had evolved. The evolutionary hypothesis of animism suggested that belief in spirits originated in experiences that primitive peoples could not explain; naturism conjectured that belief in gods or divine agents came about as a result of attempts by primitive peoples to gain some control over natural events. These theories are no longer considered viable explanations of religion, as sociologists have come to realize that generalizing from the situation of primitive peoples to our own situation can be misleading at best, particularly since the predicted withering away of religion has not happened.

Durkheim and Freud also looked to the childhood of the human race to formulate their theories of religion. From Durkheim's study of totemic religion he concluded that religion is a concrete expression of the world of social forces that we feel, so that, at root, religion is society worship. Freud postulated that religion is the result of a primal Oedipal crime, and that religion can justify acts of self-denial and play a part in protecting the individual from neuroses.

Modern theorists of religion in society have abandoned the search for religion's origins in primitive times and have sought instead to explain its causes and operation in our own place and time. Marx and Engels saw religion as part of the alienating effects of the capitalist mode of production and as a way for the ruling class to keep the proletariat oppressed.

Functionalism views society as a carefully balanced system of parts all aimed at solving basic problems of survival; according to the functionalists religion plays an integrating role. Conflict theory, on the other hand, maintains that societal processes are dominated by conflictual power struggles and sees religion as a source of conflict and a tool of a powerful elite. By using these two theoretical approaches, we can demonstrate that under certain conditions religion functions to aid the individual's adjustment to a socially constructed world and helps society maintain itself as a more or less integrated system. We can also demonstrate that religion is dysfunctional, under certain circumstances, for both the individual and for society.

Symbolic interactionism, which developed in part from the social psychology of Cooley and Mead, focuses on the way we develop a self-concept in social interaction at the level of intimate communication. It sees religion as providing a reference group for our development of a religious self, a generalized other from which we internalize rules of social conduct, and a way for us to define situations so that we know how to act. Viewing religion from the microtheoretical perspective, symbolic interactionists regard religion as the result of societally constructed meanings based on shared understandings of symbols. The sociology of emotions provides an extra dimension to symbolic interactionism by demonstrating how our feelings are connected to social structures; ergo, emotions, while often thought of as phenomena of the individual, are possibly the truest form of "social" forces. Thus religion provides a reference group that helps us define ourselves in terms of a generalized other against which we measure our social conduct and religious beliefs.

Finally, phenomenology conceptualizes religion as the structurally created meanings by which we face our sense of anomie and the inevitability of death. All these theoretical approaches to the study of religion in society can be seen as complementary, and taken together can provide us with a fuller sociological understanding of religion.

PART TWO

The Social Organization of Religion

3.

Becoming and Being Religious: Socialization and Religious Behavior

How did you come to be religious—or not religious, for that matter? How do people come to hold the religious values they have? These questions get different answers, depending on where they are asked and of whom. In some areas of the United States, it is almost assumed that you will be religious, at least to the extent of identifying with a particular religious group. In one southwestern city, for example, a family's religious affiliation is routinely printed in the city directory along with other items of personal information. Being religious is simply part of being a member of the community, despite the dominance of a "born again" tradition in the area.

Answers to the questions posed above depend on the religious orientation of the individual and the particular religious group involved. Members of small conservative or fundamentalist groups, for example, generally insist that becoming religious is a matter of a dramatic conversion experience and that only through an intense personal and emotional experience can an individual be "saved." For such Christian groups, conversion is the result of being born again by "receiving the Holy Spirit." On the other hand, members of large, middle-class groups are more inclined to see religious affiliation as a series of natural steps in the process of growing up. In these groups the members simply grow up as a Christian—never knowing they were anything else, as Horace Bushnell suggested (see Fowlkes, 1988:128).

Neither perspective gives us a total picture. Becoming religious is seldom the thundering experience of being grasped by the Spirit, nor is it simply the inevitable and automatic progress of the young into the religion of their parents. Research on religious and moral development provides conflicting findings about the actual process (see Oser and Reich, 1990; Hyde, 1990). However we conceptualize the process, potential converts do undergo some period of instruction (usually both formal and informal)—learning by word, observation, and experimentation with ritual, the ideas, and practices of their faith. In this chapter we will look first at that period of instruction and what it means.

SOCIALIZATION AND RELIGION

When sociologists examine the process of becoming religious, the key concept is *socialization* (see Finney, 1978; Hyde, 1990; Chalfant and LaBeff, 1991). Long and Hadden (1983:5) note: "[S]ocialization is the process of creating and incorporating new members of a group from a pool of nonmembers, carried out by members and their allies." To be religious, in a sociological sense, is to internalize the norms, values, beliefs and behavioral expectations of the particular religious group. Without such intense learning, smooth and efficient social interaction could not go on, a social fact as true for religious groups as it is for other aspects of society (Osmer and Gmunder, 1988).

A distinction is made between two types of socialization: primary and secondary. Primary socialization occurs during childhood as one is becoming a participating member of society. Significant others during this period, principally parents, impose definitions of reality which the child internalizes; the roles and attitudes of these others become the child's world. In this process the religious orientation of parents is the most important factor in the child's orientation toward religion (Hunsberger and Brown, 1984).

Secondary socialization takes place when the institutional, generalized world, with its roles and expectations, influences the individual and is internalized. Thus we come into contact with formal learning which is lifelong and may involve a series of affiliations and disaffiliations (Richardson, 1984: 108). Through such religious socialization, then, the individual forms a religious identity. It generally proceeds without much conscious notice, although it is constantly in the process of change as we mature.

At a time, for some, there comes a moment we call *conversion*. Sociologically it can be seen as a time of *resocialization*, a period when previous socializations are discarded for those newly learned. As we shall see later in this chapter, even a conversion experience must be viewed as the result of the internalization of the perspective of some significant other.

In our eagerness to make the sociological assertion that our individual lives are strongly affected by the group, we should not make the mistake of seeing the interaction as a one-way street. As you read this chapter, remember that the structures of society, even though they may come to have great influence over the individual, originate in the activity and interactions of individuals. And, although we can describe religious socialization as a phenomenon brought about by external agents, the individual plays an equally important part in the meaning he or she attaches to the private, emotional side of religious life and in the differing degrees of susceptibility to religious socialization that he or she exhibits at different stages of the life cycle. Far from being an automaton directed by society, the individual takes a very active part, through questioning and testing beliefs, in the development of a religious faith (Ozorak, 1989).

AGENTS OF RELIGIOUS SOCIALIZATION

Agents of religious socialization are all of the means—persons, groups, media, institutions—by which the individual is influenced to accept the values and rites of a particular religion. In reality, any member or group in society may be a socializing agent, intentionally or not. Generally, however, our concern is with those agents that provide important and purposeful social learning about religion (Hyde, 1990). The more intimate the relationship between the socializing agent and the person being socialized, the more enduring is that which is learned.

Hence, it follows that the family is the most effective socializing agent and has the longest lasting effects on our religious *persona*. Still, socialization experienced in the family during childhood is not the only influence on religious development. People experience a sequence of different statuses as they move through the life cycle. The demands of our variant role sets, as well as the results of both social and geographical mobility, may call for some type of resocialization. Thus both the peer group and the religious organization become important as agents of socialization. In this section of the chapter we will discuss the three most significant agents (see Erickson, 1992).

The Family.   The influence of the family pervades every aspect of our lives, from the day we are born until we die. No other group has the lasting impact of the family on religion, as well as on all aspects of our lives. Hyde (1990) refers to it as *the* primary influence and a number of studies bear out this contention. For example, Bahr and Chadwick (1985) compared religiosity in "Middletown" (Muncie, Indiana) in the 1920s and the 1970s. They found little change over this fifty-year period and suggest that the continuing influence of religion in the city can largely be attributed to the closely intertwined strength of family ties and religious belief. Other researchers (e.g., Grasmick, Patterson, and Bird, 1990) point to the strength of family structure in fundamentalist, patriarchal families and suggest that this assists the family in "holding" their children in their faith. Finally, Mosely and Brockenbrough (1988) contend that the family's level of religious activity is most important in the relative development of faith in younger children.

The importance of the family in the process of becoming religious can be seen in the many traditional rituals focusing on the home—the formal religious ceremonies involving family life, the practices of parents in the home setting, and, in some cases, special family ceremonies.

Jewish faith provides an example of the role of the family in traditional rituals having their focus in the home rather than in the synagogue or the church. One of the holiest of all times in the Jewish faith is the Passover season. Central to this is the seder meal, a meal reenacting the events of the first Passover in Egypt when, the Jewish people believe, Yahweh (God) delivered the Hebrew people from Egyptian captivity. Although for some the meal takes place in the synagogue or temple, this is a poor substitute for the home meal: The *seder* best takes place in the heart of the family. There, in a dialogue between the youngest child and the father of the house, the events and symbols of that first Passover are recited. Clearly, in this ritual the family is engaged in teaching or socializing the children into the basic tenets of the faith. No corresponding Christian practices are so focused in the home, although the practice of home devotions or of Christmas services in many homes serves the same purpose. Certainly religious groups—Catholic or Protestant, liberal or conservative—continually mount campaigns aimed at increasing such family-based expressions of religious faith as a testimony to their perception of the importance of such acts.

Many of the formal religious ceremonies attempt to tie the young person to the religious community through the family. Infant baptism, with its attendant responsibility for the parents and, in some communions the godparents, ties the family into the religious training of the child in religion. The implications of infant baptism are so important that many of those congregations that do not practice the rite have instituted "dedication" ceremonies. These ceremonies perform the same function in encouraging parents to undertake responsibility for passing on religious beliefs to their children. Confirmation, First Communion, and other practices that vary from group to group also involve the family formally in such training. It is significant that even in the "atheistic" former East Germany a ceremony, *Jugendweihe*, was instituted to mark this point of passage in the life of the young—and continues even in the reunited Germany as an important milestone for the young (Beckley, Chalfant, and Johnson, 1994).

Other rituals of the religious community take place with some kind of family reference. Weddings as well as funerals guide the family into a situation where its actions reinforce religious socialization. Scarcely any stage in human maturation is neglected in the procession of religious rituals. In such events the family reaffirms its religious beliefs and values.

The extent to which the family effectively forms the religious orientation of its members is dependent on the level of family integration. Families with considerable integration are more likely to produce strong individual religiosity (Michalet, 1990). In a sense, however, the pattern is reciprocal: Highly religious families tend to have the strongest family bonds (Bahr and Chadwick, 1985).

The influence of parental religious activity on that of both male and female adolescents is most strongly influenced by the religiosity of the father. Only paternal religious activity was significantly related to participation in religious activities by teenage offspring. The greater the father's involvement in religion, but not necessarily the mother's, the more likely it is that adolescents will remain religiously active (Kieren and Munro, 1987). This effect is strongest in families where paternal authority is high (Grasmick, Patterson, and Bird, 1990).

What is learned in early family life is never totally lost, but other socializing agents assert an increasing influence on the religious orientation of the individual, even though family does remain a dominant influence. Erickson (1992) notes that investigators give a crucial place to the religiosity of the social networks of adolescents in determining continuing activity (see also Benson et al., 1989). Erickson (1992) proposes that while all three agents of religious socialization play a part in adolescents' religiosity, the combined effect of religious education and peer values plays an increasingly important part in the development of religious values.

The effect of the family on religious development in an individual's middle years is largely that of support. The extent to which belief and commitment are maintained is related to how other members of the family practice religion. As old age sets in, the family may no longer be present in an effective sense, but rather remains in an internalized set of beliefs and values. The aged do experience a diminished social contact (Christiansen, 1978) and are most frequently disengaged from their families (Bernholz, 1960). Using a deprivation model for religiosity, Johnson and Mullins (1989) attempted to understand the relationship between loneliness and religiosity among the elderly. Their research showed that social involvement in religious programs led to lower levels of loneliness. In fact, religious participation was more important than family and other friendship relationships.

The Religious Organization.   Although the family is clearly the most important agent of religious socialization, it is certainly not the only influence. All religious groups seek to foster, emphasize, and initiate the internalization process, conveying the institutionalized roles and attitudes of the particular faith. Like all organizations, church programs have a hidden agenda—teaching the values and behaviors in which they seek to envelop their members (Johnstone, 1992). The development of friendships, for example, forges a strong link between the individual and the organization (Cornwall, 1987). Many activities of the congregation, such as potluck suppers and other social events, are aimed at building such links. However, congregations need to remember that there is danger when ties among older members make newcomers feel unwelcome (Olson, 1989).

Like all groups, religious ones attempt to enforce their norms of behavior. Individual religiosity is simply the consequence of the extent to which the group norms are internalized by the individual. In fact, the product of such interaction is a most important factor in the acquisition of a *particular* faith. Once acquired, that faith is best maintained when the individual is more or less isolated from other religious ideas and groups that might challenge it (see Ammerman, 1987, 1991).

In some religious organizations, the attempt at socialization is broadened to include the whole educational experience for the young through parochial schools. Greeley and Gockel (1971) discussed the impact of parochial education on Catholics; they measured the extent to which the religious faith of those attending parochial schools was strengthened as well as the extent of their continuing participation in the church's rites. They found that parochial schools were only effective when the family was active in religion. In 1966, Johnstone studied

Lutheran parochial education in St. Louis and Detroit, and found a significant association between such education and the tendency to continue to attend church schools and to become involved in a variety of church-related organizations.

Most studies of the effect of parochial education on religiosity have emphasized the fact that the family's involvement in religion is really the key issue in the effect of church-related education (White, 1985; Ridder, 1985). The rapid growth of "Christian Academies" or conservative Protestant schools has yet to be measured, although Minder (1985) has shown that students whose undergraduate education was entirely in Adventist schools were more likely to continue in that denomination. As Ammerman (1991) notes, such schools have been founded on the principle that public schools are hostile to their children's faith. "Christian" schools seek to envelop their students in the fundamentalist ideology.

The literature on the aged and religious organizations is extensive. Atchley (1991) cites the religious organization as the principal one in which the elderly are involved. Research, however, provides few clear conclusions. On the one hand, some (such as Blazer and Palmore, 1975, 1976) conclude that the elderly are very active in religious groups, with as high as 90 percent reported to be participating members. Yet other investigators (e.g., Mindel and Vaughan, 1978) have reported that the elderly tend to be disengaged from the programs of the group.

These contradictory findings may be resolved if we distinguish between types of religiosity. While the aged may remain members of their religious group, their activity is decreased by the limitations aging imposes. Thus the aged may find religion more important (Payne, 1980) but tend to express their faith in private devotional activity more than in organizational participation (Finney and Lee, 1977). As Hadden and Swann (1981) comment, the elderly may be more likely to find the "electronic church" sufficient to satisfy their religious needs.

In a review of research on religiosity and aging, Cox and Hammond (1988) identify several common patterns of church attendance related to age: belief in God, life satisfaction, and personal adjustment. Church attendance hits a low point between ages 18 and 24, remains relatively stable between 25 and 54, rises slightly after 54, then drops slightly after 80. A majority of older age groups believe that religion is important in one's life. Also those persons who attend church report greater life satisfaction and are better adjusted than those who do not. Church becomes a focal point of social integration and activity for the elderly, providing them with a sense of community and well-being.

Ainlay, Singleton, and Swigert (1992) also examined the relationship between aging and participation in religious activities. Focusing on changes in formal participation for older people, they found that participation in formal rites lessens in later life. However, it is not a matter of being "put off" by the group, but of the limitations imposed by declining health and mobility. Thus, for these authors health is an important mediating variable in the religious participation of older people:

> Not only are people's desires to participate in the life of the church unaffected by aging per se, hence raising questions about the assumptions of disengagement theory, but also we find evidence that people with lower rates of attendance at religious services are precisely the ones who wish they could be more active in the church thus signalling the importance they attach to such activity (p. 185).

The Peer Group. The peer group takes on special importance during adolescence. At that time in the life cycle, peer pressures are probably more influential in determining religious participation than at any other time. Peer-group acceptance is one way by which youth loosen the bonds of parental restriction. Acceptance by peers becomes a goal for the adolescent transitory. Thus, as Hernandez and Dudley (1990) note, religious commitment among the respondents is strongly related to the quality of primary group relationships and the level of assimilation with the peer culture. Of course, the nature of the peer group's religious commitment in such cases helps determine the adolescent's religious beliefs (Stark, 1984).

In his book on religious development, Hyde (1990) cites several studies which emphasize the importance of peer groups. A study of New York Catholic youth, for example, found that, despite the influence of parents, attitudes of peers had the strongest impact on religious practice (Pazhaypurakal, 1989). As Kane (1988) notes, the adolescent years are crucial for spiritual growth. Thus, religious groups seek to create a sense of belonging and friendship in their youth programs. It has been found (Willits and Crider, 1989) that regular attendance of one's peers is the best predictor of continued participation in religious rites.

Although we tend to think of peer groups as primarily a matter of one's adolescence, such is not the case. The business associates we have and the friendships we form in the middle years of life are also important factors in shaping religious beliefs and values. Young adults entering the business world, for example, have been known to change religious preference to conform to the image they feel their employers favor. Thus, young adults from working-class backgrounds who obtain college degrees and enter the world of business administration may seek out more mainstream religious groups than the sectlike groups of their childhood.

The effect of peer groups on individuals in their late middle years is less well known. We can assume that at this stage peer groups reinforce already internalized beliefs and values in general. Just as we tend to seek out friends who share our political beliefs, we also seek out those whose religious values and beliefs are consonant with our own. On the other hand, Hadaway and Roof (1979) found that individuals who have been nonreligious most of their lives tend eventually to identify with a religious organization. They reported this to be particularly true in the case of individuals moving from urban to more rural areas where religious participation is the norm for their new friends and associates. The authors refer to this as a switching toward consistency in which the newcomers adopt the norms of new peer groups. In contrast, Welch and Baltzell (1984) have suggested, on the basis of an analysis of geographical mobility and affiliation in three states, that such mobility may actually disrupt previous ties with religious groups where individuals maintain friendship ties with those in the places from which they moved.

Research on the development or maintenance of faith in the last stages of life has been thoroughly studied. Stark (1968) has reported evidence suggesting that cohort or peer influence affects piety among the aged. Returning to our comment concerning the religious organization and the aged, the effects of peers seems to mainly apply to frequency of religious participation. Those elderly persons who have friends and associates with whom they can participate in religious activities are more likely to participate themselves.

Regardless of the exact stage at which a person feels "significantly religious," one common mechanism, especially among some groups, is the rather problematic and increasingly controversial concept called *conversion*. The fact that such "turn arounds" (Roberts, 1990) do occur, and are increasingly emphasized, is an aspect of becoming and being religious with which we must now deal.

CONVERSION

As indicated, becoming religious is generally a subtle part of one's socialization, acknowledged generally only through formal rites of passage. But some individuals appear to experience a comparatively sudden change in religious orientation. When this happens, we refer to the experience as a conversion.

There are several opinions about what actually constitutes conversion. There are also questions as to the source and degree of change involved in a true conversion. Some insist that we frequently misuse the term *conversion* because of the stereotype we have of the sudden and dramatic way in which conversion "ought" to take place. Conversion as a dramatic, transforming experience within Christian belief is exemplified by the incident where Saul is thrown into the dust of the Damascus road by a brilliant light from heaven and through Christ's words comes to know the truth of God. Such dramatic instances, in which one's total life and ways of knowing are changed, may be described by the converted one as happening in a flash, or as being a gift from heaven, a newfound touch of grace, or as an immediate insight into the nature of existence.

Religious events that come out of the blue and radically change the total direction of an individual's life *do* occur. But the extent to which they occur and the efficacy of the transformation is still questioned by many who study the process systematically, although systematic study in itself poses problems. If conversion is "a dramatic form of religious internalization" beyond empirical investigation (Johnstone, 1992:73), then it would seem to be beyond the realm of systematic sociological study. Still, exploring the social psychology of conversion is enlightening, even though it may fall short of total illumination.

Tom Robbins (1988) provides us with a very thorough examination of the phenomenon of conversion. He again calls our attention to the difference between conversion and recruitment, as well as between conversion and commitment. *Recruitment* means being convinced to join a group while commitment deals with degree of involvement. *Conversion,* according to Robbins, should be reserved for a "radical transformation of identity or orientation" (Robbins, 1988:64). It is a change in an individual's general "universe of discourse" with one that was previously not relevant to the life of that individual (Snow and Machalek, 1983, 1984).

Lofland and Sknovd (1981, 1983) suggest that there are actually five "conversion motifs" which differ with regard to the social pressure involved in the conversion, the time the conversion experience lasted, the emotion involved, the content of the experience, and the relationship between belief and participation.

They label the five types of conversion: intellectual, mystical, experimental, and revivalistic. In the intellectual conversion the individual investigates a new religion on his or her own and comes to accept it through reading and other media. Let's take the example of those who converted from Campus Crusade to Russian Orthodoxy. (Campus Crusade is an evangelical college-oriented group unaffiliated with any specific denomination.) These students began their conversion by reading and studying the beliefs and observing the rites of the Orthodox faith (Gillquist, 1989).

The mystical type of conversion is mainly subjective, and little social pressure is involved. Although society's effect cannot be negated, the decision is basically made on the basis of personal experience. Experimental conversions occur when a person begins to take part in a group's life without being fully committed to it—Lofland and Sknovd refer to them as "converts in progress." A number of those involved with the Moonies really come under this category (Barker, 1981). Conversions of the affectional motif are strong on the creation of interpersonal bonds that tie people to a group. Lofland's description of the Divine Precepts movement (1966) stresses the group's effort to create such bonds.*

Finally, revivalistic conversion involves managed arousals of ecstatic feelings in which crowd behavior has an effect on the potential convert's feelings. The revival service conversions clearly follow this type.

Johnstone (1992) contends that conversion experiences are related to social-psychological factors. He lists three such variables:

1. The group context (older group members lead younger ones to expect to experience conversion).
2. The age factor (conversion is primarily an adolescent occurrence and may be prompted by several factors attendant to adolescence, such as nascent sexuality and the often corresponding themes of sin, guilt, anxiety, tension, and, tellingly, forgiveness).
3. Stages or progressions from one level to the other (a socialization process may be at work whereby potential converts proceed gradually to the status of the converted by, for example, associating with others in anticipation of learning group secrets or expecting to further explore religious beliefs with already committed group members).

These findings lead some to consider conversion a part of becoming religious and, as such, to be subject to the same scrutiny as any type of socialization. They seem to contradict the idea that conversion is a radical, thundering transformation. In fact, some researchers have suggested that we can look at the process of conversion as a matter of

---

*The Divine Precepts movement is the fictitious name used by Lofland (1966) and Lofland and Stark (1965) for the Unification Church, more popularly known as the Moonies.

resocialization—that is, an instance of socialization in which the individual unlearns old ways while learning new ones. Thus we can see conversion as a dual process of learning the beliefs, values, and attitudes of a new group while unlearning or altering those of previous religious reference groups or those obtained in a nonreligious milieu. Let us look more closely at this idea of conversion as a type of socialization, by focusing on how people are converted to specific religious groups. We will then speculate about the role of the convert in conversion.

Conversion and Prior Socialization

In reality, aspects of previous socialization generally lead a prospective convert to an interest in new values and beliefs of particular kinds, and circumstances in the immediate social situation of the individual trigger the new declaration of faith. This is what Lofland (1966) and Lofland and Stark (1965) reported concerning their study of the Divine Precepts movement, that is, the Unification Church or the Moonies (see also Barker, 1984; Robbins, 1988).

They noted, first, that converts to this radically different view of religious faith were predisposed by factors in previous socialization to some kind of change in religious direction. Three things seemed to characterize their situation prior to their conversion. First, they tended to be persons who for some time had felt frustrated, deprived, and under tension and strain. Second, they were individuals who were oriented to look for religious solutions to felt problems. Third, they tended to define themselves as religious seekers.

But this predisposition was not sufficient to bring about the conversion; something in the immediate situation had to trigger acceptance of the new religious perspective. Again, Lofland and Stark (1965) suggested some of the situational factors operating in the lives of the converts to the Divine Precepts movement. First, these converts had reached what they felt to be a turning point. Their old ways of dealing with their problems were no longer workable. At this time they made contact with members of the *DPs* (as Lofland and Stark referred to the movement). Second, feelings of liking, or friendship bonds, developed among members of the DPs and the preconvert. Third, as these new friendships developed, older ties with those not among the DPs weakened, or at least were neutralized. Fourth, the interaction with members of the DPs became more and more intensive until the new recruit was able to make the final, full commitment and convert, becoming an active member and recruiter for the DPs in his or her own right.

In a classic statement, Lofland (1978) modified his account of the steps in this resocialization process. Feeling that the terminology in the older study was not particularly incisive, he has suggested five new terms for the stages in the process: picking up, hooking, encapsulating, loving, and committing. Following his work, we can describe each of these stages in the route to conversion as they were manifested in this one movement.

The term *picking up* refers to that time in the life of the preconvert when contact was made with the movement. DPs spend much time trying to make just such pick-ups through a variety of means, as Lofland (1978:11) indicates: "Indeed, DPs spent time almost daily giving hitchhikers rides and approaching young men and women in public places. Display card tables for front organizations were regularly staffed in the public areas of many campuses as a way to pick up people." According to Lofland, when contact was made, it was usually followed by an invitation to some social gathering or to a DP lecture.

Hooking was the stage wherein the prospective convert was brought more under the influence of the DP movement with elaborate promotion tactics. Lofland reports one instance of such hooking where the prospect was invited to a dinner and on arrival found a large crowd of very personable, outgoing young people. The prospect was assigned a "buddy" and then (Lofland 1978:13) reports that "various people stopped by [his] table, introduced themselves and chatted. They seemed to be circulating like sorority members during rush." The DP members were taught to find out all that they could about prospective members and pass it on. They were told to "write down their hooks so that the whole center knows in follow up" (Lofland 1978:13). The prospects were made to feel that they were being served and were the full center of attention.

The next step is referred to as *encapsulating,* and involved enveloping the prospect with both ideology and "affective bonds" during a workshop or retreat when outside interference was minimal. Lofland suggests that this total immersion was accomplished along basically five lines: absorption of attention by scheduling every moment of the prospect's time; focus on collective activities; limitation of conversation and other inputs to the preconvert to matters of the DP movement; creation of fatigue in the prospect; and presentation in lectures and discussions of the beliefs of the DPs.

Loving was the movement of the prospect into a feeling of being loved and, as Lofland puts it, a desire to "melt together" into the embrace of the total group. One precept recalled the following (Lofland 1977:311):

Whenever I would raise a theological question, the leaders of my group would look very impressed and pleased, seem to agree with me, and then give me a large dose of love—and perhaps say something about unity and God's love being most important. I would have an odd, disjointed sort of feeling—not knowing if I'd really been heard or not, yet aware of the attentive look and the smiling approval. My intellectual objective had been undercut by means of emotional seduction. Unfortunately, I succumbed to this many times without learning what was happening.

The final stage in the process (that point that popularly would be seen as the conversion) is referred to as *committing*. Gradually, the convert was drawn more and more into the enveloping atmosphere of the movement. He or she at this stage expressed commitment by doing such work as street peddling and became a full-time, believing participant in the DPs.

Of course, to suggest that the description of conversion to the Moonies is one that fits every conversion would be misleading. According to Lofland, the basic fact is that most conversion experiences do not represent a complete turning-around so much as they do an alteration of the perspective from which an individual already tends to view the world. Travasiano (1969) suggests, in fact, that we need to make a distinction between conversion as a total change in perspective, and what he refers to as *alternation*. The latter is what happens when individuals do not change the general orientation through which they approach problem solving, but simply change a particular solution within that general orientation.

Greil and Rudy (1984a, 1984b) found difficulties in applying Lofland's patterns to other religious groups. In examining ten case studies, they concluded that each group can be taken as the point of analysis. The individuals who join any particular group do *not* form a homogeneous whole. The appearance of consensus is really a product of pressure for the individual to "construct" testimonies in line with the ideology of the group.

The one point in Lofland's pattern which they found to be supported was the idea that converts are people who have a religious problem-solving orientation or a predisposition to finding religious answers. They stress the importance of "boundary maintenance" by the group to keep the convert believing the particular religious answer found in the group.

Alternation appears to have been operating in conversions of young people to the Jesus movement, which was at the height of its popularity in the sixties, although it continues to live in such organizations as the Grapevine movement (Perrin and Mauss, 1991).

Richardson and Stewart (1978) found that the majority of members of the Jesus movement were, in fact, "returning fundamentalists." That is, they tended to be individuals with conservative religious backgrounds who had drifted into drug use and a hippie lifestyle. Similarly, Bibby and Brinkerhoff (1974), in their study of evangelism and conversion in fundamentalist churches in a metropolitan area, concluded that most of these conversions were the result of a good deal of predisposition and may have represented alternation more than actual resocialization to a totally new worldview. They found that the majority of the converts were actually already insiders, that is, they were the children or other family members of people who were already inside the fundamentalist, evangelical religion.

The Role of the Convert

The *world-saver model* proposed by Lofland and Stark (1965) views the convert as a person who is essentially static or passive, whose thinking is influenced by and whose life is taken over by the conversion process. However, this model may be too simplistic and places the convert in too passive a stance (Richardson and Stewart, 1978). Even Lofland (1978:22) has modified the notions involved in the theory by stating:

> Stepping back yet further, I have since come to appreciate that the world-saver model embodies a thoroughly "passive" actor—a conception of humans as "neutral medium through which social forces operate," as Blumer (1969) has so often put it…. It is with such a realization that I have lately encouraged students of conversion to turn the process on its head and to scrutinize how people go about converting themselves.

Thus, the convert may be more than putty in the hands of a molding society and may actually become an active participant in seeking out religious conversion. Even questioning traditional religious values and vaguely looking around for new ideas may constitute "seekership" or "creative bumbling" (Straus, 1976), which eventually allows one to push oneself into a newly found ideology or religious belief system.

Richardson, Stewart, and Simmonds (1979:256–74) have further focused on the role of the convert in conversion by suggesting in their general model of conversion processes the importance of the individual's (1) prior socialization (which provides general orientations and perspectives); (2) perceived personal difficulties (felt tensions of a general or specific nature); (3) ways of resolving perceived difficulties (which differ according to a host of biographical and cultural features and which may prompt "conversion careers" or "trajectories" because of continuous problem solving); (4) loss of meaningful ties with society; and (5) the pulling effect of intensified interaction with persons already belonging to the group. More recently, Richardson (1984) has asked us to seriously consider changing our ideas about the nature of conversion to more fully embrace its activist and volitional aspects. His analysis suggests that some people try out in serial fashion a number of the myriad lifestyles and beliefs that our pluralistic society makes possible. If, as he asserts (1984:103), "an ideological and behavioral mobility is typical as individuals move through many different groups," the study of conversion may ultimately come to mean the study of conversions experienced by persons during their life spans.

Roberts (1990:101–22) treats conversion and commitment along the same lines as previous scholars but suggests that additional attention be given to cognitive structuralism. This approach proposes that intellectual development is the product of a sequence of stages (apart from cultural influences), from concrete to more abstract thought processes. Moral development becomes increasingly complex, and each stage prompts further questions. At different developmental stages people are more proposed to seek out particular groups which fit their "stage specific" values.

We will return to these ideas in Chapters 8 and 9 of this book, which deal with the New Religious Movements. For now, however, we turn to a discussion of being religious. We will look at the variability of religiosity as well as the impact of secularization.

PATTERNS OF RELIGIOUS BEHAVIOR

Different people express their religious faith in quite different ways. Consider your friends and coworkers. Some may carry a Bible with them at all times, others may cross themselves before an important exam, and still others whom you know to be regular churchgoers may give no outward sign of this aspect of their lives.

A discussion of religion will bring forth a variety of doctrinal beliefs as well as a difference in the intensity with which these are held. In such a discussion you may note that some seem well informed while holding only moderate views, while others less well versed in the tenets of their faith may be quite definite about their belief in them. Some of your friends or coworkers may practice dietary restrictions related to their religion, such as not eating pork if they are Jewish or not drinking coffee or Coke if they are Mormons. Others, no matter how religious they may be, probably feel no religious restrictions on their diet, including their use of alcoholic beverages.

No single way of behaving or level of intensity of belief characterizes religious persons. Religion is not an either/or proposition. We must look at religious behavior, beliefs, and attitudes as varying along a continuum, or perhaps several such continua. Indeed, religiosity has many different facets, and many contend that religious behavior is multidimensional. In this chapter we will explore some of the dimensions of religiosity, and seek to understand the different ways in which individuals express their commitment to a religious path.

Dimensions of Religiosity

To understand general patterns of religiosity, we can start by asking whether distinctive categories of religious behaviors, beliefs, and attitudes exist. Sociologists have, in fact, concerned themselves with this question for some time. In *The Elementary Forms of Religious Life* Durkheim (1947) simply distinguished between two types of religious behavior—beliefs and rites. Wach (1944) added a social or fellowship aspect to being religious. These distinctions provide one way of comparing patterns of religious behavior, based on the activities involved in believing, ritual, or social life.

Another way of comparing patterns of religious behavior is by looking at how people practice their faith in terms of attending church and other observances expected of members. Fichter (1951, 1954) made an early attempt at delineating categories. On the basis of a study of Roman Catholic parishioners in the South, he suggested that members could be categorized as nuclear, modal, marginal, or dormant, according to their degree of participation. Nuclear Catholics are very active in parish life and attend mass every week. Modal Catholics meet the minimum requirements of participation in their parish, and live their religion in a moderate way. Marginal Catholics, though they do consider themselves members of the Catholic Church, do not meet such standards as attending mass or participating in confession, nor do they send their children to Catholic schools. Dormant Catholics are those who were born Catholic and baptized in the church and who might ask for a priest when death approaches, but otherwise are not members of any parish in a formal sense. This distinction between types of members helps us understand religiosity, but considers only one dimension.

The difficulty of finding any single measuring stick or continuum along which all religious behavior can be arrayed leads to the proposition that religiosity has a number of different dimensions. Further, these dimensions do not, in fact, correlate with one another in any discernible way. That is, people who behave as if they are religious in some respects may not be at all religious in others. For example, individuals who regularly attend Sunday morning worship services may, in reality, be using their attendance to boost a political career or an insurance business, and may not know much about the principles of their particular faith or have any commitment to it.

The search for elements in religious life has been extensively explored. For example, Furnham (1985) found five dimensions of religiosity, a finding supported by much of the exploration in the study of religion. DeJong, Faulkner, and Warland (1976) found similar results among German and American students, and identification with six dimensions of religiosity that were closely tied to the Glock/Stark pattern. Religious knowledge and social consequences appeared as separate dimensions while religious practice was a second-order factor. Beliefs, especially, were a residual category. In other words, consequential aspects of religiosity were not integral.

One of the earlier attempts to outline the dimensions of religiosity was made by Glock (1959), who suggested that religiosity could be divided into four separate aspects: the experiential, the ritualistic, the ideological, and the consequential. For Glock, these referred, respectively, to religious feelings, practices, beliefs, and works, and included the major ways in which church members could be said to be religious. Glock later (1962) added a fifth dimension—the intellectual—to include dealing with information about one's religion.

Fukuyama (1961) reformulated and elaborated on Glock's proposal. He suggested that religion can be described in terms of at least four major dimensions: the cognitive, the cultic, the creedal, and the devotional, which roughly parallel Glock's categories. The cultic dimension has to do with the practice of faith, the creedal with what a person believes, the cognitive with what a person knows about religion, and the devotional with feelings and experience.

To this day, the most often-used statement of the dimensions of religiosity is found in Glock and Stark's book *Religion and Society in Tension* (1965) and is based on Glock's five dimensions. We'll consider each of these dimensions in turn—the experiential, the ideological, the ritualistic, the intellectual, and the consequential.

The *experiential dimension* concerns the direct experience individuals have of the sacred, and the emotions accompanying that experience. This dimension of religiosity includes all the feelings, perceptions, and sensations experienced by an individual or defined by a religious group as involving some communication with the sacred.

If a person has ever felt that God was somehow especially present with him or her, we would say that the individual has had a religious experience. Members of charismatic groups who feel filled with the Holy Spirit and begin to utter strange words or sounds (known as *speaking in tongues*) certainly are having a deep religious experience (Poloma, 1982). But the experiential dimension not only involves such extreme cases of persons experiencing a sense of standing outside themselves—it also includes quite mild feelings of awareness of the sacred.

Glock and Stark have attempted to describe this experiential dimension in terms of increasing levels of intensity. The least intense kind of religious experience is what they term the *confirming experience*. This is the most general kind of religious feeling, the one most frequently reported by individuals—a sudden feeling, knowing, or intuition that one's beliefs are real. Two subtypes of such experience exist: a generalized sense of sacredness and a specific awareness of the presence of divinity.

The next level of intensity in religious experience is termed *responsive*, and includes times when the individual feels touched by the sacred in one of three ways: salvational, miraculous, and sanctioning. When individuals feel that they have been chosen by the divine, they can be said to be having a salvational experience. *Miraculous experiences* are those in which individuals perceive divine intervention as when one believes that healing has occurred because of faith. *Sanctioning experiences* are those that are perceived as divine retribution for some transgression. Many conservative groups stress the possibility of such negative sanctions, producing in their members the feeling that God will "get" them if they do not obey religious injunctions. For instance, fundamentalists have been found to believe that if they drink alcohol and then drive, they will be punished in some fashion (Peek, Chalfant, and Milton, 1979).

The third level of intensity is designated as ecstatic; it includes all of the less intense experiences plus a deepening of awareness of the divine. One example of *ecstatic experience,* noted above, is the speaking in tongues (glossolalia) common to Pentecostal groups and the current charismatic movement. Another example is what has been called *holy dancing,* in which people move in rapid dancelike ways as they feel the Holy Spirit directing them.

The most intense religious experience is one in which a *revelation* comes to the individual. The sacred, in this case, not only responds to the individual but also provides a confidential message or special knowledge. Frequently such messages, as reported by those who have had revelations, involve the day and the time of the end of the world. Obviously, not all revelations prove to be true.

The *ideological dimension* involves the individual's beliefs. Every religious group sets forth some range of beliefs to which its followers are expected to adhere. Sociologists generally measure this dimension, in terms of standard church doctrine, along a continuum from liberal to orthodox beliefs, with those professing the greatest number of traditional or orthodox beliefs being seen as having higher religiosity. To gauge the orthodoxy of a Protestant individual's beliefs, for example, sociologists might ask questions concerning belief in the virgin birth, the literal truth of Scripture, and the necessity of belief in Christ as savior. Questions asked of Catholics or Jews would vary to include elements of doctrine for those groups.

One obvious shortcoming here is that nonorthodox individuals are frequently classified as low in belief, even though they may have strong (albeit liberal) religious beliefs. Another problem is that belief may be professed but not practiced—one may profess to believe a number of things but place little importance on them in daily life—and practice of belief is seldom measured. Most Americans profess a belief in God, but what this means in terms of how they live their lives is difficult to gauge.

The *ritualistic dimension* deals with those activities performed in the name of religious faith or belief. We sometimes think of ritual as meaning acts of worship involving elaborate ceremonies, costumes, and practices. Here, however ritual means the routines or acts through which individuals attempt to come in contact with the sacred, strengthen their faith, call down the favor of the divine, and so forth. In practice, it is the dimension of religiosity most frequently measured, as it includes such easily quantified matters as religious affiliation, church attendance, participation in church activities, and practice of prayer and family devotionals.

A great variety of activities are included in the ritualistic dimension. Prayer, fasting, carrying a religious charm or Bible, and the like are all included. We can think of the Episcopalian attending a Christmas Eve mass, the Roman Catholic going to confession, the member of a charismatic group speaking in tongues, the Southern Baptist coming forward to the altar to be saved, or the Presbyterian sitting quietly in the church pew as the bread and wine of Holy Communion are passed by the elders. We can think also of the family saying grace at the dinner table, the baseball player crossing himself as he comes up to bat, the business person attending a prayer breakfast. In short, anything we do in the name of religion is part of our ritual.

Ritualistic behavior is not always consistent. Dukes and Johnson (1984) found that among Mormons at least, those who are not active participants in church activities tend to engage in private prayer fairly often, while those who are regular church attendants are less likely to practice private prayer.

The *intellectual dimension* concerns the individual's level of knowledge about Scriptures and other basic matters of religious faith. This dimension is clearly related to the ideological dimension, but here the concern is with the actual knowledge of Scriptures, creeds, doctrines, and perhaps the history of the group, rather than belief in them. In short, this dimension concerns what people know about the religious faith they profess.

For members of the Christian faith, this dimension would probably be measured by such things as knowledge about the Bible and its contents—for example, the number of books in the Old Testament— or the ability to identify such biblical characters as Abraham, Moses, Zacharias, and Joseph of Arimethea. We could also ask individuals about the official creeds and histories of the religious groups to which they belong. However, knowledge of unrelated facts is not really the whole of this dimension. Understanding of religious facts in terms of their meaning as a whole is also important, but is, of course, more difficult to measure than knowledge of facts about the Bible or church creeds and histories.

The final dimension, the *consequential,* is of a somewhat different type than the first four. It is concerned with the effects of religious belief, practice, experience, and knowledge in the secular world. In this dimension are all those things one ought to do in daily life and the attitudes one should hold as a result of being religious. We will take a closer look at this dimension later in this chapter.

Some, including Glock and Stark, question whether the consequential dimension should be seen as a dimension of religiosity, or as the outcome of it. Robertson (1970) has contended that as important as the question of the effect of religious commitment in the day-to-day world may be, to include the results of a process as part of the process itself does not seem logical. As he puts it, something "cannot be both an aspect of x and at the same time be a consequence of x" (p. 53).

Meaningfulness of the Dimensional Approach

Research has demonstrated the usefulness of the dimensional approach of Glock and Stark. Nelsen, Yokeley, and Madron (1971), for example, made use of the concept in assessing rural/urban differences in religiosity. To discover whether urban residence created a different view of the nature and importance of religion, they defined religiosity in a rather literal way in terms of four of Glock and Stark's dimensions. They measured the ideological dimension in terms of four beliefs that they saw as orthodox: belief in life after death, hell, heaven, and the devil. They gauged the intellectual dimension by simply counting how many factual questions individuals could answer about rather basic Christian beliefs. Experience was measured by response to a direct question, while prayer activity and church attendance provided the ranking for the ritualistic dimension. From the results of four surveys in the fifties and sixties, they were able to show that residential differences occurred only on the ideological dimension—that is, in terms of orthodoxy. Urbanites were less likely to be orthodox than those from rural areas. Thus, these researchers were able, through the dimensional approach, to pinpoint which aspects of religiosity really did differ for rural and urban residents.

The statement of the five dimensions has become standard in the sociology of religion, but it is not without questioners. These questioners do not so much disagree with the idea that religion is multidimensional as they disagree about whether Glock and Stark, or any of the many others who have dealt with the problem, have really come up with meaningful dimensions. Robertson (1970), in particular, has raised this question and that of the connection of any set of dimensions to a religious system as a whole. As he contends, so far the dimensions have been developed in a fairly ad hoc manner, using what could reasonably be conceived of as part of religiosity and what was measurable, a point supported in part by the large number of dimensions found by some (for example, King and Hunt, 1967, 1969, 1975). Robertson also raises another question: Can we sum individual responses and come up with a measure of the religiosity of a particular society? He thinks not, since to do so on the basis of church attendance would lead us to find Britain and Russia equally religious!

If we see religion as multidimensional, we should understand that the dimensions do not directly correlate, as mentioned earlier. Davidson (1975) found some intriguing relationships between dimensions. For instance, based on his sample of Baptist and Methodist church members, he concluded that the ideological and intellectual dimensions are not only separate but are negatively related to one another. That is, members who had very strong orthodox beliefs tended to be the ones who knew the least about their faith in terms of its content. Thus the person who believes in the Bible from cover to cover may know little of what is actually between those covers!

Somewhat differently, Davidson found that the ritualistic and experiential dimensions, while separate, are positively related to each other. Thus members who regularly performed acts of religious practice were those most likely to report having had religious experiences. Obviously, in many cases the scene of religious ritual—the praise service of a charismatic group, for example—is fertile ground for the occurrence of a religious experience. On the other hand, Davidson found the consequential dimension unrelated to the other dimensions. In short, being religious in any of four ways did not seem to relate to church members' attitudes and behaviors in everyday life in the world.

In summation, although some continue to see religiosity as unidimensional (see, for example, Mueller, 1980), the consensus is that several dimensions are involved in being religious. However, the exact nature and number of such dimensions remain unclear. Despite this, the concept of religion as multidimensional has served as an important guide in uncovering aspects of the social nature of religion.

Having suggested that the consequential element of religion may be just that—a consequence rather than a separate dimension—we turn now to look at how religion affects (or does not affect) the behavior of individuals. As we do so, keep in mind the separate dimensions of religiosity and their content. As we shall see, people vary in the extent to which their religion influences their actual behavior.

INDIVIDUAL CONSEQUENCES OF RELIGION

In his study of suicide, Durkheim (1951) proposed that the strength of religious communities has an influence on the morality of individuals. He concluded that the weakening of moral communities leads to increased rates of suicide. His work suggests that religious groups create moral communities, and that the stronger an individual's relationship to a religious group is, the higher that individual's morality will be, or in sociological terminology, the greater that individual's adherence to the moral standards of the community will be.

Certainly, a general belief exists that religion should lead to higher standards of morality and social justice. Yet innumerable examples show that such is not always the case. Recent scandals involving television ministries have shown that greed can invade religion. Other examples of insensitivity to human need appear not infrequently and involve people who see themselves as religious but who are actually blind to human needs (Curry and Chalfant, 1991).

Most of us know of examples of this kind of feeling. We also know that those who go to church regularly do not necessarily practice justice, compassion, or honesty when they operate in the business or academic world. Of course, we cannot judge all religious groups and churchgoers on the basis of the isolated examples of hypocrisy with which we are familiar. But what is the truth about how religion affects people's behavior? This question has interested sociologists of religion for some time, and no clear answers have been forthcoming. In the following section we will examine the correlation between religiosity and other aspects of life, such as obedience to laws, social attitudes, and value formation.

Religion and Delinquency

Analyses of the relationship between delinquent behavior and religiosity have led researchers to contradictory conclusions. Since there has been a tendency to use self-reports as our data on delinquency, this is not surprising. Like the evidence gathered from official records, self-reported information leads to mixed conclusions concerning the retarding effect of high levels of religiosity upon delinquent behavior. Conger and Peterson (1984) warn, also, that we must also be wary of assuming that membership in a group or subgroup necessarily leads to the same delinquency rates for all members.

A major study of religiosity and delinquency was done by Hirschi and Stark (1969). As Stark (1984) pointed out, they began with the expectation that the commonsense relationships would be found—religious adolescents are less likely to be delinquent. But their findings did not affirm popular conceptions. Young people active in religious organizations were no less likely to commit delinquent acts than those who were not active. Stark went on to note that these findings were quickly taken up by sociologists as "revealed truth" and the relationship between religion and deviance was broadly proclaimed *nil*, especially as similar findings were reported in another study (Burkett and White, 1974).

Yet two studies that appeared in the seventies rejected the Hirschi/Stark findings. Higgins and Albrecht (1977) studied teenagers in Atlanta, while Albrecht, Chadwick, and Alcorn (1977) sampled young Mormons. Both reported that church attendance was negatively related to delinquent behavior. Yet another study (Jensen and Erickson, 1979) confirmed these findings. But to further confuse the situation, Elinson, Peterson, and Hadaway (1983) showed that when controls (e.g., parental background, peers, grade average) were introduced, any relationship between religion and delinquency disappeared.

What, then, do these findings mean? Stark (1984) contends that no single conclusion has emerged because sociologists have been looking at the wrong thing. He claims that looking at the religious attitudes and behaviors of individuals will never lead to an explanation of the social effects of religion; instead, researchers need to look at a *sociological* explanation. Stark recants his earlier ideas that religion affects the behavior of the individual through the threat of hellfire or the production of guilt. As he puts the matter: "It is not whether an individual kid goes to church or believes in hell that influences his or her delinquency. What is critical is whether a majority of the kid's friends are religious" (275). He goes on to note that social life is made up of daily interactions with friends, and that these friends have more to do with our morality or values than does religion. If our friends are religious, religion plays a role in determining our behavior; if they are not, religion plays little part in our decisions.

Tittle and Welch (1983) underscore this argument. They show that for adults, too, the effects of religion on behavior are lessened when consensus exists in a community that a particular act (such as drinking alcohol) is really not wrong, regardless of what a particular religious group may say.

Stark's conclusions are convincing but they do not answer still another question about religion and delinquency. Peek, Curry, and Chalfant (1985) asked whether involvement in a religious subculture, where all or most of one's friends are religious, has a lasting effect and what happens when it does not. Following a cohort of students during their four years of high school, they found, in support of Stark's theory, that as long as the students remained within a religious subculture, they were deterred from delinquent behavior because the fear of divine punishment was supported by the group. But when individuals broke away from the religious subculture, the deterrent effect of religion was lost. In fact, as if they were making up for lost time, such students were even more likely to commit delinquent acts.

Some other studies of the relationship between crime and religious behavior have shown that the level of participation in the church is the important variable. For example, Ellis and Thompson (1989) found that measuring church attendance, rather than other variables, provided the strongest inverse relationship between the tendency to crime and religiosity. They concluded that those who were active in church were finding relief from boredom, a boredom that led to deviant behavior in others.

Cochran (1987) notes that types of delinquency (for example, alcohol use as opposed to marijuana) were differently affected by religious behavior. However, when methods and statistical measures are controlled, religious behavior tends to have a strong negative association with all deviance (Sloane and Potvin, 1986).

Substance Abuse.   One of the fullest examinations of religiosity and teenage drug use is provided by Hadaway, Hackett, and Miller (1984). In a study of nearly thirty thousand high school students in Atlanta, they found that the relationship between alcohol use and religion was weaker than for other drugs, supporting the idea that community definitions of such behavior may reduce any influence of religion. In the case of other drugs, they found the importance of religion to the teenagers and belief in prayer to be most strongly related to the nonuse of drugs. On the whole, their analysis provides evidence that religion does have an independent and constraining influence on drug use and attitudes. Again, however, this relationship varies according to the particular drug being considered and community definitions.

Brownfield and Sorenson (1991) confirm that adolescents identified with a religious group were less likely to use drugs than those without such affiliation. Once again, the social support of the peer group was found to be an important factor in determining the use or nonuse of drugs.

Amoetang and Bahr (1986) found that parental religiosity was related to lower use of alcohol and marijuana in all cases, although it varied by denomination. Controls for parental education and other aspects of the family did not destroy the relationship. Kent (1987) concludes that substance abuse in adolescents is inversely related to religious practice. The relationship with the mother's and the father's sense of control as well as the religious practice of the family had an effect on use.

Sexual Behavior.   Woodruff (1984) sampled adolescents between the ages of seventeen and nineteen who actively participated in religion. He found that their religious beliefs led them to accept traditional values and reject premarital sexual behavior. It appears that belonging to religious groups promoting such values provides role models that lower premarital sexual behavior.

Thornton and Camburn (1989) found a connection between religious affiliation and sexual practices of the adolescent. Their findings are consistent with other research, which has shown that religious involvement and the sexual attitudes of adolescents were strongly related to religious participation, a finding supported by Beck, Cole, and Hammond (1991). In all cases the more conservative the group with which the adolescents were affiliated, the less likely they were to engage in premarital sexual behavior.

Religion and Social Justice

Every religious denomination, regardless of size or theological persuasion, includes as part of its faith and practice some level of commitment to righting the injustices ingrained in the life of our society. Each makes certain pronouncements concerning the religious response to issues of racism, poverty, oppression in the developing world, sexism, and other problems in today's world. Although disagreement exists on some issues, and approaches to the problems vary, all churches and synagogues feel compelled, in the name of their faith, to make such statements. Embodied in the annual statements of these denominations are high and lofty sentiments about the way God's people should respond.

Research indicates, however, that not all of God's people are terribly impressed by the admonitions of denominational boards and leaders. Indeed, a number of books were written in the late sixties and early seventies about the growing split between liberal clergy and denominational policy on the one hand and the members of congregations on the other (for example, see Hadden, 1969; Hoge, 1976; Roof and McKinney, 1987; Wuthnow, 1988). Politically conservative members of the churches are not easily led into the liberal causes espoused by their national bodies. As we shall see in Chapter 6, many of the denominations that were the most outspoken on liberal issues during the sixties suffered direct retribution from their members in the form of church transfers and loss of contributions.

Neal (1984) and her fellow graduate students investigated the reaction of pastors in Little Rock, Arkansas, when faced with the issue of desegregation of the high school there. As Neal tells it:

> All the Christian churches at the time, in their national organizations, had taken a clear position that segregation was sin. Local churches were resisting integration for various interest reasons. We posed the question: how would the local ministers in Little Rock respond to their national church mandates to integrate? We hypothesized that those who were secure enough would do so. The actual occurrences proved us wrong. The conclusion of the study was that money and members took precedence over the mandated church directive and the secure ministers with churches and relatively permanent appointments were the most resistant to integration. We also found, however, that a number of ministers without that security risked their future careers by supporting the local integration effort.... We felt our work was done in having proved that churches can be co-opted into local interests of wealth, power, and security.

A more current picture of this conflict between secular and sacred interests can be found in the confrontation between church members and their national bodies over membership in the National Council of Churches and the World Council of Churches. At the local level, members have seen these groups as contributing to causes that are socialist or communist in nature (Moberg, 1985). Issues of social justice seem to be viewed in a different light from the pew than from the pulpit or denominational board office.

Analyses of national poll data (National Opinion Research Center, 1992) reveal that little relationship exists between religious affiliation and concern for social issues. With the exception of two groups, Episcopalians and Jews, most religious adherents are conservative, to varying degrees, on such issues as abortion, suicide, race relations, and freedom of speech. Data have also shown that with such factors as social class controlled, racial attitudes and stance with regard to both the Equal Rights Amendment and other feminist issues are little affected by religious preference, except for Jews and Episcopalians. In point of fact, the most liberal views are held by those who claimed no religious affiliation at all.

Chalfant and Heller (1985) confirm this basic lack of concern among most church members for the social welfare of others. Curry and Chalfant (1991) also found different attitudes on concepts of social justice among the "religious." In agreement with other findings, they reported that members of more conservative religious groups were more likely to see economic justice than were their more liberal (and more affluent) counterparts in other religious groups.

However, on balance, we should note that not all members of religious groups and congregations are unconcerned about issues of social justice. Although the audience for the message of liberal religion has diminished (see, for example, Johnson, 1985), numerous individuals and groups continue to pursue social justice in the name of religion. For many, involvement in the movement to provide sanctuary for refugees from Central American rightist governments is a witness to their religious faith. The movement, which seeks to protect and support the refugees, includes both Catholics and Protestants, and is not limited to small churches in the Southwest. For example, the First Methodist Church of Germantown, Pennsylvania, has a very elaborate program for helping refugees (Ramsden, 1985). Many others are protesting the nuclear arms race in the name of their religious faith. The Catholic bishop of the small west Texas diocese of Amarillo has gone so far as to urge Catholics in that area to leave their jobs with the Pantex Corporation, which assembles nuclear missiles. In support of this, he has dedicated money to provide job counseling for those who wish to leave Pantex. We discuss church involvement in both the sanctuary movement and the antinuclear movement in more detail in Chapter 12. Perhaps the most extreme example of church involvement in issues of social justice is found in the movement known as *liberation theology,* which blends Marxism and Christian faith in protest of the conditions under which many Latin Americans live.

Table 3.1   **Comparison of Religious Preference at Time of Interview and at Age Sixteen (by Percentage)**

Preference at Interview	Preference at Age Sixteen							
	Catholic	Baptist	Methodist	Lutheran	Presbyterian	Episcopalian	Other	None
Catholic	89.9%	2.4%	1.7%	1.4%	1.3%	0.4%	1.4%	1.5%
Baptist	2.3	83.3	6.0	0.5	1.4	0.2	5.0	1.3
Methodist	3.6	9.1	72.1	2.6	2.5	0.3	8.2	1.6
Lutheran	5.6	4.6	6.4	73.7	2.6	0.1	5.0	2.4
Presbyterian	6.0	8.4	11.0	73.7	2.6	0.1	5.0	2.1
Episcopalian	8.2	4.3	7.9	1.4	6.1	64.5	6.5	1.1
Other	7.3	14.7	8.5	3.0	2.9	1.1	58.4	4.1
None	26.2	13.9	9.9	5.7	4.8	2.0	14.0	23.5

Total $N = 11,498$.

Source: Adapted from data by National Opinion Research Center, 1992.

CONTINUING RELIGIOUS PARTICIPATION

Each religious group, through its socialization, attempts to instill loyalty not only to religious faith in general but also to the specific symbols and values of that group. Thus, one measure of the consequences of religion for the individual is in the extent of loyalty over the years to one particular religious group. Table 3.1 provides some information about the extent to which members of different communions continue a preference for that group from the age of sixteen into adult life. Data are drawn from the General Social Survey of the National Opinion Research Center (NORE) (1992) for the years 1984–91.

The greatest consistency in preference is found among Jews. But since this might also be seen as an ethnic identification from which one escapes only at the cost of group pride, it is hard to tell how much religious socialization has to do with loyalty to this group. Thus we have not reported figures on either table for the Jewish. We can simply note that more than 95 percent of those who "preferred" the Jewish faith at sixteen still did at the time of the interview.

Some Christian groups are less successful in holding their young than are others. Roman Catholics keep nearly 90 percent of those who were Catholic at the age of sixteen. Lutherans (a broad spectrum) retain 71.3 percent of their sixteen-year-olds. At the other end of the spectrum are the Presbyterians who hold only 56 percent of their sixteen-year-olds. The Episcopalians do only a bit better, holding 64.5 percent of their youthful adherents. However, both groups lose sig-

Table 3.2 Comparison of Church Attendance and Religious Preference (by Percentage)

Reported Church Attendance	Religious Preference							
	Catholic	Baptist	Methodist	Lutheran	Presbyterian	Episcopalian	Other	None
Never	8.3%	9.5%	10.7%	10.1%	8.9%	11.3%	11.1%	65.8%
Less than once a year	5.4	7.5	8.6	6.2	8.5	7.7	8.0	10.8
About once/ twice a year	13.9	11.7	14.9	14.1	15.3	15.1	9.9	13.2
Several times a year	12.7	14.6	15.3	13.1	15.7	20.4	9.2	5.6
About once a month	8.7	8.6	10.0	10.1	7.8	10.6	6.5	1.7
2 to 3 times a month	8.4	13.4	11.5	13.9	11.4	9.5	7.1	1.0
Nearly every week	5.0	6.1	6.3	7.0	7.4	5.6	5.3	0.3
Every week	33.7	17.9	18.6	24.0	21.4	18.0	24.9	1.1
Several times a week	3.8	10.7	4.1	1.5	3.6	1.8	18.1	0.3

Total N = 11,498.

Source: Adapted from data by National Opinion Research Center, 1992.

nificant numbers to other religions and to no religious affiliation. Those who cited their affiliation as "other" at sixteen were most likely to have chosen some other specific affiliation by the time they were interviewed. It is interesting to note that only one-fourth (23.5 percent) of those having no affiliation at sixteen had one at the time of the interview, and more than one-fourth of these had become Roman Catholic (26.2 percent). Many of those listed as others at sixteen eventually became Baptists in their later years.

As to the maintenance of ritual behavior and other religious practices several kinds of evidence exist. Some indications come from studies on the effects of parochial education. Greeley and Rossi (1966) found relatively little relationship between the formal socialization of the parochial schools and later religious practices. The example set by parents, however, did seem to have a strong effect on the chances that individuals would continue the practices of their religious faith in their adult years.

Attendance does vary from group to group (see Table 3.2). Roman Catholics most frequently attend at least once a week (33.7 percent) and 3.8 attend several times a week. Baptists are also likely to attend once a week or more (28.6 percent) with 10.7 saying they attend more than once a week. On the other hand, Methodists and Episcopalians are least likely to attend once a week or more, followed closely by the Presbyterians.

There is some regional variation in attendance patterns. For the groups in which this variation exists, all except Catholics show the most frequent attendance rates in the South, with the Midwest providing the next highest rates, except for Baptists. Catholic attendance rates are highest in the Northeast and Midwest, probably reflecting the larger percentage of Catholics in those populations. Baptist attendance is poorest in the Northeast, a finding that probably reflects the differences in emphasis on attendance between the more liberal American Baptist Convention, which is strong in the Northeast, and the Southern Baptist Convention, which has more influence elsewhere. Except for those giving Baptist as a preference, the West shows the poorest attendance rates. Even for Baptists, the greatest percentage in the West indicates that they attend rarely. In short, with some variations, some regions of the country, such as the South, do appear to provide an atmosphere that is more conducive than that of other regions of the country, such as the West, to the continuance of a regular pattern of church attendance (NORC, 1992).

Why, beyond variations in socialization and aside from the influence of the particular religious group one belongs to or region of the country in which one resides, do some people take an active part in the church to which they belong, while others do not, or show only moderate interest? Hoge and Carroll (1978) have pointed to five different answers to that question proposed by social researchers. First is deprivation theory, which holds that individuals who suffer from some form of dispossession are more likely to participate in religious activities than others as they seek to compensate for their felt deprivation. Second, the desire to give one's children some form of ethical and religious training has been seen by some as an adequate explanation; these researchers have held that the presence of young children in the family causes parents to become more active in the affairs of the church so that their children will receive the desired training. Third, the particular kinds of beliefs an individual holds and the strength of these beliefs, particularly as they relate to the church, are the important determinants of religious participation, according to some claims. Fourth, participation in a religious group enhances one's status and offers an opportunity for identification; some say these are the reasons for taking an active part in a church. Fifth, Roof (1978) has suggested that participation in a religious group is related to having a local rather than a more cosmopolitan view as the point of reference for one's life; thus, localism gives greater support to participation in the life of the church.

Hoge and Carroll could not find strong support for the first four of these theories. Indeed, deprivation theory, which has frequently been advanced as *the* explanation for participation, seems to contribute nothing to explaining variation in participation. Why does this favorite theory, as well as the other theories, not really explain religious participation? The answer, suggested in part by Hoge and Carroll, may lie in the fact that the meaning of membership and the obligations that attend it vary from group to group, and any attempt to explain participation that does not take the norms of particular churches into account has relatively little explanatory power. We will focus more attention on norms of participation for various churches in Chapter 6.

In short, we cannot really explain the degree and continuity of participation by any single theory, not only because individuals differ in their reasons for participation, but also because each particular religious group requires different things of its members. And the motivations that lead individuals to undertake these different duties may well vary from group to group.

SUMMARY

In this chapter we have first focused upon the process of becoming religious from a social-psychological viewpoint. Becoming religious, and staying religious, depends upon the process of internalization of attitudes, beliefs, expectations, and values known as socialization. The major agents of religious socialization are the family, religious organizations, and the peer group. Each of these agents not only provides information (and misinformation) but also offers it within a human context—within a milieu that interprets and attaches meaning to the information. These agents thus provide a definition of the religious situation for an individual engaged in religious seekership. In addition, religious activity and experiences roughly correspond to stages in the life cycle.

Just as Durkheim demonstrated that social influences intrude upon the seemingly private act of suicide, so several researchers claim that even the most personal phenomenon of becoming religious—conversion—can be analyzed from a sociological standpoint. Such research has indicated that a host of variables are related to experiencing conversion (for example, the group context, the age factor, predisposing and situational factors, and the intensity with which beliefs are presented and reinforced by others). Systematic study has shown that conversion is seldom a stereotypically radical, thundering transformation, but is more often a process with predictable stages. Research involving the Moonies and the Jesus movement, among others, has suggested that conversion is often a process of resocialization—unlearning old ways while learning new ones—or alternation—changing particular solutions to problems while maintaining the same general orientation.

Researchers have recently turned their attention more to the role of the convert in conversion. They theorize that the convert may be more than a passive person at the mercy of a molding society and may in fact be an active agent in seeking out religious conversion, or may at least be predisposed by psychological factors to conversion. Indeed, individuals may try on a number of belief systems and lifestyles in the course of their life span, thus experiencing a number of conversions. Finally, cognitive structuralists have suggested that intellectual and moral development proceeds through a sequence of stages and that conversion may be related to a person's stage of development. If this line of research stands up to critical testing, we may be able to differentiate types of conversion.

People express their religiosity in a variety of ways; no single pattern for practicing religion fits all people in society. Some are more devout in holding to the beliefs of their parents than others; some feel a deeper experience of God than do fellow believers. In turn, the consequences of religion vary, with some continuing in the faith of their youth throughout their lives and others continuing to profess such faith but following few of its principles.

For some time sociologists have suggested that religious behavior cannot be measured along any single continuum. Instead, it consists of several dimensions, with individuals varying as to their level of religiosity in each of these. Five dimensions have found wide acceptance: the experiential, the ideological, the ritualistic, the intellectual, and the consequential. While some debate continues over the number and meaningfulness of these dimensions, it is generally accepted that several dimensions are involved in being religious.

4.

The Organization and Leadership of Religious Groups

Some longtime favorite "gospel" songs, such as "My God and I" and "In the Garden" stress a private, personal faith. An extreme example of this feeling is expressed in the lyrics of a cowboy gospel song:

> Well, me and Jesus, got our own thing going,
> Me and Jesus, got it all worked out;
> Me and Jesus got our own thing going,
> We don't need anybody to tell us what it's all about (Hall, 1971).

This attitude blends well with the theme of rugged individualism that permeates our society's value system. Many feel that religion is something so essentially personal and individualistic that organizational structures are more likely to get in our way than to help.

Such an individualistic approach may be appealing, but it is far from realistic. Religion, like all human behavior, is essentially a group product. As humans, we are never truly alone. All that we do, even when we are physically separated from others, is deeply influenced by present and past actions of some group or groups within our society. Even to think of God is to use a gift of the group—the language by which we are enabled to think. Simply put, the group is a basic necessity for the existence and maintenance of belief, practice, values, and ritual. As it is through the group that we become truly human, so it is in interaction with the religious group that we become truly religious.

In this chapter we will first consider two aspects of the life of religious organizations: (1) the development of groups and problems attendant to that development; and (2) how we might categorize religious organizations, with special emphasis on sectarian development. We will then turn to patterns of both clergy and lay leadership in congregations.

GROWTH AND DEVELOPMENT OF RELIGIOUS GROUPS

All human groups face problems in their growth and development. Religious groups have some particular problems arising out of the nature of its goals and values. Three questions arise with regard to the development of such groups: (1) Is there any pattern of development that is shared by the groups? (2) What dilemmas are confronted as the group grows? and (3) How does the developing group relate to the broader society?

Patterns of Development

Religious groups do share some broad patterns of development. Although each faces different problems and solves them in its own way, they share clear stages in development. The first period, marking the emergence of a new movement, is characterized by informality of leadership and operation. New groups arise from the leadership of a strong individual(s) who by the power of personal gifts (charisma) attracts supporters to his or her particular program—a call to a "purer" form of belief, a new interpretation of the faith.

To illustrate from the history of our nation, we may take one example of sectarian development on the western frontier. In the wake of a period of tremendous revival, one movement took a firm hold on the beliefs of many. Known to some as the *Campbellite movement*, it was initiated by two Presbyterian ministers, Alexander and Thomas Campbell (father and son), who sought to call frontier Christians back to a "true" Christianity, unfettered by the rules, creeds, and structures of the established religions of the East. In its beginning, the movement centered on the personal gifts of these leaders. This new religious movement progressed as a result of the personal ability of these and fellow leaders to attract followers to the cause. There were no rules, no legislation, no elections—in short, no formality; only what they deemed to be the "simple" gospel.

But religious movements do not stand still; they either grow or wither. If a group does continue, it generally faces a crisis of leadership as the original leader or leaders die or otherwise leave active direction of the movement. The tendency is to resort to what is called traditional leadership—there are still no rules or creeds, but the teachings of the charismatic leader become policy, and interpretations of these teachings become the benchmark for the group. Such interpretations are needed, of course, because as the group has grown and matured new problems have arisen. For example, the original followers have families and a desire that their children be brought up in the faith, so education may be needed to instruct the new generation in the tradition.

In the case of the so-called Campbellite movement, this was a time of schism, or separation of different segments from one another. Two large factions in the movement (then calling itself simply Christian) could not agree on what the tradition said about the seemingly minor issue of the use of instrumental music in church. Over this issue the two groups split, the Churches of Christ declaring musical instruments to be unbiblical and the Christian Church (Disciples of Christ) allowing such use. The point for understanding this stage is that although there were still no official rules, tradition and its interpretation were used to decide this issue.

Usually, if a religious group continues into the second and third generation, it takes on a much more formal leadership style—one we refer to as *legal-bureaucratic.* Now the rules, laws, and strictures against which the movement first protested become a part of the group's life. Although a variety of terms may be used to disguise the fact, the movement is now established; its policies are routinized; and official rules and channels exist for making decisions. This appears to happen even to those groups that protest that they are not so formally controlled.

The Churches of Christ, for example, claim to be free of the twin "error" of distinctions between laity and clergy and connections beyond the local congregation. Yet a body as strong as this group is in such areas of the country as Texas cannot exist without routinizing and formalizing its patterns of operation. Thus, for example, "Christian" colleges have been established to train the leaders of the group and pastors have assumed official positions that in large congregations may take on a hierarchal nature. Also, congregations do, indeed, cooperate with one another according to unwritten, but acknowledged, rules.

Dilemmas of Growth

Growth for a new religious group creates a set of dilemmas, particularly for its original members. With each step a diminution of the original spirit of the movement occurs. Further, the message of the movement may seem less unique and inspiring when used to attract more converts. O'Dea and Aviada (1983) list a number of choices that maturing religious groups must make.

First, there is the matter of structure. If a group is to function as it grows larger, it must have structure; however, the effort to maintain that structure may displace basic principles. A formal organization can be an end in itself. Those with vested interests seek to maintain the status quo, which may, however, alienate rank-and-file members. For example, the demand for strict adherence to the traditional system of authority in the Roman Catholic Church has alienated large numbers of the laity in this country and diminished their loyalty to the organization.

A second dilemma arises with the introduction of formal positions which have powers and privileges. This is necessary for the functioning of the group, but again may draw the group from its ideal goals. What occurs is that leaders, now occupying positions with some payoff, may seek such positions out of motivations that are less than pure. Certainly, in a number of instances the motives of professionals in religion have been questioned. The leaders of the Protestant Reformation saw the motivations of the Roman Catholic clergy of that time as far from pure. To some, the motives of any full-time church workers are suspect; especially doubtful are the motives of the seemingly compromising pastor of the Church of the Blessed Rich or the television evangelist hawking healing with deliverance on a quasi-commercial basis.

The final dilemma is related to the way in which new recruits are attracted. Clearly, such recruits are necessary for growth, but the very lack of the group's original inspiration in these recruits may mean the necessity of watering down the strict doctrine of the original followers. To have any impact on the outsiders the group seeks to attract, it must make modifications in both its program and structure. Generally, this means that aspects of discipline and belief have to be relaxed. Also, the more extreme aspects of its general program or message must be changed so that it seems less strange to nonmembers. But if standards are lowered, the goals and ideals of the organization may be so changed that it no longer meets the needs of the original or existing membership (Nottingham, 1971). This dilemma appears to have been faced by those groups whose main focus was originally on a healing ministry. To become successful numerically, they relinquished some of their major emphasis and turned to a message promising success in a number of other areas.

Relating to the Larger Society

A critical problem faced by religious groups today is that of relating to a disinterested, even potentially hostile, secular world. In simple societies, the religious institution and the society are so nearly identical that little question exists about how one shall relate to the other. As societies become complex and institutions differentiate, the religious group must face the problem of dealing with these other, now differentiated, parts of society. Because of this, as Demerath and Hammond (1969) suggest, religious groups in contemporary society face functional problems. The religious organization in today's world can be viewed as deviant. That is, while religion may be seen as the repository of basic societal values, the values tend to be ideal ones that are no longer completely consistent with the society's real values. Indeed, a number of authors (see Marty and Appleby, 1991) suggest that many holding traditional beliefs do see themselves as outsiders with regard to the rest of the world.

To the extent this is true, religious groups must deal with this situation. Demerath and Hammond (1969:168–73) note several problems that must be faced. One is maintaining the traditional patterns of the group. How, for example, can the religious emphasis on revealed truth be maintained in a society that increasingly stresses the importance of empirical verification as the means to knowledge? It is not a question of whether the two are actually or even necessarily opposed. But to a number of persons science and religion seem to be at odds.

This challenge has been handled in a number of ways, as Demerath and Hammond indicate. The most radical is exemplified by those who, in the early 1960s, proclaimed "the death of God." Their strategy was to radically alter the symbols and belief system of Christianity to make it as compatible as possible with contemporary thought. And, more recently, the Episcopal Bishop of Newark, New Jersey, has proclaimed that we need not worry about deviance or contradictions between modern ideas and traditional theology as little of "traditional faith" should be taken as literal.

A related but less extreme strategy attempts to modernize doctrine to make it more appealing and less obviously at odds with contemporary thought. This led to the highly philosophical theology of Paul Tillich, which borrowed heavily from the existentialist movement in philosophy and redefined God as the "Ground of All Being."

Similarly, scholars like Rudolf Bultmann conceptualized biblical narratives as myths—that is, stories that contain divine truth, but should not be taken as literal accounts of reality.

A more popularized (some would say vulgarized) version of this approach can be seen on the shelves of many religious bookstores. Here God and traditional doctrine take on an extremely familiar tone, and we are asked not to believe in abstract doctrine but in our "old Daddy God," who just wants to help us if we will only plug in. Such approaches are illustrated in the approach of televangelists from Robert Schuller's happy faith to the promises of material wealth hawked by a number of those who have appeared on the "tube."

By far the most common organizational strategy, at least in mainline denominations, is to underplay traditional doctrine by leaving it understated or unmentioned whenever possible. Thus, the group or its leaders may appear to be maintaining the pattern while actually not accepting the traditional meaning of the words.

Ironically, the most effective strategy is to make a virtue of holding on to the "old time religion." Many note the continuing success of fundamentalist and Pentecostal groups as an example of the effectiveness of this strategy. While the death of fundamentalist doctrine has been confidently predicted by liberal theologians for some time, it has simply refused to die. Indeed, as Roof (1978) and Stark (1985) have pointed out, while the liberal groups (those trying hardest to be consistent with contemporary thought patterns and values) are steadily decreasing in membership, fundamentalism is flourishing, and born-again Christians appear to dominate media reports on the religious world, even if they do not really constitute a majority of Christians. While there is some reason to doubt the more extravagant claims of fundamentalist growth (see Smith, 1992), it cannot be denied that fundamentalism has attained a high profile in contemporary society (Ammerman, 1991).

Still, what appears to be a contradiction may not be as real as it seems. Some indication exists that the increasing numbers embracing a fundamentalist view consist of a hard core of true believers, while the masses are simply dropping out (Hoge and Roozen, 1979). In fact, some have noted that affiliation with liberal churches may represent a move away from a religious perspective. The seemingly successful strategy of attracting converts with old-time religion, then, may only work on a limited audience; the others are buying none of the strategies.

A second problem for the growing religious group is that of convincing the prospective clientele that religious goals are attainable and worthwhile. Organizations need to have goals related to the values of the society. Traditional religious values, such as that of ultimate, otherworldly salvation, face difficulties here. For more and more people, such values seem unsuitable or at least unimportant in light of many contemporary values: "Salvation is not so much spurned as it seems to be losing any sense of urgency" (Demerath and Hammond, 1969:174).

Goals are also better pursued when they are concrete. But it is just this sort of objective attainability that religious goals lack. They are otherworldly and unattainable in this order of existence. For this reason, religious organizations have sought more proximate goals. For example, clergy and others who supported the civil rights movement in the 1950s could be seen as substituting the concrete, obtainable goal of civil rights for the less vague one of otherworldly salvation. Likewise, those waging an antiabortion campaign may see this as an attainable goal to demonstrate the validity of belief.

Another way of dealing with this problem is goal displacement—that is, making the original programs or procedures intended as a means to an end a goal in themselves. An example is the way in which attendance often becomes the real goal. Thus, having the biggest Sunday school attendance becomes the goal of the church, rather than teaching people religious doctrine. Large churches have been known to wage intercity contests to see who could reach this sort of goal most effectively. Similarly, specific subgroups within the congregation can often take on the character of ends in themselves. The women's organization in many congregations has taken on such a complexion; its success has become a sign of the vitality of the whole group.

A third problem involves adapting to the surrounding environment while maintaining the strength of the group. Demerath and Hammond (1969:180–87) approach this problem in terms of the need of religious organizations both to recruit new members and to maintain the interest of those already in the group. Since individuals can be members of just so many groups and can only give so much of their time to religious activity, real competition takes place among religious and nonreligious organizations. Insofar as competition with other religious groups is concerned, the available pool of potential members may be so small that denominational types are led to make comity agreements. That is, areas of a city may be assigned to one denomination, with others agreeing not to establish congregations in that area. Denominational mergers are another way in which denominations seek to deal with competition, and recent history has seen a number of such mergers.

Competition still exists, however, and groups may be driven to extreme attempts in seeking to attract new members. Competition with secular groups can be even more fierce. The service club, the family, the political party, occupational and professional associations, and many other interests all demand the time and effort of members. In some smaller communities this contest is handled by establishing an understanding among community groups that a specific time is set aside for religion; for example, Sundays and one night of the week may be cleared of nonchurch activities.

A final functional problem for religious organizations is that of integrating the roles and positions in the organization to accomplish necessary tasks. It can mean the problem of integrating the various roles of the official full-time clergy. We will discuss some of the dysfunctional aspects of the clergy's role in today's church in the next section, but it's useful to mention it here as a major problem. The varying demands of parishioners on the church and its officials, as well as demands from denominational authorities, may be so severe that members of the clergy suffer a great deal of role strain leading to burnout, departures, and early retirements (Carroll, 1992).

It also means the need to integrate the church's parishioners and their various viewpoints into the denomination's program to ensure loyalty to the organization. Religious organizations also face the problem of allocating roles—that is, integrating people rather than roles. No religious group, not even the small sectarian one, is completely homogeneous. Important differences exist in the religious needs and inclinations of various members. One congregation in the inner city of Chicago presented an extreme example. It drew its diverse membership from residents of the area around the church, who were black, Italian, and Puerto Rican. But the church was near a large medical and professional center associated with a state medical school and several large hospitals; as a result, parishioners also came from the student body of the school, the faculty, and practicing medical people who lived in nearby luxury apartments. Then, too, old-time residents now living in the suburbs as well as liberals from other parts of the city came to make the church their religious home. Imagine the problems of devising a program that would suit such a variety of social statuses, ethnic groups, educational levels, and interests. Just to decide at what level to aim a sermon was a major problem for the pastor of the church.

In summary, like most groups, the religious association faces a number of problems and is confronted with dilemmas of growth. Solutions offered frequently draw the group away from its original pure ideals and drastically change its nature. The results of these changes are so significant that the group sometimes takes on a totally different character.

Differing ways of solving problems are also related to a variety of types of church organizations; each type solves them differently. Sociologists have developed several typologies to describe these different patterns of organization.

TYPES OF RELIGIOUS ORGANIZATIONS

In everyday language we tend to refer to any religious group as a church, but such an unreflective designation is not precise enough for sociological study. Actually, such groups may vary in a number of ways: the effect of being religious, the relationship between the group and the world, the involvement of the membership, and attitudes and beliefs. All these differences are significant in understanding the social aspects of religiosity and its institutional setting. In this section we will examine classifications developed to indicate these differences.

The Traditional Dichotomy: Church and Sect

The earliest attempt to differentiate between types of religious organizations divides them into two polar types called the *church* and the *sect*. This distinction is generally attributed to the German sociologist and theologian Ernst Troeltsch, and also appears in the work of his teacher, Max Weber, whose concepts of the role of the prophet and the priest were influential in the development of the classification. Although this simple dichotomy is not applicable to the contemporary religious world, its basic formulation of polar types helps us think about the differential nature of religious groups.

As Troeltsch (1931) defined it, the church is a type of religious group at peace with the ways of the secular world. It neither rejects the values of the world nor denies their power; rather, it attempts to have an influence in secular matters through its very acceptance of the secular realm. In brief, the church is built on compromise and accommodation with the secular power. Membership in the church is by virtue of birth, and all those living in a particular region are considered to be members. What Troeltsch had in mind was the Roman Catholic Church of the thirteenth century: at that time one simply was Catholic by virtue of being born and living in a particular region where power was shared by both secular and religious authorities. Although the church exercised universal domination in religious matters, it was closely aligned with the secular world; it was more concerned with correct ritual, rightly administered sacraments, and an orthodox creed than with ethics and behavior.

The sect reflects one part of what Troeltsch conceptualized as a perpetual dialogue in the history of the Christian church: a dialogue between the tendency of religion toward accommodation with the secular world and its tendency toward protest against such accommodation. The sect is essentially a protest movement. Its chief tenet is objection to the church's surrender to the secular authorities (as sectarians view it). The sect can also be seen as the failure of the church to meet the needs of its total membership, usually of its less prestigious segment. For Troeltsch (1931:336), the sect is characterized as follows:

> ...lay Christianity, personal achievement in ethics and in religion, the radical fellowship of love, religious equality and brotherly love, indifference toward the authority of the State and the ruling classes, dislike of technical law and of the oath, the separation of the religious life from the economic struggle by means of the ideal of poverty and frugality...the directness of the personal religious relationship, criticism of official spiritual guides and theologians, the appeal to the New Testament and the Primitive Church.

In actuality, almost no agreement exists about how the dichotomy should be understood and how we can properly use it today. Because Weber and Troeltsch formulated the theory for specific purposes at a particular time, it seems inappropriate to apply it directly to religion in the United States. Some (Eister, 1967, 1973; Goode, 1967) have suggested that the concept is worthless and sterile today. But even though we cannot use the concept per se, a long heritage in the sociological study of religion has found that with some modifications, the basic principle of differentiation between groups can provide the student with a useful tool.

Contemporary Typologies of Religious Groups

Several attempts have been made to adapt the church/sect dichotomy to apply to variant religious groups in contemporary society. The church/sect dichotomy was first applied to the religious scene in the United States in the work of a theologian with an interest in society, H. Richard Niebuhr. He wrote *The Social Sources of Denominationalism* (1932) as an exploration of the problem of differences in religious groups. Using the term *church* in a sense much modified from that of Troeltsch and Weber, his work implicitly polarized the two terms. That is, he saw church and sect at opposite ends of a continuum of religious organizations, with most of the existing religious bodies falling in between.

Becker (1932) suggested that four basic types of religious organizations are found in contemporary society: the ecclesia, the denomination, the sect, and the cult. Yinger accepts much of this, but has made a few useful additions (1946, 1969, 1970). To the rest of Becker's typology he adds a new category of sect—the established sect—and also differentiates between types of sects: acceptance sects, aggressive sects, and avoidance sects. We will use Becker's four types to consider the problems of differentiating among various kinds of religious groups in society today before turning to a closer consideration of sects and Yinger's typology of them.

The Ecclesia.   The ecclesia is a religious association attempting to expand its realm to claim as members everybody within the boundaries of a particular society. However, it is unable to make such a widespread appeal; for example, the ecclesia is not totally effective in dealing with the sectarian tendencies of those groups in society who feel that they have been deprived in some way.

Becker summarizes the characteristics of the ecclesia as including the following features: (1) inclusion of all members of society in its membership; (2) a sense of monopolistic right to the religious realm within the society; (3) a close alliance with the power of the secular world; (4) a social organization that is quite formal and in which there is detailed specification of roles and relationships; (5) leadership by an officially designated, full-time clergy who alone have rights over the sacramental means of grace; and (6) membership based more upon birth and socialization than upon the conversion of individuals, whether children or adult, to its particular perspective.

True examples of the ecclesia are rare in modern society. Until the nineteenth century the Church of England would have fit this category, but since the Act of Toleration in 1689 it has become more like a denomination, even if a dominant one. The Lutheran Church in Sweden is an official religion, as is the Lutheran Church in portions of Germany, but neither of these churches is free of sectarian competition. If the model can be applied outside Christendom, the fundamentalist Muslim countries provide the best contemporary illustration.

The Denomination.   The denomination, sometimes referred to as the *class church,* is certainly the most common organizational form found on the religious scene in the United States. Yinger (1970:264–66) has defined the denomination as a type of religious group that does not have general appeal to the total society, that is, it has attraction for only a limited segment of the population. The denomination is limited by the boundaries of class, race, ethnicity, and sometimes by regional area. For example, the African Methodist Church is limited mainly to blacks; the Episcopal Church draws its participation largely from the upper classes; and the Baptists have their greatest concentration in the South. While membership in denominational bodies is, clearly, not strictly limited to particular social classes, the attitudes and styles of the middle class tend to influence the life and order of the denominational religious bodies.

The major characteristics of the denominational type are (1) compromise and accommodation with the secular world and the authority of the state; (2) heavy reliance on birth (infant baptism) and socialization as a means of increasing membership; (3) more liberal (less literal) interpretation of doctrines, (4) more or less formal worship services with varying degrees of ritual and standardization; (5) leadership through a formal, trained clergy where members are usually approved by denominational bodies and persons operating from a headquarters, (6) tolerant and even friendly relationships with similar religious bodies, frequently involving a great deal of cooperation and joint efforts; and (7) a membership dominantly drawn from the middle and upper classes.

In defining and discussing both the denomination and the sect, we should remember that no existing group matches either type perfectly. Some, such as the Presbyterians and Episcopalians, fit the denomination type more than others, such as the Baptists and members of the Church of the Nazarene. The concept of a continuum stretched between the two extremes, with actual organizations ranged between them, has a great deal of validity.

It is important to note the wide range of variation within the denominational type of religious group. Tolerance is a key characteristic of such groups, but varying levels of tolerance can be found in different congregations; the degree of formality may also differ widely from one group categorized as a denomination to another. Thus, while both the Baptist Church and the Episcopal Church are classified as denominations, the formality of the worship service in a Baptist congregation differs considerably from that of an Episcopal service. Again, the degree of liberality in the interpretation of doctrine varies between congregations of the Church of the Nazarene and those of the United Church of Christ. All of these are denominations (at some point along the continuum), but they are really quite different from one another. And even *within* denominational churches, considerable variation exists. The variation is related to the region of the country in which the congregation is found, to the socioeconomic level of the group, and even to whether it is a rural or urban group.

Most frequently, the variation can be traced to the history of the particular congregation.

The key distinguishing characteristic of the denomination has always been accommodation—to the state, the secular power, and other religious groups. The denomination is comfortable in its world. However, Johnson has argued (1971:131–35) that we tend to overplay the accommodation as if it were a one-way street. He contends that denominations can gain some of their own goals through the process of working out a compromise. After all, compromise does imply give-and-take from both sides; it does not mean that the denomination is totally swallowed up by the society.

The Sect.   As we have noted, the sect is characterized, above all, by protest. It is generally a group or body that has seceded or withdrawn from a more traditional, accommodated, or compromised group. For example, the early Methodist movement protested against the formality of the established Church of England. But when the Methodist Church itself became accommodated to the dominant values of the society, sectarian groups such as the Wesleyan Methodists and the Free Methodists seceded.

A standard list of the characteristics of the sect would include the following: (1) opposition to the world and refusal to compromise, (2) a sense of elitism in which the sect is seen as stressing the pure doctrine, calling people back to some original set of principles; (3) informal, often emotionally directed services, worship, or gatherings; (4) leadership by means of lay people, with no formal clergy, and a de-emphasis on organization as such; (5) few members; (6) emphasis on coming into the group by conversion rather than by birth; and (7) members drawn largely from the lower socioeconomic strata. It has been suggested that tension with society is the single most important factor in distinguishing the sect from the denomination, with sects being in higher tension with the world than denominations (Bainbridge and Stark, 1980; Stark and Bainbridge, 1985).

As in the case of the denomination, no real group matches exactly all characteristics of the sect. Some, such as small Holiness groups that engage in exotic practices like snake handling, are very close to the ideal type. They protest the values of the secular world, and have small, poor congregations and no specified leadership. The Jehovah's Witnesses, on the other hand, have moved in some ways from the strict sectarian stance where they started. Still, the group can be classified as a sect because it remains in a state of high tension with the standards of the world. A comparison of the denomination and sect is presented in Table 4.1.

Table 4.1   Comparison of the Sect and the Denomination

Characteristic	Sect	Denomination
Size	Small	Large
Relationship with other religious groups	Rejects—feels that the sect alone has the truth	Accepts other denominations and is able to work with them in harmony
Wealth (church property), buildings, salary of clergy, income of members	Limited	Extensive
Religious services	Emotional emphasis—try to recapture conversion thrill; informal, extensive congregation participation	Intellectual emphasis—concern with teachings; formal, limited congregational participation
Clergy	Unspecialized; little if any professional training; frequently part-time	Specialized, professionally trained, full-time
Doctrines	Literal interpretations of Scriptures; emphasis upon otherworldly rewards	Liberal interpretations of Scriptures; emphasis upon this-worldly rewards
Membership recruitment	Conversion experience; emotional commitment	Born into group or ritualistic requirements; intellectual commitment
Relationship with secular world	"At war" with the secular world, which is defined as evil	Endorses prevailing culture and social organization
Social class of members	Mainly lower class	Mainly middle class

Source: Vernon, 1962:186.

Some, however, have called attention to the possibility that the differences are overrated. The tendency to polarize two groups has blurred some of the ways in which they are not so completely opposite. Demerath (1965) has demonstrated that even the most churchlike groups contain members with a sectlike orientation. Snook (1975:203) has suggested that what really differentiates the sect from the denomination is the ability of the sect to gain a higher degree of commitment to its authority and positions than do the denominations. In short, we need to guard against reifying the concepts of sect and denomination. While clear differences exist between the denomination and the sect, probably as many similarities exist. Both are, after all, organized for the same general purpose. Further, if we are correct in suggesting that religion is deviant in our society, it may be that protest is only a matter of degree.

It is important to remember that the relationship between church and sect are influenced by national history. As noted in Chapter 1, the

United States has provided fertile ground for sectarian development. Such has not been the case in other parts of the world. Nielsen (1989) contends that church/sect relationships are influenced by traditional relationships between church and society. For example, he suggests that sectarian development can only occur against a background of rationalizing civilizations. In Russia, where the range of cultural options are less than in the West, sects have not developed to oppose the mystically and ritually oriented Orthodox Church.

The Cult.   One final type of religious body remains—the cult. Yinger (1970:279) has contended that such a group develops where alienation from the traditional religious system as well as alienation from society itself exists. In such a situation, new religious systems or movements borrowing principles from other religious systems often appear.

Wallis (1975:91) has argued that the new religious movements we call cults represent way stations toward becoming sects. According to him, cults take form out of a broad background or milieu offering a range of possible ideas and practices. The new cult draws from their reservoir in merging a more or less defined group of seekers around one or several common interests. He notes several features typical of the cult: (1) focus on individual problems; (2) loose structure; (3) tolerance of other religious groups; (4) nonexclusion; (5) no clear distinction between members and nonmembers; and (6) no clear focus of authority.

Today when new religious movements spring up often and most of them soon fade away, some confusion between the sect and the cult exists. Stark (1985) has suggested a simple distinction: Cults, or cult movements, are in high tension with society and in a deviant religious tradition, at least so far as their society is concerned; sects, on the other hand, are also in high tension with their society's standards, but resolve this tension through a renewal, as they see it, of the society's traditional religious system. As we use the term *cult,* it should not be taken as a negative term but as a descriptive one.

Wallis (1975:92) has suggested that cults are subject to a number of problems not necessarily faced by other groups. Cults do not have much control over their members. Cults tend to be transient, and different leaders may attempt to change cult activities, bringing about dissension. A central problem of the group is that members share relatively few beliefs. Further, the beliefs of a specific cult generally differ little from a general cultic milieu; thus there can be little loyalty to specific beliefs. Finally, the level of commitment of cult members is relatively low as these followers tend to be seekers who can visualize a number of paths to truth or salvation. In short, members of cults may see any number of beliefs as legitimate, making allegiance to a particular cult exceedingly ephemeral. Swatos (1981:29) may have best defined the cult as simply a group focusing on the teachings of some real or legendary figure in the hope of finding a better life for themselves.

Providing examples of more or less pure cults is more difficult than it is for the denomination or sect. Because cults are transitory, almost by definition, they either pass from the cultic phase before they can be described in their pure state or fade from the religious scene. Christian Science, for example, was in its beginning close to the cult type in that it centered on a single idea, had no formal membership, tolerated other religious groups, and attracted a middle-class group of seekers. Today, of course, it has moved toward something like an established sect. Robbins (1988) includes contemporary groups such as the Unification Church (Moonies), Hare Krishna, and Scientology in his definition of the cult.

Because of the many difficulties involved in classifying specific religious groups, some have suggested that we should abandon these distinctions. Certainly, one is tempted to suggest the use of a number of continua along which to array the various groups rather than a rigid classification of specific types. However, the classification does provide a way of thinking about the differences between groups and helps us to understand the meaning and nature of these variations.

A Closer Look at the Sect

Sects have long captured the attention of the sociologist. This polar type of religious organization attracted Troeltsch's attention to variation in religious groups, and the protest orientation of such groups raises the issue of a differentiation unique to the contemporary world. At the same time, this orientation provides us with insight into the processes whereby religious organizations develop. Sects are deviant religious groups and the deviant type tells us more than does the expected pattern.

Deprivation and the Rise of Sectarian Groups.   How do sects actually come into being? An obvious answer is that they develop out of protests against theological "impurity." Public pronouncements of sectarian leaders play up the lack of spiritually, the perversion of beliefs, and the low level of commitment found among members of dominant religious groups. In fact, no topic seems closer to the heart of the sect member than the evils and waywardness of the more "respectable" churches.

But are the reasons for their rise totally religious? Sociologists cannot fully answer such a question, but some factors seem to be social. For one thing, religious disagreement and even protest need not mean a break or schism in the organization. The rise of the charismatic movement in the 1960s and 1970s (not to be confused with the charismatic activity long present in Pentecostal sects) could certainly be viewed as a protest against the supposed lack of fervor and shallowness of traditional religious groups and their leadership (see Poloma, 1982). Yet no new charismatic or Pentecostal sects have been formed as a result of the increased charismatic activity. Staid Presbyterians, wealthy Episcopalians, conservative Baptists, ritualistic Catholics, and formal Lutherans have all felt the force of the "new charismatics," but have contained the movement *within* their organizations.

Customary wisdom in sociology is that such groups arise among the poor, who are seen as cut off from the mainstream of society and for whom the establishment doctrine is inappropriate. In other words, economic deprivation and its attendant problems are seen as the root cause of the development of new sectarian groups. The poor protest their economic plight by seeking in a moral realm that status they cannot find either in the secular world or in the spiritual world of the established churches.

The majority of members of sectarian groups do come from the lower classes, and sectarian groups are generally located in the lower-income sections of the community. Also the ethos of many such groups decries worldly wealth and possessions and looks for ultimate rewards in a future realm—a heaven with ivory palaces and streets of gold. In such groups the secular status system is reversed and the first become last. To indicate that economic deprivation has played a major part in sectarian protests from the Middle Ages to the present is by no means wide of the mark. A striking example of the class nature of Pentecostalism is Latin America. Here these sectarian groups are clearly protest movements against a repressive class structure (Deiros, 1991).

But can we say that economic matters alone encourage the rise of sects? Clearly not, for not all sectarians are bitterly poor, not all sectarian groups hold to a doctrine of "pie in the sky by and by," as we shall see, and not all of the poor are members of sect groups—both the Roman Catholic and Episcopal churches have numerous lower-class members.

Culture shock, the threat presented by either geographical or social situations that are unfamiliar, has been suggested as one reason for the creation of sects (Holt, 1940). Emerging sects are seen as means for dealing with a new life condition by providing a sense of security in the unfamiliar situation. Sectarian terminology even emphasizes familylike terms (*brother, sister*), which lend an air of support for the newcomer.

Johnstone (1992:90–92) has gone beyond the economic situation as explanatory in noting that while deprivation may be the cause of the development of new sects, such deprivation need not be economic. He would add social, organismic, ethical, and psychic deprivation, each contributing to the felt need for protest. Actually, the type of deprivation felt also influences the type of sect formed to deal with it. Those who feel ethical deprivation are more likely to belong to a sect with a program for reforming the world here and now; those experiencing economic deprivation may join a sect that displaces rewards from the secular realm to a more heavenly place.

Types of Sects.   Different kinds of needs and different sorts of deprivation lead individuals into different types of sects. Thus, sects have a variety of forms and contents. Clearly, we cannot conceptualize under one umbrella the whole vast array of groups we classify as sects; they are far from homogeneous. Looking at such varied groups as the Amish, Jehovah's Witnesses, Quakers, the Pentecostal Holiness Church, and the Church of the Foursquare Gospel, we find much more diversity than similarity. We could well say that the sect is a genus with many species that need to be distinguished from one another.

To say that distinctions are needed is a good bit easier than making them. The array of such groups is so great, especially when the definition of sect is broad, that most typologies or classifications fall under their own weight. However, it would be useful to look at two attempts that contribute to our understanding of the sect. First, Yinger (1970) has analyzed sects in terms of their approach to dealing with the secular world. Second, a typology presented by Wilson (1963) seeks to classify sectarian groups in terms of their central means for adapting to deprivation.

Yinger's typology. Yinger's classification (1970:257–78) basically deals with the manner in which sectarian groups relate to the secular world: Some accept that world and its values; others aggressively seek change in that world; and still others avoid or withdraw from it. Table 4.2 presents an overview of the characteristics of the three categories.

Acceptance sects are those whose members believe they face significant problems not solved by the established religious organizations. However, they do not interpret these problems as resulting from bad social structures. Members of this type of group are primarily from the middle or upwardly mobile lower class. Their protest is

Table 4.2   Yinger's Typology of Sects

	Type Name		
	Acceptance	Aggressive	Avoidance
Characteristic form of deprivation	Individual morale	Structural	Cultural values
Characteristic type of leadership and experience	Mystical	Phophetic	Ascetic
Strategy toward society	Disregard or accept	Attack	Withdraw
Principal objective	Individual poise and participation	Power	Achievement of values
Extreme or "pure" expression	Downgrading of normal sense experience	Religious military movement	Communist community
Illustrative groups	Early Christian Science; League for Discovery	Munsterites Ghost dance	Hutterites; Amana community

Source: Yinger, 1970:279.

not so much against the principles of the world as it is against the shortcomings in it that produce alienation, meaninglessness, and suffering. Christian Science provides a good example of this kind of sect. Sin is seen as a lack of faith, and such lack is the reason for the individual suffering that the world calls sickness.

Aggressive sects are oriented toward the use of power to change the world—either through changes in individuals or by some drastic alteration in society. Yinger places both the Salvation Army, which seeks to convert people to a new way of life, and Jehovah's Witnesses, which looks for a coming of a new world, in this particular category. Such groups are often responses to economic deprivation. They give religious answers to the powerlessness and apathy that result from poverty.

Avoidance sects are most likely to be found in developed nations. Although they do not seek to reform the world (or they have little hope of that), neither do they accept the values of the secular world. Their approach is to transform the values of this world, devaluing the meaning of success symbols and focusing their hopes on a kind of success that will come in a future existence to those who have "kept the faith." Logically, they can be expected to appear among groups who have little hope that life will get better. Underprivileged minority groups—blacks, Chicanos, Puerto Ricans, Appalachian whites—

provide fertile ground for the development of this kind of sect. A drive through the main thoroughfares of any urban slum or the back alleyways of the poorer sections of smaller cities gives ample evidence of the existence of avoidance sects, indicated by crudely lettered signs and storefronts turned into "temples."

Wilson's typology.   Yinger's typology does not provide all of the meaningful distinctions we might make in looking at sect life in this country. Wilson (1963), examining mainly the sectarian scene in England, has distinguished seven types of sectarian groups. While each of these types is clearly valid, sect groups in the real world tend to cross the boundaries of this topology. For our purpose, it is important to look at four types derived from Wilson's categories based on how the sect group deals with the problem of adjusting to its environment.

Some sects are interested in *reforming the present order.* The focal point of sects thus classified is to somehow change the world so that it will be a better place, more in accord with God's will. This might be done in two ways: through converting individuals or through changing the world itself. Many sectarian groups in this country follow the former option. These groups tend to embrace an evangelical, fundamentalist approach to Christian faith, and feel that the world is an evil place because individuals are corrupt.

Other sects prefer *withdrawing from the present order.* These groups, retreatist in some ways, are like Yinger's category of avoidance sects. They deny the validity of the present world and look for an existence better than the one they feel they have found in the secular world. Again, two major types exist, depending upon the extent and kind of withdrawal made. One type retreats into pietistic and ascetic practices to declare its superiority to the ways of the world. Through a lifestyle of self-denial and avoidance of many of the pleasures of the world, members of this type of sect attempt to develop personal holiness as the means to a new kind of security, a spiritual security with which to face the world.

Still other sects are interested in *managing the present order.* Wilson's manipulation sects fit into this category. These sects believe that they have a hold on some special ability, some unique knowledge, that enables them to manage problems confronting the secular world. They do not deny the ideals of the world, but lift them to a higher category and offer special techniques for assurance of success in certain areas of life.

And some sects involve themselves in *creating a new order.* Such sects propose to be rid of the present social order when the appropriate time comes, whether by violence or the intervention of divine power. Adventist groups, such as Jehovah's Witnesses, which look for the immediate, usually dramatic Second Coming of Christ or the establishment of a divine order on earth, fit into this category.

Any attempt to categorize sectarian groups is, of course, eventually inadequate, for two reasons. First, sectarian groups, if they persist, tend to undergo change. As they are never totally cut off from the world, they cannot totally ignore its impact upon them. Further, internal factors, such as a change of leadership when charismatic leaders die, bring about changes. In short, almost by definition, sects are unstable groups and cannot be put into a category once and for all. Second, the sectarian protest is far from formally organized and cannot be neatly shoved into any particular pigeonhole. That is, sectarian groups tend to borrow from more than one strategy and use more than one approach.

For some time, the common assumption has been that sects that persist for more than a generation will move toward the denominational end of a sect/denomination continuum. In an early study of sect groups, Pope (1942) bluntly stated that such is the inevitable fate of the sect: It either dies or becomes more accommodated to the secular world. In Pope's formulations, the direction is always one-way. Sects arise through schism from a church, but never as result of the decline or reconstitution of a denomination or church. He suggested that, in their desire to achieve some measure of success, new groups lose their extreme sectarian qualities and perspectives. They build more expensive and permanent buildings, insist on a full-time, educated clergy so that it becomes necessary to build training schools, and develop tolerance of older denominations and community leaders. All of these represent attempts to achieve more prestige and power in the world, and, thus, a move away from the sectarian spirit of protest.

Clearly, a large number of sectarian groups have undergone this kind of transformation. The Church of the Nazarene, some Pentecostal Holiness groups, and the array of Assemblies of God seem to have followed such a path to some degree. Even the branch of evangelical Christianity that emphasized faith healing and seemed so sectarian in nature has undergone a process of compromise and accommodation to the world.

But a number of scholars have questioned the orthodox conclusion that such movement is inevitable and in one direction only. Wilson (1963) contends that such a movement is only characteristic of those kinds of sects he calls *conversionist*, and that it tends to be true only where an expanding economy gives sectarian members hope of improving their economic status. In other situations, the groups may evolve into other kinds of sects rather than into denominations.

Established sects. For the sect, an alternative to moving toward being a denomination is to develop into what Yinger (1970) has called an established sect. In fact, Redekop (1974) argues that this is especially likely to occur when the sectarian group's protest is aimed at the basic norms of the society. Yinger (1970:266) defines the established sect as a group that has grown out of the less stable sectarian movements and has become "somewhat more inclusive, less alienated, and more structured than the sect." However, it does not make the full change into a denominational type of group. As he notes, while the Methodists and Quakers both began as sectarian protests, and while both have since moved away from the extremes of such protest, they clearly cannot be considered similar today. The Methodists have gone the full route of transformation to take their place with the denominational groups of today, but the Quakers have not made this change. They cannot be comfortably classified as a denomination, but they do not fully fit the sect category either. The Quakers, then, are an example of an established sect, as are several Amish and Mennonite groups and the Hutterites. In each case, these groups have accommodated to the world to a degree, but *only* to the degree essential for survival.

GOVERNANCE AND LEADERSHIP IN RELIGIOUS GROUPS

Religion, as we have emphasized, is a group activity. Group activities require organization and leadership. Therefore, religious groups, regardless of size or wealth, must have some form of government, or polity. The polities of different religious groups vary, and the ways in which they vary are important to the life of the group.

Our attention is now focused on issues of governance. First, we will look at various means by which religious group are governed, and at the tendency of these organizations toward bureaucratization. Then we will discuss the formal leadership role of the clergy as well as that of lay members.

The Forms of Religious Governance

Three common organizational forms, or polities, have been delineated: congregational, presbyterian, and episcopal. The main difference among them is the location of the focus of control. Congregational polities place ultimate authority in the congregation itself; presbyterian polities locate control in the hands of the clergy and elders, who are elected lay leaders; and episcopal polities give final authority to a hierarchy of bishops. Despite their original form, the polity of any group in the contemporary world tends toward bureaucratization. Also, local parishes do not necessarily operate as the constitution of the parent body would prescribe.

The Congregational Polity.   In the ideal type of congregational polity, each separate congregation is the ultimate and essentially only source of authority. Churches with this type of polity may belong to conferences or conventions, but each separate congregation is theoretically a law unto itself. Further, in such groups, although an official board of some kind generally exists, all *major* decisions are theoretically made by the total congregation. The role of the minister is that of democratic leader, subject to the will of the congregation. Conferences or convention boards may make recommendations about standards for clergy and may circulate the names of pastors looking to make a move, but they have no control over such matters. In some extreme forms of this polity, the minister's contract is up for renewal every year.

The Congregational Church of New England was an example of such a polity, but since its merger with the Evangelical and Reformed Church to form the United Church of Christ, it has evolved a form of polity that gives more control over local affairs to outside bodies. The Southern Baptist Convention, largest of all Protestant bodies in the United States, is a current example of congregational polity in its purer form, as is the Christian Church (Disciples of Christ). In both cases, despite the presence of regional and national associations, the congregations, in theory, make their own decisions, and pastors are really only the leaders of these officially independent fellowships. Most sectarian groups are also organized according to this congregational type of polity. In general, groups so governed de-emphasize the importance of formal creeds and confessions.

The Presbyterian Polity.   The presbyterian form of polity takes its name from a Greek word, *presbuteros*, meaning *elder*. Presbyterian churches are organized so that authority resides in a session composed of lay representatives, known as elders, and the pastor, titled *Minister of the Word*. With some exceptions, including hiring of pastors groups and approval of the annual budget, authority at the local level rests in this group of representatives of the congregation. As in the form of democracy embodied in the U.S. Constitution, elected representatives in the presbyterian polity are free to act in accordance with their own consciences and wisdom. However, the local session is also subject to a higher body, generally called a *presbytery*, composed of all ordained clergy and ruling elders representing each congregation. Much of the authority in such churches rests in this group, which has some of the powers given the bishop in the episcopal type of polity.

The session of the local church in the presbyterian system has control of that congregation, but this authority is subject to the review of the higher courts or judicatories of the church, particularly the presbytery. When trouble or complaints occur in such congregations, the presbytery may exercise its authority and actually take over the duties of the session. In churches governed by such a polity, the minister is typically called (hired) by the church, but the local congregation must have the approval of the presbytery, which ultimately has the authority to maintain or dissolve the relationship between the pastor and the local congregation.

The Presbyterian Church in the United States of America, as well as most smaller bodies with *Presbyterian* in their names, have some variation of this form of organization. Generally, churches with the term *Reformed* in their names also have such a form of government.

The Episcopal Polity.   The episcopal form of polity also takes its name from a Greek word, *episcopus*, literally *overseer*, which became *bishop* in English. Thus episcopal churches make provision for some form of bishopric in their structures. Episcopal polities are theoretically dominated by a hierarchy that controls the appointment of local clergy and exercises much authority over the local congregation. Although authority clearly flows from the top, some room for decisions remains at the local congregational level. Ultimately, however, the bishop and other higher church officials can overrule the congregation.

Local clergy in the pure type of episcopal polity are almost totally dependent upon the hierarchy; technically, clergy are appointed to parish positions by the bishop's office and at the will of the bishop. The Episcopal Church, as might be obvious, has such a polity, as does the Roman Catholic Church. The official polity of the United Methodist (formerly Methodist Episcopal) Church is also of the episcopal type, although with much modification.

Mixed Polities.   Denominations have blunted some of the extreme features of each type of polity, and some represent a mixture of the pure types. As an example of the former case, the United Methodist Church seems to be moving away from episcopal authority in the matter of appointing pastors and adopting a style more like the presbyterian polity. Some Lutheran churches in this country have also tended to have a mixture of polities, combining elements of the presbyterian and congregational approaches. The models of government that we have described really represent extreme cases, and a given denomination or group does not necessarily follow one to the exclusion of elements of the other.

Both congregations and governing bodies often subvert official policy. Beckford (1985) has noted that problems of organizational size lead to policies of rationalization and bureaucratization. Depending upon the level of resources available and size of the organization bureaucracies then tend to expand (Johnson and Chalfant, 1993). These, in turn, lead to a greater professionalization of the ministry and the development of religious specialists who make autonomous decisions for the boards, agencies, or programs they direct. In most cases, the autonomy of such boards does not follow denominational policy. Bureaucratization may also lead to a sort of "organizational transcendence" (Wood, 1981), where national or regional bodies take stands on social as well as theological issues that may not be in harmony with the views of the majority of church members. This, in turn, poses a problem for members of the clergy. Should they follow the demands of the particular congregation or those of denominational leaders?

Ingram (1980) has indicated that the ideal of congregational polity breaks down at the local level, too, where a minister with charismatic qualities may become an autonomous source of authority. Given the sense of vocation implicit in leading a congregation, the high visibility of the pulpit, and the general role conception of the ministry, the pastor in such polities can be the one member of the congregation with the prominence to lead. This leadership may actually be more autocratic than that of ministers in other, more structured forms of church government because of the lack of controls beyond the local congregation.

The Bureaucratic Tendency

The fact that pure embodiments of the various ideal types of polity do not actually exist can be attributed partly to the real problems of operating a church in contemporary society. Churches, beyond the early sectarian stage, are corporations (most are, in fact, legally so), and they have problems not unlike those of any complex organization.

Thus, the most striking feature of church life in the contemporary United States has to be its increasing bureaucratization. More and more, denominations and their congregations are being operated (regardless of polity) on models approximating the bureaucratic ones used in governmental agencies, businesses, and other large-scale organizations. In this regard Demerath (1974:23) has noted that "the romantic Norman Rockwell portrait of Americans at worship in the neighborhood church of their choice must now be placed side by side with an image of denominational headquarters as a business enterprise and a portrait of the clergyman as a harassed professional torn between different roles and conflicting demands."

The best-known study of the bureaucratic tendency, especially as seen in a denomination with a congregational polity, is Paul Harrison's *Authority and Power in the Free Church Tradition* (1959). In this study of the American Baptist Convention (sometimes referred to as the Northern Baptist Church), Harrison claimed that the "fences" built to control central authority had been futile, and that the attempt to maintain the pure congregational ideal had led to a situation in which some leaders of the convention had appropriated extralegal, personal power.

Echoes of Harrison's study are found in Ammerman's recent study of the Southern Baptist Convention, *Baptist Battles* (1990). While the focus of the book is on the struggle between moderates and fundamentalists in this free church type of denomination, she shows how that battle has actually been carried out in the struggle to control its elaborate bureaucratic structure. In spite of the historic noncreedal character of Southern Baptists, by controlling major offices in the bureaucratic structure of the Convention, fundamentalists have been able to force denominational workers to adhere to this strict creed or face being fired.

FORMAL LEADERSHIP IN RELIGIOUS ORGANIZATIONS

Religious groups are composed of people who, from the sociological perspective, occupy various status-roles. The most frequent is that of church member, and the nature of that particular position varies considerably from group to group. Some members take on roles of formal leadership, such as steward, deacon, elder, or vestryperson. Of course, the most highly specialized position is that of a member of the clergy, a position that takes different shapes from communion to communion but is almost always central.

The Role of the Clergy

Most religious organizations in our society give the major leadership role to full-time, formally appointed ordained pastors or priests (as well as to other religious professionals) who stand as symbols of the sacred engaged in using their expertise to interpret that sacred (Carroll, 1992). The nature of such a leadership role obviously varies from one type of religious group to another. Sectarian groups of the pure type have no formally appointed functionaries such as pastors, ministers, or rabbis, although such groups probably have one or several members who, in reality, assume what amounts to pastoral leadership. Frequently, such groups are led by what is referred to as a *charismatic leader*, someone who claims power on the basis of personal characteristics. Nevertheless, in groups with a formal clergy, that is where the burden of leadership lies.

The problem that arises in attempting to describe the role of the clergy is that not just *one* role, but a multiplicity of them, exists. Blizzard (1956, 1958, 1985), who wrote the first major work on this issue, has contended that ministers are expected to play five basic roles. First, the minister is expected to be a preacher, composing and delivering fifty sermons a year. Second, he or she operates as a priest, conducting worship services properly and performing the various rites of the particular communion with some skill and familiarity. Third, community relations—in many formal as well as informal ways—must be maintained. The minister is really a spokesperson for the congregation. Fourth, many members (increasingly, it seems) call upon the minister for pastoral counseling, and the expectation is that he or she will have skill, with insights from psychology, in this rather difficult task. Finally, administration of the church's program, finances, and other aspects of the group are usually left almost entirely in the hands of the minister.

This list of duties is interesting in that its order corresponds to the amount of time spent on each of the roles during ministerial training. Indeed, in accredited seminaries, the bulk of the education centers on biblical studies and theology, with much less attention paid to other areas. Administrative skills are seldom taught, although the need to perform such tasks is frequently bemoaned. According to some indications, seminaries are making adjustments to this need, though those who regularly visit seminaries to interview students report that changes seem more cosmetic than real.

The difficulty comes in the fact that the order of this listing of ministerial roles is directly opposite to their order in terms of the amount of time ministers end up spending on them in the actual parish experience. Blizzard's research showed that 40 percent of the parish minister's time is spent in the somewhat distasteful task of administration; 25 percent is devoted to pastoral counseling; 15 percent to operating in the community as agent of the congregation—and only 20 percent, together, on the most favored roles of preacher and priest. In other words, what the seminary trains the minister to do is precisely those tasks that take up the least of the parish minister's time, and what takes up most hours of the clergy's day receives little, if any, attention during the seminary years. What seems particularly frustrating is that the laity are no more satisfied with the minister's spending time on such things as administration than is the minister (see Glock and Ross, 1961). The parishioners, too, would prefer their minister to be primarily a preacher and a priest, but bow to the need to have certain tasks done.

Corresponding research on the role of Catholic priests has been done by Reilly (1975). She determined that the priest plays six prime roles: priest and teacher, prophet, pastor, administrator, organizer, and priest-ritualist. As she notes, great similarities exist between these roles and those Blizzard described. The only role not described by Blizzard is that of prophet, that is, someone who seeks to call church members to social justice, a role suggested by Fichter (1968), Hall and Schneider (1973), and Koval (1970). Reilly found that perceptions of the priestly role varied strongly by age. Younger priests were heavily committed to action for social justice and were dissatisfied with traditional clerical roles. Trained at the time of Vatican II and the emphasis on social action, these young priests were further influenced by the currents of social action that also deeply affected Protestant churches. Priests in their early middle years still looking for advancement were more completely organization-type people and more concerned about their futures. Most priests over forty-five were pastors and were probably versed in routines established over the years.

Conceptions of the minister's role underwent change especially during the sixties and seventies, leaving both the clergy and those who train them in a quandary (see Mills, 1985; Nelsen, 1985). To answer the question posed by active clergy about what is expected of them, the Association of Theological Schools in the United States and Canada commissioned a thorough study of the ministry (Schuller, Strommen, and Brekke, 1980) in the forty-seven denominations that it represents. The study obtained responses from a sample of more than five thousand laypeople, ministers, seminary students, and ordained clergy in nonparish positions; it isolated seven factors that, across the entire sample, were rated as quite important for the minister (Aleshire, 1980:25): (1) an open and affirming style; (2) an ability to care for persons under stress through counseling; (3) an ability to administer the congregation in a manner indicating willingness to share power; (4) a general knowledge of theology and reflection of it in one's life, (5) a personal commitment to the faith in a life of biblical affirmation, and a strong sense of evangelistic priority; (6) an ability to communicate a sense of community, both in worship and the ongoing life of the congregation; and (7) knowledge and acceptance of denominational priorities, and a sense of belonging to the group. Of course, these seven items, although quite important in the opinion of all members of the sample, varied from one denomination to another in the relative importance attached to them. For example, Anglican-Episcopal respondents all were most interested in the ability of the minister to perform well in interpersonal relationships (Richards, 1980), while Southern Baptists stressed evangelistic ability above all else (Songer, 1980).

More recently, Jackson W. Carroll (1991, 1992) has noted significant changes occurring in clergy authority and leadership. In his book *As One with Authority* (1991), Carroll contends that the authority of the clergy is more cultural than social, and that just that type of authority is being eroded in times of high modernity. He cites three influences contributing to this erosion: a crisis of belief in which many ministers question fundamental assumptions about their faith; the movement of the religious institution from the center of social life to its periphery; and the voluntarism of contemporary life, which leaves the minister dependent on members who have variant and conflicting demands.

Elsewhere (1992) Carroll writes of these changes as a restructuring of our view of the religious leader. He cites three ways in which the ministerial role is being reshaped. He notes, first, that the male image of the ministry is being altered because of the increasing number of women now involved in the active, ordained ministry. Second, he suggests that there is a blurring of the separation of pastoral and lay roles as there is a renewed emphasis on shared ministry in both Protestant and Catholic churches (see Schoenherr, 1987; D'Antonio et al., 1989; Russell, 1987; Hornsby-Smith, 1991). While consistent with our democratic principles, such a movement reduces a power that many clergy covet, even if covertly. Finally, clergy face the erosion of certainty in our time. Carroll suggests that these factors contribute to the strains and conflicts in the ministry which result in burnout, low morale, and leaving the ministry.

Strains and Conflict in the Ministry

The effects of strain and conflict upon the clergy have long been a matter of concern (Mills, 1985). The unusually high number of clergy leaving the pastorate today is one evidence of such felt strain. What is the source of this defection? Older studies (such as Fichter, 1961) explained defections in terms of spiritual deficiency in the individual.

More recent work, however, lays much of the responsibility on a lack of clarity in the role of the minister or priest (Schoenherr and Greeley, 1974; Potvin, 1976; Hoge, Dyble, and Polk, 1981). According to some, the Catholic priesthood is in a state of near crisis (Schoenherr and Sorenson, 1982), resulting in large part from confusion over what services the clergy are to render, especially with regard to others who hold professional roles. Others (such as Hadden, 1969) suggest that the current instability of our society's norms and values often leaves clergy with little idea of how to define, sustain, and transmit values. Thus, even the ministry as a profession has its problems. Suggesting that the occupation is totally filled with such strain and conflict would be an exaggeration, but many pushes and pulls clearly operate on the person occupying that status in contemporary society.

At the center of these strains and conflicts might well be the difficulty that the minister has in developing an appropriate professional identity and self-image. Carroll (1991, 1992) comments on the increasing ambiguity of the role. The minister no longer is able to clearly determine what should be done and how it should be accomplished.

With regard to role strain in the ministry, Whitley (1964) has pointed to three studies that have emphasized different kinds of conflict faced by the clergy. The first of these studies (Wilson, 1958–59) dealt with the special strains faced by ministers in a sectarian group (in this case the Elim movement, an English Pentecostal group) that, by official ideology, found the presence of a formally appointed pastor an embarrassment, even if it was a necessity. The problem, of course, is that in a Pentecostal group, the idea of a trained and appointed person as a minister is out of keeping with the pure Pentecostal spirit, which says that only a spirit-filled person can occupy such a role. However, the minister in the Elim movement was trained, specialized, and paid. As Wilson summed up (1958–59:504), "The status of the Pentecostal minister is contradictory because of a lack of consensus among those for whom his role has significance.... The contradictions in his status arise from the marginality of his role both within the profession and within the movement." Thus the minister is a living contradiction of the values of the movement. In addition, and again contrary to Pentecostal tradition, the minister must represent the group's headquarters, while at the same time trying to build up a primary group feeling among the members of the congregation. In a sense, the Elim minister described by Wilson was cut off from professional identification because of the structure of the movement, but he was also in touch with the status of the ministry in the surrounding community.

A study by Burchard (1954) explored a second sort of conflict— one due to the contradiction between two roles played at once. His study dealt with the potential problem a military chaplain has in balancing the two statuses of minister and military officer with regard to a possible conflict between military regulations and religious ideology. He did, indeed, find such a conflict, and determined that the chaplains tended to handle it through a process of compartmentalization. That is, they saw themselves in the moral context of religious ideology only when they were actually performing clerical tasks; at other times they considered themselves to be in a nonreligious situation, and dealt with the situation in terms of military ideology. However, considerable ambiguity existed in their minds concerning their status as military officers. While they felt that this cut them off, to some extent, from enlisted personnel, they also had a considerable interest in maintaining the officer status.

A third kind of conflict can occur when the beliefs and values held by members of the clergy are opposite to those of the general community. An example of this was reported in Pettigrew and Campbell's (1958–59) study of ministers in Little Rock, Arkansas, at the time of the school integration crisis. Clergy members who held integration to be a desirable Christian end got some support from the official boards of their denominations, but this support was not adequate or even very strong. These clergy had most difficulty dealing with members of their congregations, who represented the general position of the Little Rock community. The clergy found that any position that would upset members' prosperity represented a danger. How, then, did these ministers deal with the conflict? Basically, those clergy interested in integration tended to placate their values by simply calling attention to the need for brotherly love but not getting involved in action. Similar conflicts were faced by many ministers at this time (cf. Carroll, 1991), and as new social issues come to the fore they will probably continue to be sources of conflict.

Schuller (1980) has gone on to point out that many clergy in the sixties and seventies made an implicit decision to minister to the structures of society rather than simply to individuals, and their excitement about this social activist approach brought about alienation from their lay membership; a gathering storm seemed to loom, in Hadden's phrase (1969). In the studies of Hadden and others (Quinley, 1974; Hoge, 1976), two almost opposite factions appeared to emerge in the church—one that stressed the need for personal evangelism and the maintenance of moral standards, and another that saw social activism as the real purpose of Christian faith as expressed through the church. The main battle was really over the protection of commitments to the middle-class values of family, career, and standard of living (Hoge, 1976).

Actually, the rank-and-file membership of these churches never have accepted an active public role for the clergy or the organized church. They have not accepted the social action mission as having high priority, nor have they felt it the church's mission to provide leadership on such issues as race, poverty, and peace. In sum, then, the "gathering storm" seems to have passed through mainline churches without changing their basic conservative nature, although it has driven many more conservative members from the congregations of the more liberal denominations. With the passing of this storm, ministers inclined to see social action as having high priority for the church are caught in an increasing conflict. The lay backlash demands conformity to a priority these clergy do not respect, thus creating feelings of guilt and disenchantment.

The Role of the Laity

The extent to which laypersons participate in a particular religious group, both as members and as leaders, depends somewhat upon the type of group and its organizational structure. To a certain extent, the degree of participation expected of members of different religious groups varies along the continuum stretching from church at one pole to sect at the other. Sect members certainly have heavier obligations than do those who belong to established denominations— obligations ranging from ascetic regulations for daily life to time spent in doing church work and attending the various services and activities of the group. But the difference between participation in churches and sects isn't quite that simple. The kind, number, and intensity of requirements imposed upon the lay member vary from group to group within each category. What is expected of the Roman Catholic layperson is quite different from what is expected of the devout Presbyterian; a member of the Churches of Christ is obliged to give far more time to church activities than is even a conservative counterpart in a Southern Baptist congregation; and so it goes from group to group.

With regard to participation in the more specialized roles involved in running the organization, groups differ here, too, in the extent to which they allow the layperson power in the process of governing. Actually, religious groups in the United States have exemplified all possible variations in the amount of power permitted the laity. Those who first came to this country were strongly influenced by the Protestant doctrine of the priesthood of all believers. Thus they felt the laity was endowed with the same priestly authority as the clergy and should have a strong, if not dominant, voice in the operation of the religious group. Some, indeed, felt that there should be no control beyond that of the local democratic assembly in which all laypersons have an equal voice. Most of the original religious groups in this country had such a view. At the opposite end of the spectrum, the Catholic tradition has always stressed the authority of its hierarchy. Indeed, the authority of the Catholic hierarchy was originally the source of great distrust of the Catholic Church by Protestants, who saw the hierarchy as exercising foreign control over the affairs of the church.

Today most Protestant groups provide for a considerable amount of voluntary leadership by laypersons and are generally governed by some official board with lay members, such as a session or board of stewards or deacons. Recently, the Catholic Church has relied more on lay advice, if not rule, in the operation of its parishes. In addition, many other part-time roles are played by members of the laity in the religious organization, and persons filling roles such as Sunday school superintendent occupy a special status within the group. In practice, of course, most groups fall at different points on a continuum of lay participation in leadership. No church seems to be totally congregational in its form of leadership, at least if it has gone beyond the early sectarian stage. Nor is the Catholic Church so totally hierarchical in government as to leave the laity no place in its decision making. The real situation seems to be that in almost all instances of bureaucratic organization, the formal structure is frequently abrogated, and people with no place in the formal organization have real power in the operation of the group. This is what Chalfant (1967) found for those small churches that he described as failing to live up to all the rules of the Book of Order of the Presbyterian Church (U.S.A.). In those congregations, individuals without formal leadership roles had much influence: The husband of an elder, for example, could really determine the school curriculum of the church; the couple who gave the most money, although neither held any position in the congregation, had to be consulted on most decisions; and the old-time member who had literally established the church still determined much church policy, even though he had not served on the official board for years. At times the unofficial leadership seemed to have virtual veto power over areas of congregational life.

This kind of informal power has been noted by others. Hougland and Wood (1979) have referred to the "inner circles in social churches"—groups of individuals who actually exercise considerable control over the affairs of a local church, despite the fact that this control is not in line with the church's constitution. Hougland and Wood studied a sample of fifty-eight Protestant churches in the Indianapolis area that included congregations from what could be considered mainline denominations. They found that inner circles did exist in a large number of these congregations, and that these circles had real power in the management of the congregation. Far from seeing some conspiratorial plot aimed at subverting the rules, Hougland and Wood seemed to feel that the inner circles operated in the absence of other strong leadership as well as in cases where the size and complexity of the congregation, in terms of members and budget, made control by official boards difficult. In such instances, control by this inner circle was possible, if not necessary. Only in cases where the minister's activism offended some in the inner circle could this circle be accused of attempting to exercise ideological control. The authors noted (1979:235):

> Inner circles seem most likely to develop when relatively little control is being exercised elsewhere in the church and when ministers lack attributes that would expedite their exercising strong leadership. Thus, inner circles may be particularly likely to emerge in organizations when other potential mechanisms of control (ministerial leadership, united congregational action, etc.) are not performing effectively.

Thus, these authors tend to see inner circles as a means for filling a leadership vacuum.

In the Roman Catholic Church, the assumption has generally been that a definite hierarchical structure exists that officially leaves lay members with activities but little power. However, the influence of American voluntary associations has brought about some movement toward more lay participation in decision making, as have the principles set forth at the Second Vatican Council (1962–65), an ecumenical gathering of the Roman Catholic bishops that brought about a number of liberalizing reforms. As Rosenberg (1979) has pointed out, a movement has taken place toward a shared responsibility in the Catholic Church that involves a lessening of the traditional barriers between clergy and laity, as well as between nonclergy in religious orders and laity. Another reason for fuller lay participation in leadership is the growing shortage of full-time clergy and religious,* and the need for lay people to take over new responsibilities. More opportunities have been made available to the laity on ideological grounds,

---

*Members of religious orders, including priests, brothers, and sisters.

also. Catholic laity are now performing such functions as reading parts of the mass, distributing the elements in Communion, doing pastoral counseling, and working with other groups.

SUMMARY

We have been concerned in this chapter with the religious group as an organization that takes form and structure in society and with leadership roles in that structure. Two aspects of this structural existence have been discussed: (1) the development of religious groups and the problems attendant to such development, and (2) the various types of religious groups that emerge.

Religious groups, if they persist over time, seem to follow a broad general pattern. Basically, the pattern is a movement from an informal, charismatic style of leadership and a loose structure to a formal, bureaucratic style of organization. This pattern presents four dilemmas to developing groups, dilemmas which involve changes in the group that may lessen its original purpose and involve it in many changes that sometimes alienate older members.

The religious group is also faced with the problem of relating to the larger society. In many ways, religious values are deviant in contemporary industrial society. This deviant status may make it difficult for the religious group to solve the functional problems of maintenance of traditional patterns, tension management and goal attainment, adaptation, and integration.

The classification of religious groups into types has fascinated students of religion since the time of Ernst Troeltsch, who first divided Western Christianity into two types—the church and the sect—largely on the basis of whether the particular group's values were harmonious with the secular world or protested against it. Contemporary students of religious groups, however, have found this dichotomy inadequate and have suggested four types of religious groups: ecclesia, denomination, sect, and cult. In the United States most attention focuses on the differences between the denomination and the sect; they are seen as something like polar types, with the denomination accommodating to the secular world and the sect making a religious protest.

We have also drawn attention to the development of sectarian groups. The common rule has been that sects, if they last, give up their protestant stance and become like the accommodating denominations. A number of researchers, however, have raised doubt that such is necessarily the case, although it does seem to occur with great frequency. These researchers have suggested that if sects change at all, they simply change into other kinds of sects. Also, some sects seem to change in only relatively minor ways. Thus Yinger has suggested that we need to talk about established sects.

Religious groups can be classified as having one of three forms of government or polity—congregational, presbyterian, and episcopal—although a number combine elements from each of these polities. The congregational form places rule and authority in the local congregation; the presbyterian form locates authority in the pastor and representative lay people; the episcopal form vests power in a hierarchy of bishops. Regardless of actual polity, most religious organizations operate on bureaucratic principles.

Religious organizations are structured around a number of different roles: member, clergy, officer, teacher, et cetera. Although laity participate in some governmental activities of the congregation, frequently informally, the major leadership role belongs to the clergy. Members of the clergy play not just one role in their churches but many. We note five major roles, ordered by increasing amount of time devoted to them: preacher, priest, community relations spokesperson, pastoral counselor, and administrator. A major problem for the clergy is that this ordering is exactly opposite to the training and desires of ministers for spending their time. Currently clergy face a crisis of authority which involves considerable role strain and conflict.

PART THREE

Diversity and Change in Religious Expressions

5.
The Development of
Religious Pluralism

The enormous diversity of religious life in the United States is obvious. Almost any almanac lists hundreds of separate religious groups, and the telephone book's Yellow Pages present a variety of groups sufficient to satisfy almost anyone's religious tastes. We wander through any community and observe churches and faiths of all sizes holding public services and sessions of religious instruction. We see ornate Gothic cathedrals, simple colonial-style buildings, and storefront churches all housing religious groups. We also see Islamic centers and Hindu temples in our larger cities. We can choose to follow the faith of the Catholics, the Jews (Orthodox, Conservative, or Reform), the more than two hundred varieties of Protestants, the Muslims, and the Hindus—or choose to give allegiance to no religious faith.

Diversity of belief is widespread, and the various groups live with each other in harmony. But such has not always been the case. Pluralism in religion in the United States—the concept of coexisting different groups—evolved historically from a colonial situation dominated by "state" colonial churches. In today's language, religion in America was *deregulated*. In this chapter we will present a topical and chronological summary of this historical development.

EARLY FOUNDATIONS OF DIVERSITY

That religious pluralism would eventually hold sway in our country was not apparent at the outset. Toleration for religious dissent was low in the colonies, with church domination of government the rule rather than the exception. Still, early circumstances such as the Great Awakening (the religious revivalist movement that spread across the colonies in the eighteenth century), the separation of church and state established by the Constitution, and the consequent church reliance on voluntarism to spread religion to the frontier—all these factors set the stage for the later acceptance of religious pluralism. We will briefly summarize these early circumstances in this section.

Church Domination in the Colonies

Finke and Stark (1992) contend that all Christian religions since the Protestant Reformation began as sects and generally evolved into denominations. This seems to hold true for the most of the religious groups found in the United States. The first English colonists, the Pilgrims, came to the New World ostensibly to escape religious persecution because of their sect's Calvinist beliefs. They were followed shortly by the early settlers of the Massachusetts Bay Colony, the Puritans, who made a serious attempt to enforce religious uniformity (Hudson, 1981). This theocracy mixed religious law and secular law; dissenters from the Puritan religious point of view were dealt with swiftly and harshly.

In his search for a primitive purity characteristic of early Christianity, Roger Williams (1603?–83) found himself in opposition to Puritanism. In the wilderness area of Rhode Island to which he fled from Massachusetts, he attacked Puritan idolatry. Soon he established the first Baptist congregation in the New World (Marty, 1984:76–77) and argued for the establishment of God-given natural rights.

Religious dissenters from the Church of England also settled in other areas: notably the Quakers in Pennsylvania. In addition, Roman Catholics founded Maryland. On the other hand, in the proprietary colonies of Virginia, the Carolinas, and Georgia, the Church of England became the state church (Littell, 1962:12). New York began as a Dutch colony with the Dutch Reformed Church as the state church, but later became English and Anglican. In 1689, Anglicanism was established in Maryland and, as a result, Catholics were persecuted there. Littell (1962:17) has summed up the colonial religious order as an oppressive establishment of mixed Congregational and Presbyterian groups in New England and the dominant Church of England in the southern colonies. Only in Pennsylvania, New Jersey, and Delaware was the shift to religious liberty and voluntary church support accomplished without severe readjustment. In fact, Pennsylvania was considered a "swamp of sectarianism" by New Englanders and Southerners. To this "swamp" migrated the German lowland Lutherans, the Moravians, the Dutch Calvinists, and the Amish. In 1707, the Baptists chose Philadelphia as their headquarters (Hudson, 1981). Religious ferment in the middle colonies provided the basis for the First Great Awakening, which further developed the concept of religious pluralism.

The First Great Awakening

The First Great Awakening was an emotional religious revival that swept the colonies beginning in 1734. Littell (1962:19) has described it as "the first major manifestation of a motif that, more than any other, has shaped modern American church life: mass evangelism." The evangelical message emphasizes earning salvation through a personal commitment to Christ, supports the authority of the Bible, and is delivered through preaching rather than ritual. The first evangelical preaching in the colonies was done by Theodorus Freylinghausen, a Dutch Calvinist. Jonathan Edwards (1703–58) was influential in New England, and George Whitefield (1714–70) an English Methodist, preached the message of evangelicalism among all the colonies from New Hampshire to Georgia. In spite of Calvinists' involvement in the evangelistic efforts of these men, the Congregationalists of New England and the Presbyterians of several colonies divided as to the propriety of such "mass evangelistic efforts." The revivalists prevailed, however.

Beginning with the Great Awakening, the revivalist wing of the Presbyterians (the New Side) and the Methodists began to play an important role in American religious life. The Methodists were most effective in the mission to those without a church in the Anglican-dominated southern colonies. During the same period, Baptists also became more prominent with their revivalistic message. Under the Puritan-Congregationalist establishment of New England, they suffered whippings, jailings, and other persecutions. But during the Great Awakening, many Congregationalists and Anglicans were forced out of state-church parishes and joined the Baptists. Ammerman (1990:24) states that the Baptist revivals continued in North Carolina and led to the establishment of forty-two Baptist churches in the surrounding territory. This contributed to a spirit of pluralism that saw old denomination affiliation as less important than religious fervor.

This spirit of pluralism was advanced by revivalist preachers, who were ready to deliver their messages in the meetinghouses of any denomination in order to reach the religiously indifferent colonial population. These preachers emphasized that the true church was not to be identified exclusively with any single ecclesiastical body, and that no denomination could claim to represent the whole of Christianity; they made clear that they regarded each denomination as constituting a different mode of expressing in its outward forms of worship and organization the larger life of the universal church in which they all shared. John Wesley's famous quote sums up this early spirit of pluralism (cited by Hudson, 1981: 45):

> I...refuse to be distinguished from any other men by any but the common principles of Christianity.... I renounce and test all other marks of distinction. But from real Christians, of whatever denomination, I earnestly desire not to be distinguished at all.... Dost thou love and fear God? It is enough! I give the right hand of fellowship.

This early pluralistic idea, though expansive in concept, was applied in rather limited ways: Only evangelical Christians granted each other tolerance. The few Roman Catholics in the colonies were disenfranchised; Jews were so few in number that they were almost invisible. The religion of black slaves was of almost no concern until the first Great Awakening (Baer and Singer, 1992). When the conversion of the slaves began, these new "Christians" were overseen through white paternalism (Rabateau, 1978:66). The communal settlements of the Moravians and Amish were self-contained, and so posed no threat to either the established or evangelical Protestants. Nevertheless, this early concept of pluralism allowed for the development of religious tolerance, religious liberty, and later the formal separation of church and state. These revolutionary religious principles provided the base from which religious pluralism evolved.

The Separation of Church and State

Even though many of the settlers had come to the English-speaking colonies in search of religious freedom, they had, in many ways, become a religious establishment. At the time of the Declaration of Independence in 1776, there were thirteen small nations trying to become one out of many. Nine of these former colonies recognized official establishments of religion, but all of the colonies had a significant number of religious dropouts and dissenters. Between the time independence was won from Britain and the framing of the U.S. Constitution, no single church body had enough strength to prevail in the new country (Marty, 1970:36).

Formally, the new nation was Christian. (For most Americans this meant Protestant Christian: out of a population of approximately 3.5 million, only about twenty thousand were Roman Catholic and only about six thousand were Jewish.) But actually, in 1776 only about 10 to 20 percent of the colonial population were adherents of religion, according to church historians (Ahlstrom, 1975; Hudson, 1981). As a result of examining religious censuses and denominational data sources, Finke and Stark (1992:26–28) believe that the figure was closer to 17 percent. In a very real sense, organized religion in the United States was weaker at our national beginning than at any other time in its history. This was the result of both philosophical beliefs from the age of the Enlightenment and a general indifference to the practice of religion (Turner, 1985). Yet the influence of religion was deeply stamped on colonial institutions and minds. And although few people really bothered to observe religious customs and practices, few citizens wished to harm religion. Apathy, not antipathy, was the rule (Marty, 1970:38–39). Members of the huge unchurched majority in the new nation had to find a way to assert their freedom *from* religion; people who were churchgoing wished to preserve this right; and the few passionate defenders of religion needed a formulation they could endorse (Marty, 1970:37).

Some of the political leaders of the new nation, notably James Madison, took comfort from the division of churches. He and fellow framers of the Constitution were nominal church members, but they embraced the Enlightenment beliefs of the eighteenth century, including the religious philosophy of deism. Deism viewed God as a benign Spirit who was content to let the world be controlled only through the natural law, which the Deity had fashioned. At the same time as Benjamin Franklin, John Adams, James Madison, and particularly Thomas Jefferson wished to prevent the churches from "meddling in civil affairs," evangelical church leaders and dissenters from the established religion were pressing for a method to guarantee freedom from governmental intrusion into religion (Marty, 1970:35–39). Shortly after the ratification of the U.S. Constitution in 1789, the first ten amendments, or Bill of Rights, were added. Included was the important First Amendment guaranteeing freedom of religion. It was a unique feature that the new nation, which was officially nonreligious, guaranteed religious tolerance and freedom. The compromises of the political intellectuals and the proponents of religious tolerance gave rise to what we now refer to as the historic *separation of church and state.*

Wilson (1978:194) has listed ten reasons for the development and implementation of the separation of church and state, ranging from the fact that the United States was originally settled by those seeking freedom from religious persecution to the fact that Freemasonry, which strongly advocated religious toleration, was popular among many moving spirits of the American Revolution. Three of Wilson's reasons seem particularly relevant to the establishment of church/state separation. First, the dominant values in the infant nation were liberalism and pluralism. Both emphasized freedom of choice and individual responsibility, an emphasis that extended into the area of religion. Second, the First Great Awakening had strengthened the nonconformist spirit in the American colonies and had helped break down the constraints of the old parish system upon which the Anglican Church largely depended. Third, the sheer number and variety of religious groups present by the time of the nation's founding made some sort of accommodation to pluralism necessary if the nation were not only to become united but also to remain united. In addition, the voluntarism of most of these groups paved the way for religious pluralism and militated against the establishment of a nation in which citizenship and religious affiliation would be synonymous.

As we stated earlier, religious toleration, chiefly among Protestants, had begun before the ratification of the first ten amendments to the Constitution. Even in the colonies dominated by Anglicans and Congregationalists, other religious groups had not only coexisted with the established churches, but had begun to rival them in size (Finke and Stark, 1992:24–25). The religious groups that had gained most from the Great Awakening—the Methodists and the Baptists— felt that the separation of church and state gave them a new charter that elevated their status and enhanced their sense of mission to the unchurched masses (Marty, 1970). Soon after the nation's founding, they began to move west to the frontier in an effort to fight religious apathy.

The Birth and Development of Voluntarism and Religious Competition

Established religion in the colonies as well as in Europe depended upon financial support from the state. But in exchange for the right to remain free from state control or interference, the churches of the United States had to become self-supporting and self-perpetuating. An emasculated religious establishment continued for a while in three New England states, with each taxpayer assigning his taxes to the church of his choice. But the other ten states of the new nation incorporated the principle of separation of church and state into their constitutions. Only with voluntary support could the revivalist churches (the Baptists, Methodists, some Presbyterians, and later the Disciples of Christ) attempt mass evangelism on the expanding frontier. Voluntary support from the wealthy planter class of Virginia saved the newly named Protestant Episcopal Church (the American successor to the Anglican Church) from oblivion. When state support of the Congregationalists finally came to an end in New England in 1832, the Congregationalist churches also survived through voluntarism.

Hudson (1981) reports that voluntary societies sprang up first in New England and later in other seaboard states. Sunday schools, religious tracts (or pamphlets), religious periodicals, schools, colleges, and missionaries to the frontier territory were the beneficiaries of these voluntary societies. The American Home Missionary Society, founded in 1826, had as its stated purpose the promotion of "home missions" essential to the moral advancement and political stability of the United States. A series of frontier campaigns stressed the need of a Bible for every family, schools for all, and an abundance of pastors for the western settlers. The few frontier churches, as well as the more established ones in the original thirteen states, depended heavily on voluntary support.

The primary basis of religious growth after the establishment of the nation was an increase in religious mobilization. Much of the success of the Methodists and Baptists was due to their gathering in large numbers of the previously unchurched, particularly in the expanding frontier regions of the new nation (Finke and Stark, 1989:29). The older more established churches did not move rapidly to the frontier in spite of their involvement in voluntarism.

Finke and Stark (1989:30–31; 1992:54–59) also report that between 1776 and 1850, while the Baptists achieved a subtantial growth through conversion, the Methodists showed a *meteoric* rise. In 1776 Methodists accounted for only 2.5 percent of all religious adherents in the thirteen colonies, but by 1850 they numbered 13,302 congregations with more than 2.6 million members. Thus, the Methodist Church accounted then for 34.2 percent of all U.S. church members. Although Methodist and Baptist memberships increased rapidly, those of the Congregationalists and Episcopalians had only a modest growth. The Presbyterians also increased at a moderate rate.

These successes and failures caused the Congregationalists and Episcopalians to lose ground in what Finke and Stark (1992:59–60) call the rise of a "free-market religious economy." In spite of a commitment to voluntarism by all the leading denominations, the

Baptists and Methodists utilized their organizational structure (denominational polity), their "sales representatives" (clergy), their "product" (the religious message), and their "marketing techniques" (evangelism) to win the religious market in an expanding nation (Finke and Stark, 1989:32; 1992:71–86).

Specifically, the Baptists were democratic in polity; on the frontier, the Methodists were *locally* democratic as well. In terms of clergy, the Baptists utilized "farmer preachers" and the Methodists depended on "circuit rider preachers." These clergy (who were, for the most part, undereducated) preached a simple Christian evangelical message and employed revival techniques to add people to their denominational rolls. The Baptist and Methodist clergy were *of* the people, not *above* the people whom they served.

By contrast, the Congregationalists, Episcopalians, and Presbyterians were not so aggressive in moving westward. Congregationalists lacked a truly national organizational base. Although the Presbyterians and Episcopalians had national and regional organizations, each confronted unique problems. The American Revolution had severely weakened the American version of the Anglican communion. Presbyterians worked for unity (particularly with Congregationalists), but their efforts to promote strict standards in polity and doctrine led to regional schisms (Ahlstrom, 1975; cited in Finke and Stark, 1989:34).

So the concepts of voluntarism and competition in a "free-market religious economy" were necessary complements to the separation of church and state. According to functional theory, this separation contributed to the nation's stability by neutralizing any potential conflict that might have been caused by religion. The churches that flourished supported the nation, its leaders, and its new political system—all in all, the status quo. Voluntarism balanced this religious reinforcement of the political status quo by allowing some accommodation of more peculiar religious groups such as the Moravians, Amish, and Mennonites, whose exclusivity and communitarian characteristics stood in direct contrast to the more established and culturally approved Protestant denominations. Voluntarism also allowed for the founding of separate black Protestant churches, beginning in 1816 with the African Methodist Episcopal Church. Although white slave owners and nonslave owners alike agreed that black Americans were not equal to Anglo-Saxon whites, the whites' feelings of paternalism led them to give financial support for a separate denomination for free black Americans (Marty, 1970:27–38).

As the republic moved into its second half-century, religious pluralism had been tenuously established. Voluntarism and religious competition had proven successful, allowing influential but uneven

Protestant expansion into the western territories of the nation. The separation of church and state seemed to pose no threat to either party, since the state did not actively discourage religious beliefs and practices. "Freedom of religion was seen as belonging to the *individual* rather than to any religious group to which he might or might not belong," according to Pfeiffer (1974:13). Genuine diversity existed in American religious life, but within a framework of Protestant unity. Real religious diversity, which would test the boundaries of pluralism, church/state separation, and voluntarism, was about to unfold. The tensions produced by conflicting religious groups, a civil war, internal Protestant bickerings, and a visible philosophy of religious nonbelief were about to begin.

LATER FORCES FOR RELIGIOUS DIVERSITY

Four major historical processes led to the present religious diversity in the United States. The first was the influx of a largely Roman Catholic immigrant population. The second was the Civil War, which divided many of the major Protestant denominations into northern and southern branches and led to the further creation of separate churches for blacks. The third process was the division within Protestantism brought about by (1) the Unitarian schism in New England, (2) competition and differences among the frontier revival churches, (3) the millenarian movement within Protestantism, and (4) liberal theological developments that led to the Social Gospel and the fundamentalist/modernist controversy. Finally, the immigration of large numbers of Jews, with their refusal to believe that Christ was the Messiah, provided another foil to Christianity. Within the Protestant-dominated religious establishment, these historical processes created conflicts during the nineteenth century that did not begin to subside until the 1930s and 1940s. In addition to these major historical processes, the persistence of fringe sects, the recurring awakenings and revivals in religion, and the ebb and flow of dominance by one particular religious group or another have also contributed to religious diversity within the United States.

We can look at this religious diversity from the perspectives of functionalism and conflict theory, which we outlined in Chapter 2. From a functionalist theoretical perspective, the religious pluralism in the United States that allows for religious diversity promotes social integration. No single religious group does, or can, dominate, and religious diversity diffuses moral and ethical values throughout the various social classes. Functionalism tends, then, to play down social conflict, particularly that of an earlier era, which seemingly has worked itself out. The competing (or complementary) conflict perspective plays up the potentiality for conflict caused by religious differences. The historical events described in the following subsections will provide data for an analysis based upon conflict theory; this can provide an alternative explanation for religious diversity.

From the viewpoint of conflict theory, then, the presence of a dominant Protestant establishment that equated itself with national expansionism, laissez-faire capitalism, industrialization, and Christian Manifest Destiny provides some evidence that religious differences were used as tools to keep the growing numbers of urban workers economically depressed. It can also be demonstrated that religious arrogance and paternalism maintained the economic and political oppression of black Americans, even after the same paternalism had precipitated the abolition of slavery. The assumption of conflict theory—that conflict is a major source of social change—can help explain competition between Baptists and Methodists on the frontier and the established churches in the East.

About the same time, the following other battles took place within American Protestantism:

1. Millenarian groups began to make gloomy predictions that the end of the world was imminent;
2. Other Protestants embraced the idealism of the Social Gospel movement that claimed that society rather than individual souls could be saved; and
3. Many church believers were torn by the struggle to reconcile the new discoveries of science with the tradition of the Bible's inerrancy.

All these conflicts altered the overwhelming dominance of the U.S. social structure by a rather monolithic Protestantism. Finally, conflict theory assumes that religion can operate to mask real divisions (such as economic and political divisions) by substituting racial and ethnic "differences" that are specious. Thus we can see anti-Semitism that has surfaced from time to time in the United States as a means of preventing domination by Jews of parts of the economic order.

But conflict theory does not explain why the conflictual historical processes that furthered religious diversity finally resulted in what seemed like a peaceful, religiously diversified nation with some members of most religious groups within the higher levels of the stratification system. A closer look at these processes reveals both conflict and consensus, both intolerance and real accommodation. We will turn to that closer look now.

The Growth of Roman Catholicism

At the time the nation began, Roman Catholics numbered only twenty thousand and had but fifty-six parishes (Hudson, 1981). Their numbers did not begin to increase until the first immigration of Irish and continental Europeans, which began in the 1830s. After that time, American Protestants did not take long to strike out against this other branch of Christianity. Politically, the Know-Nothing party sought to prevent economic and political pluralism insofar as it applied to Catholics. Several prominent citizens, including the inventor of the telegraph Samuel F. B. Morse (1791–1872), published anti-Catholic tracts and made anti-Catholic speeches, the main theme of which was that Roman Catholics constituted a foreign conspiracy. Most of these anti-Catholics believed in the Manifest Destiny of a Protestant Christian United States; in the words of Marty (1970), they sought to extend the "righteous empire" of Protestant Christianity.

Most historians of religion in America (Marty, 1970; Hudson, 1981; Littell, 1962) have assumed that Catholic immigrants brought with them a steadfast belief in the "one true church." Because of this, the Protestant establishment reacted swiftly. Yet Finke and Stark (1992:109–144) have challenged this collective point of view. They demonstrate that the number of Catholic immigrants was probably exaggerated, particularly that of Irish Catholics. Many of the Irish were from the predominantly Protestant northern Ireland. Catholics who came from central, eastern, and southern Europe were products of a state church which required only nominal participation on the part of the laity. In other words, they were neither particularly committed to the church nor pious in their beliefs.

Furthermore, the waves of immigrants included continental European Protestants (Lutheran and Reformed church members), Jews, and infidels. These groups had been assimilated into the national consciousness before the Civil War. Nevertheless, many Protestant spokespersons believed that Catholic "hordes" posed the main threat to the Protestant establishment. Between 1815 and 1845, about 1 million Irish people entered the United States. German immigration was smaller, but did include a sizeable portion of Catholics (Marty 1970:124–28; 1984:272). By 1850 there were 1,088,016 Catholics in this country, or 13.9 percent of the population (Finke and Stark, 1992:55). Obviously, this percentage was not particularly significant, but it *seemed* an ominous growth rate. As a result, many within Protestantism would spend years fighting for immigration laws and other attempts to place legal limitations on Catholicism.

Proper evangelical Protestants were offended by the Germans' observance of the continental Sabbath, which included beer drinking and other robust entertainments, all held on Sunday. The Irish were viewed as poor, undependable, and untrustworthy drunkards. In general, the alien culture of a vast majority of Catholics provided a convenient target for blame for the increasing problems of poverty, unrest, and crime in the expanding population of the nation. The Know-Nothing party (properly named the American party) disclosed lurid information concerning alleged illicit sexual activities behind the doors of Catholic convents. The best known of these phony exposés were *Six Months in a Convent* (1834) and *The Awful Disclosures of Maria Monk* (1836) (Myers, 1960:92).

Shortly thereafter, in 1844, the Methodist bishops announced that "Romanism is now laboring, not only to recover what it had of its former supremacy before the Reformation, but also to assert and establish its monstrous pretensions in countries never subject either to its civil or ecclesiastical authority" (Marty, 1970:129). These bishops and other Protestant clergy appear to have joined in the anti-Catholic crusade with almost as much vigor as the extremist Know-Nothings. Protestant alarmists greatly exaggerated the numerical strength of the Catholics as well as their organized efforts to convert Americans to Catholicism. Typical is this quote from the *Protestant Vindicator* in 1834 (cited in Marty, 1970:129–30): "Jesuits are prowling about all parts of the United States in every possible disguise…to disseminate Popery…including puppet show men, dancing masters, music teachers, peddlers of images and ornaments, barrel organ players, and similar practitioners."

Even though Catholics arrived in greater and greater numbers, they were not automatically drawn to the Roman Catholic Church. In fact, Finke and Stark (1992:115–123) describe Catholic variants of "evangelism and revivalism" efforts aimed at keeping newly arrived immigrants within the Catholic fold. As early as 1829, the Catholic bishops began to advocate the formation of parochial schools, and by 1840 there were over two hundred Catholic schools in the United States. By 1850 the Roman Catholic Church had become the third-largest single church in the country (Finke and Stark, 1992:113). Despite this fact, Protestant alarmists often portrayed Catholics as the *largest* denomination (Marty, 1984).

As a result, the political power marshaled against Roman Catholic immigration reached a frenzy during the 1850s. For example, in 1854 the Know-Nothing party seated 8 out of 62 United States senators and 104 out of 234 U.S. representatives; the party also controlled the governorships of nine states (Myers, 1960:144). The party's extremist viewpoint failed, however, to halt the Catholic increase, and the extremist rhetoric of the Know-Nothings proved too much for the majority of Americans. Moreover, the events leading up to the Civil War preoccupied most citizens. Protestant fanatics failed to prove that a vast majority of the foreign-born Catholics were un-American (Marty, 1970:130).

In addition to the early Catholic influx from Europe, the predominantly Protestant nation also "inherited" Roman Catholics. The Louisiana Purchase included territory with a large Catholic population. The annexation of Texas added Hispanic Catholics, as did the Treaty of Guadalupe Hidalgo (1848), which made California, New Mexico, and Arizona a part of the nation. In methods parallel to those used by Baptist "home missionaries," Catholics used railroad cars converted into "chapel cars" to travel through the newer western states and to bring a Catholic evangelistic message to an expanding nation (Finke and Stark, 1992:141–43; 123–24).

After the Civil War, immigration continued at an even more rapid pace. As in the preceding decades, the cities became the respositories of the alien populations. Between 1820 and 1900, 19 million immigrants arrived; one-fourth of these were Irish who settled in the cities of the East (and later the Midwest). Although their muscle built much of the cities and fired the industrial machines, most Protestants despised them. Because these immigrants made up the bulk of the urban working class, it was inevitable that they would be implicated in agitation for unionization. When the highest-ranking Catholic cleric, Cardinal James Gibbons of Baltimore, refused to condemn the Knights of Labor in 1887, he thereby gave tacit approval for Catholics to join in labor organizing. Affluent Protestants, who in large part were antilabor, mistrusted and feared the Catholic masses even more after this event.

The immigrant nature of the Roman Catholic Church made it an "outsider" religious group, but one differentiated from other outsider groups. The typical American Catholic in mid-nineteenth-century America began life as either a foreigner or an annexed citizen. "Immigrant Catholics brought with them not only their strong sense of cultural differences between Catholicism and Protestantism but also their sense of the differences between their own national identification and that of other nineteenth-century immigrants to America" (Moore, 1986:51).

Because of religious (and ethnic) prejudice, most of the foreign-born stayed close together, particularly the Irish Catholics. In Ireland, the Catholic Church, the major force against British Protestant dominance, found itself in tension with the British government. Because of this, Finke and Stark (1992:136–38) describe much of early American Catholicism as an Irish "sect movement." Irish Catholics, particularly Irish priests, found a continuation of that tension with American Protestantism when they arrived in the United States. Although many Catholics had been indifferent about the church in Ireland, they contributed pennies and nickels from meager wages to build the imposing parish churches of urban Catholicism in the United States. The church became the center for neighborhoods under local Irish control. The Catholics continued to build parochial schools to avoid excessive Protestant influence upon their children (Marty, 1970:150; 1984:273–75). Other Catholic immigrant groups followed these exclusive patterns, which were due in large part to the Irish dominance of the Catholic hierarchy and priesthood.

The extent to which Protestants feared, mistrusted, and resented Roman Catholics was revealed in *Our Country*, a book written in 1891 by Josiah Strong, a public relations agent for the Congregational Church and a Protestant moderate. According to Strong, Catholicism opposed the bases of our national life: It was critical of popular sovereignty, free speech, free press, free conscience, free schools, and the separation of church and state. Strong had heard the Catholic archbishop of St. Paul, Minnesota, announce his desire to make the United States a Catholic nation. Such inflammatory statements suggested to Protestants that Catholics were out to destroy church/state separation. Further, the decree of papal infallibility issued in 1870–71 made Protestants suspect that Catholics would be more responsive to an infallible foreign religious leader than to the civil leaders of the United States. Catholic numbers were estimated by spokesmen of the Catholic hierarchy at anywhere from 9 million to 13 million in 1889–90. Strong reported that there was, on average, 1 Protestant church organization to every 438 people in the United States in 1890; by way of contrast, in the Roman Catholic enclave of Boston the ratio was 1 to 1,778; in St. Louis, it was 1 to 2,662; and worse of all, in Chicago, the ratio was 1 to 3,061 people (Marty, 1970:155–60).

At the same time that Catholic numbers in the United States were swelling, Roman Catholics were facing an internal struggle over the issue of Americanization. Irish Catholics, under the leadership of Cardinal Gibbons, advocated a united Roman Catholic Church free of ethnic divisions. Other Catholic ethnic groups, notably the Germans, opposed this diffusion of national values, customs, and language. The disputes within the American Roman Catholic Church were not over the question of whether immigrant Catholics should Americanize, but about how they should do so (Moore, 1986:51). However, in the end the bond of Roman Catholicism and Americanization prevailed over the more narrow focuses of various ethnic groups (Marty, 1984:280–85).

The efforts of Protestants first to prevent and later to temper Catholic influence can be seen as attempts to preserve Protestant hegemony. Catholics were mainly city dwellers and industrial workers. This made them an easy target of the anticity bias of Protestants that lingered in efforts to preserve the rural presence in the political realm even as native-born rural Protestants were also moving into cities to work in the factories and businesses of the evolving industrial system. This also made Catholics an easy target of the Protestant antiunionism that sought to preserve owner-dominated capitalism at the expense of the masses of the urban working class. As Hunter (1983:24) has stated, a distinct element of the nineteenth-century Protestant world was an ethical orientation expressed in self-discipline, frugality, industry, and pragmatism. The growth of Roman Catholicism not only threatened the numerical dominance of Protestants but also this deeply held ethical orientation.

The Civil War and the Growth of Black Churches

The second major historical process that contributed to religious division and diversity in the United States was the conflict that divided North and South. Slavery and the economic system that spawned it were attacked by abolitionist religious leaders in the North and defended by proslavery clergy in the South. Marty (1970:57–58) has stated that southern church leaders defended the two-nation theory of the secessionists as "God's plan for America." God was seen as a proslavery Deity by Southerners and as an antislavery Deity by Northerners.

Historically, the influence of the Episcopal Church and the eighteenth-century deistic philosophy had contributed to the preeminence of the southern colonies (and later states) in American politics and intellectual leadership. As we have shown, however, Methodists, Baptists, and other more evangelical religious groups became the dominant churches of the southern states. Baptists and Methodists were able to achieve great success in converting slaves from their African religions to Christianity. The best estimates of these successes state that 12 to 15 percent of the slaves were church members by the middle of the nineteenth century (Moore, 1986:176). In addition, many of these African-American Christians knew not only the tenets of Christianity but also some of the finer points of doctrine (Rabateau, 1978:209–10).

Revivalism was as strong in the southern region as in the new territories of the country. In spite of the common mission of revivalism,

sectional differences developed between and within the revivalist denominations (Finke and Stark, 1992:92–108). Breakdown of communications between the sections of the country was also foreshadowed
by a breakdown of communication within the Methodist, Baptist, and
Presbyterian churches. This created a situation in which the most
strenuous efforts were made to suppress discussion concerning slavery, pro or con, culminating in 1832 in the passage by the U.S. House
of Representatives of the Gag Law, which tabled without discussion
all petitions against slavery (Littell, 1962:62).

Other religious issues entered the argument between regional
branches of the different Protestant denominations, but the issue of
slavery and the economic survival of the agrarian South was always
present. For example, Presbyterians in the southern states split initially concerning the propriety of revivalism, but slavery soon entered
into the discussion.

Methodists and Baptists did not mask the issue of slavery as well
as Presbyterians did. Even though most Southerners did not own
slaves, they saw the perpetuation of this "peculiar institution" as necessary, and at the root of their defense was the fact that the Bible did
not proscribe slavery. As the growing and exporting of cotton continued to increase in the South, the association of religion with race came
to be a distinctive feature of southern thinking and economic rationalization. It contributed to the defense of the southern way of life
(largely agrarian) and to the isolation of the rural South from the ur-
banizing and industrializing North (Marty 1970:63–64). In 1845 Southern Baptists withdrew from their northern counterparts over the
question of slavery and control of missionary efforts in the two regions of the country (Ammerman, 1990:31–32). In that same year the
Methodists in the South became the Methodist Episcopal Church,
South. In 1857 the Old Side alliance between Presbyterians of both
sections of the country gave way to a separate branch of the Presbyterian Church within the southern states, calling itself the Presbyterian Church in the United States.

The Civil War exacerbated these divisions. During the war the
Emancipation Proclamation added further fuel to the split. Abraham
Lincoln's religious language perpetuated the idea within the Union
that the war was a holy war to preserve the common society; this belief was countered by the South's version of a holy war to create two
distinctive nations (Marty, 1970). Although President Lincoln wanted
the victorious northern states to heal the deep wounds inflicted by the
war, his death resulted in the ascension of radical Republican leaders
who implemented vindictive reconstruction policies. As a result, the

economically devastated South suffered even greater personal and political humiliation than would have occurred under Lincoln. In addition, the emancipation of slaves left the South with about 4 million largely untrained freed people (Marty, 1970:134).

Northern church people saw their abolitionist cause as vindicated; southern church people could only be confused and make vague references to "God's will." Largely left out of the religious thought of the South were the newly enfranchised black citizens. The northern churches began concentrating on educational missions among blacks. Previously, Protestant churches of the South had provided for the spiritual needs of the slaves through the establishment of some separate slave churches, but largely through segregated seating in their own church buildings. During the Civil War, however, a mass exodus of blacks from the dominant southern churches began. In 1860 there had been 207,000 southern Methodist blacks; in 1866, there were only 78,000 still on the church membership rolls. Southern Presbyterians experienced a 70 percent decline in black membership during the war years. Southern Baptists saw a similar black exodus, but because of the local autonomy of Baptist churches, their statistics were more tenuous (Marty 1970:137).

For the remainder of the nineteenth century, and well into this one, the split between northern and southern Protestants continued to further divide the Protestant religious community in the United States. The two dominant southern denominations, the Methodists and the Baptists, became heirs of the evangelical and revivalistic traditions of nineteenth-century Protestantism after the Social Gospel debates and the fundamentalist/modernist doctrinal controversy of the 1920s. Rural Protestantism was the legacy left to southern Protestants after the Civil War and Reconstruction.

During the same period, the new status of African-Americans as officeholders in southern states aided in the further establishment and growth of all-black churches. As stated earlier in this chapter, the African Methodist Episcopal Church was founded in 1816, and a rival group was formed out of the denomination a few years later. However, these churches were predominantly northern with members who were freed blacks. After the Civil War, the black exodus from southern Protestant churches was welcomed by whites; the black person in the South was seen by the Protestant establishment as an ally of Republican Reconstruction. Separate African-American denominations began with help from Northerners (Lincoln and Mamiya, 1990). Any mission to blacks was largely abandoned by southern church people, who established the policy of segregation in religion as well as in all other areas of social life (Marty, 1970:140). African-Americans who remained within the Presbyterian and Methodist churches were members of segregated congregations. The emergence of a separate black religious community followed this rigid segregation in the South and subsequent discrimination against blacks in the North. It also gave rise to African-American religious and political subcultures (Lincoln and Mamiya, 1990). The African-American church is examined in greater detail in Chapter 12.

We can say, then, that the economic and political conflict that resulted in the Civil War had a divisive effect upon the dominant Protestant religious establishment. A division almost as deep as that between Roman Catholics and Protestants developed as a result of the slavery issue before the Civil War and the racism that developed in the South after the conflict. This division resulted in a separate kind of culture in the southern states that emphasized segregation in religion, education, and daily social contacts. The evangelistic tradition of nineteenth-century Protestantism remained firmly embedded in the religious consciousness of Southerners, both African-American and white. Although Reconstruction ended in 1876 when the South was fully restored politically to the Union, in the realm of "religious reconstruction" African-American Protestants did not win full participation in the religious affairs of either the South or the rest of the country. In a real sense, this further diversity in American religious life has perhaps perpetuated the caste system affecting African-Americans by providing "caste churches" for this largest of American minorities (Wilson, 1978:322).

Thus the Civil War created more religious organizations, particularly African-American churches, and further divided white Protestants into northern and southern groups. For better or worse, religious diversity continued to expand. Meanwhile, other events that had begun before the Civil War continued to divide the dominant Protestant establishment of the United States.

Divisions within Protestantism

The evangelical fervor of the Great Awakenings had become the dominant feature of Protestantism in the United States by the early part of the nineteenth century, but the revival techniques characteristic of evangelicalism were not universally accepted. Even during the First Great Awakening of the late colonial period, the Puritan Congregational establishment divided into prorevival and antirevival segments, as did the Presbyterians, who then suffered another schism following the Second Great Awakening of the early nineteenth century. As we stated earlier in this chapter, the primary participants in these evangelical efforts were the Baptists, the Methodists, and the newly formed Disciples of Christ churches.

When the American frontier became the arena for Protestant revival efforts, the common purpose of evangelizing people in the new territories united divergent Protestant groups for several decades. Even the introduction of millenarianism—the belief in the imminent return of Christ to Earth—into most American Protestant denominations did not fragment them at first. However, differences did develop both in theology and in the nature and purpose of the Christian tradition that ultimately divided the Protestant denominations and weakened their dominance of the U.S. religious realm. The first of these was the doctrinal dispute concerning the concept of the Trinity—God the Father, God the Son, and God the Holy Spirit.

The nineteenth century opened with anti-Trinitarianism enjoying rather widespread support in the new nation. The thinkers of the eighteenth-century Enlightenment had partially embraced Unitarianism through their infatuation with deism. Many prominent political leaders, including Thomas Jefferson and John Calhoun, believed that Unitarianism was the "wave of the future" for Americans.

The rejection of a Trinitarian formula as a test of religious orthodoxy brought together not only intellectuals and New England elitists but also many who opposed the rigid theological scholasticism of Calvinist doctrine. As early as 1785, the historic King's Chapel (Episcopal) in Boston altered its prayer book and embraced Unitarian ideas (Chorowsky and Raible, 1975:274). As we mentioned earlier, Congregational churches in Massachusetts began to embrace Unitarianism while still supported by state monies, prompting orthodox Congregationalists to press for disestablishment. In 1819 William Ellery Channing delivered a sermon entitled "Unitarian Christianity," and more churches joined the exodus from Congregationalism. The final result was the end of state support of churches in New England and the division of the old established church in New England into two smaller denominations, Congregationalism and Unitarianism (Marty, 1970:70).

Elitism was to become the Unitarians' hallmark. They remained centered intellectually in eastern cultural circles and became dominant in literary and philosophical interests. They refused to participate in missionary activity both in the eastern states and on the frontier because such activity seemed incompatible with their views on the dignity of man (Littell 1962:44–45). A kind of religious toleration was a permanent part of Unitarianism, but it did not quickly spread to the more exclusive denominations. The doctrinal controversy between the New England Trinitarians and Unitarians was a hint of what was to develop within the ranks of Protestantism. On the frontier, a similar controversy further divided Protestantism.

In the movement that began under Thomas Campbell (1763–1854) and his son, Alexander Campbell (1788–1866), the goal was a restoration of primitive Christian unity. The Campbells believed that sectarian divisions among Christians were un-Christian and that the cure for such divisions was the restoration of the New Testament church. After attempts at Christian unity failed, this Cambellite movement became known as the Christian Church. The movement became more settled in the form of a brotherhood of locally organized churches whose members viewed the Bible as the chief cornerstone of faith and truth. Although these churches were confined almost entirely to the Ohio River Valley, their zeal in opposing an educated clergy and their opposition to the missionary societies of the more established religious groups were an early sign of later Protestant fragmentation over the fundamentals of the faith (Hudson, 1981).

As these attempts toward Protestant unity disintegrated, the support of a united Protestant ministry in the expanding nation fragmented into more sectarian voluntary efforts. Baptists, Methodists, Presbyterians, and the weakened Congregationalists pursued similar but nonetheless different paths in extending Christianity. At the end of the Civil War, few attempts toward reunification of the split evangelical denominations were successful. The Northern Baptists made efforts toward reconciliation with Southern Baptists, but were rejected (Ammerman, 1990:37). As a result, the defeated South became firmly entrenched in a religious culture that included the isolated traditions of rural Protestantism but excluded the participation of African-Americans in the religion of white Southerners.

A different kind of religious culture developed in the northern tier of states. As immigrants (largely Catholic) poured into the cities, so also did rural native-born citizens. The virtues of the work ethic and laissez-faire capitalism were the features of this transplanted urban Protestantism. The unique and obvious destiny of a Protestant United States in the world provided a common goal for Protestant denominations in the last three decades of the nineteenth century. To limit Catholic influence and to convert as many Catholic immigrants as possible were publicly stated aims. However, even these common efforts did not prevent further division within Protestantism.

As Protestant immigrants came to the Midwest, they were also viewed as somehow different and threatening to the evangelical denominations. Lutherans from the German states and members of European Reformed churches practiced the customs of the continent.

Sabbath, just as did Roman Catholics. Furthermore, the Lutherans sought to preserve their liturgical traditions. Although Germans had been well regarded in the school textbooks of America, their arrival in large numbers made them hard to absorb or to comprehend. Marty (1970:126) quotes a Methodist mission superintendent on the need to proselytize these Lutherans:

> The Germans almost all belong to some church, and are strongly attached to what they call their faith. Hence, we have to preach their religion out of their heads in order to preach Bible religion into their hearts.

These efforts largely failed, for few German Lutherans—particularly those who had settled in cities—converted to evangelical denominations. But Lutherans from the Scandinavian countries also came to the upper Midwest and the Great Plains; among those immigrants an alliance with the larger evangelical bodies did develop. Their fear of Catholics and of sinfulness in the urban areas led them to adopt much of the Protestant religious culture of the day. Still, the Lutherans, who were largely divided along ethnic lines, remained apart from the Methodists, Baptists, Presbyterians, and other evangelicals.

Another source of divisiveness in Protestantism during this same era was the *millenarian movement* within the United States. Millenarians believe that Christ's return to Earth is imminent, and that when he does return, holiness will prevail and he will reign on Earth for a thousand years. This concept is based, in part, upon the twentieth chapter of the book of Revelation. This movement attempted to function as a correction to "perverse beliefs" in different Protestant denominations. It possessed a distinct identity and all the characteristics of a new sect, developing as a "church within a church" (Sandeen, 1970:xv). The leadership for this apocalyptic vision of society's destiny came largely from the Episcopal, Presbyterian, and Baptist clergy of good standing and considerable pulpit abilities. This group, which believed in the imminent Second Coming of Christ, spread their doctrinal interpretations through annual summer conferences, periodicals, and winter conventions. Sandeen (1970:xvii) has stated that their aim was to "awaken the sleeping church to the imminence of judgment and to call sinners to repentance before the day of salvation had passed away." They campaigned against biblical liberalism and for belief in the "infallibility of the Holy Scriptures," which they saw as tools for the salvation of the masses.

Within the ranks of Southern Baptists, the millenarian movement eventually led to a schism. Although about 95 percent of Southern Baptist ministers rejected biblical criticism as ungodly, they were not as united in interpreting certain portions of the New Testament, and in particular those portions of the Scriptures underscoring the millenarian position in various ways. The millenarians within the denomination were vocal critics of the nonmillenarians. Many churches left to become "independent Baptist churches," in what was a prelude to twentieth-century millenarian divisiveness.

Also within the more established evangelical churches emerged the major issue that would fragment Protestantism in the United States for many decades. That issue consisted of two parts: a doctrinal dispute concerning biblical inerrancy, and an internal dispute over the mission of the church. The doctrinal dispute, known as the *fundamentalist/modernist controversy*, emerged when the rise of science and scientific discovery led to disagreements over the creation of humankind and the universe. While biblical literalists insisted upon the accuracy of the account given in the book of Genesis, proponents of biblical criticism argued that this need not be a test of orthodoxy. These disputes within Protestant evangelical bodies continued into the twentieth century. The second part of the major divisive issue was also a result of the rise of science, or more specifically, the applications of science that developed the mighty industrial machine in the cities. Proponents of the Social Gospel advocated ministering to the economic, political, and social needs of the rising number of the urban poor. Complacent and conservative Protestants, however, saw this as a subversion of the gospel; the old evangelical mission was concerned first with the salvation of the individual, not with the improvement of his or her living conditions.

We will discuss these two disputes in greater detail in Chapter 7. For now, suffice it to say that ultimately the Protestant world split into two distinct groups, which Marty (1970) has labeled *public* and *private Protestants*. Public Protestants sought to improve conditions within the social order, and gradually rejected more and more the techniques of revivalism and personal conversion as they became more politically involved. On the other hand, private Protestants cherished the evangelical traditions that had characterized all Protestants early in the nineteenth century. These church members and clergy accented individual salvation, or personal moral life characterized by piety, and heavenly rewards (Marty, 1970:179).

The inability of these two factions to reconcile their internal differences contributed to further diversity in the religious life of the United States. Minor splits involving holiness in living occurred within Methodism. Baptists in both the North and South suffered schisms involving doctrinal disputes. The Campbellite movement split into two camps, one conservative and the other moderate: the present-day

Churches of Christ are the extremely conservative group, and the Disciples of Christ are moderate to liberal in their theological and social stances. In the end a "third force in Christendom" (McLoughlin, 1967) developed, composed of conservative Protestants in mainline denominations, fundamentalists, and members of small sects. Together these formed, at the beginning of the twentieth century, a pietistic religious culture that has competed, however unequally, with mainstream Protestantism in this century.

Thus, these internal conflicts created deep and permanent divisions within Protestantism in the United States. Although some of the wounds healed, Protestant battles against each other, particularly those of conservative and fundamentalist bodies versus the more moderate churches, were only slightly less intense than the Protestant battle against the Roman Catholics. The absolute dominance of the nation's religious life by Protestantism was permanently weakened by this internal divisiveness and would continue into the first four decades of the twentieth century (Marty, 1991). No longer able to stand united against Catholic growth, Protestantism was faced with a fourth historical process that further promoted religious pluralism. Hunter (1983:27) has called this the beginning of the disestablishment of American Protestantism.

The Growth of Judaism

When the colonial state churches of the United States were disestablished, Jews were present in the new nation but numbered only one-twentieth of 1 percent of the citizenry. Most were of Spanish, Dutch, German, and Portuguese descent. Before the Civil War, they made little impact on the national consciousness, and by 1848 only fifty congregations of Jews existed. Although anti-Semitism was a feature of the early post–Civil War Ku Klux Klan, this anti-Jewish prejudice did not fully bloom until much later. In the 1880s the first large migration began to occur from Germany. Soon many other Jews migrated from Russia in the wake of anti-Jewish pograms in that country. Almost all the Jewish immigrants gravitated to urban areas. Most of them were secularized as a result of their Russian and eastern European experiences. Some, but by no means all, were politically radical. They did not embrace the rural American virtues sustained by Protestants (Marty, 1970:38, 124–25, 160–61). Judaism offered the benefits of a homogeneous community struggling against ethnic and religious bigotry; as a result, Judaism in the United States has always seemed to be an ethnic subculture as well as a religion.

The formation of this ethnic subculture was aided in large part by the fact that not all of the many immigrant families were orthodox Jews. Most of the almost 2 million Jews who came between the end of the Civil War and the outbreak of World War I (1914) were influenced by the ideals of the European Enlightenment of the eighteenth century. In America Jews could pursue opportunities unavailable in the European countries from which they came. Not only were economic opportunities available but so also were the benefits of democratic idealism and humanitarianism (Moore, 1986:73–74). These rather secular Jews had undergone considerable emancipation from traditional Jewish observances. The earlier-arriving German Jews, through their rabbis, had developed what is now known as *Reform Judaism*. The appeal of this branch of the Jewish faith to the secularists among the migrants lay in its emphasis upon liberal humanism and its adaptation of certain features of American Protestantism, notably the religious education of the young (McNamara, 1974:211). However, this dose of humanism did not satisfy all the newly arrived Jews. By the end of the nineteenth century, a reaction had developed among Jews dissatisfied with such an amalgamation of liberalism and Protestantism. This produced the branch of that faith now known as *Conservative Judaism*. Emphasis was upon Jewish traditions but not upon strict orthodoxy. While fidelity to Jewish law, literature, and language was preeminent, flexibility concerning American traditions was also included (Sklare, 1971:269).

The Conservative position, however, was not the compromise that would provide a unification of the growing Jewish population in the United States. The eastern European Jews who formed the second wave of Jewish immigration at the end of the nineteenth century were a mix of people who adhered to both religious orthodoxy and political radicalism, such as socialism and anarchism (McNamara, 1974:212). The more orthodox among this group desired to continue the strict observance of Jewish law and dietary customs ("keeping kosher"). This desire, as well as the emphasis on national origin, impeded the absorption of most eastern European Jews into the existing religious structure of Judaism in the United States. Thus began Orthodox Judaism, with its own organizational forms and synagogues. Bitter arguments occurred among the branches, but the kind of permanent alienation characteristic of the relationship between fundamentalist and nonfundamentalist Protestantism never developed. By 1924 Jews in the United States, despite their internal divisions, constituted a well-defined ethnic group and this ethnicity often overshadowed the religious aspect of Judaism. In addition to other social sources, the Yiddish language (a mixture of High German and Hebrew), remained a cultural mark of Jewishness, particularly for immigrants from eastern Europe (Goldscheider and Neusner, 1990).

Both the orthodoxy of some of these eastern European Jews and the widely publicized unorthodox political views of other Jews impeded their assimilation in the United States. The strict customs of Orthodox Judaism seemed repugnant to both Protestants and Catholics. Because the Roman Catholic Church still blamed the death of Christ upon all Jews, tensions quickly developed between Catholic and Jewish enclaves within the growing cities. The increasing presence of Judaism, particularly in the cities, added fuel to the smoldering fires of anti-Jewish prejudice.

Throughout history, the form and substance of anti-Semitism has varied. The long association between Jews and banking and finance in certain European nations was certainly a factor in much of the anti-Semitism directed against them as more and more Jews arrived in the United States. This was particularly true of the anti-Semitism demonstrated by other European immigrants. As early as the 1880s, Jews were suspected in some quarters of economic manipulation and exploitation. Curiously, the later immigrants were relatively poor, and most were crowded into tenement houses in New York City's Lower East Side and other urban areas. Several decades passed before the upward mobility of Jews took place on a large scale. Nevertheless, anti-Jewish prejudice, so long a part of Western civilization, became a part of the religious as well as the economic and political fabric of the United States.

In summary, although no European-style pogroms occurred against Jews in the United States, their acceptance by Protestants and Roman Catholics was long in coming. Partly as a reaction to these hostilities, American Jews, unlike the majority of Catholics who came from Europe, rejected the idea that assimilation was the end toward which they should strive (Sklare, 1971:4). Thus, although fewer public conflicts took place between Jews and others than between Protestants and Catholics, the addition of this third dimension to religious diversity did not come easily.

The Growth of Exclusive Religious Groups and Sects

A final process contributing to religious diversity in the United States was the ebb and flow of communitarian experiments, religious sects adhering to particularistic beliefs, and the development of three uniquely American sects—Mormonism, Christian Science, and Jehovah's Witnesses. In addition, many new smaller bodies split off from the larger Protestant groups; within Judaism, smaller exclusive groups developed that adhere to its historical traditions more than do most American Jews; and even within Roman Catholicism, old-order churches such as the Polish Old Catholics and the Byzantine Rite Church maintained separate identities. But the three groups of American origin are generally seen by religious historians as the best examples of this country's religious originality in the infinite variety of the world's religions (Littell 1962:83).

Exclusive religious communities date back to colonial times. Mennonites and Amish arrived in Pennsylvania in the late 1600s. Moravians (or German Pietists) migrated to Pennsylvania in the early 1700s, and later to North Carolina. During the early decades of this country, several communitarian experiments with religious overtones were established. The Shakers, Rappites, and Owenites as well as the Zoar, Oneida, and Amana communities, plus others, tested the limits of religious consensus and encountered various degrees of ostracism, persecution, and martyrdom (Marty, 1970:123).

None of these communities, however, was as disturbing as Mormonism, which began in western New York state. According to Littell (1962:83–84), it is best understood as one of the many variant movements emerging out of theocratic Puritanism. Its founder, Joseph Smith (1805–44), advocated polygamy because it was present in the Old Testament. Latter-day revelations extending biblical teachings became a part of the tradition of Mormonism. The early Mormons viewed America as the continent upon which the ten tribes of Israel would be restored and would be reigned over personally by Christ. When the followers of Smith were driven from New York to Illinois, many establishment Protestants viewed them as a greater threat to America's religious life than the Roman Catholics (Marty, 1970:124–25). Smith was killed by an armed mob in Carthage, Illinois, in 1844; his successor, Brigham Young, led the group into the Salt Lake Valley of the Utah territory in 1847. During the 1850s and 1860s, some eighty thousand Mormon pioneers migrated west. Of these, more than six thousand died en route (Evans, 1975:187–88).

The enemies of Mormonism believed that the Mormons were morally and ethnically peculiar. In a fashion also used against other minorities, these individuals tried to validate claims that Mormons had lied, stolen, sworn, and fornicated. A number of charges accused them of theft and murder against their neighbors (Moore, 1986). However, other persecuted subcultures responded in much the same manner against their persecutors. In the end, however, the Mormons' commitment to hard work and their sense of communal values allowed them greater acceptance by the general population (Moore, 1986:43–44).

The Church of Jesus Christ of Latter-day Saints (the Mormon Church) now claims almost a monopoly in the political, economic, and religious spheres in Utah, southern Idaho, and most of Nevada.

With this kind of power have come dominance and affluence (Shupe, 1989). This dominance was facilitated by the church's giving up its belief in polygamy in exchange for Utah statehood. Through extensive proselytizing, the Mormon church has increased its membership not only in those states but throughout the United States and most of the world. The church's emphasis upon large families, the subservience of wives to husbands, and the virtues of the work ethic have attracted many converts to this conservative approach to life.

Christian Science, by contrast, does not proselytize but claims that its possession of an esoteric body of knowledge will lead people to a new vision of the world. Intellectually, it is based on a simplified reading of the tenets of German idealism: Evil has no real existence, and the attainment of a positive, manifest prosperity is the mark of triumphant living and divine favor. When Mary Baker Eddy (1821–1910) founded this movement in 1875, she had only a small number of followers in a poor suburb of Boston (Littell, 1962:89). The textbook of the new religion was Mrs. Eddy's book *Science and Health* (later published as *Science and Health with Key to the Scriptures*). She and her followers stressed the reinstatement of primitive Christianity and its lost element of healing; unity of mind between God and people became the chief tenet of the faith—a kind of simplified transcendentalism (Stokes, 1975:69–70). Moore (1986:106–8) points out that writers in the nineteenth century were alarmed by Mrs. Eddy's doctrines and accused her of "occult practices." He further states that she was responsible, in large part, for her reputation as an eccentric. In the end, her quiet zeal led to the formation of churches in all of the major cities of the United States and Europe. Her stress on the evidence of spiritual well-being, as well as on spiritual healing, fit in with an upper-middle-class belief in prosperity.

Christian Science grew rather slowly in the first half of the twentieth century, but its influence now extends far beyond its estimated three hundred thousand members. For example, *The Christian Science Monitor* remains an influential newspaper. The legality of Christian Science practitioners' forms of healing is now unquestioned, since fees paid to them are tax-deductible as medical expenses. But in spite of its influential role in our country's religious development, Christian Science maintains an exclusive attitude, shown by its lack of interdenominational cooperation and its attempts to suppress books and articles deemed unfriendly to its cause (Littell, 1962:90). In the last decade, its practices have been subjected to several court challenges, both civil and criminal. In addition, the church is generally regarded as on the edge of bankruptcy because of its membership loss and the purchase of an unprofitable cable television network.

The third American contribution to religious bodies is Jehovah's Witnesses, a millenarian movement founded by Charles Taze Russell in 1872. In 1881 this former Congregationalist incorporated the group as the Watch Tower Bible and Tract Society. Like Mormonism and Christian Science, Jehovah's Witnesses claimed to represent a restitution of primitive Christianity; its teachings included an imminent Second Coming of Christ followed by a millennium, or thousand-year reign of Christ upon the Earth (Littell, 1962:90–91). Jehovah's Witnesses were proletarian in their beginnings—their original appeal was to dispersed working people and the poor—and they have remained so throughout their history. According to Zygmunt (1970:926–48), the Witnesses have maintained and intensified their opposition to worldly life. They have always cited biblical authority for their name and particularly for their belief that only 144,000 people will ultimately be saved and permitted to live in heaven (Henschel, 1975:132). The central preoccupation of this sect was, and is, proselytizing. Their evangelism has become a warning-and-rescue operation, with deliverance from the world as a major theme (Zygmunt, 1970:946).

In a way similar to the Mormons, the Witnesses have experienced organized opposition by government and private groups. Their refusal to salute the flag or do military service has aroused particular hostility. During 1940 alone, more than 335 cases of mob violence against Jehovah's Witnesses in forty-four states was documented. Arrests of group members were widespread and, because of this, court action was sought by the sect. In 1943 they finally won the right not to salute the United States flag (Wilson, 1978:197). Thus, their right to exist as an alternative to traditional forms of Christianity has been hard fought. More than most millenarian organizations, Jehovah's Witnesses have survived organizationally, have maintained their "last days" appeal, and have continued to convert thousands of people to their beliefs (Zygmunt, 1970:947).

THE ASCENDANCE OF RELIGIOUS PLURALISM

By the twentieth century Protestant dominance of religious life in our country was almost at an end. Roman Catholic populations in the cities had begun to exercise political power through urban Democratic party machines. This culminated in the largely anti-Catholic temperance movement as a reaction against the growth of Catholic power. The coercive side of this crusade drew a heavy line between the Anglo-Saxon Protestantism of rural and small-town America and the non-Anglo-Saxon Catholicism of the cities. "Rum, Romanism, and rebellion" were pitted against the slogan "Prohibition, Protestantism, and patriotism." The passage in 1919 of the Eighteenth Amendment to the Constitution enacting prohibition was the last time that Protestants were to attempt to preserve their brand of American morality (Wilson, 1978:313–14). Prohibition, of course, was a failure almost from the start. In addition, the Prohibition decade saw an upswing in overt anti-Catholicism: Catholic ethnic differences continued to make middle-class Protestants uncomfortable, and they continued to view the Roman Catholic Church in the United States as a church made up mainly of immigrants (Finke and Stark, 1992).

The Protestant middle class also gave its support to a revived Ku Klux Klan during the 1920s, partly as an outgrowth of the extreme xenophobia that arose during World War I and partly out of a continuing fear of Catholics' foreign allegiances and their perceived desire to unite church and state. By 1922 the Klan was operating in all the states; and by 1925 it had grown to a membership of 8 million (Wilson, 1978:314). Roman Catholic leaders reacted to that atmosphere in one of two ways. While a minority of them tried to further Americanize the church, emphasizing freedom and democracy as a climate in which Roman Catholicism would flourish, most Catholic leaders reacted much more defensively. They sought to protect Catholics from the continuing Protestant hostility and warned their members against cooperating with non-Catholics in political and social ventures. Parochial schools were continued, the ethnic diversity among Catholics was encouraged through the maintenance of neighborhood parishes, and ties to Rome and international Catholicism were stressed. Social, charitable, and religious activities were the features of the typical urban neighborhood parish. All in all, a separate American Catholic front against Protestant prejudice was the dominant response of American Catholicism until World War II (Finke and Stark, 1992:126–39).

The Protestant middle class also continued some of its hostility toward Judaism. The Ku Klux Klan was anti-Semitic, both for religious and economic reasons. Beginning in the 1920s, Jews in the United States became upwardly mobile. Using the mechanism of higher education, they began to enter many professions and occupations formerly closed to them. Still Jews had difficulty in gaining entrance into top corporate management positions, governmental posts, and political offices (Wilson, 1978:317). Covenant agreements in exclusive neighborhoods and suburbs prevented Jewish home ownership. Private clubs and resorts often were closed to Jews. The reaction of Jewish Americans was usually withdrawal. The synagogue became more and more a social as well as a religious meeting place. In ways similar to those of the Roman Catholics, Jews began their own charitable or-ganizations, social service agencies, and social clubs (McNamara, 1974:212–13). It was not until World War II and the subsequent knowledge of Nazi atrocities perpetrated against European Jews that anti-Semitism in the United States became more muted.

In the midst of anti-Catholic and anti-Jewish sentiment, Protes-tantism continued its internecine struggles. The temporary victory by "modernists" in the fundamentalist/modernist controversy of the 1920s resulted in a complacent moderate-to-liberal Protestant religious culture dominating everywhere but in the South (Marty, 1991). South-ern Protestantism, along with the fundamentalism of the North, contin-ued to emphasize narrow doctrinal views, personal evangelism, and piety. One exception to this legacy of the Civil War and Reconstruction was the reunification of three branches of the Methodist Church. In 1939 the Methodist Episcopal Church, the Methodist Protestant Church, and the Methodist Episcopal Church-South reunited. A separate all-black conference, the Central Jurisdictional Conference, was created for African-American Methodists—a necessary compromise for southern Methodists. Except for this action concerning black Methodists, black Protestant churches were largely ignored in all parts of society.

Protestant mainline denominations at first fought Roman Catholics and fundamentalist groups for dominance in the use of radio for reli-gious programming. Later, they successfully won free radio time for themselves and Catholics at the expense of fundamentalists and Penecostals (Finke and Stark, 1992:218–23; Voskuil, 1989:72–92). For those groups, radio time had to be purchased from one of the four radio networks. This dominance of media access by mainline Protes-tants and Catholics continued well into the era of television.

During the 1920s the role of women in religion created controversy in three mainline Protestant denominations. One group of Presbyterian women ordained as elders were elected as commissioners to the Pres-byterian General Assembly in 1930. However, this event did not open the door for full participation by women in the life of either the Presby-terian Church or other mainline denominations. For most of the first sixty years of this century, women remained subordinated insiders in religion (Brereton, 1989:143–67). Only in Pentecostal churches did women seem to have a status equal with men, and that status was usu-ally reserved for the wife of the pastor, who served as his "copastor."

During the 1930s the Great Depression preoccupied most Ameri-cans. Wuthnow (1988:25–26) states that most churches were weak-ened by this economic catastrophe. Expenditures for both Catholics and Protestants declined an average of 36 percent. Denominational workers were without work, and needed repairs on church buildings were postponed. The outbreak of World War II further delayed these rebuilding efforts.

With the outbreak of World War II, religion once again supported the national war effort. Persecution of fringe sects such as Jehovah's Witnesses did take place, but by the end of the war, religious diversity was a permanent reality in the United States. Loyalty to the nation had been demonstrated by Catholics, Jews, African-Americans, and even by Japanese-Americans whose religion was outside the Judeo-Christian tradition. At the end of World War II, the stage seemed to be set for a religious renewal and growth (Wuthnow, 1988). As the 1950s began, a new religious culture popular with almost all segments of the population emerged. Three key religious leaders were involved in this popularization of religion. For moderate Protestants, Norman Vincent Peale, a Reformed Church minister, was the chief proponent of "religious positive thinking"; for Roman Catholics, Bishop Fulton J. Sheen of New York used the new medium of television as a vehicle for popular inspiration and advice; and for conservative and fundamentalist Protestants, Billy Graham used the techniques of revivalism to further promote the religious heritage of the United States and its need for continuing religious commitment. Brotherhood Weeks and interfaith observances included Jews as well as Christians.

At no time in the history of the United States had people demonstrated so much overt, yet benign, religiosity. By 1950, 57 percent of Americans were church members, up from less than 50 percent in the 1940s, and by 1960, 63 percent were members. Polls revealed that by the late 1950s, almost 50 percent of the American people attended religious services weekly, up from 35 percent in 1940. Although Roman Catholic attendance increased, Protestant churches were the chief beneficiaries of this apparent religious revival.

All the major religious faiths concurred in the dominant theme of American moral, ethical, and political superiority. Soon the menace of the Soviet Union and worldwide communism were denounced by Catholics, Protestants, and Jews. The peace won by the concerted actions of the Western allies during World War II appeared fragile. Spiritual values seemed a proper complement to a defensive military posture. Indeed, the nation looked united in terms of a common, pluralistic religious stance, or as Wuthnow (1988) put it: "three cheers for America."

CIVIL RELIGION

Civil religion, a term that can be traced to French philosopher Jean Jacques Rousseau (1712–78), has been used by Robert Bellah (1967) to describe "a set of religious beliefs, symbols, and rituals growing out of the American historical experience interpreted in the dimension of transcendence." Beginning with the words of the founding fathers and early presidents of the United States, Bellah cites historical examples of statements that refer to Providence, the Deity, the Almighty Being, and God as guiding the destiny of the United States. Bellah (1967:7) states that the "God of the civil religion is not only rather 'unitarian'; he is also on the austere side, more related to order, law, and right than to salvation and love.... He is actively interested and involved in history, with special concern for America." Bellah continues his argument by pointing out that there has been, from the early years of the United States, a collection of beliefs, symbols, and rituals with respect to sacred things that have become institutionalized. American civil religion, Bellah states, makes reference to God's special concern for the "chosen people" of the United States (1975:36–40). Furthermore, this civil religion celebrates "the American Way of Life"—economic, political, and ethical.

Bellah views the Civil War as an important milestone in enhancing the moral and intellectual meaning of an American civil religion. The Civil War raised very deep questions concerning national purpose and meaning; subsequently, Abraham Lincoln became a high priest of this religion. For him, the issue was not slavery but "whether that nation, or any nation so conceived and so dedicated, can long endure." Bellah states also that the two national cemeteries that were the product of the Civil War, Gettysburg and Arlington, have become shrines of civil religion. Memorial Day and Thanksgiving Day have become sacred days in the celebration of this civil religion, as have Independence Day, Veterans' Day, and Presidents' Day. Less frequent, although just as important, are the celebrations of civil religion in the inaugurations of American presidents.

In his initial article concerning civil religion, Bellah (1967) drew attention to the religious solemnity of John F. Kennedy's inaugural address, which pointed to the religious aspect of the Declaration of Independence; Bellah also noted the references to God and his approval of American causes in Lyndon B. Johnson's 1964 inaugural address. Other ceremonies are also crucial but unpredictable. For example, funeral ceremonies for national figures are a time for national mourning and for a reaffirmation of our country's commonly held values. Bellah (1967) and Cherry (1970) have both acknowledged this quasi-sacred phenomenon. In recent decades the funerals of John F. Kennedy, Martin Luther King, Jr., Robert F. Kennedy, Dwight D. Eisenhower, and Lyndon B. Johnson have demonstrated civil religion in operation. Wilson (1978:178), in discussing civil religion, has pointed out that true civil religion is present in the minds of all who have faith in democracy as defined by the American system. In this faith, the goals of freedom, equality, and justice are sacred. "Sacred ceremonies" simply undergird this faith.

In their exposition of civil religion, Bellah and others have referred to this concept in the context of Durkheim's (1974) premise concerning religion and societal integration. According to this thesis, civil religion embodies the symbols of cohesion and unity in American society. Winter (1977:88) has stated that the existence of such a civil religion supports Durkheim's notion that religion has an eternal quality. In an advanced industrial society like that of the United States, the religious function identified by Durkheim is performed with the help of political symbols and content more than through traditional Judeo-Christian symbols and ceremonies.

Since the concept of civil religion tends to be defined in rather vague terms, it has been the subject of much discussion and disagreement (see, for example, Hammond, 1976, 1985; Bellah and Hammond, 1980; and Gehrig, 1981). Evidence of civil religion *has* been found by researchers in this country; in particular, Wimberly and various associates (Wimberly, 1979, 1980; Wimberly and Christenson, 1980, 1981) have validated the presence of a concept like civil religion in the minds of a large segment of people in the United States. And Bellah and Hammond (1980) have found various forms of civil religion in Japan, Mexico, and Italy.

Yet many scholars question the validity of the concept. The problem is that this concept, for many, rests too heavily on the presumption of a societal consensus that perhaps no longer exists. There are certainly signals of a breakdown in a common set of beliefs and values in our society. Bellah (1975) speaks of a now "broken covenant"; that is, the common sense of unity remembered from past days has been shattered into personal and private concerns that, by definition, lack the presumed consensus of civil religion. Jews may indeed have a special sense of civil religion that includes (but transcends) the synagogue, which has its own separate beliefs, myths, and rituals (Woocher, 1986). Followers of Islam, Hinduism, Eastern religions, and ethical philosophies may *not* share in the kind of civil religion about which Bellah and others identify. In short, as Chalfant (1984) has suggested, the cluster of beliefs that make up civil religion support the ideology of the dominant power structure, and are not shared by all segments of society.

At the very least, social differentiation and pluralism probably reduce civil religion to a far less important role in societal integration than that suggested by Bellah. Civil religion may exist, but only on the periphery of a society whose integration is very functional in nature (Winter, 1977:88–89). Or as Bellah (1974, 1975) has stated, perhaps the content of contemporary American civil religion is no longer as adequate to its integrative task as it once was.

CONTEMPORARY FORCES OF DIVERSITY

In the last two decades, religious pluralism has been extended to include groups outside the Christian and Jewish faiths. Protestant denominationalism has been challenged by independent Bible churches. Even within Roman Catholicism, splinter groups have developed which include practitioners of the ancient Tridentine mass, gay Catholic groups, Catholic cells presided over by female priests, and small parishes with married priests. At the present time, this society appears to be more religiously pluralistic than at any other period in its history.

Islam is firmly established as another monotheistic religion in the United States. This has occurred in two ways. First, the Black Muslim movement converted a sizeable minority of African-Americans during the 1960s, 1970s, and 1980s. Second, immigrants from the Middle East and certain parts of Asia brought traditional Islam with them in much the same manner that earlier immigrants brought Roman Catholicism and Judaism with them. As was true for earlier groups, most Iranians, Saudis, Jordanians, Egyptians, and even Iraqis demonstrated loyalty to this nation when the opportunity arose (in this case during the Persian Gulf military action of 1991).

Hinduism and other religions from Asia and Southeast Asia are also found in increasing strength in the United States. Variants of Hinduism have gained converts outside of Asian Indian groups. Buddhism has also made converts within the United States, as have other Eastern ethical religions. As is true for Islam, both Hinduism and Buddhism have been brought by immigrants from India and other countries of Asia. These individuals make up the majority of the followers of the Eastern religions. All of these new religious expressions will be discussed in Chapters 6, 8, and 9. We will take up so-called Bible churches in greater detail in Chapter 7.

SUMMARY

Religious pluralism implies the coequal existence of diverse religious groups within one society. Such coequality, however, has not always been characteristic of America. During the colonial period, for example, there was widespread discrimination against dissenters both in New England and the southern colonies. After the Revolution, the early political leaders of the new United States favored religious freedom for two reasons: (1) Many Americans, including most of the founding fathers, were suspicious of the political influence of the state-churches; and (2) there was considerable agitation on the part of the nonestablishment religious groups which wished to see their rights protected by law. As a result, the First Amendment to the U.S. Constitution stated that "Congress shall make no law respecting the establishment of religion, or prohibiting the free exercise thereof...." Voluntarism—a necessary complement to the separation of church and state—allowed any and all churches to spread freely to the frontier and take root there.

Yet the legal guarantee of the First Amendment did not automatically assure the coexistence of different and unique religious groups. The citizens of the early United States were overwhelmingly Protestant, and to them religious diversity meant Protestant diversity. Not until Catholics began migrating to the United States in increasing numbers after 1830 were religious persons within the United States faced with the necessity of accepting this other branch of Christianity. This acceptance was slow in coming, even if aided by the preoccupation of native-born Americans with the Civil War and Reconstruction.

As a result of the debate over slavery, several Protestant denominations split into northern and southern bodies. The southern groups for the most part excluded the freed slaves, who were overwhelmingly Protestant. This resulted in the formation of more separate African-American Protestant denominations, continuing a trend that had begun with free blacks forming separate Methodist churches before the Civil War.

Intra-Protestant divisiveness over orthodox doctrine, scientific versus biblical explanations of creation, and revivalism versus social action further contributed to religious diversity. So also did the formation of groups that either rejected or modified traditional Christian doctrine, such as the Unitarians, Mormons, Christian Scientists, and Jehovah's Witnesses. Each of these unorthodox bodies overcame hostility from traditional American Protestants and took their place within the religious realm of the United States.

Finally, the influx of large numbers of Jews, first from Germany and subsequently from Russia and eastern Europe, added another dimension to the religious scene. Though Judaism split into three groups—Reform, Conservative, and Orthodox—Jews in the United States, unlike Protestants, were able to maintain a sense of community that was both ethnic and religious.

CHAPTER

6.
Contemporary Trends in Religious Life

If the 1950s seemed like a golden age for religious unity and popularity in the United States, the social turmoil of the 1960s and 1970s presented new challenges that caused rifts in some churches even while contributing to further unification of others. During the 1980s the growth and visibility of many conservative and fundamentalist Protestant churches further changed the landscape of the religious life of the United States. In this chapter we will trace the beginning of these trends and their results and provide a close look at the distinctive features of the major religious groups in the United States today.

THE SUCCESS AND THE LIMITS OF ECUMENICAL MOVEMENTS

One important response to religious pluralism that emerged after World War II was the ecumenical movement. *Ecumenism* can mean a number of things, from interdenominational cooperation to common work through federations or corporate bodies to an organic union of separate denominations (Wilson, 1978:424). The ecumenical movement has encompassed all of these trends. Ironically, it has also caused a further division within Protestantism, as some churches have joined the movement and others have not. In this section we will examine some of the manifestations of ecumenism and some of its limits.

The reversal of the nineteenth-century pattern of divisiveness within Protestantism began with the establishment of the Federal Council of Churches in 1908. This interdenominational organization made little historical impact in its early years, however, because of continuing Protestant infighting. In the 1930s the theological position known as *neo-orthodoxy* gained a wide following among Protestants in the United States. Under the leadership of the theologian Reinhold Niebuhr (1892–1971), this doctrinal interpretation became a synthesis of the socioeconomic liberalism of the Social Gospel and the doctrine of the fall of man and the judgment of God (Rosten, 1975:619). Its acceptance led to the reduction of theological differences characteristic of Protestant denominationalism.

In 1950 and 1951 the moribund Federal Council of Churches was supplanted by the newly formed National Council of Churches in Christ. In addition to the original twenty or more Protestant denominations that were members of the old Federal Council, some of the Lutheran bodies also joined. Between 1951 and 1968 ten more denominations, including the Eastern Orthodox Church, became members of the council. Previously independent ventures in missions, education, stewardship, and mass communications were absorbed by the new council (Wilson, 1978:427).

The ecumenical spirit of the National Council of Churches also furthered the development of the World Council of Churches, which was a larger but more loosely knit world federation of cooperating denominations. Even more than the national federation, this example of international ecumenism has concentrated on the practical side of church work: missionary work in the non-Christian world, disaster relief and charity, and attempts at doctrinal agreement (Wilson, 1978:428).

Denominational Mergers

As we stated in Chapter 5, the reunion of the three major Methodist denominations in 1939 served as an example to other Protestant Christians, and a uniting trend was evident throughout the 1950s and 1960s. It began with the merger of the Congregational Christian Churches (the modern successors to the churches of the Puritans) and the Evangelical and Reformed Church (the transplanted European Reformed Church). Although the merging denominations had different traditional policies, the local autonomy of the Congregationalists and the synodical relationship of the Evangelical and Reformed congregations became a loosely knit, connected system known as the United Church of Christ.

In 1958 two of the four Presbyterian bodies united. The Presbyterian Church in the United States of America and the United Presbyterian Church became the United Presbyterian Church in the United States of America; the Presbyterian Church in the United States (the southern branch of Presbyterianism) and the rural Cumberland Presbyterian Church remained separate denominations at that time. It was not until 1983 that the United Presbyterian Church in the United States of America and the Presbyterian Church in the United States finally reunited, resulting in the formation of the Presbyterian Church (U.S.A.). However, this reunion of Presbyterians caused the exodus of many local Presbyterian congregations to the Presbyterian Church in America, a denomination formed in the 1970s that is conservative both theologically and politically.

Lutheran churches of Norwegian, Danish, and German background united in 1960 to form the American Lutheran Church. Two years later the United Lutheran Church, whose history traced back to colonial times, joined the Augustana (Swedish) Lutheran Church and smaller synods of Finnish and Danish backgrounds, to become the Lutheran Church in America. In 1987 these two denominations became the Evangelical Lutheran Church in America. The Lutheran Church–Missouri Synod joined with the other two large Lutheran bodies to form the Lutheran Council in the United States of America in 1965, but it has not participated in larger ecumenical activities (Raff and Standerman, 1975:157). It also did not join in the most recent plan of union.

In 1961 the two most liberal religious groups joined together: The American Unitarian Association merged with the Universalist Church of America to become the Unitarian Universalist Association (Rosten, 1975:620). This religious community stresses liberal humanism and generally liberal political activities.

The decade of the 1960s also saw the merger of the Methodist Church with the smaller but similar Evangelical United Brethren. In 1967 the two denominations became the United Methodist Church. An important feature of this unification was the elimination of the All-Black Central Jurisdiction of the Methodist Church. That internally segregated component of Methodism was a necessary compromise with Southerners in the original Methodist merger of 1939.

As important as these church unions have been, they have usually involved the reuniting of similar groups, with the United Church of

Christ as the exception. A more dramatic plan of union was proposed at the close of the 1950s. In 1960 the Consultation on Church Union (COCU) was initiated by the Presbyterians, Episcopalians, Methodists, and the United Church of Christ, with its goal the organic union of mainline Protestantism. In 1962 the Disciples of Christ joined in, and formal negotiations began. The Presbyterian Church in the United States affiliated with COCU in 1966. In that same year and the next, two large black Protestant denominations participated in the discussions: the African Methodist Episcopal Church and the African Methodist Episcopal Zion Church. They were followed by the third largest black Methodist body, the Christian Methodist Episcopal Church, in 1967. At present little discussion concerning the Consultation of Church Union is going on, but its goal remains the same.

Interfaith Ecumenism

Because of interfaith prejudices fostered by the historical process of immigration and its threat to Protestant hegemony, ecumenism among three of the major faiths in the United States—the Protestants, Catholics, and Jews—has proceeded cautiously. The defensive response of ethnic Catholics to Protestant suspicion and overt discrimination precluded any rush toward an embrace. Likewise, the subcultural aspects of American Judaism minimized religious fraternization for many decades. Joint charitable endeavors and symbolic days of interfaith cooperation were about the only examples of ecumenism among these faiths until the 1960s. However, the gradual lowering of religious barriers in the 1950s, the eventual tolerance of Billy Graham by the Roman Catholic hierarchy, and the end to the political intolerance of Protestants toward Catholics through the election of Catholic John F. Kennedy to the presidency in 1960 set the scene for Christian interfaith cooperation.

The Catholic Church sent its first official observers to the assembly of the World Council of Churches in 1961. Protestants were official observers at the Second Vatican Council, 1962–65, which fostered new Catholic and Protestant working relationships at an institutional level; the hierarchy of the Roman Catholic church moved closer at this time to the position that church divisions are harmful not only to Protestants but also to Catholics. Vatican II also affirmed support for the World Council of Churches and acknowledged the ecclesiastical reality of non-Catholic denominations (Wilson, 1978:429–30). The translation of the Catholic liturgy from Latin into the vernacular languages made Catholic observances and services more comprehensible to non-Catholics. Also, the end of the practice by which a non-

The middle class and upper-middle class membership of the Protestant mainline seems less committed to the necessity of church membership. Roof and McKinney point out that the newer secular unchurched part of the population is as much in the cultural mainstream as any of the mainline Protestant groupings (1987:147). In this cultural mainstream, the affinities of the mainline Protestant and nonreligious secular constituencies converge. Roof and McKinney's research points out that these denominations stress issues of tolerance (civil liberties and racial justice) and issues of liberal morality (women's issues, including a pro-choice stance on abortion—and less restrictive views on sexuality). These are essentially the same issues that nonreligious groups in society tend to endorse. This stands in marked contrast to conservative and fundamentalist Protestants and to traditional Catholics (1987:186–228). Roof and McKinney conclude that these issues, along with the demographic variables will "split" the already fragmented Protestant mainline. They predict that the liberal Protestant denominations will experience further decline and will end up at the margin of the American religious mosaic. At the same time, they predict that the moderate Protestant denominations will inherit the role of redefining the middle part of the mosaic, which will be inherited by the conservative and fundamentalist Protestant denominations (1987:236–43).

2. Wuthnow's analysis of the decline of mainline Protestantism locates the cause in a profound "restructuring" of religion in the United States. Although he acknowledges that the cleavage between Protestant liberals and conservatives can be traced in part to the fundamentalist/modernist controversy of the 1920s, he points to events, activities, and processes of the 1950s, 1960s, and 1970s as the underlying causation of this phenomenon. What appeared to begin as a post-World War II era of unprecedented religious cooperation gradually disintegrated into an era of competitiveness and recrimination between different camps of Protestants.

The denominational mergers discussed earlier in this chapter are seen by Wuthnow as contributing to denominational weakness. The distinctiveness of belonging to one denomination as compared to another was de-emphasized by many leaders within the National Council of Churches denominations. There were, however, important exceptions to this. Southern Baptists, even when compared to other Protestants only in the South were far more likely to emphasize the importance of denomination. This is seen as important since people in the American South are more likely to attend religious activities than those in the Northeast, on the West Coast, or even in the Midwest (Wuthnow, 1988).

Those for whom denominational identification carried great weight, in some cases, moved to denominations that emphasized this point. Others felt increasingly uncomfortable in the more liberal denominations of mainline Protestantism, particularly as they de-emphasized restrictions concerning the sacraments of the church. The ecumenism from which such shifts evolved created a new tension between liberals and conservatives within denominations and between denominations (Wuthnow, 1988).

In addition, the more conservative Protestant denominations produced a more trained leadership corps than in the past. No longer could mainline Protestantism claim the only (or even the best) theological training that produced the best clergy. In the more independent conservative Protestant denominations, interdenominational ties developed between these churches for the exchange of information and the marshaling of resources. The conservatives gained greater access to the media and became less sectarian and less exclusive than the Protestant fundamentalists of the past (Wuthnow, 1988).

During the 1960s and 1970s, the political interest groups aligned with mainline Protestantism embraced the liberal social causes of those decades: civil rights, opposition to the war in Southeast Asia, sexual freedom, feminism, support for a women's right to abortion, and liberal government-sponsored social programs. As a reaction to this, conservative Protestantism developed its own interest groups in opposition to these stances. For religious and political conservatives, these organizations offered a powerful and seductive alternative to the perceived secularized message of mainline Protestantism. Furthermore, they brought into the open the differences and hostilities existing between Protestant liberals and conservatives (Wuthnow, 1988).

As a result, the religious political right was able to mobilize its resources to oppose the liberal social agenda of the mainline churches and to attract some lapsed members of these denominations. It also was able to redefine the nature of America's civil religion to emphasize conservative and traditional values, such as an antiabortion stance, limits to governmental intervention in social problems, opposition to pornography, opposition to increased rights for gay men and lesbians, and an emphasis on traditional family values. In the process, the more liberal mainline denominations continued to embrace the pluralistic stances of tolerance, cultural diversity, and inclusiveness. It is not so much that these values are rejected by a majority of society, but instead it seems that the very diversity and pluralism embodied in the mainline churches prevents a countermobilization on their part.

3. Finke and Stark offer a third explanation of the mainline Protestant denominational decline. Their analysis points out that *religious organizations are stronger to the degree that they impose significant costs in terms of sacrifice and even stigma upon their members…* (1992:238). They further argue that the more "mainline" the denomination is, the lower the value of belonging to it is, since it does not demand great costs in return for the respectability of membership. As a result, people have found it convenient (and easy) to leave mainline Protestant congregations.

The cultural revolution of the 1960s brought about an interest in alternative religious groups, including Eastern religious mysticism. According to Kelley (1972), membership growth in the conservative

Table 6.2   Market Shares: Members per 1,000 Church Members, 1940–1985

	1940	1960	1985	Percentage Loss or Gain
Mainline				
United Methodists	124.7	93.0	64.3	–48%
Presbyterian, USA	41.7	36.4	21.3	–49%
Episcopal	30.9	28.6	19.2	–38%
Christian (Disciples)	25.7	15.7	7.8	–70%
United Church of Christ				
(Congregationalist)	26.5	19.6	11.8	–56%
Evangelicals				
Southern Baptists	76.7	85.0	101.3	+32%
Assemblies of God	3.1	4.4	14.6	+371%
Church of the Nazarene	2.6	2.7	3.7	+42%
Church of God	1.0	1.5	3.6	+260%
Roman Catholics	330.0	367.9	368.4	+12%

Source: Finke and Stark, 1992:248.

churches also took place at this time. In the 1980s new religious movements gained prominence. (We shall speak at some length about this phenomenon in Chapter 8.) All these cults and religious groups, quite obviously, competed in the religious marketplace with mainline Protestantism. Yet as Finke and Stark argue (1992:249), the decline of the mainline churches is the result of a long and steady trend. This trend had even become evident before the *numerical* decline of the mainline groups, which began in the 1960s.

As shown in Table 6.2, all five mainline Protestant denominations have lost in their percentage share in the religious population of the United States. Why have these groups faltered even as more sectarian denominations prospered? To answer this question, Finke and Stark (1992: 252–55) have advanced their hypothesis about *costly faith*. According to this concept, religious groups—like all organizations—have to make initially some demands of their individual members for the collective good of the whole membership. We need to keep in mind that all groups include some "free riders," that is, individuals who wish to reap the benefits of their voluntary association without contributing much, if anything, in time, effort, or money. The result can be fewer participants in relatively empty church buildings.

According to Finke and Stark, *costly demands* offer a solution to this dilemma. The demands consist of sacrifices (in time, money, or materials) to gain and maintain church membership. While conservative/fundamentalist Protestantism makes and requires such a commitment of its members, mainline Protestantism has not done so for many decades. As shown in Table 6.3, many of the conservative denominations are smaller in numbers than many mainline denomina-

Table 6.3   Recent Growth and Decline of Protestant Church
            Membership

	1983 Membership	1991 Membership	Change
Conservative/fundamentalist denominations			
Southern Baptist Convention	14,185,454	15,038,409	+6%
Church of Jesus Christ of Latter-day Saints	3,593,000	4,267,000	+19%
Assemblies of God	1,879,182	2,181,502	+16%
Seventh-day Adventists	623,563	717,446	+15%
Mainline Protestant denominations			
United Methodist Church	9,405,083	8,904,824	−6%
Presbyterian Church (U.S.A.)	3,157,372*	2,847,437*	−11%
Episcopal Church	2,794,139	2,446,050	−12%
Evangelical Lutheran Church in America	5,327,916†	5,240,739*	−2%
Disciples of Christ (Christian Church)	1,156,458	1,039,692	−11%

* Communicant or confirmed members, rather than inclusive members.

†Combination membership figures of the former American Lutheran Church, Evangelical Lutherans in Mission, and the Lutheran Church in America, which merged to form the Evangelical Lutheran Church in America.

Source: Data from the *Yearbook of American and Canadian Churches,* 1984; 1991.

tions. Yet the percentage growth of the conservative churches, as well as their market share, is greater, as Table 6.2 shows.

All three of these explanations for the decline of mainline Protestantism are different, although the first two are complementary of each other; the third explanation (by Finke and Stark) challenges the interpretations of the data utilized by the first two analyses. In spite of this difference, all three offer *valid reasons* for the changed religious landscape in the United States.

Other Characteristics of Mainline Protestantism. Many of the reasons for the decline also provide a partial portrait of the characteristics of these mainline denominations. They have embraced most of the liberal and progressive social agenda of the 1960s, 1970s, and 1980s, although variations by denominations exist. The mainline can be subdivided into liberal and moderate churches, with the latter group showing more tentativeness toward many of these issues.

In a series of studies addressing the dilemma of the Presbyterian Church (U.S.A.) in dealing with the decline (1990), six authors found strengths and weaknesses in this denomination, which is one of the original mainline churches. Wuthnow (1990), in his analysis of the Presbyterians, suggests that Presbyterian feminists serve as one source of replenishment of the liberal wing of the denomination. Farley (1990) states that contemporary Presbyterianism has moved away from being a traditional Calvinist/Reformed religious community to one characterized by "critical modernism," that is, a viewpoint that stresses pluralism, the validity of scientific explanations, and a consistency with the Christian Gospels as well as a Christian Gospel "social" in character. He states that a majority of Presbyterians (and other mainline Protestant clergy and lay people) believe in "critical modernism." This belief has nurtured a less traditional morality that tolerates abortion, changing gender roles, and sexual activities outside marriage, for example (Roof and McKinney, 1987). Furthermore, articles making up the study discuss other issues characteristic of Presbyterians and other mainliners. These include an increasing presence of women clergy and a commitment to racial and ethnic tolerance.

In addition to these issues, several mainline denominations have debated the question of gay and lesbian clergy. Twice the Presbyterian Church (U.S.A.) debated and then reaffirmed the traditional prohibition against the ordination of openly gay men and lesbians to the ministry. The last prohibition was affirmed in 1991 at that denomination's General Assembly (Minutes of the General Assembly, 1991). The Episcopal Church and the Evangelical Lutheran Church in America also debated this issue in 1991. In 1992 the United Methodist Church reaffirmed its stance against such ordinations. In 1992 the highest judicial court of the Presbyterian Church (U.S.A.) overruled lower rulings and prohibited an openly lesbian minister from accepting a pastoral position in Buffalo, New York (*Presbyterian News*, 1992).

Ease of changing membership from one denomination to another is also a characteristic of most denominations within the National Council of Churches. Although the completion of an inquirers' or communicants' class is required for membership in the Episcopal and Lutheran churches, such extended sessions are not generally necessary for membership in the other Protestant bodies. Transferring church membership between denominations is often as easy as transferring membership within congregations of the same denomination. This ease of affiliation has further blurred the distinctive doctrinal beliefs and religious practices of mainline Protestantism. The phenomenon of the cultural community church, chosen more for its convenience, the verbal skills of its minister, its music, or its educational and social programs for the young, continues today within mainline churches.

Conservative/Fundamentalist Protestantism

In contrast to the churches of mainline Protestantism, Protestant denominations outside the National Council of Churches in Christ (and thus outside the ecumenical movement) have more distinctive doctrinal beliefs, a higher level of church attendance, and more exclusive requirements for church membership. Sometimes such groups are referred to as evangelicals. However, as Ammerman (1991:2) states, not all conservative or evangelical Christians are fundamentalists. Often the common point between these religious groups is that they tend to reject the liberal, middle-class social action policies of the mainline Protestant denominations. The approximately 41 million people who belong to these denominations are generally of a lower social class than are the members of the predominantly white mainline Protestant churches.

Some important exceptions to this general social-class ranking do exist, however. In the South, Southern Baptists have more middle- and upper-middle-class members than do Baptists in other areas of the country. Ammerman (1990) states that this upward mobility has occurred since World War II and is affected mostly by the urban, better-educated Southern Baptist constituency. With approximately 15.7 million members, the Southern Baptist Convention accounts for almost one-half of all conservative and fundamentalist Protestants.

Likewise, churches of the Lutheran Church-Missouri Synod have more middle- and upper-middle-class members than do most conservative and fundamentalist groups. Another large group of conservative and fundamentalist Protestants is the Churches of Christ, which split early in this century from the mainline Disciples of Christ. Most of the congregations forming the Churches of Christ are located in the South and Southwest. Although these congregations have many middle- and upper-middle-class members, more of their membership is lower-middle-class and lower-class than is the case for both the Southern Baptists and Missouri-Synod Lutherans. Another larger religious group generally included with conservative and fundamentalist Protestants is the Church of Jesus Christ of Latter-day Saints (the Mormons). In states where Mormons are the dominant group, they are likely to come from all social classes. On the other hand, Pentecostal and Holiness groups, groups identifying themselves as Bible churches and groups emphasizing a new revelation, such as the Jehovah's Witnesses, include a preponderance of members from the lower social classes.

In general, conservative-fundamentalist Protestants show more commitment to religious practices than do mainline Protestants. Gallup and Castelli (1989) report that 65 percent of those who label themselves as members of conservative Protestant denominations attend religious services either often or regularly. Likewise, 57 percent of Baptists attend either often or regularly. Groups with a preponderance of members from the lower social classes tend to require more commitment of their members; consequently, a higher proportion of their membership is regular in attending religious services, often more than just once a week.

Fundamentalist Protestant denominations (and independent fundamentalist churches) share in some of what Ammerman (1991:4–8) calls central features. These are evangelism (revival techniques to reach the unchurched and the unsaved); biblical inerrancy (a belief that the Bible is the *exact* word of God, not just the *inspired* word); premillennialism (a belief that the end of the world is imminent); and separatism (a practice of excluding those whose religious beliefs are not correct). However, churches which are evangelical, conservative, or both, do not necessarily have all of these central features. In addition to these beliefs, fundamentalist, conservative, and evangelical Protestants generally adhere to a faith that moral truth is unchanging, universal, and divinely sanctioned (Hunter, 1991). Since this view is opposite to the one held by progressive religious forces, Hunter believes that the more conservative Protestants are engaged in a cultural war. That war is being waged over the control of education, the mass media, politics, and the family. Religious organizations, according to Hunter's thesis, provide the rallying points for conservatives and fundamentalists to mobilize for this cultural war.

The crusading issues of the religious right in contemporary American politics are the catalysts for this ideological battle. These include the restoration of prayer in public schools; opposition to abortion-on-demand; opposition to civil rights for gays and lesbians; opposition to sex education within the public school curricula; opposition to realistic attempts to educate the adolescent population concerning AIDS and the use of condoms; and general opposition to feminist perspectives and agendas. In Chapter 7 we will examine this agenda in greater detail.

Historically, less internal cooperation has taken place within the conservative and fundamentalist sphere than within mainline Protestantism. However, cooperative efforts, such as conservative interdenominational seminaries, the evangelical journal Christianity Today, and the National Association of Evangelicals, do exist. Organizations representing the newer religious-political right also draw from many of these denominations. As we shall see in Chapter 7, however, division often supplants unity.

In general, intensity of religious beliefs, exclusivity of membership requirements, the emphasis upon salvation, and the suspicion of any religious compromise are the hallmarks of conservative/fundamentalist Protestant denominations and sects. Several researchers firmly believe that these denominations have grown because of these features. In fact, some of these denominations have recently increased in membership, as Table 6.3 demonstrates. In the selected denominations shown, the growth rates ranged from 6 percent for the Southern Baptist Convention to 16 percent for the Assemblies of God. However, as Smith (1992) demonstrates, this "growth" may be misleading.

Smith states that focusing on the *relative* growth of fundamentalist versus nonfundamentalist Protestant church membership is too narrow, since Protestants account for only 60 to 65 percent of the population. Of this number, only about 70 to 75 percent are church members. Changes in church membership involve only a minority of adults (42 to 49 percent). Even if fundamentalists are gaining among Protestant church members, they are not necessarily gaining ground in the total population (Smith, 1992:306–7).

According to Smith, data from church membership statistics and reports of church affiliation in surveys are often different. Generally, the surveys overreport church affiliation. He suggests that the mobilization by fundamentalist Protestants for political action, their use of televangelism, and the media's "discovery" of fundamentalist Protestants caused an overestimation of their real size and influence in the religious realm (Smith, 1992:318–25). On the other hand, conservative/fundamentalist Protestants feel that the evangelical movement is a vindication of their exclusivity and their emphasis upon personal salvation. In Chapter 7 we will examine the beliefs and ramifications of contemporary fundamentalist and evangelical movements in greater detail.

Roman Catholicism

If Finke and Stark (1992) are correct in their analysis that Roman Catholicism began as a sectlike religious movement in the United States, then the present-day situation of Catholicism is a logical outcome of a sect becoming a mainline denomination. On the other hand, Roman Catholics in America are part of a truly international church, unlike Protestants or Jews. Because of this, the tensions existing among the clergy, the various religious orders, and the laity within Catholicism extend beyond the United States. Roman Catholicism is

Catholic marriage partner agreed that the children of such a union would be reared in the Catholic faith diminished Protestant prejudice toward Catholics. Finally, the participation of Catholics in Protestant and Jewish services promoted interfaith ecumenism.

Jews have remained the weakest of the three interfaith partners. Protestant-Catholic cooperation has seemed to progress at a more rapid pace than has Christian-Jewish cooperation. Whereas serious discussion concerning doctrinal reconciliation between Protestants and Catholics is occurring, only cultural and charitable ventures are conducted jointly by Jews and Christians. Limits to interfaith ecumenism obviously exist, as do limits to interdenominational ecumenism within Protestant Christianity.

Limits to Interdenominational and Interfaith Ecumenism

Although mainline Protestant denominations do exhibit a cooperative spirit, significantly large minorities of Protestant Christians do not share in this venture. The largest Protestant denomination, the Southern Baptist Convention (with 15.2 million members), remains outside the National Council of Churches. Likewise, another strong evangelical body, the Churches of Christ (with 2.4 million members), believes that it is the only real New Testament church and therefore refuses cooperation with other Protestants except in certain local situations. The Lutheran Church–Missouri Synod (with 3 million members) also exhibits almost no interdenominational cooperation because of beliefs concerning biblical literalism and orthodox Lutheran doctrinalism. All the sectarian bodies (such as the Seventh-day Adventists, Pentecostal groups, the Assemblies of God, and the independent fundamentalist Protestant churches) that have been classified as growing conservative churches (Kelley, 1978; Smith, 1992) are also outside the ecumenical movement. To some extent, the ecumenical movement is a social class movement, reflecting a division between mainline Protestantism and the evangelical lower class (Wilson, 1978). Thus, even within Protestant Christianity, serious divisions remain. Among those who express support for Christian unity, some pessimism concerning ultimate union remains.

Since the ecumenical movement has been generally identified with cooperative social activism, members of the laity who are more conservative in both doctrinal beliefs and political beliefs tend to show less enthusiasm for ecumenical activities. While such individuals are not necessarily opposed to interdenominational cooperation, they simply are more cautious concerning an expanding (and less controllable) religious bureaucracy that is responsible to a variety of religious denominations. They view such an organization as more likely to promote liberal causes, such as increased welfare spending, support of women's rights, abortions, and international religious co-operation (Wuthnow, 1990). Consequently, conservative lay organizations have developed within the United Methodist, the Presbyterian Church (U.S.A.), and the Episcopal denominations in order to slow down ecumenical cooperation, to re-emphasize denominational distinctiveness, and to promote more traditional moral and spiritual values. Wuthnow (1990) reports that within the Presbyterian Church (U.S.A.), for example, the lay leadership is more conservative—both in theology and in politics—than are the Presbyterian clergy. Because of these pressures by the laity, the ecumenism of the 1970s began to emphasize the compatibility of personal evangelism and social concerns. The rise of contemporary evangelicalism (which will be discussed in Chapter 7) has no doubt been influential in this new convergence.

Finke and Stark (1992) believe that denominational mergers take place only when one or more of the denominations is in decline or when the denominations are within the same "family." Thus the re-unification of Presbyterians can be interpreted as either a marriage of two declining mainline Protestant denominations or as the blending of two partners within the same extended family. The same interpretation can also be used for the recent Lutheran mergers.

If Finke and Stark are correct, then the findings of Kelly (1972) two decades ago remain essentially true: Limits to ecumenism between Protestants and Catholics remain strong. In a study of attitudes toward interfaith ecumenism, he found the majority of each congregation questioned, with the exception of Jews in two synagogues, accepted the convergence theory of Protestant and Catholic doctrinal development. This theory simply states that the Protestant/Catholic dialogue will produce agreement on religious essentials and freedom to differ on religious nonessentials. The first statement to which people responded said, "It seems to me that Protestants and Catholics are becoming more and more alike in their religious beliefs and practices." All Protestant and Catholic respondents overwhelmingly agreed with the statement. But the issue of future Protestant/Catholic union produced a different response among the survey population. To the statement, "Unity among Protestant, Roman Catholic, and Eastern Orthodox churches will always prove to be impossible," a great majority of sect members (72 percent) and a slight majority of Unitarians (54 percent) and of Jews (54 percent) agreed. Mainline Protestants were uncertain on this question. A sizeable plurality (48 percent) agreed; the majority of Protestants either expressed uncertainty (22 percent) or disagreed (30 percent). By contrast, Roman Catholics either felt that church union is possible (48 percent) or expressed uncertainty concerning it (22 percent) (Kelly 1972:341–51).

One final issue also suggests either a limitation to ecumenism or the actual decline of this cooperative effort. This issue is the National Council of Churches itself. In 1983 some of the news media through programs and articles reported that the National Council of Churches supported Marxist regimes in different parts of the world under the ideology of *liberation theology*. Money, most of which came indirectly from member denominations, was supplied to the regimes and guerilla movements. Many conservative clergy and laypeople within some of the member denominations voiced protests to such expenditures.

Finke and Stark (1992) report that in 1988 the National Council of Churches issued a lengthy confession of its failures, which included the decline of support from its constituent members and the inability to "embody the ecumenical vision." They also report that between 1976 and 1989 the National Council had reduced its staff from 187 to less than 70 people. In addition, the National Council of Churches in Christ now represents only 40 percent of all American Protestants within 32 of the several hundred Protestant denominations and groupings. There is a developing point of view both within the mainline denominations and the more conservative/fundamentalist denominations that the National Council of Churches does not usually reflect the views "even of the leaders of its member denominations, let alone the rank-and-file" (Billingsley, 1990; as cited in Finke and Stark, 1992:224).

LIMITS TO THE THREE-CULTURE HYPOTHESIS

A popular thesis advanced by Will Herberg (1960) explained the strides made by various ethnic groups toward religious assimilation by the 1950s. According to Herberg, the bond between religious affiliation and ethnic identity had loosened, and, consequently, second- and third-generation immigrants were expressing more generalized feelings of religious identification with one of the three major American faiths—Protestantism, Catholicism, or Judaism. For Herberg, the three major faiths were different cultural manifestations of a basic American unity; central to this unity was a common set of values related to the American way of life. Thus the religiosity characteristic of that era was a way of sociability and belonging. Herberg's thesis attracted much attention since interfaith cooperation was increasing and church attendance was high, in spite of the fact that church members' knowledge of specific and individual religious beliefs was low.

Although Herberg's analysis appeared to apply to all Americans, it was most directly applicable to the largely eastern and southern European ethnics. Among those ethnics of the second generation, differences did *seem* to be disappearing. But many divisions within Roman Catholicism remained fixed along ethnic lines, particularly in the large eastern and midwestern cities. Also contrary to the thesis is the fact that Protestant denominational differences have remained important to many in spite of the developing ecumenicity. To be sure, a kind of melting-pot Protestantism exists, as exemplified by community megachurches such as Robert Schuller's Garden Grove Community Church (California); the nationwide telecasts of his "Hour of Power" attest to the appeal of this kind of religious culture. But Schuller's popularity does not lie with the more evangelical Protestants of the 1970s and 1980s, but instead with the heirs to Norman Vincent Peale's religious culture of the 1950s (Mariani, 1979). To be a Baptist or a Presbyterian or a Lutheran still means something to many people in the United States. This something may be a class identification, a regional identification, or an ethnic identification. It may even be a theological identification, as in the case of a Pentecostal.

Furthermore, Herberg's thesis tends to ignore racial differences. During the civil rights revolution of the 1960s, an African-American Methodist or Baptist was something greatly different from his or her white counterpart. And for Jews, Herberg's thesis seems to apply least of all. To be a Jew in the United States is something vastly different from being a Protestant, a Catholic, a Hindu, or a Muslim.

Regardless of whether or not the three-culture hypothesis *was* the "correct" analysis of religious pluralism, it *did help* to explain the relatively peaceful coexistence of diverse religious bodies in the United States. Tensions among Roman Catholics, Protestants, and Jews still exist. Old hostilities and suspicions can at any time be resurrected, particularly by fundamentalist Protestants and particularly concerning political ideologies and their "crusading issues." It is also within the realm of possibility that the newly emerging Islamic population within this society can threaten this coexistence.

CONTEMPORARY PROFILES OF MAJOR RELIGIOUS GROUPS

Contemporary religious life in the United States is paradoxical: Cooperation and conflict are both present, products of the process of religious pluralism. Protestant denominations hold the allegiance of a majority of our country's population; Roman Catholicism commands

the second-largest membership and constitutes the largest single religious body; Jews form a small but affluent minority of citizens who
claim religious affiliation. Data also indicate a growing presence of
adherents to Islam. All of these major faiths have minority group
members, but racial minorities constitute only small proportions of
the membership of the predominantly white denominations. Because
of this, Winter (1977:265) suggested that their religious organizations
and religiosity constitute another major religious community. We will
discuss the African-American churches and religious organizations in
Chapter 12, but for now, we will focus attention on profiles of the four
major religious faiths in the United States. For each of these groups,
we will look at their social characteristics, their central tenets of belief,
and the extent to which their members practice these beliefs.

To put the these major faiths in perspective, we should note first
that there are well over two hundred different denominations and
sects with more than one thousand members in the United States, and
total church membership in 1992 (according to the *Yearbook of American and Canadian Churches*, 1992) was more than *132,694,380*. For our
purposes here, we will discuss mainline Protestant bodies (those that
belong to the National Council of Churches in Christ) separately from
conservative/fundamentalist Protestant bodies (all those religious
groups such as the Mormons, Jehovah's Witnesses, and Churches of
Christ members that consider themselves to be either the only true
church or more perfect than other churches and who thus are not ecumenical in orientation). By this definition, the Eastern Orthodox
Church and the predominantly black churches that are members of
the National Council of Churches are part of mainline Christianity.
However, the nation's largest Protestant denomination, the Southern
Baptist Convention, is not. Table 6.1 shows 1992 membership for the
four major religious groups we profile in this section. We should note
that verifying the accuracy of these figures is difficult because different
groups have different ways of counting members. Some include infants
and young children; others enumerate only teenage and adult members.

Mainline Protestantism and Its Decline

The popular religious culture of the 1950s blurred denominational differences, and promoted the practice of comity, or avoidance of
proselytizing members of another denomination among the participating council denominations. In many ways the National Council of
Churches member denominations defined the religious landscape for
four decades through these practices. This "staking out of the territory" also fostered denominational switching by an increasingly

Table 6.1   Membership in Major Faiths in the United States, 1989–1992*

Religious Group	Membership
Mainline Protestants (members of the National Council of Churches in Christ)	46,829,961†
Conservative/fundamentalist Protestants (nonmembers of the National Council of Churches in Christ)	23,405,099
Roman Catholics	58,568,015
Jews (Orthodox, Conservative, and Reform)	5,500,000
Muslims	(no data available)

* Some of the data included in the *Yearbook* were reported in 1989, 1990, and 1991.

† These figures are for "inclusive membership which would, in many cases, include baptized children who are not full members of the member denominations. Also, these figures exclude the 141,315 members of the Unitarian-Universalist Fellowship.

Source: Data from the *Yearbook of American and Canadian Churches,* 1992.

mobile and suburban people. The mainline Protestant churches de-emphasized membership requirements and promoted common points of unity in the form of ecumenical Thanksgiving services, World Communion Sundays, and occasionally the creation of union community churches with pan-denominational support. Data available suggest that these practices have been responsible *in part* for the decline of mainline Protestant membership and support. Denominational loyalty, so long a part of religious identification through religious socialization, has also weakened when compared to past decades. Roof and McKinney (1987) suggest that this has been replaced by what they call a *new voluntarism,* which provides for less loyalty to a particular religious institution.

Thirty-two Protestant and Orthodox denominations belong to the National Council of Churches in Christ; of these, the United Methodist Church is the largest. Mainline religious bodies show varying degrees of ecumenical cooperation, as we mentioned earlier. For the most part, their membership is middle-class and above, although some members belong to the lower classes. This is particularly true for the largest of the African-American Protestant denominations that belong to the council. However, mainline Protestantism is predominantly white. In addition, there seems to be a common doctrinal perspective shared by most mainline Protestants.

Some data indicate that there exists a core set of generalized beliefs concerning the existence of God (Gallup and Castelli, 1989; Finke and

Stark, 1992). Gallup and Castelli (1989) also found, however, that there is a lack of consistency concerning ritual practices similar to that noted by Stark and Glock (1968) in their study of religious beliefs and practices in the San Francisco area. They found that only the more liturgical Protestant denominations (Episcopalians and Lutherans) placed great emphasis upon baptism and the Sacrament of the Lord's Supper (or the Eucharist). The United Methodists, the United Church of Christ, the Disciples of Christ, the Presbyterians, and the American Baptists tended to de-emphasize such ritualistic practices (Stark and Glock, 1968).

Mainline Protestants show less commitment to religious practices than do either conservative/fundamentalist Protestants or Roman Catholics. For example, Stark and Glock (1968) found that between 41 and 49 percent of the membership of denominations within the National Council of Churches attended services weekly or almost weekly. This percentage remained about the same throughout the 1970s. More recent survey research data from the National Opinion Research Center (1992) indicate that most mainline Protestants still do not attend religious services regularly. Among Methodists, 46 percent indicated that they attend often or regularly; 44 percent of Presbyterians stated that they attend often or regularly; and 42 percent of Episcopalians indicated that they attend often or regularly. Even the contemporary evangelical movements within the mainline Protestant churches have failed to increase this proportion except in localized instances. Neither an emphasis on sociability nor on revivalistic evangelism have changed significantly church attendance patterns.

In addition to efforts to redirect mainline Protestantism toward individualistic evangelicalism, most of these denominations have experienced varying degrees of the charismatic renewal movement known as *neo-Pentecostalism,* involving *gifts of the spirit* and glossolalia (speaking in tongues). Most of the churches in which this movement has occurred have adopted a tolerant attitude on the denominational level, but in local congregations and parishes animosities between procharismatics and anticharismatics have developed.

Reasons for the Mainline Protestant Decline. Both the decline in membership and the lack of renewed participation by members of these denominations have been the subject of significant research during the 1980s and the first two years of the 1990s. Some of this research was commissioned by several mainline denominations. Three tentative conclusions can be drawn from these research efforts: (1) Roof and McKinney (1987) suggest as a cause of the decline religious voluntarism (or privatism) as well as demographic variables, such as a low birth rate and the loss of the so-called Baby Boomers within the mainline churches; (2) Wuthnow (1988) points to the decline of denominationalism, the formation of religious/political special interest groups (mostly from the political and religious right), and the cleavages that have developed between religious liberals and conservatives; and (3) Finke and Stark (1992) conjecture that the decline is a continuation of forces which began in the nineteenth century and are still in operation today. These forces give the conservative Protestant denominations a greater stake in the market economy of the religious realm through their successful "marketing" efforts.

No one of these three interpretations contains the *definitive* reason for what Roof and McKinney refer to as the "disestablishment of mainline Protestantism." Each gives a part of the picture and suggests that the growth or decline of the remainder of the religious realm is related to the decline of the Protestant mainline. We will briefly examine the three analyses.

Survey data have long suggested that most of the denominations within the National Council of Churches have fewer adherents who, in turn, demonstrate less loyalty to their congregation and denomination. The reasons behind these data offer a richer picture of this shrinkage and its effects. Let us now summarize the main points of these researches:

1. Roof and McKinney (1987) contend that the 1960s caused a collapse of the "religious middle." By this they mean that religion was strongest at the religious and political fringes (1987:25–33). Liberal pronouncements by mainline denominational leaders called for further social action against injustices within American society. Many young, well-educated individuals experimented with "new religions" outside the traditional Judeo-Christian tradition. On the other side of the political and theological spectrum, conservative denominations and groups continued their stance of traditionalism both in religious faith and morality. In addition, mainline Protestants were unable to hold on to their younger members as they graduated from college and took their places in the occupational world. Unlike past generations, these Baby Boomers did not immediately return to the religions of their parents. According to some observers, they still have not. By contrast, the same age group whose religious background was within the conservative Protestant denominations remained more loyal to their faith. Furthermore, these more youthful members did not abandon their denominational roots as rapidly as previous generations had done when their educational and occupational status increased (Roof and McKinney, 1987:106–47). Class, region, ethnicity, and race lost some of their force in shaping religious and cultural identities. Conservative Protestant denominations (such as the Southern Baptist Convention) provided more urban congregations for a more urban constituency.

headed by a conservative pope, John Paul II. His spoken and written statements often chastise American Catholics for not obeying the teachings of Rome, particularly on contraception and abortion.

Today there are essentially no differences between Catholics and members of other religious groups on contraception (D'Antonio, Davidson, Hoge, and Wallace, 1989). Even on a constitutional amendment to prohibit abortion except in the case of rape, incest, or danger to the mother's life, Catholics supported this initiative by 59 percent as opposed to 51 percent support by Protestants (Gallup and Castelli, 1989:168). Yet this support among Catholics is at a much lower level than the Catholic Church's teachings would seem to desire. Furthermore, only 49 percent of Roman Catholics expressed opposition to the *Roe* v. *Wade* Supreme Court decision (Gallup and Castelli, 1989:168). It seems that the church whose members were taught to "pray and pay" can no longer enforce such subservience. Profound changes have taken place in the Roman Catholic Church in the United States. Much of this can be explained by the social, cultural, and demographic characteristics of American Catholics.

Since World War II, the "church of the immigrants" has become more and more the church of native-born Americans (McNamara, 1984:144–45). Whereas Roman Catholicism was once characterized by a majority of working-class and lower-class members, it is little different today in class representation from mainline Protestantism. With few exceptions, the proportionate distribution of Catholics by education, occupation, and income parallels that of the United States population at large (Greeley, 1989). Like both the mainline Protestant churches and conservative/fundamentalist Protestant churches, the Roman Catholic Church has a very small number of African-American members.

Although Catholicism remains distinctively different in terms of doctrine and religious practices from Protestant Christianity, the Second Vatican Council caused profound liberalizing changes within the church (Dinges, 1992). These changes resulted in the church's beginning to officially recognize the existence of other Christian bodies and giving up exclusive claim to all religious truth. Celebrating the mass in vernacular languages, introducing broader congregational participation through the use of hymns and musical liturgies, allowing communicants the option of taking the wine as well as the host (or bread)—all these developments are also major innovations in the public religious rites of the Roman Catholic Church. In addition, the proscriptions against eating meat on Friday and making significant sacrifices during Lent blurred some of the outwardly visible differences between Catholics and Protestants (Finke and Stark, 1992: 263–64).

These changes have given rise to a resurgence of Roman Catholic traditionalism. This traditionalist movement is a response to the perception that the papacy has capitulated to the influences of liberalism, communism, socialism, modernism, and Zionism (Dinges, 1992:66). However, many women within the Roman Catholic Church in America continue to call for the ordination of women to the priesthood, which the traditionalist movement also opposes. In 1992 the National Conference of Catholic Bishops failed to adopt a major statement on the status and role of women within Catholicism, and this amounted to a reaffirmation of the traditional status of Catholic women: no ordination to the priesthood and subservience to an all-male hierarchy.

There are other divisions within the Roman Catholic Church. Catholic conservatives *do* oppose abortion and participate in the contemporary antiabortion movement. Hitchcock (1991:101–3) refers to this as Catholic activist conservatism in which some of both the clergy and laity participate in illegal acts against abortion clinics and physicians and other health-care workers who provide abortion services. He further demonstrates that these conservatives subscribe to a conservative social agenda which includes proscriptions on pornography; opposition to gay and lesbian rights; opposition to most sex-education programs; government aid to private, religiously oriented schools; and support for nondenominational prayers in public schools (Hitchcock, 1991:110). A majority of Roman Catholics do not subscribe to most of the items on this social agenda (D'Antonio, Davidson, Hoge, and Wallace, 1989). Instead, they display the same kind of general opposition to this conservative agenda as do most mainline Protestants (Gallup and Castelli, 1989).

In another area, the Roman Catholic Church has groups urging charismatic renewal within the church. These scattered groups began to form in 1960 and came together for the first time in 1967. From a total of one hundred people attending the first conference, attendance increased to twenty-two thousand at the 1973 meeting, reportedly drawn from 1,250 separate Catholic neo-Pentecostal groups around the United States (Harrison, 1974). Fichter (1975:33) has stated that the Catholic neo-Pentecostals generally appear to be uninterested in affecting structural reform within the church; instead, they are rather conservative both theologically and socially. Bord and Faulkner (1985) have reported that Catholic charismatics are actively involved with their religion, often attending weekly meetings, engaging in public religious behavior, and attending mass frequently. Participants can be described as highly orthodox, and their charismatic involvement tends to reinforce involvement with the formal church and respect for church authority.

In her study, Poloma (1982:16) found that the Catholic charismatic renewal movement differs from the neo-Pentecostal movement of conservative Protestantism. The Catholic movement emphasizes houses of prayer (retreat centers), Pentecostal religious communities, and prayer groups. Furthermore, it is firmly rooted in the Roman Catholic Church and its history. In fact, Poloma (1982:119) reports that the Roman Catholic Church has established organizational structures that allow for the growth of the charismatic renewal movement. Because the church has a centralized structure, the movement has a legitimate place within it. Also Pope John Paul II and the American Catholic bishops have endorsed it; thus, individual Catholics who oppose the charismatic renewal movement cannot actively work against it without challenging church authority (Poloma, 1982:120).

During the 1980s the mainstream of the Catholic charismatic movement became increasingly conservative in its beliefs (Hitchcock, 1991:125–26). Participants emphasized the need for balance between the guidance of the Holy Spirit and the teachings of the church. On the other hand, Catholic charismatics have much in common with conservative Protestant charismatics, relying on biblical authority for guidance and forming religious communities featuring hierarchical control (Hitchcock, 1991:125). Personal piety, similar to that exhibited by Protestant charismatics, became a hallmark of Catholic charismatics.

In terms of basic beliefs, Roman Catholics still overwhelmingly subscribe to the orthodox and traditional doctrines of their faith. Gallup and Castelli (1989:56–64) found that 90 percent of Roman Catholics in their sample never doubted the existence of God, 91 percent believed in the divinity of Christ, and 71 percent believed in life beyond death.

A Gallup poll utilized by D'Antonio, Davidson, Hoge, and Wallace (1989) revealed change among Catholics in the United States in their willingness to accept the more exclusive teachings of the church, particularly those related to social issues. A majority viewed moral authority not as the reuslt of church teachings but as the result of personal autonomy in decision making. They found further evidence that the moral authority of the Roman Catholic Church is being called into question by Catholic laity. Such findings may be the result of the conservative nature of the Roman Catholic hierarchy. Reese (1989) demonstrates that very little has changed in the selection of bishops during the last century. The prospective candidate must show adherence to the doctrine and *magisterium* of the church and must concur with papal pronouncements on the priestly ordination of men (as opposed to women), on marriage, on sexual ethics, and on social justice.

A variety of studies continue to show that a majority of both priests and lay people within Roman Catholicism believe that priests should be permitted to marry (D'Antonio, Davidson, Hoge, and Wallace, 1989; Siedler and Meyer, 1989). The continuing inability of the Catholic hierarchy to address these and other issues partially accounts for the shortage of priests within the church (Finke and Stark, 1992:259–61). In addition to the issue of marriage and sexuality for priests, a recently revealed scandal has caused further erosion of the reputation of priests: the continuing revelations of sexual abuse of children and adolescents by priests. Allegations have been lodged against about four hundred priests since 1982. Only recently, however, has the hierarchy of the Roman Catholic Church firmly responded to this problem. A *Newsweek* public opinion poll indicated that about 66 percent of American Catholics who were questioned believe that the church has treated abusive priests too leniently. Most of those polled think that priests found to be abusers should be defrocked immediately (Press, 1993:42). The archbishop of Chicago, Cardinal Joseph Bernardin, and the archbishop of Boston, Cardinal Bernard Law, have ordered searches of personnel files of priests in their dioceses and have proposed faster procedures for rooting out those clergy against whom there is evidence of abuse (Press, 1993:42–44).

This problem and the seemingly related issues of marriage and sexuality for priests have caused members of the Catholic clergy—like their Protestant colleagues—to perceive their priestly authority eroding. This recent development is in sharp contrast to the past situation when, as Ebaugh reported (1991), Roman Catholic laypeople highly respected their priests as persons of superior authority and as interpreters of papal pronouncements and church teachings.

In recent works, Greeley (1990; 1991) views the declining loyalty and church participation of Roman Catholics as a result of an eroding confidence in church leadership and growing differences between the church hierarchy and the people over several social issues such as birth control, poorly run parishes, and "poor preaching and religious instruction." However, he points out that a majority of Catholics choose to remain *in* the church in spite of these problems. Other studies conducted during recent years suggest that these "Catholic problems" are perhaps the result of the changing demographic profile of Roman Catholics. Roof (1979), Mosher and Goldscheider (1984), and Lane (1984) all have shown that few differences exist between Protestants and Catholics concerning marriage patterns, frequency of divorce, use of birth control, family size, and attitudes toward abortion. D'Antonio (1985:339) suggested that Catholics, particularly younger

Catholics, have become more personally autonomous and less subject to traditional religious social control mechanisms. Fee et al (1981:19) found that young Catholics seem to have rejected the church as a teacher, signifying that the church's position as a moral force has been weakened. Only those young Catholics who attended parochial schools showed any variation from this overall rejection pattern, and that variation was slight. In their later study, D'Antonio, Davidson, Hoge, and Wallace (1989) suggested that democratization within the Roman Catholic Church could result in a greater commitment from the Catholic laity.

These changes in attitude and belief within the membership of the largest single religious body in the United States have come about as Catholics have achieved virtual parity with Protestants in educational attainment, occupational prestige, and income. The ethnicity so characteristic of Catholics before World War II has not been a barrier to these achievements (Greeley, 1977). However, the ethnicity of many Roman Catholics *does* still make for a difference between family units of various ethnic identities, such as Italian, Polish, and Irish Catholics.

In spite of such findings, Greeley (1977) has stated that more similarities than dissimilarities of moral style exist among Protestants, Catholics, and Jews. Additionally, many of the religious activities— devotions and observances of certain holy days—that Catholics formerly participated in and used to define themselves as distinctively religious as compared to Protestants have been eliminated. Nevertheless, in the practice of religion, Roman Catholic attendance at religious services still exceeds either Protestant or Jewish attendance, in spite of an overall decline in Catholic attendance. In 1973, 55 percent of Catholics attended church in a given week, as compared to 37 percent of Protestants (Rosten, 1975:431). Data analyzed by Gallup and Castelli (1989) show that in 1980, 53 percent of Roman Catholics attended services weekly, compared to 39 percent of Protestants. In 1988, the data indicated that 48 percent of Catholic and 45 percent of Protestants attended church services weekly.

The Roman Catholic Church in the contemporary United States is a church in transition—less traditional than in the past, less influential in terms of moral authority, containing a neo-Pentecostal (charismatic renewal) movement, and both conservative and radical priests and nuns. While acknowledging that many of these changes are a reaction to the conservatism of the Vatican, Finke and Stark (1992:271–72) suggest that the Roman Catholic Church has become another mainline denomination. As a result, it will continue to show a decline in attendance at services and in adherence to the traditional Catholic moral authority. Still, it is a tremendously important religious body with parishes representing all social classes and a stable membership.

Judaism

As we learned in Chapter 5, a sizable migration of Jews into the United States between the end of the Civil War and the end of World War I resulted in the expansion of religious pluralism to include a third faith, Judaism. During the early decades of the twentieth century, Conservative Judaism became the target of the three branches of Judaism, mainly because it appealed to the sons and daughters of immigrants with its emphasis on liberalism in politics, human rights, and religious rights. Today, however, the largest membership (3 million members) is found within the 3,000 congregations of the Union of Orthodox Jewish Congregations of America. Conservative Judaism is known as the United Synagogues of America and has 835 congregations with 1.5 million members. The most "American" of the branches, the Reform branch, counts 1 million members in the 686 congregations of the Union of American Hebrew Congregations (Bedell and Jones, 1992).

The relative smallness of both Conservative and Reform Judaism as compared to Orthodox Judaism probably reflects the secularization of many Jews who have simply left Jewish religious organizations while maintaining Jewish cultural ties. For example, some Jewish people, because of their humanism and political liberalism, have become Unitarians, while others may observe the high holy days of Judaism but not participate regularly in weekly synagogue or temple activities. All the same, these people do express their Jewishness, do identify with Jewish people, and do carry on the Jewish tradition (Lasker, 1971). This phenomenon is viewed by Winter (1991:47–59; 1992: 349–63) as a characteristic of *ethnoreligion*. Many Jews are members of a community with both religious and ethnic concerns. The American Jewish community incorporates support for Israel but not necessarily for Zionism. This is in contrast to the view suggested by Levine (1986: 323–43), which sees Judaism as a religion as separate from Jewish ethnicity. The transformation of American Jews is due largely to the forces of industrialization, urbanization, modernization, and secularization (Goldscheider, 1986).

By contrast, Orthodox Jews observe religious customs and practices on a much more regular basis. In a study of motivations for attending high holy day services, Lasker (1971) found that his subjects who were Orthodox ranked "relationship with God" and "influence on God" as their highest motivations for attending, and considered as a very important reason for observing the holy days their desire "to comply with God's requirement that we observe Rosh Hashanah and Yom Kippur." Such expressions reflect both the Orthodox emphasis upon a personal God and his requirements for the Jewish people to practice the religion legalistically. These tenets of faith are less emphasized in both Conservative and Reform Judaism.

Recent studies suggests that there is a re-emphasis on orthodoxy. Included in the debates concerning Orthodoxy is the fundamental question of "*Who* is Jewish?" Orthodox Jews apply a strict test to determine adherents to the faith. Heilman (1990) believes that while this debate could lead to a schism between Orthodox Jews and members of the other two branches, a serious division is a more likely outcome. This Orthodox movement is similar to Protestant fundamentalism and Roman Catholic traditionalism. It emphasizes allegiance to Jewish religious practices, unquestioned support for the Jewish state of Israel, support of a hierarchy, and the subordination of Jewish women to Jewish men.

In spite of predictions that Jewish Orthodoxy would decline because it seemed out of step with modernity, it has enjoyed a renaissance based partly upon a successful *recruitment effort*. Danzger (1989) illustrates various innovative teaching efforts directed at nominal, nonorthodox Jewish young people—particularly those who have visited Israel. Although he argues that returning to Orthodox Judaism is not the same as being converted in a radical Christian "revival meeting," the two events do share similarities.

Two other studies examine the status of Orthodox Jewish women in the United States. Kaufman (1991) states that these women, particularly the "converts," are celebrating traditional femininity and the life cycle of women. Davidson (1991), in a study of two synagogues, points out that some of the women see their "return" to orthodoxy as a result of free choice, while others see it as an inevitable step in fulfilling the requirements of Judaism. Heilman and Cohen (1989) demonstrate that, contrary to predictions, Orthodox social institutions are growing both in number and influence. This has given Orthodox Jews a stronger voice in the American Jewish community—a community that has often been dominated by Reform and Conservative Jews.

The inconsistency in the regular practice of religion among American Jews is reflected in weekly attendance rates at synagogues and temples. In 1973 a Gallup poll found that only 19 percent of Jews in the sample attended services in a typical week, as compared with 17 percent in 1964 (Rosten, 1975:565). Gallup and Castelli (1989) reported similar attendance figures. In 1989, 21 percent of Jews reported weekly attendance at religious services. Only 44 percent of people identifying themselves as Jewish claimed synagogue membership. In spite of this, Jewish identity remains strong. The attendance for high holy day services is much higher, sometimes as much as 57 percent. This identity is also reflected in the Bar Mitzvah of young Jewish males and similar ceremonies for young Jewish females.

In parallel fashion to Protestantism, religious affiliation as well as attendance for Jews seems to vary according to location. The overwhelming majority of Jews in the United States live in urban areas, where synagogue affiliation is lower than in smaller communities. While in 1966, 84 percent of Jews lived in the northeastern area of the country, by 1989, only 56 percent did so. The Jewish population has increased dramatically in the South, Midwest, and West (Gallup and Castelli, 1989:116–18). As this population shift occurred, Jews often found themselves in smaller communities of the South, Midwest, and West, where synagogue affiliation commonly reaches 80 percent of all Jews in the area (Sklare, 1971). This development reflects the fact that as the number of Jews forming a Jewish community decreases, synagogue affiliation increases. A recent study shows similar findings (Raffkind, 1993). Significantly, the rate of affiliation among foreign-born Jews is no higher than it is among the native-born (Sklare, 1971). Sklare has observed that the lack of affiliation or the lack of regular attendance does *not* reflect opposition to synagogue life or activities; instead, it probably reflects secularization on the part of the unaffiliated. In those larger communities where affiliation and attendance are lower, many organizations and causes of a specifically Jewish nature are available outside the orbit of the synagogue.

Affiliation and attendance patterns also relate to differences in beliefs and rituals among the three branches of Judaism in the United States. Orthodox Jews regard their faith as the maintream of a tradition that has been unaltered for three thousand years. They see the Hebrew Bible (the Old Testament of the Christians) as the revealed word of God. For the Orthodox, the Sabbath is strictly observed: No work, no travel, no writing, no business dealings, and no carrying of money are allowed. The Orthodox observe all details of the dietary laws, segregate women from men in synagogue seating, and use only Hebrew in prayer and ceremonial services. Furthermore, the men wear a hat or skullcap at all times. Conservative Jews follow the pattern of traditional Judaism, but regard the religion as evolving and ever-growing. They follow the dietary laws, but with minor relaxations. They observe the Sabbath and the high holy days, but the Sabbath observance is likely to be late on Friday evening. Also, many Conservative congregations use English in the prayers. Reform Jews are quite different in their practice from the Orthodox and somewhat

different from the Conservatives. In matters of the revelation of the will of God to humanity, the Reform branch accepts as binding only the moral laws of the Bible and the ceremonies that elevate and sanctify the lives of people. A rational religious faith capable of withstanding the scrutiny of reason and science is the goal of Reform Judaism. In the temple complete equality of sexes prevails, prayer is largely in English, and flexibility in the choice of prayers is great. Organs, and sometimes choirs, are used in worship services. Rarely do worshippers cover their heads during prayer (Kertzer, 1975).

Despite these differences in beliefs and worship practices, Orthodox, Conservative, and Reform Judaism share some common beliefs. The Torah, consisting of the five books of Moses in the Bible (Genesis to Deuteronomy), and the Talmud, consisting of sixty-three books of legal, philosophical, ethical, and historical writings of the ancient rabbis, are accepted by all three branches. The Jewish prayer book also speaks of three basic principles of Jewish faith: The first is the love of learning; the second is the worship of God; and the third is the performance of good deeds. Jews are also generally in agreement in not accepting the principle of incarnation (God becoming human). In contrast, a cardinal tenet of Jewish faith is that God is spiritual and has no human attributes.

A more recent group within Judaism, the Reconstructionist Movement, attempts to reconcile the different beliefs and practices of Judaism—both in the United States and other parts of the world. A worldwide Jewish perspective and belief system is its goal. Reconstructionists can be found both in separate synagogues and in the three established branches of Judaism. Obviously, Jews reject the divinity of Jesus Christ, and Judaism does not accept the principle of atonement by Christ for the sins of the whole world (Kertzer, 1975). In spite of this rejection of Christianity, contemporary American Judaism is not a proselytizing religion. However, converts to the Jewish faith are welcome. (Many of these converts are the non-Jewish spouses of an interfaith marriage.) These commonly held beliefs, along with a strong sense of Jewish community and culture, unite Jews in the United States in a way that few other religious faiths in our country experience.

Like immigrant Catholics, American Jews of the second and third generations have achieved much upward social mobility. Thirty-six percent of American Jews were found by a 1989 Gallup poll to be in the top income bracket and 60 percent in the two highest-income levels, a much higher proportion than all Protestants and Roman Catholics in the two highest-income levels (Gallup and Castelli, 1989: 117). Glazer (1972) has asserted that this overrepresentation in the higher socioeconomic levels is one reason for the decline in Jewish radicalism and some dimunition of the traditional Jewish political and economic liberalism. Since their stake in the economic (and political) system in the United States is so great, American Jews have looked with dismay as younger secular Jews (as well as black militants and white radicals) have advocated a radical economic and social reform of our society.

The sense of community that solidified among Jews as a result of the Nazi Holocaust was further strengthened with the formation of the nation of Israel following World War II. An overwhelming majority of Jews in the United States support Israel emotionally, and many support its defense efforts financially. More recent accounts of human rights violations against Jews in the former Soviet Union have also promoted Jewish unity.

Still, important differences remain between American Judaism and Christianity. Although the Roman Catholic Church has officially renounced its anti-Semitic accusation of deocide against the Jews, little substantive rapprochement between Catholics and Jews has occurred, except for ecumenical Thanksgiving services and the like. Protestant-Jewish relationships are more relaxed, except between fundamentalist Protestantism and Judaism. But still, according to Himmelfarb (1967), American Jews who are traditional or Orthodox in the observance of their faith feel that the overt and covert Christian symbols and practices of the United States erode Jewish religious faith; as a result, these Jews promote further secularization.

Nevertheless, to be Jewish and American means something unique in the history of Judaism. It means a sense of loyalty to a religious and an ethnic heritage; it means a historical identification with the oppressed; and it means perseverance in overcoming a vast social, economic, political, and religious discrimination. Today's American Jews are no longer subjected to covenant restrictions that exclude them from neighborhoods or from social clubs. Jews experience only sporadic outbursts of anti-Semitism—usually only from fringe political groups like the Ku Klux Klan, the John Birch Society, and neo-Nazi groups. Still, Jewish representation in the highest echelons of predominantly Gentile corporate organizations remains low. Certain country clubs still admit no Jews or only a few Jews. Because of these exceptions to the complete acceptance of Jews in our society, the three branches of American Judaism remain a solidified religious community in the United States.

Islam

Of all of the recent religious groups and movements found in the United States, none is faster growing than Islam, the third monotheistic religion of the world. Much of this growth is from the immigration of Muslims into this country and from higher birthrates among Muslims than among Protestants, Roman Catholics, and Jews. Demographically, adherents of Islam are found in urban areas—particularly New York City, Detroit, and Los Angeles. In almost all major cities with populations of 500,000 or more, there is either a mosque or an Islamic worship center. The most prevalent Islamic group in the United States is the Sunni sect, although Shiite Muslims are also present. The best estimates of Islamic membership is 1,300,000, although accurate data are not available (Bedell and Jones, 1992).

To lead an Islamic life in a non-Muslim society is somewhat difficult, since Islam has reaffirmed the essential unity between religion and the state. In a way similar to the black Muslims (who will be discussed in Chapter 12), non-African-American Muslims are still viewed with some hostility and suspicion. During the 1991 Persian Gulf War, Muslims in the United States were quick to affirm allegiance to this society. In spite of those affirmations, some acts of violence were directed at various Islamic communities in this country.

Haddad and Lummis (1987) examined the Islamic community and its integration (or lack thereof) into the larger society. They reported that Muslims in the United States often modify the basic tenets of the faith, even those that demand strict compliance. This enables the followers of Islam to blend into American society and its cultural demands. In essence, they move between their religious world and the perceived secular world of Western society. One example is the observance of national holidays. Those stressing family relations and values—Thanksgiving Day, Valentine's Day, Mother's Day, and Father's Day—are often observed. Obviously, Christmas and Easter are not. In some ways Muslims are treated as Jewish immigrants were in the nineteenth century: with ambivalence. The fact that Allah is often referred to as "God" emphasizes the monotheistic nature of Islam. Islam's recognition of Jesus and Abraham as historical persons and prophets allows more toleration for Sunni Muslims than for members of other non-Western religions. On the other hand, the militancy and anti-Western campaigns of the Shiite fundamentalist sects still cause aversion and sometimes hatred on the part of Protestants, Catholics, and Jews in the United States.

Haddad and Lummis (1987) suggest that as more Muslims immigrate to the United States and as more and more Islamic worship centers spring up, our level of public tolerance should become more like that demonstrated in the United Kingdom. Already Sunni Muslims are consolidating strength through intermarriage and networking.

One aim of this is to enhance the validity of Islamic law in the United States so that it will influence the social regulation of marriage and divorce. In addition, it is probable that second- and third-generation Muslims will show more assimilation into the religious landscape of America.

SUMMARY

By the middle of the twentieth century, religious diversity seemed a stabilizing force in the United States. Church attendance had reached an all-time high. The mainline Protestant denominations promoted unity by reorganizing the old Federal Council of Churches into the National Council of Churches in Christ and by continuing the denominational mergers that began in 1939. The ecumenism in the Roman Catholic Church that resulted from the Second Vatican Council brought Protestants and Catholics into new dialogue and closer cooperation. Conservative/fundamentalist Protestant bodies, however, remained outside this new expression of cooperation and ecumenism.

The three-culture hypothesis advanced by Herberg saw the three major faiths—Catholicism, Judaism, and Protestantism—as different cultural manifestations of a basic American unity. It also viewed religious affiliation as more important than ethnic identification for the third generation of immigrant families. But Herberg's thesis ignored ethnic, class, regional, and theological differences that continued to exist both among and within the three faiths.

Mainline Protestant bodies have a predominantly white middle-class membership, and show less commitment to religious practices than do conservative/fundamentalist bodies or Catholics. During the 1960s, the liberal social activism of mainline Protestantism in the arena of civil rights and opposition to the Vietnam War resulted in a conservative reaction within these churches and in declining membership. This began in the 1970s and continues today. Neo-Pentecostal and charismatic renewal movements have occurred in mainline Protestant churches, and for the most part have been accommodated, although some animosities have developed at the local level. Conservative/fundamentalist Protestant churches, characterized by intensity of religious belief, exclusivity of membership requirements, a higher level of church attendance, and emphasis upon individual salvation, have grown in membership in recent years. However, this growth may or may not be at the expense of the mainline churches. We will look more closely at this particular expression of Protestantism in the next chapter.

Roman Catholicism in the United States more and more resembles mainline Protestantism in terms of class representation, ecumenism, more liberal doctrinal interpretations, and religious practices since Vatican II. It also has a sizable charismatic renewal movement. The church membership has been characterized in recent years by changing attitudes, by declining loyalty and church participation, and by a traditionalist movement that seeks to return the church to its pre-Vatican II state. Roman Catholicism also has a conservative activist movement whose primary goals closely resemble those of conservative/fundamentalist Protestantism. The most prominent social agenda item is the elimination of most abortions in the United States. This is countered by the continuing efforts of Catholic moderates and liberals to bring more democracy into the church and to bring about the ordination of women to the Catholic priesthood.

Though the practices and beliefs of Orthodox, Conservative, and Reform Jews differ, and though many Jews have become secularized and do not affiliate with any synagogue, Jewish ethnic and cultural identification remains strong in the United States, and the Jewish community remains unified. Of the three branches, Orthodox Judaism continues to attract new adherents, particularly young people.

Islam is more and more a visible religion in the United States. In terms of members, Islam is next in size after Judaism. Its ritual beliefs and ideologies are often at odds with the cultural and religious pluralism of the United States. However, Muslims living in America seem to have adapted a dualism that allows them to practice most of the strict requirements of a non-Western religious faith and to coexist in the secular Western world.

7.

Fundamentalist and Evangelical Resurgence

"There is a religious and cultural war being waged for the soul of the nation," declared conservative television personality and newspaper columnist Patrick Buchanan at the Republican Convention in August 1992. Although Buchanan is a Roman Catholic, his speech reflected the social and political agenda of most Protestant fundamentalists and many Protestant evangelicals. His political speech listed a long list of the issues important to fundamentalists and evangelicals: support for traditional family values, opposition to civil rights for gays, opposition to abortion on demand, support for a constitutional amendment for voluntary prayer in public schools, opposition to pornography, and opposition to realistic sex education concerning the spread of AIDS.

Within the convention hall in Houston thousands of delegates cheered; hundreds remained silent. The television audience watching the Republican Convention were equally divided, as Buchanan and other speakers accused Democratic presidential candidate (and now President) Bill Clinton of supporting all of the political positions opposed by traditional religious folk. In addition, other speakers, including Marilyn Quayle, wife of the then vice president, attacked Hillary Clinton as the antithesis of what an American wife and mother should be. It would be easy to say that the presidential election of 1992 laid to rest the social and political agenda of conservative and fundamentalist Protestants. Both President Bill Clinton and Vice President Albert Gore are Southern Baptists, members of the largest Protestant denomination known for its conservatism and fundamentalism. Such would not seem to be the case. In California over three hundred local and state political offices were won by religious evangelicals and fundamentalists. Consider also the natural history of this textbook in describing this subject. In the first edition (published in 1981), this chapter was titled "Fundamentalism as a Social Movement." In the second edition (published in 1987), it was "The Fundamentalist and Evangelical Movement." This edition's chapter title is "Fundamentalist and Evangelical Resurgence." Obviously, fundamentalism and evangelism remain an important part of the religious realm. The loss of one presidential election is not the end of the fundamentalists' and evangelicals' battle for "America's soul." In fact, this loss seems to serve as a rallying cry for continued diligence on the part of fundamentalists and evangelicals. Both groups have powerful allies among Roman Catholic traditionalists and conservative activists as well as sympathetic members of mainline Protestant denominations. Protestant fundamentalism and evangelicalism remain a force in the religious, social, and political life of the United States.

How did a social movement which seemed doomed by the end of the 1920s make such a remarkable comeback during the 1970s and 1980s? What salient religious, social, and political issues sustain its momentum? As a movement, Protestant fundamentalism began with an agitation to return to the fundamentals of the Christian faith as expressed in the Bible. This biblical literalism, coupled with an emphasis on personal salvation through Jesus Christ and a reliance on preaching to convey the message, has characterized mass evangelism since the urban, small-town, and frontier revivals of the early days of this society.

Chapter 5 briefly mentioned the major controversies over modern progress that caused a rift between fundamentalists and more progressive Protestants as the 1800s gave way to the 1900s. Chapter 6 touched on the opposition of conservative/fundamentalist churches to the ecumenism and social activism of the liberal and moderate churches in the years since World War II. In this chapter we will focus on the continuing presence of the fundamentalist and evangelical movement—the phenomenon that continues to fragment the Protestant establishment of the United States and to enjoy continued vitality even as the influence of mainline Protestantism has recently declined.

HISTORICAL FOUNDATIONS OF FUNDAMENTALISM

Various historians, sociologists, and journalists view the decade of the 1920s as the time when fundamentalism asserted itself most vehemently in the public eye in a debate called the *fundamentalist/modernist controversy,* which was mentioned briefly in Chapter 5. But an analysis of this portion of American religious history from a sociological perspective indicates that the social processes that led to this public religious battle—organized evangelism in urban areas and on the frontier, urbanization and industrialization, and the Social Gospel debate—began early in the collective life of the United States. In this section we will discuss the most important historical trends and events that led to the growth of southern fundamentalist churches and the decline of others, to the influence of evangelist Billy Graham, and eventually to the present vitality of evangelicalism in the United States.

The Legacy of Urban and Frontier Evangelism

Early in the nineteenth century, Lyman Beecher (1775–1863), a distinguished Congregationalist minister in New England, wrote an eloquent appeal to the churches to recognize that "the religious and political destiny of the nation" would be decided "in the continually multiplying frontier communities" (Hudson, 1981). On the other hand, the same Lyman Beecher severely criticized fellow Congregationalist Charles Finney for his evangelistic crusades in the cities and towns of the new nation (Finke and Stark, 1992:85–86).

These awakenings, revivals, and frontier camp meetings were viewed by many as spontaneous outbreaks of religious fervor. Doubtless some were. For the most part, the evangelism of nineteenth-century America not only was well organized but also became routine (Finke and Stark,1992:87–92; Ammerman, 1991:18–20). Ammerman points out that Finney "was the first to articulate the goal of revivalism as 'winning souls' and the first to set out a step-by-step method for achieving that goal and calculating its success" (1991:18). As a result, the evangelistic crusades took on a life outside organized religion. Finke and Stark (1992:90) note that Finney also recruited large numbers of lay workers and arranged for local clergy and laypeople to be trained for ministering to the "sinners" who would repent during these revivals. Furthermore, he believed that routine revivals were necessary for religion to remain healthy.

On the western frontier, revivalism was institutionalized in camp

meetings which might last one or two weeks. Finke and Stark (1992: 92–96) describe such meetings as both religious revivals and recreational opportunities. Like the urban revivals of Finney, they were carefully planned. For many settlers living in isolated areas, the camp meetings provided opportunities for socializing with other adults.

Without question, some of the churches were better prepared than others to fill the religious vacuum existing in the new frontier communities in the early 1800s, and thus to influence the nation's religious and political destiny. In particular, the churches that followed people westward to the new frontier were the Methodists, the Baptists, the missionary-minded New Light Congregationalists, and the New Side Presbyterians. They were joined by the newly formed Christian Church that had grown out of the Campbellite Movement (Finke and Stark, 1992:87–98).

As mentioned in Chapter 5, these were precisely the groups that had been prominent in the First Great Awakening in the colonies (with the exception of the Campbellite Movement, which was founded on the frontier by Alexander and Thomas Campbell). The revival emphasis of these groups was eminently suited to work under frontier conditions as the new nation expanded westward, and the home missionary societies they founded provided financial support as well as personnel for mass evangelism. The Baptists' farmer-preachers and the Methodists' camp meetings and itinerant preachers who rode the circuit among settlements brought the kind of fervor necessary to awaken settlers from their religious apathy. In addition, the closeness of the members of these groups and their emphasis upon personal redemption appealed to the needs of those living on the frontier.

By contrast, the concerns of religious groups established in the coastal states and especially in New England were order, tradition, propriety, and education (Littell 1962:18–22). Most Congregationalists, Presbyterians, and Episcopalians disapproved of evangelistic tactics. As a result, the old-line denominations stopped participating in the camp meetings, leaving the pulpit time to the Baptists and Methodists (Finke and Stark, 1992:99–101). Because of the success of the Baptists, Methodists, and Campbellites, the old-line churches tried to persuade local officials to ban camp meetings as "disturbances of the peace." Sometimes these tactics worked, but often they did not. Thus the split between evangelical and mainline Protestantism was already clearly in evidence.

Just as the revival emphasis during the First Great Awakening was more successful in the southern colonies than in the New England colonies with their staid religious establishment, so it was most successful on the frontier with those who had migrated from the southern states. These frontier folk were characterized by lower educational and cultural standards and by more religious apathy than were the New Englanders, who had settled the upper Midwest and the Mississippi River Valley (Hudson, 1981). Thus, the frontier people from the South were more susceptible to the emotional, personally oriented, simplistic message of the frontier evangelists. The seeds of fundamentalism had been planted in the fertile soil of the frontier. By the middle of the nineteenth century, revival churches predominated and had put their indelible imprint on public life.

Urbanization and the Social Gospel Dispute

The shift from a rural to an urban emphasis in the United States in the late 1800s set the stage for the fundamentalist movement to emerge as a rural reaction against the cities and their immigrant populations. As a steady stream of largely Catholic European immigrants settled in the industrial cities of the East and Midwest, biblical orthodoxy became a tool for opposing the social and political accommodation of urban industrial workers, for preserving the political power of the rural segments of the nation, and for standing against improving the economic position of working-class Americans, regardless of their religious identification. The Social Gospel was the focus of controversy between fundamentalists and more liberal Protestants as the nineteenth century ended and the twentieth century began.

The Social Gospel came onto the scene as the methods of mass evangelism were being adapted for an urban setting. In particular, Protestant evangelist Dwight L. Moody (1837–99) aimed his conservative biblical message at urban Catholics and native-born citizens who had traded the farm for the factory or urban business. In revival meetings, he treated the urban masses to large doses of descriptions of Christ's Second Coming, emphasizing that only this would bring in a new order and that until the Advent occurred, Christians should occupy themselves with saving the souls of others and tending to their own souls (Marty, 1970:162–63). Further, Moody stressed that people would survive the harshness of city living largely by coming under the care of the Great Shepherd (Marty, 1970:162, 1984:315–19). In short, Moody adopted a stance of protecting the faith from reformers and their theological questioning of Holy Scriptures. In his meetings, Protestants from almost all denominations were present and in agreement as to the need for personal salvation and piety (Ammerman, 1991:19). But Moody's preaching fame overshadowed his programs for the urban masses, and the Social Gospel began to challenge his view that individual salvation and concern for our own soul were the keys to the kingdom, both on earth and in heaven.

The Social Gospel emerged from those branches of moderate and progressive Protestantism that sought to reconcile the message of Christianity with the social, economic, and political needs of the urban population. It became first a complement and later an alternative to mass evangelism and revivalism. Those who promoted this movement tried to redress urban social ills brought about through overcrowded living conditions and poverty. Fair labor practices and provisions for decent health became as important as frequent church attendance (Ammerman, 1991:12–13). Leading advocates of the Social Gospel were Baptist minister Walter Rauschenbusch (1861–1918), who became aware of social problems in the poverty-stricken immigrant neighborhood of Hell's Kitchen in New York City; Washington Gladden (1836–1918), a Congregationalist minister in Columbus, Ohio; and Reinhold Niebuhr (1892–1971), a pastor in Detroit, Michigan. These men believed that Christianity should work to change the laws so that all persons, rich and poor, would be treated in a humane way. Although they advocated reshaping the collective social condition of urban dwellers, their methods were an extension of earlier evangelical traditions. They saw social involvement as a complement to concern with individual salvation and viewed cooperation among Christians as essential.

The capstone of the Social Gospel movement was the issuance of a social creed in 1908 by the newly founded Federal Council of Churches. The creed called for equal rights for all people, child labor laws, laws against the liquor traffic, protection for workers in their place of employment, old-age benefits, labor arbitration, the reduction of working hours, a guaranteed living wage, and "the application of Christian principles to the acquisition and use of property." Although these positions seem rather mild by contemporary standards, a majority of the affluent Protestant laity saw them as inflammatory. Many of these church members identified the labor movement and unionization with socialism and feared that the churches were supporting these movements (Olmstead, 1961).

The conservative alternative to the Social Gospel remained a kind of Christian social service that was individual-oriented. Notable was an import from England, the Salvation Army. Founded in 1878 by William Booth, its program stressed witnessing to Christ by informal preaching and outdoor evangelistic missions that featured brass bands. Its theology was conservative, emphasizing sin, redemption, and holiness in living. When the Salvation Army reached the United States in 1889, it began its ministry in the tenement sections of cities through its highly publicized Slum Brigades. These "troops," organized along quasi-military lines, went into the deteriorating city neighborhoods, held services in saloons, brought relief to the destitute, and preached against sinful vice (Olmstead, 1961). Since this kind of approach was in line with the evangelical style of church ministry, it gradually won the support of conservative Protestants and served as a foil to the Social Gospel.

Although proponents of the Social Gospel hoped to build a broad base of support through all of Protestantism, it gained only limited acceptance within the Presbyterian, northern Baptist, Congregationalist, Methodist, and Disciples of Christ denominations. As the Social Gospel movement came to be perceived as a genuine threat to conservative Protestant Christianity, southern Protestants, who were largely rural, allied themselves with northern fundamentalists. Foes of the Social Gospel continued to view it as an unscriptural perversion of the gospel and as an extremely liberal political philosophy masquerading as religion. Proponents of the Social Gospel, on the other hand, pointed out that private Protestants (those who stressed individual salvation, pietistic personal behavior, and the future benefits of heavenly life) also meddled in politics by constantly taking stands against gambling and drinking and for Sunday closing laws and other similar issues. Furthermore, these conservative Protestants supported the laissez-faire economic system and, in general, the status quo. The only issue on which the two camps could agree was the temperance movement, but this issue alone was not strong enough to keep together both fundamentalists and progressives within the mainline Protestant denominations. In the end, the Social Gospel movement helped drive fundamentalist Protestant clergy and laity further into intransigence regarding orthodoxy, piety, and personal evangelism.

Thus, during the first two and a half decades of the twentieth century, fundamentalist Christians emerged as different kinds of believers from their less conservative counterparts. They were anti-Social Gospel, anti-intellectual, and anti–biblical criticism. Some were ardent millenarians who believed that God would end the evil world momentarily; others were conservatives who believed that humans should not tamper with the revelations of God to humanity recorded in the Scriptures. Still others, a broad-based plurality of Protestants, simply believed that religion should consist of living a holy and pietistic life, of saving the souls of unbelievers through the techniques of revivalism, and of working hard during our earthly life in order to obtain heavenly rewards. Such beliefs were the older, familiar tenets of Protestantism in the United States, and, in the eyes of many, fundamentalism preserved these familiar frontier and rural beliefs.

The Fundamentalist/Modernist Controversy

The growing rift between fundamentalist and progressive Protestants reached a crisis as the impact of science and the philosophy of skepticism began to permeate all aspects of intellectual life. About the middle of the nineteenth century, German scholars began to use the same critical tools to study the Bible that they had used for scrutinizing other ancient texts. Their message was that the Scriptures were neither unique nor historically accurate (Ammerman, 1991: 11–12).

This *higher criticism* (as the process came to be known) was to traditional biblical interpretation what contemporary theories of sociobiology are to the more traditional theories of *learned behavior*. By 1910 the clash concerning nonliteral biblical interpretations, the Social Gospel ideology, and liberal theology had erupted into open controversy. The fundamentalist movement became an organized campaign against urbanization and the impact of science upon biblical truths.

Between 1910 and 1912, twelve paperback pamphlets, *The Fundamentals,* were published and distributed by two wealthy brothers from California. These pamphlets gave sober and serious defenses for the main beliefs of conservative Protestant Christianity; virtually all the contributing writers were scholarly students of the Bible. Over three hundred thousand copies were distributed, serving to bring the issues involved in the controversy over fundamentalism out into the open (Goen, 1959:88). But *The Fundamentals* failed in their primary purpose of checking the spread of modern and liberal theology, according to Sandeen (1970). He views the writing as the "last flowering of a millenarian-conservative alliance dedicated at all costs to the defense of the cardinal doctrines of nineteenth-century American evangelicalism" (1970:206–7).

Nevertheless, conservative Protestants who subscribed to the doctrinal points outlined in *The Fundamentals* began a movement within the organized churches (which later would lead to a parting of the ways for many of them). Revivalism continued to enjoy success in the years leading up to World War I. Billy Sunday (1863–1935), a baseball player turned evangelist, followed in the footsteps of Dwight L. Moody. When prohibition became the law of the land through the Eighteenth Amendment to the U.S. Constitution, conservative Protestants felt that traditional Christianity had been preserved. In 1919 the World's Christian Fundamentals Association was founded by a prominent Baptist minister from Minneapolis, William Bell Riley. Represented were theological conservatives, millenarians, and a few people from the Holiness or Pentecostal sects; their common bond was a holy war on modernism within the organized churches and their theological schools. Over six thousand people gathered at the first meeting in Philadelphia. The organization was never successful because it became involved in one controversy after another (Ammerman, 1991:23–24).

As the decade of the 1920s opened, two significant controversies began to unfold. The first was a northeastern urban tempest, while the second was a southern rural storm. The former was precipitated by the famous sermon entitled "Shall the Fundamentalists Win?" preached in 1922 from the pulpit of New York's First Presbyterian Church by liberal Baptist pastor Harry Emerson Fosdick (1878–1969). Fosdick's controversial message flung down the gauntlet to fundamentalists, daring them to fight to the finish. In the ensuing uproar Baptists demanded Fosdick's resignation from the ministry, and Presbyterians urged his removal from the pulpit of the New York church. Instead, the Presbyterian Judicial Commission ruled that since Fosdick was a Baptist, they could not judge him. Furthermore, Fosdick chose *not* to become a Presbyterian (Ammerman, 1991:25). This prevented fundamentalist victories in both these battles. Fosdick became the minister of New York City's Riverside Church, built by John D. Rockefeller, and also gained national acclaim as a radio preacher. However, the controversy concerning fundamentalist doctrine continued in several denominations, including the Presbyterians, for several more years.

The second controversy concerned science and religion. Since fundamentalists viewed the theory of evolution as a direct threat to belief in the omnipotence of God and the Genesis account of the creation of the universe, they sought to uproot this theory from the public schools. The antievolution campaign concentrated mostly upon the southern states and drew rather strong support from Methodists and Disciples of Christ as well as from southern Presbyterians and Baptists. All in all, thirty-seven antievolution bills were introduced into twenty state legislatures between 1921 and 1929 (Sandeen, 1970: 266–67). The climax of the controversy occurred in 1925 in the small town of Dayton, Tennessee. Known as the "monkey trial," it involved the prosecution of John T. Scopes for teaching evolution in the local high school in direct violation of a Tennessee state law against promoting evolutionary theory. William Jennings Bryan (1860–1925), the three-time presidential candidate, was the special prosecutor. Clarence Darrow of Chicago was Scopes' defense attorney. Bryan, a conservative Protestant, defended Christianity as he understood it, and was in turn attacked by the agnostic Darrow. Scopes was convicted, but the "war against modernism" was not won with this one victory. In fact, both of these controversies simply added to the intransigence of the fundamentalists in their defense of conservative Protestantism.

In 1929 the Presbyterian Seminary at Princeton University became the object of a last-ditch effort for control by fundamentalist J. Gresham Machen. In 1923 he had published a volume entitled *Christianity and Liberalism,* whose formulation of fundamentalism has been paraphrased by Goen (1959:91) as follows:

> Christianity must be defined in terms of doctrine from the Bible.... The Bible represents the essentially trustworthy transmission of the message—it is the Word of God. Its central truths are the transcendence of the living God, the special creation of man as a moral personality, the universality and power of sin, the historical redemption provided by Jesus Christ the Son of God, the need of every person for cleansing and quickening by the Holy Spirit, the incompleteness of time forms, and the necessity for a final consummation. Machen and those who agreed with him viewed these central truths as necessary; the dilution of any one would allow the concept of biblical fallibility to prevail, which, in turn, would humanize God and deify man.

By 1930 the mainline Protestant faiths had repudiated the narrow stance of fundamentalism. Fundamentalist Presbyterians, as a result, withdrew and formed Westminster Seminary in Philadelphia, and extremely conservative northern Baptists likewise established the Eastern Baptist Seminary (Goen, 1959:89). Although many fundamentalists remained within the established denominations, their influence was diluted. Outside the South, Protestant denominations began to substitute a broad community religion in place of the older nineteenth-century model of evangelical revivalism and tended to minimize doctrinal differences. Glorification of the destiny of the United States and its prosperity prevailed, and occasional intra-Protestant fights occurred (Marty, 1991). Mainline denominations in the northern tier of states seemed to close the door on the fundamentalist/modernist controversy. The heritage of evangelical Protestantism remained with the Protestants of the South: Methodists, Baptists, Presbyterians, and the Disciples of Christ.

The Growth and Decline of Southern Churches

Fundamentalism remained very much a restricted movement in northern Protestant denominations from the 1930s on, although its southern counterpart continued to flourish and to carry on the tradition of evangelism. Warren A. Candler, a famed bishop of the

Methodist Church for whom the Candler School of Theology at Emory University is named, stated southern Protestantism's evangelical mission as follows: "The hope of mankind is in the keeping of the Anglo-Saxon nations, led by the United States; and evangelical Christianity, with Methodism in the forefront, is the hope of these nations" (Candler, cited in Marty, 1970:222–23). Although Candler did not represent all of southern religion, he did give eloquent support to the widely shared religious symbols of the South: the Bible, the hymnal (or songbook), the revival, and the prayer meeting.

The Methodists, Baptists, Presbyterians, and Disciples of Christ kept the revivalistic tradition alive in the South. This revivalism emphasized personal redemption, pietistic living, and evangelistic fervor, and communitywide cooperation prevailed among these churches during seasonal evangelistic efforts. To "save the lost" was a common goal for southern Protestants. Though no evangelist of national prominence emerged to succeed Billy Sunday during the thirties and forties, there were many Southern Baptist ministers whose preaching reputations were regional or statewide. A major part of southern Protestantism had always involved the pulpit appeal of the clergy, and Southern Baptists continued this legacy. One well-known Baptist pastor, Joseph M. Dawson, who served the historic First Baptist Church of Waco, Texas, for over thirty years, said that the ability to bring in converts during a revival was a primary measure of a minister's worth.

This spirit of revivalism and growth lived on among Southern Baptists in spite of the intradenominational doctrinal disputes that had begun in the 1800s. The first of these controversies was the *Landmark Movement*. Its proponents believed that there were certain landmarks of faith that could be traced to the apostolic era, the most important of which was baptism by immersion. Those not properly baptized were not worthy to take communion. Landmark Baptist churches also limited communion to members of the *local* congregation (Ammerman, 1990:33–34). Finke and Stark (1992:178) point out that the Landmark Movement was the belief that Baptists were the only *authentic* Christian churches and should not cooperate with other Christians. Although most Southern Baptists rejected the most radical Landmark ideologies, the superiority of Baptists became a denominational hallmark.

A second controversy involved seminary education, evolution, and modernism. The best-known Southern Baptist pastor involved was J. Frank Norris of Fort Worth, Texas. Norris was constantly attacking fellow clergy for not becoming involved in the fundamentalist/modernist controversy. He also attacked the efforts of the

Southern Baptist Convention to centralize benevolences and doctrinal beliefs at the expense of Baptist local autonomy (Ammerman, 1990: 48). Norris attacked what he perceived as the lack of orthodoxy at Southwestern Baptist Seminary and the teaching of evolution at Baylor University in Waco, Texas. However, since most Southern Baptists subscribed to fundamentalist beliefs, his blustery attacks seemed hollow and shrill. As a denomination, the Southern Baptist Convention was largely committed to revivalism, doctrinal orthodoxy, and a feeling of moral superiority.

In their analysis of church growth and decline from colonial times until the present, Finke and Stark (1992) assert that the decline of Methodists as the largest Protestant denomination began shortly after 1850. However, they also indicate that Methodists continued to grow in the South, although at a slower rate than did the Baptists (Finke and Stark, 1992:146–48). Still, the trappings of southern revivalism remained a part of "southern" Methodist religious culture not only in rural areas and small towns but also in southern cities.

After the southern branch of the Methodist church merged with the northern Methodists in 1939, evangelistic preaching and revivals gradually became less important. In the 1930s Methodist seminary students began to be exposed to a less conservative theological education as the preaching mission of that tradition gave way to a community religious culture characteristic of the church's northern branch. The affluence characteristic of northern Methodists became a characteristic of southern Methodists as well. In spite of this change, Methodism continued to grow, as did other southern churches. Although the Orthodox Presbyterian Church (one of the sectlike groups formed out of the fundamentalist/modernist controversy) attracted only a few thousand members, the conservative Southern Baptist Convention experienced a rapid growth between 1930 and 1950. Other conservative religious groups such as the Churches of Christ also expanded in the southern and southwestern regions of the United States. Pentecostal and Holiness sects, some of which were heirs to the pietism and holiness once present in Methodism, likewise flourished in the South. The exclusivity of all these groups and their narrow doctrinal beliefs became the symbols of southern fundamentalism.

In the 1950s the Baptist revival technique continued to flourish, and Southern Baptists exported it to other parts of the nation, opening churches in the West, the Midwest, and even in the Northeast. This ended an informal demarcation between them and their northern Baptist counterparts that had prevented competition between the denominations (Ammerman,1990:50–52). Since many of those who left the South were skilled and semiskilled laborers, most of the Southern Baptist churches built in the northern and western states were working-class congregations with a strong emphasis upon distinctive doctrines, exclusiveness, and political conservatism.

Southern Baptists aimed for bigness and growth, building upon a bureaucracy dating back to the 1890s when they had established their Baptist Sunday School Board. During the 1920s this trend toward bureaucratization continued with the establishment of the Cooperative Program—a unified system of benevolence and mission support. Despite the Southern Baptists' loosely knit system of congregational autonomy, regional and denominational pride melded the local congregations together. Thus, when their drive for expansion began in earnest in the 1950s, the organizational machinery was already in place.

In short, the once regional, provincial, and fundamentalist Southern Baptist Convention successfully combined the organizational techniques of mainline Protestantism, and modified them for their own use with the techniques of mass evangelism. The result was an unprecedented growth, an elevation in the prestige of the denomination, and an increased commitment from active members. During the sixties and the seventies, the Southern Baptist Convention continued a steady and rapid increase in membership. In 1967 the church, with more than 11 million members, surpassed in total membership its longtime rival, the Methodists. Although a majority of Southern Baptist Churches were in rural areas (54.7 percent), a majority of the members were in urban churches (72.5 percent) as the 1970s began (Ammerman, 1990:53).

Other evangelical sects and denominations also grew throughout the sixties and seventies (Kelley, 1972). However, not all of these groups expanded as rapidly as Kelley reported (Smith, 1992). But those that did experience growth did so without abandoning fundamentalist doctrine, conservative political stances, or their exclusivity. As the more liberal Protestant denominations asserted themselves in the realm of civil rights and protest against the Vietnam War, the conservatives and fundamentalists, for the most part, maintained the stance of private Protestantism referred to earlier. They continued to oppose political issues involving private morality—legalized gambling, liquor by the drink, and the repeal of Sunday closing laws—but they remained virtually silent regarding the rights of minorities and the issue of the war in Vietnam. Clergy from the Methodist, Presbyterian, United Church of Christ, and Episcopalian denominations spoke out and demonstrated on behalf of these national issues. In contrast, only mild resolutions endorsing desegregation were adopted by the Southern Baptists. The mainline churches' preoccupation with social and political issues led many of their leaders to predict fragmentation and decline for the fundamentalists, but the continued success of the fundamentalists would prove them wrong.

The Rise of Billy Graham

The rise of Billy Graham kept evangelism before the public eye even as it was quietly maintaining itself and growing in the South. From the late 1930s to the middle 1960s, fundamentalism reached radio listeners nationwide through the "Old-Fashioned Revival Hour" of Charles H. Fuller, a moderate spokesman for the conservative Protestant cause. Like the mass evangelists who had preceded him, Fuller used gospel music and a theme song; he also read letters and testimonies from listeners that further personalized his evangelism. While Fuller's success with radio evangelism led to numerous imitators, none were as successful as Billy Graham (Martin, 1991).

In the late 1940s the man who was to become the most widely known evangelist in the world seemed to be just another revivalist who moved his "tent cathedral" from one city to another. Graham's preaching was predictable and typical for someone who had attended Bob Jones University and had graduated from the conservative Wheaton College: a millenarian message of Christ's imminent return to earth and the need for repentance before this happened. He married the daughter of A. Nelson Bell, a well-known conservative southern Presbyterian missionary. Then, in a California evangelistic tent meeting, Graham received nationwide publicity through the conversion of two Hollywood personalities: actress Coleen Townsend and songwriter Stuart Hamblin. As the result of his experience, Hamblin wrote a song—"It Is No Secret What God Can Do"—that became a nationwide hit by the early 1950s (Martin, 1991:106–20).

Soon Billy Graham's crusades were attracting overflow crowds in arenas, coliseums, and stadiums in cities throughout the country. Motion pictures, beginning with *Oil Town, U.S.A.*, were produced to further promote the fundamentalist/evangelical cause. A nationwide program, "The Hour of Decision," began its broadcasts (Frady, 1979:194–96, 231). Very quickly his one-week and two-week evangelistic meetings demonstrated remarkable organizational skill reminiscent of Charles Finney's urban revivals of the 1800s. Graham organization always utilized local clergy and laypeople. He would not schedule an event in a city in which there was a lack of local church support (Martin, 1991:123–41). At the end of a crusade, Graham urged converts to join a local church.

As Graham became more successful, he became more respectable. Although his message remained basically millenarian and biblically literal, his cooperation with nonfundamentalists incurred the wrath of established fundamentalists like Bob Jones, the founder of Bob Jones University (Martin, 1991:204–24). On the other hand, Graham's success won him respect not only from evangelicals but also even from mainline Protestants and Roman Catholics. He became an invited guest of American Presidents, beginning with Dwight D. Eisenhower. The National Prayer Breakfast held annually in Washington usually featured a Graham talk. Though Graham gradually modified his timetable for the Second Coming of Christ, he never abandoned the basic millenarian belief (McLoughlin, 1967; Martin, 1991).

That Graham's evangelical approach flourished in the 1950s is something of a paradox. While the United States was more visibly religious than at any other time in its history, this religiosity thrived mainly upon a religious culture that stressed progress, positive thinking, the spiritual and material blessings of God, and cooperation among religious groups. In contrast, the evangelical Graham preached repentance from sins, pietistic living through Christ, and the heavenly life. Still, Americans of the 1950s seemed to thrive on both these religious themes. Although his crusades were attended mostly by white audiences, he did insist that audiences be integrated after a Supreme Court decision in 1955 pronounced an end to school segregation. The phenomenal success of Billy Graham's mass evangelism served to reassert fundamentalist and evangelical theology. His fame and his acceptance by national leaders gave evangelicalism a respectability it had lacked for twenty or more years. This success would continue until the present time as Graham became the Christian world's best-known clergyman and one of the world's most admired men.

CONTEMPORARY EVANGELICALISM

Contemporary evangelicalism is a present-day expression of both the fundamentalist and conservative Protestant traditions. In a real sense, it was born out of the frustrations of the 1960s. Although the nation made real gains in the area of civil rights and finally disengaged from the Vietnam conflict in 1973, the liberal influence of mainline Protestantism failed again to produce the Kingdom of God on earth. A sizable minority within the mainline denominations called for a return to theological conservatism, personal evangelism, and biblical enlightenment. The United Methodist Church saw the formation of clergy and laity groups that called for a return to the personal evangelistic techniques that had caused Methodist growth in earlier times (Wilke, 1986). No denomination within Protestantism escaped these pressures. By the mid-1970s, most had reached accommodation with their own evangelicals, who saw themselves as the vanguard of a genuine Christian renewal of nationwide size. Popular journals, religious journals, and scholars call this renewal movement the contemporary evangelicalism.

Who Are the Evangelicals?

As stated in Chapter 6, fundamentalists and evangelical Protestants are not necessarily a monolithic group. They often disagree on points of doctrine, millenarian issues, cooperation with other churches and denominations, and certain political issues. Almost all African-American Protestants seem to be evangelicals, but the black churches are different in terms of their experiences of slavery and segregation and political efforts to bring about desegregation. Charismatic Christians are also different from other evangelicals in their emphasis on the "gifts of the spirit" (Ammerman, 1991:2–3). Also included under this umbrella are members of the Church of Jesus Christ of Latter-day Saints (the Mormons). Although Mormons have a reverence for Scripture, they are not biblical literalists since they have "extended" scripture through *The Book of Mormon* (Ammerman, 1991:4). They do share the same social and political agenda of most evangelical and fundamentalist Protestants.

The main point of agreement between the many present-day evangelicals of various denominational affiliations is a subjective experience of personal salvation that they describe as being *born again*. This generally means conversion or regeneration; more particularistic interpretations vary from one group to another. For example, members of the churches of the Southern Baptist Convention have always emphasized the idea of being born again; the baptism of infants has never been a part of their tradition, but the conversion of children, teenagers, and adults has. By contrast, many Missouri Synod Lutherans embrace the authority of the Bible—a major tenet of the evangelicals—but keep the tradition of infant baptism. United Methodist, Presbyterian, and Disciples of Christ congregations that are evangelical are more likely to embrace conservative doctrine, personal morality, and biblical authority as an alternative to the social activism and involvement of their parent denominations. They stress what was once an integral part of their tradition, particularly in the South: making a "conscious, personal commitment to Christ," a spiritual encounter that can be either sudden or gradual.

Furthermore, as we stated in Chapter 6, contemporary evangelicals can be identified doctrinally by their adherence to some or all of the following beliefs: the Bible as the inerrant work of God, the belief in Christ's divinity, and the truth of Christ's life, death, and resurrection for the salvation of humankind (Hunter, 1983:7). This loosely knit minority within Christianity in the United States numbers an estimated 47 million people. Unlike the successors to the fundamentalist controversy of the 1920s, many of these newer evangelicals are prosperous business and professional people. They are not exclusively confined either to the southern or midwestern Bible Belts. Many of fundamentalists belong to independent Bible churches that are loosely linked to similar congregations. Some are in denominations that belong to the umbrella organization, the National Association of Evangelicals, while others are members of congregations within the Southern Baptist Convention and the Lutheran Church-Missouri Synod which remain independent of interdenominational organizations. Some remain a vocal minority within mainline Protestant denominations with the aim of correcting the liberal and inclusive trends in those churches.

However, certain demographic characteristics are important in understanding who the evangelicals are. Hunter's (1983:49–60) analysis of data from a survey conducted by the Princeton Religious Research Center showed that 88.2 percent of evangelicals in the survey were white and 59.9 percent were women; their mean age was 48.4 years. Interestingly, the mean age of liberal Protestants and Catholics was within two years of the evangelical average; by contrast, those in the survey who classified themselves as secularists had a mean age of 34.3. Furthermore, 77.2 percent of the evangelicals were married as compared to 69 percent of Catholics, 72.9 percent of liberal Protestants, and 57.6 percent of secularists. Geographically, the greatest percentage of evangelicals—45 percent—is in the southern region of the United States. However, 25.7 percent of liberal Protestants (the largest regional group) are also in the South. Also, evangelical Protestants are disproportionately represented in rural areas (43.7 percent) and in towns and cities whose populations are between 2,500 and 50,000 (28.4 percent). Gallup and Castelli (1989) offer more demographic information about evangelicals. Only 13 percent are college graduates compared to 25 percent of the general population. More evangelicals are not high school graduates (29 percent) than the general population (22 percent).

Hunter (1983) also reports that the survey data show that evangelicals are overwhelmingly literalistic in interpreting the Bible. They believe in the doctrine of the Trinity, the personification of evil in

Satan (or the devil), the beginning of human life through God's creation of Adam and Eve, and God's intervention in history. Furthermore, evangelicals are far more involved in religious activities than are other Protestants; they surpass all other groups in weekly church attendance, with 62.2 percent attending once a week or more.

In a more recent study, Hunter (1987:24–27) found some differences in the biblical literalism beliefs of evangelicals. Only 38 percent of evangelical college students and 43 percent of evangelical seminary students embraced biblical inerrancy. On the other hand, 78 percent of the evangelical college students and 79 percent of the evangelical seminary students believed that human life began with God's creation of Adam and Eve.

One appeal of the fundamentalist and evangelical movement seems to be in its promotion of the sense of a close-knit community. This, along with the reaction against the public activism of mainline Protestantism, accounts for the continuing success of born-again Christianity. The new respectability of the evangelicals has been aided also by large numbers of business and professional people who engage in organized Bible study, smaller prayer meetings, and personal evangelism.

A further example of the symbolic community aspect of the evangelicals is the use of certain phrases that indicate (1) intimacy with each other, (2) piety as a demonstration of religiosity, and (3) the necessity of evangelism. For example, "God loves you," "Jesus loves you," and "Praise the Lord" repeated to each other serve as means to show familiarity. Phrases such as "surrendering to the Lord," "under conviction of the Holy Spirit," and "my life has been changed by Jesus Christ" tell others of a new-found personal faith and relationship. Evangelicals also use slogans and phrases that stress the importance of mass evangelism and personal evangelism, such as "witnessing for Christ," and urging someone to "let Jesus come into your heart."

Some of the evangelical communities are more close-knit than others. Fundamentalist Bible churches tend to be extremely exclusive, even at the expense of other evangelicals. Those involved in the Reconstructionist Movement have as a goal the purging of all secular ideologies and activities in American society. Their vision of society is that of a theocratic community. Brief descriptions of both Bible churches and the Reconstructionist Movement illustrate this viewpoint.

The Independent Bible Church

Independent Bible churches began to appear in sizable numbers during the 1930s as one response to modernism in mainline Protestantism (Ammerman, 1991:29–31). Many of these local autonomous congregations used Baptist as part of their name; others did not since they were not Baptist in background. A few belonged to the National Association of Evangelicals, but most existed without extraorganizational ties. These churches provided their members with an ideological home in which morality, decency, and biblical authority were reinforced within the community of fundamentalist believers. These fundamentalist churches offered their members a local, visible, supportive community (Ammerman, 1991:30).

In her participant-observation study of a fundamentalist church, Ammerman carefully differentiates fundamentalism from evangelicalism: "Fundamentalists are considerably more sure that every word of scripture (often found in the King James Version) is to be taken at face value. Evangelicals are more comfortable with ambiguity of translation and interpretation that arise when scripture is subjected to critical analysis..." (1987:5). In addition, fundamentalists are much more likely to make their beliefs about the imminent return of Christ to earth central to their understanding of biblical truth and their preaching of the Gospel.

Ammerman likens the role of the fundamentalist Bible church in the life of its members to that of the medieval parish church—the center of all community activities. The Bible church stresses the dominance of men over women, the subservience of children to parents, and the paramount importance of a "Christian home." It undergirds the notion that religious liberals are not really Christian and that liberal churches are not true churches.

In describing "Southside Gospel Church" and those who make up its membership, Ammerman compares the organization, its services, and its members' views with those of more liberal Protestant churches and their constituencies. "Throughout the service, although everything is led by those on the platform, there is a feeling of spontaneity and participation. There are no recited prayers or responses, no prayer of confession or words of assurance, no formal call to worship or prayer for the world..." (1987:37). Controlled emotions, rather than intellectual thought, dominate the services.

Important also is the way children are raised in "the nurture and admonition of the Lord" at home, at church, and in the fundamentalist school operated by the church (if possible). The children and adolescents of "Southside Church" live apart from their unchurched peers. They learn the ideal standards for Christian families: priestly fathers, full-time mothers, and daily family devotions. Additionally, most of the members buy reading materials at Christian bookstores and listen to Christian radio programs (1989:173–74).

Finally, Ammerman discusses the tension between fundamentalists and the modern world. Their world, according to the fundamentalists, contains order while the outside world is chaotic. Fundamentalists believe that God has a plan for all of life's details and that they can find meaning for their lives if only they try to follow this plan within the context of the fundamentalist community.

The Reconstructionist Movement

Reconstructionists believe that the nation has drifted into a secularized situation in which Christian principles of nationhood no longer exist. More than the Bible church members, reconstructionists view the world as ungodly and in need of restoring Christian civilization and the eventual victory of God over the forces of Satan. The "golden age" to which reconstructionists look is the seventeenth century of the heroic Puritans of the Massachusetts Bay Colony. In that theocracy, the laws of the Bible became the laws of society (Ammerman, 1991:49–50).

The modern state is viewed as a culprit, for it has usurped the power of God and has grown beyond its rightful boundaries. They see government as a substitute for God's imposing a secular philosophy designed to make men "good" rather than restraining evil. However, reconstructionists do not necessarily agree that Christians should take the law into their own hands in order to combat evil government through acts of civil disobedience like Operation Rescue (Ammerman, 1991:52). Instead, they believe in an informed Christian citizenry that will counter humanistic ideology. Reconstructionists advocate a philosophy of "Christian dominion" over the forces of secularism (Ammerman, 1991:54).

Both of these exclusive manifestations of Protestant fundamentalism represent the extremes of the movement. Most evangelicals would feel uncomfortable in either fundamentalist Bible churches or in the Reconstructionist Movement, even though they share some of the same crusading issues that participants in these organizations have.

Involvement in Social and Political Issues

In the opening paragraph of this chapter, we spoke of a "cultural war being waged for the soul of America." Although Patrick Buchanan used the phrase in the context of partisan politics, Hunter (1991) speaks of a cultural war in the context of religion and its relationship to other aspects of society. He views the struggle as a battle between conservative and progressive forces in the United States both in the realm of everyday life and public policy. The core of truth and morality is unchanging for fundamentalists and most evangelicals, a view not necessarily shared by religious or secular progressives. For fundamentalists and evangelicals, there are *crusading issues* worth fighting against: abortion, gay rights, sexually explicit material, the prohibition against voluntary school prayer, special treatment and disability funds for people with AIDS and HIV-positive individuals who are gay or bisexual, certain kinds of overtly sexual programming on television, federal funding for the arts and humanities when the subject matter is considered sexually explicit or otherwise provocative, the legalized sale of pornography, and the proliferation of what they regard as secular humanism. To evangelicals, secular humanists are those who are pluralistic in their concept of morality and in their economic and political ideology and practice (Shupe and Stacey, 1982: 321–33); secular humanism is the result of a decadent society, the salvation of which is seen to be directly correlated with the morality of its public and private behavior.

A spirit of cooperation between various fundamentalist and evangelical groups has existed since the 1970s in common efforts to influence the nation through politics, to publicize social issues, and to influence consumer patterns. As early as the 1976 presidential campaign, both Gerald Ford and Jimmy Carter emphasized their evangelical beliefs. In that same election year, an estimated thirty congressional candidates, including several members of the clergy, sought office on political platforms that stressed evangelical Christianity—particularly its commitment to traditional morality. In 1980 several groups from the Christian right endorsed Ronald Reagan, repudiating born-again evangelical President Jimmy Carter. Reagan emerged as the hero of a large segment of the religious conservatives in the United States; they seemed to view him as God's man for that hour in the nation's life (Hill and Owen, 1982:14–15). To many, this candidate (and, of course, later presidents) would preside over a late-twentieth-century theocracy dedicated to conservative religious, political, social, and economic values. Their support for President Reagan would continue in his successful bid for reelection in 1984 (Jorstad, 1990), and would be transferred to George Bush in the 1988 presidential election (Guth and Green, 1991). This support was also given to Bush in the 1992 presidential election but was not enough to overcome the victory of Bill Clinton (Guth, 1992).

This political involvement is ironic for many evangelicals, since they have benefited from the religious pluralism in the United States that resulted from early separation of church and state. On the other hand, as we mentioned earlier in this chapter, fundamentalists and evangelicals have always participated in political campaigns involving issues of personal morality. These groups became further involved in social and political issues through such organizations as the Moral Majority, Roundtable, and Christian Voice, which we will describe more fully in Chapter 10.

Evangelicals and fundamentalists are also involved in a concerted effort to once again debunk the evolutionary theory of human creation. Finally, they continue to support a constitutional amendment to restore some version of voluntary prayer to public school classrooms. These efforts will also be discussed more fully in Chapter 10.

Past relationships between fundamentalists and right-wing political extremists have been analyzed by Redekop (1969:159–78). He saw a simplistic dualism as characteristic of both groups: Fundamentalists recognize only two categories of thought and people, good and evil, while right-wing radicals view citizens of the United States as either loyal Americans or communists. Redekop also characterized fundamentalism and right-wing extremism as sharing a conspiratorial view of the world: The devil causes people to detour from righteous living, while communism causes people to detour from Christian belief and the capitalistic philosophy. Finally, the concept of the individualistic nature of salvation in fundamentalism was usually connected with the fundamentalist's disapproval of social action and public welfare programs and was parallel to the right-winger's philosophy of laissez-faire economics. The issue of America versus communism had waned, but new "devils" have replaced the communist threat, not the least of which is the secularization of all aspects of society.

The causes espoused by fundamentalists, each of which can be seen as part of a movement to resist new or prevailing points of view, are from time to time skillfully promoted by evangelicals through the mass media. The widespread use of television and radio is another characteristic of contemporary evangelicalism.

EVANGELICALISM AND THE MASS MEDIA

Television evangelism has become a booming business. As we stated earlier, the success of Billy Graham's "Hour of Decision" and Charles H. Fuller's "Old-Fashioned Revival Hour" demonstrated the power of radio as an evangelistic medium. Although most mainline Protestant denominations were content to present television and radio broadcasts of worship services, the evangelicals have used further deregulation of radio and television to buy access to local radio and television stations, networks, and cable channels. Evangelicals and fundamentalists have built up a substantial number of listeners who are willing to make financial contributions to fulfill this goal (Finke and Stark, 1992:223). In the late 1970s these groups began presenting full-scale productions that use not only worship-service formats but also variety-show and talk-show formats. In their book *Prime Time Preachers* (1981), Hadden and Swann used the term *televangelists* to categorize those who not only present an evangelical message but also raise millions of dollars for their operations and often for financing conservative political lobbying and campaigns.

Other studies during the 1980s indicated that many viewers of the televangelists and other religious programming often make sophisticated distinctions among televangelists as to their formats, styles, and religious messages (Frankl, 1987; Hoover, 1988). Also, the more a televangelist builds the programs around his or her personality, the greater will be both the audience ratings and the program's financial success. Modern computers allow the televangelist's staff to "personalize" responses to viewers. It is often that personal touch that keeps the viewers' contributions flowing in (Bruce, 1990).

That kind of personal touch served as a barrier to competition from mainline Protestant denominations and the Roman Catholics. Liberal and moderate Protestants as well as Catholics do not feel comfortable asking for donations from viewers. However, some mainline denominations did join together with the Roman Catholics, Mormons, Jews, and Orthodox groups during the late 1980s to create a multidenominational programming cable network called VISN (Jorstad, 1990:98). Still, VISN failed to capture the kind of viewing audience enjoyed by televangelists and other evangelical programs. Many of these programs began appearing on the ACTS cable network run by the Southern Baptist Convention. By 1988 there were 336 religious television stations on the air, compared with 92 in 1985. In addition, marketing became highly competitive among the evangelical broadcasters (Jorstad, 1990:98–99).

This growth did slow down after the scandals involving Jim Bakker and Jimmy Swaggart became known. Bakker was accused of extramarital sexual affairs with one of his secretaries. Later, he was accused by fellow televangelist Jerry Falwell of homosexual encounters. Swaggart confessed to using the services of prostitutes. Although Falwell stepped in to clean up the financial chaos of Bakker's PTL organizations, this effort failed (PTL stands for "People That Love or Praise the Lord.") Later Bakker and his colleagues were indicted by a federal grand jury in North Carolina for misusing contributions sent by viewers of the "PTL Club" to buy vacation apartments and homes in a Christian theme park known as "Heritage, U.S.A." Bakker was convicted on several federal counts and is serving time in a federal prison. The more than $50 million yearly contributions that Jim Bakker, Jerry Falwell, Pat Robertson, and Jimmy Swaggart were each bringing in dropped dramatically (Jorstad, 1990:67–68; 99–100). Even televangelists not involved in these scandals were hurt financially by them, notably Oral Roberts, Robert Schuller, and James Roberson. In 1991 two Texas-based televangelists were "exposed" on the ABC-TV program "Primetime." Evidence presented indicated they were involved in questionable financial practices. One went off the air, but the other, Robert Tilden, still syndicates his program. This added to what Hadden and Shupe (1990) said was the dominant persistent image of televangelists: the Elmer Gantry stereotype.

Because of these problems, the leading religious programs have either disappeared or have curtailed the number of stations and cable systems on which they broadcast. Gone is the "PTL Club," and greatly reduced in terms of outlets is Jerry Falwell's "Old Time Gospel Hour," The Jimmy Swaggart Show," "The Rex Humbard Show," and several other less-watched programs of the early and mid-1980s. On the other hand, Pat Robertson's "700 Club" is still seen by a large audience. It is the flagship program of his Family Channel, which was formerly known as the Christian Broadcasting Network. Oral Roberts' programs and James Roberson's evangelistic programs are still seen. Robert Schuller's modified worship service, "The Hour of Power," also enjoys a large viewing audience. James Kennedy's modified worship service from Coral Ridge, Florida, is still on the air, along with a music series hosted by that church's organist.

One controversy that has emerged concerning evangelical programming involves its role in the coalition of conservative political and religious groups (Crawford, 1980). Hadden and Swann (1981:144) noted early on that "the shift [among televangelists] from a generally negative or neutral posture toward political activism…is an important step in developing support for a broad-based movement." Throughout the 1980s, televangelists cleverly utilized their programming to promote Christian political action and to endorse conservative Christian political candidates. Direct mailings, telephone solicitations, and political information mailings were utilized by Jerry Fallwell and the Moral Majority and by Pat Robertson of the "700 Club" in his unsuccessful bid for the Republican presidential nomination in 1988 (Johnson, Tamney, and Burton, 1992; Bruce, 1990; Guth and Green, 1991). Since many in the contemporary evangelical movement are involved in direct political action, their use of television for this purpose has alarmed not only mainline Protestant denominations and Jewish groups but also the less politically involved within evangelicalism.

Hadden (1987) believes that the political activities of televange-lists and other religious broadcasters is part of a genuine social move-ment in the process of legitimation and institutionalization, and that these activities are not likely to disappear in the near future. In an ar-ticle assessing the political activities of religious broadcasting during the 1980s, Hadden states that seldom in modern history has the emer-gence of interest groups like the Moral Majority generated so much attention. This was followed by a premature obituary of its demise when it did not produce significant evangelical election results in 1982. However, Hadden cites exit poll data from the 1988 presidential election indicating that George Bush received 80 percent or more of the evangelical vote (Hadden, 1990:463–72). He also notes that the po-litical organizations which utilize religious broadcasting as a means of influencing voting are more pragmatic than earlier waves of conserv-ative Christian activists during this century. According to Hadden, directly or indirectly televangelists will contribute to the mobilization of fundamentalist and evangelical Christians in efforts to turn back the tide of secular humanism.

In their pioneering work on televangelism, Hadden and Swann (1981:60–61) pointed out that the televangelists drew a disproportion-ate percentage of their audiences from the South. Furthermore, nearly all of the syndicated programs had audiences of which two-thirds to three-quarters were fifty years of age or older. In addition, a majority of the viewers were female. Finally, the amount of money raised by the electronic church also seemed to be exaggerated. More recent data confirm this finding. Ableman and Hoover (1990) show that it is a myth to think that the electronic church robs from the established churches. True, viewers send in millions of dollars, but thus far their contributions have not significantly affected contributions to estab-lished churches and denominations.

THE CHARISMATIC RENEWAL MOVEMENT

Media use by evangelicals is likely to remain controversial for some time. So also is the charismatic renewal movement, which we will dis-cuss next. For many fundamentalists and evangelicals, this phenome-non is a perversion of biblical truth; others, however, embrace it as the ultimate spiritual experience.

Pentecostalism, the original name associated with glossolalia and faith healing, began to emerge at the end of the nineteenth century in the United States. Finke and Stark (1992:163–66) point out that some reformers within Methodism sought a return to the "old-time

Methodist enthusiasm," which had begun to disappear as Methodists became more affluent and sedate. This sought-after enthusiasm evolved into what became known as the *Holiness Movement,* which was linked to camp meetings and revivalism and placed great emphasis on the Wesleyan commitment to "sanctification through baptism of the Holy Spirit." As the movement grew, the hierarchy of the Methodist Church sought to limit the use of their facilities for these activities. In response, spokespersons for holiness activities called for like-minded Christians to leave the Methodist Church. One of the first sects to evolve was the present-day Church of the Nazarene. Later other Pentecostal sects appeared, notably those that would eventually become the Assemblies of God Church and the United Pentecostal Church.

The one common bond between these groups was their belief that "baptism of the Holy Ghost, accompanied by speaking in tongues, was the final, and Pentecostal, work of grace to be sought by every Christian" (Harrel, 1975:11). Harrell reports that this "amorphous movement" slowly took shape in the 1920s as a "confusing patchwork" of small sects frequently divided by seemingly trivial points of doctrine. Pentecostal religion was especially successful in the South, but small churches began to spring up throughout the United States, drawing members from the poor and from those discontented in more traditional Protestant churches.

Because of their emphasis upon faith healing, glossolalia, and Jesus (as opposed to the Trinity), Pentecostal bodies were refused admission to the World's Christian Fundamentals Association in 1928. Still, the traditions associated with Pentecostalism and the Holiness Movement continued, although various sects split and resplit because of internal divisions over interpretations of Scripture on marriage, divorce, and other moral issues. These relatively poor and obscure churches—the Pentecostal Church, the Assembly of God, and the Church of the Nazarene—offered distinctive alternatives to other Protestant churches, liberal and conservative, through the emotionalism of their music, glossolalia, and healing activities.

After World War II two prominent Pentecostal evangelists gradually dominated the entire movement: A. A. Allen and Oral Roberts. Both continued the Pentecostal tradition of the tent revival meeting featuring both personal salvation and personal healing. Loose affiliations with local congregations were present, but these evangelists ran their own operations. Even though they were prosperous enough to purchase radio time, Allen, Roberts, and lesser Pentecostal evangelists continued to suffer the same skepticism and derision from the major Protestant denominations that had been leveled at earlier evangelists of their type (Harrell, 1975).

During the 1960s, however, Pentecostal religion began to appeal to certain members of traditional Protestant churches and the Roman Catholic Church, as we mentioned in Chapter 6. These people, most of whom were affluent and educated, chose to remain in their respective churches. In Protestant denominations, however, certain congregations and parishes came to be known for their charismatic or neo-Pentecostal emphasis. Liturgical denominations, such as the Lutheran and the Episcopal churches, have gradually adopted a tolerant attitude toward their charismatics. The Presbyterians, United Methodists, and Disciples of Christ have studied the issue and are, at least, benign toward manifestation of the movement within their congregations. On the other hand, the Southern Baptists and the Churches of Christ have been generally intolerant, condemning charismatic activities as unscriptural.

Poloma (1982) has studied the charismatic renewal movement as both a sociologist and a participant. She pinpoints the services of 1960 in St. Mark's Episcopal Church in Van Nuys, California, as the start of the movement in mainline Protestantism. The rector's charismatic activities so outraged some members that they transferred to St. Luke's Church in the same city. Poloma further states that this current phenomenon is in reaction to the secularization of much of mainline religion in the United States (1982:29–32). As such, it can be classified as a countermovement within a presumably secularized world. Her analysis also claims that the charismatic renewal movement represents a process of sacralization for large segments within society. She sees sacralization and secularization as coexisting phenomena reflecting different views of the world; furthermore, she describes the charismatic renewal movement as part of the larger sacralization process that is contemporary evangelicalism (1982:38–39).

More recently Poloma (1991) has analyzed the largest of the charismatic denominations, the Assemblies of God. Her work is unique in that she is both a participant (a member) and an observer (a sociologist). She believes that *charismatic experience* is the traditional core aspect of Assemblies of God religious identity and the essential factor in the denomination's rapid growth. She found that these experiences are highly associated with evangelistic activities, not with the demographic characteristics of local congregations; the local pastor is the key to the encouragement of charismatic experiences. Furthermore, according to Poloma, the Assemblies of God congregations, while wounded by the scandals of Assemblies' televangelists Bakker and Swaggart, have sufficient organizational structure to weather that crisis.

Not all charismatics embrace the fundamentalist aspects of traditional and Protestant neo-Pentecostalism, and other points of disagreement exist, as well, within the general charismatic renewal movement. When some forty-seven thousand charismatics from traditional Pentecostal sects and denominations, including mainline Protestant denominations, and the Roman Catholic Church gathered in Kansas City, Missouri, in 1977, their common interest and belief in the "gifts of the spirit" were their major points of unity. Still, the sacramental nature of the Catholic and Episcopalian charismatic experience is basically incompatible with the spontaneity of the same phenomenon for a Pentecostal or a charismatic Presbyterian. The music of the Catholic folk mass, which includes speaking in tongues after receiving the Eucharist, is not an emotional experience for the charismatic of the Assemblies of God tradition.

Finally, some charismatics have adopted an attitude that has become a point of controversy between them and non-charismatic Christians. Many who share in the beliefs of neo-Pentecostalism are adamant about its rightness, and they question not only the beliefs but also the sincerity of noncharismatics. Such people believe that no religious experience is valid unless it is charismatic. This exclusivity has threatened the unity in not a few congregations and parishes that have neo-Pentecostal groups. This attitude, coupled with the ideological opposition of most Southern Baptists, has made the charismatic movement a subject of controversy in contemporary evangelicalism.

DIVISIONS WITHIN CONTEMPORARY EVANGELICALISM

The charismatic renewal movement is not the only issue that divides evangelicals. Those predisposed toward extremely conservative political, economic, and social views remain skeptical of the more socially activistic, born-again believers, as represented by the radical evangelical journal *Sojourners*. The Chicago Declaration of 1973, held by an ecumenical group of evangelical scholars and activists, called for a greater commitment to social reform in the tradition of the great reforms in England that followed the Wesleyan awakening. Many younger evangelicals agree with U.S. Senator Mark Hatfield that political liberalism is scripturally sound. This zeal for social reform stands in direct contrast to the right-wing political ideology of fundamentalists like Carl McIntyre, founder of the Orthodox Presbyterian Church, and W. A. Criswell, senior pastor of the largest Southern Baptist church—the First Baptist Church in Dallas. It is also far more activistic than the political and economic conservatism of the Presbyterian Lay Committee—the conservative movement within the Presbyterian Church (U.S.A.)—and the evangelical and fundamentalist Presbyterian Church in America.

Even within the rather culturally isolated Southern Baptist Convention, diverse opinions concerning social activism have existed for several decades (Ammerman, 1990:63–71). The Christian Life Commission promoted desegregation and held seminars and workshops concerning a variety of controversial social issues (poverty, situational ethics, and sexuality). However, each of these events always provoked reaction from fundamentalists and traditionalists within the denomination. So also did information that the six Southern Baptist seminaries were using the techniques of biblical higher criticism in theological courses. Earlier, one seminary professor at Midwestern Baptist Seminary was publically rebuked after the denominational press published what was seen by fundamentalists as a controversial book, *The Message of Genesis*. As the 1960s gave way to the 1970s, these controversies began to build up within the denomination. The fundamentalist takeover of a basically conservative and evangelical religious body is, in and of itself, interesting as a successful social movement. It is also interesting because the controversy generated by this takeover seems so "typical" of past fundamentalist internal divisiveness. It is of paramount interest because the Southern Baptist Convention with its 15,038,409 members is the largest Protestant denomination in the United States. Thus, the future of this denomination has implications for other evangelical groups as well.

Southern Baptist Controversies

Several key fundamentalists within the denomination established an independent group named the *Baptist Faith and Message Fellowship*, which began publishing *The Southern Baptist Journal* in the early 1970s. They began to warn rank-and-file clergy and laypeople about "liberal tendencies" within Southern Baptist seminaries and agencies (Finke and Stark, 1992:194). Still, without control over administrative procedures or seminary and agency trustee selections, these fundamentalists could effect little change. In 1977 Paul Pressler, a state judge in Houston, Texas, and a Sunday school teacher in the conservative Second Baptist Church, heard from some of his former students that they were confused by their religion course at Baylor University, the largest Baptist university in the country. Pressler decided to take some kind of action. He created an alliance with Paige Patterson, the president of Criswell Bible Institute (a Bible college connected with First Baptist Church in Dallas, Texas). Patterson was the son of Dr. T.A. Patterson, the retired executive secretary of the Baptist General

Convention of Texas and a highly respected pastor. The younger Patterson was well connected but immune to denominational sanctions since he was in an independent institution (Ammerman, 1990). He and Pressler engineered a plan to wrest control of the presidency of the Southern Baptist Convention from the denominational moderates. Along with other fundamentalists, Patterson and Pressler began to implement a ten-year plan to take over the leadership positions within the convention and to name a preponderance of fundamentalists to the boards of trustees of Southern Baptist agencies and seminaries. In 1979 they achieved their first victory (Ammerman, 1990:173; Finke and Stark, 1992:195).

By continuing to elect a fundamentalist to the denominational presidency, they would eventually be able to fill a majority of vacancies on the trustee boards of the agencies and seminaries. This would allow the fundamentalists to purge the denomination's seminaries, colleges, commissions, and agencies of those who did not subscribe to biblical inerrancy (Ammerman, 1990). In June 1985 the largest number of delegates in the history of the annual meetings of the Southern Baptist Convention cast their ballots for president, giving 55.3 percent of the votes to incumbent president Dr. Charles Stanley (a fundamentalist) and 44.7 percent to Dr. Winfred Moore (a conservative) (Beckley, 1985). Moore, who was later elected first vice president of the Southern Baptist Convention, pledged to work to head off the impending Baptist schism. In 1986 Moore again lost the presidency to Dr. Adrian Rogers (a fundamentalist) by about the same percentage. By then, fundamentalist ascendency seemed inevitable, and in 1991 the moderates did not field a candidate for president.

To an outsider, the logical solution to the fundamentalist control of the Southern Baptist Convention for nonfundamentalists would be withdrawal. However, the religious culture of Southern Baptists remains a strong unifying force. As Ammerman (1990:59–60) demonstrates, the similarity of Southern Baptist worship services since the 1950s assure both moderate and conservative Baptists that familiar hymns, biblical sermons, choral anthems, and informality will be found in an overwhelming majority of local congregations. Formality versus informality will vary depending on geographical location, the size of the congregation, and the affluence of the local membership. Although Southern Baptists claim to be free of liturgy and ritual, the typical service is a liturgy as predictable as any church with a prayer book. Additionally, Southern Baptists have also been unified by successful evangelistic efforts that resulted in impressive church growth.

Thus far, this common religious culture has allowed most of the subgroups (or ideal types) within the Southern Baptist Convention that Ammerman (1990:78–79) has identified to remain within the extended Southern Baptist family. These subgroups include the following: self-identified fundamentalists (those holding strong fundamentalist beliefs, such as the leaders of the movement); fundamentalist conservatives (those who are conservative denominational "loyalists" interested in preserving the Convention, but who adhere to a basic fundamentalist perspective; conservatives (those who are quite conservative in theology but fully committed to the conservative denomination in which they came to maturity); moderate conservatives (those who reject the fundamentalist perspective but choose to label themselves as conservative); and self-identified moderates (those who hold more progressive theological beliefs and strongly disapprove of fundamentalist beliefs and tactics). According to Ammerman's research, 83 percent of all Southern Baptist clergy are found in the first three subtypes. The conservatives are the pivitol group who make up 50 percent of those surveyed.

Still, the crusading issues of the Baptist fundamentalists make it difficult for even some among the conservatives to remain loyal. These include a strong belief in pastoral authority at the expense of lay authority; support for an amendment to the U.S. Constitution for the restoration of school prayers (a reversal of the historic Baptist belief in the principle of church/state separation); the antiabortion campaign and other conservative social issues; support for the traditional roles of husband, father, wife, and mother; opposition to the ordination of women to the offices of pastor and deacon; and unswerving support for the concept of biblical inerrancy.

During the late 1980s some of the moderate factions among Southern Baptists joined together in the Southern Baptist Alliance as a supplemental organization for programming and for joint mission efforts (Ammerman, 1990:282–85). In the early 1990s many more congregations became involved in the Cooperative Baptist Fellowship for joint mission efforts while maintaining ties with the Southern Baptist Convention through minimal contributions to the Baptist Cooperative Program.

Another significant part of this religious drama occurred in 1990. The Board of Trustees of Baylor University in Texas implemented a charter change devised by Baylor's president, Herbert Reynolds, that in effect removed Baylor from the direct control of Texas Baptists by limiting the number of trustees that the state convention could name (Finke and Stark, 1992:197). Immediately, the fundamentalists in Texas cried foul and threatened court action. A special committee was appointed to negotiate with Baylor and report back to the Texas Baptist Convention's annual meeting in November. Baylor was able to have elected enough "messengers" (voting delegates) who were alumni or sympathetic to Baylor to fight off these attempts (Beckley, 1990). In 1991 the convention's annual meeting was held in Waco, Texas—the home of Baylor. During the summer the fundamentalists reserved a majority of the hotel and motel rooms in an attempt to shut out moderates. Again a vote on whether or not Texas Baptists would approve the final "plan of separation" and minimal funding for ministerial students enrolled there was scheduled. In a spirit of cooperation rarely seen between evangelicals and mainline Protestants, members of Episcopal, Methodist, and Presbyterian churches—along with members of moderate Baptist churches—provided accommodations in their homes for "moderate messengers." Again, Baylor University supporters won the crucial votes, dealing the Texas fundamentalists a major setback in their attempts to control Baptist higher education in Texas. Baylor University is now "Baptist related" rather than "Baptist controlled" (Beckley, 1991).

What does the future hold for society's largest Protestant denomination? Ammerman (1990) estimates that about 20 percent of Southern Baptists are in churches willing to formally sever ties with the Southern Baptist Convention. Many more are in denominationally loyal congregations which would split if formal separation occurred. Still that 20 percent would translate into a new 3 million member denomination, larger than both the Presbyterian Church (U.S.A.) and the Episcopal Church. Although many fundamentalist churches are "superchurches," far more of the moderate churches have provided a bulk of the funding for the cooperative mission endeavors of the Southern Baptist Convention. Their departure would drastically impact Southern Baptist finances. The future of the Southern Baptist Convention as it used to exist remains uncertain.

Thus, disunity within the evangelical ranks continues. The inerrancy of the Bible remains a smoldering issue, one that caused a schism within the Lutheran Church–Missouri Synod during the early 1970s and a potential schism within the ranks of Southern Baptists in the 1990s. More traditional and fundamentalist evangelicals, particularly those with a Calvinist theological framework, are still fighting among themselves on the literalness of the Bible. All of these issues—social activism versus conservatism, charismatic renewal versus conservatism, charismatic renewal versus noncharismatic renewal, biblical inerrancy versus errancy—are similar to the doctrinal, political, and social issues that divided the fundamentalists toward the end of the 1920s. These internecine battles demonstrate continuing ferment more than the solidification of like-minded groups who are bringing about a genuine revival and renewal within Protestantism in the United States.

The ecumenical spirit of contemporary evangelicalism remains tenuous, and the aloofness of many within the Southern Baptist Convention, the Churches of Christ, and the Lutheran Church–Missouri Synod from other conservative and evangelical Christian groups seems to preclude any genuine pan-church movement of Great Awakening proportions. The two camps of American Protestantism, private and public, are still present, and each group sees its purpose as preeminent. Public Protestants still practice their historical toleration of private Protestants' piety and conservatism, but no real rapprochement between the private Protestant groups and the more liberal mainline denominations has yet to emerge.

SUMMARY

The roots of fundamentalism and evangelicalism extend back to the beginnings of the United States. The First and Second Great Awakenings in the eighteenth and nineteenth centuries provided a tool, revivalism, through which the expanding nation could be made more religious. This religiosity was of an evangelical Protestant kind, stamped by the frontier revivals of the Methodists, Baptists, Disciples of Christ, and certain groups of Presbyterians and Congregationalists.

The relative success of evangelism on the frontier produced a comfortable Protestant religious culture complete with the idea of Protestant manifest destiny. However, the immigration of vast numbers of Europeans, mainly Roman Catholics, to the expanding industrial cities threatened the dominance of the evangelicals. Native-born Americans who migrated to the cities brought their revivalistic religion with them. The latter decades of the nineteenth century saw a continuation of revivalism with an element of millenarianism included.

Protestants who challenged the complacency of fundamentalist Protestantism by advocating a social gospel as well as an individualistic gospel met with resistance not only from the pietistic revivalists of the North but also from almost all of southern Protestantism. The Social Gospel, along with scientific knowledge that contradicted biblical literalism, created strife and division within the Protestant ranks in the early twentieth century. In the 1920s Harry Emerson Fosdick preached a famous sermon entitled "Shall the Fundamentalists Win?" In a real sense, these liberal views set the stage for a fundamentalist withdrawal from mainline Protestantism outside of the South.

In the South, fundamentalism and evangelicalism continued to flourish as the chief characteristics of Protestantism. Southern churches regularly held revivals and kept fundamentalism alive. This, in part, accounted for the steady growth of the most evangelical of the southern Protestant denominations, the Southern Baptists, a denomination that eventually surpassed the rival Methodists as the largest Protestant body. While many other Protestants within the southern region deemphasized revivalism, the Southern Baptist Convention used it, exported it to other regions, and increased its membership in this way.

When a renewed interest in evangelical Christianity appeared in the late 1960s, Southern Baptists provided a model for many to follow. The born-again Christian, new to mainstream Protestants of the twentieth century, has always been a conventional idea to Southern Baptists. Fundamentalist and evangelical Protestantism skillfully used religious media programming to promote a conservative religious, social, and political agenda during the 1980s. The charismatic renewal movement, which is a subject of controversy in contemporary evangelicalism, has introduced another dimension of personal piety into Christianity. Ideas once rejected by more moderate and liberal Protestants have created a renewed interest in the tenets of evangelicalism: piety, revival, witnessing, and conventional morality. That this movement will become a more permanent facet of Christianity seems likely, in spite of continuing infighting within its ranks.

8.
The Emergence of New Religious Movements

Since the social upheaval of the 1960s we have become increasingly aware of the emergence of religious groups having little in common with the mainline denominations that have dotted the landscape since before the American Revolution (Finke and Stark, 1992). The strangeness of the rituals and beliefs of some of these new religious groups, along with their aggressive and sometimes deceptive recruiting techniques, have combined to produce suspicion, fear, and distrust among many religious leaders, parents, and laypersons in the United States and abroad. While new religious expressions are a reality, and while they proliferated, particularly in the United States, Canada, and England in the 1960s, much media attention, popular writing, and attention to the novelty of these movements gave them a prominence that outweighed their actual numerical impact on the national religious scene.

We will explore the issues mentioned above in this chapter. We will also discuss the overall concept of New Religious Movements (NRMs) and articulate some of the theoretical approaches to the study of NRMs. Chapter 9 will present a more in-depth treatment of NRMs by focusing on specific examples of such movements and discussing some of the major controversies surrounding their emergence.

The term *New Religious Movements* requires some qualification. It is used in order to avoid some of the difficulties and controversies surrounding the designation *cult* as well as popular confusion over the differences between cults and sects. We will discuss this issue fully later in the chapter, but at this point feel it necessary to qualify the term because of the ambiguity surrounding its meaning. It is true that some of the movements we refer to as new religious movements are not really new; they may just be old wine in new bottles. Further, some groups or movements we will refer to as NRMs, like New Age expressions, are scarcely organizations. We will use the term to refer to what might variously be seen as new religious expressions as well as new religious movements. We will also use specific terms for new groups when such usage illuminates changes in religious ideation, emotion, and behaviors. Barker (1989:145–46) suggests that such a general use of the term will not necessarily distort our discussion of the various religious movements that have emerged during the past three decades or so.

One reason for using the term *NRM* is that *cult*, as used by the media and the public, has become a pejorative term. In popular usage the word can have extremely negative connotations. Melton (1992:3) notes:

> The term "cult" is a pejorative label used to describe certain religious groups outside the mainstream of Western religion. Exactly which groups should be considered cults is a matter of disagreement among researchers in the cult phenomema, and considerable confusion exists.

There is a tendency to term any religious group that is deviant or threatening a cult or NRM. To many, particularly to family members of those who have joined cults, these groups are sufficiently dangerous to justify using any means to destroy them. As van Driel and Richardson (1988:172) point out:

> Putting a label on something has social even political significance. This is particularly true if that label has negative connotations. If the word we use to describe something implies that it is a bad thing, those who hear and accept the label will perceive the person, object, or organization named as threatening and dangerous.

Thus, they reaffirm that when media and public alike use the term in a negative sense, anything to which it is applied is viewed negatively.

Thus we feel there is value in using the more general term *NRM* where it seems appropriate. In fact, many of the organizations that have risen in the past three decades do not fit the social scientific definition of a cult (see Chapter 4). The reader should be reminded, however, that when we do use the term, its use is not meant to carry a negative connotation but only to refer to a particular type of religious group without any evaluation of its goodness or badness.

Another caveat to be made is that some of what we call new expressions, or NRMs, have roots that go back many centuries in other societies. While recent expressions connected to New Age have put a contemporary twist on ideas which embrace spiritualism, reincarnation, and metaphysics, these ideas are certainly not new in the history of spiritual beliefs (cf. Melton, 1991:x1). However, contemporary activities, personalities, publications, organizations, and the media present these age-old concepts as if they were new. Similarly, while Hare Krishna certainly was a new experience for Americans, it actually has its roots in a centuries-old variation, or sect, of Hinduism.

We can also point out that even the seemingly unique and bizarre mass suicide/murder of 913 People's Temple devotees at Jonestown, Guyana, on November 18, 1978, was unique only in terms of the circumstances and personalities involved. At the time of the event, reporters noted that other masses of people had taken their lives when faced with tense circumstances involving their religious beliefs. Morrow (1978:30), for example, wrote:

> Jonestown, for all its gruesome power to shock, has its religious (or quasi-religious) precedents.... The Jewish Zealots defending the fortress of Masada against the Roman legions in A.D. 73 chose self-slaughter rather than submission; 960 men, women and children died.... In the 17th century, Russian Orthodox dissenters called the Old Believers refused to accept liturgical reforms. Over a period of years some 20,000 peasants in protest abandoned their fields and burned themselves.

Others were reminded of the fact that hundreds of Japanese civilians jumped to their deaths off the cliffs of Saipan as American forces approached in World War II, and that Japanese kamikaze pilots routinely gave their lives for their beliefs. Wooden (1981:204–5) contended that Jonestown's People's Temple was not unique in methods of manipulation and that other people had died in U.S. cities "as a result of fanatical cults ceremonies or at the hands of a lunatic prophet."

Regardless of echoes of age-old currents of common human activity concerning the mysteries of life and death, new religious movements seem to have exploded in this age of high modernity (Giddens, 1990; 1991). The reality of the expansion of religious groups is documented in a number of sources. For example, when J. Gordon Melton (1991) updated his *Encyclopedia of American Religions* and chronicled the existence of religious organizations, he named 1,588 denominations, sects, and/or cults. This was 388 more than he had counted in the 1986 edition of the encyclopedia. In addition, Saliba (1990) summarizes 2,219 entries on cults alone in his *Social Science and the Cults: An Annotated Bibliography*. Further delineations of the spread of new religious movements in late twentieth-century America are provided in two other books: Robbins (1988) *Cults, Converts and Charisma* and Galanter (1989) *Cults: Faith, Healing and Coercion*. Tim Stafford (1991), in his work on the Spiritual Counterfeits Projects, writes that the 1988 *Directory of Cult Research Organizations* has grown from 305 entries in 1988 to over 500 in 1991.

Activities of some of these groups capture the attention and imagination of those interested in the variety of innovations demonstrated by NRMs and new expressions of religious beliefs. The Church of the New Song, for example, emerged in 1970 among those incarcerated in U.S. penitentiaries. Melton (1991, Vol. 3:301) states:

> In February 1972 a federal court recognized the church as a legitimate body, and ordered prison officials to permit it to meet and hold services. After that decision the church spread rapidly and became the focus of controversy. It was accused of causing a work strike at San Quentin, and its sincerity was questioned because of a claimed specification that porterhouse steak and Harvey's Bristol Cream were its communion elements.

The Tribe of Judah, founded in 1980 by a former outlaw biker by the name of Ben Priest, represents a new twist to preaching the gospel. This group, along with the Full Gospel Motorcycle International, the Righteous Riders, and The Christian Motorcyclists Association, travels the roads, ready to proselytize stranded motorists and others they meet on the nation's highways. According to Crandall (1992:60):

> Their handlebars are their pulpits. Their vestments, black leather. They are Bikers for Christ, and they want to save the godless motorist—not to mention all those wayward Hells Angels types out there.... The spiritual awakening began 12 years ago, when an epiphany struck a drug-ingesting, shotgun-toting biker named Ben Priest. After attending a service in a Houston church, he says, "Jesus fixed my life." He felt the call to minister to outlaw bikers....

Another recent phenomenon surrounds the amount of attention that can be produced by mass marketing even a parody of new religious expressions. Ivan Stang, a Dallas radio announcer and film producer, has long studied nonconventional religious groups. He co-founded the Church of the Subgenius to call attention to the gullibili-ty of Americans when it comes to religious broadcasting, mail order tracts, and media evangelism. Levine (1988:67) mentions that while the church started as a comic parody of some of the religious fringe groups in this country:

> Its 3,500 dues-paying followers, mostly baby-boomers reared on the '60s counterculture, "worship" a smiling, pipe-smoking salesman named J. R. "Bob" Dobbs, and proselytize with such slogans as "Eternal Salvation—or triple your money back." Despite its comic intent, the church has been plagued by some overzealous followers mockingly dubbed "Bobbies" by church leaders, who urge them to rebel instead and form their own schisms.... Ironically, the church is as big as many genuine cults. The group's "bible," *The Book of the Subgenius,* has sold about 30,000 copies. Cult-monitoring organizations even report occasional worried inquiries about it. The group's most sacred ritual: Hitting a plastic bust of Arnold Palmer across a room while prostrate members listen to an impassioned minister inveigh against the "anti-Palmer," Lee Trevino.

Another marketing strategy is being planned for the merger of vegetarianism, magic, and meditation. Lustgarden (1992:12) reports that the vegetarian magician and TV performer Doug Henning and the guru of Transcendental Meditation, Maharishi Mahesh Yogi, are planning the opening of a $1.5 billion theme park in Ontario, Canada, close to Niagara Falls. The park will be called Maharishi Veda Land and will, according to Henning (Lustgarden, 1992:12):

> "...stimulate the visitors' intellects, arouse their emotions and even awaken the human consciousness...." Henning is banking on 33 "won-drous" high-tech family attractions—such as the world's only levitating building, floating 15 feet over water—to draw in visitors. Besides the re-sort, Veda Land hopes to attract crowds with its business conference cen-ter, health center, 1,000-unit residential development, Tower of Peace for reconciling international conflicts, even a proposed university able to ac-commodate 7,000 students of yogic flying, the highest level of Transcen-dental Meditation.

Another meditation-centered, new religious expression currently on the American scene uses a mind-awareness tract written by psy-chologist Helen Schucman titled *A Course in Miracles.* This book is the centerpiece of more than 1,000 study groups based on its introspective program (Smilgis, 1991). Gardner (1992:17;21) says that Schucman:

...was short, slight, and a professed atheist. Suddenly in 1965 a strange thing happened. A silent "inner voice" commanded her to take notes for a "course in miracles." For almost eight years (1965 to 1973) the Voice dictated at intervals.... If a phone call interrupted the channeling, the Voice would stop and later take up where it had left off.... Some converts to the *Course* are loath to admit that the Voice was the voice of Jesus, but passages in the *Course* make this clear, and Helen Schucman was openly frank about it.

Marianne Williamson has one of the most successful of the new groups based on the course in miracles. She rents the St. Thomas Episcopal Church in West Hollywood each Saturday morning and ministers to celebrities and others alike with a think-positive message about love, self, and happiness (Smilgis, 1991). Her presentation "has the rapid-fire delivery of a televangelist" and she claims that "nothing occurs outside our minds.... Time does not exist...we're always perfect...[and] Sickness is an illusion and does not actually exist" (Gardner, 1992:20–21). Williamson has also been interviewed on TV programs, has become a fund raiser for Project Angel Food, a civil program that delivers gourmet meals to those with AIDS, and is well known for officiating at Elizabeth Taylor's marriage to Larry Fortensky. Recently Williamson has attracted negative press for her apparent temper tantrums and hostile reactions to board members who have helped bring millions of dollars to her projects. In regard to her own definition of the situation, she is quoted as calling herself "a bitch for God" (Gardner, 1992:23).

One last set of events should sensitize the reader to the events, movements, and activities that fall under the rubric of NRMs. When the Soviet Union began dissolving and eastern Europe began changing rapidly in the late 1980s, many NRMs quickly responded to the newly created market for religious expressionism. Mainline Christian denominations were also drawn to the area but few could compete with the flexibility, zealotry, and quick pace of some of the NRMs. An article by Maxwell (1992) states that Hare Krishna posters now fill Moscow's subways; Soviet Armenian psychiatrists are already recommending Transcendental Meditation for stress and pain relief; and Unification Church founder Sun Myung Moon flew 1,400 students from Moscow and other cities to the United States for field trips that included Moon's teachings. Maxwell also reports that the Children of God are working the streets in Bulgaria with posters and thousands of leaflets; L. Ron Hubbard's *An Introduction to Scientology* has been translated into Czech, Polish, Serbo-Croatian, Hungarian, and Russian, and a magical order is now initiating members in the former Yugoslavia. In Poland he found (Maxwell, 1992:37) the following NRMs:

Twenty-two Zen Buddist organizations; thirteen Hindu organizations; two Theosophical organizations; Hawaiian Kahuna, a magic movement; Ordo Lux, a Pagan occult movement; two esoteric Yoga groups; a Sikh group; a Baha'i group; a Rastafarian group.

As indicated above, NRMs can be quick to move proselytizers, zealots, true believers, and "advance men" to situations and places where persons are available to hear their words and/or to where active or passive seekership is occurring. Cold war rhetoric preached to the United States that Russia, in particular, was an atheistic country. However, Lefevere (1991:11) quotes Archpriest Vladimir Sorokin, rector of the Russian Orthodox Theological Academy and Seminary, as saying that the 6 million population of St. Petersburg (formerly Leningrad) is 60 percent Orthodox, about 10 to 15 percent "militantly atheists," while the rest are Catholic, Protestant, Jewish, or Muslim. The rector further said (Lefevere, 1991:11):

For us it's clear that Russia is not a non-Christian country. We have had a millennium of rich iconography, of church architecture, history and liturgy...yet many American preachers treat us as if we were a "wild, unchurched land...." Sorokin was referring to televangelists, Campus Crusaders, Moonies, Mormans [sic], Krishnas, New Age and other gurus, some of who are selling their religious wares on Soviet television at a cost of five-six million rubles per minute ($165,000–$200,000).... The [Russian] Orthodox church has no funds to compete with such efforts....

Our point here is that these events and situations demonstrate that something radical has happened in the past three decades to give religious life and expression in the United States, as well as other parts of the world, a flavor unlike that of the immediate past. These NRMs have seemingly proliferated to the point that many can now branch out internationally to proselytize, evangelize, and organize new followers. TV reports as well as numerous popular magazines and periodical articles now underscore the existence of something new on the religious scene in the United States and elsewhere, as mentioned above (cf. Behar, 1991; Groothuis, 1991; Krajick, 1992). Just what is going on, and what are the reasons for this proliferation?

In the remainder of this chapter we will address two basic issues. First, how much do we actually know about the extent of participation in these new religious movements? Second, what are some of the underlying reasons for what appears to be their rapid growth and the involvement of individuals in them. We will look at models of how these movements have emerged, focusing on three models proposed by Bainbridge and Stark (1979), cultural explanations of the growth of such movements, and an analysis of other factors that may influence the tendency of individuals to participate in religious expressions so different from those in which they were raised.

EXTENT OF PARTICIPATION IN NEW RELIGIOUS MOVEMENTS

Estimates of the number of new religious groups in the United States and the number of participants in these groups vary tremendously. Difficulties with definitions of terms, as mentioned above, make clear conceptualization problematic. Still, the often unorganized, informal, and flexible nature of many of these new groups makes obtaining precise and valid data on their membership difficult—if not impossible. Keeping books and rolls, in other words, may seem too traditional or mainline to leaders who might otherwise be able to provide fairly accurate membership profiles of their groups.

Leaders may also feel that letting outsiders know too much about their internal affairs might be detrimental to the group's operations. For example, if membership figures were known by the public, the group might not be able to claim widespread support; taxing agencies might also hamper the operation should membership be reported to governmental agencies, because of the unclear nature of the separation of church and state definitions vis-à-vis cults. Struggling organizations may also *want* to project a negative financial situation and waning membership in order to attract contributions. In other words, accurate membership figures may not be available or the movements may be reluctant to admit how small their impact has been.

Researchers, therefore, deal with less than reliable figures on the extent of such groups, regardless of their efforts to be precise. The resulting imprecision appears frequently in statements about the "thousands" of members of groups or the "several hundred thousand" persons (Richardson, 1978) who have had meaningful experiences within a particular organization or movement. Thus, we have to expect discrepancies in reports of membership in new religious groups and may have to settle for the imprecision such organizational styles necessitate.

Barker (1989:vii–viii) provides insight into some of the basic sources of information we have about NRMs: (1) The movements themselves provide information about their organizations, in some cases including membership information that may be accurate but may also be selective or misleading, as we have noted above; (2) ex-members as well as relatives and friends of members—these people are rich sources of qualitative information about their experiences but may be unable to provide quantitative data about numbers in the movement; (3) specialized organizations collect information about NRMs, but these vary widely in scope and reliability of data collected—some of these organizations are "cult-watching" groups that stand to benefit from alarmist claims and/or exaggerated membership data; (4) the electronic and print media also provide information about NRMs but can seldom provide independently collected primary aggregate data of high reliability; and (5) academic research and data may be fairly accurate but buried in sources not generally available or attractive to the general public. For these reasons and others, the reader is urged to recognize the difficulty researchers have in obtaining accurate, reliable, and current information about NRMs. What is seemingly a mass movement may be neither a "mass" nor a "movement."

Researchers, however, press for clear answers and contact various spokespersons for the groups, asking specifically for membership information. Appel (1983), curious about discrepancies in membership reports, contacted sources within various groups by telephone: These sources revealed an overestimation of size when taking into account differences between full-time (or "staff") and part-time members.

Another reason for distorted data concerns the level of participation required to be counted a "member" of an NRM. For example, Hare Krishna (International Society for Krishna Consciousness—ISKCON) was credited with approximately twenty thousand members in the United States in the early 1980s (Barker, 1982:340), but a Krishna spokesperson told Appel (1983:13) that there were five thousand full-time members in the United States, and that full-time membership was "waning a bit." Melton (1991, Vol. 3:206) states that the Krishna group reported 3,000 core community members in 1984 but also claimed 250,000 "lay constituents." Another compounding problem is presented by Barker (1989:147):

> ...although most Westerners would consider *Western* Krishna devotees to be members of an NRM, they might be less certain whether to label as "cultists" the far larger number of worshippers in ISKCON temples in Britain who are drawn from the Asian community and are regarded as little more or less than members of one Hindu tradition among many by most of their fellow Asians. ISKCON is, indeed, a respected member of the National Council of Hindu Temples.... [R]espectability or "cause for concern" are sometimes drawn into the definition of what constitutes an NRM (or "cult").

The million plus membership number used for the Church of Scientology shrinks drastically when the level of participation is controlled (Appel, 1983). Melton (1991, Vol. 2:312) states the following:

> The church reported that in 1987 there were 4,959,433 Dianetics and Scientology books sold, and that it had a total of 6,598 staff members delivering Scientology services to its parishioners in its 673 churches, missions, and groups worldwide. No precise figure of its total membership currently exists; however, church statistics of its membership were reported in 1977 to be more than five million worldwide with more than three million of those in the United States. Those figures represent a cumulative number of people who have participated in one or more of the church's programs or availed themselves of the church's services over a period of several years.

Barker (1989:152) comes to much the same conclusion. She points out that the Church of Scientology has claimed that one hundred thousand people have paid for one or more of the church's introductory courses since the church started offering them in Britain during the 1950s. However, only about 250 full-time staff members appear to be at the Church of Scientology's East Grinstead headquarters. According to Behar (1991:50–51), the group "boasts 700 centers in 65 countries…[but] has about 50,000 active members, far fewer than the 8 million the group claims."

Melton (1992:7–8) contends that the number of new religious movements in the United States has grown to between 500 and 600 since World War II. However, the actual membership in such movements has been greatly exaggerated by the press. Only a few of the older movements (e.g., Jehovah's Witnesses and the Latter-day Saints) maintain a broad membership. The more publicized groups (e.g., the Unification Church and Hare Krishna) claim less than ten thousand members. Most groups count their actual members in the hundreds rather than the thousands.

Regardless of the exact number of groups and participants (whether full-time, part-time, lay constituents, or other peripherally connected individuals), the last three decades have seen a rapid growth of diverse religious and quasi-religious organizations. The religious map of the United States and other Western countries has been significantly redrawn.

Stark, Bainbridge, and Doyle (1979), cognizant of the problems with data distortion, provide an important summary of information on the demographics of 501 new religious movements in the United States during the late seventies, based on information contained in

Melton's (1978) *The Encyclopedia of American Religion.* For each group, Stark et al. (1979:349) coded the state where its headquarters was located, indicating that for most cults this state was also where the group originated and where most, if not all, of its members resided. States having 15 or more cults were California (167), New York (59), Illinois (34), Florida (20), Pennsylvania (18), and Colorado and Missouri (15 each). Alaska, Delaware, Maine, Mississippi, Montana, North Dakota, South Dakota, Vermont, and West Virginia, among others, had none.

These researchers also divided the number of NRMs located in a state by its population and found that the following five states had more than five cults per million residents: Nevada (10.0), New Mexico (9.1), California (7.9), Colorado (6.0), and Arizona (5.9). This listing is particularly interesting as these states are in what is sometimes known as the "unchurched" West. And these states retained this ranking in a later study by Stark and Bainbridge (1985). Actually, according to this report, the District of Columbia had a higher rate of cult *headquarters* per million residents than any of the states. This may, however, simply represent the convergence of organizational headquarters at the nation's capital rather than a peculiar attraction for residents of that district.

Looking at NRMs or cults by region of the country, per million residents, Stark et al. (1979:350) found the Pacific region highest in the number of NRMs (6.9 per million inhabitants), followed by the Rocky Mountain region (3.5), the Southwest (2.1), the East (2.0), the Northeast (1.9), East Central (1.6), West Central (1.4), and the South with the lowest (0.9; with Florida omitted, 0.6). Using thirteen categories representing fundamental divisions among NRM or cult members, these researchers (Stark et al., 1979:352) arrived at the data on cult composition of regions of the United States presented in Table 8.1.

Stark (1992:423) used census data to measure occult practitioners per 100,000 individuals in the labor force for the year 1920 and found that the same geographic areas of the nation were represented by NRMs then as now. Thus, regional variation in the emergence of NRMs appears to be constant over seventy years of history.

Because of the volume (or sometimes scarcity), diversity, and complexity of data available on new groups, we cannot deal with many of these groups in detail. Hence our discussion of a few of the more prominent groups in the next chapter will remain somewhat limited. In this chapter we consider it important to reflect upon the reasons these new religious groups have surfaced and proliferated in recent decades. How do they get started? How do they draw and maintain members? Under what societal and cultural situations might

Table 8.1   Cult Composition of Regions of the United States
(by Percentage)

Kind of Cult	Pacific	South-west	Moun-tain	West Central	East Central	East	North-east	South	National*
				Region					
Mormon groups†	0	8	0	24	3	3	0	0	3
Cult communes	5	3	0	0	4	1	5	4	3
New thought	6	10	11	7	3	6	21	5	7
Theosophy and spiritualism	26	31	21	4	24	21	21	36	25
Occult orders	4	2	5	0	4	3	0	0	3
Flying saucers	6	2	5	3	3	1	0	7	4
Psychedelic	2	5	0	0	0	1	0	0	1
Psychic	12	15	10	17	0	8	16	12	11
Magick, witches, and Satanists	7	8	16	21	16	11	16	24	12
Pagans	7	3	0	7	7	1	0	0	4
Asian faiths	20	8	32	3	22	37	21	12	21
Jesus people	4	0	0	4	7	0	0	0	2
Miscellaneous	1	5	0	10	7	7	0	0	4

* Washington, D.C., included.
†Utah Mormon groups omitted.
Source: Stark et al., 1979:352.

we expect the emergence of religious movements to flourish despite their opposition to the normative religious traditions wherein they have emerged?

HOW AND WHY NEW EXPRESSIONS EMERGE

Numerous conceptual frameworks have been advanced to explain the emergence of religious expressions. One classic and rather exhaustive work by LaBarre (1971) points to the complexity of the question of how religious movements get started. Centering his attention on *crisis cults* and addressing theories of causality, LaBarre (1971:36) concludes that no particularist explanation can be given for cult formation and/or transformation, and that we should guard against reductionism. Before reaching this conclusion, LaBarre lists several theories or approaches that various writers have used in an attempt to further our understanding of certain religious and quasi-religious movements. Some of these theories can be classified as political, military, economic, or messianic; others emphasize factors such as the emergence of a "great man," acculturation, or psychological stress. Each of these emphases, separately or together, may offer important clues to the causes of new movements, religious or otherwise, and provide us with a wealth of variables to consider in analyzing new religious expressions.

Robbins (1988:11–13) urges us to look at the recent history of spiritual ferment in attempting to understand NRMs in the United States. Defining the initial period as lasting from the middle sixties through the early seventies, he describes this as a time of "diffuse countercultural protest: student protest, psychedelic utopianism, hippies, etc." As student protest diminished, certain religiotherapeutic movements emerged as "successor movements" to the broader countercultural protest. The second period started at the end of the sixties and is now waning, with the latter half of this period marked by controversies over destructive cults. This is when the anticult movement emerged and *deprogramming* was applied to deconversion from NRMs. According to Robbins, the third period, which continues through to the present, is characterized by "charismatic-fundamentalist renewal… televangelical right-wing politics…patriotic revitalization and moral agitation."

As we will see in the next chapter, some of the most recent (1988–1992) NRM activities are concerned with New Age expressions which may have had connections to the self-help agenda and advanced materialism of the eighties. The NRM scene today is still attracting middle- and upper-middle-class individuals in disproportionate numbers (Barker, 1989:14). Stark (1992:430) reaffirms this position by stating that "the average cult convert these days is not a social outcast lacking education and good job prospects." Popular periodicals also draw attention to the notion that middle-aged and older women as well as older and complacent parents are potential candidates for cult involvement. Claire Safran (1990:46) declares, "If you're mid-life or older, feeling a little vulnerable and have some money, you're a candidate for a cult." Thus, the middle-aged as well as the young may now become involved in new religious expressions.

Further theoretical insights are relevant to the formation and functioning of NRMs. One explanation for the emergence of NRMs in such profusion today may well lie in the conditions of advanced modern society (Giddens, 1990; 1991). Some theorists (see, e.g., Jameson, 1991; Crooks, Pakulski, and Waters, 1992) contend that world society is undergoing a phase change as we move from "modern times" to postmodernity. Such a phase change is particularly troubling as the "traditions of modernity," which have ordered our lives for two centuries, are being pulled apart, resulting in a fragmented and atomized world. Mestrovic (1992) argues that we have arrived at a *fin-de-siècle* as significant as that which Durkheim faced as he wrote.

As Giddens (1991:20) has put it, the characteristics of this society "propel social life away from the hold of pre-established concepts or practices." In such a situation our certainty is threatened and doubt becomes more a part of our life than belief. Everything is open to revision when the all-encompassing traditions and sureties of previous decades have been removed. Thus, we are on our own as we "ride the juggernaut of modernity" (Giddens, 1991:28).

In what may be seen as a crisis of belief, several options are open. One that has received much attention is the so-called resurgence of fundamentalism. But another way to recapture the "sacred" can be found in the ideologies of NRMs. In the wide variety of forms of religious thought, NRMs offer new certainties to replace those shattered by the disruptive nature of society in the last decade of the twentieth century.

Several models and explanations of the emergence of NRMs have been presented by sociologists. No one model appears to explain fully the movements, yet each contributes something to our understanding of the phenomenon. We will review some of the more noteworthy contributions below in greater detail.

NRMs as Compensator Systems

In writing about cult formation, Bainbridge and Stark (1979) have proposed three different, but compatible, models of how religious ideas are generated and made social: (1) the *psychopathology model*, (2) the *entrepreneur model*, and (3) the *subculture-evolution model*. Viewing religions as exchange systems, these two authors (1979:284) rely heavily upon their concept of compensators, stating that "faced with rewards that are very scarce, or not available at all, humans create and exchange compensators—sets of beliefs and prescriptions for action that substitute for the immediate achievement of the desired reward." Thus these models focus on possible psychological, social, and cultural factors in the formation of cults.

The main ideas of the psychopathology model (Bainbridge and Stark, 1979:285) are the following:

1. Cults are novel cultural responses to personal and societal crisis.
2. New cults are invented by individuals suffering from certain forms of mental illness.
3. These individuals typically achieve their novel visions during psychotic episodes.

4. During such an episode, the individual invents a new package of compensators to meet his own needs.
5. The individual's illness commits him to his new vision, either because his hallucinations appear to demonstrate its truth, or because his compelling needs demand immediate satisfaction.
6. After the episode, the individual will be most likely to succeed in forming a cult around his vision if the society contains many other persons suffering from problems similar to those originally faced by the cult founder, to whose solution, therefore, they are likely to respond.
7. Therefore, such cults most often succeed during times of societal crisis, when large numbers of persons suffer from similar unresolved problems.
8. If the cult does succeed in attracting many followers, the individual founder may achieve at least a partial cure of his illness, because his self-generated compensators are legitimated by other persons, and because he now receives true rewards from his followers.

Therefore, this model deals with cult founders who invent compensator systems for their own use.

On the other hand, the entrepreneur model emphasizes cult formation and organization as a business. Bainbridge and Stark (1979:288) identify the following ten points of the entrepreneur model:

1. Cults are businesses which provide a product for their customers and receive payment in return.
2. Cults are mainly in the business of selling novel compensators, or at least freshly packaged compensators that appear new.
3. Therefore, a supply of novel compensators must be manufactured.
4. Both manufacture and sales are accomplished by entrepreneurs.
5. These entrepreneurs, like those in other businesses, are motivated by the desire for profit, which they can gain by exchanging compensators for rewards.
6. Motivation to enter the cult business is stimulated by the perception that such business can be profitable, an impression likely to be acquired through prior involvement with a successful cult.
7. Successful entrepreneurs require skills and experience, which are most easily gained through a prior career as the employee of an earlier successful cult.
8. The manufacture of salable new compensators (or compensatorpackages) is most easily accomplished by assembling components of preexisting compensator-systems into new configurations, or by the further development of successful compensator-systems.
9. Therefore, cults tend to cluster in lineages. They are linked by individual entrepreneurs who begin their careers in one cult and then

leave to found their own. They bear strong "family resemblances" because they share many cultural features.

10. Ideas for completely new compensators can come from any cultural source or personal experience whatsoever, but the skillful entrepreneur experiments carefully in the development of new products and incorporates them permanently in his cult only if the market response is favorable.

Both the psychopathology and entrepreneur models concentrate on the innovative behavior of an individual, while the subculture-evolution model stresses group behavior. The nine points of the subculture model mentioned by Bainbridge and Stark (1979:291) are the following:

1. Cults are the expression of novel social systems, usually small in size but composed of at least a few intimately interacting individuals.
2. These cultic social systems are most likely to emerge in populations already deeply involved in the occult milieu, but cult evolution may also begin in entirely secular settings.
3. Cults are the result of sidetracked or failed collective attempts to obtain scarce or nonexistent rewards.
4. The evolution begins when the group of persons commits itself to the attainment of certain rewards.
5. In working together to obtain these rewards, members begin exchanging other rewards as well, such as affect.
6. As they progressively come to experience failure in achieving their original goals, they will gradually generate and exchange compensators as well.
7. If the intragroup exchange of rewards and compensators becomes sufficiently intense, the group will become relatively encapsulated, in the extreme case undergoing complete social implosion.
8. Once separated to some degree from external control, the evolving cult develops and consolidates a novel culture, energized by the need to facilitate the exchange of rewards and compensators, and inspired by essentially accidental factors.
9. The end point of successful cult evolution is a novel religious culture embodied in a distinct social group which must now cope with the problem of extracting resources (including new members) from the surrounding environment.

Cultural Factors

These models articulate some of the processes in cult formation but do not address completely the ways in which cultural factors can facilitate the emergence of new religious expressions. White (1959) has indicated that until the cultural base is sufficiently developed to allow something to come into being, it will not gain fruition in society. Thus many of the factors possibly involved in the creation and fulfillment of new expressions in religious life have a decidedly cultural or social basis. Many new expressions arise because of a need for something innovative to meet expectations and desires not being met by existing societal arrangements. Many people rejected several of society's institutions during the 1960s in part because they perceived them as archaic, ineffective, discriminatory, rigid, and unfulfilling. As Tipton (1984:30) has pointed out:

> In the atmosphere of disappointment and depression that followed the conflicts and failures of the sixties, many youths sought out alternative religious movements. Disoriented by drugs, embittered by politics, disillusioned by apparent worthlessness of work and the transiency of love, they have found a way back through these movements, a way to get along with conventional American society and to cope with the demands of their own maturing lives.

The concept of anomie or normlessness, in addition, has sensitized us to the fact that the relationship of an individual to societal mores depends in part upon the social forces acting upon the person at any given time. The more anomic the society, the greater the possibility of searching for novel expressions of individuality and, therefore, the greater the likelihood that new religious expressions will form.

The interplay between the individual and his or her cultural milieu has been the focus of many studies of religion. Such studies lead to an analysis of how the group affects the individual and of the impact of individuals upon the group. Given this perspective, in looking for elements instrumental in the emergence of new expressions, we may find it difficult to completely separate the individual from society. In a review of theory and research on new religions, Robbins, Anthony, and Richardson (1978:95–99) identified four basic variables explaining the why of recent religious movements. These are secularization, the quest for community, the value crisis, and the increasing need for holistic self-definition in a differentiated society.

Secularization refers to the breaking up of society into various parts that do not have a religious ideology as a guiding principle. In fact, the sacred and the secular are often contrasted as opposites. But secularization means more than just antireligion; it refers to some extent to society's becoming complex, bureaucratized, fragmented, and impersonal. Since persons in a society are not encapsulated by a set of traditional sacred rules and principles, they are diverted to seek out new ways of psychological and social expression.

As Wilson (1975:80) has contended, secularization produces "a supermarket of faith," where a number of groups coexist and compete for consumers' attention, but where these groups are, nonetheless, "relatively unimportant consumer items." Thus, if a society becomes secular, we can expect that traditional religious values will lose some of their strength and a certain kind of social and religious experimentation will take place.

Stark (1992:427) presents an argument that this is true in many European nations, and that "contrary to popular wisdom, North America is not the land of cults. Cults are much more plentiful and successful in most of northern Europe and Great Britian than in the United States or Canada. Indeed, this is even true of groups that originated in the United States...." Even after hearing this argument, however, we should remember that no society is in reality purely sacred or purely secular; societies vary along a continuum from more sacred to more secular. For this reason, among others, secularization is not a necessary and sufficient condition for the emergence of new religious expressions.

We must mention that secularization, which was once an all-pervasive concept for many sociologists of religion, is now being questioned (see Chapters 1 and 14). Today secularization is seen as more limited. That is, in the sense that the church as an institution, and particularly mainline churches, are losing influence in society there is secularization. As a result, there is a vacuum in our complex, bureaucratized, and fragmented society which needs to be filled. However, individuals are no longer fully encapsulated by traditional sacred rules. Religious belief and activity are based on voluntarism (Roof and McKinney, 1987), and people are free to pick and choose their religious beliefs, making up a bricolage of unassorted items from the belief systems that compete for their attention (see Dobbelaere, 1990).

Similarly, the second factor mentioned by Robbins et al. (1978), the quest for community, does not alone explain religious change. The quest for community on the part of individuals supports the idea that as societies become more impersonal, persons seek to establish (or perhaps reestablish) a feeling of belonging to certain groups and ideas. As the family becomes less traditional and encompasses less of the individual's field of experiences, and as primary groups lose out in importance to secondary concerns, the individual may have vague feelings of frustration and aloneness, and may try to ease these feelings through involvement with a primary surrogate, which may be a new religion. This thesis, again, is not comprehensive, but it buttresses the notion of the interplay between societal conditions and individual action as one seeks a place in society.

The third and fourth themes identified by Robbins et al. (1978) continue the basic social-psychological perspective of the first two. Individuals who undergo a crisis of values and search for groups offering a more holistic conception are reacting to a set of social circumstances. Because of social change, their old belief systems may break down, and these persons may question the appropriateness of their traditional ways of thinking. As these individuals become more aware not only of alternative values but also of the plethora of such values, they may try to reorient themselves to particular beliefs that give meaning to their lives.

Other Possible Factors

Let us think together now about other possible factors related to the formation of groups such as the Jesus movement, Hare Krishna, the Unification Church, and Scientology. For one thing, a political climate that allows expression is essential; the agents of social control have to permit such expressions, and entrepreneurs have to simultaneously press for the right to engage in innovative behavior. Religious freedom from a purely sociological perspective is as dependent on freedom as it is on religion. Political ideology, then, must be less than totally repressive to tolerate new religious ideas.

Another variable to consider surrounds the needs of the recruits. Rather than being lured away by a religious Pied Piper, many persons (particularly the young) seek out excitement, emotion, and a new way when the old ways do not satisfactorily address these needs. MacCannell (1973) claims that Westerners are searching for authenticity of experience. Derber (1979:6) speaks of an individualistic psychology formed when the self is "cut adrift from any enduring community." For the community to endure, it must meet, at least minimally, the needs of significant numbers of participants. Some members, particularly in a pluralistic system, may venture into marginal religious groups without threatening the societal fabric and may actually provide a mechanism of vicarious participation for the more conformist members of the religious community. Societal change necessitates innovative expression, whether in art, science, technology, or religion. Likewise, individual creativity and freedom of expression necessitate an ability to search for psychic nurturance within the conventional or within the unconventional.

A similar vein has to do with privatization, which McGuire (1992:43) defines as "the process by which certain spheres of life become removed from effective roles in the public sphere." Joining a collectivity professing nontraditional values can be, to the recruit and to the group as a whole, a way of engaging in privatization of a belief system and a lifestyle, as several of the new religious groups on today's scene possess numerous features of the secret society. Connected to a need for validation, a search for authenticity, and a need for excitement and new experiences, the privatization produced by belonging to a unique and marginal (if not secret) religious group can fill one's life with both psychic and social energy. This may manifest itself by producing both psychological commitment and the expenditure of personal resources necessary to stay in the group.

Of course, those who choose the unconventional route are faced with resistance from some individual and social control agents if their search proves too threatening or becomes labeled sinister by public opinion or by powerful members of vested interest groups, some of whom may actually be in competition with the new group (see Robbins, 1984). When this occurs the recruit may have to deal with labels such as *brainwashed, youthfully rebellious, mentally incompetent,* and *led astray.* The point is that societal agents create part of the problem by their attempts to control behavior through informal and formal mechanisms. Unconventional behavior of most kinds threatens not the physical well-being of society but the symbolic order (which, as mentioned above, is not unyielding to change). Therefore, societal reaction perpetuates some of the unconventional religions by pushing them into a deviant status (Lemert, 1951:76). Barker (1989), in particular, has drawn our attention to the overreaction we often demonstrate when it comes to NRMs.

The reasons mentioned above, and numerous others, do not completely explain the creation and maintenance of new religious expressions. Werblowsky (1982:43) has sanely advised that to fully understand these new groups, we should look at local and regional variations. Thus we clearly do not have all the information necessary for a full understanding. Recall, also, that within sociology alone, three basic theoretical perspectives (functionalism, conflict theory, and symbolic interactionism) exist; each may contribute to understanding the emergence of different religious expressions or different aspects of a religious movement at different points in its evolution. Barker (1982b) has called for an approach to the study of new religious movements that compares different groups to each other and investigates the same movement at different times or in different societies. Melton (1992:10) mentions that many "mundane causes," such as immigration laws and restrictions, the merging and maturing of various social and historical trends, and population shifts influence new expressions of religious beliefs. Consider for yourself the numerous social, psychological, and historical routes you have traveled to arrive at your present religious beliefs (or lack of them). As you do this, you should be better able to recognize the complexity of religious phenomena and gain additional insight into the development of novel religious expressions.

SUMMARY

This chapter suggests that numerous factors contribute to the creation and maintenance of new religious expressions. Sociologists often begin their analyses with attempts to conceptually distinguish between major concepts, such as sects, cults, and NRMs, as we have done. This allows us to better explain how certain factors influence the phenomena under investigation; it also lets us show how the terms themselves can be used in connotatively imprecise ways by the media and the general public. Such imprecision can lead to the distortion and exaggeration of the extent of participation in NRMs and can label participants incorrectly regarding their degree of involvement and commitment to the group under question.

We have also explored in this chapter some rather basic models concerning the creation of NRMs. The psychopathology, entrepreneur, and subculture-evolution models offer a wide range of possible explanations for the formation of novel religious expressions. Religious expressions are also tied to the overall social and historical fabric of a particular era and are influenced by its culture base. The complexity of the culture base surely has a bearing on the types of expressions that can originate and flourish in a society. We mentioned a few of the more recent novel groups to appear on the American scene, such as the Bikers for Christ, the Maharishi Veda Land, and groups centered around *A Course in Miracles* as well as the new religious activities currently taking place in the former Soviet Union. Many of these activities are attractive to individuals who use them as compensators and substitutes for other rewards not immediately achievable. Thus, religious activity is often dependent upon the characteristics of several other social forces operative in a society at a given time (e.g., the degree of secularization, the nature of the economy, the amount of political freedom, etc.) as well as the more personalistic models of actual cult formation mentioned above. Finally, we have pointed out that a variety of mundane factors, such as the need for excitement and new experiences, the official quotas on immigrants from other countries, regional variations and occupational subcultures, and population shifts may influence the creation of NRMs. The next chapter will provide more details on the exact nature of some of these NRMs.

9.
New Religious Movements: Contemporary Examples

New religious movements are intriguing. They conjure images of weird practices, strange garbs, and sometimes bizarre beliefs. Clearly they represent a break with "stuffy" tradition. As we consider the nature of some of these groups it is well to remember that Christianity was a new religious expression two thousand years ago.

> *All religions begin as cult movements.* All of today's great world religions were once regarded as weird, crazy, foolish, and sinful. How Roman intellectuals in the first century must have laughed at the notion that a messiah and his tiny flock in Palestine, an obscure corner of the empire, posed a threat to the might pagan temples [emphasis in original].

Moving to the history of movements within Christianity, Finke and Stark (1992) describe the early history of religion in the United States as one of "upstart sects" challenging the established big three of the colonial era—the Episcopalians, Presbyterians, and Congregationalists. And how the elitists mocked the "crudities" of the Methodists and Baptists, among others! But the "laughable" challengers soon outpaced these "elite" religious groups, becoming themselves part of the establishment—only to be confronted with newer movements which, again, seemed strange and uncouth to the "establishment," yet they flourished and began to erode the strength of the new mainline.

Keeping this history in mind, we will look briefly in this chapter at selected new religious expressions to determine their basic characteristics—beliefs, histories, and ramifications for the lives of their adherents. As we describe the requirements and activities of some of these groups, think how *you* would fare as a recruit.

Many new expressions we discuss here came to our attention in the 1960s. Religious change appeared to accelerate in that decade as part cause and part effect of sweeping social upheavals, although Finke and Stark (1992) would contend that it was simply an accentuated form of processes occurring throughout the history of pluralistic religion in the United States. Indeed, Robbins (1990) contends that such new religious movements have existed since the beginning of the concept of religion and are peculiar to our time only in the attention they receive from the media.

Still at this time the Western world did become enamored of Eastern thought and self-help movements as the drift to experimentation with various locations of the sacred became acceptable, even encouraged, as part of a "liberated" lifestyle; Hammond (1985) termed it "the escape of the sacred"—escape, that is, from traditional institutional sites. Some emergent religious groups prompted converts to radically alter their spiritual consciousness. Converts embraced new living arrangements, new levels of physiological, and new psychological awareness as well as publicly proclaiming the error of their past lives.

Some of the new religious expressions emerging in the United States in recent decades have been homegrown, other have been imported. In the former group, the Jesus movement and People's Temple grew from Christian roots, while Scientology has its roots in science fiction. In the latter group, the Hare Krishna movement, Unification Church, and cult of Rajneesh all have Eastern roots. New Age expressions are a mixture of Western and Eastern influences. And most recently the focus on Satanism, inspired both by fundamentalists and some police called *cult cops* (Crouch and Damphousse, 1991), has captured our attention. This brief overview will give some idea of the great diversity of new religious expressions appearing in the United States. We will now turn to a closer look at these groups and then end with a discussion of the programming-deprogramming controversy surrounding some of these groups.

THE JESUS MOVEMENT

In considering the New Religious Movement (NRM), the Jesus movement is primarily seen as a social phenomenon involving a number of diverse, loosely organized groups whose "peculiar unifying characteristic is the belief that man can overcome his alienation and find real meaning in life only through a personal relationship with Jesus Christ" (Balswick 1977:167). Various writers have questioned the exactitude of referring to this as a social movement. As Enroth, Ericson, and Peters (1972:11–12) pointed out, "There is so much diversity within the movement that some elements of it consider others non-Christian, even demonic." Nevertheless, write Enroth et al., "There are some unifying threads that run through all segments and make it proper to consider the Jesus People as one movement." Although different organizations may require different regimens for their members and place different emphases upon Scriptures, some of the "unifying threads" of the Jesus movement are the following: (1) an experiential relationship with Jesus, (2) emotional religious services, (3) belief in the power of prayer, (4) belief in the healing powers of Jesus, (5) denunciation of the secular world as evil, (6) anti-intellectualism, (7) belief in the Bible as inerrant, (8) witnessing for Jesus, (9) proselytizing, and (10) speaking in tongues, or glossolalia.

As a new religious movement, the term *Jesus movement* is most often used to describe groups that grew out of the counterculture during the United States in the mid-1960s and that involve mainly young people. Known variously as Street Christians, Jesus Freaks, and Jesus People, these movements were largely made up of "survivors" of the counterculture. Some of the organizations deemed part of this movement are the Children of God/Family of Love/The Family; the Texas Soul Clinic; the Christian World Liberation Front; the Jesus People's Army; The Way; Tony and Susan Alamo's Christian Foundation; His Place; the East Coast Jesus People; the Jesus People Church, Inc.; Calvary Chapel; Jews for Jesus; and many other communal and localized organizations throughout the United States and rest of the world.

The Children of God/Family of Love/The Family

The Children of God (COG), which was renamed the Family of Love at the end of 1970s (Barker, 1989:172), is an antiestablishment form of Christianity. The sect was formed in 1968 in Huntington Beach, California, by an itinerant evangelical preacher named David Berg (Van Zandt, 1991). Originally Berg called his movement Teens for Christ. Members of the movement see themselves as true followers of God and they adhere to a belief in the King James version of the Bible as the only "authoritative" translation. According to Davis and Richardson (1976:321), by mid-1976 the COG claimed approximately 4,500 full-time members (not counting some 800 young children of members), and they had organized into more than 600 colonies in over 70 countries."

Early activities of the Children of God in California included descending *en masse* on services conducted in other churches and generally disturbing them. Leaving California, the COG wandered about the country until it finally camped out at Fred Jordan's range in Texas, which was the home of Jordan's Texas Soul Clinic. After a conflict with Jordan, the COG moved on to several new locations, including San Diego; Boulder, Colorado; Austin and Dallas in Texas. When two other groups—the Jesus People's Army and the House of Judah—joined up with the Children of God, the movement began to spread to other countries. Barker (1989:172) asserts that members of COG appeared in Japan and Australia as well as Third World nations, including India, Thailand, Hong Kong, mainland China, and some Latin American nations. They can be seen today on the streets of Britain as well.

The Children of God profess the following beliefs:

1. They are the only Christians who have "sold out one hundred percent" for Christ.
2. They are to separate themselves from the world through communal living and give up all their worldly possessions to the elders of the group.
3. Witnessing and memorizing Scripture are essential activities.
4. They must destroy their former identities and aggressively recruit new members as well as protest against events in the world with which they are not in agreement.
5. The COG movement is receiving the correct interpretation of the Bible, and its members are to recognize the fast-approaching doomsday.

Enroth et al. (1972:44) point out that at least four types of young people are particularly susceptible to the Children of God's message:

1. Those desperately seeking meaning or fulfillment in life after unsuccessfully trying many other "trips."
2. Those coming from a fundamentalist background who do not have sufficient biblical knowledge to feel confident of their position.
3. Those who strongly need a sense of belonging.
4. Those who have come from a permissive background and feel a need for discipline.

As Van Zandt (1991) comments, the beliefs and practices of the COG appear strange to the uninitiated. However, they play a role in structuring the daily life of its members. Their ideology, according to Van Zandt, flows from the interaction of members with one another. Three types of ideology are used within the movement in different settings: the formal ideology, the practical ideology, and the kerygma (18). The first of these ideologies consists of the teachings of the movement, particularly as expressed in the Mo letters (produced by David Berg) and the Bible (Neitz, 1987:7). As is true in more standard belief systems, members often have a more implicit system of beliefs that derive from their understanding of what is needed to perform their mission. Such beliefs are "often a mere shadow of the more systematic and articulated formal ideology presented in COG publications and by group ideologists" (19). The third type of ideology has to do with the doctrine offered potential converts. As Van Zandt (1991) puts it, these belief systems gave prospects only "milk" since they could not readily digest the "meat" of the ideology.

Flirty Fishing and the Family of Love

On March 13, 1974, Berg and his followers left England for the COG colony at Tenerife in the Canary Islands. They wanted to try out a curious practice called *flirty fishing* in an isolated area. Surrounding themselves with some of their most trusted women members, they began to refer to themselves as the *Family of Love*, the name later adopted by the whole group. Melton (1986:156) describes how Berg "ordered the women of the group to use their natural sexual appeal and talents to gain new members, to become fish bait, hookers for Jesus." Frequenting discotheques and bars, the women slept with a number of men in flirty fishing attempts. This colony at Tenerife was considered *selah* ("secret"). Most COG members had no idea of its existence or activities until the formal introduction of flirty fishing in 1976 (Van Zandt, 1991:46).

According to Barker (1989:173), Berg's authoritarian leadership, secrecy about group activities, and employment of sex for manipulative purposes have caused problems for the movement. In fact, a group of parents organized an anticult group know as FREECOG (Free the Children of God). Melton (1986:158) contends that the sexual exploitation of the movement's members as well as the publication of an exposé by one of Berg's daughters have made it difficult for the Children of God/Family of Love to "regain any respectable place in the larger religious community.

In still another shift The Children of God/Family of Love/The Family, operating from headquarters in Whittier, California, has begun a campaign to gain respect and freedom to practice their faith (Family, 1993). An overview of their beliefs and practices states that David Berg has disclaimed all responsibility for past indiscretions and mismanagement in the movement. Extreme practices, e.g., flirty fishing (to some extent because of the AIDS epidemic), have been abandoned. According to their press releases, The Family claims that its members have always been committed to proclaiming the whole Gospel message. They portray themselves as an independent Christian missionary community. As such, they are pursuing an aggressive campaign of evangelism to their faith because they believe we are living in the "end time" and therefore the final harvest must be as full as possible (Niebuhr, 1993).

The impact of the Jesus movement has not yet been assessed. Some contend that the whole enterprise is faddish and will fade away without lasting consequences. Recent TV programs showing the trickery and insincerity of people who beg for money to support starving children in the name of Jesus but who then deliver only a pittance, if anything, to the orphans demonstrate that the religious field is ripe for hucksters. This, along with the notoriety of some of the money-making schemes of televangelists, may be decreasing the overall credibility of the Jesus movement. However, more hopeful critics contend that the movement has produced new recruits for mainline Christianity after they have "burned out" on the intense emotionalism of a Jesus movement experience. Others maintain that the movement has scarred young people for life and done irrevocable psychological damage to the participants. Still others predict that the movement will continue to splinter and form more established types of religious expression akin to a real spiritual awakening.

The Vineyard Christian Fellowship

The spirit of the Jesus movement, as a counterculture event, does continue to live on in such groups as the Vineyard movement (Perrin and Mauss, 1991, 1993). The Vineyard Christian Fellowship (VCF) was founded in the early 1980s. While its roots are in the countercultural Jesus movement, the VCF emerged in 1982 as the result of a merger of two groups: Chuck Smith's Calvary Chapel and Ken Gullickson's Bible study fellowship. Both of these had been part of the Jesus movement in southern California.

John Wimber, the leader of the VCF, combines evangelical and charismatic theological and worship styles in his ministry. His original congregation in Anaheim, California, has built up a membership of approximately 5,000, and Wimber plant to "plant" 10,000 other congregations. At this time more than 250 Vineyards are operating, and the total membership is estimated at 50,000 with congregations in twenty-eight states and five other countries (Perrin and Mauss, 1993). While some of the congregations are relatively small, others have a substantial membership.

Perrin and Mauss expect that the membership will be drawn from *outside* the evangelical community of churches rather than from within it. That is to say, Perrin and Mauss believe that the new recruits to VCF are seeking a more "serious" religion and for this reason will be coming from the mainline Protestant churches, the Roman Catholic Church, or the unchurched rather from other evangelical churches as predicted by Bibby and Brinkerhoff (1983). In general, Perrin and Mauss' findings support the contentions of Dean M. Kelly (1978). Recruits to the Vineyard Christian Fellowship clearly see it as more "serious" than their previous religion—a factor that strongly influences their desire to convert.

People's Temple

The first People's Temple was opened by James Warren Jones in Indianapolis in 1956 when he was twenty-five (Hall, 1990:272). Though Jones's work for racial equality and his faith-healing demonstrations drew hostile reactions from some in Indianapolis, his church became a Disciples of Christ congregation in 1963, and he was ordained as a Disciples of Christ minister in 1965. Soon afterward he moved to Ukiah, California, with several members of his congregation. Some say he left to escape mounting financial and political problems, while others contend he went to Ukiah because it was supposedly one of the safest places in the world in the event of a nuclear war. Jones and his followers lived and worked there until 1972, when he moved his headquarters to San Francisco. He soon attracted local blacks to his church with a soup kitchen, faith healing, religious revivals, and a style of emotionally pitched sermonizing influenced by Father Divine. Soon blacks, women, and elderly persons were migrating to California from the South to join People's Temple as their religious and social base.

In 1973 Jones and a few followers visited Guyana and leased twenty-seven thousand acres of land (Hall, 1990:274); in the following year they established a modest commune and cleared several fields for agricultural production. When Jones began to attract negative media attention in San Francisco (culminating in a damning article in *New West* magazine in August 1977), he and approximately eight hundred followers migrated to the Guyanese jungle and expanded the commune. By the spring 1978, reports that all was not well in the commune spurred relatives of People's Temple members to form a committee that contacted Congressman Leo Ryan, who was already interested in People's Temple. Its members convinced him to lead an investigation. Ryan and his party flew to Jonestown in November 1978 and talked to members of People's Temple, several of whom indicated that they wanted to leave. When Ryan and his party attempted to leave with the defectors, they were ambushed, and Ryan and four members of his party were killed. That evening more than nine hundred members of People's Temple, including many children, were murdered or committed suicide by drinking or injecting themselves with poison.

Does the founding, development, and demise of People's Temple qualify as a new religious expression? As suggested in the introduction to this chapter, some aspects of this phenomenon were not new in form but only in circumstance. Also, Richardson (1979), in a critique of the journalistic and psychologized interpretation of Jonestown, has warned that it is questionable to assume that People's Temple shared crucial features with the new religious groups of the 1960s and 1970s. Hargrove (1979a:14–15) stated that this group was not primarily made up of young people seeking alternatives to established institutions; she contended that although "Jones may not have fit many scholars' definitions of the ideal Christian minister,...it is hard to say that he led a new religious movement." Nevertheless, People's Temple did evolve from its Christian fundamentalist roots into something quite different, certainly outside the mainstream of Christian expression. Scholars from a variety of theoretical perspectives, some emphasizing psychological and psychiatric explanations and others employing sociological and sociopolitical frameworks, have attempted to explain this phenomenon. We'll look briefly at some of these perspectives for the light they can shed on the mechanisms of this particular new religious expression.

Earlier we presented the three models of cult formation developed by Bainbridge and Stark (1979): the psychopathology, entrepreneur, and subculture-evolution models. Probably only the most cynical observer would place People's Temple in the entrepreneurial classification (cult formation as a business), even though People's Temple at the time of the Jonestown suicides reportedly had a budget running into the millions. People's Temple probably is best categorized as having some elements of both the psychopathological and subcultural models, with different factors being more dominant at different points in the Temple's chronology. Bainbridge and Stark (1979) characterize the Temple as a group that began as an extreme but culturally traditional sect and then evolved into a cult as Jones's radical vision progressed. Indicating that the members probably encouraged Jones by requiring him to accomplish impossible goals, Bainbridge and Stark (1979:293) summarize as follows:

> Even when a single individual dominates a group, the subculture-evolution model will apply to the extent that the followers also participate in pushing the group toward cultism. In this case, the needs of the followers and their social relationships with the leader may have served as a psychopathology amplifier, reflecting back to Jones his own narcissism multiplied by the strength of their unreasonable hopes.

Johnson (1979) explained many of the happenings surrounding Jonestown in terms of the "dilemmas" of charismatic leadership. Johnson's central thesis is that charismatic leadership is tenuous and precarious and is in continual need of reinforcement. Assuming that the charismatic leader seeks to continue and strengthen his or her leadership position and power, Johnson (1979:316–19) outlines several strategies useful to the leader: (1) creating member dependency; (2) seeking organizational growth; (3) delegating authority to trusted close associates; (4) establishing contact with representatives of the wider society (which may be perceived as hostile); (5) seeking an isolated environment; (6) modifying and strengthening the ideology that justifies the group's existence, goals, and strategies; (7) establishing a sharp break between task activities and socioemotional activities; (8) developing special rituals that reaffirm or dramatically express member commitment; and (9) insuring that the rituals are so dramatic and overpowering emotionally that they appear sincere.

Johnson realized that the application of this model to the Temple involves an ex-post-facto interpretation, and so he fleshed out the model with information about Jones, his followers, Temple activities, and defectors. First, Jones created dependency in his followers by requiring them to contribute their resources to the Temple, and later by requiring them to sign incriminating statements about themselves. Next, he promoted organizational and political growth by moving to California, involving himself and the Temple in community activities, road trips, and recruitment drives, and in establishing contact with numerous state and national political figures. This expansion also required more coordination and led to a division of labor involving an inner circle. Possibly losing part of his control (due to size, defections, and a bad press), Jones decided to migrate with his followers to an extremely isolated environment (creating even more dependency), where he could more readily control daily activities and communications with the outside world. At least two accounts indicate that Jones was conscious of the relationship between an isolated environment and increased control.

That the ideology supporting the Jonestown migration was strengthened and modified is indicated by numerous published reports. The idea of Jonestown as a "promised land" free from governmental interference and a place of "brotherly love" signaled a more intense ideology. Socialistic rhetoric also became more prevalent after the relocation, as indicated by Jones' contention that the group was being persecuted from all sides, and that the United States was a hopelessly racist and imperialistic society. To differentiate between the grueling work activities required of members to provide food, clothing, and shelter in a hot, humid jungle and the socioemotional (religious) motivation of members, Jones used marathon sessions of preaching and testimonials. He intensified the ritualistic practices of "emergency sessions," "education hours," and "white night drills." This ritualistic behavior became more and more dramatic and overpowering within a milieu that surely would have seemed bizarre to outsiders. Jones's claim to supernatural powers may have persisted right up until the end. His admonitions to his followers to commit "revolutionary suicide," and his promise that they would meet in "another place," indicates this, as well as his prophecy that Representative Ryan's airplane would "fall from the sky." (The plane, of course, never left the ground.)

Journalistic accounts, in a less abstract mode, have indicated several reasons for members joining the Temple and accepting the influence of Jones. Kilduff and Javers (1978:68–69), for example, stated that, at least initially, Jones was a kindly preacher, a warm soul who addressed the old ladies as "dear" in a soft baritone voice. He also was a caring humanitarian who was working toward social change and a new and better world. Like Father Divine, Jones provided physical comfort and help with financial matters such as paying the rent, utilities, and food bills. Jones provided "miracles" in terms of faith healing to alleviate the health problems of those who might not have understood the aloofness of a modern physician or the scientific nature of modern medicine. Jones offered a simplicity of lifestyle for some and excitement for others. As Wooden (1981:57) proclaimed, "Those who came under the spell of this man were made to order for his cult gospel. 'Racial equality' and 'social justice' were music to their ears." Whether Jones was a concerned humanitarian, as his followers at first must have believed, or a crazed drug-addicted con artist and charlatan, as others have claimed, makes little difference in the end. According to the theorem of W. I. Thomas, if people define situations as real, they are real in their consequences. The consequences of following Jones to Guyana were certainly real.

It is a mistake, Barker (1986) asserts, to compare new religious movements with one another. For example, the charge of brainwashing simply does not find support in research on Jonestown. Wright (1984) also warns against overreliance on brainwashing theories. These two observers note that believers in such movements willingly committed themselves.

A different view of the Jonestown episode is provided by Hall (1988, 1990). Directing attention to the brainwashing charges against People's Temple, he contends that such charges are not sufficient explanations of what happened on that fateful day in Guyana. Since this process is evident in a number of other organizations, it must be considered a necessary but still not a sufficient cause to explain the mass murders and suicides. Such an explanation does not answer the question of why suicide became a "rational" course of action. Hall calls the People's Temple Agricultural Project an apocalyptic sect. Such sects tend to move to one of three "ideal" possibilities: (1) Adventism of the preapocalyptic type, (2) preapocalyptic war, or (3) postapocalyptic Adventism. Hall argues that Jonestown was caught in a dilemma. The origins of Jonestown were deeply imbedded in a rather vague apocalyptic evangelism. The Guyanese settlement attempted to transcend the apocalyptic claim by creating a "heaven on earth." As this was frustrated, members of the People's Temple were drawn into the imagery of a preapocalyptic war against the forces of established religion. According to Hall, when this view was aborted, the Jonestown group had to retreat to war with the established order. In this context, revolutionary suicide was seen as a way of responding to the frustration of going beyond apocalyptic conflict with the establishment. Revolutionary suicide was a way of overcoming frustration and moving beyond the earth to heaven, albeit not an earthly existence. As Hall (1990) puts it:

> Though they paid the total price of death for their ultimate commitment and though they achieved little except perhaps sustenance of their own collective sense of honor, those who won this hollow victory cannot have it taken away from them (288).

We may never be completely satisfied with explanations for the Jonestown tragedy. Attempts are still being made to fit it more accurately into a theoretical framework and to draw upon the raw data in an effort to formulate new insights into the phenomenon. As it stands, we must guard against the tendency to place Jonestown upon a Procrustean bed to make it fit one schema or another. As with all human behavior, religious behavior is sometimes more complicated than the categories we develop to explain it.

Although the spirit that guided the Jonestown tragedy seems alien to our idea of religion, it was by no means unique. Consider, for example, the tribulations and problems of the Branch Davidians of Waco, Texas, in 1993, which seem to reflect to some degree the spirit of Jonestown (see *Time*, 1993). The arsenal of weapons accumulated by members of the Branch Davidian movement and the costly battles they waged with agents of the Bureau of Alcohol, Tobacco and Firearms as well as the Federal Bureau of Investigations seem reminiscent of the People's Temple and its troubles with the U.S. government, which the courts have decided were the fault of the government. After a siege of fifty-one days, the confrontation ended with a deadly conclusion; approximately eighty-one members of the group, including their leader David Koresh, died in a fire apparently set by the group itself. However, we should not take this incident as normative of all the new religious movements referred to by the media as *cults*. As James Beckford points out (1993), the media focus on the newsworthy and the scandalous and thus report on such incidents. But probably more than 95 percent of the activity of the new religious movements is relatively harmless, despite its deviance from what we usually call the normal.

SATANISM

As a response to Christian beliefs, Satanism is the worship of the devil. Some forms of Satanism are as old as the Middle Ages. However, they may not be directly tied to the "Christian" variety but may be called Luciferism and may use the name of Satan in their practices but do so without connection to any religious theology (Barker 1989:199). Melton (1986:76) provides an insightful summary of Satanism:

> Traditionally associated with Satanism are a number of practices including: the black mass, the essence of which is the performing (usually through parody) of Christian worship (e.g., repeating the Lord's Prayer backwards) and/or the desecration of sacred objects (i.e., trampling a sacramental host underfoot, spitting on a cross, etc.); the ritual slaughter of animals, usually a dog or cat; the murder, mutilation and/or rape of a human victim; and black magic, the invocation of Satan for the purpose of working malevolent sorcery.

While the gruesome nature of these rituals make for good TV plots and a theme for novels, some say that true Satanism has failed to grow into the status of a movement and has been perpetuated more by anti-Satan writers than by adherents to satanic precepts. Melton (1986:76) makes this point, as do Forsyth and Olivier (1990:287), who state that there is no "clear support" for accepting either an increase or a decrease in satanic activity. What has definitely increased recently is media attention to Satanism and "rumor-panics" about satanic activity. Victor (1990) located twenty-one sites of rumor-panics since 1984 and found that almost all occurred in economically declining small towns and rural areas. He (1990:290) is disturbed about the amount of money being made by those on the lecture circuit who are:

> ...cultivating fear about satanic cults. Many of these same Satan-hunters have broadcast their claims to national audiences on the television talk-shows of Geraldo Rivera, Oprah Winfrey, and Sally Jessy Rafael. Their wild, unsubstantiated claims about Satanism have the effect of inflaming passions. Many innocent people can be victimized by their appeals to the scapegoating hysteria.

Bromley (1991:49) summarizes the elements of "media Satanism" in several distinct elements. First, there are local instances such as the desecration of graveyards or animal mutilation. Second, there are attacks on heavy metal music as containing hidden satanic messages. Third, there are confessions by "survivors" of occult rituals which include tales of cannibalism.

In another study Victor (1991) found that not only those in economically depressed areas are affected by rumors of satanic activity. He describes his participant observation of a psychiatric seminar titled "Culture, Cults and Psychotherapy: Exploring Satanic and Other Cult Behavior" sponsored by Harding Hospital in a suburb of Columbus, Ohio, in March 1990. The main speakers, a social worker and a clinical psychologist, presented materials on satanic cults and the ritual torture of children and on the testimonies of patients diagnosed as having multiple personality disorder and supposedly "survivors" of satanic cult torture as children. The seminar included 370 social workers, nurses, psychiatrists, psychologists, clergymen, and counselors. When the speakers were pressed for external corroborating evidence for a satanic cult conspiracy they referred to the pop-culture books on Satanism as useful sources of information and then asked members of the audience to raise their hands if they had encountered cases of "ritual abuse" in their practices. About two-thirds of the audience raised their hands. Victor (1991:276) contends that the process of "group-think" operates on professionals to make them accept the satanic cult stories as true when many are without corroborated substantiation. Victor (1991:279) gives the following description of a conversation he had at the seminar:

> A psychiatric nurse who worked at Harding Hospital was seated beside me. I asked her if she believed what the presenters had reported about satanic cults, including the idea of an international network of criminal Satanists? She responded, "Definitely!"… I then asked her how she could be so certain that Kaye's and Kline's presentations were true. What she told me reveals the crux of the whole satanic-cult phenomenon. She quite candidly said that the existence of Satanism confirms her belief in God. Being a bit mystified by this response, I asked, "Why?" She said: "Anyone who is Christian and believes in God must also believe in the existence of Satan. Satanists believe in Satan and work for him, just like people who believe in God work for God. So I know that God and goodness really exist.

Hicks (1991) notes that the police are giving satanic crime presentations which resemble the offerings of a huckster. Elsewhere (1990) he has also outlined how the mechanics of law-enforcement training seminars lead to exaggerated claims of satanic activity and unsubstantiated claims of the incidence of satanic crime. He states (1991:276–77):

> I argue that the current preoccupation of law-enforcers with satanism and cults has not been prompted by anything new: the phenomenon has a firm historical and cultural context. Further, I suggested that the news media are largely responsible for the law-enforcement model of cult activity, since the evidence officers cite for cult mayhem is generally based on nothing more than newspaper stories.… I suggest that for police the actual problem with cults, in terms of their threat to public order, is very small, has nonsupernatural explanations, and requires no new law-enforcement resources.

It may be that law enforcement officials and news reporters have an interesting symbiotic relationship when it comes to accounts of satanic and other cult activity. For example, van Driel and van Belzen (1990:87) contend that reporters go to police headquarters, city hall, and federal courthouses in an attempt to get news most efficiently. These authors contend that this may be the reason that the United States, when compared to the former West Germany and the Netherlands, has the most negative coverage of cult activity. This includes a "crime approach" which often contains a "mafia scenario" complete with conspiracy, national organization, brutality, and strong-arm tactics as components.

One approach to understanding the Satanism scare is known as *constructionist* (Richardson, Best, and Bromley, 1991:3ff.) This approach is in direct contrast to perspectives that see social problems like Satanism as objective, that is, as perspectives which take for granted the reality of these phenomena. The constructionist perspective questions this reality; its suggests, instead, that such problems are not natural phenomena but the product of social processes. Attention, thus, is focused on understanding how these processes have constructed a certain kind of reality. Thus, in the constructionist view, Satanism is the result of social processes; it is important to discover who is making the claims, why they are being made, what is their content, and what is the response of others.

According to these authors, several sources of appeal contribute to the construction of the myth of a satanic "epidemic":

> During the 1980s, elements of apparently unrelated social movements converged in the cause of antisatanism. Each movement brought its own set of concepts and concerns. Five precursor movements—fundamentalist Christianity, the anticult movement, the development of "satanic churches," the new wave of child saving, and the survivor/recovery movement—made particularly important contributions to social construction of the satanist menace (Richardson, Best, and Bromley, 1991:5–6).

A particularly important aspect in the construction of a Satanism scare is the association of presumed satanic activity with the endangerment of children (cf. Nathan, 1991; Best, 1991). According to Nathan, concern for the exploitation of children began in the late 1970s. During that decade women diagnosed as having multiple personality disorders began to "remember" being sexually assaulted as children by adults involved in sadomasochistic sex, in many instances this abuse was associated with "satanic ritual." This anti-Satanism movement was given added fuel in the early 1980s with charges of massive child sex abuse at a preschool in a Los Angeles suburb. Pupils at the school spoke of sacramental animal killings as well as sexual activity in churches and graveyards. Upon the heels of these assertions, similar reports came from across the country. The claims suggested a widespread, organized movement, identified by many with Satanism. Yet there were numerous inconsistencies in the reports, and legitimate researchers failed to validate them. In addition, some children who had reported abuse indicated that they had exaggerated or lied.

Bromley (1991:95ff.) points to the claim that the satanists make children their target as powerful in building up both the myth of and resistance to satanic cults. He contends that the link between Satanism and sexual abuse of children is what makes the image of Satanism acceptable in a basically secular age. The charges made against satanic cults is validated by connecting them with *real* problems. The reports of so-called occult survivors (Jenkins and Maier-Katkin, 1991) also fuel the flames of the satanist scare. The claims of survival by those involved in a twelve-step group, *Overcomers Victorious,* is part of the foundation of the dangers of Satanism.

These arguments are not presented to the reader to indicate that Satanism is a total fabrication. Traditional satanist groups tend to be quite small, consisting of three to five people, and to have a short life span, usually a few weeks or months (Melton 1986:77). Similarly, Barker (1989:48) contends that there have been several instances of young people who experimented with satanic practices but that:

> Most people who dabble in satanic or black magic rituals quickly get bored and pass on to less unsavory pursuits, but there seems to be little doubt that certain aspects of Satanism appeal to some psychopaths with sadistic tendencies, and, obviously enough, 60 crimes involving Satanism is 60 crimes too many [referring to a five-year period from 1983 to 1988 wherein only 60 crimes in the U.S. were listed by the police as involving Satanism].

Cultic Satanism, however, is not the same as that practiced by several well-known organizations, chief among them the Church of Satan. Founded in San Francisco in 1966 by Anton S. LaVey, a consultant to the police department and later to the movie industry, this group (which may have never had more than five hundred active members) promotes the practice of selfish values as long as they do no harm to others.

The Church of Satan has recently decreased in size; the Temple of Set was one of the few satanic groups in the LaVey tradition that lasted into the eighties. Schisms in the church and the growing reclusiveness of LaVey led to a vanishing membership. Some leaders of the LaVey tradition formed the Church of Satanic Brotherhood in 1973, but this group lasted only a short time. One incident was staged in St. Petersburg, Florida, at which John DeHaven, a former leader of the Detroit, Michigan, Church of Satan, professed his conversion to evangelical Christianity (Melton, 1986:78).

Since part of the egocentrism of the Church of Satan can be related somewhat to the self-centeredness of the New Age movement, we may return to certain aspects of Satanism when we describe New Age occultism. For our purposes, Satanism as a movement has recently received much more attention than other movements because of the intrigue associated with some reported practices and rituals of certain of its members.

THE NEW AGE MOVEMENT

Nearly any work attempting to corral the definition and number of New Age organizations will start with a statement that *New Age* refers to a nebulous set of ideas, groups, and publications. The terms *human potential, self-help philosophy, occultism, neo-paganism, creativity, mysticism, crystalogy, spiritualism, channeling, psychic counseling, parapsychology, astrology,* and many others are associated with the term *New Age.* Paul Kurtz (1989:365) has given a good introduction to the New Age in a special issue of the *Skeptical Inquirer:*

> The "New Age" is an amorphous term used to designate a range of popular beliefs and attitudes. It includes under its banner widely disparate individuals and points of view. Broadly conceived, it is a protest movement, expressing a distrust of science and seeking to develop new levels of "spiritual" awareness.

Similarly, Barker (1989:189), after pointing out the New Age label has been applied rather loosely by proponents and opponents of the movement alike, states:

> Most people connected with the New Age would see themselves as seekers who are exploring new and exciting frontiers. Several individuals belong to a number of different groups—some will also belong to a more traditional religious group, but be wanting to open themselves up to new ideas and experiences; others are "New Age" through having rejected traditional religious and philosophical options as bankrupt…. There is no central organization.

Maureen O'Hara (1989), in a theoretical piece which explores the increase in attention being given to New Age activities, says that scientific materialism has weakened religion's ability to soothe the nonmaterial ills and needs of contemporary folk. She states (1989:371) that New Agers enter into a miasma of myths, pseudopriests, pseudoscientists. Her interpretation of the movement makes it equivalent to drug dealers, psychotherapists, and fundamentalists preachers who "spin" out meaning to those suffering the fragmentation of the late modern age.

This movement has some identifiable spokespersons. Kurtz (1989:365) states that these are "'Baba Ram Das,' David Spangler, Judith Skutch, and George Leonard.... The New Age, in its rejection of the establishment, is a continuation of the counterculture of the 1960s and early 1970s, although today it goes beyond the ideological protests of that era. It has penetrated many aspects of American culture: the publishing industry, the mass media, and even corporate America has embraced its techniques and values."

One of the aspects of the New Age movement that has received much media attention is *channeling,* a term describing "what supposedly occurs when an individual serves as a conduit for some otherworldly entity to communicate with people of this world. It can take many forms: The channeler might be wide awake, in a trance, or even asleep ('dream channeling'). The channeler may speak or produce automatic writing, or even operate through a Ouija board" (Alcock, 1989:380).

Alcock (1989) identifies several well-known modern channelers (e.g., Penny Torres, a California housewife who channels a 2,000-year-old woman called Mafu; J.Z. Knight, who channels Ramtha, a native of Atlantis who conquered the world 35,000 years ago; Elwood Babbitt, who channels Einstein, etc.). Some channelers believe that there are historical entities who served as mediums, including the Oracle of Delphi, Moses, and Jesus Christ. In the not-to-distant past Emanuel Swedenborg (1688–1772) was known for this mystic abilities to converse with the souls of departed men and women. Helene Petrovna Blavatsky (1831–91), the founder of the Theosophical Society, claimed to have astral access to Tibetan mahatmas. Recently, Jane Roberts (1929–84) supposedly presented the communications of Seth, an unseen entity, in such a fashion that her husband, Robert Butts, could take down the utterances verbatim using his own type of shorthand. Alcock (1989:382) connects much of the interest in channeling and New Age occultism to the popularity of a contemporary movie star:

> The interest produced by Seth developed to the level of frenzy when Shirley MacLaine began her New Age writings about entities, channeling, and related themes. Like a latter-day Madame Blavatsky, MacLaine has ranged the world in search of spiritual understanding. In 1983, her book *Out on a Limb* became a best-seller, with more than four million copies being sold. Because of her fame, this book brought many people to the occult bookshelf who otherwise might have stayed away. Three years later, her ABC-TV miniseries introduced millions of others to the notion of unseen entities.

In another view of channelers, Babbie (1990) participated in the presentation of one person in the Los Angeles area. Babbie contends that channeling is not new. He views the current interest in the process on the fragmentation of modern society and the way in which many create their own religious reality (262):

> Commensurate with the view of God residing within us and the view that our physical reality is an illusion is the view that each individual creates his or her own reality. This applies most specifically to our life experiences and altogether denies the notion of victimhood or martyrdom. If someone is experiencing difficulties at work or in a relationship, for example, the entities I've studied are quite consistent in suggesting that he or she look to him or herself for explanations and solutions—rather than blaming problems on the others involved.

Graham Reed (1989) has asked the straightforward yet complex question about channelers, "What makes them do it?" He says (1989:387–88) that the activity meets a variety of needs, among them:

1. Ego-enhancements… It produces, at least among believers, attention, respect, gratitude, and even affection.…
2. Compensation. Engagement in channeling provides a counterweight against the perceived drabness and lack of excitement of the individual's everyday life. The individual is elevated to the position of seer, oracle, and spiritual advisor.…
3. Material Rewards…the successful channeler can give high monetary return for minimal training and capital investment.

Reed says that some observers claim that channelers are mentally ill people. While he cautions (1989:388–89) about attaching diagnostic labels, he nevertheless contends that the behaviors exhibited by channelers during their séances resemble certain psychotic symptomatology, including systematized delusions, formal thought disorders characteristic of schizophrenia, and the blurring of ego boundaries. If the channelers are not psychotic (in the sense that they may be able to turn the "symptoms" off and on at will), then what about channelers who are neurotic or suffer from a personality disorder? Reed outlines the activities of channeling and contends that, from a clinical perspective, one can identify the following components: depersonalization, ego-splitting, hysterical amnesia, trances, and trancelike states. According to Reed, these classical examples of dissociation are listed in the *Diagnostic and Statistical Manual of Mental Disorders* (DSM III) under the heading "Dissociative Disorders." He ends (1989:390) his argument by stating that channelers:

...may reasonably be regarded as persons of hysterical personality, displaying classical dissociative features. Their motives are characteristic of their personality type, including ego-enhancement and a need for attention.... The reiterativeness, diffuse structure, and trite content of these statements place them well within the intellectual capacity of any fluent but uninhibited individual, without any assistance from occult or other sources.

This description and evaluation of New Age channeling contains the seeds of much of the debate about New Age activities, whether they involve crystal power, pyramid power, spiritualism, possession (demonic or otherwise), psychokinesis, creationism, vibrational oscillation, and what Gordon (1989) calls the "Shirley MacLaine phenomenon" known as "sharing." Reed's analysis is bounded by systematic thought and concepts. New Age philosophy contends that such systematization is too narrow, too constraining, too objective, and too Western a paradigm.

In 1972 Ted Schultz (1989:375) dropped out of college, left his home in Illinois, and set out in search of the New Age movement. He immersed himself "in the whole range of twentieth-century mysticism, spirituality, and alternative culture: yoga, Tai Chi, Buddhism, Taoism, meditation, vegetarianism, and various occult and psychic practices." Later as a graduate student at Cornell studying insect evolution, Schultz (1989:376) contended that New Age adherents are not drawn to it in search of objectivity and systematic knowledge, but mostly for "the tangible effects on their lives generated by 'subjective arts' like trance induction, meditation, physical therapies, (like yoga and massage), psychological counseling, and the pleasure of love and friendship within a shared social context." He further contended that there are a number of things that can be done to mend the rift between those subjectively inclined and those concerned more with "rationally comprehensible realms." First, he pointed out (1989:379) that we need to accept that both views are important. "It's easy to mock New Agers, but I think a far more profitable enterprise would be to research and understand those unmet human needs that are compelling tens of thousands of people to turn to the New Age for satisfaction. We must somehow learn to nourish these nonrational dimensions in ways that are not antithetical to rationalism and science."

Second, Schultz also believes that we need to continue to empirically test claims of New Agers—particularly those beliefs espoused by tens of thousands of people. Third, Schultz (1989:378) is of the opinion that we have to offer people something better than what they currently have because our culture has outgrown the mythologies of the past:

In the light of modern science and society, these ancient world-views no longer hold any explanatory power—but they still hold emotional power. Since we haven't replaced the old myths with new ones, some of our contemporaries periodically reconstruct hybrid mythologies out of the rubble of the old stories, investing them with belief and then dogmatically defending them. This is as true of the current wave of Christian fundamentalism as it is of the New Age.

Schultz reminds us again that religious activities of various kinds appear on the scene to compensate for some unmet needs of groups of people. The New Age conglomeration also reminds us of Stark's (1992:416) adage that all religions start as cult movements. Even though there is no central organization to the New Age movement, Barker (1989:189–91) identifies several resource centers in Britain that specialize in books, candles, crystals, and other "curiosities" associated with New Age thought. She also mentions the Findhorn community in the north of Scotland and the Farm in the United States as New Age communities, contending that there are "hundreds" of other such groups scattered around Europe and North America. Since New Agers are not aggressive proselytizers and are unlikely to be under the control of authoritarian leaders, the New Age movement will probably not command the attention other new religions have had in the past three decades.

THE HARE KRISHNA MOVEMENT

The Hare Krishna (spelled Krsna in Sanskrit) movement began in this country with the arrival in 1965, at the age of the seventy, of Abhay Charan De, also known as His Divine Grace A. C. Rhaktivedanta Swami Prabhupada. As Judah (1974:464) has told it:

When he [the swami] arrived in New York he began chanting the names of Krishna to the rhythm of his kartals (small Indian cymbals), while sitting beneath a tree in Tompkins Park on the Lower East Side. Soon, however, he attracted many about him, a number of whom were hippies. The following year a temple was established in New York. Other centers soon appeared, close to the hippie community in the Haight-Ashbury of San Francisco, in Los Angeles, Berkeley, and elsewhere.

Swami Prabhupada offered his followers a connection to Krishna, one of the most widely revered of Hindu divinities, through a chain of "disciplic succession" (Daner 1976:107). He taught devotion to Krishna and translated the *Bhagavad-gita* (the sacred book of the Vedic tradition) under the title *The Bhagavad-gita as It Is* (published in 1968 by Collier-Macmillan). This book, along with the *Bhagavatum,* outlines the philosophy for devotees of Hare Krishna to follow.

Devotees are required to try to obtain Krishna Consciousness through *bhakti,* or loving service to the deity Krishna. According to Daner (1976:35), eight acts are meant to bring about the proper feeling of humility and self-surrender to *bhakti:*

1. Recognizing Krsna as one's only refuge.
2. Service to spiritual master (guru).
3. Reading and listening to the *Bhagavad-gita* and the *Srinad-Bhagavatum,* Krsna's pastimes, and the writings of the guru.
4. Sankirtana, that is, singing the names and praises of Krsna.
5. Thinking constantly of the name, form and pastimes of Krsna.
6. Serving the feet of the deities, seeing, touching, and worshiping the deities.
7. Performing rites and ceremonies learned from the guru, such as putting *vaisnava* signs on one's body, taking the remains of an offering to the deity as *prasada* [usually food], drinking the water used to wash the deity, and so on.
8. Prostrating before the deity forms and the spiritual master.

In addition to these aspects of *bhakti,* devotees entering a Hare Krishna temple are to turn over all their worldly possessions to the temple and follow four prescriptive rules listed by Daner (1976:60–61) as (1) no gambling, (2) no intoxicants, (3) no illicit sex, and (4) no eating of meat, fish, or eggs.

The International Society for Krishna Consciousness (ISKCON) has become an international organization, and maintains financial stability through a variety of techniques. In addition to requiring the surrender of its adherents' worldly possessions, including money and bank accounts, the movement teaches devotees to beg for money or donations in return for copies of *Back to Godhead: The Magazine of the Hare Krishna Movement.* Another venture, which Daner (1976:59) considers the "real backbone of ISKCON's economic success," is the Spiritual Sky Incense Company. While incense manufacturing is done in Los Angeles by devotees, sales are handled mainly by computer and by persons outside of Hare Krishna. Other scented products made for ISKCON by Avon, such as oils, shampoo, and soap, are sold to businesses and boutiques throughout the country. This type of economic activity was positively sanctioned by Swami Prabhupada.

The swami died in 1977. According to early reports from ISKCON, "his disciples are carrying forward the movement he started" (*Back to Godhead*, 1978, vol. 13, no. 4); the succession of authority within the movement was thought out before Prabhupada's death. As to the future of ISKCON, some researchers have indicated that as the group's novelty wears off, its appeal to young people will dwindle. This, along with a more "introversionist position" and civil suits against the organization for invoking emotional distress (see, for example, *People*, September 12, 1983:108, 112), may have produced a reduction in membership and less visibility for the group as a whole.

Barker (1989:147) points out that many ISKCON devotees consider their religion to be an ancient and traditional one; they regard the Prabhupada organization as the only "new" part of the whole movement. Barker calls our attention to the difficulty of including the large number of worshipers in ISKCON temples in Britain as members of a cult. In fact, most of their fellow Asians in Britain regard these devotees as little more than members of simply one Hindu tradition among many traditions. Nevertheless, recent reports (Rochford, 1989) show that there are continuing internal conflicts within the Western Hare Krishna organization, and the its organizational structure is crumbling. Its members have been prohibited from soliciting airports, have admitted to having weapons stored at some of their farms (where they had been harassed), and have been involved in civil suits and other difficulties involving charges of harboring a child snatched by a noncustodial parent (Melton, 1986:163–64).

Recent research has shown, however, that the effects of membership in ISKCON are not so detrimental to adherents' mental health as its opponents claim. Barker's work (1989) tones down the reports of hysteria associated with cult brainwashing, kidnapping, and claims of torture and abuse of members ISKCON and other cults. More specifically, Weis and Mendoza (1990:173) reported on their use of standard personality scales and a 38-item Mental Health Inventory with a sample of Krishna devotees. The researchers found that "greater degrees of acculturation were associated with greater subjective well-being," and that "no evidence was found that adverse personality traits are associated with greater acculturation into the movement" (181). The future of the Hare Krishna movement may well rest with these devotees who have become integrated into a movement that no longer experiences the level of hostility and criticism that it once faced. The future of the overall group, however, is still hard to predict.

THE UNIFICATION CHURCH

Probably one of the best-known new expressions in religious life to develop in this country in the past three decades is the Unification Church and its adherents—the "Moonies." The mass media have extensively covered this movement and its involvement in religious and legal controversy stemming from accusations of brainwashing of converts, illegal solicitation of funds by members, questions about the tax-free status of the church, and, in perhaps a more crucial domain, the issue of whether guarantees of religious freedom extend to the varied activities of the Unification Church. The church as also been investigated by the Internal Revenue Service, Justice Department, and Immigration Service (Lofland 1977:334), and has run afoul of the law in Britain and other countries (Barker, 1984).

The leader of the movement, the Reverend Sun Myung Moon, was convicted of federal income tax evasion in 1982 and sentenced to eighteen months imprisonment in the federal correctional institution at Danbury, Connecticut. He served from July 20, 1984, to July 4, 1985, received early release for good behavior, and was allowed to satisfy part of his sentence by spending nights at a halfway house in Brooklyn, New York. After leaving the halfway house on August 20, 1985, the Reverend Moon was given a welcome-home party in Washington, D.C., where he told more than sixteen hundred members of the National Committee for God and Freedom that he held no bitterness because of his imprisonment. Some federal and state officials and numerous religious leaders rallied around Moon, contending that his imprisonment was unjust and a prime example of government intrusion into religious matters.

Just who is this man, and how has his movement become such an unlikely *cause célèbre* in American religious circles? Robbins et al. (1976:114) report that Moon is a Korean evangelist who suffered imprisonment by the Communists in North Korea in 1947 and was liberated by the Americans during the Korean War. Seeing himself as the Messiah, he received a divine revelation embodied in his book *Divine Principle* (1974). Moon, who founded the Unification Church in Korea in 1954, first visited the United States in 1965. The movement, however, had already begun before his arrival here. Sociologists as well as others are fortunate that the early history of the church was chronicled in an ethnographic description by John Lofland in his book *Doomsday Cult* (1966), which was later updated and enlarged (1977). We are equally fortunate to have a recent and exceptionally well-documented account of the Moonies in Britain, the United States, and other countries by Barker in her book *The Making of a Moonie* (1984).

In their early days in the United States, the Moonies were a small group of persons who made up the American wing of a larger group of millenarians in Korea. They believed that Sun Myung Moon was a "Christ-Messiah," who taught that the world was to be transformed and made perfect by 1967. In his descriptive introduction to the DP or Divine Precepts cult (Lofland's pseudonym for the Moonies), which Lofland originally studied from 1959 through mid-1963, the researcher (1977:4) gives the following account of "Mr. Chang" (Lofland's pseudonym for Moon):

> During the late 1940s and early fifties, a young Korean electrical engineer, Mr. Soon Sun Chang, received a series of what he took to be messages from God, acknowledging him as none other than the returned Christ, the Lord of the Second Advent. Chang was also convinced that through these divine encounters, a new body of knowledge, the Divine Precepts, was being revealed to him. This doctrine unveiled the laws or principles by which God governs man...and disclosed the manner in which the perfected and eternal kingdom of God would shortly be established on earth.

From this start the Moonies grew to several hundred in and around Seoul, Korea, by the late 1950s. In 1959 Moon sent one of his earliest followers, an English-speaking former university professor, to the United States. Her efforts resulted initially in only a few converts; numerous problems arose in the course of establishing the cult. Lofland's (1977) "Postscript" stated that the DPs had grown to only thirty-five places in these two countries. According to Barker (1984:64), by 1969 the number of Western converts to the Unification Church probably did not exceed 250.

The Unification Church's belief in the establishment of the Kingdom of God on earth (originally predicted for 1967) apparently changed in 1964. The year 1967 now became the target date for the appearance of the "Spirit of Truth," which would appear in the sky and be visible to everyone in the world simultaneously. Upon its appearance, "low-level" spirits would descent to earth as "black blobs" and "hairy things." To interpret these creatures, people would have to turn to the DPs for understanding and guidance toward perfection, and would then convert to the church. As Lofland (1977:268) states, however, this would "only be the beginning of restoring the world to perfection. The actual work of making the entire world perfect would take until about the year 2000."

One important finding during the 1972–74 period of the movement was that the DPs used a polished recruitment method consisting of the strategies and components already described in Chapter 3. To review, Lofland (1977:305–14) outlines these steps as (1) picking up, (2) hooking, (3) encapsulating, (4) loving, and (5) committing. Barker (1984:94) believes that these practices may currently "persist to some extent," but she also describes recruitment processes much more resistible (1984:233) and less coercive than those used in the past.

The movement is based upon the ideas and revelations of the Reverend Moon. Primary principles (Lofland 1977:15–16) are that (1) creation consists of three stages (formation, growth, and perfection); (2) things exist in complementary association (male and female, positive and negative); (3) an action of give-and-take exists between complementary associations; (4) God created man so that he could exist in complementary association and experience the energy of life and the joy of love; (5) a spirit world and a material world exist, and man has a spirit body and a material body; and (6) Lucifer thwarted God's plan for man's spirit to grow through the three stages of development to perfection. According to Robbins et al. (1976:116–17):

> The goal of Reverend Moon's ministry is to enable man to overcome his "fallen nature" and to re-unite mankind into God's family, all of which is possible if enough persons internalize Unification principles.... Harmonious "give and take" (a key term) must prevail among family members, peers, social classes, and nations, and between God and man. When this prevails man will fulfill his true purpose of constituting God's perfect creation.

Another perspective is presented by Barker (1984), who contends that the sinister descriptions of life as a Moonie as controlled and regimented are not exactly what she found in her studies. She argues (258–59) that while Moonies do change after joining the movement, the change is not nearly as drastic as the anticultists contend. While some members do become "burned out" after long hours of fund raising, they are no more likely to do so than commuters traveling the monotonous routine of the white-collar world. Converts will have a wide variety of emotional and intellectual experiences as they go through victories and disillusionments similar to those of their non-Moonie counterparts. In the end, however, Barker, believes that the vast majority of Moonies will leave the movement on their own within a couple of years after their conversion.

In 1977 Lofland predicted that the Unification Church in the United States would become a has-been movement in the eighties. Leaders of the movement have not remained passive, however, and the imprisonment of the Reverend Moon may have given the movement new visibility and new allies if we can judge by the response to his release from prison. He may have gained new legitimacy by being the target of the government in the continuous battle over the principles of the separation of church and state.

The Unification Church has diversified its financial holdings and sent its members as missionaries all over the world. Increasingly common is member participation in one of the organization's numerous businesses. Bromley (1985:272) outlined in detail the economic structure of the Unification movement and identified the ways in which it "has created an economic conglomerate to underwrite its theological agenda." He further contends (273) that the movement is "a creature of the age in which it was wrought." Proof of this adaptability is the quickness the Unification Church to move into Moscow amidst the recent radical changes in the former Soviet Union.

However, the Unification Church, which has never had more than ten thousand members in the West, has fallen on hard times and lost a large proportion of its membership (Barker, 1989:216). Its supposedly vastly profitable enterprises are no longer making money and accusations of connections to foreign criminals, for example, the Japanese "mafia," have been raised. It is interesting to observe, as Parsons (1989) points out, how such a movement simultaneously encourages separation from the secular world while adapting to the elements of secular culture that will lead to success, and perhaps acceptance, in the religious market of the society. While rejecting some elements of the secular culture, movements like the Unification Church engage in a dialectic which alternates between deviance from worldly norms and adjustment to them. In this way such movements gradually become more compromised with the world.

SCIENTOLOGY

Scientology would not qualify for religious status according to some observers' definitions of religion. In fact, we might say that Scientology has created more controversy than any other new religious movement. Certainly it has been involved in numerous legal problems (Passas and Escimilla, 1992).

Nevertheless, Scientology bills itself as "an applied religious philosophy" in the small print of magazine advertisements, along with statements that "the Church of Scientology of California is a non-profit organization." Writings on new religious expressions give various figures for the size of the organization. Whitehead (1974:548) estimated the number of active Scientologists in America in the mid-70s at approximately thirty thousand, and the number of people touched by Scientology at approximately 2 million.

Scientology is the creation of L. Ron Hubbard, a writer of adventure and science fiction stories. According to one account (*Time*, December 11, 1978:36), Hubbard once said to a colleague, "Writing for a penny a word is ridiculous. If a man wanted to make a million dollars, the best way would be to start his own religion." Hubbard, who died in 1986, was also an explorer, a daredevil glider pilot, and an accomplished mariner who saw naval duty in World War II. His estranged son, Ronald E. De Wolf, has claimed that his father was a con man, and that his church is a sham.

The church has been plagued with internal rifts, IRS scrutiny, and the aftermath of the conviction and imprisonment of Hubbard's wife, Mary Sue, and several other Scientologists for bugging and burglarizing the Washington offices of the IRS, Federal Trade Commission, Drug Enforcement Administration, and the Justice, Treasury, and Labor departments. Another problem faced by Hubbard's Scientology organization is civil suits brought against the church. One suit resulted in an amazing award (in May 1985) of $39 million in punitive damages to a former Scientologist who claimed she had been duped into giving the organization money and into enrolling in fraudulently described engineering courses (*People*, June 10, 1985:59).

Scientology started out as Dianetics, a movement introduced to the world in 1950 by John Campbell, Jr., then editor of *Astounding Science Fiction*. Campbell began his writing career while still student at the Massachusetts Institute of Technology in 1928. Upon assuming the editorship of *Astounding Science Fiction*, he recruited and cultivated numerous writers, among them L. Ron Hubbard, who published a book entitled *Dianetics: The Modern Source of Mental Health* in 1950.

Originally Dianetics involved a theory of the mind that divided the psyche into two parts: the analytic mind and the reactive mind. The analytic mind is operative when people are fully conscious and rational; it contains information readily available to our awareness. The analytic mind may mislead us if it has obtained incorrect information; this, however, can be corrected by training and reeducation. The analytic mind sorts, assesses, and explores information, and comes up with interpretations and judgments appropriate for the situation. Like the analytic mind, the reactive mind aids the survival of the individual, but does so through conditioned reflexivity or reaction. Such conditioning is usually inaccessible to awareness and is not consciously learned. As Whitehead (1974:574–75) explained:

The engram, which is defined as an incident containing pain and uncon-
sciousness, is the basic building block of the Reactive Mind. All of man's
apparently inappropriate or "irrational" behavior which cannot be explained on the basis of false analytic information...stems from the engramic contents of the Reactive Mind. These engrams are stirred into
action...by any stimulus in the external world that resembles or is the
same as something in an engram. When such a stimulus appears, the Reactive Mind "keys in" and causes the individual to react in a manner
which would be appropriate were the present-time situation the same as
the past-time situation of the engram...the contents of the Reactive Mind
are responsible for neuroses, psychoses, and psychosomatic illness.

Therefore, if one is to become "cleared" of irrationalities and neuroses, one has to consciously confront past engramic incidents and
allow them to discharge their force and influence. For Dianetics, the
way to discharge engrams is through a process of auditing or listening; auditors question and command in an effort to allow the subject,
called the *preclear*, to recognize and recall past incidents. Through the
processing of the preclear through these incidents, the person theoretically becomes "clear," or a totally rational person.

Whether we evaluate Scientology as a hucksterism in which basic
concepts of psychology are woven into an argotic style of expression
and ontology or as the ultimate technique for arriving at the truth, the
fact remains that for many people Scientology is religion. As Whitehead (1974:565) proclaimed, "It is part of Hubbard's genius to have
invented a system which, like Alchemy, can move from the mundane
to the mystical with a good long stretch of wizardry in between."

Stark and Bainbridge (1985) alluded to the fact that Scientology is
continually increasing the number and stretching the conceptualization of the *statuses* its members can attain. A constantly expanding set
of statuses provides continual opportunities to progress, grow, and
get closer to a perfect state of being. In 1950 Dianetics offered two statuses to members (preclear and clear); in 1954, six; in 1965, eight; in
1970, after clearance had been attained, forty-one statuses; and in the
1982 booklet *From Clear to Eternity*, sixty-four statuses were offered.
Part of the alchemy of Scientology, then, relies on a system that "*always* includes statuses that no member has yet attained" (Stark and
Bainbridge 1985:276).

Melton (1986:132) says that the estimate of Scientology's active
membership is in the tens of thousands, and that approximately 3
million persons worldwide have received some kind of service from
Scientology. More recently Scientology has claimed 8 million members and over 1,100 churches, missions, and groups in 69 countries

(*USA Today*, August 2–4, 1991:6A–7A). The movement has also continued its hostile stance toward the Internal Revenue Service, a fight that started in the 1950s when Scientology first had its tax-exempt status revoked by the IRS. Typical of these ads, presented as a "Public Service by the Church of Scientology International," is the one that appeared as a full-page in *USA Today* (September 3, 1991:8B), of the alleged physical, verbal, and vindictive abuses leveled against U.S. citizens by IRS agents and U.S. marshals carrying out attachment and eviction orders. The banner headline reads, "Don't you kill my Daddy!" It is accompanied by a color picture of a young girl, mouth open as if screaming and clinching her fists in apparent distress.

Scientology, like the Unification Church, has expanded into several economic areas, but it continues to receive much of its money from fees charged to interested persons and the appeal of Hubbard's *Dianetics,* which is advertised on late-night television and through the print media. The current life of Scientology appears linked to the success of these advertisements and the support it is able to generate by fighting the IRS. This is particularly true in light of a study by Ross (1988) on forty-eight longtime members of Scientology which reports no negative findings about the effect of membership on individuals. Using standard scales form the Minnesota Multiple Personality Inventory (MMPI) and other well-known measuring devices, Ross (1988:635) assents that "the belief that membership in the Church of Scientology invariably leads to personality disintegration and mental illness cannot be confirmed by the present study: if any conclusion is to be drawn, it may be in the opposite direction." Ross further contends that joining Scientology has produced an increase in social ease and in the effectiveness of goal-directed behavior, and that its joiners were unlikely to have been unhappy or unstable prior to joining the movement.

TRANSCENDENTAL MEDITATION

Transcendental Meditation (TM) was started in this country by the Hindu teacher Marharishi Mahesh Yogi in the last sixties. His followers included the Beatles, the Rolling Stones, and Mia Farrow (Needleman, 1970). Transcendental Meditation is based upon the idea that one can become more in tune with cosmic consciousness and obtain a happier state of mind or inner peace by meditation during which one repeats a mantra. The mantra is a word, phrase, or sound given to a recruit by an initiator. According to Needleman (1970:137):

Initiation is the procedure whereby the mantra is imparted. To receive this initiation, the aspirant need only attend two introductory lectures and be interviewed. He is requested to refrain from drugs or any spiritual practice for a period of about two weeks both before and after being given the mantra. This is so he will be clear in his own mind as to the results, or lack of results, of transcendental meditation.

Mantras are privatized in that initiators or instructors "interview" initiates and give them the mantra that "best fits their personality." These judgments are made on information obtained about the person's health, education, profession, and marital status. After receiving the mantra, initiates are instructed to sit quietly and comfortably for about twenty minutes in the morning and in the evening. They are to repeat the mantra quietly to themselves, and if the mind begins to wander, they are to slowly bring their attention back to the repetition (Needleman, 1970:138). They are also encouraged to keep the mantra to themselves, for to tell it to someone would possibly destroy its impact. Stark and Bainbridge (1985:288) have suggested that "in fact, the mantras were assigned purely on the basis of the new meditator's age and were taken from a list of just sixteen Sanskrit words," and that one reason for the secrecy surrounding the mantra may be to keep initiates collectively ignorant. The theory behind TM is that persons will become more relaxed, easier to get along with, and happier by meditating each day. Furthermore, "[N]o problems of human life would remain if only enough people practiced transcendental meditation. War, poverty, injustice, and crime would vanish, permitting humanity happily to fulfill its function in the cosmos..." (Needleman, 1970:134).

Even though TM has died down in the United States (see, for example, Stark and Bainbridge 1985:384–403 in their chapter titled "The Rise and Decline of Transcendental Meditation"), the Maharishi has recently been rekindling the movement with organizational changes and a renewed geopolitical zeal to reduce global violence. To accomplish a heaven on earth, TM leaders called for conferences labeled a "Taste of Utopia." Two conferences were held in Fairfield, Iowa, in January and July 1984, where Maharishi International University (MIU) is located. Over seven thousand followers, representing approximately the square root of 1 percent of the world's population, attended sessions at which they collectively meditated and hoped that their harmonious cohesive minds would mute world violence (*Esquire*, April 1985:72). Such meditative efforts are said to have produced reductions in aggression among groups of prisoners who practice TM, so why would they not have a similar effect for the world (*New Republic*, April 22, 1985:13–15)? By creating a "unified field of enlightenment" (*U.S. News & World Report*, June 25, 1984:60–61), meditators hoped to reduce world hostilities. Whether or not such collective transcendental mediation can bring about the intended results is debatable (*Newsweek*, January 2, 1984:31). But such massive collective events show that predicting the complete demise of a particular cult is a precarious business; predictions can be upset by a host of situational factors.

THE CULT OF RAJNEESH

The appeal of new religious groups did not disappear with the 1960s and 1970s, as we can see from a look at one of the latest religious groups to develop in the United States. This movement gelled around the personality of Bhagwan (The Blessed One) Sri Rajneesh, a former philosophy teacher from India who became a freelance guru in the United States. According to *Newsweek* (December 3, 1984:34), he blended "Eastern religion and pop psychology into a body of thought that was irresistible to many Westerners. In 1974 he opened an ashram in Poona, India, and welcomed more than 50,000 visitors a year—mostly well-heeled Americans and Europeans drawn to his encounter therapies and free-love reputation." After the ashram came under attack in 1981 for prostitution and drug dealing, the Indian government revoked Rajneesh's tax-exempt status, whereupon he came to the United States on a three-month medical visa.

Rajneesh established a sixty-four-thousand-acre commune near the town of Antelope, Oregon, where he built a modern hotel, airport runway, and shopping center. According to *Maclean's* (December 1985:74), Rajneeshpuram (the name of the commune) developed in four years to an estimated worth of $275 million. "It has more than 40 businesses, including pizza parlors, a hairdresser and a gambling casino. Many of its citizens are well educated and affluent; they use Rajneesh checking cards, drink alcohol freely and fly on Air Rajneesh's aircraft. At last count, cult members had given their leader 90 Rolls-Royce cars."

The town of Antelope, Oregon, became embroiled in numerous political squabbles with commune members. These battles were won by Rajneesh followers, who were elected to town council offices and who planned to incorporate the area so that urban growth could begin in earnest. The Rajneesh followers soon ran afoul of environmentalists and others who wished them out of Oregon. These clashes gained attention as the followers began to arm themselves against invasions from local, state, and federal officials attempting to contain the growth of the movement. Internal squabbles began and the bhagwan's top aide, Ma Anand Sheela, was charged with assault and attempted murder before fleeing to West Germany.

According to van Driel and Belzen (1990) the media had an important effect on the fate of Rajneeshpuram. Coverage of the movement in the United States was particularly destructive. The media portrayed the movement within a criminal model. The movement was, to some extent, described as mafialike in its organization and activities. Members were delineated in the media as potential assassins of those who disagreed with or opposed the religion.

Latkin (1991) contends that the social-psychological dynamics of the movement were, in part, responsible for its demise. A major problem was that of ambiguity—situational ambiguity and control. "The lack of structure and the absence of a codified belief system gave those in power a free hand in designating the commune's culture. Since norms, even if arbitrary, tend to take on a life of their own, members are highly susceptible to them." Several factors contributed to social control: the unacceptability of negative feedback, the emphasis on positive demeanor, and a Rajneeshee device for personal growth. "Structural characteristics, such as isolation, contributed to the leader's power and to the conflict with the surrounding community, as did methods of internal control. Within the community, maladaptive norms took on a life of their own and aided in the demise of the movement."

In November 1985 the bhagwan and a few followers left Oregon in two Lear jets ahead of charges from the United States Attorney's office that the bhagwan was in violation of immigration laws at the commune, and that two Oregon prosecutors were targeted in murder plots by members of the group (*Newsweek*, November 11, 1985:26, 31–32). The entourage was tracked to Charlotte, North Carolina, where they were arrested aboard two charter planes allegedly bound for Bermuda. The guru was jailed and then taken back to Oregon, where he pled guilty to the immigration charges and agreed to pay a $400,000 fine and accept a ten-year suspended sentence. Bhagwan Rajneesh then flew to New Delhi, India, where he was reportedly met by more than five hundred disciples strewing rose petals and chanting welcome to their guru. Followers still at Rajneeshpuram vowed to continue the commune (*Newsweek*, November 25, 1985:50).

Rajneesh was arrested on March 5, 1986, by Greek authorities on Crete, only two weeks after his arrival. He had supposedly angered bishops of the Greek Orthodox Church by advocating free sex and the abolition of religion. He and five of his followers were ordered to leave by plane after being labeled a "public menace" (*USA Today*, March 6, 1986 2A). After traveling to Spain and other countries, Rajneesh returned to Poona, where he has continued to attract devotees. Barker (1989:204–205) says that "centers presenting Bhagwan's philosophy, and offering the full range of therapies and avenues to self-enlightenment, have started opening up again and, it would appear, reassembling in North America, Europe, the UK, Australia, New Zealand and other parts of the world."

These sketches, of course, could go on endlessly. We have not mentioned Rastafarianism, Zen, Meher Baba, Subud, witchcraft, Nichiren Shoshu, 3HO, est, the Japanese Golf religion, yoga, and numerous other aspects of the occult. You are referred to John Saliba's (1990) annotated bibliography for a fuller appreciation of the extent to which new religious movements have influenced the world in the past three decades. Our remaining space can be better used in a brief analysis of a "problem" constructed by those who oppose several of these new expressions. The problem involves conflictual relationships among individuals, group, and corporations as well as between a government and its citizenry; it is best conceptualized as a conflict over "programming" and "deprogramming" people into and out of religious beliefs and organizations.

THE PROGRAMMING/DEPROGRAMMING CONTROVERSY

Most of the new expressions we have described have run into conflict over their recruiting tactics, lifestyles, fund-raising techniques, and belief systems, which some have felt overstep the freedoms granted to persons in our society. Groups of people opposed to the new expressions have formed coalitions and started their own anticult movement, based on the premise that various marginal religions "present a clear and present danger, not only to the integrity of basic American values such as individualism, but also to the safety of individual cult members" (Shupe, Spielmann, and Stigall, n.d.:8). Their major claim has been that cult members are in some way duped, brainwashed, or programmed by some bizarre techniques, and do not operate of their own free will. This claim was seemingly bolstered by the Jonestown massacre. Cults, on the other hand, have charged that in deprogramming attempts by anticult groups, cult members have been kidnapped or stolen and brainwashed out of their cultic beliefs.

Programming and deprogramming, along with the occupation of a professional deprogrammer, emerged as controversial topics in the seventies.

One of the first anticult groups was started by angry parents determined to find their children and expose the Children of God. At a meeting of like-minded families in San Diego in 1972, the FREECOG (Free the Children of God) organization was founded. In the mid-1970s the Moonies became a target of anticult groups, who claimed that devotees were brainwashed and described them as "love-bombed," "blissed-out," "vacant-eyed," "glassy-eyed," "duped," "entrapped," "psychologically enslaved," and in "mental bondage."

The anticult movement, as documented by Shupe et al. (n.d.) eventually consolidated efforts in an attempt to "rescue" cult members and to bring about official investigations, if not control, of the cults. Although many small groups developed independently (and later aligned with larger groups or dissolved), the anticult movement was at its height basically and ideologically represented by the following anticult organizations: Citizens Engaged in Reuniting Families, Inc. (CERF); the Individual Freedom Foundation (IFF); Return to Personal Choice, Inc.; the Citizens Freedom Foundation (CFF); the Spiritual Counterfeits Project; Love Our Children, Inc.–Citizens Organized for Public Awareness of Cults; Free Minds, Inc.; Committee of the Third Day, the International Foundation for Individual Freedom (IFIF); and the National Ad Hoc Committee Engaged in Freeing Minds (CEFM).

An analysis of the anticult organization (Shupe et al., n.d.) found that the groups functioned in three specific roles. First, as disseminators of information, they provided descriptions of the beliefs, structures, and geographical movements of the cults. Pamphlets included information on the last-known locations of the cults as well as the names and addresses of specific persons to contact for more information on each group. Other memos contained the names of front organizations for the different religious cults as well as bibliographies of printed materials (books, articles, and newspaper stories) on the cults. Second, the organizations functioned as lobbyists, seeking to convince legislators and executives at the local, state, and federal level that the cults were dangerous. Third, many anticult organizations functioned in a referral role, maintaining files on successful deprogrammers and others who were able to help locate and detain members until deprogramming could occur. Certain groups also gave specific advice and checklists to families who suspected their children had been kidnapped by religious groups.

A central issue in the programming/deprogramming controversy was the nature of the conversion that new recruits undergo. The anticult movement argued that recruits undergo "capture" and "programming" rather than "normal" socialization into a religious belief structure and lifestyle. Cult spokespersons asserted that there is no difference between what they do and what parents and "legitimate" society do all the time: Do parents not program their children into a set of beliefs (which the cult may see as "plastic," false, or materialistic)? Why, then, the cults have asked, cannot our system be just as true, important, and sacred as the ones parents promote for their children? The counterargument from parents was that they train their children, but do not force or coerce or trick them into believing a certain way; the children do it of their own free will. But cults pointed out that trickery and deception, if not outright kidnapping, has been used on cult members who have been taken to motel or hotel rooms or to houses with the windows nailed shut, for deprogramming. Shupe et al. (1978:156) stated that "it is ironic that while modern anti-cultists perceive commitment to cults' doctrines as the result of brainwashing, their own attempts to restore their loved ones to 'normality' closely resemble the very phenomena they profess to despise." Some researchers (Conway and Siegelman, 1982) claimed to show a relationship between the psychological trauma experienced by cult members and the amount of time spent in indoctrination rituals in the cult, while others (Kilbourne, 1983) found no support for such claims.

Barker (1989) does not argue that the impact on new recruits to a new religious group is minimal—she argues for reason and perseverance, and outlines a host of things parents and others can do to relate successfully to a cult member. Recent studies by Ross (1988), Weiss and Mendoza (1990), and others have shown less pathology associated with cult membership than was originally thought to occur. The tone of the 1990s is one in which persons are balancing more the costs, or potential costs, of deprogramming efforts against the benefits of relating to persons more on their own terms, possibly even tolerating their behavior with the hope that time will bring about changes in the person. This seems to us to be one of the most important recent changes in the programming/deprogramming controversy.

The controversy over the definition of religion is, in essence, a controversy over the rights and liberties guaranteed by the Constitution of the United States (Slade, 1979). This legal dispute is simply an indication that in the social evolution of a society, new expressions serve as a change agent and a reflection of the times, as well as a molder of social structures and human activities.

SUMMARY

This chapter has discussed a few of the aspects of some of the new religious expressions and presented several theoretical perspectives related to the formation, maintenance, and operation of these religious groups. We have concentrated on some of the better-known Christian and non-Christian organizations to document some of the ways in which new religious expressions, rituals, and beliefs can emerge.

The Jesus movement is a new religious expression with Christian roots. Members of the counterculture branch that emerged in the 1960s, usually young persons, appear to be searching for transcendental experiences consisting of personalized relationships with Jesus and religious experiences they can *feel* as part of their religious identities. (In this sense, some of these Jesus People and some of the New Agers are on the same quest.) Some of this religious fundamentalism is also a part of the media branch, often associated with television and radio broadcasts produced by formally organized and financially successful religious groups. In this branch, fundamental Christianity has taken on a new form as some use the *born again* label as a business calling card, refusing to do business with those not of like persuasion.

People's Temple was different in important respects from the other new religions. It consisted mainly of blacks, females, and elderly persons who migrated to California from the South and used People's Temple as a religious and social base. They supported the activities of a white man some claim to have been a crazed, drug-addicted con artist and charlatan, and whom others describe as a concerned humanitarian. Scholars have approached Jonestown with a variety of theoretical perspectives, some emphasizing psychological and psychiatric explanations and others employing sociological and sociopolitical frameworks. Probably all have some utility. We are still learning from and about Jonestown.

We also provided vignettes of Satanism, the New Age movement, the Hare Krishna movement, the Unification Church, Scientology, Transcendental Meditation, and the cult of Rajneesh, and we have sought to convey something of the theological and philosophical underpinnings of these groups' beliefs. Through an examination of recent happenings and trends within these groups, we have indicated that the futures of some groups are, at best, uncertain. Some organizations are apparently losing membership while others are dispersing to other parts of the country and to different nations. Still others are diversifying their economic holdings and may be stabilized. Still others were never that big and were never centrally organized.

Finally, we have cursorily examined the anticult movement and have shown that some of these groups have employed several of the same techniques, possibly even more harshly, as have the cults used in the "battle of the minds." These battles will probably continue for some time into the future and may eventually result in landmark legislation regarding religious liberty for American citizens.

PART FOUR

Religion and Society in Interaction

10.
Religion and Institutional Arrangements

Religion and family life seem so intertwined that to question the relationship between the two seems superfluous. The belief that religion promotes family solidarity is widespread. Obviously religious affiliation is important in mate selection; it also has been linked to marital happiness, marital stability, and marital dissolution. Patterns of sexual behavior and attitudes toward contraception and abortion can also be influenced by religious beliefs and practices. Furthermore, the socialization process, particularly the learning of gender-role behavior, can be directly and indirectly influenced by religion. Historically, monogamous marriage and the sanctity of family life have been supported by virtually all religious groups in the United States. Groups advocating polygamous marriage forms (notably the Mormons) have quickly found their religious right to such practices condemned by other Christian bodies and outlawed by federal court decisions.

The quality of education has also been a much debated issue in the United States in recent years. Part of this controversy is religiously connected. Conservative Protestants and Catholics seem unhappy with part or all of the curricula in public education. As a result, President George Bush proposed a *voucher system* that would allow parents to use public money to send their children to religious or other

301

private schools. Although this seems like a radical idea in today's multicultural society, there is a long tradition for religious involvement in education. Historically, religious groups have been involved in establishing both private and public educational systems. Much of what is taught in the classrooms is of deep concern to various religious groups—particularly to conservative and fundamentalist religious groups.

Politics and religion are not nearly so separate as the First Amendment would suggest. Almost all the major religious groups (and most of the minor groups as well) in the United States view their existence, their purpose, and their mission as harmonious with our country's economic and political arrangements. The virtues of a capitalist economy and democracy have been extolled from Protestant pulpits, Catholic chancels, and Jewish sanctuaries.

But occasionally religion comes into conflict with these institutional arrangements. Military service, for example has been shunned by Quakers, Mennonites, Seventh-day Adventists, and Jehovah's Witnesses. Even during the recent Persian Gulf War, certain religious groups in the United States questioned the motives of our government's actions. Some African-American religious groups continue to challenge the economic disparities between minority and majority groups. During the 1960s declarations by the National Council of Churches and by several mainline Protestant denominations condemned the United States' involvement in the Vietnam War. During the 1980s America's Catholic bishops wrote pastoral letters opposing the nuclear arms race and perceived inequitable economic arrangements.

However, interinstitutional conflict involving religion has been far less characteristic of religion in the United States than has interinstitutional cooperation and accommodation. In this chapter we will examine the relationships between religion, on the one hand, and family life, education, and politics, on the other. In addition, we will look at the connection between religion and health care, using the contemporary epidemic of AIDS as an example.

RELIGION AND THE FAMILY

Any thorough study of the family as a social institution finds that many of the norms concerning the structural family type, marriage ceremony, and procreation are interwined with religious beliefs and practices. An overwhelming majority of marriages—whether they take place in a church, synagogue, hotel ballroom, home, or garden—are presided over by ministers, priests, and rabbis. Religious norms also stress having children and rearing them in conjunction with religious norms. Organized religious groups also discourage divorce or other forms of marital dissolution—although with less condemnation than in the past.

From a functionalist perspective, religion supports the institution of the family as a basic agent of socialization, as the "correct" location of procreation, and as a stabilizing force for society, insofar as religious beliefs and practices have generally undergirded traditional family norms. On the other hand, from a conflict theoretical perspective, religion undermines the legitimation of women as equal members of society by preserving the status quo. The traditional subjugation of wives to husbands continues to be justified by many conservative and fundamentalist groups as "biblically correct." Organized efforts defeated the ratification of the Equal Rights Amendment. At present campaigns to enact "profamily" legislation enjoy support from some evangelical Christians and most fundamentalist Christians. Similarly, these same religious groups oppose most abortions on the grounds that abortion prohibits the natural process of procreation biblically commanded for Christians as well as for Jews.

For better or for worse, then, marriage and family life have traditionally been closely related to religion in the United States. In this section we will look at the effects of that relationship, and at how it is changing.

Influence on Marriage and Family Life

Several aspects of marriage and family life are related to religion. Religious socialization begins with the family, and religious preference is important in the choice of a marital partner. In their replication of the "Middletown" studies (the studies of Muncie, Indiana, conducted more than fifty years ago by the Lynds), Bahr and Chadwick (1985:407–14) found that those who reported no church preference were more likely to have never been married, to be remarried, or to be divorced or separated. Of course, it is possible that this may be true because those without a preference are more likely to be young or that the nonmarried may not be as religious as the married. Also, specific groups differ in terms of the rate of marriage. Catholics, Lutherans, Presbyterians, and Jews are most likely to be married, while Episcopalians have the highest percentange of those currently divorced, according to data from the National Opinion Research Center's General Social Surveys, 1987–91.

Generally speaking, religious preference tends to define the pool from which one chooses a partner for marriage. Although this is not so true as it once was, a strong tendency still exists to marry within one's broad religious group—Protestant, Catholic, or Jewish. Norms prescribing marriage within the religious group do vary with the different organizations. Both the Jewish and Catholic faiths have strong norms of endogamy, as do several conservative Protestant groups. As Wilson (1978) has pointed out, such norms have a dual purpose: They make a contribution to family solidarity, and they also increase commitment to the particular religious group. Despite the norms discouraging interfaith marriage, the number of such alliances has increased steadily over the last half century.

Among the different Protestant denominations, some variation exists in the rates with which individuals marry outside their group. Recent studies show that this is still true. When Presbyterians do marry outside their faith, they are less likely to remain Presbyterian than are members of other religious groups. The reason for this is that the religious socialization in more liberal Protestant denominations emphasizes an inclusiveness toward other religious traditions (Roof and McKinney, 1987).

Whether or not a marriage ends in divorce is also related to religious preference. According to National Opinion Research Center data (see Table 10.1), those without any religious preference are most likely to have divorced at some time, which might lead to the suggestion that being religious binds families together. However, three of the more traditional religious groups—Baptists, Catholics, and that loosely defined body known as the sects—have nearly as high a percentage of adherents who have been divorced as the group of those with no religious preference.

Table 10.1   Religious Preference and Divorce (by Percentage)

	Divorce Status		
Preference	Never Divorced	Divorced	Total *N*
Catholic	89.2	10.8	3021
Jewish	91.7	8.3	298
Baptist	86.9	13.1	2586
Methodist	89.1	10.9	1202
Lutheran	90.3	9.7	790
Presbyterian	89.4	10.6	538
Episcopalian	88.4	11.6	284
Sectarian	88.4	11.6	2349
None	85.3	14.7	884

Source: Adapted from data by National Opinion Research Center General Social Surveys, 1986–91.

Both socioeconomic status and particular religious norms concerning the family are certainly involved to some extent in these varying divorce rates. Both Catholics and Jews stress family solidarity, with Catholics maintaining rigid norms prohibiting remarriage of those who are divorced. The high divorce rates for members of conservative Christian groups are probably related to the lower socioeconomic status of these groups, as marital dissolution is generally associated with lower status.

McCarthy (1979) noted that traditionally Catholics have been far less likely to divorce than non-Catholics. More recent studies have shown convergence of these differences, with Catholics becoming more like Protestants with regard to divorce rates (McRae 1977; D'Antonio, 1985; D'Antonio et al., 1989). Still, although rates of dissolution of marriage—both through divorce and separation—have increased more for Catholics than for Protestants, Catholic rates have not yet reached the level of Protestant rates.

D'Antonio (1985) has indicated that all the studies showing a convergence between Catholic and Protestant rates of divorce are accurate, and this convergence is happening in spite of the teachings of the Catholic Church concerning marriage, family life, procreation, and human love. These teachings—particularly concerning birth control and divorce—are followed by only a minority of Catholics, and an overwhelming percentage of Roman Catholics support the right of divorced Catholics to remarry (D'Antonio, 1985:400–401). D'Antonio suggests that one reason for this is the weaker tie between younger Catholics and the institutional church. Both the percentage of young Catholics identifying themselves as members of the church and the percentage indicating regular church attendance decreased between 1970 and 1980 (D'Antonio, 1985:398–99).

Finally, we can look at the relationship between (1) religious preference and (2) happiness in marriage and satisfaction with family life. Does being religious have an effect on such happiness and satisfaction? As Table 10.2 indicates, those with no preference are least likely to describe their marriage as very happy. Actually, little difference exists among the groups, although Jews and sectarians are somewhat more likely to see their marriages as very happy. Bahr and Chadwick (1985:407–14) also reported that in their Middletown study, religious affiliation per se, regardless of the type of religion, is the characteristic related to marital satisfaction. Furthermore, they found that church attendance is positively associated with marital satisfaction.

Looking at satisfaction with family life in general, we see a similar pattern (Table 10.3). Those with no preference are least satisfied with their family life; Episcopalians, sectarians, and Presbyterians are the

Table 10.2   Preference and Marital Happiness
             (by Percentage)

| | Marital Happiness | | | |
Preference	Very Happy	Fairly Happy	Not Happy	Total N
Catholic	63.2	33.9	2.9	1,642
Jewish	68.3	29.7	2.0	170
Baptist	60.3	35.9	3.8	1,280
Methodist	64.0	34.4	1.6	675
Lutheran	58.8	39.7	1.5	469
Presbyterian	65.9	32.5	1.6	320
Episcopalian	63.5	32.5	4.1	148
Sectarian	64.0	32.7	3.3	1,371
None	56.0	38.7	5.3	377

Source: Adapted from data by National Opinion Research Center General Social Surveys, 1986–91.

Table 10.3   Religious Preference and Family Satisfaction
             (by Percentage)

| | Family Satisfaction | | | |
Preference	Very Great	Great	Fair	Some, Little, or None	Total N
Catholic	42.7	33.7	10.3	13.0	3,407
Jewish	43.2	31.6	14.7	10.5	232
Baptist	38.5	34.4	11.0	15.2	1,868
Methodist	41.8	35.7	10.2	12.3	844
Lutheran	41.0	34.9	11.3	12.7	556
Presbyterian	45.3	33.2	8.9	12.6	382
Episcopalian	47.2	29.2	10.8	12.8	179
Sectarian	43.8	32.9	10.4	12.8	1,690
None	32.9	29.9	13.6	23.6	638

Source: Adapted from data by National Opinion Research Center General Social Surveys, 1986–91.

most likely to report that they are happy with their family life although the differences are rather small. Again, the factor of socioeconomic status probably plays a fairly important part in these findings, and may be more influential than religious belief. Certainly, the groups reporting the greatest family happiness are those that generally have a higher socioeconomic status, and it seems reasonable that such high status would incline one to more family satisfaction.

Obviously, religious values and beliefs as well as demonstration of religiosity (as measured by attendance) are important determinants of family happiness. D'Antonio's (1980) research on both the meaning and importance of love demonstrates this. He clearly indicates that for many, love in the social realm cannot be separated from the love that possesses a divine element. He further reports that many young people are dubious about religions that do not help people to love other people. In fact, Thomas and Henry (1985:369–79) report that the issue of the religious valuation of love, as well as other social-psychological aspects of religion and family life, has gained new attention within the social sciences. More attention began to be paid to how religious institutions provide social support for family life rather than to how these institutions' rules function to control family life (D'Antonio, Newman, and Wright, 1982). Traditional gender role definitions have been strongly influenced by the Judeo-Christian tradition, as we will demonstrate in Chapter 13.

Changing Families, Changing Churches

Until recently, conventional wisdom linked successful family relations with religious norms—such as "till death do us part." Today, however, many first marriages do not last, and an increasingly significant segment of families in the United States consists of second spouses and children from previous marrages or families headed by single parents. Most religious groups are attempting to adjust to these new trends, to two-income families, to single parenthood, and to gender-role changes.

Virtually all churches in the United States—including many conservative-fundamentalist Protestant groups and the Roman Catholic Church—have examined their traditional teachings and policies regarding family life, and virtually all have modified their stances on specific issues, although some have done this more quickly than others (Thornton, 1985:390). The Roman Catholic Church, although never publicly wavering from its antidivorce, antiabortion, and anti–birth control positions, has nonetheless really lost the battle on divorce and birth control (D'Antonio, 1985:402). Although most conservative and fundamentalist Protestants identified with the religious right publicly condemn both divorce and the changing relationships between men and women as they promote "family values," some of their pastoral and counseling materials recognize these societywide changes. Even within the evangelical framework, compromise, negotiation, and mutual adjustment can take place in husband-wife relationships (McNamara, 1985:456). Still, many conservative religious groups try to stop—or to slow down—the changes occurring within the family unit through political action and other forms of pressure.

Whether or not the reciprocal influences between religion and family will remain steady, grow stronger, or grow weaker is still to be seen. In many places, churches seem to be holding their own as important influences on family life. Middletown may or may not be representative of other cities and towns in the United States, but Bahr and Chadwick (1985:413) have reported the following about churches and family life there:

> The Lynds said that, in 1935, Middletown's churches were only partially filled and that most regular attenders were women and old people. Our survey data and our personal observations during two years of residence in Middletown indicated that, if that were ever so, it is so no longer. In the late 1970s Middletown's churches—Catholic and Protestant—catered to youth and young families, as well as to the middle-aged and older citizens. Programs for children, for teenagers, and for young adults were prominent in most of the churches, and young children were much in evidence in most worship services. From our perspective the profamily values of Middletown churches include the having and rearing of children and the rearing of children includes a variety of church-related activities.

RELIGION AND EDUCATION

The relationship between education and religion in our country is best understood as a multifaceted association. This association, like the relationship between religion and the family, has generally been harmonious, but not always. Historically, established religious groups gave rise to our educational system, private and public. Those religious organizations that most valued learning also established colleges and universities. As a consequence, a religious and educational elite developed early in the United States. But as the state took responsibility for education, schools became increasingly secular, even while still dominated by Protestant culture. Conflict arose between church and state over education. Churches reacted to the secularization of education in a number of ways, from founding parochial schools and developing religious organizations for students to withholding support from public education, especially higher education.

Religious Origins of Our Educational System

From colonial times through the early decades of our nation's history, religious groups in the United States were largely responsible for education. The most prominent source for the present forms of U.S. education was Puritan New England. Its Calvinist commitment to the universal education of believers and potential believers gave rise to local schools under control of the Puritan theocracy. Though religion was the primary topic of instruction, reading was also taught since it was perceived as necessary to improve the quality of Christian life. In the southern colonies, largely Anglican in religion, school curricula were less focused on religion and more oriented toward training the Anglican elite to govern the uneducated masses.

In a relatively short time colleges developed. Harvard, Yale, and Brown were extensions of the two dominant religions in New England: Congregationalist and Baptist. The College of William and Mary in Virginia was officially English and Anglican. After Scottish Presbyterians settled the middle colonies, Princeton was founded. Even though the Great Awakening stressed personal piety rather than religious knowledge, formal education was not denounced by the growing number of Baptists and Methodists. For the most part the colonies enjoyed an educational system more universal in its scope than the system then in operation in Europe. As the frontier expanded, education moved into the newer regions of the nation.

When a public school system emerged from the New England tradition and was extended into the western areas of the country, the Protestant religion remained an integral part of the curriculum. As Catholic immigrants began to arrive, they considered this Protestant-dominated educational system to be anti-Catholic. As a result, the Catholic Church established parochial schools serving as fortresses against this bias so as to insure the teaching of Catholic beliefs along with reading, writing, and arithmetic. From its beginning, then, the parochial school has been a religious alternative to both the public and private systems of education.

As the nation became more and more education-conscious, compulsory and universal education became public policy. Because of the historic separation of church and state, education became more secular. As this secularization of public schools began to occur, Protestant churches established Sunday schools, religious retreats, and church-related colleges to supplement public education (Hargrove, 1979b:180). Jews also followed this pattern by forming Hebrew or Sabbath schools. Eventually, the secularity of public education was extended by court decisions concerned with abolishing prayers and Scripture readings in public schools.

In recent years the number of students enrolled in Protestant and Jewish parochial schools has increased dramatically, even while Catholic schools have shown some decline in enrollment, perhaps because financial crises have forced the closing of some Catholic schools. In both central city areas of the Northeast and Midwest and in recently integrated cities of the South, Protestant families are abandoning the public school systems. Although much of this flight is a response to white fears of forced busing, some of it is attributable to a desire for a more religiously oriented education. Fundamentalist conservative Protestant parents continue to enroll their children in increasing numbers in private Christian schools as a protest against the notions of secular humanism, cultural relativity, and biological evolution that are taught in public schools (Hargrove, 1979b:188). In addition, some fundamentalist Protestant parents are opting out of public education in favor of *home schooling* (Bates, 1991). This has become a more viable option as more and more states allow this practice if the parent is a certified teacher. So although education and religion were once intimately related in our country, this relationship has grown more and more distant in the public schools, and in many private schools also, leaving the church-related schools to combine religious education with education for the worldly life.

Church-State Issues in Education

The desire of many parents for more religious education for their children than that provided by the state has raised a number of issues. One of the earliest issues was the question of compulsory school attendance versus religious freedom. Because of the states' policy of compulsory and universal education, smaller sects with an informal educational tradition, such as the Amish, were required to attend formal schools—public, parochial, or private. The Amish often were able to maintain their own elementary education by having a few members of the sect become qualified teachers, but most states demanded that Amish youth also attend high school as the age limit for compulsory attendance rose (Hargrove, 1979b:182). The Amish resisted, took their case to court, and eventually won this battle in Wisconsin through a 1973 Supreme Court decision, *Yoder v. Wisconsin.* The Court acknowledge that the Amish refusal to send their children to school beyond eighth grade was based on a desire to retain a simple, primitive Christian life by insulating themselves from the modern world; their concept of life aloof from the world and its values was central to their faith. Believing that compulsory high schol attendance would destroy this aloofness and ultimately the Amish faith, the Court exempted Amish youth from Wisconsin compulsory education beyond the eighth grade (Winter, 1977:249–50).

The rapid increase of enrollment in recent years in both Protestant and Jewish private schools has led to a reexamination of the question of public aid for religious schools by those who formerly opposed it, including its most vocal opponents, the Southern Baptists. All parochial schools, regardless of their faith, face a similar dilemma: insufficient funds with which to compete with public education. Ammerman (1987) points out, for example, that the fundamentalist Christian school operated by the Bible church she studied had inferior and insufficient supplies, equipment, and books. Public schoolteachers are better paid than parochial school teachers, and laboratories and other facilities in public schools are generally better equipped. Religious schools must rely on tuition for their income, but parents whose children attend them contend they are paying for education twice: through taxes supporting the public schools and through their children's tuition. Such an economic burden for middle-income families is often unmanageable, and parents have demanded relief from the rising costs of public and private education. As a result, some of the past Protestant opposition to public aid for religious schools has evaporated. President George Bush's proposal for tuition vouchers to be used at either private or parochial schools is a more recent example of tuition equalization. Few, if any, conservative or fundamentalist Christians opposed his plan. Most opposition came from mainline Protestant denominations, Jewish groups, secular groups, and public education interest groups.

Another church-state issue that emerges repeatedly with regard to education is the amount of religion allowable in public schools—in the curriculum, in textbooks, and in school prayer. As mentioned in Chapter 7, fundamentalist groups in the 1920s successfully lobbied for legislation in a few states that required the account of creation in the book of Genesis to be taught in the schools; the Scopes monkey trial tested whether a biology teacher could teach evolution in direct violation of Tennessee state law against promoting evolutionary theory. Now that the widely accepted scientific perspective of the beginnings of life prevails in the schools, fundamentalists have renewed their efforts to have their viewpoint taught and included in textbooks. The creationist position, which never really died out among fundamentalists, has achieved today a new sophistication. Those who support this perspective tend to be self-identified fundamentalists. Higher levels of education attainment are most often associated with acceptance of scientific evolution (Eve and Harrold, 1991). Several public school systems, including the Dallas Independent School District, now provide for the use of a textbook that presents the creationist point of view along with textbooks that subscribe to the evolutionary point of view. In 1982, a lawsuit was filed in the Little Rock, Arkansas, federal court challenging state legislation that mandated the teaching of both theories in public schools; the judge ruled against proponents of the creationist viewpoint. Still, many fundamentalists and evangelicals continue to lobby for an equal hearing for creationism, and many private Christian schools teach the creationist understanding of the origin of the human species, refusing in the name of religious freedom to submit to state guidelines on the curriculum (Ammerman, 1987; Wilcox, 1989). During the 1992 general elections, several candidates whose hidden agenda called for the promotion of a conservative-creationist ideology in public schools won election to local school boards in California. These individuals were labeled *stealth candidates* because their true beliefs and agendas were hidden from the general public.

In public education, the conservative religious reaction against secularism is perhaps most apparent in repeated attempts to secure passage of an amendment to the U.S. Constitution allowing school prayer. Two Supreme Court decisions served as a catalyst for this movement: *Abington School District* v. *Schempp* (1964) and *Murray* v. *Curlett;* the latter case had been brought by atheist Madalyn Murray O'Hair. Of the two suits, *Murray* v. *Curlett* has had by far the greater impact. Its outcome established a "wall of separation" between religion and the state in the 1960s, when the majority opinion of the Court held that public schools in the United States were essentially agencies of government and should not be involved in the business of selecting prayers or Bible passages (Winter, 1977:240–41). At the same time, however, the Court did not endorse complete neutrality by government in matters of religion, pronouncing in the *Schempp* decision that "today, as in the beginning, our national life reflects a religious people" (United States Supreme Court, 1964:853).

In response to these court decisions, local and national movements were begun to promote a constitutional amendment that would permit Bible reading and prayer in public schools. Although legislators introduce these amendments each year, thus far the legislation has failed to achieve the necessary two-thirds majority in both Houses of the United States Congress.

Church Support for Higher Education

Are church-related colleges and universities faring well in an era that is less overtly religious than in the past? At a time of increasing educational expense—both for students as well as for institutions—

many of these colleges are experiencing enrollment increases. Catholic Notre Dame University in Indiana draws a large student population from across the nation. Baptist Baylor University in Texas also enjoys flourishing enrollments. Both universities can be highly selective in their acceptance of students. Regardless of the distance or closeness of the school's relationship to its parent denomination, that denomination is contributing *some* funds to the ongoing operation of the school. Similarly, most religious organizations in the United States continue to support church-related higher education.

But not all religious groups are supportive of higher education. Some, like the Amish, are suspicious of education beyond its rudimentary elements. Others see no value in higher education. This is true, primarily, for sects that have a preponderance of lower-class and working-class members. Very few members of Pentecostal and Holiness sects have college educations, and neither do most of their ministers. As a result, both clergy and laity are somewhat suspicious of higher education. Roman Catholics, at one time predominantly working-class, have used education as a mechanism of upward mobility. As a consequence, the Catholic laity is better educated than in the past, and Catholic priests are more likely to have a college degree as well as seminary training. American Jews, more than any other group, have been upwardly mobile through education. However, Jews have depended more on the public education system than have either Protestants or Catholics. Not until after World War II, when Brandeis University was founded, was there a Jewish university.

Today the degree of commitment to education is related to the relative social class levels within religious bodies. Groups that have larger proportions of members in the upper and middle classes have the highest level of educational attainment. These organizations support education not only in church-related colleges and universities but also in the public sector of education. While the upper classes have traditionally used private schools, the upper-middle and middle classes have usually supported public education. The Jews, Episcopalians, Presbyterians, the Congregationalist part of the United Church of Christ, and Methodists generally have little quarrel with secularized education. To a lesser extent, the Lutherans, Disciples of Christ, Baptists, and Roman Catholics have made accommodations with secular education also. This is particularly true of the middle- and upper-middle-class members of these bodies. By contrast, fundamentalist Protestants, lower-class Baptists, and Pentecostal and Holiness groups demonstrate the least support of education, particularly of its most secular aspects. If education continues to be the primary mechanism for upward mobility in the United States, however, members of religious groups appealing to the lower class will probably demonstrate stronger support for education in due time.

RELIGION AND POLITICAL ARRANGEMENTS

As was pointed out in Chapter 5, the First Amendment to the Constitution states that "Congress shall make no law respecting an establishment of religion, or prohibiting the free exercise thereof...." This guarantee of official neutrality toward religion emerged, as you will recall from Chapter 5, from a context in which state churches were the norm. In the Massachusetts Bay Colony, for example, government officials were required to be members of the official church. In Virginia, the colonial government established the Church of England as the state church, required all citizens to attend Anglican services, levied taxes to support the church, and prohibited non-Anglican clergy from functioning as ministers and priests (Johnstone, 1975:180–81). Even after the Constitution became the law of the land, tax-supported churches in some states remained as late as 1832, when Massachusetts cut off support to both Trinitarian and Unitarian Congregational churches.

Nevertheless, the disestablishment of state religion by the framers of the Constitution seemed to reflect a separationist stance held by many in the colonies. According to this viewpoint, the proper duty of government toward religion is to provide a situation in which various religious traditions can be freely practiced. Thus, separation of church and state became a foundation of the new nation, and much has been made of this supposed separation. Recall that a major factor in the anti-Catholic sentiment in this country in the 1800s and early 1900s was suspicion of the Catholic tradition of a close relationship between church and state.

In reality, however, the separation of church and state in the United States is not absolute, but only partial. The United States government has incorporated religious mottoes (for example, "In God We Trust") into official materials, has taken care of the religious needs of the armed forces (for example, providing chaplains and chapels at military and naval bases), and has generally supported conventional and established Christian and Jewish religious groups. On the other hand, it has brought legal action against churches that did not conform to the laws of the state. Churches have a latent effect on government by influencing their members' voting behavior; they have a more blatant effect in efforts to lobby and exert pressure for various causes, from legislating individual mobility to urging social reform.

Thus, in practice, the boundaries between church and state are often blurred. In this section we will focus on some of these blurred areas.

State Prosecution of Religious Groups

The government's early orientation toward established religions disposed it to favor religion, particularly Christianity. As the Protestant establishment sent out clergy to the frontiers, the state tolerated this one-sided expansionism. Later, when violence by members of Protestant denominations against the Mormons flared, the government did little to protect Mormon beliefs and believers. Court decisions in church-state disputes often reflected this Protestant viewpoint, and it was not until this original bias was challenged by the influx of millions of Roman Catholic and Jewish immigrants that the courts began to rule more evenhandedly on church-state cases (Hargrove, 1979b:210). Still, churches that have run afoul of the state have generally been minority groups.

For example, minority churches such as the Mormons, Jehovah's Witnesses, and the Amish have been accused by the government of not conforming to the laws of the state. In 1870, the Supreme Court unanimously ruled in *Reynolds* v. *United States* that Mormons were free to believe anything they desired concerning the virtues of plural marriage, but that their actions must stay within the laws of the state (Hargrove, 1979b:211). In a subsequent case, *Davis* v. *Beason*, a Mormon challenged an Idaho law that, in exchange for the right to vote, required a person to swear that he was not a member of a group that teaches, counsels, or encourages polygamy. In this instance, the Supreme Court upheld the law, using the *Reynolds* case as a precedent, even though the plaintiff had not engaged in the action of plural marriage (Hargrove, 1979b:211). The strongly held bias against Mormons at that time probably influenced the Court's decision.

The state has prosecuted the Amish to make them conform to laws requiring high-school-age children to attend schools, as described earlier in this chapter. Both the Amish and Jehovah's Witnesses have been engaged in court action concerning their right not to salute the national flag or to repeat the pledge of allegiance to the flag. Their claims to conscientious objection to military service have been met with both governmental skepticism and majority church disapproval. On the other hand, the government has acknowledged some respect for religious prescriptions against killing by establishing a conscientious objector status for young men who are drafted.

Interestingly, many of these actions have been initiated or influenced by majority churches trying to use the political machinery of the state to limit minority religions and movements that threaten cherished religious as well as family and political values. The anti-Catholic sentiment of the 1840s and 1850s found political expression in the Know-Nothing party. Outcries for immigration limitations against southern and eastern European Catholics and Jews and for prohibition of parochial schools came from Protestant groups like the American Protective Association. In the 1920s the American Protestant Alliance lobbied for a constitutional amendment that would deny citizenship to anyone who acknowledged allegiance to the pope (Wilson, 1978:203). Recently, a number of mainline Protestant denominations, the Roman Catholic Church, and Conservative and Orthodox Judaism have supported legal action against the Unification Church and the Children of God sect (Davis and Richardson, 1976:324). And since World War II, as Demerath (1983) has pointed out, various groups, including religious groups, with single-issue agendas have used the courts as the principal arena for finding political solutions to disputes.

Many clergy from a wide variety of denominations seem to understand the implicit limits to sectarian religion in a pluralistic society, even though many of the laity (and some clergy) do not support the actual practice of church-state separation. This is clear from the extent to which religious groups have attempted to exert pressure on the political process, both in the past and in more recent times. We will turn our attention now to the influence of these religious lobbies and pressure groups.

Religious Lobbies and Pressure Groups

Hargrove (1979b:212–13) has identified two types of religious pressure groups: *transformationist* and *separationist*. Transformationist groups become involved in politics to sway public policy toward religiously sanctioned ends, seeing this as part of the "prophetic ministry of the church." Historically, the involvement of religious groups and their leaders in projects of community betterment, the advocacy of the Social Gospel by some Protestants, and the endorsement of union-organizing activities by the Roman Catholic Church have been within this tradition. More recently, efforts to enact civil rights legislation, to end the war in Vietnam, to restore prayer in public schools, and to outlaw abortion by constitutional amendment demonstrate the same transformationist philosophy. On the other hand, separationists advocate a pragmatic separation between church and state, and become involved in politics in order to insure this continued separation. Their activity is conservative in nature, in contrast to the reform-oriented action of transformationist pressure groups. The effects of Protestants and Other Americans United for the Separation of Church and State (POAU) opposing state aid to parochial schools are in the separationist tradition.

A number of well-organized church lobbies representing both the transformationist and the separationist stances exist to exert pressure on legislators both in Washington, D.C., and in the state capitols. According to Hertzke (1988), these lobbies give political expression to a variety of concerns, particularly those with moral content. These concerns would otherwise be neglected by more traditional lobby groups attempting to influence economic policy. Mainline Protestant denominations have recently been more interested in international and broad humanitarian issues such as peace, curtailment of nuclear weapons, world hunger, economic sanctions against South Africa, and human rights. Most of these groups have also continued to lobby against the school prayer amendment and for the continuation of the present abortion policy.

By contrast, Protestant fundamentalist and evangelical churches concentrate more on domestic issues, such as prohibitions on abortion, passage of the school prayer amendment, and tuition vouchers for parochial schools. The newer religious lobbies (such as the now dormant Moral Majority) joined with the older, established National Association of Evangelicals to promote their religious and political agenda. Jerry Falwell, founder of the Moral Majority, has promised to resurrect that organization if President Clinton's programs are interpreted as too "liberal."

The Roman Catholic Church in its lobbying efforts often sides with the mainline Protestant denominations on world issues, but sides with fundamentalist and evangelical Protestants on the issue of limiting or outlawing abortions. Jewish groups, more often than not, come down on the side of mainline Protestantism. In addition, they lobby for continued aid to and protection for Israel.

In contrast to the lobbies of the major religious groups in the United States, transformationist religious lobbies advocate right-wing extremism in the political arena and the economic system. Generally these lobbies have been supported by fundamentalist Protestants who are militantly anticommunist. Although their strength in the 1970s and 1980s was not so great as in the previous two decades, religious organizations waging a "holy war" against "godless, atheistic communism" continue to exist and to apply some political pressure on the governmental system in our country. With the collapse of communist governments in the former Soviet Union and eastern Europe, these groups have lost their crusading political issue.

Still, much of the agenda of the political right has been carried on by a newer religious lobby that first became visible during the 1980 presidential campaign. This lobby is actually an informal coalition of a number of groups often lumped together and called the Moral Majority, though in fact the Moral Majority is only one of these groups. Known collectively as the religious-political right, the new Christian right, or the religious right, they have as their common purpose halting what they interpret as the moral and spiritual deterioration of life in the United States. Their ultimate goal is to dislodge the liberal establishment within religion and politics and to establish a traditionalist society characterized by a conservative moral and spiritual consensus. The original crusading issues of this religious lobby included (1) opposition to tolerance of abortion, (2) determination to restore the rights of public schools to have voluntary prayer, (3) opposition to the perceived weakened military position of the nation, (4) hostility to pornography, (5) opposition to the Equal Rights Amendment, and (6) determination to curtail the influence of secular humanism, which they diagnose as the number one disease afflicting the United States (Hill and Owen, 1982:17).

Characterizing the overall composition of this coalition as it gained wide-spread attention during the early 1980s, Hill and Owen (1982:32–33) stated that it is a company of American Protestants with some not-very-churched allies, who hitherto have been powerless—partly because they belonged to the working class and partly because their religion called them to repudiate entangling alliances with society. For the most part, the coalition's membership consists of devout, conservative Protestants.

In research during the 1980s, Wilcox (1989a, 1989b) has found that support for the crusading issues of the Moral Majority was best explained as a function of deeply held religious beliefs and values intertwined with similiar political beliefs and values. Wilcox has identified the following characteristics of Moral Majority supporters: those who attend fundamentalist Protestant churches and Pentecostal churches; those who identify themselves as fundamentalists; those who hold fundamentalist religious beliefs; those with higher levels of religiosity; those who frequently view televangelists; those who have antipathy toward Roman Catholics; and those who identify themselves as conservative Republicans (1989b:410).

The Roundtable, originally called the Religious Roundtable, serves primarily as an agency to coordinate and to provide resources for conservative religious leaders. The agency organized a National Affairs Briefing in Dallas in 1980 during which presidential candidate Ronald Reagan and other conservative politicians appeared with conservative religious leaders, including Jerry Falwell, James Robison, and Round-table leaders. Some 15,000 people attended this August meeting, including 250 members of the press. The Roundtable's founder, Edward McAteer, claims that the Roundtable provided educational material to over 40,000 people—the elite of the new religious-political right—between August and November of 1980 (Hill and Owen, 1982:69). It continued to give support to Ronald Reagan during the presidential campaign of 1984 and to George Bush during the presidential campaign of 1988. In 1992 it opposed the election of Bill Clinton.

Several studies done later indicate that television evangelists could influence voters. The support that Pat Robertson received in his unsuccessful quest for the Republican presidential nomination in 1988 came mostly from those who watched his "700 Club" television program (Johnson, Tamney, and Burton, 1989). Wilcox (1987) also found that the televangelists were somewhat successful in raising money for political action committees of the religious-political right, particularly those connected with the Moral Majority (1988).

In summary, some religious pressure groups and lobbies are separationist, but most are transformationist, and these transformationist groups have aligned themselves with causes at all points on the political spectrum. It is useful here to recall from Chapter 5 Marty's (1970) categorization of Protestants as either public or private: Public Protestants seek to improve social conditions through political action, while private Protestants are concerned with pietistic living, personal salvation, and heavenly reward.

Church Pressure to Legislate Morality

Religious groups and individuals have attempted to "Christianize" the political and governmental structure of the United States throughout its history by exerting pressure to legislate their own particular brand of morality. Church pressure to ban alcoholic beverages through the Eighteenth Amendment is the best-known historic example of this type of lobbying. A well-organized Protestant church lobby founded in 1895 sought to promote Protestant hegemony. The Anti-Saloon League had the express purpose of prohibiting by constitutional amendment the sale of most intoxicating beverages (Pfeffer, 1953:200). The eventual repeal of this amendment did not halt other attempts to legislate particularistic morality. Laws still prohibit liquor sales on Sundays in some states and prescribe where taverns and liquor stores can be located in relationship to churches or synagogues.

In the eyes of many people, church pressure to legislate morality violates the premises that government should remain neutral in matters of religion, and that religious pluralism in the United States allows a diversity of viewpoints on moral stances. Members of groups pressuring for legislation of morality seem at times to regard themselves as a moral elite and to believe that theirs is the only correct moral and religious position.

Church pressure to prohibit abortion on demand is a direct reaction to the 1973 Supreme Court decision (*Roe* v. *Wade*) that legalized abortion. These efforts not only continue but have intensified since the court decision. The American Conference of Catholic Bishops has been the prime supporter of a constitutional amendment to outlaw abortion except under very limited circumstances, but local and national right-to-life groups have also lobbied for the amendment. Many evangelical Protestants are strongly opposed to abortion on demand, as is the Lutheran Church–Missouri Synod. Smaller churches of the Calvinist tradition, such as the Reformed Church in America and the Christian Reformed Church, are on record as favoring a constitutional amendment to outlaw all but therapeutic abortions. The Southern Baptist Convention has passed resolutions against current abortion policy since fundamentalists gained control of the convention's policymaking.

Although support for some rights to abortion remains, more people favor restrictions than in the past, as we stated earlier. This seems to be reflected in the deliberations and pronouncements of the mainline Protestant denominations. Individual congregations of the Presbyterian Church (U.S.A.) have continued to press the issue at regional presbytery and synod meetings and at the national general assemblies. In 1992 the General Assembly of that church reaffirmed the denomination's commitment to a woman's right to abortion, but specified its concern that abortion was becoming just another means of elective birth control. Such concern had not been officially expressed in the previous ten years. Even so, the vote was much closer than in previous annual meetings. Annual conferences of the United Methodist Church have also heard from their more conservative, evangelical congregations about opposition to abortion. And within other mainline Protestant churches, most of which maintain a pro-choice stance toward abortion, grass-roots opposition to abortion exists in virtually all the denominations.

Although several restrictive antiabortion amendments have been proposed in Congress, none has yet received a majority vote. Religious lobbies will almost certainly continue to exert pressure on this moral issue. Since these groups strongly believe that legalized abortion is akin to legalized murder, it is doubtful that compromise will be reached on it. The most recent antiabortion tactic involves religious lobbying at the state level to bring about state laws placing limitations on a woman's right to abortion. In all cases, these laws are appealed by pro-choice groups to higher courts. In the four cases heard by the Supreme Court, it has upheld most of the state restrictions (*Webster* v. *Reproductive Health Services* (1989); *Ohio* v. *Akron Center for Reproductive Health* (1990); *Hodgon* v. *Minnesota* (1990); *Planned Parenthood of Southeast Pennsylvania* v. *Casey* (1992). But the Supreme Court has refused to overturn the original case that allowed abortions, *Roe* v. *Wade*.

More recently, some religious-political right groups and activist Catholic conservatives have continued their efforts to change current abortion policy through direct action. Often this involves acts of civil disobedience similar to those used by clergy and lay people during the civil rights movement. Participants have seemed willing to serve jail time in order to block entrances to abortion clinics and Planned Parenthood facilities. Other tactics include verbal intimidation and threats against physicians (and their families) who perform abortions. In 1993 these unlawful activities accelerated as antiabortionist activists murdered two physicians and attempted to murder another. The best known of these direct action groups is Operation Rescue (Hitchcock, 1991). In a study of the abortion controversy, Tamney, Johnson, and Burton (1992) gathered data in "Middletown" (Muncie, Indiana). They found that pro-life individuals had significantly different attitudes than pro-choice individuals. Antiabortionists were more likely to be traditionalists and to base their vote on a candidate's stand on the abortion issue. They also found that religion seemed to play a role immobilizing political action on this issue.

Opposition to legislated civil rights for gay men and lesbians is another issue with deep religious overtones. Many religious groups see gains in rights for homosexuals as eroding society's traditional family values. And the doctrinal positions of all but the most liberal religious bodies condemn, to some degree, homosexual activity. Catholic dogma sees it as a sin; Baptist interpretation of Scriptures allows for a similar belief, and Lutherans also disapprove of it. Conservative Christians who oppose public acceptance or tolerance of homosexuality cite Old Testament scriptural passages condemning homosexuality as a grievous sin and use the writings of St. Paul as further justification for their opposition to gays and gay rights. Gallup and Castelli (1989:94) report that only 19 percent of evangelical Protestants approve of making homosexual relations legal, compared with 42 percent of nonevangelicals. Most mainline Protestant denominations, along with evangelical Protestant denominations, continue to oppose the ordination of open and avowed homosexuals, although it has been debated by Presbyterians, United Methodists, and Lutherans.

As gay rights activists have sought to have antidiscrimination ordinances and laws enacted on behalf of homosexuals, religious opposition to such legislative acts has increased. Anita Bryant's successful campaign to repeal many of the antidiscrimination provisions enacted by Dade County, Florida, was an early example of such religious opposition. As a result, similar successes by religious pressure groups have occurred in other cities and states. The most recent success was in Colorado as a result of a referendum passed during the 1992 election. However, a more restrictive constitutional amendment was voted down in Oregon. Jorstad (1990) states that conservative and fundamentalist Protestants are solidly opposed to any legitimation of a gay and lesbian lifestyle, and that many within their ranks seek a return to restrictive criminal penalties for homosexual acts. Furthermore, he reports that many within their ranks believe that AIDS is either punishment from God for those living a gay lifestyle or is the consequence of homosexual promiscuity. We will discuss the relationship between religion and AIDS later in this chapter.

The dissemination of obscene materials is a similar issue in terms of traditional morality. Aside from the unresolved controversy concerning the effects of pornography on people, many believe that such materials—books, magazines, and movies—are immoral. Not only conservative Protestants and Catholics but also many moderate Protestants, Catholics, and Jews were disturbed by the Supreme Court's decision to protect such materials under the First Amendment. Because the decision of the Court allows local community standards to prevail in determining whether or not a movie, book, or magazine is obscene, local and regional groups, most of which have a religious base, have applied pressure to city councils and state legislatures to write more restrictive laws regulating pornography. Many states and communities have done so.

More recently, religious-political right organizations have attacked the National Endowment for the Humanities for that organization's funding of controversial art exhibits, notably the Robert Mapplethorpe photographic exhibit in Cincinnati, Ohio, which included pictures of gay men engaged in sexually explicit activities. A grand jury indicted the director of the Cincinnati museum which had exhibited the National Endowment–funded display. During the 1991 trial the museum director was acquitted of criminal charges. However, religious-political right groups continued their pressure to cut off funding for the National Endowment for the Humanities on the ground that it was funding obscene works of art and sexually explicit dramas, operas, and musicals. Obviously, the issue of pornography remains volatile.

Data from national samples indicate that a broad section of the population is also concerned about pornography. Gallup and Castelli (1989:135) report that among those claiming church membership, 49 percent favor more restrictive laws governing the sale of pornographic materials. Among those demonstrating a high level of religiosity, 60 percent favor more restrictions. In spite of this, some of the organizations whose purpose is to defend artistic expression under the First Amendment to the Constitution of the United States, continue to oppose most efforts to censor sexually explicit materials (Jorstad, 1990: 144–45).

Network television programming has also been attacked for being too sexually explicit or for using controversial subject matter. For example, in 1979 CBS-TV scheduled a movie concerning incest, and before its scheduled airing, religious groups around the country protested to the network. When CBS refused to withdraw the movie, local affiliates of the network were pressured by these groups, which were loosely coordinated by a Methodist minister from Tupelo, Mississippi, Donald Wildmon. Some stations did substitute a local program for the network movie; other stations taped it and broadcast it during late evening hours. One Baptist church in Dallas, Texas, bought a full-page ad in the Sunday edition of the *Dallas Morning News* stating that church members would boycott the sponsors of the television show and would refrain from watching most CBS-TV programs. The ad was signed by hundreds of church members.

More recently, Donald Wildmon and his organization have continued to pressure the television networks to cancel what are regarded as sexually explicit materials. His claims usually point to the fact that the program or advertisement in question goes beyond what the mainstream of America considers to be acceptable (Jorstad, 1990:145). However, a pluralistic society seems divided concerning this issue. Cable television channels and the availability of video rentals allow viewers access to the very material that Wildmon finds objectionable, even if network television forbids its transmission.

Church Pressure for Social Reform

Beginning with the Social Gospel movement, liberal Christian groups have tried to influence politics in the United States. As indicated in Chapter 6, the ecumenical movement in the churches has generally been identified with liberal social activism, and the National Council of Churches and its member denominations have supported a variety of liberal and moderate social issues. Reform Judaism and many Catholic bishops have also lobbied for many of these issues. Often such stances have alienated rank-and-file members in the denominations, but the elected and appointed leadership in the denominations has continued to involve itself in efforts for social reform. During the 1980s two such efforts sought to implement a bilateral nuclear freeze and to provide sanctuary for political refugees.

Organized efforts to implement a nuclear freeze policy came from a wide variety of liberal Protestants and liberal Catholics. Though the suggested means by which a freeze could be implemented varied, a common theme existed, stressing the inevitability of a nuclear holocaust, the economic strain of stockpiling more nuclear weapons, and the immorality of spending funds for weapons in a world characterized by poverty, famine, and injustice. Efforts to draw public attention to this cause took various forms from local actions to national pronouncements.

The American Conference of Catholic Bishops issued a policy paper against the proliferation of nuclear weapons and other armaments (Catholic Bishops of America, 1983). The bishops stated that they were following the lead of Pope John Paul II in addressing the fear and preoccupation of many groups throughout the world concerning nuclear war. They spoke out against the United States' efforts to plan for prolonged nuclear strikes and argued that if nuclear deterrence is the goal of the United States, then sufficiency rather than superiority in weaponry is adequate. Finally, they suggested that nuclear deterrence should be used to speed nuclear disarmament of both the United States and the Soviet Union.

McNamara (1984:211) stated that the Catholic bishops' efforts, along with parallel movements in many mainline Protestant churches, such as the Peacemaking movement of the Presbyterian Church (U.S.A.), seemed designed to stir thought and debate concerning the volatile issue. These statements, as well as organized actions promoting a nuclear freeze, evoked strong reactions from both conservative Catholics (D'Antonio, 1985) and conservative Protestants. Many of the governing bodies of local congregations with the Presbyterian Church (U.S.A.) refused to endorse the Peacemaking initiatives and the church's call for a nuclear freeze policy.

The end of the cold war neutralized many concerns of those advocating a nuclear freeze. However, the issue itself may have hastened the collapse of communist governments in Eastern Europe and ultimately in the Soviet Union. The knowledge of organized American opposition to the continuing nuclear buildup of the two superpowers helped to bring together peace groups, environmental groups, and prodemocracy groups in East Germany and other Eastern bloc countries (Beckley and Chalfant, 1991; Beckley, Chalfant, and Johnson, 1992). The lack of control over nuclear weapons in former Soviet Union republics and their possible sale to nations hostile to Western countries keeps the antinuclear movement alive in some mainline Protestant denominations and the Roman Catholic Church.

Some Roman Catholics and some Protestants—mainly Presbyterians and Methodists—participated in a sanctuary program for political refugees from Central America. According to existing U.S. immigration laws, these refugees were illegal aliens, and those who helped them could be subject to criminal prosecution. The issue for individuals (and congregations) giving sanctuary to the Central Americans was one of civil disobedience, not criminality. Several federal grand juries returned indictments against those harboring the refugees. In the few trials that took place, some defendants were found guilty and some were acquitted. In the guilty verdicts, a few individuals were granted probation and others were sentenced to prison. In spite of these prosecutions, the sanctuary movement did not subside. In 1992 the Presbyterian Church (U.S.A.) elected John Fyte, one of the convicted defendants in the sanctuary movement, as moderator (president) of its General Assembly.

These liberal issues involving religion in the political realm continue to cause controversy, just as the issues of the religious-political right evoke spirited debate. Catholic conservatives as well as political conservatives strongly disagreed with the bishops' positions on the nuclear freeze and on Central American policy (D'Antonio, 1985). Conservative Protestants voiced similar concerns about these issues as well as about the World Council of Churches' involvement in and allocation of funds for liberation causes in Third World countries, which they perceived and continue to perceive as anticapitalist, pro-Marxist causes. We will turn now to the question of how supportive rank-and-file clergy and laity actually are of their churches' political stances.

Clergy and Lay Support for Religious Lobbies

Although religious lobbying appears to be an ongoing concern not only in Washington, D.C., but in the various state capitals as well, religious pressure groups in the United States do not always speak together, nor do they speak for all their members and clergy. It is true that many of the issues endorsed by these political arms of the churches are supported by the rank-and-file membership of the denominations as well as by religious Americans in general. For example, since the establishment of Israel as a modern nation, Jewish lobbying on behalf of Israel has enjoyed Protestant, Catholic, and non-religious support. Northern Protestants, Catholics, and Jews seemed to approve of their groups' efforts on behalf of civil rights for southern blacks in the 1960s. Most Baptists (and quite a few Methodists) have approved of pressure tactics to limit parochial school aid, though this position is not as widely espoused by other Protestants and Jews as it once was. And a majority of Roman Catholics have generally favored efforts to outlaw abortion. However, not all rank-and-file Catholics are as committed to prohibiting abortion by amendment as is the hierarchy of the church, and neither are most mainline Protestant pressure groups or Reform Judaism. In fact, particularistic lobbying by some religious organizations has alienated other religious groups as well as members within these groups.

As mentioned in Chapter 6, the 1960s in particular were a time when some denominational bodies took liberal stances that displeased members and led to a decline in giving and some decline in membership. Early church civil rights involvement was confined mostly to the South, and thus most churches comfortably supported political solutions from afar, although some clergy and laity were involved in marches, demonstrations, sit-ins, and voter registration drives. When the black leaders of the civil rights movement began to experience overt and covert racism and discrimination in the northern tier of states, religious leaders were put on the spot. They quickly learned that an official denominational endorsement of specific civil rights issues such as reparations for blacks could result in the withholding of denominational giving by the laity and condemnation of such stands by more conservative political officials. Unified church lobbying in this arena became fragmented, as pressure mounted from conservative church members against further extension of civil rights. Similarly, church lobbying against the war in Vietnam angered many members who either were for prosecution of the war or believed that governmental policy should not be questioned by religious organizations. The controversy between church leaders at the denominational level and the laity and some clergy at the congregational and parish level over the issues of the Vietnam War and civil rights brought about much disaffection among members who felt that their careers, families, and lifestyles were threatened (Hargrove, 1979b:215).

Conservative religious lobbies may also experience less-than-full support from the laity. For example, when Shupe and Stacey (1982) analyzed survey data from samples of citizens and clergy in the Dallas–Fort Worth area, they found no evidence of any sizable or majority support for the best-known group in the new religious-political right, the Moral Majority. In fact, they found that twice as many peo-

ple opposed the Moral Majority as supported it, and the largest percentage of their sample was indifferent to it. Furthermore, they reported that not all conservative evangelicals and fundamentalists
supported its agenda, but those who did tended to be people high in
traditional Christian orthodoxy, active churchgoers, and frequent
consumers of electronic church programming. Among the clergy, the
overwhelming support for Moral Majority issues came from conservative and fundamentalist Protestant ministers. A survey of Presbyterian, Methodist, Episcopalian, and Disciples of Christ ministers in the
western and northwestern sections of Texas by Beckley and Stribling
(1981) found, similarly, that support for Moral Majority issues was
low. A majority of the mainline Protestant clergy, regardless of theological orientation or political affiliation, opposed the amendment to
restore school prayer, the amendment to outlaw abortion, and censor-
ship of television programs. They did, however, support stronger
laws against pornography. Support for the agenda of the Moral Majority came largely from clergy in small towns whose populations
were less than five thousand. Congregational size, in itself, was not
significant. Gallup and Castelli (1989:206) found that the founder of
the Moral Majority, Jerry Falwell, was *less* popular than then–Soviet
President Gorbachev among nonevangelical Christians.

Religious preference and its relationship to approval or disapproval of the promotion of social change through religious lobbying
seems to be related to other variables—notably theological liberalism
or conservatism and to some extent social class. For example, Eck-
hardt (1970:199) reported that the greater the religiosity of the typical
white church member, the less militant that person was likely to be in
promoting civil rights reforms. The personal piety of such a church
member would reflect a conservative theological orientation. On the
other hand, liberally oriented laity do exist, many of whom are affluent. These people have generally expressed approval of the reform-
oriented political tactics characteristic of the mainline American
religious groups.

In the 1980s Guth found that among the Southern Baptist clergy,
those who were most orthodox in their beliefs were most likely to be
actively involved in politics and to approve of religious lobbying efforts. He also reported that among mainline Protestant clergy, those
who were the most liberal were most involved and most likely to support religiously oriented lobbying efforts (Guth, 1992). According to
another study, the Protestant clergy are characterized by at least two
separate "issue agendas." One is advocated by the more liberal clergy
and consists mainly of economic, welfare, and foreign policy issues.
The other is advocated by the more conservative clergy and consists

mainly of social issues such as abortion, school prayer, pornography, and antiwelfare issues. Both agendas are found within and across denominational lines (Green and Poloma, 1990). Smidt and Penning (1990) have suggested that such partisan and ideological orientations of the Protestant clergy could be contributing to a realignment of both Protestant clergy and laity into opposing ideological camps oriented to specific issue agendas. However, as Hunter (1987) demonstratred, not all younger evangelicals are conservative in terms of the crusading issues of the religious-political right. Furthermore, as the 1992 presidential election indicated, economic issues remain salient for a majority of American voters, in spite of the religious-political right's organized efforts to make their conservative social agenda the main issue. This raises the issue of the influence of religion on *actual* voting behavior.

Religious Influence on Voting Behavior

It is apparent that religion has some influence on voting behavior in the United States. Perhaps the most blatant example of this is the fact that until 1960, all the presidents of the United States were either members of some Protestant body or sympathetic to the Protestant religion. Protestant fears of "papal domination" of the presidency played no small part in the defeat of Catholic candidates, although this bias was more apparent in some elections than in others. We have already mentioned the anti-Catholicism of the Know-Nothing party in the mid-1800s. Another campaign in which anti-Catholicism played some part was the 1928 presidential campaign, in which a Catholic candidate, Al Smith, was opposed to the Eighteenth Amendment. Protestant extremists spoke out against Smith's perceived subservience to the Roman Catholic Church, and although newspapers and other periodicals did not overdramatize this facet of the election, the Catholic and liquor issues were on the minds of the electorate. On the other hand, evidence indicates that no Democratic candidate could have defeated Republican Herbert Hoover in that election, so that then, as now, other factors were important in the voting patterns of the electorate.

Historically, a link has existed between Roman Catholics and the Democratic party in the United States. As we mentioned in Chapter 5, the presence of urban Catholics who were voting for Democratic machine candidates greatly disturbed the Protestant establishment and caused an overwhelming majority of Protestants to begin the historical trend of voting for candidates of the Republican party. Only in the South did the Democratic party command a majority of Protestant voters. These patterns held true until recently when whites in south-

Table 10.4   **Religious Preference and Political Ideology (by Percentage)**

Preference	Political Ideology			
	Liberal	Moderate	Conservative	Total *N*
Catholic	27.4	41.9	30.6	2,147
Jewish	46.1	34.7	19.2	167
Baptist (excluding Southern Baptist)	33.0	33.9	33.0	221
Southern Baptist	22.2	41.3	36.5	820
Methodist	23.3	43.5	33.2	623
Lutheran	25.6	43.3	31.1	586
Presbyterian	24.8	35.9	39.2	395
Episcopalian	23.1	39.4	37.5	208
Sectarian	22.8	36.0	41.2	1,945
None	44.6	31.0	42.4	630

Source: Adapted from data by National Opinion Research Center General Social Surveys, 1986–91.

ern states began to abandon the Democratic party and Catholic voters voted for Ronald Reagan in large numbers.

Table 10.4 shows that political liberalism is not the ideology for a majority of members in any major religious denomination. Jews, however, are far more liberal than either Catholics or Protestants, and in fact are the most liberal group in the sample. These data also indicate that Protestant denominations with a higher proportion of members in the upper and upper-middle classes also have fewer members who embrace liberalism. The least liberal are the Lutherans, who have a majority of members in the middle class. However, more Methodists and Lutherans state that they are moderate than do either Presbyterians or Episcopalians. A moderate political ideology is characteristic of a plurality of Catholics and all the major Protestant groups, but Presbyterians and Episcopalians are less moderate and more conservative politically than other Protestants.

One valid conclusion seems to be that although one's religion does correlate with political liberalism and conservatism, so also does one's social class level. The exception, of course, is that Jews, who are relatively high in our stratification system, continue to reject political conservatism as an ideology. Catholics, by contrast, seem to be following more closely the Protestant pattern of political ideology, one that is understood by viewing social class and religion together as these variables relate to political liberalism and conservatism.

Analyses of presidential voting shows similar relationships between social class level, religious preference, and reported voting behavior. The 1980 election was somewhat different, but the traditional political alignments of various denominations still held up, for the most part. Certainly, the Iranian hostage crisis hurt Carter among members of all social class levels and all religious groups. Table 10.5 presents the findings for the 1980 race between Carter and Reagan. Small majorities of Catholics and Jews voted for the liberal candidate. Among Baptists (including black Baptists), the preference for Carter remained high. Once again, a majority of people from middle-class, upper-middle-class, and upper-class denominations reported a conservative preference by voting for Reagan. Both Presbyterians and Episcopalians voted in about the same proportions for Reagan as they did for Ford. However, more people indicating no religious preference voted for Reagan than voted in the previous election for Ford. Methodist voting was less evenly divided than in 1976, with the percentage preferring Carter declining. Lutherans reported an almost complete reversal. Although Carter's religiosity was questioned by the new religious-political right in 1980 (in spite of his evangelical Baptist membership), and several groups within the new religious-political right claimed that their voting provided Reagan's margin of victory, the religious issue, in the end, was probably not the most important determinant of the election's outcome.

The 1984 presidential race is more difficult to discern as to religious influence. Menendez (1988) states that an overwhelming majority of the fundamentalist and evangelical vote went for President Reagan, but so also did majorities and sizeable pluralities from most religious groups, as indicated in Table 10.6. Nevertheless, the religious-political right claimed credit for Reagan's reelection. Their presence on the contemporary scene does raise the question of the impact of religious bloc voting. To what extent can religious groups, like ethnic and racial groups in the past, use bloc voting to impose their viewpoints on the entire pluralistic electorate?

Table 10.7 shows the breakdown of votes by different religious categories. Analyses of the 1988 presidential election in a collection edited by Guth and Green (1991) show that Protestants remain an important component of Republican victories both at the presidential level and the local level. Smidt and Kellstedt (1992:332–38) observe that there seems to be a growing divergence between the voting patterns of white evangelical Protestants and nonevangelical Protestants within the South. As a result, southern evangelicals show voting patterns more characteristic of nonsouthern evangelical and fundamen-

**Table 10.5   Religious Preference and 1980 Presidential Voting
(by Percentage)**

Preference	Preferred Candidate		
	Carter	Reagan	Other
Catholic	51.7	39.7	8.6
Jewish	54.3	29.8	15.9
Baptist	69.5	28.9	1.6
Methodist	43.2	51.5	5.3
Lutheran	36.6	56.0	7.4
Presbyterian	30.8	61.0	8.2
Episcopalian	32.9	63.4	3.7
Sectarian	46.8	48.4	4.8
None	33.7	57.7	8.6
Total N = 2,872			

Source: Adapted from data by National Opinion Research Center General Social Surveys, 1979–84.

**Table 10.6   Religious Preference and 1984 Presidential Voting
(by Percentage)**

Preference	Preferred Candidate			
	Mondale	Reagan	Anderson	Other
Catholic	38.9	59.7	0.6	0.7
Jewish	60.9	37.9	1.1	—
Baptist (excluding Southern Baptist)	57.3	42.7	—	—
Southern Baptist	44.1	55.1	0.6	0.3
Methodist	30.4	68.7	0.3	0.6
Lutheran	32.7	66.0	1.3	—
Presbyterian	28.6	69.8	1.6	—
Episcopalian	27.8	70.4	1.9	—
Sectarian	31.4	67.9	0.5	0.2
None	50.9	44.5	2.3	2.3
Total N = 3,500				

Source: Adapted from data by National Opinion Research Center General Social Surveys, 1986–91.

talist Protestants. This indicates a voting pattern that emphasizes domestic social issues rather than economic issues. Menendez (1988) also concludes that the evangelical vote provided the margin of victory for George Bush in 1988 in several close states.

Table 10.7   Religious Preference and 1988 Presidential Voting
(by Percentage)

Preference	Preferred Candidate		
	Dukakis	Bush	Other
Catholic	40.5	58.7	0.9
Jewish	74.3	25.7	—
Baptist (excluding Southern Baptist)	62.3	36.1	1.6
Southern Baptist	38.3	61.3	0.4
Methodist	32.4	67.6	—
Lutheran	37.1	62.9	—
Presbyterian	31.1	68.9	—
Episcopalian	33.7	65.1	1.2
Sectarian	35.1	68.8	1.2
None	57.1	40.4	2.6
Total N = 2,409			

Source: Adapted from data by National Opinion Research Center General Social Surveys, 1986–91.

In spite of the attempts of the Republican presidential campaign to emphasize many of the crusading issues of the religious-political right during the 1992 presidential campaign, Bill Clinton won in a campaign that stressed the economic morass and hope for economic growth. As stated in Chapter 7, Bill Clinton was portrayed as the candidate on the wrong side of the "culture war battle line." In that election, the religious-political right was unable to provide the margin of victory for George Bush in several closely contested states that those groups had done in 1988 (Guth, 1992).

The religious-political right groups have laid claim to a significant role in defeating liberal politicians, yet little evidence exists that they have actually been responsible for most of these election outcomes during most of the 1980s. Congressional elections tend to focus mostly on the records of the incumbents or the promises of the challengers and only occasionally on religiously oriented issues.

The influence of religious bloc voting on state politics is somewhat different from its effect on national politics. Menendez (1977:15–16) reported that in twenty-two states, one religious tradition accounts for more than 50 percent of the total church membership; in twenty-five states, two religious groups comprise over 50 percent of the religious membership; and in only three states, at least three churches are required to form a majority of the religious membership. This still holds true. Clearly, the potential for religious influence in state polities is great. As stated in Chapter 7, three hundred local races were won by religious-political right candidates. There are also organized efforts by the religious right to take over control of the Republican party since the defeat of George Bush. Since President Clinton has stated that he plans to undo many of the conservative policies of President Bush, these efforts may dramatically increase. The crusading issues of the religious-political right will no longer enjoy the support they once had from George Bush.

In summary, religious groups have attempted to influence politics and governmental activity throughout the history of the United States, demonstrating the less-than-absolute boundary between church and state. Some of their efforts have succeeded, while others have failed. Protestant attempts to curtail Catholic and Jewish immigration were failures. Denying state aid to parochial schools was for many years a successful lobbying effort. Prohibition was both a success and a failure: The amendment was ratified, but its intent was never realized. Religious lobbying against the Vietnam War was perhaps one small factor in its eventual truncation. The religious-political right has had mixed success in influencing election outcomes. In the end, only those issues that have been perceived by a majority of politically involved citizens as good or necessary have been enacted into law or policy, and only those candidates whose appeal extends beyond the religious sphere have been elected, regardless of religious pressure tactics and religious influence on voting behavior.

RELIGION AND ECONOMIC ARRANGEMENTS

As we pointed out in the introduction to this chapter, religious organizations in the United States have more often supported than opposed the capitalist economic system. As the nation has prospered economically, so have the churches and their members. The importance of occupation and income for an American cannot be underestimated; along with educational attainment, these are the major indicators of social class level. In the next chapter we will show that social class and religion are highly associated with each other: Affluent individuals generally participate in religious organizations that have other affluent people as members, while poor persons generally belong to religious groups whose members are also poor. On a less individual level, the relationship between the economic system and religion in a society offers insight into the interrelationships of all social institutions.

In terms of sociological theory, two generalizations have offered basically different interpretations of the association between religion and economics. One is the thesis of Max Weber and the other is the theoretical viewpoint of Karl Marx. In the next section we will take a look at these interpretations.

Weber's Analysis of Protestantism and Capitalism

Max Weber (1958) believed that a set of religious ideas could profoundly influence secular economic behavior. His analysis was concentrated on the doctrines of John Calvin, usually referred to as Calvinism. Weber's argument was that Calvinist doctrine determined the content of a unique system of ethics that led to the creation of an ideal character type important in stimulating the development of rational capitalism.

Briefly stated, Weber's analysis began with the Calvinist conception of God, which emphasized his glory and holiness and his freedom and sovereignty. Since humanity exists for the pleasure of God, everything we humans do should be for his glory. Weber also demonstrated that these conceptions of God and humanity led to the doctrine of predestination, the belief that God selects certain individuals for heaven and others for hell, and that nothing individuals do during their lifetime can affect God's decision. This absolutism of God had an important implication for the Calvinists: A person had to go through life all alone to meet his ultimate destiny. Weber saw this as producing a tremendous psychological pressure on Calvinists to live righteously to convince themselves that they could be among the elect destined for eternal salvation.

These doctrines created a set of ethical standards. In addition to honoring and glorifying God through the sacraments and on Sundays, people had to glorify God through their labors during the week. Working for the glory of God required nothing less than the best efforts of believers. The emphasis was upon individualism in all social relationships, including work. Those individuals who worked hardest would do the most to glorify God. Additionally, economic achievement would occur, but the use of the money had also to be for God's glory. Wealth must not be spent frivolously. Hence, it must be saved, even invested, in order to demonstrate further a person's dedication to hard work by enabling the production of more goods, which would then create more profit and, in turn, more investment.

Weber did not attribute the development of all forms of capitalism to Calvinist doctrine. He did, however, hypothesize that modern rational capitalism was a product of the Calvinist tradition of the Reformation. In what Weber called the emergence of *ascetic Protestantism*, or devotion to a life of discipline and hard work, religious doctrine produced the enterprising attitude required by modern rational capitalism. Thus Calvinism, in Weber's view, hastened the development of capitalism in the countries where Calvinist influence was greatest—England, Scotland, the Netherlands, and English colonial America. Capitalism rapidly became the dominant economic activity in the Western world.

Critics of the Weberian thesis point out that the Catholic spheres of influence in Europe also allowed the development of capitalism. Others argued that later interpreters of Calvin's writings, and not Calvin himself, rationalized economic success and interpreted the accumulation of wealth as virtuous. Hammond and Demerath (1969:150) have written that the advent of Protestantism was the beginning of the breakdown of medieval Catholic control, and this resulted in greater freedom to experiment with new political and economic forms, one of which was capitalism. The debate over the correctness of Weber's thesis has raged for many decades. Who is right—Weber or his critics? The answer is not clear, but the questions raised by Weber's thesis are useful for analyzing the relationship between religion and the economy in the United States. In particular, we can ask (1) to what extent the religious dimension influences capitalist economics, or vice versa, and (2) to what extent the *Protestant work ethic* exists in our country.

Weber's Thesis and the United States

If the United States is Protestant in orientation, in spite of its religious pluralism, does Weber's thesis find validation here? The answer to this question is a qualified yes. The history of the relationship between organized religion and the economy shows that almost all religious bodies have supported the capitalist economic system of the United States. The dominant Protestant denominations of the nineteenth century strongly supported the emerging industrial economy, and the large Catholic and Jewish immigration supplied the workers for that system. As we said in Chapter 7, the evangelical preachers of the 1800s, notably Dwight L. Moody, proclaimed a message stressing the harmonious relationship between industrial capitalism and Christianity.

Today the major churches and synagogues of the United States are primarily attended by individuals who are business people, professionals, or workers. Almost all have profited financially from the capitalist economic system. On an institutional level, organized reli-

gion is intimately involved in the economic system, both as a producer and as a consumer. As a consuming unit, religion depends upon
the voluntary financial support of its constituency. The millions of
contributors to religious causes and enterprises are given a tax advantage: Religious gifts are tax exempt. Religious organizations themselves are granted a tax-exempt status for all operations except those
that are obviously commercial. Literally billions of dollars worth of
church property and other assets are exempt from local, state, and
federal taxes. As a producing unit in the economy, religious groups in
the United States employ thousands of workers. Not only are professional ministers, priests, and rabbis paid, but auxiliary personnel,
such as educational directors, musicians, secretaries, and clerks, are
salaried employees of religious bodies. Investments in the form of
time deposits, stocks, and bonds are made by Christian churches and
Jewish bodies to increase the monies available for employees' pension
funds and for denominations' capital funds. Like private corporations
and government agencies, the major religious traditions have denominational bureaucracies whose tasks include the preparation, printing,
and distribution of religious literature, distribution of church funds, and
coordination of denominational schools, seminaries, and programs.

So it would seem that the religious and economic dimensions do
influence each other in the United States. As far as the Protestant
work ethic goes, the ethics of our religious traditions generally lends
support to the dominant capitalist economic system. In addition,
many business people attribute their success to God. Although this
was at one time more of a Protestant phenomenon than a Catholic or
Jewish one, the other two religious traditions generally support capitalism as much as do the Protestant denominations. Protestants occupy the highest echelons of business, government, and education in
greater proportions than do either Catholics or Jews, but Greeley's
(1977) data on Catholics in the contemporary United States suggest
that economic gains made by members of that tradition have created
a situation of parity with Protestants. Jews have outstripped both
Protestants and Catholics in general economic gains, but still are behind Protestants in access to the highest positions in the economic
sphere. What was once the Protestant work ethic has become a generalized work ethic, followed by a majority of members from all three
major religious traditions as well as by the religiously nonaffiliated.

Marx's Analysis of Religion and the Economic Order

Although religious beliefs and practices do draw Americans together politically and economically, some evidence exists that the eco-

nomic cleavages present in the social class system of the United States are related to our religious traditions. In Chapter 1, we stated that Karl Marx believed that religious institutions played a pivotal role in sustaining the vested interests of the dominant capitalist class within society. According to Marxist theory, religion contributes to the class structure, and aids in perpetuating an unequal distribution of wealth. A Marxist analysis also views religion as another force that alienates individuals from their true humanity. The masses in society are not only denied the wealth and prestige available to a select few but they are also encouraged by the dominant religious system to accept this position in the stratification system.

Marxist theorists see economic strife and conflict in the United States attributable in some ways to religious institutions as much as to economic and governmental arrangements. All denominations and religious groups of any size are culpable. Because no one powerful state church dominated the economic system, and virtually all religious groups include *some* members from the lower-class as well as the upper-class levels, almost all religious organizations in the United States support the capitalist economic system. Religion, then, is viewed as an extension of a dominant and propertied social order by those who subscribe to a Marxist perspective. Some evidence exists to support this view, but the collapse of totalitarian socialist governments and economic systems in central and eastern Europe and in the former Soviet Union has diminished the viability of a Marxist analysis of the institutions of society.

Religion and Health Care

Religion and health care have always been intimately related in this and other societies. In medieval times, hospitals were built by the church to provide assistance for the sick and needy (Kurtz and Chalfant, 1991). Some of the first hospitals were built and operated by Catholic religious orders as places for the poor to die. In 1737 the Roman Catholic Church founded Charity Hospital in New Orleans. By the beginning of the twentieth century, most cities of medium size had a hospital, usually operated by some religious order or denomination. Thus, Christianity has for centuries been involved with medicine, carrying on the tradition of medical healing through miracles and prayers.

In the United States, the successor to this tradition of healing has been the faith healer who claims to be God's medical representative. Denton (1978) stated that two basic beliefs are common in faith healing. One belief stresses that faith healing mostly involves psychologi-

cal processes and can only be effective with psychophysiological illnesses. The second belief emphasizes the healing intervention of God
as a modern-day miracle. Not only is faith healing a part of the Pentecostal Protestant tradition but it is also one of the central tenets of
Christian Science. During the 1980s there was a resurgence of interest
in the supernatural aspect of health care. Part of this is due to the influence of "holistic" health care orientation in medicine and in counseling techniques (Schaller and Carroll, 1976).

In hospital settings, chaplains, chapels, and prayer rooms are
found, regardless of whether or not the hospital is governmental, private, or religious. Clergy are notified when their parishioners are admitted and when someone from their denomination is hospitalized.
Obviously, religion plays an important role in illness and in life and
death matters connected with illness. Furthermore, when an illness is
seen as the result of an individual's actions, the judgmental nature of
religion can come into play. The appearance of AIDS as a life-threatening illness linked to an individual's actions provides an example of
both the positive and negative consequences of the association between religion and medicine.

Religion and AIDS

Throughout history, medical crises and diseases have challenged
societies and their institutions. In the United States as well as in Canada and Europe, religion has been confronted and challenged by AIDS
and the social effects upon those who have this disease and those who
have tested positive to the acquired immunodeficiency syndrome.
These effects are generated and sustained because AIDS continues to
be seen more as a stigmatized illness than as a terminal disease. Consequently, this stigma of AIDS as an illness overshadows the medical
and scientific aspects of AIDS as a disease.

The initial appearance of AIDS as a "new" terminal disease during the early 1980s attracted widespread public attention because sexual transmission of HIV was identified as the primary way the virus
spread from one person to another. By 1985 the overwhelming proportion of deaths from AIDS and known HIV-positive individuals
was from the ranks of gay and bisexual men. In 1988 an estimated 70
percent of the AIDS sufferers were gay or bisexual men or gay or bisexual men who were also intravenous drug users (Heyword and
Curran, 1988). The proportion of heterosexual individuals (including
drug users, women, adolescents, and children) gradually increased.
In 1990 the United States Public Health Department estimated that 63
percent of all known cases involved gay and bisexual men, whose

rate of infection began to decline by 1991 as the rates for the other groups began to climb (U.S. Department of Public Health, 1992). Still, the majority of known cases of AIDS and known HIV-positive individuals are from the original high-risk groups in society. This is in sharp contrast to Africa and to Asia, where the majority of cases are found among heterosexuals.

Almost from the beginning of the AIDS crisis in the United States, the controversial issue of gay sexuality and sexual behavior became issues for most Protestant denominations, the Roman Catholic Church, and Judaism. Gallup and Castelli (1989:190–92) reported that those least likely to favor gay rights (Protestant fundamentalists and evangelicals) are most likely to "blame" people with AIDS for their plight and for the spread of AIDS. They also found that mainline Protestants, Catholics, and Jews are less likely to see AIDS as the "wrath of God visited on homosexuals." However, even among those claiming membership in the more moderate and liberal denominations, Gallup and Castelli discovered people who held those views. Still, for many AIDS was a disease with little impact upon them personally. Many Americans saw AIDS as an illness affecting primarily people in urban areas with sizable gay and lesbian populations (San Francisco, Los Angeles, New York City, Houston, and Dallas). As a consequence, organized religious groups reacted rather slowly to the growing number of diagnosed AIDS cases and HIV-positive individuals, with two important exceptions.

These exceptions to a rather slow religious involvement were the Metropolitan Community Church and the Episcopal Diocese of San Francisco. The Metropolitan Church, with its predominantly gay and lesbian membership, began to minister to "its own" who were dying. The Episcopal bishop in San Francisco urged parishes within his dioceses to offer pastoral care and other services for AIDS sufferers. Other clergy and congregations seemed willing to help—but often only if asked.

Beckley and Chalfant (1988a; 1989) found that while a majority of Protestant clergy did not believe that AIDS was the "wrath of God," 97 percent reported that at least some members of their congregation thought that it was. In spite of their nonjudgmental attitude, only 29 percent of the clergy had actually dealt with an AIDS sufferer. In another study of the Presbyterian clergy, Beckley and Chalfant (1988b; 1990) found that 5 percent of these mainline pastors did believe that AIDS was the "wrath of God," and that 15 percent thought that inappropriate sexual behavior on the part of people with AIDS was to blame for their illness. For the most part, churches and clergy did not take an active role in providing either pastoral counseling or other

forms of care to people with AIDS. However, a variety of denominations made pronouncements, issued position papers, and published
resources for congregations. Some of the pronouncements were neither comforting nor supportive of people with AIDS. Jorstad (1990:
143–44) reports that the founder of the Moral Majority, Jerry Falwell,
blamed homosexuals for their illness and for the spread of the HIV
virus. Other Protestant fundamentalists and evangelicals opposed efforts to provide better sex education to impede the spread of AIDS
and to make condoms more readily available to both adults and adolescents.

Kowalewski (1990:91–96) examined statements on AIDS from a
variety of religious denominations and groups and found that there
were three types of statements and pronouncements. The first response type engaged in "blaming the victim" and defined AIDS as a
divine punishment. Jerry Falwell's statements fell into this type, as
did a 1986 pastoral letter from the Vatican sent to all Catholic bishops.
The second engaged in "embracing the exile." These statements and
writings viewed AIDS as a disease which could be prevented by
avoiding certain behaviors. AIDS, however, was separated from sexual morality. Most mainline Protestant denominational materials and
some individualistic Catholic statements and writings were representative of this type. The third type promoted "helping the victim" and
attempted to reconcile the two polar types by defining AIDS as a public health crisis while maintaining the traditional religious norms
against homosexuality. Literature of this type showed ambivalence
concerning the proper religious response to AIDS. Some of the pronouncements advocated "caring for sinners," while others stressed
"curing the sick." Much Catholic material fell into this category.

In addition to these materials, several writers, most of whom
were directly involved in ministering to people with AIDS, wrote articles and books attempting to reaffirm religion's need to minister to
people with AIDS in the same way that religion ministers to all
among the powerless and outcasts of society (Flynn, 1985; Casto,
1987; Shelp and Sunderland, 1985; Shelp and Sunderland, 1987; 1991;
Amos, 1988; Goss, 1989). Also, several publications affirmed the necessity of religiously oriented gays in ministering to persons with
AIDS (Kayal, 1985; 1992). In spite of these advocacy statements and
practical guides for pastoral care and care teams, most congregations
and clergy remained slow in responding to people with AIDS. As a
result, more activist congregations and clergy began to set up AIDS
interfaith networks, denominational specific networks, hospice programs, and laity care teams. At first these were available only in larger metropolitan areas.

Their success led to the formation of a National Interfaith AIDS Network, a National Catholic AIDS Network, and several Protestant Denominational AIDS networks. As AIDS became an illness seen in cities of medium and small size, religious organizations there began to organize AIDS interfaith networks and hospices, providing more options for religiously oriented care for people with AIDS. In follow-up interviews conducted in 1991, Beckley and Chalfant (1992a; 1992b) found that 94 percent of the clergy originally interviewed in 1987 and 1988 had now provided some spiritual care and counseling to people with AIDS and HIV-positive individuals, as compared to 29 percent four years earlier. Ninety-four percent stated that more resources were now available to them in terms of counseling and support services. Only 4 percent of these clergy still felt either hostility toward or inadequacy in dealing with AIDS-related illness or HIV-positive individuals. Forty percent of these Protestant ministers reported they had utilized one or more acts of worship in ministering to people with AIDS. Furthermore, more Catholic priests and Jewish rabbis were involved in AIDS ministries in 1992 than four years earlier.

AIDS remains a stigmatized illness that is on the increase. It is one of those diseases that is morally suspect, like leprosy, epilepsy, mental disorders, and venereal diseases. Those who suffer from such a disease are subjected to stigma or moral shame (Conrad, 1986). Stigmatized illnesses are in some way linked to deviant behavior and seen, at least to some degree, as the fault of those who have them. Deaths reported to be AIDS-related between 1981 and 1992 numbered 241,000. The Center for Disease Control estimated 50,000 additional deaths for 1991 and 1992. Public health authorities believe that as many as 1.2 million people in the United States are carrying the HIV virus. More and more, most people will know someone who is living with AIDS or is HIV-positive. Clearly, religious organizations will become more involved in pastoral care, in support services, and perhaps in advocacy roles for those who are HIV-positive. Still, it is likely that Protestant fundamentalist and evangelical congregations will be the least involved as long as statistics suggest that premarital, extramarital, and gay sexual behavior are the primary means of HIV transmission. Such religious groups are also unlikely to show compassion for intravenous drug users who become infected.

SUMMARY

Traditionally, marriage and family life have been closely related to religion. In the United States people have believed that family relations are closely linked to religious norms. However, single-parent families and serial marriages have presented religious organizations with new challenges. No longer do marriage and family life mean a lifetime commitment.

Several aspects of marriage and family life are related to religious socialization. Religious preference tends to define the pool from which one chooses a marriage partner. Whether or not a marriage ends in divorce is also related to religious preference, although less so today than in the past. Today there is a convergence among Catholic, Protestant, and Jewish divorce rates. To some extent religious preference seems to be associated with marital happiness. In addition, those with no religious preference seem least satisfied with their family life. There are difference between the major religious groupings as to the proper roles of husbands, wives, and children. Mainline Protestants, most Roman Catholics, and Jews have modified their views concerning the subjugation of wives and children to fathers. However, the more conservative religious groups hold more traditional opinions on this subject. Despite these differences, most religious groups within the United States have responded to changes in family structure. Both teachings and policies regarding divorce, single-parent families, and two-income families have been modified.

The relationship between education and religion is best understood as a multifaceted association. Religious organizations have promoted education since the colonial era, with some exceptions. For the most part, private, parochial, and public education coexist peacefully. Some tensions continue between conservative and fundamentalist Protestants and state-supported public education. The number of private Protestant schools has increased, as have the number of children being schooled at home by religiously conservative parents who mistrust public education. In addition, the issues of prayer in schools and the teaching of creationism and perceived "secular humanism" remain smoldering questions for many who do not accept the contemporary church-state policy.

Religion and other social institutions in American society share a common culture and norms. The unique religious pluralism in the United States has, by and large, been encouraged by our political institution. Occasionally though, religious groups and the government have seemingly overstepped the blurred boundaries separating church and state. When such conflicts occur, the federal courts have attempted to define what is religious (and thus protected by First Amendment rights) and what is secular (and thus governed by the laws of the United States). In more recent years the courts have protected the rights of the nonreligious as well.

Most religious groups lobby both the federal and the state governments to make their positions known on legislation with religious or moral implications. The religious right has opposed many "status quo" government programs on the ground that they are "un-Christian" and "prosecular." Abortion rights are one of the most emotional of their crusading issues. Religious groups which are more moderate and liberal continue to lobby for pluralistic positions which recognize the diversity of the U.S. population and respect the constitutional and individual rights of all citizens, regardless of religious preference.

Religion in America has historically supported capitalism. This situation appears to conform to Weber's contention that Protestantism, by encouraging a work ethic, set the stage for modern rational capitalism. Most major religious groups have profited institutionally from our capitalist economic system. So, too, have most individual members of these groups. According to Marxist theory, economic strife and conflict in the United States are just as much caused by our religious institutions as by our economic and political systems.

Religion and health are closely related. The earliest hospitals and other places of health care were begun by religious organizations, and this tradition is still alive today. Since illness and death are major life crises, the religious institution provides chaplains in health care settings. Spiritual healing is also important to many people in our society, both as a supplement to modern medicine as well as an alternative to it.

The emergence of AIDS as a new life-threatening illness has become a challenge for both medicine and religion. Since the majority of deaths and HIV-positive diagnoses have occurred among gay men, bisexual men, and intravenous drug users, AIDS remains a stigmatized illness. Many religious groups are reluctant to provide the normal spiritual support and counseling given to those suffering from other illnesses. Some conservative and fundamentalist Protestant groups have condemned the sufferers as "sinners suffering from the wrath of God visited on homosexuals." However, most religious organizations and their clergy do respond to the need of people with AIDS and HIV-positive individuals.

11.
Religion and Social Stratification

I sing a song of the saints of God…
Patient and brave and true,
Who toiled and fought and lived and died
For the Lord they loved and knew.
And one was a doctor, and one was a queen,
And one was a shepherdess on the green;
They were all of them saints of God—
and I mean, God helping, to be one too.

They lived not only in ages past;
There are hundreds and thousands still.
The world is bright with the joyous saints
Who love to do Jesus' will.
You can meet them in school, or in lanes, or at sea,
In church, or in trains, or in shops, or at tea,
For the saints of God are just folk like me,
And I mean to be one too.

Episcopal hymn / Lesbia Scott, 1929

Have you failed in your plan of your storm-tossed life?
Place your hand in the nail-scarred hand;
Are you weary and worn from its toil and strife?

Place your hand in the nail-scarred hand.
Are you walking alone thro' the shadows dim?
Place your hand in the nail-scarred hand;
Christ will comfort your heart, put your trust in him,
Place your hand in the nail-scarred hand.
Place your hand in the nail-scarred hand,
Place your hand in the nail-scarred hand;
He will keep to the end, he's your dearest friend,
Place your hand in the nail-scarred hand.

Baptist hymn / B. B. McKinney, 1924

Clearly, these two hymns differ greatly in both tone and message. One seems to express a confidence in this life and our part in it; the other gives the impression that this life is a time of pain and suffering from which the only relief is to be found in another existence. The difference is not simply accidental. Each hymn is more or less unique to its denomination; and each denomination, while having members from all walks of life, is dominated by a different socioeconomic stratum or social class. The tone of the Episcopal hymn, primarily a children's hymn, expresses the secure place in life of the upper-class members of that denomination, while the message of the Baptist hymn seems attuned to the needs of the large number of lower-class persons belonging to that group. Although we may seek to avoid the knowledge, we need not look closely to notice that our churches are stratified, just like other aspects of society.

This should come as no sudden revelation to the student of society. The totality of the stratification system's effects on our lives is perhaps the best-established and most reliable social fact we have. Although sociologists may argue about the necessity, inevitability, and value of stratification, none deny its omnipresent consequences. The partitioning of society into groups ranked by power, prestige, property, and/or psychic reward touches every corner of our lives, and our religious lives are no exception. The effects of social stratification (the system of social class) are felt in every aspect of the operation of religious organizations, and in the ways in which their members express their religiosity. In this chapter we will consider these effects of the stratification system on religion and religiosity.

SOCIAL CLASS AND RELIGIOUS AFFILIATION

Church membership can mean a variety of things to individuals, such as commitment and devotion to a specific set of beliefs and val-

ues, continuance of a family tradition, opportunity for business contacts, or simply maintenance of a routine. From the sociological perspective, yet another meaning attaches to membership in a specific
denomination (or sect) and in a particular congregation. Membership
endows the individual with some measure of social status, either
higher or lower, depending on the church. Whether or not we are
consciously aware of this symbolic link of church and class, subcon-
sciously we do seem to know that those people who belong to "Old
First" have higher status than those who attend "Faith Tabernacle."
Gilbert and Kahl (1993:130), in their work on American class structure, tellingly state:

> Even churches—institutions supposedly rejoicing in the common broth-
> erhood of a common Father—are class typed. In most American towns,
> the people of higher status belong to those Protestant denominations that
> feature services of quiet dignity and restrained emotion, such as the Epis-
> copal or Unitarian groups. The common men are more often seen at the
> Methodist and Baptist churches, where the services are more vigorous,
> or in Catholic churches (reflecting their origins as part of the "new" im-
> migration from southern and eastern Europe).

Membership in or preference for a particular denomination or
sect is related, then, to socioeconomic status, according to all indications. Of course, no church is totally homogeneous as to class (see
Roof and McKinney, 1987:68), but the different groups do tend to
have certain social class profiles. In Chapter 5, while discussing the
various types of religious organizations, we noted that the most certain generalization that we can make about the differences between
the sect and the denomination is that the former is basically lower-
class in membership, while the latter is overwhelmingly made up of
middle- and upper-class individuals. On balance, however, Demerath
(1965:xxi) has pointed out that although it has been commonplace for
studies to make a distinction between the low-status sects and the
higher-status denominations, the membership pattern of religious
groups in the United States is extremely heterogenous, with the particular religious groups having considerable diversity within as well
as among themselves. With that caveat in mind, we can look at the
generalizations arrived at by a couple of different studies of church
affiliation and social class.

At the middle of this century, Schneider (1952) provided a sketch
of the distribution of members by social class for the major religious
groups of that time. Groups such as the Episcopal and Presbyterian
churches, as well as the Jewish faith, tended to have higher proportions of members from what Schneider called the upper class. On the

other hand, about two-thirds of members of the Roman Catholic, Baptist, and Mormon groups came from the lower class, and more than 60 percent of those belonging to small sectarian bodies were also in the lower class. While each of these religious groups had members from all classes, including the upper or upper-middle class, the percentage of members of different status groups varied.

A recent portrait of the social class composition of religious groups in our society is provided by data from the General Social Surveys conducted by the National Opinion Research Center (NORC) from 1986 through 1991 (see Table 11.1). The four socioeconomic status groups, referred to as upper, middle, working, and lower class, are based on a combination of income, education, and occupation, and correspond generally to the classes used by Demerath (1965) in a general study of social class and Protestantism in the United States.

As this table indicates, the relationship between social class and religious affiliation remains similar, though not identical, to that found in the fifties. The three groups that had a preponderance of upper-class members in 1952 (Jewish, Episcopal, and Presbyterian) still have far the greatest proportion of higher-status members. Nearly 45 percent of those indicating affiliation with the Jewish faith are upper-class, as are nearly 40 percent of those affiliated with the Episcopal church. Presbyterians have nearly 35 percent upper-class members. The Baptists continue to have over two-thirds of their members from the working and lower classes, and the sectarian groups have more than 50 percent of members from these two groups.

Table 11.1   Religious Affiliation and Socioeconomic Status (by Percentage)

| | Socioeconomic Status | | | | |
Affiliation	Upper Class	Middle Class	Working Class	Lower Class	Total N
Catholic	26.1	27.4	22.3	24.3	2,238
Jewish	44.4	25.1	7.6	22.8	171
Baptist	11.7	20.9	28.7	38.7	230
Southern Baptist	21.0	26.8	29.6	22.6	868
Methodist	30.6	23.5	21.1	24.8	648
Lutheran	31.1	26.1	20.7	22.1	598
Presbyterian	34.2	24.9	17.5	23.4	406
Episcopal	39.7	21.5	20.1	18.7	214
Sectarian	22.8	24.2	28.1	25.0	2,069
None	29.8	25.6	22.3	22.3	668

Source: Summary Data from National Opinion Research Center General Social Surveys, 1986–91.

The major change, at least for the limited number of groups considered here, involves the Roman Catholic Church. Since Schneider's study, the status of those indicating a preference for the Roman Catholic Church has risen overall. While only a very few (8.76 percent) upper-class individuals indicated affiliation with it in 1952, today all levels of the status continuum are nearly equally represented in the Catholic Church. It, like the Methodist Church, appears to have equal appeal for all groups in society. Roof and McKinney (1987:110) also show that the Catholics have moved into this middle range. They note that other groups formerly in the bottom rank now fall into the middle of the status hierarchy, e.g., the Mormons as well as miscellaneous evangelical and fundamentalist groups. According to Roof and McKinney's analysis of NORC data, only the Christian Scientists have fallen from the top rank while Unitarian-Universalists have risen to that rung.

We can also note that sectarian groups have a higher percentage of upper-class members than do the Baptists. This figure is double that found by Schneider and may mean that many groups once seen as sectarian should no longer be classified as such. Interestingly, sectarians and Southern Baptists are very similar in class composition. Additionally, Stark and Bainbridge (1985) have found that many recruits to cults, often classified as sects, are the children of upper-class families. Another change of note is the fairly equal spread through the various social classes of those claiming "none" as religious affiliation (see also Roof and McKinney, 1987:114). Despite these changes and the continuing presence of members of all status groups in each religious organization, stratification patterns are still discernable for the majority of religious affiliations.

Data from NORC used in the first two editions of this book (1981; 1987) revealed significant differences in intensity of religious preference by social class. Current data (Table 11.2), however, show that differences in intensity are not statistically significant. The pattern is for all classes to be about equally split between categories of *strong* intensity and *not strong* intensity of preference. The largest differential revealed for any class is that of the working class, where 46.1 percent indicated a strong religious preference compared to 53.9 percent who indicated that their religious preference was not strong. The fact that nearly 50 percent of all class members indicate a strong preference may denote what Roof and McKinney (1987:247) refer to as a type of *individualism* in religious preference. They say (1987:248):

Table 11.2   Socioeconomic Status and Intensity of Religious Preference (by Percentage)

Intensity of Preference	Socioeconomic Status			
	Upper Class	Middle Class	Working Class	Lower Class
Not strong	51.3	51.7	53.9	50.2
Strong	48.7	48.3	46.1	49.8

Note: Differences not significant at $p.<0.05$.

Source: Summary Data from National Opinion Research Center General Social Surveys, 1986–91.

By the turn of the century, many religious groups may have a clearer religious and cultural identity than they now have.... More voluntary patterns of religious switching in the future will contribute to more homogeneous orientational and behavioral styles. As church affiliation ceases to fulfill a vaguely perceived social obligation, and as the choice of a church ceases to express one's social standing and cultural background, individuals will "sort themselves out" more on the basis of personal preference. As a result, ideological differences between the churches could become more pronounced.

This interesting phenomenon is also connected to larger societal changes. While people of all classes are now in the process of sorting themselves out more on the basis of personal preference, the strength of religious preference has increased for all groups since the 1970s.

SOCIAL CLASS AND RELIGIOSITY

As religious preference is related to social class, so also is the degree of religiosity related to socioeconomic position. Yet, as Demerath (1965) has pointed out, the relationship is not clear: Some investigators have found that religiosity is highest for upper-status individuals while others have found just the opposite. Demerath goes on to suggest, in effect, that since religiosity is not unidimensional, persons may be religious to different degrees on different dimensions of religiosity. That is, individuals express their religiosity not only to varying degrees but also in varying ways. Socioeconomic status, thus, affects not just the degree but also the form of religiosity.

An investigation by Stark (1972) into the nature of this difference found it to be quite complex. He, too, sees the class difference in religiosity as one of kind rather than degree. As he has noted (1972:496), "The poor are not just more or less religious than the rich, or even more or less religious in different ways, but they are more religious in some ways under some circumstances, and less religious in some ways under other circumstances." Stark, along with Bainbridge (1985), feels that socioeconomic status is related to what individuals look for in religion. Identifying power as the important element in status, they propose that those with power, that is, upper-status individuals and groups, look for rewards of a more immediate type from their religious groups than do those with less power. Similarly, those with little power seek compensation for this lack of power from their religious involvement. Thus the kind of religious involvement differs by status group. Since not all members of a particular religious group are from the same class, as we have seen, this proposition means that individuals in the same group may well be seeking different things from their religious participation.

The question of social class and religiosity can be approached in several ways. We will look at two aspects of this matter of difference in kind rather than degree of religiosity by socioeconomic status: (1) attendance at church services and (2) churchlike and sectlike religiosity in the same groups.

Church Attendance

Stark (1972), as well as others, has indicated that persons from the upper class are more likely than lower-class persons to participate in such public rituals as Sunday morning worship services, saying grace before meals, and other organized activities of the group. Researchers have noted that attendance at formal Sunday worship services is a middle-class and upper-class phenomenon.

Certainly evidence from the past has supported this contention. The data presented in Table 11.3, however, do not do so. According to these data, small differences do exist in the tendency to attend religious services regularly. But, despite statistical significance, they are small in terms of substance. The major indication is that those we classify as *working class* are most likely to attend rarely. It may be that the resurgence of fundamentalism over the past several years has impacted more heavily on the lower class than on the upper or middle ranks. Or, conversely, the decline of the mainline churches may also signal a decline in the attendance of the upper- and middle-class people who are the major support of such congregations.

Table 11.3   Socioeconomic Status and Attendance at Religious Services
(by Percentage)

Attendance	Socioeconomic Status			
	Upper Class	Middle Class	Working Class	Lower Class
Barely	18.0	21.3	24.5	22.6
Some	27.3	27.1	24.1	24.1
Often	18.4	17.1	18.6	18.0
Regularly	36.3	34.5	32.8	35.3
Total N	2,342	2,278	2,239	2,249

Note: All differences significant at p <0.001.

Source: Summary Data from National Opinion Research Center General Social Surveys, 1986–91.

Churchlike versus Sectlike Religiosity

As Stark and Glock (1968) have noted, sectlike elements can be found in even the most formal denominations, and some churchlike tendencies appear in the most sectlike groups. Further, they suggest that lower-class members of more middle-class groups are responsible for what sectlike practices are found in such churches. Demerath (1961, 1965) has worked on this assumption and studied churchlike versus sectlike religiosity as it relates to differences for the four socioeconomic status groups. For Demerath, churchlike religiosity is suggested by such behavior as frequent attendance at Sunday morning services, taking part in the activities of the church, and belonging, in addition, to a number of voluntary organizations other than the church. Sectlike religiosity, on the other hand, is marked by communal involvement in the religious group and is measured by having a number of close friends in the congregation, finding religious rewards paying off in secular areas of life, and the tendency to disapprove of the pastor's participation in community affairs and controversy (1965:82).

Using these behaviors as measures of the two types of religiosity, Demerath looked at the involvement of members of four West Coast denominations (the Congregationalists, Presbyterians, Disciples of Christ, and Baptists) by social class. The data showed that the upper-class members were consistently more likely to be churchlike than were other members classified as lower-class; indeed, the upper-class members were more frequently churchlike in their religiosity than any of the other three groups. The corollary held also: Lower-class members were more likely to report a sectlike religiosity than were those from the other classes in Demerath's analysis.

The tendency to express religion in a sectlike fashion was also somewhat tied to the denomination insofar as Congregationalists and Baptists in Demerath's study were concerned. The Congregationalists, occupying the highest status of the four groups studied, had, in comparison, relatively few members *in any status group* who expressed their religiosity in a sectlike fashion. Similarly, the lowest-status group, the Baptists, had a higher proportion of those with sectlike religiosity than any other group. Thus, sectlike religiosity, like the churchlike variety, is tied to both social class and denomination.

Another way to look at the matter is to focus on the relationship between socioeconomic status and the tendency of church members to report having felt a religious experience, such as sensing a divine presence. Stark (1972) found social class differences in the tendency to report such religious experiences. While a sizable proportion in all four groups in his study reported a religious experience (even 38 percent of the liberal Protestant upper-class members reported such experiences), a clear tendency existed for lower-class members to report more religion experiences. This difference was small only in the case of the conservative churches, where a greater emphasis is placed on such emotionality in religious behavior. And this difference in religious experience by socioeconomic status continues to hold somewhat today. Data from the National Opinion Research Center indicate that members of the working and lower classes are more likely than members of other classes to have experienced often a sense of the supernatural, though these differences are not statistically significant (see Table 11.4).

Table 11.4   Socioeconomic Status and Experience of the Supernatural (by Percentage)

	Socioeconomic Status			
Frequency of Experience	Upper Class	Middle Class	Working Class	Lower Class
Often	4.1	3.6	5.7	5.4
Several times	9.3	6.9	7.6	10.0
Once or twice	20.6	18.6	15.6	15.4
Never	66.0	70.9	71.1	69.3

Note: Differences not significant at $p < 0.05$ level.

Source: Summary Data from National Opinion Research Center General Social Surveys, 1986–91.

Another measure of religious experience is the sense of closeness to God. As Table 11.5 shows, lower-class respondents to the NORC surveys were much more likely than upper-class respondents to feel extremely close to God. Similarly, lower-class respondents were the least likely to feel not close at all to God. And the prayer life of those in the lower class appears to be more frequent, if not richer, than that of the other classes. As Table 11.6 shows, lower-class respondents to the NORC surveys were somewhat more likely than those in other classes to pray once or several times a day. They were also less likely to pray less than once a week or never at all.

Table 11.5 Socioeconomic Status and Feelings of Closeness to God
(by Percentage)

	Socioeconomic Status			
Feelings of Closeness	Upper Class	Middle Class	Working Class	Lower Class
Extremely close	26.3	30.5	34.4	39.7
Somewhat close	55.7	54.7	50.2	49.3
Not very close	9.5	8.6	9.7	6.3
Not close at all	6.2	5.0	4.6	3.3
Do not believe	2.3	1.2	1.2	1.4

Note: All differences significant at $p < 0.001$.

Source: Summary Data from National Opinion Research Center General Social Surveys, 1986–91.

Table 11.6 Socioeconomic Status and Frequency of Prayer
(by Percentage)

	Socioeconomic Status			
Frequency of Prayer	Upper Class	Middle Class	Working Class	Lower Class
Several times a day	22.3	22.6	26.8	31.6
Once a day	27.5	32.7	31.6	34.2
Several times a week	16.1	15.0	12.5	14.6
Once a week	8.5	7.8	7.3	5.3
Less than once a week or never	25.5	21.9	21.8	14.2

Note: All differences significant at $p < 0.001$.

Source: Summary Data from National Opinion Research Center General Social Surveys, 1986–91.

Summarizing the differences in kinds of religiosity by social class, Stark (1972:494) has posited three types of religious commitment that are churchlike and have a positive relationship with socioeconomic status—public ritual involvement, religious knowledge, and participation in church organizations and activities—and three that are sectlike and have a negative relationship with social class—orthodox belief, the feeling that one's own group is the only means to salvation, and religious experience and devotionalism—as well as other factors. For Stark, the difference in religiosity among socioeconomic statuses, at least as far as church members are concerned, is more of kind than of degree: The poor participate most fully in those activities that meet the needs arising from their deprivation; the middle and upper classes participate to a greater degree in those activities that confirm their worldly success.

Thus, notes Stark (1972:495), participation in church rituals demonstrates for the middle and upper classes "that one is respectable, substantial, responsible, and proper." Firm, traditional faith and orthodox belief, as well as involvement in prayer and other emotional experiences, provides answers to the needs of the lower-status individual. The Lynds (1929:329) found this to be true in their study of "Middletown," noting that "members of the working class show a disposition to believe their religion more ardently and to accumulate more emotionally charged values around their beliefs. Religion appears to operate more predominantly as an active agency of support and encouragement among these sections of the city." While this trend continues, our data from NORC also support Roof and McKinney's contention that we should recognize the somewhat attenuated ties between religion and class. They state (1987:144–45):

> The nation's faith community continues to be divided along lines of social class, ethnicity, region, and race.... We should not, however, minimize the changes that have occurred during this time [from the 1950s to the 1990s]. The religious map of America is much different today from the time when Niebuhr wrote, nor has it lived up to the predictions of the theorist in the 1950s and early 1960s.... [T]he ascriptive bases of the religious communities have declined, creating a more fluid and voluntary religious system. Class, ethnicity, region, race—all have lost force in shaping religious and cultural identities.

Keeping this prediction in mind, let us now turn to some of the earlier studies of religion and class that demonstrated a more definite and crystalline connection between these two variables. From these earlier studies we may establish a point of comparison from which to view today's class/religion connection and the significant changes in American culture in these late modern or postmodern times.

COMMUNITY STUDIES OF RELIGION AND CLASS

During the first half of this century, a number of community studies served to demonstrate, among other things, that the choice of a religious affiliation and style of religiosity is closely linked to one's position on the socioeconomic ladder. In this section we will report on two of these studies: Hollingshead's study of "Elmtown" and Pope's study of Gastonia, which we mentioned briefly in Chapter 4. Although these studies were confined to particular places and times, the fact that other studies in other places and other times have consistently found a link between religion and the class system provides convincing evidence that such a link has existed for our society as a whole and throughout most of our history.

Class and Religion in Elmtown

A. B. Hollingshead studied the lives of the young people of "Elmtown," a small northern Illinois community in the 1940s. His findings concerning religion and the lives of these youth is of particular interest to us here. According to Hollingshead (1949:243), a young person in Elmtown learned from his parents to place different valuations on the different congregations in the community: "He ... learns in his home that to be Catholic, Methodist, or Pentecostal is desirable or undesirable socially." That the young people tended to early identify specific churches with levels of socioeconomic prestige is a good indication that social class had a powerful influence on the religious life of Elmtown.

Hollingshead also noted several important differences in the religious behavior of persons in the different social classes. For example, he noted that all families designated as being in the upper class belonged to a church, and more than half of these belonged to the Federated (probably Presbyterian and Congregationalist) Church. Despite the fact that they tended to contribute financially, they did not attend church with any great regularity. Likewise, almost every family in the upper-middle class was affiliated with some church and was the group upon which the church relied most heavily for all kinds of support. Membership in this class was heavily Protestant, with the majority (60 percent) belonging to the Federated Church. Members of the lower-middle class belonged predominantly to the

Federated and Methodist churches. For this group, regular attendance at church services appeared to be a mark of respectability in the community, and both men and women from this class tended to make up the bulk of those who taught church school classes in their respective churches.

The religious situation in the working class was confused by the ethnicity of members of this group, and there was also the problem of claimed versus real church affiliation, further confounded by the fact that members of this class avoided participation in some of the community's churches while being extremely active in other organizations. Membership in the higher-status Federated and Methodist churches seemed to be perfunctory for those members of the working class who belonged to them; those who belonged to lower-status churches were much more involved in church activities. Overall, members of this class were not as active in church as were higher-status church members.

For members of the lower class, ties to religion were frequently nonexistent and often extremely loose. Hollingshead reported that nine out of ten lower-class families did not have an active connection with a church. Indeed, he (1949:117) quoted a woman who said bitterly, "The Everyone Welcome signs in front of the churches should add except people like us—we're not wanted." Hollingshead went on to point out:

> She was right… several of the ministers of the high-prestige churches (Federated, Methodist, and Lutheran) indicate they have no objections to [lower-class] persons coming to service and participation in church activities, but they know that members of the congregation resent the presence of these people so they do not encourage their attendance.

In sum, Hollingshead's study of young people in Elmtown amply demonstrated, although this was far from its central premise, that religious organizations and the social stratification system were inextricably linked.

Gastonia's Churches

Another classic study that has contributed to our understanding of the complex association between religion and the social stratification system is Liston Pope's *Millhands and Preachers* (1942). Pope not only described the numerous ways in which the religious group and social class intersected but also described in some detail the lifestyles of various churches in the mill community of Gastonia, North Carolina. In the mid-1970s a group of researchers revisited Gastonia to replicate Pope's study and determine what changes, if any, had occurred in the religious community since World War II (Earle, Knudsen, and Shriver, 1976).

Although obvious changes had taken place in the North Carolina community and its religious situation, the variety in lifestyles for the different religious associations apparent in Pope's study remained. The authors of the later study note that the single most important sociological change was that the millhands who used to live in mill villages and belong to mill churches had moved outward from their local communities and were now living all over Gastonia, so that their class could no longer be identified by where its members lived and worshiped. While the large uptown churches had maintained their social prominence, they did not dominate the religious life of the community as totally as they had done at the time of the original study. Formerly rural churches had been incorporated into the city and had taken on some of the aspects of city churches. Some of the formerly sectarian mill churches had made the transition typical of sectarian groups that survive into a more denominationlike religious organization. All in all, researchers were able to delineate five sociologically significant categories of religious groups in the community at the time of their study: uptown, transitional, middle-class, sect, and black. Table 11.7 presents the occupational distribution of the membership of these churches.

Table 11.7 Occupational Distribution of Membership by Type of Church, Gastonia, 1976 (by Percentage)

| Occupational Category | Type of Church | | | | |
	Uptown	Middle Class	Transitional	Sect	Black
Professional, technical, and kindred	16.6	7.5	3.6	0.7	14.8
Managers, officials, and proprietors	32.7	21.0	13.5	6.4	3.5
Sales	16.0	11.0	9.2	2.1	3.5
Clerical and kindred	15.5	11.3	13.5	8.5	2.3
Craftsmen, foremen, and kindred	11.2	20.4	24.4	18.4	9.6
Operatives and kindred	3.0	11.6	17.7	44.7	8.1
Service: all types	3.0	6.8	6.6	7.1	34.7
Laborers	2.0	10.4	11.5	12.1	23.5

Source: Earle, Knudsen, and Shriver, 1976:109.

As the table shows, persons with higher-status occupations were concentrated in the uptown and middle-class churches. By the same token, as the authors point out, three-fourths of the membership of the white sectarian groups were drawn from those who had lower-status occupations. As is the case in all studies of church and class, no church was without either upper- or lower-status members. Nevertheless, we can clearly put a status or class tag on the particular church types or categories. We will now briefly examine each of these types.

The Uptown Church. The uptown church went back in its origin to the very founding of the city. As the established church in the community, it drew its membership from residential areas throughout the entire city. The most prominent civic leaders were likely to be found on its membership roles. It was characterized by an extensive church plant or building and tended to have two or more full-time ministers on its staff, scholarly persons who had the responsibility of teaching religion (as interpreted by the denomination) to the members of the church.

Families involved in the church were drawn disproportionately from the upper- and upper-middle class in the community. That is, the members of the congregation frequently had professional, managerial, and proprietary occupations, and those persons dominated the congregation. Further, a large proportion of the members of this church had college educations—a fact, the authors note, that was reflected in the formal, intellectually oriented services that characterized worship in the uptown church.

> On Sunday morning a visitor to an uptown church walks up concrete stairs flanked by neatly sculptured shrubbery. He or she is greeted at the door by an usher and escorted to a seat. The sanctuary has stained glass windows, carpeted floor, padded pews, and elaborately decorated pulpit furniture. About 500 people, most of whom are middle-aged or older, all well attired, are present for the prelude, written by a classical composer and skillfully played on a pipe organ. The printed bulletin indicates the order of service, but also lists a large number of board meetings and interest groups scheduled for the coming week. During a processional hymn, the robed choir enters, followed by the ministers. The service follows the printed program without introduction and is conducted with quiet dignity and formality. The atmosphere of the service is suffused with a sense of stability, permanence, and devotion to time-honored truth (Earle et al., 1976:111).

It is not surprising that the uptown church represented and undergirded the basic values of Gastonia's dominant culture. In fact, a large number of the community leaders were in its membership and, in reality, the church had been instrumental in the shaping of that general culture throughout its long years as a part of Gastonia's culture.

The Middle-Class Church. The middle-class church was a relatively new form of religious organization in Gastonia that had emerged in the period of rapid industrial and economic expansion following the Second World War. All the middle-class churches were affiliated with one of the major denominations of American society. The congregation of this church represented a cross section of the occupational groups in the neighborhood in which it was located. Buildings were relatively new but were not as adequate as those of the older, uptown churches. Members of the middle-class church were better educated, as well as younger, than members of the transitional church, but they were also less likely to be permanent or long-term residents of Gastonia. The professional staff generally consisted of a full-time pastor who perhaps had a seminary student as a part-time assistant.

> A visitor to a middle-class church service finds it akin to the uptown church but on a much more informal level. The sanctuary is pleasantly if modestly decorated, with some carpet and modern furnishings. The bulletin indicates a formal order of worship reflecting the high educational level of the pastor and the congregation. The 200 people in attendance tend to be young—mostly in their 30s and 40s, well dressed and attentive (Earle et al., 1976:111).

The distinctive feature of the middle-class church was that it came into being as a separate religious denomination without having the sectarian beginnings characteristic of most new religious groups in our society. It resembled the program of the uptown church in many ways, but the mixture of blue- and white-collar members in the congregation distinguished it from the uptown church and kept it from being an institution that always supported the cultural status quo. Nevertheless, such a congregation did not likely pose any serious challenge to the established order.

The Transitional Church. The transitional church had its beginnings in the mill villages during the early half of the century (1920s and 1930s). It had had a continuing existence since that time and was generally associated with either the Baptist or Methodist denomination. The dominant group in this type of church, so far as class was concerned, came from what can be called an upper-blue-collar occupational class, and was varied in both income and education. Younger members of this church were generally high school graduates, in contrast to only half as many of the older members of the congregation who had achieved this level of education. The homes of the church's members were located throughout the community; however, its leadership roles were generally held by members living in the outlying areas of the community. In a sense the transitional church, in its shift from a mill church, had become a smaller-scale version of the uptown church.

The staff of the transitional church was smaller than that of the uptown church, generally including one pastor, or at most two, with a full-time secretary. The pastor of such a church was not viewed as an educator, but rather as a spiritual leader and guide. The role of the pastor, as the members of this church saw it, was to cultivate and maintain the loyalty of the members of the church and their involvement in it.

> The visitor approaches the building from a paved parking lot, is greeted by several people at the door, and is directed to a seat by an usher. The decor of the sanctuary indicates the moderate prosperity of the congregation. In addition to an organ, there is carpeting, a divided chancel, unpretentious but attractive stained glass windows, overhead medieval-style lights, and modern, simple, pulpit furniture. Present are about 250 well-dressed persons, mostly in their 30s and 40s. The mimeographed bulletin describes a rather formal structure for the service, with written and pastoral prayers, public affirmation of faith and scripture reading. In spite of the formal character of the order of service, it is frequently interrupted for announcements or other concerns. The sermon is well prepared and delivered with enthusiasm by the pastor (Earle et al., 1976:113).

What the authors call the transitional church was no longer a mill church, but neither did it yet have the status of the uptown church. Actually, it incorporated some elements of the styles of both the uptown and old mill churches. Its members seemed to attend because, while they sensed the need for some kind of religious experience, an experience typical of the nonsectarian type of religious group, they had outgrown the totally emotional service of the sect. Thus the transitional church did not go in for the kind of emotional conversion typical of the sectarian group. It was transitional in the sense that it mixed the traditional religious themes characteristic of the older mill sectarian church with the more formal patterns of the uptown church.

The Sect. We have already discussed the general nature of sectarian groups. Gastonia's sects had been a part of its religious community since its founding days and were similar to such groups everywhere. Regardless of the denominational affiliation of the old mill churches, they tended to have a sectarian character about their organization and life. In addition to the older churches, new religious groups with a sectarian tone had continued to emerge among the poor and those outside Gastonia's general social structure.

In a geographical sense, these religious groups were generally found in or around the older mill villages, and were located in areas of low-income housing. Services in the sect were generally attended by people living in the immediate vicinity of the sect building and attending this particular church for that very reason. Unskilled workers in the mills, as well as in related industries, made up the dominant portion of the sect group. The buildings in which the mill workers worshiped were often made of concrete blocks and tended to consist mainly of an auditorium, without extensive provisions for educational purposes. The services of the sect group were long. Frequently they were led by one of a number of persons, although there was generally a preacher who had had only an elementary school training and possibly some correspondence courses from a Bible institute. There was little formal organization in such congregations:

> A visitor to a sectarian service climbs three wooden or cinder-block steps to enter a small, bare room which has old, unmatched pews seating 150 people. On one Thursday night in the middle of a week-long revival, about 60 people—including 10 children—are present at the time the service is scheduled to begin. Drums, a guitar, a piano, and an electronic organ are being played, the songs having pronounced rhythms which involve the audience almost involuntarily in clapping of hands, tapping of feet, or movement of the body. The mood of those in attendance is informal. A dozen teenagers sit together and talk, while the older people move freely about the room to talk to others.
>
> A crudely constructed pulpit and a speaker's pew are on the platform at front.... The preacher and his two associates move to the platform from the audience where they have been talking and shaking hands, and the service begins. After announcing the song, one of the men moves about, all the time singing into the microphone which he holds close to his face. The beat of the music is pronounced, and the people present respond with a rhythmic clapping. A prayer follows, accompanied by shouts of "Hallelujah," "Praise God," "Yes, Jesus," "Glory," and is followed by another hymn, and then another, again with rhythmic participation by the audience....
>
> The sermon begins with the preacher describing the "foolishness of

most people in the world" and their careless disdain of the "fact that Jesus died for them, to deliver them from hell." Certain themes appear repeatedly in his sermon: "salvation," "punishment of the evil in these days," "the danger of giving in to the world," "God will see you through," "open your heart to Jesus." The faithful of God are pictured as being free from the bonds of religious doctrine and tradition, and willing to "let God go" by shouting, clapping, dancing, and singing (Earle et al., 1976:116–17).

Obviously, the service or meeting of the sect group was in direct contrast to the kind of service that went on in the uptown church. No attempt was made to communicate any sort of intellectual message in the meeting; it was an emotional religious experience for those who attended it, and this was their goal. To the outside observer, their services may well have appeared crudely contrived and manipulated to bring about this emotional experience. However, this experience was clearly an outlet needed by the people who attended this particular church.

The Black Church. In as much as blacks tended to represent a separate status hierarchy within the community of Gastonia, their church also was outside the status rankings of the white churches. Although the black church was found to be more prominent in the community in 1976 than it was at the time of Pope's study, its prominence did not develop as a result of the support of the civil rights movement. In reality, the black church crossed most of the sociological boundaries of the white churches, since the members of the black church had chosen it for its racial identification rather than for any class concerns.

A visitor to a black uptown service enters the building and is seated by an usher. The sanctuary is large, old, and in need of repairs. At the front is a large choir loft and a pulpit, with a piano on the side being played by a young woman. The entrance of the choir and the minister signals the start of the service, which follows a regular pattern of hymns, prayers, special music, ordering, and scripture reading. The service is similar to that in non-sectarian white churches but is conducted with greater vocal participation by the congregation. Shouts of "Amen," "Yes, Lord," and "Yes, Jesus," punctuate the minister's prayers. In the sermon, as well as in the prayers, emphasis is placed upon the ability of the people to endure. The entire service gravitates around the capacity of the individual, with God's help, to resist evil and overcome personal problems (Earle et al., 1976:119).

The authors point out that the church continued to have strong influence in the lives of the blacks in the community. They note, how-

ever, that the heavy emphasis on individualism evident in the services may have led unintentionally to support of the status quo en-
forced by the community's white leaders. The pastor of the church,
who was typically the only staff except for a secretary, was generally
not in opposition to the views of these white leaders.

THE MEGACHURCHES OF THE NINETIES

Dotting the current national landscape are large churches with membership and attendance reaching into the thousands. These congregations represent a distinctive new note in the religious landscape. They
underscore points made by Roof and McKinney (1987) about the at-
tenuation of social class ties and religious affiliation. Where distinct
denominations once, and still in most cases do, represent distinct class
locations, the megachurches combine within their boundaries a variety of social classes, offering to each on a "cafeteria" basis that which
fits their particular location in the social structure. They offer many
things to a variety of people, who have only to choose what they
want—ignoring aspects of the congregations that are irrelevant or
even offensive.

Ostling (1992:63) reports that over 40 congregations in the United
States claim 5,000 or more Sunday worshippers, while Stewart
(1989:128) says that over 10,000 churches in the country have an average attendance of 1,000 or more. Most of these are Protestant but many
are inter- or nondenominational. They have grown by using marketing, media, and demographic research strategies ranging from phone
bank ("boiler room") surveys and computerized data bank manipulation, including mass mailings and computerized phone surveys, to
door-to-door canvassing in middle-class suburban neighborhoods.

The largest of the U.S. Protestant supercongregations (Ostling
1992:63) are: First Baptist Church in Hammond, Indiana (attendance
20,000); Willow Creek Community Church in South Barrington, Illinois (attendance 13,000); Calvary Chapel in Santa Ana, California (attendance 12,000); Second Baptist Church in Houston, Texas
(attendance 11,500); Thomas Road Baptist Church in Lynchburg, Virginia (attendance 11,000); and First Assembly of God in Phoenix, Arizona (attendance 10,000). Sidey (1991:46), in an interview with Carl
George, director of the Charles E. Fuller Institute of Evangelism and
Church Growth, provides evidence of how these large churches can
function and grow without necessarily producing alienation and im-
personality among the members. Recognizing that a single pastor, or
even a larger pastoral staff, cannot provide the personal attention de-

sired by modern parishioners, the pastorate ministers to fellow staff members and to a group of key lay coaches. The formula is based upon small cells of 10 or more individuals who attend the celebration of a public worship service but who practice religiosity in home discipleship centers. According to Carl George (Sidey 1991:46), these centers are "affinity based, spiritual-gift dependent, lay shepherded, supervised, evangelistic, and self-reproducing. Virtually all ministry is decentralized to these groups." Thus *cells* plus *celebration* equals *church,* and the notion of congregation as a part of the formula has been dropped in these megachurches (Sidey, 1991:46).

Such huge churches are not arranged like the churches in Gastonia or Elmtown. Arrival by automobile at the superstructures is aided by their location near interstate or limited-access highway intersections in growing middle-class suburbs. One of the first activities is to find a parking space. Ostling (1992:62) describes the situation at the Willow Creek Community Church northwest of Chicago: "So many people turn up...[that] a traffic controller atop the building is needed to supervise the uniformed attendants who direct cars across the acres of asphalt. Befuddled visitors are greeted with information booths in the lobby." Once inside these buildings, members then go to a variety of breakout and specialized rooms offering a variety of services. Ostling (1992) mentions that churches may contain movie theaters, weight rooms, saunas, indoor gardens, roller rinks, and racquetball courts. Rooms are available for meditation, Sunday-school classes, organizational activities, and planning sessions. Attendance at these preworship service meetings may be stratified by a variety of factors. Ostling (1992:62) explains the situation:

> Along with enthusiastic, often entertaining worship, a major attraction is the churches' spiritual equivalent of one-stop shopping. They provide not only Sunday School but also long lists of elective courses for adults or specialized ministries, for instance for the hearing impaired or developmentally disabled. Groups can be targeted to Vietnamese immigrants, young divorcees, 50-plus singles or compulsive eaters....[Some churches have] programs for AIDS patients, the wheelchair users, transients and alcoholics.

The actual worship services at these megachurches may involve not so much ritual or liturgy as listening to a biblically based sermon in an acoustically perfected grand room capable of seating thousands. Stewart (1989:120) states:

> Now Willow Creek's three weekend services draw up to 13,500 people altogether.... Newcomers hear that the church doesn't want their money

until they've decided they want the church. The minute Hybels [the pastor] finishes preaching a sermon, tape-duplicating machines in the basement crank out 3,000 copies, which are stacked in the lobby by the time the service ends and which the departing congregation can buy for $2 a piece.

Megachurches may benefit in their planning, management, and growth strategies by a group called the Leadership Network, founded by Texas businessman Robert Buford in 1984. Buford arranges seminars and meetings of those involved in running the ten thousand churches in the United States that have an average attendance of one thousand or more. According to Stewart (1989:128):

> In Buford's view, denominations and seminaries support an obsolete 19th-century model of church organization. That Church, he says, was "like a corner grocery store." It served a blue-collar or agricultural constituency that had little free time, and it had one pastor for 200 or fewer people "because that was as many as the pastor could keep up with...." [Today's megachurch] "is like a shopping mall. It contains all the specialized ministries of parachurch groups under one roof." It is often suburban, and its members are looking for a sense of community in a place that is often far from where they grew up.... [According to Fred Smith, a member of the Leadership Network], "These churches grow because they have identified their business differently. They see themselves as delivery systems rather than as accumulators of human capital...." [O]ne thing they deliver better than small churches, paradoxically, is intimacy. Says Smith: "Large churches are honeycombed with small groups—cells, sharing groups, discipleship groups—organized around a subject like caring for small children or growing older" (see *Religious News Services* 1990:71 for a similar report).

Of course, some believe that the small neighborhood church which reflects the social class expectations of its members provides the true religious family upon which most U.S. religiosity is based. Some argue that small faith communities are becoming increasingly important as new building blocks of the church. Jones (1992:4) states, "Small communities are becoming so integral a part of the Catholic scene these days that there are three national organizations...sharing information and organizing programs...." These independent small Christian communities or ecclesial base communities are similar in functioning to the cells mentioned above in regard to the megachurches, but are not contained is the same type of superstructure. Many of these *communidades* operate under the following premise: "It's better not to measure success by quantity" (Jones, 1992:4), and "We can belong to the parish, yes, but Jesus called the

Twelve. We need that small group to go with, to pray with, to share" (Jones, 1992:5).

A final example about megachurches and stratification points out that some church activity is directed not only to particular social classes but also to particular age groups within, say, the lower middle and professional classes. Berkley (1991) provides an interesting case study on how to market a large church to Baby Boomers (those born between 1946 and 1964), some of whom could be classified as yuppies. Berkley chronicles the activities of pastor Leith Anderson who came to Minneapolis/St. Paul in 1977 to serve the Wooddale Baptist Church. The church, called a *Boomer church*, has now doubled in size, dropped the word *Baptist* from its name, moved to a modernistic building in a prominent location, and advertises on billboards and in other media. The growth strategy for Wooddale Church involved a number of assumptions made about the target group, the Baby Boomers. Berkley (1991:34–35) describes in detail the operative strategies adopted by Pastor Anderson. We will summarize and paraphrase these below:

1. *Understand Baby Boomers.* "A notable boomer characteristic is a lack of institutional loyalty. 'The loyalty of a baby boomer must be won on a weekly basis....' If you've gained the loyalty of people born in the first quarter of this century, generally they'll stick with you. But the boomers, raised on consumerism, will switch brands if they find a better deal." Pastor Anderson used this assumption when he dropped the word *Baptist* from the church name. Research showed a positive connotation for the word *church* but *Baptist*—a brand name—was found "to be an impediment to some boomers. People these days do not so much want a church of a particular denomination; they want a good church. And will easily cross denominations to find it."

2. *Maintain credibility.* Anderson is careful when using illustrations in his sermons. "For instance, if I misuse a medical illustration in my sermon, medical personnel... may lose confidence and walk away." Anderson says that credibility has to be earned week by week because titles and educational degrees by themselves will not guarantee today's Boomer pastor respect. It is the product that is important, more so than the label on the package. Anderson maintains credibility by being careful not to use sexist and/or stereotypical language, using the vocabulary of the targeted generation, and by microactions such as reading Scripture from a paperback—such books being familiar to Boomers.

3. *Meet needs.* Many Boomers have needs exacerbated by their generation. "Many have grown up in alcoholic families. Infertility may reach 20 percent. The divorce rate haunts them. The church that will reach

baby boomers must provide something to meet these needs." Consultants to Pastor Anderson tell him that, unlike those born before World War II who were brought to the church through worship services, Boomers enter the church through entry points of services provided by the church, such as youth activities or divorce-recovery workshops (cf. Stewart, 1989; Ostling, 1992; Sidey, 1991).

4. *Offer options.* Being part of a consumer oriented culture, Boomers are accustomed to options, even in their churches. "Wooddale provides a Saturday-evening worship service for those who would not consider going to one of the four on Sunday. While the Sunday Services incorporate use of a massive organ, the Saturday service leans toward using synthesizers and drums. On Sunday, Anderson wears a business suit; on Saturday, a sweater and jeans."

Wooddale Church and Pastor Anderson are aware of the criticisms lodged against the pragmatic strategies employed to gain members and reinvigorate church activities. He was perceived as being disloyal to the Baptist denomination by removing *Baptist* from the name, yet he maintains ties to that denomination. In a rush to reinvigorate, has the church lost touch with the true meaning of Christian worship? Anderson counters with "three methods to beat the hip-but-specious 'trendency.' The first is commitment to Scripture..." (Berkley, 1991:35). Anderson also counters with a second method which embraces openness and critical examination of the missions of Wooddale. This involves inviting "consultants and critics to evaluate it" (Berkley, 1991:36). Finally, recognizing the hazard of total idepedence, Wooddale "remains attached to its denomination and to the National Association of Evangelicals. Pastors...[associate] with the local ministerial association and with other fellow pastors" (Berkley, 1991:36).

Interestingly, the superstructure of the megachurches may bring together Boomers and persons from many different worship styles, ethnic and racial groups, and linguistic cultures. Yet while under the same roof, these groups may still maintain their basic heterogeneity. The late Donald McGavran, an early leader of the church-growth movement in the 1970s, wrote, "People like to become Christians without crossing significant linguistic, ethnic, or cultural barriers" (Sidey, 1991:46). Thus, megachurches, like suburban shopping malls, may meet numerous specialized needs under one roof but fail to integrate people from different social, racial, and economic groups. The megachurches and Boomer churches of today may be just as stratified, internally, as the churches of Gastonia and Elmtown were yesterday. But such stratification is obscured by the overall presentation of a community of faith—with options to suit any status level.

Additionally, in a related but somewhat more morbid vein, Specter (1993:194) tells us that Baby Boomers are buying cemetery plots in record numbers. "[Y]uppies have seen the future, and it is death.... Americans of the 20th century are still among the first people routinely to die far from where they were born. So naturally we are among the first to go house-hunting for our sacred resting place." Specter's (1993) article takes a rather lighthearted approach to the trials and tribulations of yuppies attempting to find the "hot" properties of graveyard realtors, but his message is realistic when one thinks about the option orientation and selective consumerism described by Berkley (1991) above. Likewise, Specter's (1993:196) observations on stratification are apropos for yuppies, Boomers, or other Americans:

> Cemeteries traditionally have been repositories of class structure. In Europe it wasn't until a few hundred years ago that they were even acceptable for upper-class burials. Until then the sacred and the noble were buried in the church. The dregs got dumped in the fields. Although most cemeteries still break down along religious, ethnic, or class lines, the distinctions are often far more subtle these days...in death American democracy remains happily intact. There, after all, everyone has the right to do with himself as he sees fit.... Money might not get you into Harvard anymore, but it can still get you buried next to its alumni.

This lengthy summary of Gastonia revisited, as well as the earlier comments on Elmtown, and the treatment of the megachurches offered above give us a holistic view of how the structure of socioeconomic status affects, as well as is affected by, the structure of the religious institution as it appears in the world. We will now consider an intriguing question about the mutual influence of religion and social class.

SOCIOECONOMIC AND RELIGIOUS MOBILITY

Although it may seem to some that social class and religious affiliation are statuses in which individuals remain for life, mobility can and does occur in both realms. And mobility in the socioeconomic realm often affects religious affiliation, and religious affiliation may affect socioeconomic mobility. So which comes first, religious affiliation or socioeconomic mobility? Does one experience socioeconomic mobility because one is a member of a certain church or faith, or does one join a particular church because one moves to a certain socioeconomic group? No simple answer to this chicken-or-the-egg question has been found, but different researchers have studied both possibilities. We will briefly consider these studies here.

Religion's Effect on Socioeconomic Mobility

The notion that religion might be implicated in social mobility and orientation toward achievement was implicit in Weber's major work, *The Protestant Ethic and the Spirit of Capitalism* (1958). As we saw in the last chapter, Weber suggested that the values and norms of Calvinist Protestantism led to a rational, this-worldly asceticism that encouraged the development of a capitalist economy. As Riccio (1979:200) noted:

> Weber claimed that, even within the European capitalist societies of his time, religious affiliation was associated with attitudes toward economic behavior. This, he thought, explained the differential socioeconomic achievement that existed among certain religious groups. For example, he observed a greater tendency for Protestants, as compared with Catholics, to be owners of capital, business leaders, and more highly skilled laborers.

Do Protestants, in Western society, have an economic advantage over other religionists, particularly Catholics? Are Protestants more likely to have an achievement orientation that leads to, or maintains, a more prestigious position in the economic system? Or have the religious differentials with regard to economic behavior actually declined? These questions were addressed directly by Lenski in a study of *The Religious Factor* (1961) in Detroit, Michigan. He reported that, at least for the males in his probability sample, a significant difference existed in occupational achievement among members of different religious groups. His study demonstrated that, at least for Detroit at the time of the study, Weber's thesis continued to be true. Catholics were still lower in occupational achievement than Protestants.

But a variety of criticisms have been leveled at the study and its conclusions, criticisms that suggest that the religious differences in socioeconomic standing have disappeared or even been reversed. Bouma (1973) and Gaede (1977) both reviewed a number of studies that assessed socioeconomic mobility for Protestants and Catholics and concluded that little evidence exists that any real variation based on the difference in religious affiliation remains. Bouma assessed ten research reports, in addition to Lenski's, and found inconsistent results. What differences appeared did not seem to be due solely to religious affiliation. The findings with regard to intergenerational mobility were also complex, with some indication that any previous differences in mobility for members of particular religious groups were diminishing or had disappeared.

In a later review, Gaede (1977) looked at several studies not considered by Bouma, and found the same mixed results, which were probably due to the way in which the investigators controlled for intervening variables. According to Gaede, factors that seemed to have a consistent influence on the occupational mobility of individuals were ethnicity, the generation of immigration, age, the region reared in, and the size of the community reared in. However, the most important variables in mobility were the size of the community of residence, the region of the country in which it was located, and educational attainment. When these factors were controlled for, no differences were found in the occupational mobility of Catholics and Protestants. However, a Protestant advantage was found in studies that controlled for the father's occupation, the generation of the individual in this country, the region of the country reared in, ethnicity, and community size.

In still another attempt to unravel the link between religious affiliation and the socioeconomic status, Riccio (1979) looked at seventeen studies, eight of which had not been considered in the other two reviews. He looked at four aspects of socioeconomic mobility: occupation, income, education, and achievement orientation. With regard to occupation, six of the studies showed an advantage for Protestants, and three found no difference between Protestants and Catholics. When the other variables were considered, the results were equally mixed. The studies he considered were equally divided in finding Protestants socioeconomically superior to Catholics or in reporting that no differences existed. Two studies did report an economic advantage for Catholics (Greeley, 1963; Greeley and Rossi, 1966), particularly for those who had had a parochial school education.

One particular difficulty with research on differences in Protestant and Catholic socioeconomic mobility is that Protestantism is by no means a monolithic religious structure. The present social statuses of different Protestant groups are probably the most significant factor in the mobility of members of these groups. Thus, for example, the already upper-status Episcopalians are more likely to have upward occupational mobility than are the lower-status Baptists or Pentecostals. In short, if Protestants are considered as a whole, Protestant-Catholic differentials in socioeconomic mobility are mixed. However, when Protestantism is considered as a number of different status groups, rather than as a single whole, many of the disputes disappear (Lauer, 1975). Catholics are less upwardly mobile than some Protestant groups and more mobile than others.

Socioeconomic Achievement's Effect on Religious Mobility

That religious mobility follows socioeconomic mobility is a tenet common to both popular and sociological thought. That is, as individuals move up the socioeconomic status ladder, they tend to shift religious affiliation to a denomination that enjoys higher prestige; Baptists become Methodists, Methodists join the Presbyterians, and Presbyterians turn into Episcopalians. Berger (1961:74) has asserted that "we are all familiar with the young Baptist salesman who becomes an Episcopalian sales executive," and Demerath (1965:71) has described this phenomenon as "playing musical church to a status-striving tune." In short, a new socioeconomic status, whether higher or lower, seems to call for a new religious status also. Such an assertion seems perfectly sensible. Religious affiliation not only symbolizes a new position but also tends to speak to the particular needs of the social status. This sensible assertion may be supported, however, more by inference than by empirical evidence.

One study by Lauer (1975) does provide some support for the idea of a relationship between social and religious mobility. Although, in general, religious mobility was not always attendant on social mobility in the small midwestern community he studied, such mobility did occur under some conditions. Where mobility in occupational status was extreme—that is, where the old and the new occupational status differed considerably—individuals tended to shift religious affiliation. In addition, Lauer found that educational attainment had an independent effect on religious mobility; attainment of a higher educational status did lead to movement to a more prestigious religious affiliation. These findings support the "up and out" idea proposed by Glock and Stark (1965): For the majority of those who are religiously mobile, the tendency appears to be a switch to a high-status denomination or to stop practicing the Christian faith, at least in traditional ways.

Nelsen and Snizek (1976) studied the same phenomenon, referring to it as *musical pews*. Analyzing data from a national election sample that included intergenerational measures of both religious and occupational mobility, they found no evidence to support the thesis that religious mobility follows socioeconomic mobility. Instead, they concluded that it is the stable workers at either the white- or blue-collar level who feel free to make a change in their religious affiliation. They did find a closer relationship between religious and occupational mobility for rural residents, and suggested that this may be because religion has a greater possibility for conferring prestige in an atmosphere where ties are close and the behavior and affiliations of individuals are more a matter of public knowledge. Thus it may well be that playing musical pews is related to particular localities; it seems reasonable to suggest that such mobility is more likely where religion is important enough to confer meaningful status on the individual. In a large metropolitan area, little is to be gained in community status by shifting religious affiliation, so little impetus exists to do so. In a smaller community, however, a change in affiliation can give a new status, and thus may well result from a change in socioeconomic status.

Another suggestion concerning religious and occupational mobility is that religious mobility does follow occupational mobility, but *within* rather than *among* denominations. Kaufman (1972) found, for example, that Mennonites in one small community with a number of Mennonite congregations had made just such movements. Within the Mennonite community, the congregations were status-typed; as individuals became upwardly mobile, they tended to shift affiliation to the most liberal and prestigious Mennonite congregation. Informal observation of the memberships of Southern Baptist and Church of Christ congregations in the Southwest indicates a similar kind of religious mobility. Congregations of these groups clearly show differences in status, and membership does appear to be aligned, to some extent, with class. This could be related to the change in residence that usually accompanies occupational and status mobility, but that is just another aspect of the total status game.

Data on sectarian groups presented by Stark and Bainbridge (1985) seem to bear out this suggestion of mobility within the particular group. In addressing the question of how sects come to change from groups in high tension with the world to denominational lower-tension groups, they concluded that sects are transformed into churches because their older members have attained a higher status. Thus, the "succession of generations" is all that is needed to change a sectarian group or congregation into a churchlike organization.

In summary, religious mobility probably does follow occupational and other types of status mobility, but the relationship is more complex than a simple shift in denomination. While such shifts certainly do occur, a tendency also exists for lower-status groups in high tension with the secular world to change their level of tension to the needs of their upwardly mobile members. Also, such sectarian groups or conservative denominations may, as in the case of the Mennonites, develop some congregations in which the upwardly mobile members can find a religious haven without changing religious affiliation.

SUMMARY

In our society, religious organizations are as subject to the effects of the social stratification system as are all other aspects of social and economic life. Denominations (and sects) are generally perceived as having different levels of prestige, and their memberships are drawn disproportionately from the various socioeconomic levels. For instance, Episcopalians are disproportionately drawn from the upper classes, but Baptists and sectarians are drawn more frequently from the lower rungs of the status ladder. Further, the strength of one's affiliation with a particular church may also be affected, to some degree, by social status.

The ways in which people are religious also vary with social class. Many studies report that higher-status individuals are more likely to attend church than are individuals from the lower class. Participation in the public services or organizational life of the group are more characteristic of higher-status individuals, as is possession of greater knowledge about the religious group. On the other hand, orthodoxy in religious belief and attributing ultimate meaning to religious faith are characteristic of the lower class. We can summarize these connections by saying that although sectlike and churchlike characteristics are found in the religiosity of members of each socioeconomic group, upper-class members tend to display churchlike religiosity while those from the lower class are more likely to display sectlike characteristics in their religiosity.

During the first half of this century, a number of community studies gave evidence that the choice of a religious affiliation and style of religiosity are closely linked to socioeconomic status. Most notably, Hollingshead's study of Elmtown youth identified class differentials in religious affiliation and expression, and Liston Pope's *Millhands and Preachers* described the memberships and lifestyles of religious groups in the North Carolina community of Gastonia. Returning to Gastonia in the late 1970s, another group of researchers found that specific differences among the churches had changed, although a strong socioeconomic impact could still be seen in the life of each church—whether uptown, middle-class, transitional, sect, or black. Each had its own style, reflecting the majority socioeconomic status of its membership. However, today Megachurches are inclusive bodies that speak to the needs of various social classes.

The link between socioeconomic mobility and religious identification is a complex matter. Some evidence exists that Protestants are more upwardly mobile than Catholics, but such generalizations are probably meaningless without taking other variables into account. Upward mobility appears to affect religious affiliation in two ways: In some cases individuals who are upwardly mobile switch to more prestigious denominations, although in other cases religious groups that have been in high tension with society change as their members succeed, or such groups may develop higher-status congregations that meet the needs of the higher-status members.

In this chapter we have really discussed only one kind of stratification—that based on socioeconomic factors. Stratification also exists in our society on the basis of racial and ethnic group memberships. We will next consider how racial and ethnic status affects religious beliefs and participation.

12.
Religion, Race, and Ethnicity

Just as the values of certain socioeconomic classes are reflected in religion, so also are minority group values reflected in the religious beliefs and practices of minorities in the United States. But there is a difference: The emergence of the largest minority religious organization, the African-American church, was more than just a reflection of the social differentiation between the majority and the minority groups imposed originally by the white Anglo-Saxon population. The African-American church developed as a result of white supremacy, slavery, segregation, and discrimination. It endures as a repository of cultural traditions and pride. African-American religious traditions reflect society's precarious racial and ethnic relations and challenge the moral consciousness of the religious realm in society.

Evidence and data indicate that racial and ethnic prejudices are sometimes related to certain religious beliefs. Often religious beliefs benignly tolerate the prevailing prejudices and discriminatory practices of society. Some have charged that the eleven o'clock worship hour on Sunday morning is the most segregated time period each week. Even though this may be an exaggeration, religious groups do mirror the attitudes and practices of their members, regardless of the idealistic beliefs of the organization.

In this chapter we will examine African-American churches as the model of a minority group's religious expression and discuss other minority expressions of religion. In addition, we will analyze the phenomenon of anti-Semitism—the hostile attitudes and behavior directed against Jews. Since anti-Semitism is deeply entrenched in the history of Western civilization, it has special significance in our discussion of religion and ethnicity.

THE AFRICAN-AMERICAN CHURCH

During the civil rights movement of the 1950s, 1960s, and 1970s, sociologists focused on black Protestant churches as both religious institutions and political institutions. The validity of these studies still holds true. Even today, the black churches are more than houses of worship and places for social events. For millions of African-Americans, they are still catalysts for political and economic reform. In this section we will consider the historical development of the various African-American churches, their present-day characteristics, and their place within African-American communities.

Historical Development

As we saw in Chapter 5, the all-black Protestant church began early in the nineteenth century as a result of discrimination by white Protestants against free blacks. This was preceded by separate religious meeting places for slaves in the late 1700s (Baer and Singer, 1992). However, the growth of the African-American church as a separate religious group did not gain momentum until after the Civil War. The rejection of black Baptists and black Methodists by white Southern Baptists and white Southern Methodists was the major impetus for the evolution of separate minority Methodist and Baptist churches. As part of the southern white backlash to the policies of Reconstruction, African-American Protestants in the South were encouraged to form separate denominations. The "Christian" paternalism of the antebellum South toward slaves in matters of religion was replaced by a caste system in all realms of social life, including religion, which resulted in segregation between whites and blacks. For the most part, the freed slaves were either uneducated or undereducated, but the disenfranchisement of whites during Reconstruction did allow some blacks to achieve political and economic advantages.

These gains, however, were cut short when white Southerners reclaimed their political rights. As a result, the euphoria of Reconstruction was short-lived for a vast majority of African-Americans. As economic, social, and political subservience replaced parity in these aspects of societal life, the religious aspect of black life took on increasing importance. African-American religion filled the vacuum in education, social identity, and social prestige. An overwhelming majority of institutions of higher learning for African-Americans were church-related, educating not only ministers but also teachers.

During the closing decades of the nineteenth century and the early decades of this century, African-Americans could establish a social identity within a segregated community as members of the Zion Methodist Church or the Bethel Baptist Church. Although the Presbyterians and Disciples of Christ did not encourage African-Americans to form separate denominations, what few African-Americans belonged to these denominations were, for the most part, members of segregated congregations. The few African-American Catholics in the southern states were also relegated to segregated parishes. In general, African-American Protestantism and Catholicism became separate expressions of Protestantism and Catholicism. Sometimes these religious expressions were parallel, but at other times elements of a separate African-American culture permeated this religious realm.

Lincoln and Mamiya (1990:2–7) state that a black sacred cosmos is related both to an African heritage, which sees the whole universe as sacred, and to African-Americans' conversion to Christianity during slavery and its aftermath. They also contend that the relationship between the horrors of slavery and the idea of divine rescue permeated the theological beliefs of the laity and the preaching themes of the clergy. *Freedom* became a dominant theme of both the spoken word and the music within African-American spirituality. The themes of freedom, justice, and equality—often denied to African-Americans during (and even after) the era of segregation—were legitimized by the black sacred cosmos.

The African-American churches, particularly those which were Protestant, were the principal source of leadership development for blacks (Frazier, 1974). This happened largely because of the absence or weakness of black educational and other socializing institutions outside the home. The *invisible religious institution* of the plantations during slavery allowed slaves to hear preachers, and thus the leadership position of the African-American clergy began early in the religious traditions of African-Americans. Because religion provided the earliest attempts at higher education for blacks, the minister was often the most educated or the only educated person in the southern rural communities of African-Americans.

According to Frazier, the rural and urban congregations for African-Americans in a segregated South and a discriminating North served as agents of social control (1974:37–40). These congregations could sanction, as well as reward, behavior within the community; they could withhold, as well as confer, social prestige and identity. In the rigid days of segregation, the African-American church in the South engaged in a kind of political holding action, although, even then, it was usually the center of political life (Washington, 1964). Mostly as an organized entity, the minority church adapted itself to the customs of segregation, and the minister was often the go-between for the white political structure and the African-American community.

In spite of these limitations, the local congregation in the rural South represented the largest social group in which blacks could find an identity in an otherwise alienating society. (Frazier, 1974:49). Participant observation studies done in the 1930s and 1940s also suggest that this function was of vital importance in the maintenance of an African-American religious community (Winter, 1977:275–76). Generally speaking, then, a sense of community that cut across denominational lines emerged as black religion developed in the United States (Winter, 1977:277). Washington (1964:31) described black religiosity as uniting all blacks "in a brotherhood or sense of community which takes precedence over their individual patterns for the worship of God." Lincoln and Mamiya (1990:7–10) describe the black church as the "central institutional sector" of the African-American community. Much of African-American culture was honed in black religion and the black church.

Winter (1977:271–73) argued that a religious community need not have a firm origin. He cited Herberg's three-culture hypothesis concerning immigrant Catholics and Jews as evidence that the religious community was a new and unique social structure that developed under uniquely American conditions. The grandchildren of the immigrants (the third generation) identified themselves as members of a religious community, whereas the immigrants had viewed themselves as members of village communities and the children of immigrants saw themselves as members of ethnic communities. Winter further argued that a religious heritage is what makes for the maintenance of a religious community. Such a religious heritage is, for blacks, rooted deep within an overall black heritage based upon the experiences of being black in the United States. Williams (1971:267) also lent support to this idea by claiming that blacks view themselves as a community in which religion is a source of a sense of oneness that overrides the difference among denominations, creeds, and religious practices. Washington (1964:30–31) cited the presence of a black *folk religion* that unites all blacks and transcends all religious and socioeconomic barriers. In this regard we must also remember that, until very recently, African-American Catholics were members of segregated parishes served often by black priests. Joseph Fichter's *Southern Parish* (1951) gives a detailed description of this southern Catholic practice in Louisiana.

In addition to the dominant African-American Protestant denominations, black sects and cults, including the Black Muslim movement, have stressed the heritage of African-American oppression and the necessity of overcoming such conditions by uniting religiously. In spite of the traditional accommodation by African-American churches to social and economic discrimination, the more effective political assertions of African-Americans in the arena of civil rights have had their origins in the black churches of southern cities and towns. The great prestige of the religious institution within the African-American community in the United States has definitely contributed to the economic and political gains made by African-Americans by providing a base of social solidarity as well as effective moderate leadership. Obviously, Black Muslims and black Christians disagree over basic religious beliefs. Other areas of disagreement among blacks, in general, involve political militancy and the separatist movement endorsed by some African-Americans. The black church is both praised and condemned for its role in these issues. Nevertheless, the points of agreement among African-Americans in reaction to the conditions of life in the United States and the dual role of religion as both comforter and innovator do support Winter's view of a separate and distinct religious community among African-Americans. Religion, be it Christian or Muslim, still remains important for African-Americans in the rural South and in the inner-city areas of large metropolitan centers.

In acknowledging Winter's hypothesis, we do not imply that white Protestantism and Catholicism are permanently separated from African-American Protestantism and Catholicism. Instead, we recognize that the black churches have distinctive identities and purposes apart from the common identities and purposes shared with mainline Protestantism and the Roman Catholic Church. The continuing struggle for social and economic parity with whites remains an issue with which African-American religious leaders must deal. The historical processes that gave rise to black religion in the United States—slavery, the Civil War, emancipation, and segregation—are still influencing factors in the beliefs and practices of African-American churches.

Characteristics of the African-American Church

If a layperson were asked to differentiate between the religion of white Americans and African-Americans, that individual would probably identify the highly expressive qualities of a typical religious service in a black church as compared to the orderliness of such a service in a white church. Of course, he or she would be referring to a black Protestant service. To a large extent, this stereotype is true, but many exceptions to this picture exist. For example, African-American Catholics, in terms of liturgy, worship in much the same manner as do white Catholics, particularly when they attend mass in an integrated parish. However, in a manner similar to Hispanic Catholics, African-American Catholics who attend mass in a predominantly black parish often incorporate more emotional music and other aspects of African-American culture into the liturgy.

Black Protestant congregations within predominantly white denominations largely follow the liturgies and rituals of the Presbyterian Church (U.S.A.), the United Methodist Church, the Episcopal Church, the United Church of Christ, and so forth. It is, then, the black denominational church to which the stereotype of expressiveness applies in preaching, in other aspects of worship, and particularly in music (Lincoln and Mamiya, 1990:19). Since an overwhelming majority of blacks who espouse and practice religion in the United States are members of black denominations, we must direct our attention primarily to these congregations.

Lincoln and Mamiya (1990) identify seven historic African-American denominations: the National Baptist Convention, U.S.A., Inc.; the National Baptist Convention, Inc.; the Progressive National Baptist Convention, Inc.; the African Methodist Episcopal Church (A.M.E.); the African Methodist Episcopal Church Zion; the Christian Methodist Episcopal Church (C.M.E.); and the Church of God in Christ (a black Pentecostal denomination). Smaller African-American Baptist, Methodist, and Pentecostal groups also exist, but their membership numbers are small when compared to the seven large Protestant denominations. In addition, there are African-American members in predominantly white American Baptist, Southern Baptist, United Methodist, Episcopal Church, and the Presbyterian Church (U.S.A.) congregations. Baer and Singer (1992) classify African-American religious organizations as mainstream churches (Baptist and Methodists both in African-American denominations and in predominantly white denominations; Presbyterians and Episcopalians in predominantly white denominations), messianic-nationalist sects (Black Muslim sects, black Jewish sects, etc.), and conversionist sects (the Church of God in Christ and other Pentecostal sects).

Table 12.1 shows selected black denominational membership, using data from the *Yearbook of American and Canadian Churches* (1992). African-American denominational leaders suggest that a small proportion of all African-Americans are members of the predominantly white mainline Protestant denominations; Baer and Singer (1992) report this proportion to be about 10 percent of church-going African-Americans. Of all the predominately white Protestant denominations, the United Methodist Church has the largest number of African-American members. Of the 9.4 million United Methodists, 360,000 are African-American. Eleven of the forty-six United Methodist bishops are African-American (Lincoln and Mamiya, 1990:65–68). Society's largest Protestant denomination, the Southern Baptist Convention claims to have around 200,000 African-American members (Fitts, 1985:305–6). The Roman Catholic Church has 722,609 black communicants, and a very small 1 percent of African-Americans are Jewish. In addition, blacks account for a small percentage of the members of predominantly white Holiness and Pentecostal sects, and for approximately 30 percent of the members of Jehovah's Witnesses (Rosten, 1975).

Table 12.1   Membership in Major African-American Denominations

Denomination	Number of Members	Number of Churches	Number of Pastors Serving Parishes
National Baptist Convention, U.S.A., Inc.	7,800,000 (1991)	30,000	30,000
National Baptist Convention of America	2,668,799 (1956)	11,398	7,598
Progressive National Baptist Convention, Inc.	2,500,000 (1991)	1,400	1,400
African Methodist Episcopal Church	2,210,000 (1981)	6,200	6,050
African Methodist Episcopal Church Zion	1,200,000 (1991)	3,000	2,500
Christian Methodist Episcopal Church	718,922 (1983)	2,340	2,340
Church of God in Christ	5,499,875 (1991)	15,300	28,988

Note: Dates in parentheses are the years when the denominations reported data.

Source: Data from *Yearbook of American and Canadian Churches*, 1992.

As with white denominations, African-American denominations (and their congregations) reflect the boundaries of social class, geographical region, and, of course, race. Affluent congregations and parishes reflect a more middle-class approach to religious observances than do those congregations with a preponderance of working-class members. That is, affluent churches are more likely to have formal services, a vested clergy, and a robed choir. In addition, the leadership positions are filled by a more educated laity. In contrast, the poorer black congregations are less formal in their religious services and more expressive (Lincoln and Mamiya, 1990).

Lincoln and Mamiya state that the sermon and the music of the black Protestant church is one of its great heritages:

> The sermon, or more accurately, the *preaching* is the focal point of worship in the Black Church, and all other activities find their place in some subsidiary relationship. In most black churches music, or more precisely, *singing* is second only to preaching as the magnet of attraction and primary vehicle of spiritual transport for the worshiping congregation... (Lincoln and Mamiya, 1990:346).

Both worship activities are African in origin and represent a holistic approach in expressiveness. The black spirituals began during slavery and emphasized *otherworldliness* as a foil to the oppressions of slavery. After the Civil War, spirituals began to share the music stage with social salvation hymns, most of which were written by white hymn composers influenced by the Social Gospel movement. Finally, Gospel music became the most characteristic sacred music of African-Americans (Lincoln and Mamiya, 1990:348–62).

The "golden age of gospel music began around 1930 and was characterized by such songs as 'Precious Lord, Take My Hand.'" The contemporary Gospel age began around 1970 and resulted in Gospel music being exported from the church sanctuaries to the larger world. It has become the most important staple in black Pentecostalism, where it is the customary denominational music (Lincoln and Mamiya, 1990:361–64).

Equally important have been the "freedom songs" of African-American religion. The freedom songs of the civil rights movement built upon a tradition that began during the abolitionist movement. Some of the freedom songs were composed specifically for the civil rights movement, but most were adaptations of existing black spiritual songs. The best known of these is, of course, "We Shall Overcome," which is an adaptation of "I'll Overcome Someday" (Lincoln and Mamiya, 1990:368–70).

All in all, music in black churches provides cohesion between African-American denominations, regardless of social or economic characteristics. It also is a constant reminder of the heritage of African-Americans, which includes the oppressions of slavery and segregation and the continuing phenomenon of discrimination.

St. George and McNamara (1984) found that African-Americans' sense of well-being seems markedly enhanced by both religious attendance and the strength of religious affiliation, even among upwardly mobile blacks. These authors believe that their research demonstrates that black Americans differ from other Americans in terms of their degree of reliance on the value of the church and religious beliefs. For African-Americans, religion is a major source of psychological well-being, regardless of age, education, and income.

To a large extent, the congregations of these Protestant denominations practice an ecumenism that minimizes denominational differences and magnifies the common purpose of religion for African-Americans (Frazier, 1974). The denominations we previously listed as containing a majority of black members are all members of the National Council of Churches of Christ. By such membership they are also involved to some extent in the larger ecumenical movement within the United States. However, attempts to bring about merger within the black Baptist denominations as well as within the three black Methodist denominations have repeatedly failed (Lincoln and Mamiya, 1990). This is due, in part, to the fact that all of the large black Baptist groups began as schismatic groups from the original black Baptist denomination.

By contrast, those sects that appeal to African-Americans are similar to sects that appeal to whites—that is, they are either of the avoidance or the aggressive type. The avoidance sects remain aloof from the secular world and stress rewards in the life to come, since they perceive little chance that life on earth will get better. In ghettos or the black areas of smaller cities, storefront churches and "temples" are representative of these sects. Aggressive sects that appeal to blacks offer change either in the individual or in a drastic alteration of the world. Jehovah's Witnesses appeal to African-Americans by offering such an opportunity. Baer and Singer (1992:107) state that Jehovah's Witnesses seem to have a larger percentage of African-Americans than any of the white-controlled Protestant denominations.

By and large, however, religious life for African-Americans has offered solace and has accommodated its members to a mostly prejudiced society. Examples of advocacy for social reform as well as for an end to segregation and discrimination have always been present, but only since the 1960s has this advocacy become more public. Because of these churches' accommodation to the social and institutional arrangements in the United States, critics have charged that African-American Christianity has historically been an "opiate of the black masses."

OPIATE OF THE BLACK MASSES?

Karl Marx's thesis that religion serves as an "opiate of the masses" by supporting the existing economic (and political) order is seen by some as an explanation for the lack of radical black revolt against segregation and discrimination after the triumph of white supremacy near the end of the nineteenth century. As early as 1900, W. E. B. Du Bois, one of the founders of the National Association for the Advancement of Colored People (NAACP), wrote that the black denominations gave social and economic concerns less priority than maintaining moral standards, engaging in charity work, engaging in social activities, and maintaining their membership. Because of these denominations' dependence on white funds, they did little to assert moral leadership against the subservient role expected of black organizations and black people (Du Bois, 1971:77; first published in 1899).

Others have said that this accommodative function of religion began during slavery and that the black slaves were given biblical commands that they should be obedient to their masters in order to obtain freedom in the afterlife (Stampp, 1956:158). In his analysis of race relations in the United States, Myrdal (1944:851–53) stated that after the Civil War and well into the twentieth century, the black church in the South sublimated frustration into emotionalism, and lack of opportunity into a fixation on the afterworld. Dollard's study of a small southern town reached a similar conclusion: "Religion can be seen as a mechanism for the social control of Negroes" (Dollard, 1937:248). Lincoln (1974:108) has written that because the black denomination was the one institution under black control, black religious leaders did not want to jeopardize the autonomy of the black church by challenging the segregation of the southern states. He and Mamiya (1990) contend that this interpretation is still valid.

The presence of African-American conversionist sects is perhaps another example of religion's accommodative function. This return to an "old time religion" is seen by Baer and Singer as a struggle to make an oppressive situation better without openly challenging the oppressive structures that society has used against African-Americans. Compared to the mainstream black denominations, most of the conversionist sects remain apolitical in their relationships with larger society. The one exception is the largest of these, the Church of God in Christ (Baer and Singer, 1992:147, 177–78).

On the other hand, as Gary T. Marx (1967) has pointed out, the apparent acceptance by religious blacks of the prevailing social order was not without its protests historically. Marx (1967:66) states that "all Negro churches first came into being as protest organizations and later some served as meeting places where protest strategy was planned, or as stations on the underground railroad." In other words, the black church occasionally protested, but usually advocated gradualism in the arena of race relations and civil rights until the desegregation decision of the United States Supreme Court in 1954 (Glenn, 1964).

Marx's empirical study sheds some illumination on the charge that the black church has served as an opiate for African-Americans. He first considered the effect of particular denominations on militancy and then examined the relationship between religiosity and militancy. His study found that those blacks who were members of sects and cults were the least likely to advocate militancy in the struggle for civil rights. Members of predominantly black denominations were not as militant as were blacks who were members of largely white denominations. In measuring the degree of association between expressions of religiosity and militancy, Marx reports that militancy increased significantly as the importance of religion for respondents decreased. Thus, he suggests, piety and protest seem basically incompatible (Marx, 1967:64–72).

Another study, by Johnstone (1969), focused on the types of ministers in the black church and their advocacy of gradualism or activism in the civil rights movement. Johnstone indicated that there are three ideal types of black Protestant ministers: the militant, the moderate, and the traditionalist. In his study, which consisted of interviews with a 25 percent random sample of all black clergymen in Detroit, Johnstone found that the traditionalist minister "is passive with regard to challenges to the prevailing social order. His attitudes and thoughts will rarely be framed in protest even to himself, nor will he join in attempts at aggressive action." Traditionalists see their religious task as solely spiritual—preaching, converting people, and leading their people to heaven. In Johnstone's study, these ministers were older, less-educated pastors of small congregations (predominantly Baptist and Pentecostal), and came from a low socioeconomic background. We can conclude, then, that religion is an opiate for escape from the conditions of poverty experienced by congregations served by traditionalist preachers.

However, the presence of moderates and militants among black ministers indicates that religion for blacks can and does serve another purpose. The moderate clergyman is well aware of the conditions of blacks and is much more inclined to do something about the plight of his people than is the traditionalist. Still, the moderate's methods include being a peacemaker, a gradualist, and a "treader-down-the-middle-of-the-road." He or she does not see religion as completely involved only with spiritual affairs but also with the social concerns of church members.

Those ministers who can be classified as moderates and militants have, since the inception of the civil rights movement, included advocacy of political and economic rights as a part of African-American religion. In a sense, these religious leaders have sought to return their religious organizations to positions they held when African-American churches began as organizations protesting the racism and discrimination of the white church (and white society in general). Hargrove (1979b:148–49) has reported that the local black church became an important forum for the development and expression of opinion in the black community, provided an arena for leadership and authority when few other arenas existed, and served as a welfare agency to the poor, disabled, and ill.

Baer and Singer (1992) suggest that African-American churches, particularly in the South, also served as politicoreligious organizations. Because all of these activities were part of the black church, the leaders in the struggle for civil rights, particularly in the South, used these structures for advocating resistance, nonviolence, and even militancy. The historical role of black churches in providing African-Americans with training for leadership skills has contributed to the lessening of political alienation among African-Americans (Lincoln and Mamiya, 1990:214). Furthermore, Sawyer's analysis of the Congressional Black Caucus revealed that all fourteen members who served between 1952 and 1982 stated that they were religious. All but two had strong ties to black churches. The other two ascribed to the tenets of civil religion (Lincoln and Mamiya, 1992:215–17).

African-American Religion and Social Action

Martin Luther King, Jr., is, of course, the best known of all African-American civil rights leaders. He combined the moral principles of Christianity with effective political action in behalf of civil rights. Since hs was trained in theology and was pastor of a Baptist church in Montgomery, Alabama, King effectively marshaled support from a large segment of the black religious community to sustain a boycott against the city bus company in 1955. The boycott was successful, and segregation in that public transportation facility was ended.

Out of this success grew the Southern Christian Leadership Conference, which used both the symbols and the rhetoric of black Protestantism as an underpinning for its philosophy of nonviolence in effecting social and political change. Joining King in the leadership roles were several other black ministers, most notably Ralph Abernathy, Andrew Young, and Hosea Williams. These leaders stressed the immorality of segregation and discrimination, offering as an alternative integration and brotherhood. King was particularly effective in using the preaching style of black Protestantism with its cadence that allows the audience to verbally agree and show support. To this he added rich allegories from black religion: "the promised land," "a new Jerusalem," "going to the mountaintop." These phrases took on a new political and social meaning, particularly for southern blacks.

Thus, Martin Luther King was most successful in appealing to southern African-Americans steeped in black religion. Although he offended hard-core white segregationists in the South, his religiously oriented movement gradually gained widespread acceptance with white moderates and liberals throughout the country. In addition, individual church people were prominent in rallies and marches, and individual congregations gave food and shelter to civil rights workers (Wilson, 1978:376). These efforts reflected the white philosophy that in the end the white majority in the United States would morally support the political and economic plight of African-Americans.

In retrospect, King and the Southern Christian Leadership Conference were only mildly militant. Lincoln and Mamiya (1990) argue that, despite criticisms that African-American churches are inherently antipolitical, they have been somewhat effective in their long struggle against white domination. This has occurred because the churches have engaged in community building and empowerment as well as in direct protest activities. In spite of early successes in the civil rights movement, a militancy among blacks more harsh in rhetoric, more laced with demands, and more antiwhite emerged after the earlier years of the civil rights struggle. In 1967 civil rights activist James Forman startled the liberal white Protestant denominations by asking for "reparations" to pay for past economic exploitation of blacks, obviously speaking for a group of blacks unwilling to settle for moral support from white Christianity. The Black Economic Development Council, a subsidary of the National Committee of Black Churchmen, demanded that white churches make a significant contribution to show good faith in the civil rights movement. This manifesto caused considerable conflict within the denominations that considered the idea (Hargrove, 1979b:151). However, many black churchmen opposed Forman's demands, and those who did support them chose to interpret the demands as a call for better opportunities for blacks to compete in the economy (Wilson, 1978:376).

During the campaign for the 1984 Democratic presidential nomination, Jesse Jackson again used the power of the black church to organize voter registration drives and political support. As the first black candidate to seek the presidential nomination of a major political party, Jackson proved that black religious sentiment could translate into effective political action. He counted as his supporters many black Protestant ministers. His campaign style reflected his training as a black minister and was reminiscent of Martin Luther King, Jr.'s, oratory. His respectable showing in the primary elections was due in large part to support from the African-American religious community.

New Themes in African-American Religion

Militancy. The turn toward militancy in behalf of more rapid economic change for blacks also produced a militant black theology. This new expression of religion rejected both resignation and accommodation by African-Americans. Instead, it stressed the more radical elements of the Christian faith. Although aspects of this radical impulse have been present in black religion since its separation from white religion, this liberal variant of Christianity did not receive extensive theological treatment until the 1960s. As a theological interpretation, black liberation stresses Christianity's theme of good news to the poor and oppressed, which has more relevance in the black ghetto than in the affluent white suburb (Hargrove, 1979b:151).

James Cone (1969:3), one of the spokesmen for black theology, has stated that the church must try to recover the man Jesus by totally identifying itself with the poor and the suffering, and must, therefore, identify itself with the black power movement, which advocates rights for the poor and the oppressed. This is really a variant of a larger theology of liberation and of hope. Black theology has in common with these various theologies an emphasis upon the Kingdom of God (on earth) and the place in it of the poor and the oppressed (Hargrove, 1979b:152–53).

Another expression of black theology is Albert B. Cleage, Jr.'s, (1974) call for a "revolutionary black church" totally committed to the struggle for black liberation. Cleage argues that Christianity began as one of the religions available to blacks in Africa (the Coptic Christian Church), and that whites of Europe and the United States have distorted Christianity and its message. Cleage sees the first task of a new black church as one of liberating the black person's mind away from what he calls fairy tales to thinking through solutions to everyday problems of living. He also advocates a black nationalist movement in which the black religious institution would be liberated from its historic role of comforter. Cleage's emphasis upon black separatism is akin to the more ascetic separatism of the Black Muslims.

The Black Muslim Movement. Although the Black Muslim movement began in the 1930s as the "Nation of Islam," it did not receive much attention until the 1960s. Most of the converts to this black variant of the Islamic faith are ex-Christians in the inner cities of the United States. According to Black Muslim belief, blacks in the United States are the "lost Nation of Islam in North America"; the "white devils" have been allocated six thousand years to rule, and in a short time the chosen of Allah will be resurrected from the mental death imposed on them by the white man (Lincoln and Mamiya, 1990). Elijah Muhammad, the head of the Black Muslims from the 1930s until his death in 1975, preached a militant hatred of whites. This theme was expanded by Malcolm X, and succeeded in bringing the Black Muslims many new members and national attention. An open break with Elijah Muhammad caused a bitter schism within the Muslim movement and cost Malcolm X his life (Rosten, 1975:380).

Following the assassination of Malcolm X in 1965, the Muslims retreated into the background of the black power struggle and began to practice the purities of the Islamic faith. These include a revering of Allah as God and the Koran as sacred Scripture. If Muslims are orthodox, they adhere to strict disciplines concerning food, tobacco, liquor, fasting, and cohabitation: Pork, tobacco, alcohol, and cohabitation are forbidden, fasting is encouraged, and asceticism is an ideal. Devout Black Muslims eat only an evening meal after a full day's work. Muslim recreation usually centers around temple work, proselytizing in the streets of the inner city, or reading the Koran at home (Rosten, 1975:381). The manhood of blacks and the subservience of women is preached. According to Wilson (1978:127–28), the convert to the Muslim movement is encouraged to stop seeing old friends and to make new friendships within the movement. Black Muslims encourage new members to change their names, not only to symbolize rebirth, but to deny their "Negroness." The old name is seen as a "slave name" that must be replaced with a Muslim name. Thus Cassius Clay became Muhammad Ali, and Lew Alcindor became Kareem Abdul Jabbar. Despite their stress upon living life according to ascetic principles by withdrawing from as much contact as possible with the white world, violence continues within the Black Muslim community.

The several sects within the faith have fought among themselves concerning religious differences (Rosten, 1975:381). Following Elijah Muhammad's death in 1975, an estimated 100,000 members of the Nation of Islam followed a new leader, Warith Deen Muhammad, into Sunni Muslim orthodoxy. Another 20,000 Black Muslims are led by Minister Louis Farrakhan, who continues the black nationalist teachings and retains the name Nation of Islam (Lincoln and Mamiya, 1990:389–90). In 1978 two rival sects engaged in a shoot-out that eventually resulted in several innocent bystanders being held hostage in the federal court building in Washington, D.C. Kareem Abdul Jabbar has bodyguards to protect him from possible violence inflicted by rival Black Muslim sects. More recently Louis Farrakhan has spoken out against whites in general and Jews in particular for their discriminatory practices (Cummings, 1985, as cited in Baer and Singer, 1992:123).

Although their numbers are small compared with those of African-American Christians, the Black Muslims have increased their influence in the urban ghettos. Muslim schools have achieved recognition for their stress on basic educational techniques. Seemingly, the Muslim community has chosen to work within the economic framework of the United States, and this economic prosperity has legitimized the Black Muslim faith. Non-Muslim blacks recognize their success, and many are anxious to enroll their children in Muslim schools. Theoretically, whites can now join this "Lost-Found Nation of Islam."

Both the black theology of liberation and the growth of the Black Muslim sects seem to offer alternatives to traditional expressions of Christianity for American blacks. The new theology directly challenges the historical role of accommodation and gradual reform practiced by African-American churches in their relations with whites in the United States, by advocating a religion that will actively solve the oppression of minorities through radical action. Black Muslims offer an alternative to Christianity that emphasizes African heritage, black self-help, and a new black identity for the convert.

Problems and Challenges for African-American Religions

African-American religion is not without its problems. Lincoln and Mamiya (1990:274–308) discuss the role of women within black

Protestantism. Although the number of women church members has been disproportionately high, women have never been full participants in leadership positions. The offices of preacher and pastor in the historic black denominations are still male preserves. Ironically, there were "preaching women" during slavery and in the remainder of the nineteenth century who preserved the African oral tradition of sacred messages. However, in a way reminiscent of mainline Protestantism and its earlier subjugation of women, most black denominations continue to resist full leadership participation by women, although most of the black Methodist groups and some of the black Baptist groups do allow the ordination of women. According to Gray (1992:14–15), African-American women have had to struggle against the double bind of racism and gender discrimination in society. Within the mainstream black Protestant churches, they continue to face gender discrimination. Although African-American Protestants are not "fundamentalists" in the sense of white Protestant fundamentalism, some of the conservative stances of the black denominations show an affinity to Protestant fundamentalism, including the belief that women should not be in the ministry (Ammerman, 1991).

Within the black spirtualist churches, Baer has found a reluctant acceptance of African-American women pastors (1993:65–82). He characterizes this as limited empowerment. Gilkes (1988) states that women's positions in the black spiritual and Pentecostal churches run the gamut from subordination to one preaching role in the Church of God in Christ to full equality with male leaders in some of the smaller black spiritual sects. Still, when compared to the female leadership participation in mainstream African-American Protestant denominations, leadership positions occupied by female spiritualist clergy is rather insignificant. These sects provide a spiritual escape from the social, economic, and political problems of African-American communities.

In their nationwide survey of 2,150 African-American clergy, Lincoln and Mamiya (1990:289) found that only 66 (or 3.7 percent) were women. They further estimate that fewer than 5 percent of the clergy in the historic black Protestant denominations are women. Comments made by those interviewees ranged from extremely negative to rather positive, with each opposing group of African-American clergy citing biblical support for its position (Lincoln and Mamiya, 1990:289–97). It seems that full leadership participation by African-American women in black denominations remains one of the challenges within African-American religion.

In addition to discriminatory practices toward women, African-American religion faces another dilemma. Lincoln and Mamiya (1990:

113) state that the loyalty of rural African-American church members surpasses that of almost any other religious group. By contrast such loyalty, as measured by attendance and financial support, is not as characteristic of urban African-American congregations. Rural church members are poorer than other segments of the African-American population. Urban church members, on the other hand, are more affluent, although their congregations are often in inner-city areas where poverty is all-pervasive. The rural congregation is far more likely to be the center of community activities, while the urban congregation competes with other organizations for this honor.

As a consequence, alienation and poverty, which are particularly characteristic of young African-Americans, present challenges both to urban clergy and lay members. Although the mainstream black denominations have not experienced the kinds of membership declines characteristic of predominately white Protestant denominations, there are more "nonchurched" urban African-Americans than ever before (Lincoln and Mamiya, 1990:160–61). However, a significant number of urban congregations are making efforts to "reach out" to the disaffected and alienated residents in the inner cities (Winston, 1992:2–4). One of the most difficult problems is dealing with the growing number of African-American families headed by females (Lincoln and Mamiya, 1990:402–4).

In addition to poverty and its debilitating consequences, urban African-American communities face the continuing problems of drug use and AIDS. As Winston (1992:4) reports, some African-American clergy and lay people have dismissed AIDS as a disease of gay white men, as a disease brought on by drugs and sexual promiscuity, and even as a punishment from God for these practices. Only recently have many black churches been able to move beyond the traditional antipathy toward homosexuality and drug use in order to confront the African-American cases of AIDS and HIV infection. During 1992 the African-American National AIDS Interfaith Network became operational. For the first time African-American clergy were willing to preach on this subject and to urge their congregations to become involved in AIDS ministries and other programs (South, 1993).

Another challenge for African-American religion is clergy replacement and clergy education. Before the civil rights movement, the ministry was one of the few professions available to African-Americans. Today, law, medicine, dentistry, and business careers are much more available to educated African-Americans. Lincoln and Mamiya report that there is an aging clergy in both rural and urban congrega-

Table 12.2   African-American Student Enrollment in Seminaries

Year	Number of African-American Students	Percent Change for Five-Year Intervals	Percent of Total Enrollment
1971	908	—	2.8%
1976	1,524	67.8%	3.5%
1981	2,371	55.5%	4.7%
1986	3,277	38.8%	5.8%
1991	4,582	39.8%	7.6%

Source: Data from *Yearbook of American and Canadian Churches,* 1992.

tions with a median age of fifty-two years. Although there is an increased interest in clergy careers among African-American women, the previously mentioned barriers to their full participation in religious leadership roles remain (Lincoln and Mamiya, 1990:401–2. Lumpkins (1992:10–13) believes that the expanded duties and expectations of urban clergy will continue to exert pressure for better theological education and reeducation. Table 12.2 shows the increases in seminary enrollment among African-Americans. However, we should note that a sizable proportion of African-American theological students are training for careers in church bureaucracies and in predominately white Protestant denominations.

Yet another challenge for African-American mainstream denominations is the problem of two black Americas and two black church groups—one that is quasi-affluent and supports middle-class denominations and another that is poor and feels alienated from such denominations. Lincoln and Mamiya (1990:383–85) see the possibility of continuing failure of black Protestantism in reaching down to the black underclass. If this happens, they foresee the development of an African-American "church" of the poor which will include independent, fundamentalist, and Pentecostal storefront churches. Lincoln and Mamiya point out that within the black Protestant churches, neo-Pentecostalism has appeal for many within the working poor and black underclass groups (1990:385–88).

OTHER MINORITY EXPRESSIONS

Our country's ethnic groups—European, Asian, and Hispanic—historically brought their own unique religious practices to the United

States. Catholic ethnic groups held onto many practices indigenous to their countries of origin. Many of the northern European and Scandinavian Lutheran groups maintained the practice of having services in their native languages. Gradually, however, most of these groups adapted to the prevalent customs in the United States. But even today, ethnic variations in religious commitment and in religious practices exist.

Greeley (1979) has described ethnic variations among Catholics. Based upon available data, he demonstrates that the more devout Catholic groups—the Irish, Germans, Slavs, and French—attend church regularly in greater proportion than the general American public. He reports that slightly under half of the population go to church at least two or three times a month, but that among the devout Catholic groups, approximately three-fifths attend that often. By contrast, Italian and Hispanic Catholic attendance is little different from the national average (Greeley, 1979:118–19). In summarizing data from NORC General Social Surveys, Greeley says that ethnicity seems more important than religious affiliation as a predictor of church attendance, belief in life after death, and religiously mixed marriages. German Catholics are the most likely to go to church and the most likely to believe in life after death. They are least likely to have entered into religiously mixed marriages. Irish and Slavic Catholics demonstrate less religious loyalty than Germans; and Italian and Hispanic Catholics demonstrate the least religious loyalty (Greeley, 1979:122).

In contrast to the ethnic variations in religious practices among Catholics suggested by Greeley, Anderson (1970) found white Protestant ethnic groups to be relatively well assimilated into American Protestantism. Old-world distinctiveness previously demonstrated among Lutherans, for example, has all but disappeared. Rarely is a Lutheran service conducted in German any longer, even in congregations of the Lutheran Church–Missouri Synod, which maintained its German heritage for many decades.

Distinctive religious expressions can still be observed among Hispanic Catholics. Catholics of Mexican origin incorporate many folk practices into their Sunday services and their observances of holy days. Martin (1979) described one Mexican-American church in San Antonio, Texas: A Mariachi band provided the music for the folk mass, and the liturgy, of course, was in Spanish. He also reported that the older women in the parish were more devout in observing holy days than were typical Anglo-Saxon Catholics. Much superstition and mysticism still permeates Catholicism as believed and practiced among Hispanics in the United States. In April 1980, for example, a new church and shrine (where many Mexican Americans and Mexicans believe that miracles and healing are available) were dedicated in the Rio Grande Valley of Texas. For many Hispanics, the church of their birth, even with its problems, remains the church of choice (Hughes, 1992:364–75).

On the other hand, many other Hispanic Americans have abandoned Catholicism for small Protestant sects. The number of Spanish Assembly of God congregations and Spanish Pentecostal groups is growing. Many officials within the Roman Catholic Church have become alarmed at this exodus of Hispanic Catholics and are now encouraging predominantly Hispanic parishes to place greater emphasis upon the ethnicity of their memberships. Greeley (1988) refers to the inability of the Catholic hierarchy to stem this tide as a mistake of major proportion that will cause long-term harm to Roman Catholicism. Two theories are cited for Hispanic defections from Roman Catholicism. One assumes that Hispanic converts see in Protestantism a vehicle of upward social mobility and Americanization (Greeley, 1990:122). The second theory explains Hispanic defection as a vehicle for seeking small intimate religious communities containing emotional religiosity and elements of authentic Hispanic culture (Deck, 1990).

Of all the ethnic groups that have been in the United States for some time, the Hispanic have most maintained a distinctive minority expression of religion; this is due mainly to their language difference and to their generally low level in the stratification system. In many ways Hispanic Protestants and Catholics are similar to African-American Protestants in their distinctive religious practices.

Americans of Asian origin who are members of Christian bodies frequently attend churches that are predominantly Chinese, Korean, or Japanese. Some of these congregations maintain services in the native languages while others do not. With the recent influx of Indo-Chinese refugees, many Catholic parishes in cities with sizable refugee populations offer services in the particular languages of the refugee groups. This migration has included a number of priests and nuns, particularly from Vietnam and Thailand. Many of these individuals attend to the religious needs of the Indo-Chinese. Whether or not these newest immigrants will be assimilated into American Catholicism remains to be seen.

ANTI-SEMITISM

Although the United States, on the whole, has demonstrated less religious prejudice, less economic prejudice, and less ethnic prejudice against Jews than have the nations of Europe, many American Jews believe that they are just as vulnerable as ever to anti-Semitic rampages. Furthermore, many feel that they are only a few steps removed from the blacks, Puerto Ricans, native Americans, Mexican Americans, and other ethnic minorities in terms of prejudice and discrimination (Steinfield, 1970:139).

As stated in Chapter 5, anti-Semitism developed historically as a religious prejudice. Jews were stigmatized as the killers of Christ. Official teachings of the Catholic Church and pronouncements from the Protestant churches following the Reformation laid this blame upon those who followed the teachings of Judaism. In later centuries much of the expressed anti-Semitism took on economic and ethnic overtones. This culminated, of course, in Hitler's successful scapegoating of the Jews for Germany's economic and political decline in the early twentieth century. The Nazi atrocities during the Holocaust were without parallel in the history of civilization.

In the United States, Jews have been the most successful of all ethnic groups in terms of upward mobility. The second, third, and fourth generations of eastern European Jewish immigrants have achieved economic and social mobility at a much more rapid pace than their Catholic immigrant counterparts. Yet anti-Semitism, like more generalized racial and ethnic prejudice, is still present within the United States. Steinfield (1970:140) attributes this to a confusion about who Jews are. Is a Jew a member of a religious group? Is he or she a member of a nationality or an ethnic group? Is a Jew a member of a race, chosen or otherwise? Although the religious Jewish person expresses belief in God, he and the secular Jew have in common the status of a non-Christian—a position shared with a majority of American Indians and Asian Americans. This has led to prejudice against Jews in our country in the twentieth century.

The aftermath of World War I brought a widespread incidence of anti-Semitism. Former Senator Jacob Javits of New York (1970) has blamed in part the anti-Semitism and anti-Catholicism of the Ku Klux Klan revival, but he places more blame on the vicious anti-Semitic campaign waged by automaker Henry Ford through his newspaper, the *Dearborn Independent*. For seven years, beginning in 1920, the newspaper carried on a relentless campaign against Jews that publicized numerous slanders and scurrilities. One of the chief sources for such information was a forged book entitled *Protocols of the Elders of Zion*, which British, Russian, and German anti-Semites had used. American Jewish leaders exposed the fraudulent document and also sued Henry Ford for libel. He made a complete retraction and apologized for his newspaper's false accusations.

Javits also shows that during the 1930s anti-Semitism increased under the impact of the rise of Nazism in Germany and the economic depression in the United States. New barriers against Jews were raised in employment, housing, education, and social relations. From 1933 onward the word *Jew* appeared with increasing frequency in the press, on the radio, and on the speaker's platform. Radio sermons and publications of Catholic Father Charles E. Coughlin increased anti-Semitic emotions to a fever pitch in 1939. Toward the end of the 1930s, anti-Semitism also became a factor on the American political scene, complete with dramatic attacks and denunciations by anti-Semitic representatives and senators in the United States Congress (Javits, 1970).

When the United States entered World War II, anti-Semites accused American Jews of bringing the country into conflict with Germany. Even after the Nazi atrocities became public knowledge at the end of World War II, violent attacks against Jewish people, their property, and their synagogues continued. Over six hundred such incidents were documented between the mid-1950s and the mid-1960s (Feagin, 1978:157–58). Many of those overt acts came from Nazi-type political organizations, but a pervasive underlying religious anti-Semitism is responsible for the continuation of these outbursts. Much of the stereotyping of Jews is economic and political, but historically the underlying basis for the stereotyping has been religious. To what extent, then, is anti-Semitism still a religious prejudice?

The most well-known sociological study of anti-Semitism was done by Charles Glock and Rodney Stark in 1966 and reported in their book *Christian Beliefs and Anti-Semitism*. The contradiction between Christianity as a religion of love and brotherhood and Christianity as anti-Semitic was demonstrated in the survey data obtained by the authors. Although they did not view the Christian religion as the sole cause of anti-Semitism, they saw it as an extremely important component. They concluded that at least one-fourth of the anti-Semites had a religious basis for their prejudice and another one-fourth in the United States had this religious basis in considerable part. Only 5 percent of Americans who expressed anti-Semitism seemed to lack any religious reason for their prejudice against Jews. In extrapolating the sample finding to the larger population, these researchers estimated that about 17.5 million Americans hold fairly strong anti-Semitic views that would classify them as strong adherents to religious bigotry.

In another study, Lipset and Raab (1970:441) concluded that a stronger religious commitment on the part of Protestants and Catholics correlates with stronger anti-Semitism. In spite of the fact that the Roman Catholic Church, during the Second Vatican Council

(1962–65), condemned anti-Semitism and the centuries-old teaching of Jewish guilt for the crucifixion, and in spite of similar statements issued by the major Protestant denominations, a stubborn and persistent belief in these two related factors remains. Hadden's study of clergy and lay attitudes of prejudice (1969) indicated that a minority of clergy continues to accept the notion of collective and continuing Jewish guilt. In a summary of their earlier findings concerning anti-Semitism, Stark and Glock (1973:75–76) stated that half of the Christians in the United States continue to blame the Jews for Christ's crucifixion. Also, the more conservative Protestant laity exhibit the strongest feeling against Jews for their rejection of Christ as Messiah. The fundamentalist Christian view also remains that Jews are absolutely out of harmony with God for their rejection of Jesus as the Messiah. To the fundamentalist Christian groups, this is sin, and these religious bodies remain eager to convert the "heathen" Jews (Feagin, 1978:175). In recent decades a number of Christian evangelical missionary organizations, such as the American Board of Missions to the Jews, have sought to convert Jewish people to Christianity (Strober, 1974:83, 98).

In a 1971 study Stark et al. reported that the Protestant clergy are less likely than the laity to be anti-Semitic. However, the clergy were still believed to demonstrate considerable religious hostility toward Jewish people. Glock and Stark's findings (1966) did indicate that extreme religious bigotry is correlated with anti-Semitism, but Middleton (1973:35) has concluded that this religious hostility can be counterbalanced by the acceptance of norms of religious libertarianism. He further states that "those who view the modern Jew as an unforgiven crucifier being punished by God also tend to develop similar anti-Semitic beliefs." Wilson (1978:310) concluded that the more theologically conservative clergy are, the more likely they are to express religious hostility toward Jews. He also stated that the clergy are not as likely to demonstrate secular anti-Semitism as the laity.

The most recent form of anti-Semitism—that perpetrated by blacks against Jewish people—seems to be more of an economic (and, therefore, secular) anti-Semitism than a religious prejudice. Anti-Semitic statements made by militant black leaders have sometimes caused violent confrontations. Black rioters attacked Jewish businesses in many black ghetto areas of the central cities in the 1960s, seeing these business concerns as exploitative of the urban poor (Feagin, 1978:158). This was particularly disturbing to Jewish intellectuals, as well as to the rank-and-file Jewish community, since American Jews have always supported the struggle for equal rights. Some basis may exist for viewing black anti-Semitism as partially religious: Black

Muslim antipathy toward Judaism is based upon the historic Islamic hatred of Judaism.

Jesse Jackson's unflattering remarks about Jews during the 1984 presidential primaries further substantiated the impression that anti-Semitism among black Americans is growing. Black Muslim minister Louis Farrakhan—a supporter of Jackson's presidential campaign—added more fuel to the fire. First, he threatened the *Washington Post* reporter who first reported Jackson's derisive remarks about Jews. Second, Farrakhan continued to denounce Jews and the "Jewish-influenced" foreign policy favorable to Israel.

In a fashion similar to racial and ethnic prejudice, anti-Semitism persists in our society despite official pronouncements and educational efforts against anti-Semitism by the major Christian religious bodies. While the most religiously oriented variant of this prejudice seems lodged within fundamentalist Christian denominations; a general anti-Semitism, with certain religious overtones, exists among members of *all* Christian denominations.

RELIGIOUS BELIEF: CAUSE OR COMPANION OF PREJUDICE?

Some researchers concerned with religion in American society tend to conclude that religious beliefs do indeed cause racial, ethnic, and religious prejudice. Indeed, survey data indicate that religious people are highly prejudiced. On the other hand, sociologists who have researched prejudice and discrimination have long recognized that both these attitudes and actions are caused by a multiplicity of social, economic, political, and religious factors.

In the realm of religion and religious beliefs, research findings are somewhat confusing. Historically, the Christian churches did indeed foster anti-Semitism through deliberate teachings. In addition, American Protestantism contributed directly and indirectly to the creation of separate black denominations. Protestants also exhibited prejudice toward ethnic Catholic immigrants, and on many occasions committed hostile acts against various Catholic groups. Contemporary sociological research, however, indicates that the relationship between religious belief and prejudice is associational rather than causal in most situations.

Racial and ethnic prejudice reflects a *conservative* view of the world, including that part of the world that reflects religious beliefs. Stark and Glock (1973:95) note that underlying traditional Christian thought is an image of the individual as "a free actor, as essentially unfettered by social circumstances, free to choose and thus free to effect his own salvation." These researchers interpret their finding of a significant degree of racial and ethnic prejudice among church members to mean that a great many of these people believe that men and women are really in control of their destinies, and thus the minorities themselves (particularly blacks) are to blame for their present misery. Many perhaps believe that economic and social disadvantages are the results of racial shortcomings. Stark and Glock also point to the individualistic orientation of many conservative and evangelical Protestants toward salvation as precluding their involvement in curtailing discrimination against racial groups. They call this orientation the *miracle motif,* which suggests that if all humans are brought to Christ, social evils will disappear through the miraculous regeneration of the individual by the Holy Spirit.

The more theologically *conservative* and *particularistic* a religious belief is, the more related it is to prejudice. *Particularism,* as expressed by Stark and Glock (1973:95), is the idea that a person's own religion is true while all others are false. In this view, any nonbeliever is a deviant and is subject to intolerance. Religious practices of a different racial group lie outside this solidarity of the in-group. Thus, particularism does not cause racial prejudice, but both the particularism of the religion and the expression of racial prejudice are part of the communal aspect of an in-group subculture (Wilson, 1978:331). Anti-Semitism, specifically, is also associated with highly particularistic and theologically conservative religious beliefs that view Jewish people and their religious beliefs are obviously in error.

Another factor that, when combined with religious beliefs, is associated with prejudice is *localism.* Roof (1974:661) has noted that people with localistic orientations tend to hold intolerant and authoritarian attitudes in general; religious beliefs and prejudiced attitudes are part of these more general intolerance and authoritarian attitudes. Another study that reached similar conclusions is Strommen's (1972) major study of a representative sample of Lutherans from all major Lutheran denominations in the United States. Strommen reported that Lutherans who felt threatened by diversity or change, and who rigidly adhered to religious law, exhibited higher levels of prejudice, both racial and religious, than did the less rigid and law-oriented Lutherans. In specifically discussing anti-Semitism, Strommen reported that this religious prejudice was not a separate entity, but just one facet of generalized prejudice.

Finally, although the original Glock and Stark study of anti-Semitism (1966) concluded that specific teachings of Christianity had fostered anti-Semitism and continued to do so, several studies since 1966 have indicated that this is too simplistic a conclusion. As Wilson (1978:330) has written, "There is just too much evidence of a *lack* of association between religious orthodoxy or dogmatism taken alone, and racial prejudice, for this theory to be supported." Religion is associated with prejudice against racial and ethnic minorities and with anti-Semitism, but as Hoge, Dyble, and Polk (1973:75) have suggested, the main determinants of prejudice are probably not religious beliefs so much as personal rigidity and a personal need for an unchanging cognitive, as well as social structure.

In conclusion, religious belief *alone* does not cause prejudice, except for a small minority of people. However, religious beliefs that are particularistic and conservative are a part of a constellation of economic, political, and social attitudes that are rigid and authoritarian. Prejudice against Mexican Americans, Puerto Ricans, native Americans, and other ethnic minorities can probably be attributed to this same configuration. Only the minority of "Archie Bunker" types in the United States would articulate *specific* religious prejudice against Jews, Catholics, Hindus, and nonbelievers. Even then, their list of "undesirable" Americans would probably also include blacks, Mexican Americans, Italian Americans, Polish Americans, and so on. An attitude of white Anglo-Saxon religious superiority remains, but it is manifest only when a general conservative orientation is characteristic of the individual.

SUMMARY

The emergence of a largely separate African-American church structure was a historical reflection of social differentiation in the United States. Its continuing presence reflects not only a continuation of social differentiation but also minority group values in the realm of religion. African-American denominations are Protestant and are divided along social class lines in parallel fashion to white religious groups. Although there are black Roman Catholics and black members of predominantly white congregations, an overwhelming majority of religiously affiliated African-Americans are within the black churches. In a real sense, these groups constitute a "fourth religious community."

Observers have charged the black churches with promoting an otherworldly orientation and with seeking a comfortable accommodation in a white society. This is true up to a point, but the prominence of the black church, particularly in the South, during the civil rights movement indicated a concern with social justice. In the last couple of decades, a black theology of liberation has emerged that advocates militancy on behalf of the oppressed and the poor. In addition, an alternative to Christianity, the Black Muslim sect, competes in many urban areas for the allegiance of religious African-Americans. In spite of their strengths, the historic African-American Protestant denominations face problems and challenges. These include overcoming a sexist ideology toward females in leadership roles, making the denominations meaningful and relevant for disaffected African-American youth and others in the black underclass, and insuring a continuing and better-educated African-American clergy.

Anti-Semitism, or prejudice directed exclusively at Jews, is thought to be related to both religious intolerance and hostility toward Jews in secular matters. Although the United States has never persecuted the Jews in the manner of European countries, our society has demonstrated hostility toward Jews, partly on the basis of the Jewish religion. Fundamentalist Christians are most likely to seek to convert Jews to Christianity.

Religious beliefs and prejudice are associated with each other, but other variables are usually present that affect prejudice and acts of discrimination. Particularism, conservatism, localism, and personal rigidity are usually within the consternation of attitudes of religious people who express high levels of prejudice.

13.
Religion, Women, and Religious Organizations

Like other social institutions, the institution of religion has experienced the pressures of the women's movement upon its beliefs, traditions, and practices. Wittingly or unwittingly, Judaism, Christianity, and Islam have been involved in reinforcing the inferior status of women and the traditional female role (Hargrove, Schmidt, and Devaney, 1985). Medieval church leaders debated whether or not women had souls, and far more females than males were accused of witchcraft and burned at the stake in medieval England and hanged in the seventeenth century in the Massachusetts Bay Colony. Until very recently women were denied ordination in almost all Protestant Christian denominations and the branches of Judaism. The Roman Catholic Church and the Islamic faith continue to deny women access to clergy positions. Read literally, the sacred writings of all four major faith groups subjugate women to an inferior status as compared to that of men.

In more recent years many feminists and some males have challenged the writings as well as the traditions and practices of organized religion in the United States as these relate to women and women's issues. Very few religious organizations have escaped challenges to their centuries-old practices toward women. Indeed, just as a glass ceiling seems to exist that excludes women from the highest positions in education, government, and corporations, so also does a "stained glass ceiling" seemingly exist that denies women the most important leadership roles in religious institutions. In addition, male dominance continues to be debated by many within the context of religious teachings. Many gender-related issues, such as abortion, family roles, and lesbianism, are also discussed within a religious context (see, for example, Conover and Gray, 1983; Huber and Spitze, 1983; and Minutes of the General Assembly of the Presbyterian Church [U.S.A.], 1991).

In this chapter, we will examine the ways in which religion has contributed to the subordination of women, the issues of gender as they relate to religion, the struggles of women to gain power and authority within religious organizations, women as clergy, feminist theological issues, and some feminist alternatives to traditional religious practices.

RELIGION AND THE STATUS OF WOMEN

Most literature in the sociology of religion indicates that Jewish and Christian writings and practices reflect the traditional, subservient role of women. In addition, the increasing presence of Islam in the United States adds a deeper dimension of male domination. While many ancient religions had female goddesses and did not portray women as subservient, the Judeo-Christian and Islamic traditions have seen women primarily in a domestic role. These traditions have also displayed an ambivalent attitude concerning women: They have idealized them at some points, but have seen them as the source of dangerous temptation at others (Carmody, 1979). Jewish and Christian practices have tended to deny full participation to women in the life of the religious group and have assigned them a subservient, nurturant role (Verdesi, 1976). Religion as an institution has served to legitimate women's subordinate status within the larger society and its institutions—particularly the family. Religious writings reflect stereotypical gender roles that have created and legitimated inequality between women and men (Richardson, 1988).

Both the Old and New Testaments support discrimination against women in religion, a view that eventually became dominant in the Middle East as the Judaic tradition replaced older religious ideologies. In the Old Testament women are frequently defined as the property of males (Driver, 1976). One of the Ten Commandments, for example, forbids coveting the wife of a neighbor in the same sense that his other property should not be the object of envy. The Christian Gospels do soften this harsh attitude toward women, portraying a

Jesus who treated women and men as equals. To some extent this carried over into the writings of Paul, who proclaimed that there should be neither male nor female in the church. Yet in writing to Timothy, Paul admonished women to be quiet and submissive and not to hold any place of authority in the church, as Eve had been the cause of the fall of "mankind" from grace. The early church fathers reverted to a view of women that put them in submissive roles. Some trace of an egalitarian view of the Gospels appeared in the early writings and symbolism of the Gnostic sect of Christianity (Pagels, 1970), but Gnosticism was declared a heresy; from that point on, the writings of the early church fathers returned to the Old Testament portrayal of women as property or subservient creatures. Daly (1975) contended that not a single statement favorable to women appears in all of early Christian literature.

Although early Christianity did emphasize the duality of a masculine and feminine diety, eventually the masculine side of God, so dominant in Judaism, prevailed. God appears as patriarch, king, judge, and lord of hosts. Instrumental rather than expressive attributes of God are emphasized. Although Catholicism has permitted the veneration of Mary the Virgin since the fourth century, the domination of God, Jesus, and the Holy Spirit overshadows Mary today. Protestantism eliminated Mary as an object of devotion and emphasized the masculinity of both God and Jesus (Schoenfeld and Mestrovich, 1991). Schoenfeld and Mestrovich further point out that it was the aggressive male version of God associated with Judaism and Protestantism that propelled the development of Western capitalism. Catholicism's embracing of capitalism hastened the subtle shift from the Madonna and Child to God and his Son. Women's religious orders were also relegated to an expressive and servile role in Roman Catholicism.

In addition to giving overt support to discrimination against women, traditional translations of the Bible, read literally, subtly sanction the low status of women with both its language and its symbolism (Russell, 1976). The Bible tends to portray men in a variety of leadership roles, but women are almost always portrayed in the role of servants or in a domestic role (Crabtree, 1970; Wilson, 1973; Neville, 1974). Further, the Bible seems to show a God-ordained pecking order in which women are only slightly less inferior than children (Morton, 1974; Pagels, 1970). Undergirding these messages about female inferiority is a heavily masculine system of symbols. God and Jesus are referred to exclusively in masculine terms. Two excerpts from the Bible illustrate this: "He was in the world, and the world was made through him, yet the world knew him not" (Jn. 1:10), and

"For the Son of man came to seek and to save the lost" (Lk. 19:10) (both excerpts from the Revised Standard Version, 1962). Men are also referred to in terms reflecting power and authority, such as *king*, *master*, *lord*, and *father*, seldom with terms reflecting intimacy with women, such as *husband* or *lover*.

Furthermore, these important symbols became a part of the music tradition of both Catholic and Protestant Christianity. Three hymn excerpts illustrate this. "Time like an ever rolling stream, bears all its sons away..."; "God of our Fathers, whose almighty hand..."; and "Great Father of Glory, pure Father of light..." (*The Worship Book*, 1972). Hundreds of other hymns reflect this same patriarchal view of God. Thus early religious socialization has emphasized a masculine God and, by implication, dominant males and subservient females.

Judaism and Christianity have, until recently, provided an ideology which is promale and antifeminist. Himmelstein (1986) states that religious involvement as measured by church attendance promotes antifeminism as measured by opposition to abortion. The greater the religious involvement, the greater is the opposition to abortion for Catholics and for liberal and moderate Protestants. He further argues that this high level of participation reflects a shared religious culture. Roof and McKinney (1987) also show that liberal Protestant denominations have fewer members who attend frequently than do moderate and conservative Protestant denominations. Liberal Protestants show greater support for feminist social issues than do other Protestants and Catholics. Thus religion can still offer a shared culture that accepts traditional gender roles.

Thus both the Bible and the early Christian theology contain a strong bias toward the traditional role for women, a sexist bias now woven deeply into the subcultural fabric of nearly all Christian groups. With the exception of statements of national policy by some liberal denominations, religious organizations have given little impetus for change in the status of women until recently. One analysis of leading Catholic and Protestant periodicals during the 1970s indicated that less than 1 percent of copy was given to the status of women, despite the extensive coverage given the issue in the secular media (Chambers and Chalfant, 1978). During the 1980s this began to change. Not only did religious publications contain more articles on women, religion, and gender issues but so also did nonreligious publications. Ironically, at the same time that organized religion contributed to the subjugation and oppression of women (Renzetti and Curran, 1988), it provided women with an organizational forum from which to articulate gender and other feminist concerns (Anderson, 1988).

RELIGIOUS INFLUENCE ON GENDER-RELATED ISSUES

Today Protestant fundamentalists and evangelicals seem to be spiritual heirs to the tradition of male domination and female subjugation (Huber and Spitze, 1983:169). Although the religious-political right has opposed virtually all of the feminist social agenda, many within mainline Protestantism, Roman Catholicism, and Judaism have also been against it. However, within mainline Protestant denominations, the Roman Catholic Church as well as within Reform and Conservative Judaism, sizable forces support not only a greater role for women in religion but also most feminist issues. Even within the conservative Southern Baptist Convention, there are those who support women's ordination and a pro-choice stance on abortion (Ammerman, 1990; Bonfante, Gibson, and Kamlani, 1992).

Gender-role definitions first appear in the context of family life: the basic role requirements of female and male are initially defined in this realm. Religious validation of either traditional definitions or more egalitarian definitions are often a part of this familial process. Male domination (and female subjugation) in terms of gender-role behavior can be either emphasized or repudiated—depending on the religious (or nonreligious) orientation of parents. Other gender-related issues such as the right of women to abortion and the legislation of equality for women can also be influenced by the religious orientation (or lack thereof) in family units.

Mainline Protestantism, Reform Judaism, and a sizable segment of Roman Catholicism have modified their view of traditional gender-role behavior. Most mainline Protestant denominations have supported equality for women in religious life, the failed Equal Rights Amendment, the right to abortion on demand, and an egalitarian family structure. Many Roman Catholics defy church authority and recognize the right of other female citizens to have abortions—a position labeled as pro-choice (D'Antonio, 1985). Likewise, the general public in the United States tends to support these positions or at least to have adopted an attitude of pluralism toward other citizens, according to survey data. A 1982 ABC-TV/Louis Harris poll found that 60 percent of the American people approved of abortion in general. A National Opinion Research Center survey that same year found that 80 percent of people polled supported abortion in cases of rape or incest, but only 40 percent supported it for general reasons (Brewster, 1984:241). Since then, the issue has become more controversial. In 1988, 51 percent of Americans were opposed to making abortions more difficult to obtain. Among Catholics, 48 percent were opposed compared to 41 percent who were in favor of making abortions more difficult to obtain (Gallup and Castelli, 1989:171).

In their study of mainline Protestantism, Roof and McKinney (1987:186–228) found that liberal and moderate Protestants were more likely to support limited abortion rights (in cases of rape, incest, and life-threatening situations for the mother) than were conservative Protestants and Catholics. However, liberal Protestants, Jews, and nonaffiliated Americans were the only groups favoring abortion for a married women who did not want more children. Moderate Protestants tended not to favor such abortions; Catholics, conservative Protestants, and African-American Protestants were strongly opposed to such abortions. In his study of Presbyterians, Wuthnow (1990:44–45) found that college-educated women who hold feminist views are lower in church participation rates than are other college-educated women and noncollege educated women. In contrast, Presbyterian college-educated women holding feminist views are no less likely to attend church than are college-educated women holding traditional views. Thus, such women are likely to remain active in church activities.

Cochran, Beeghley, Van Metre, and Morgan (1991) reported that women who hold feminist perspectives see other women with similar views as their reference group. If those women are in a church which is pro-choice in its stance toward abortion, they will remain active in religious activities. On other gender-related issues, religious belief and religiosity seem to account for support of two other salient feminist issues: gender equality and tolerance of lesbians and gay men. Roof and McKinney (1987) also found that support for a less traditional role for women in the world of work and in politics was higher among liberal Protestants, Jews, and nonaffiliated Americans than it was among Catholics and conservative Protestants. Felty and Poloma (1990) found that gender-role ideology has an important effect on religiosity in that the stronger the ideology, the less important is support for traditional aspects of religion such as biblical orthodoxy and the importance of prayer. Thus, women with a strong feminist ideology would be less likely to participate in traditional and conservative religious organizations.

In terms of homosexuality, a larger plurality of liberal Protestants stated that it was not "always wrong" than did conservative and moderate Protestants and Catholics. Only Jews, among the major religious traditions, indicated a majority response to this issue. Within most liberal and moderate Protestant denominations, organized groups promote acceptance of lesbians and gay men both in clergy and lay roles. Even though most Protestant denominations forbid ordination of known gay men and lesbian women, the Episcopal Church and the United Church of Christ have held such ordinations. The Evangelical Lutheran Church in America and the Presbyterian Church (U.S.A.) have attempted this, but higher authorities in both groups refused to recognize the ordinations or installations of gay and lesbian clergy.

Among those who support female subjugation and who oppose equality for women and related issues, religion can be an important variable. The traditional religious significance of the family is an important crusading issue of conservatives opposed to the feminist movement and its gains. These conservatives view the family as an institution charged with control over the "base impulses of human beings" (Hadden, 1983:254), and they view divinely inspired Scripture as the major reliable guide for human living (McNamara, 1985:456).

Since most fundamentalists and evangelicals believe in a literal interpretation of the Bible, they read the writings of St. Paul prescribing the subservience of women to men as authoritative. They see any activity that takes women away from serving their husbands as unscriptural; for them, a wife's submissiveness and obedience to her husband express the will of God (D'Antonio, 1983:81–108). Evangelical groups press for a return to what they define as traditional family roles, which they believe have a biblical basis for the exercise of male domination as head of the family and the subservience of wives and children (Hargrove, 1989:220). In this view of the role for women, great emphasis is placed on the strict discipline of children. According to evangelical groups, permissiveness in the realm of child-rearing is un-Christian, as is inattention to the moral and social needs of husbands. In her study of a fundamentalist congregation, Ammerman (1987) found many families which attempted to practice this lifestyle.

The more militant evangelicals refuse to change their views of traditional gender roles, believing that to do so would mean capitulation before a satanic attack on Christian morality (Hargrove, 1983a:21–48). Many fundamentalist and evangelical Protestant leaders continue an all-out effort in support of "profamily" legislation that would deny federal funds for textbooks that fail to support the traditional image of woman's role. They also favor legislation that would prohibit legal aid funds for abortions and divorce cases (Brewster, 1984:237–38). Their efforts to prevent ratification of the Equal Rights Amendment were successful. Their continuing opposition to abortion is a part of an overall drive to enforce a particularistic family morality. Militant evangelicals wish to preserve family control mechanisms against the pluralistic stance of other religious groups that endorse a positive view of sexuality and personal growth and a greater concern for the integrity and freedom of the individual D'Antonio, 1983:103). Overall, conservative religious groups oppose gender-related issues that they perceive as a threat to traditional family roles and stability. The religious political right—in conjunction with the secular political right—has molded this religiously based opposition into direct political action, as we saw in Chapter 10.

Some studies have analyzed the influence of traditional religious beliefs and practices on attitudes about gender-related issues. Huber and Spitze (1983:170, 207) hypothesized that Roman Catholic gender-role attitudes would be more liberal than those of Protestants and that, among Protestants, the views of fundamentalists would be more conservative than the views of others. They found that, in general, their hypotheses were supported by data from a national sample. Conservative and fundamentalist religious affiliation mainly affected items related to family life—divorce, abortion, the adequacy of lesbians as mothers, and surname choice for married women.

In another study, Brinkerhoff and Mackie (1985) examined student attitudes in Canada and the United States regarding religion and gender roles. They found that members of the Church of Jesus Christ of Latter Day Saints (the Mormons) tended to hold the most traditional attitudes with regard to gender roles; fundamentalist Protestants were also quite traditional. Those who indicated no religious affiliation were the most egalitarian, followed by Roman Catholics and mainline Protestants.

Ammerman's study of the controversy between fundamentalists and moderates within the Southern Baptist Convention showed that an overwhelming majority of conservatives and fundamentalists opposed a pro-choice stance on abortion and the ratification of the Equal Rights Amendment when it was still a viable issue (1990). Southern Baptist conservatives and fundamentalists also strongly opposed the ordination of women as deacons and pastors.

Research dealing with the specific issue of religion and abortion indicates that conservative religious beliefs are associated with an antiabortion stance. Most of this research has consistently found that those who oppose legalized abortion subscribe to traditional gender and family ideology. Most of these people believe that a woman's place is in the home, that sex education has no place in the school, and that sexual freedom, pornography, and divorce are wrong (Tamney, Johnson, and Burton, 1992; Johnson and Tamney, 1988). In a study of "Middletown" (Muncie, Indiana), Tamney, Johnson, and Burton found that religious traditionalism and political conservatism influenced individuals to consider an antiabortion stance as a salient issue in voting behavior. They found that religion does play a role in mobilizing political action on the abortion issue. Organized Catholic right-to-life groups and Operation Rescue are examples of religiously based antiabortion social and political movements, as we stated in Chapter 10.

LEADERSHIP ROLES AND WOMEN IN THE CHURCH

Although women have had a primary place in the ongoing work of churches in the United States and Canada since colonial times, they have seldom had a significant voice in authority and in making policy decisions. In this century, many, though not all, Protestant denominations have allowed women to be eligible for membership on their ruling boards or councils. Frequently, however, when women are elected to the governing bodies of their local churches, they are made to feel inferior and are treated as tokens. In 1930 the Presbyterian Church in the U.S.A. (the northern branch of Presbyterianism) voted to ordain women as elders. The next year, five attended as commissioners (delegates) to that denomination's General Assembly. However, these early ordinations were much more symbolic than substantive, since local congregations within the Presbyterian denomination could refuse to ordain women to this office (Brereton, 1989). Brereton categorized early twentieth-century women religious leaders as "outsiders" in a male-dominated religious structure. Furthermore, she pointed out that most Protestant churches were slow to grant women the right to participate in meaningful policymaking organizations within denominations. Even when lay rights were granted, the number of women in such groups remained small. However, women within Protestant churches did aid in the early years of ecumenism, particularly in the United Churchwomen movement (Brereton, 1989:145–51). In these cases the male-dominated power structure of the congregation seems to be saying, "We have to give women the impression they have a part in governing the church, but they must also understand that they are not really supposed to do anything to upset the status quo."

Even more recently the struggle for a place in denominational seats of power has not been an easy, or pleasant, one for women. Oliver (1983) described the problems of women in the Episcopal Church. The issue began surfacing in 1952, when the all-male House of Delegates of the Episcopal Church appeared to find the issue of equality for women amusing and debated the matter in a less-than-serious manner. This body decided that men and women should play different roles in the church, and that women should not seek or want representation at the highest court of the church. The matter came up again in 1967 and was again treated with ribaldry and much laughter over double entendres. As late as 1969, Oliver was refused her seat at the General Convention although she had been duly elected by her own diocese. A number of other women from other dioceses were similarly denied the positions to which they had been elected. Not until 1970 did the House of Delegates finally agree to seat twenty-eight women.

The struggle of women in the United Presbyterian Church has not been much different, according to Verdesi's (1976) account of her personal experience and that of women throughout the history of the denomination. Although women were granted the right to hold the office of ruling elder in 1930 and extended ordination in 1956, Verdesi contended that discrimination against women continued to exist. Clergywomen were not treated as the full equals of their male counterparts, and the General Assembly did not take seriously women's concerns. Even in 1971, when the first woman was elected moderator of the National General Assembly, delegates would not take seriously a proposal that the body confess its past guilt in discrimination against women; rather, a motion to that effect was defeated amidst an atmosphere of titters and embarrassment. According to Verdesi, at this point some women in the United Presbyterian Church became more radicalized, seeing that the church was involved in the same cultural bind as other institutions and that they would need to learn to manipulate power if they were to achieve any significant gains toward recognition by the denomination.

During the 1980s most mainline Protestant denominations paid more attention to the need to include women in leadership positions and to address some of the issues of the religious feminist agenda. Inclusive language in translations of the Bible, hymn texts, and prayers and liturgies became a norm for most of these denominations. Many women and men believe that sacred and secular language carries great symbolic power, and these changes were initiated to address that issue. Roman Catholics, on the other hand, made few significant changes to address the concerns of Catholic women, although pressure began to mount within the largest religious group of American society (Bonfante, Gibson, and Kamlani, 1992).

On the other hand, many women still feel that their place in the church should remain the traditional one. Such women are more frequently found in conservative Protestant denominations and the Roman Catholic Church. Ammerman (1990) found strong support for traditional female roles among conservative and fundamentalist

Southern Baptists. This carried over into opposition to the ordination of women ministers. On the other hand, 81 percent of the moderate conservatives in her study said that they would support hiring an ordained woman. In a survey done by Yankelovich in 1992, 64 percent of Roman Catholic women expressed satisfaction with their church's overall treatment of women (Ostling, 1992). However, the same survey reported that 59 percent of Catholic women favored the ordination of women to priesthood. Furthermore, a vocal blacklash against Roman Catholic women perceived as "radical" has developed. Joyce A. Little, a conservative Catholic theologian, describes "feminism as one aspect of an insidious cultural attack against all traditional restraints and beliefs in favor of asserting individual desires..." (Ostling, 1992:65). Another conservative critic of the feminist movement within Roman Catholicism, Helen Hull Hitchcock, attacks Catholic feminism as ideologies that "seek to eradicate the natural and essential distinction between the sexes...." Hitchcock is head of an intrachurch lobby called Women for Faith and Family (Bonfante, Gibson, and Kamlani, 1992:57–58). Given the fact that women are divided over the issue of women and their role within religion, controversy over leadership positions for women seems likely to continue.

But not all women accept the established order in the churches; many call for radical reform. Verdesi (1976), for example, looks for programs that will allow women more power in the church and thus the ability to transform some of its institutionalized sexism. Noting the naiveté of the women in the church in the 1970s, she calls for a better understanding of how to manipulate the power structure. Ruether (1975), from the perspective of the Roman Catholic Church, has put out a call for "radical obedience." She wants women to bring about reform within the structures of the church. Primarily this means remaining within the church but refusing to accept the passive image of women that has so long pervailed. Daly (1972, 1973, 1974, 1975), on the other hand, has issued a strong statement calling for an "exodus" from the church, with no faith in the possibility of reforming it from within. Speaking for many women, she recanted her 1968 book, *The Church and the Second Sex;* its 1975 edition systematically radicalized her point of view on every issue. She contends that no place exists in the church for women, and charges that "equality between men and women in the church is impossible." Indeed, she asks why women should want equality, seeing women's seeking such status as equivalent to blacks' seeking equality in the Ku Klux Klan.

During the 1980s, as Protestant women achieved some sense of acceptance in religious leadership roles, Catholic women took up the fight with greater energy. One organization, the Women's Ordination

Conference, makes ordination of women a top priority since all authority rests with the bishops of the church (Ostling, 1992). One study of Catholic women discusses the double bind in which Catholic women find themselves. Often they must choose between a radical feminist stance or the Catholic Church's liberal stance on most social issues. Official Catholic teaching concerning the complementary roles of women and men presents a confusing form of gender-role stereotyping. Many women leave, but others stay in order to change the conservative structures of Roman Catholism (Weaver, 1985).

WOMEN AND THE MINISTRY

In November 1992 the Church of England provided newspaper headlines and television news lead stories both in the United Kingdom and in North America in the historic two-vote margin of its General Synod to allow the ordination of women to the Anglican priesthood. As historic as that church's vote was, it was only the latest in a long list of gradual events by religious organizations to practice inclusiveness by bringing women into clergy positions. As Bonfarte, Gibson, and Kamlani (1992:54–55) point out, several important events provide a chronology of this unfolding process, beginning in the late 1940s.

In 1948 the African Methodist Episcopal Church, the largest of the predominately black Methodist denominations approved the ordination of women. Eight years late in 1956, the Methodist Church (now the United Methodist Church), the largest Protestant denomination, and the Presbyterian church in the U.S.A. (the northern Presbyterian church) also approved women's ordination to the ministry. In 1958 the Lutheran Church in Sweden allowed women to become pastors.

Ten years later, in an historic debate concerning women clergy, the Lambeth Conference of worldwide Anglican bishops ruled that the arguments against women clergy were inconclusive. In North America, however, the momentum for women clergy continued. In 1970 the Lutheran Church in America approved the ordination of women pastors. The first ordination of a female Episcopal priest occurred and was branded an irregular process by traditionalists within the Episcopal Church. In 1975 the Anglican Church in Canada allowed women to become priests. The next year, the Episcopal Church in the United States approved the ordination of women priests. On the other hand, the Roman Catholic Church's Vatican Doctrinal Office issued a decree in 1976 that continued to insist on an all-male priesthood.

The 1980s provided for the elevation of women clergy to episcopal positions in two denominations. In 1980 the United Methodist Church elected its first woman bishop, and in 1989 the Episcopal Church installed its first woman bishop. This trend continued during the early years of this decade. In 1992 the Evangelical Church in Germany (the Lutheran Church) named its first female bishop. Its counterpart in the United States, the Evangelical Lutheran Church in America, also named its first woman bishop in 1992.

If we are correct in referring to the formal role of minister, pastor, or priest as the key to leadership in religious groups, then women have had and still have an inferior role. Only in some of the more marginal religions, such as spiritualism (Haywood, 1983), and in sectarian groups, such as Aimee Semple McPherson's Church of the Foursquare Gospel, have women held power for very long. As the chronological list suggests, ordination of women is a recent phenomenon. And even though many mainline Protestant denominations now ordain women, such women are generally assigned or called to an inferior kind of ministry or to the less desirable pastorates.

Despite the obstacles, the 1970s and 1980s saw some increase in the number of women entering the ordained ministry in major denominational bodies (Carroll, Hargrove, and Lummis, 1983). In 1977 the National Council of Churches reported that 4 percent of the ministers in its seventy-six-member groups were women (Carroll and Wilson, 1980). By 1989 that proportion had increased to 7.9 percent of all clergy in the denominations that ordain women. And the proportion of women enrolled in schools of theology has shown a substantial increase. The number of women in theological schools in 1991 had increased by 445 percent over 1972. In fact, 30.5 percent of those enrolled in theological schools in 1991 were women (Bedell and Jones, 1992:286).

Even when ordained, women are less likely to obtain the more prestigious and remunerative posts. Bonn and Kelley (1973) surveyed clergy support in terms of salary, income, and attitudes and found that the average congregation served by a male minister had 313 members while that served by a female had only 128. Salary figures showed a similar discrepancy. By the late 1980s, these same discrepancies continued to exist. Carroll and Wilson (1980) have indicated that women clergy are able to find parishes or relocate only if they have no complicating factors, such as the spouse's occupation or the preference for a particular community or type of ministry.

According to Carroll and Wilson (1978), women theological students differed from their male counterparts in that 23 percent planned to become pastors, compared with 55 percent of the men. About 33 percent of the women planned to become assistants compared to 23 percent of the men. Thus, only 56 percent of women students planned to enter the pastorate at some stage, compared with 78 percent of male seminary students, perhaps because the women felt they would have fewer opportunities to assume the role. But as indicated earlier, the slowing of the birthrate and the relative lack of new church growth, along with a decline in the number of nonpastoral positions have made it difficult for mainline Protestant denominations with a dwindling membership to absorb new pastors—male or female. The Episcopal and Presbyterian churches, for example, have a serious surplus of clergy. Thus in a market where any entrant has difficulty finding a good position, women continue to be at a disadvantage.

Lehman (1985) found that resistance to women clergy remained significant because a majority of church members preferred a male pastor, if at all possible. Many expressed fear that women clergy would alienate parishioners and contribute to a decline in both membership and financial receipts. He contends that clergywomen are seen as a threat to organizational stability and to be in conflict with church officials and members. According to Lehman, churches tend to try to protect organizational stability rather than comply with denominational policy. The exception is found in declining churches, where the organization can only be maintained if the members are willing to accept a clergywoman. In addition, this study and two earlier studies by Lehman (1980, 1981, 1985) reported that women are consistently less successful than men in obtaining pastoral assignments. And when they are successful, it is because they have had strong support from the denominational executives and the positions received by the women conform to traditional role definitions for women in the ministry.

Another study of women in ministry by Carroll, Hargrove, and Lummis (1983) viewed the growing number of women clergy as a new opportunity for the churches. They point out that the seminary as a "male citadel" has slowly disappeared, and that an evolving redefinition of the clergy role is emerging. Their data indicate that women's sense of a "call" to ministry seems deeper than that of men. Furthermore, more than twice as many women as men in the seminary come from professional backgrounds. During their first and second pastoral jobs, these women find equitable work situations, although such placements for women tend to be easier to obtain than later ones. Lay leaders who have had experience with women clergy are more positive than those who have not. In many local situations, the authors report, men find women in leadership roles as an attack on their sense of masculinity.

Lehman reports in two recent studies (1993a, 1993b) that many women and men believe that there are differences in ministry style between female and male clergy. He used nine composite measures of different traits of the clergy. Some were labeled as masculine; others as feminine. These traits are willingness to use coercive power (masculine); striving to empower congregations (feminine); desire for formal authority (masculine); desire for rational structure (masculine); ethical legalism (masculine); general interpersonal style (masculine if status-conscious and formal; feminine if egalitarian and informal); orientation to preaching (masculine if authoritative; feminine if consisting of sharing experiences and feelings); criteria of clergy status (masculine if clearly defined in a traditional way); and involvement in social issues (usually feminine). He found that among men and women ordained clergy within the American Baptist Churches, the Presbyterian Church (U.S.A.), the United Church of Christ, and the United Methodist Church, gender differences did exist in ministry style. However, women did not always exhibit the feminine traits, and men did not always manifest the masculine traits of the composite measures. One of his empirical conclusions is that while there are some gender-specific approaches to pastoral ministry among female and male Protestant clergy, this is not true for all of the dimensions. Another conclusion is that the statistical strength of those differences tends to be weak, thus suggesting that the gender differences are not as great as many people believed. A third conclusion is that appearances of gender differences in ministry style depended on identifiable cultural, structural, and biographical conditions (Lehman, 1993a:1–11).

Lummis (1991) surveyed women priests in seven northeastern dioceses of the Episcopal Church. She found that 51 percent felt that their image or expectation of being an ordained leader was fulfilled. Sixteen percent reported that this was not relevant because their image or expectation had changed. According to 33 percent of those surveyed, their image or expectation had not been fully met or met at all. Lummis also reported that 75 percent of these women priests believed that it would be difficult to obtain better positions than those they now held. Thirty-seven percent stated that being a woman would make getting a better position difficult "to a great extent" or "quite a bit," and 41 percent thought that it would make getting a better position "somewhat" more difficult. On the other hand, 56 percent reported that they usually felt "joy and satisfaction" from their work in the church; another 34 percent stated that this was somewhat true. Lummis' research indicates that generally, while the role of the clergy is rewarding, career advancement for women clergy remains difficult, at least in the Episcopal Church.

This picture does have a brighter side, though. Where women have been placed in pastorates, they have generally been well accepted (Royle, 1982) and have been seen as filling the ministerial role well, once church members have had the experience of working with them (Proctor and Proctor, 1976; Lehman, 1985). In an analysis of data based on responses of women who had found active pastorates in four major Protestant denominations, Royle found that churches in which these women had been placed were not significantly less viable or poorer than churches that had called male pastors. Her results also provided little support for the idea the women only function well in traditionally female areas of work. Royle's message is that women having difficulty getting placed should take hope, as once they are placed, the path becomes much smoother. Further, she suggests that denominational executives will find the incorporation of women pastors relatively easy. In short, despite gloomy findings reported on initial placement, the acceptance of women appointed to parishes seems to be positive.

Rosenberg (1979) reported on the status of women in ministry in the Catholic Church. The fact that women cannot be ordained as priests and the apparent rigid resistance of the papacy to such a move have been issues occupying much of the attention of those investigating women's rights within the Catholic Church. But lack of progress on this point should not be taken to mean that no change has occurred in the status of women. The changes accompanying Vatican II, as well as some parish needs, have brought new opportunities for women to serve within the church or ministry, as Rosenberg defines it. Although in some parishes women are still limited to traditional tasks, in others they take part, with men, in the increasing role of the laity in leading the church. According to Rosenberg, there seems to be a trend toward expanding the participation of women in the Catholic Church. Her predictions at first seemed to be borne out to some extent by the fact that in 1982 the National Conference of Catholic Bishops seriously considered ordaining women to the office of deacon, a first step toward the priesthood ("Bishops Reviewing Question," 1982). However, this did not occur.

Since then, organized groups within the Roman Catholic Church have continued to press for women's ordination. As we stated earlier, the Women's Ordination Conference continues to exist. However, neither the American Catholic bishops nor Pope John Paul II seem inclined to allow ordination either to the offices of deacon or priest. The church's official position is that since Christ was a male, a male must administer the sacraments of the church (Bonfante, Gibson, and Kamlani, 1992).

One interesting development within the Roman Catholic Church is the use of women—either nuns or laypersons—as parish administrators. Wallace (1993) reports that these leaders are under the supervision of priests, who consecrate the Eucharist at mass. However, men or women can then administer the Eucharist. Her study of 300 such parishes indicates that 75 percent of them are led by women. Futhermore, they often perform the counseling and preaching roles as well as the administrative role. Wallace (1993) also demonstrates that one of the striking differences between these "women pastors" and the priests who formerly served the parishes was leadership style. The dominant pattern of the women was collaborative leadership, based on equality rather than hierarchy. Wallace (1993) also found that parishioners mostly responded positively when the parish administrator/pastor asked them to become more involved in helping to run the parish. Obviously many women religious (nuns) within Roman Catholicism are candidates for these positions. However, Ostling (1992) points out that women's orders are in decline in the United States; in 1964 there were 180,015 nuns, but by 1992 their numbers had dropped to 99,337. Although the Roman Catholic Church might not ordain women to the priesthood for some time yet, female members of religious orders and other women who choose to remain in the church are gaining more autonomy in their work.

Women within mainline Protestant denominations and Reform and Conservative Judaism have achieved the status of priest, pastor, minister, or rabbi. Still, conservative Protestant denominations and the Church of Jesus Christ of Latter-day Saints remain opposed to women clergy. A few Southern Baptist churches have ordained women as clergy since that denomination allows local congregational autonomy (Ammerman, 1990; Bonfante, Gibson, and Kamlani, 1992). However, the fundamentalist wing of the Southern Baptist Convention, which is now in control of the denominational agencies and seminaries, strongly discourages the ordination of women to the offices of both deacon and pastor. These exceptions to the inclusion of women as clergy are likely to remain for some time, as is the exclusiveness of the Roman Catholic priesthood and the Orthodox Jewish rabbinate.

FEMINIST THEOLOGICAL ISSUES

In mainline Protestant denominations and Roman Catholic feminist groups, feminist perspectives on ministry and theology developed during the 1970s and 1980s. Some of these perspectives focus on inclusive versus exclusive language in biblical translations, hymns, prayers, and liturgies. Other perspectives address the patriarchal images of God and Jesus and the subsequent patriarchy within both Christianity and Judaism. Still other perspectives are concerned with the roles of women members of the laity and clergy. Since this is not a theological textbook, we will examine only briefly these feminist perspectives.

Concern over exclusive language and attempts to change it can be best seen as an attempt to *reform* religious traditions and practices. Inclusive language promotes the inclusivity of women and men into the worship and activities of religion. An examination of the biblical texts and hymn texts cited earlier in this chapter illustrates. The exclusive language of the two scripture passages is easily changed to the following: "The Word was in the world, and the world was made through the Word, yet the world did not know the Word. The Word came to the Word's own home, but those to whom the Word came did not receive the Word..."; and "Jesus came to seek and save those who are lost..." (Revised Standard Version, 1991). A more progressive translation adds the concept of female to God: "Go therefore and make disciples of all nations, baptizing them in the name of God the Father and Mother and of Jesus Christ the beloved Child and the Holy Spirit..." (Mt. 28:19, United Church of Christ, 1992).

Similar changes in the language of hymn texts have been published in recent hymnals of some mainline Protestant denominations. "Time, like an ever rolling stream/Soon bears us all away..."; "God of the Ages, whose almighty hand..."; and "Thou reignest in glory, Thou rulest in light..." (Westminster/John Knox Press, 1990). Further attempts to either eliminate or limit the masculine noun and pronoun references to God, Jesus, and people continue. However, opposition to this is present in most Protestant denominations and in the Roman Catholic Church. Critics refer to such language changes as the *feminization* of religious traditions and practices. Others see references to God as "Father/Mother" as pagan rather than Christian (Bonfarte, Gibson, and Kamlani, 1992).

The theology of both Judaism and Christianity has, for centuries, reflected the male domination and patriarchy that have historically ruled Middle Eastern, European, and North American societies. The philosophical underpinnings of these societies perpetuated the superiority of men and the subjugation of women. According to this viewpoint, God is male; Jesus, his Son, is male; and the Holy Spirit is, at best, of questionable gender. The Old Testament shared by both Jews and Christian reflects patriarchy. While the New Testament, for the most part, is less partriarchial, some of the writings of St. Paul relegate women to a servile status, admonishing them to "keep silent in the churches... (1 Cor. 14:34)" and to "permit no woman to teach or have authority over men..." (1 Cor. 14:34, and 1 Tim. 2:12). For centuries, few people questioned the exclusiveness of male-dominated religious beliefs, traditions, and practices.

Feminist theologians, women clergy, and women laity have recently begun to construct a *revisionist version* of these beliefs and traditions. Christ and Plaskow (1979) point out that with the advent of monotheism, the different roles and personalities of gods (masculine and feminine) were fused into the single figure of God. Yet, according to Mollenkott (1983), certain biblical imagery suggests that God might easily be female. At times God is portrayed as merciful and loving rather than as stern and harsh. Such dualism is often interpreted as a manifestation of God's masculine and feminine qualities (Schoenfeld and Mestrovic, 1991). After all, dual-gender gods have a long history: The Canaanite society had both Baal (a male) and Astarte (a female) as its deities.

Ancient Greece had Zeus and Hera among many other gods and goddesses. Monotheism resulted in the loss of this divine dualism. Although Roman Catholicism elevated Mary to almost divine status as the mother of God as well as of Jesus, the structure of the church remained partriarchial. As we stated earlier, Protestantism reemphasized male dominance, and capitalism further marginalized women as domestic workers, subservient wives, and nurturing mothers (Schoenfeld and Mestrovic, 1991).

It is this patriarchy and its proscriptions of women that feminist theology addresses. Furthermore, feminist theology seeks, in large part, to reemphasize the dual gender of God and to break the oppression seen as the legacy of patriarchy, which includes racism, classism, sexism, heterosexism, ageism, and the abuse of children (Filippi, 1991).

Such a theology emphasizes mutuality, egalitarianism, and spirituality in relations among people and between people and God. A holistic view of religion as nurturing and compromising rather than as prescriptive and authoritarian is another characteristic of some feminist theology (Ice, 1987). It seeks to emphasize the inclusiveness of all of humankind and to break down power relationships that have historically characterized Western societies. Rhodes (1987) says that feminist ministry—the end result of feminist theology—should have as its purpose the extension of trustworthiness, resources, and strength to all in the community in times of crisis. Put another way, feminist theology exists to "cure the soul of the church..." and to "show the way during a time of declining expectations..." (Zikmund, 1990:132).

This theology suggests new or redefined roles for women clergy. Expressive, rather than instrumental needs, are better met by roles traditionally associated with women: unconditional love, mercy, and nurturing. These are also central themes in the dominant Western religions. Zikmund (1990) states that most women clergy are less interested in the power that ordination gives than in emphasizing the ministry of *all* members of a religious community. She further argues that women clergy find that the "set-apart" tradition of ordination perpetuates the hierarchial arrangements of historic traditions. One way out of this is to emphasize the *teaching* aspect over the *preaching* aspect of clergy roles. Finally, Zikmund states that female members of the clergy refuse to separate sexuality, spirituality, and power.

Ice (1987), in her study of clergywomen, found that most were oriented to responsible caring and displayed a strong identification with laypeople. Their theological perspectives, for the most part, emphasized the reconciliation of historic traditions with more immediate experiences. Spirituality was also a dominant orientation of many of the women she studied.

For some women, feminist perspectives and theology aimed at reforming or transforming a patriarchal institution do not go far enough. Residual power relationships of male dominance remain, despite the strategies and good intentions of the reformers. For some women, feminist alternatives to traditional Western religions have an appeal.

FEMINIST RELIGIOUS ALTERNATIVES

Some women have sought to establish religious organizations based on feminist ideology and addressed to feminist concerns. Some of these are extensions of the Judeo-Christian religious tradition. Others combine elements of Judaism and Christianity with different religious traditions. Still others are revivals of goddess worship and witchcraft, which can be seen as alternatives to attempts to reform or transform Judaism and Christianity into inclusive religious communities.

One extention of the Judeo-Christian tradition is Women-Church, a group of Catholic women whose goal is to produce an alternative spirituality (Trebbi, 1990). It is a coalition which evolved from the lack of success of the Women's Ordination Conference in bringing about the ordination of women to the priesthood. The Women's Ordination Conference was the first major Catholic feminist organization with both women religious and laywomen as members. In 1977 a group known as Chicago Catholic Women attracted wide support from other Catholic feminists. Its members held their first meeting in 1983. By 1987 the organization, which had changed its name to Women-

Church, attracted 3,000 women from the United States and fifteen foreign countries to a "convergence" held in Cincinnati, Ohio. Trebbi (1990) states further that for those involved, ministry had shifted from the concept of helping others to improve their lives to a commitment to transform all oppressive relationships and structures.

According to Winter (1989), Women-Church is a social movement of feminist base communities and a coalition of feminist organizations whose goal is to support each other in living out faith experiences. Any women's group with three or more members can call itself women-church. Trebbi (1990) points out that the base communities are modeled on the small Latin American communities of liberation theology. Winter (1989:260) quotes Rosemary Radford Ruether's comment concerning Women-Church: "Women-church means neither leaving the church as a sectarian group, nor continuing to fit into it on its terms. It means establishing bases for a feminist critical culture and celebrational community that have some autonomy from the established institutions." Ziegenhals (1989) further notes that much of what holds Women-Church together is its liturgies and rituals, some of which are purification rights. According to her, these celebrations are only tentatively Christian, but they fill a need not met in a traditional church.

Another feminist alternative is the goddess religion. One form of this alternative expression is neopagan witchcraft, another is the goddess movement. There is overlap between the two since the present goddess movement evolved from neopagan witchcraft. Symbols and beliefs are more important in both of these alternative religious expressions than a formal organization.

For feminist witches, the symbol of the goddess is one of empowerment for women rather than one viewing the goddess as a symbol of all that is beautiful in life (Neitz, 1990). Among feminists who embrace witchcraft, there is an appreciation for the diversity of goddess symbols. For many involved in these groups, the female deity represents *mother nature*. To honor her is one way of restoring balance in a society threatened by technological extinction. Because of this ecological orientation, neopagan witchcraft rituals have become a part of environmental and other political demonstrations. Many women "come out" as witches, but often only within a circle of trusted friends (Neitz, 1990).

The goddess movement provides a slightly different alternative. Goddess theology emphasizes "the legitimacy of female power as a beneficent and independent power..." (Christ and Plaskow, 1987: 121). Goddess symbolism also affirms the female body. Birthing and menstruation are celebrated as mysteries of womanhood. Women are encouraged to know their wills and to believe that their valid wills can be achieved. There is no subservience to the male will.

Neitz (1990) also states that the goddess movement began with "grass-roots women's circles," which emphasized *womanspirit*, a female spirituality. Out of these came a publication, *Womanspirit*, which connects the groups and promotes that spirituality. Some of the groups share and study matriarchal histories; others believe in and practice witchcraft. Diversity, though challenged by some in the neo-pagan and goddess movements, is now characteristic of these overlapping movements.

Neitz (1990) reports that the symbols of the goddess movement represent cultural change. Although relatively few people are directly involved in the goddess movement, its attitude toward nature and the accompanying emphasis on ecological issues and feminist concerns are shared by many women and are a part of a more widespread social and cultural change (Neitz, 1990:369–70).

SUMMARY

The role of women in religious organizations has been limited by a sexist bias inherent in the Judeo-Christian and Islamic traditions. Clearly, the symbol system of those traditions are replete with evidence of male domination. And the subservient status of women in religious organizations can be seen in the kinds of roles they play (or do not play) in the leadership of such groups. Some women continue to accept this inferior status while others work from within to challenge it. Another group, however, has given up on the traditional religious institution and called for an exodus.

Traditional Judeo-Christian religion has developed norms that support male dominance. Today's Protestant fundamentalists and evangelicals seem to be the spiritual heirs to this tradition; however, mainline Protestantism, Reform Judaism, and a sizable segment of Roman Catholicism have modified their views of traditional gender roles and gender-role behavior. An ongoing clash between the more conservative and the more liberal religious groups concerns the subservience of wives to husbands, the issue of working mothers, and the enactment of "profamily" legislation to curtail a woman's right to abortion, to prohibit legal aid in divorce cases, and to defeat new attempts to ratify the Equal Rights Amendment. In spite of these differences, most religious groups within the United States have responded to changes in the family structure. Teachings and policies regarding divorce, single-parent families, two-income families, and gender role have changed.

While most groups elect women to their governing boards, their positions on these boards are frequently inferior ones. Some organizations allow women in the formal role of the clergy; however, even in bodies that permit female clergy, only 4 percent of the ministers are women. Female clergy also tend to occupy subordinate roles (as assistant pastors, directors of Christian education, and so forth) or to be given pastorates too small or too poor to support a male pastor. Recent research suggests, however, that women clergy have been well accepted once they obtained an initial appointment.

Feminist theological issues have emerged during the 1970s and 1980s. Some of these involve inclusive language in Scriptures, hymn texts, prayers, and liturgies. Other issues are concerned with changing the patriarchal belief systems and practices of Western religions. Out of the concerns about transforming patriarchy have come new definitions of the clergy role for women.

Finally, alternative feminist religious traditions have emerged. Some of these are extensions of the Judeo-Christian tradition, while others are syntheses of Christian and non-Christian practices. Some involve witchcraft and goddess worship.

Changes in the relationships of women to religion have produced resistance within many religious organizations. Conservative Protestant groups and the Roman Catholic Church seem opposed to most of the feminist religious issues, particularly the ordination of women to clergy positions.

14.
Religion and Society Today... and Tomorrow

We have taken up a broad array of topics regarding religion and society in the previous chapters. In general, our discussion has been centered on religious behavior in the distant and recent past, as well as in the present. A number of points we made point to questions about what the future of religion in our society will be. In this chapter we will address that issue, drawing upon what has been said before as well as upon new considerations.

Speculation about the future of religion is certainly not new for sociologists. Given the evolutionary tone of early sociological theory, it was inevitable that consideration would be given to the evolution of religion and religious institutions—particularly since the world was drastically changing. As noted in Chapter 2, early sociologists and other scholars during the Enlightenment and at the beginning of the Industrial Revolution forecast grim times for religious faith, at least as expressed in traditional societal institutions and ideologies. Glock (1973:281) comments that such considerations were inevitable, given the thinking of the time:

> Marx made the topic salient by raising the possibility of society without religion. In the last century when evolutionary theory was having a

major impact on sociological thought it was natural to include religion in predictions about social evolution. Structural-functional theory also made the topic pertinent through its proposition that religion is a necessary condition to the maintenance of social order. And cyclical theories of human history...also included religion as an element in prognostications about where society was headed.

Along these lines of evolutionary thought, Durkheim (1951; see also Westley, 1978) made seven predictions concerning the religion of the future:

1. Given the greater specialization of human social roles in the nineteenth century, humanity would come to be the object to be worshiped;
2. The increasing diversification of society would lead to a similar diversification of society's religions; religious ideals would vary with the cultures of particular religious groups;
3. Religion would continue to exercise the function of expressing the individual to society; however, the sacred would be internal rather than external to the individual.
4. In the religion centered around the cult of humanity, science and religion would serve complementary functions; science would explain the individual's relationship to society, and religion would express this relationship;
5. Ritual life would involve *skill testing* and would relate accomplishment to positions of authority;
6. These rituals would be more private than public in nature and would focus on the development of the new sacred self; and
7. Finally, these rituals would be concerned mainly with the development of *purity*.

While the wording and particulars are different, some of these themes do seem to have taken shape in the religious life of the late twentieth-century world. Although Durkheim's predictions were written nearly a century ago, they were deeply influenced by evolutionary thought. Looking at contemporary trends, we do find that some of his predictions have been fulfilled, at least in broad terms, while others have simply not been realized.

In examining contemporary religiosity, Roof and McKinney, in *Mainline Religion* (1987:3–5), provide an insightful assessment of contrasting trends in today's religious life. They point to the fact that much of our former traditional faith, with its moral certainty, has lost its power to inform contemporary practice; in fact, the opposite may be true. For some religious groups, society informs their moral practice. Further, we are presented with ambiguous trends with regard to institutional religion. Statistics can be amassed to point to a significant upswing in religion, but they can also be arranged to indicate that secularization is far advanced and that the influence of religion over our lives is diminishing.

Roof and McKinney have given a useful six-point summary of the important changes under way in our religious life:

1. The once-privileged Protestant mainline no longer enjoys its place of power;
2. Conservative Protestants are flourishing and becoming more interested in influencing the political and moral life of this world;
3. The Roman Catholic Church is taking a more centrist position, resembling at times a denomination;
4. American Jews have become more self-affirming and less interested in assimilation;
5. Black religionists are less interested in maintaining a separatist view of the United States; and
6. Secular humanism is identified as a growing and hostile force in relation to traditional religion and morality.

Other trends are also observed. Non-Western religions, particularly Islam, are becoming numerically a force in the life of the United States. Islam, for example, is now the third-largest single religious group in the nation. As immigrants from Asia are once again welcome in the United States, Buddhist temples are almost as common as Islamic mosques in some cities. And in another trend many former "ethnic" Eastern Orthodox churches are attracting converts from such diverse origins as Campus Crusade and Roman Catholicism (Chalfant, 1992; Gillquist, 1989).

According to Roof and McKinney and others, then, the religious world is undergoing a rapid and at times confusing change. What has been the religious establishment is undergoing a profound transformation. We may be seeing, Roof and McKinney indicate, the emergence of a newly shaped religious faith that will form the core of religion as we near the twenty-first century, as what Roof (1993) calls a *generation of seekers* reworks the traditional aspects of religious life in the United States. While New Religious Movements continue to be of interest, changes at the heart of our religious life will have a more lasting impact on the patterns of religion. As demonstrated in recent battles over human sexuality in mainline denominations, the parameters of belief and morality are no longer firm. One thing we need to consider is the paradox in the midst of all this change: American life remains deeply religious while, at the same time, it is also deeply secular in orientation.

Reflecting on these trends, we need to consider the following questions: Is religion in decline, as secularization theory predicts? Or is religious life basically stable, exhibiting much less change than many have contended? Are we undergoing a renewal of religion which outshines other periods of "awakening"? Or are there underlying changes in contemporary religious life that portend a variety of alternatives to traditional concepts of the sacred? The answers to these questions are not simple. Certainly today we can only "see through a glass darkly..." when it comes to analyzing the future course of religion. We can, however, explore what is at present known and what is predicted.

One thing appears certain: The confident predictions of our classical sociological theorists, as well as those of some more recent analysts, that modern societies would be increasingly secularized as religious institutions were systematically divested of their functions and authority have not been entirely fulfilled (Finke, 1990). At the very least, if traditional expressions of religion have lost their impact, the sacred continues to be a part of societal life although it may be found in new or unexpected places. While it can be shown, through data on membership and attendance, that traditional religious institutions (most especially those termed *mainline*) have been declining, belief in the sacred in some form continues to be strong, with the vast majority of the population, particularly in the United States, professing a belief in God (NORC, 1992). However, what people mean when they say they believe in God is not clear. Respondents in the same poll do profess a broad variety of religious beliefs ranging across the entire spectrum of possible concepts.

As we consider the various developments in religious life today, it is important to keep the issues raised in mind. Debates over the meaning of shifts in church attendance and membership need to be enlightened by what facts we have. Further, we need to take into account controversies over whether invisible religions and the growth of mystic Eastern cults on supposedly secular soil suggest that predictions about new forms of religion will come to represent a loose religious core. The emergence of prominent television evangelists as pastors to many people can also be seen as part of the privatization of religious life, as can the "salad bar" approach to religion in which doctrines are selected on the basis of personal wish rather than on systematic theological belief. In fact, many take the "salad bar" approach today, constructing their own personal belief system.

What, then, can we really say concerning the future of religion? As we weigh the options presented by the questions raised earlier in this chapter, four different possibilities appear. While we will discuss them as if they were mutually exclusive, it is quite possible that people will not see them as such in the present voluntaristic religious climate. In the late years of the twentieth century, people may be able to encompass several options with regard to religion at the same time. It has been suggested by some that we should not focus our attention on the secularization of the mainline denominations or on the apparent upsurge in evangelical or fundamentalist faith. Neither, for that matter, should we concentrate on the New Religious Movements. The major factor in contemporary religious life, according to such observers, is a type of syncretism which merges various aspects of religious belief to formulate—often for single persons—an individual concept of the sacred.

Focusing on a tendency we have already noted, Dobbelaere (1981, 1984, 1990) has pointed to the trend in contemporary society to erect a religious faith which is in truth a bricolage of numerous items of faith which may or may not go together, much like the items on a plate filled at a smorgasbord restaurant. As Giddens indicates in his critique of postmodernist theory, religion in contemporary society is characterized by duality rather than dualism (Giddens, 1979, 1984, 1990). We can comprehend several seemingly incompatible ideologies without great discomfort or realization of the ambiguity involved. Thus, we can combine both traditional and new religious ideas without strain. In the modern age, then, implicit religious beliefs can mix with and perhaps be more powerful than the orthodoxies of our forbearers.

Keeping these cautions in mind, let us examine each of the following four possibilities presented by our earlier questions. In doing so, we should be aware that some answers may be appropriate for one segment of the population while others will better fit different people. Here are the four possibilities:

1. Religion—at least religion as we have known it—is declining as forces of modernization result in some form of that secularization foretold by early sociologists and much favored by many sociology of religion scholars;
2. Despite apparent fluctuations, religion is basically about as strong as it has been throughout our history and will probably continue in this path;
3. The strength of fundamentalist and Pentacostal churches is increasing and this form of religion may become the dominant or core religion, shoving aside the "tepidness" of the old mainline;
4. Life in late modern or postmodern society is so radically different that we can expect religion—or the sacred—to appear in new and, in part, yet unheard of forms.

We will look at each of these options in turn, reminding ourselves that consistency is not necessarily the benchmark of contemporary religious patterns.

THE TRANSFORMATION OF TRADITIONAL RELIGIOUS BELIEF

The first possibility to be discussed is that religion will be so changed by the forces of modernization that it will no longer be recognizable as what it has traditionally been. In one sense, this prediction claims that the forces of secularization may not totally destroy religion, but that in accommodating to modernization, religious faith will become a new creation.

As we observed in Chapter 5, the beliefs and rewards offered by traditional religious systems are, to many, somewhat discordant with the value system of a larger society perceived as secular. Because of this discordance, traditional religious groups in our society appear to have a much diminished influence in the contemporary world, being reduced to individual piety or public ceremony (Berger, 1967). Such an observation is in line with the early predictions of the evolutionary school of social thought (see Chapter 2) and cited in the speculations of Durkheim that religion was only a vestige of humanity's primitive ignorance—a remnant that would vanish as human knowledge increased and the need to explain unexplained facts decreased. Actually, attempts to conform to the secular world with accommodation seem to have resulted in a loss rather than a gain, as those denominations espousing conformity have seen their membership rolls dwindle.

As mentioned previously, there is a long tradition in the sociological study of religion which looks for either the demise of religion or its nearly total transformation. The central concept or hypothesis guiding these assumptions is *secularization*.

Secularization

The assumption of decline in the centrality of the religious institution has led many to view religion as if it were a patient with a terminal disease. The diagnosis is secularization, a concept we have mentioned but not thoroughly discussed up to this point. Although secularization has many forms and definitions, its chief symptom is the gradual erosion of religion's authority in the face of society's devotion to science as the basic epistemology, or way of knowing.

The disease has resulted, as those who support the secularization theory say, in divesting religion of more and more spheres of influence to the point that it now stands at the periphery of society, relegated to only the most public of affairs or life's most private moments (Berger, 1967).

In England, where the Industrial Revolution began, the thesis of the secularization of society has been vigorously asserted. Some scholars there have rushed to administer last rites to the religious institution (for example, Wilson, 1966, 1975, 1982). Figures on church attendance, particularly for the Church of England, seem to bear out the prognosis. Religion can be seen as either a private or a *very public* matter, as in the royal ceremonies. However, others (for example, Martin, 1978) resist the notion that England is a truly secular nation, finding signs of religious faith still very much a part of British life.

In the United States many people are now more cautious in pronouncing secularization a terminal condition for institutional religion than might have been true a decade or two ago. Such observers contend that secularization is viewed too narrowly, and that while many traditional beliefs have been recast and the church as an institution may be ailing, a religious belief system or a sense of the sacred still exists in the secular world (see Hammond, 1985). Thus some scholars, while agreeing that secularization exists, contend that it always has been an element in human society and does not justify the diagnosis of a terminal disease (see, for example, Daniel Bell, 1971; Stark and Bainbridge, 1985). While Novak acknowledges (1967:237) that the "transformation that Christianity, in particular, is now experiencing is unique in its rapidity, profundity, and intensity," there is the sense of a continuing vitality which continues to rise through the changes.

Secularization is a complex concept. To help us understand it, we may begin with the three brief propositions in explanation of the term offered by Hadden (1986:599):

> Once the world was filled with the sacred—in thought, practice, and institutional form.
>
> After the Reformation and the Renaissance, the forces of modernization swept across the globe and secularization, a corollary historical process, loosened the dominance of the sacred.
>
> In due course, the sacred shall disappear altogether except, possibly, in the private realm.

While this is a seductively easy explanation of the concept, few, including Hadden, would seriously see the matter in more simplistic terms. Karel Dobbelaere, a Belgian sociologist, points out that secularization is a multidimensional process. In a sweeping article on the subject (1981), he notes three basic meanings of the term:

1. In one sense secularization refers to a diminishing role for institutional religion in providing legitimation for society while such other institutional areas as education and politics take over the functions and authority of religion;
2. Another sense of the concept is that church beliefs become adjusted to the world. In this sense secularization refers to the replacement of church religion with a cultural religion; and
3. Secularization is simply a sensitizing concept that alerts us to the direction religion is taking.

In a later article (1984), Dobbelaere attempts to refine the issues involved in defining the concept of secularization. Trying to give a summary statement, he indicates that the term refers to the reduction of an overarching religious system to a subsystem of society—one that operates on an equal basis with other subsystems. In other words, religion does not disappear but becomes only one of several segments of society.

A broad concept like secularization, with so many definitions, really cannot be proven or disproven. Rather, we tend to observe features of modern life which appear to be secularized. One of these indications is the reported decline in membership in some of the mainline denominations in the United States.

Early support for the notion of an ever-diminishing role for traditional religion was provided in a 1960s study of religion in America. The view that religion is being slowly abandoned is represented by Stark and Glock's study, *American Piety: The Nature of Religious Commitment* (1968), which sees religion as moving away from its customary patterns in a direction that will end up with the eventual abandonment of traditional religion. Based on data from a sample of California church members, these researchers asserted that "a profound revolution in religious thought is sweeping the churches." Their findings concluded that the major result of this transformation in attitudes toward religion would be first a movement toward liberal church membership and eventually a significant lessening of the degree to which individuals in society commit themselves to the more orthodox religious faiths. Such a diminishment could mean a weakening of the influence of traditional faith in society and, eventually, the demise of religion in any commonsense meaning of that word.

As they viewed the responses of church members in the San Francisco Bay area, Stark and Glock found an interpretation of Christian faith and its symbols that was so different as to be unrecognizable as traditional Christianity. They contended that this radically altered version of religion was the dominant view, not only for the occasional skeptic on the fringes of the religious organization but indeed also among the religious institution's brightest theological minds and its ablest clergy. Although the data did not indicate that a basic belief in a personal God had disappeared, they did show that a number of such basic beliefs regarded as fundamental to Christian belief seemed to have been discarded; at the very least, such beliefs were viewed in only the most symbolic of fashions. In the liberal churches which Stark and Glock saw as dominant (especially among church members under the age of fifty), orthodox views such as the belief in Jesus' divinity and the reality of physical miracles were accepted as myths reflecting some philosophical truth but not empirical accounts of reality. Whether wishful thinking or scientific miasma, the picture painted does not seem accurate today.

Actually numerous studies have criticized these researchers' methods and challenged the conclusion that liberal churches would initially be the ones to grow (Roof and Hadaway, 1977; Hadaway, 1978). A major criticism of Stark and Glock's findings (Hadaway, 1978) is that the sample upon which they based their conclusions was by no means representative of society as a whole, if only because the level of migration into California from other parts of the country is so high. Because some denominations, like the Southern Baptist Convention, were poorly represented in California in contrast to other areas from which people move, a good deal of denominational switching obviously took place; this switching perforce favored the more liberal groups that were better established in California. Such switching, however, did not necessarily indicate a preference for the more liberal theology of, for example, the Presbyterian church. Rather, it was most likely a matter of choosing a church reasonably close to the residence of the switcher. And, with the influx of Presbyterian pastors trained at the conservative Fuller seminary, church doctrine might have been transformed by the switchers rather than vice versa.

Another factor in the growth of membership in liberal denominations—leading to an assumption of increasingly liberal theology for the laity—was the socioeconomic climate of the 1960s. This was a time when many people experienced an upward occupational and economic mobility. Many individuals from blue-collar backgrounds (and blue-collar religious groups) obtained a college education and entered the white-collar world at that time. The religions of their youth did not fit their new statuses and some of them did join mainline denominations (see Chapter 11). But this did not necessarily mean an ideological switch. The more conservative beliefs of those individuals' early socialization came with them into their new affiliations.

Thus, another element was added to the misperception of trends. The transformation to liberal ideology was only apparent, not real. And, as the leaders of the mainline denominations took it for real, they contributed one of several factors in the decline of the mainline denominations in the 1960s and 1970s.

Decline in the Mainline

What then can we say about secularization? Instead of the transformation seen in the growth of liberal denominations in the fifties, they have experienced sharp decreases in membership. This raises the possibility that secularization, insofar as it means a decline in institutional religion, is limited to these denominations.

Before continuing our discussion of this decline, we need to be sure what we mean by the term *mainline*. As we have indicated the terms *mainline* or *mainstream* generally indicate the religious groups that have been culturally dominant since the beginning of the nation. They are the established middle-class religions (Roof and McKinney, 1987). Originally, they were the Congregationalists, Episcopalians, and Presbyterians. Over the course of the nation's history other groups have been added to this list—including Catholics and Jews, as well as former "upstart" sects, like the Methodists and Baptists (Finke and Stark, 1989). The beliefs of the mainline, as Roof and McKinney comment, can be summarized in three points: (1) Beliefs and styles tend to cluster around a broad central theme (one that can be shared by many groups); (2) there is almost total acceptance of the social world in which the groups find themselves; and (3) while innovations may begin at the fringes, if they are to find acceptance they must make their way to the center.

Roof (1993) suggests that when analyzing religious life today it is important to focus on this core, rather than on what is happening in the marginal sects and cult groups. He contends that the extent of secularization in the society cannot be adequately measured by looking at the growth of the New Religious Movements or the revitalization of evangelical groups. Rather we need to look at what is happening in the mainline core since this is still our cultural center.

To the extent that secularization can be equated with a decline in church membership (a claim disputed by many), it is primarily in these mainline groups that its effects have been most keenly felt. Beginning with the work of Kelley (1972), the plight of mainline churches has been brought forcefully to our attention (see Chapter 6). As we have seen, he outlined the rise of the conservative groups; more particularly, he detailed the decline of the mainstream, ecumenically oriented groups. In these groups the sixties marked the first time that their membership actually declined numerically, as opposed to proportionally. While the old mainline felt the pinch, Catholicism also felt the strains and tensions of a decline in its numbers and power.

Actually, according to Finke and Stark (1989), the decline of the mainline did not begin in the 1960s. Although that was the point in national history when precipitous drops in the actual number of members began to occur, the proportion of the population affiliated with mainline groups was already declining early in the nineteenth century. What they refer to as the "upstart" sects—the Methodists and Baptists—early on seriously challenged the position of the mainline churches. The clergy of the Anglican, Congregationalist, and Presbyterian churches had become persons of learning who did not speak the language of the common people, particularly as the migration to the frontier increased. It was the Methodists and Baptists who carried the faith into these parts and who were able to win members. Actually the Methodist spurt sputtered out soon, perhaps not coincidentally with the rise of learning among the Methodist clergy. Thus what alarmed those in the mainline in the sixties and seventies was only the end result of a longer process in which the mainline had been losing proportionately since the Revolution.

Of course, there are many strands in this puzzling situation. Roozen and Carroll (1979) noted that trends in church membership may be due to the result of institutional factors, to the societal context, or to both these factors. First we can look at trends that may be the result of the actions of church bureaucracies. For example, much of the decline in mainline membership appears to have resulted from the liberal stands taken by denominational executives (Hadden, 1969; Hoge, 1976). The home offices of the United Church of Christ, for example, took the most liberal positions of any denomination, but apparently could not lead their "flock" with them as that denomination suffered the greatest decline in membership among the mainline churches (Kelley, 1977; Roof and McKinney, 1987).

In the summer of 1991, Presbyterians, Methodists, and Episcopalians faced a crisis over attempts to change traditional standards of sexual morality. In many ways the more liberal leadership of the denominations, which was often in control of key bureaucratic positions, was leading in a way the denominations did not want to go. Had those in executive positions in the denominational headquarters prevailed, it seems certain that further defections would have occurred.

But contextual factors, such as the social climate, also have an important effect on changes in church membership. Hoge (1979) reports that for the period from 1955 to 1975, denominations grew or declined at rates consistently relative to one another, suggesting that these changes were the result of external factors common to many denominations rather than to specific groups. This points to a gradual, pervasive effect at work with regard to membership trends. The main contextual factors that seem to explain growth and decline are socioeconomic status, the culture of the society, birthrates for the nation, and changes in values about such matters as having children.

Along these lines, McKinney and Hoge (1983) found congregational youthfulness to be a key factor in growth, even though the main reason for church growth or decline appeared related to the nature of the community in which a particular church was located. Likewise, Hadaway (1981) has commented on the importance of the demographic environment for church membership. Thus trends in church membership are not merely extensions or artifacts of socioeconomic status, family size, or region of greatest strength for the denominations. Hoge concludes that contextual factors explain more than half of the variations found in the growth or decline of denominations.

A finding of particular importance is that factors that most affect membership impinge most heavily on denominations with the highest percentage of members of upper socioeconomic status. Indeed, the higher the status of the denomination's membership, the smaller its growth is likely to be. The encroachment of secular-humanistic views into the thinking of upper-status persons may be the most important factor in changes in membership growth along with low birthrates.

These considerations lead us to look at *how* the growing churches obtain new members. For example, Bibby (1978) contends that Kelley has not proved that the growth of the conservative churches is the result of their conservative beliefs and the attraction of members from outside the conservative Christian community. Rather, the growth has perhaps been the result of proselytizing adherents from other fundamentalist or conservative Christian groups, as well as from the fact that such groups hold onto members better than do the more liberal denominations. Actually, Bibby finds that mainline and conservative Protestant groups do not differ greatly in the number of outsiders they are bringing into the faith. That the conservatives draw members away from the liberals is not true; indeed, the opposite actually appears to be the case. However, in terms of percentage, the conservatives have more children and also have better success in holding these children as members of the particular group. Conservative churches, then, may really be growing because of their higher birthrates and the more effective socialization of their children rather than because of some vast turning toward orthodox belief. In a later study of conversions to conservative churches, Bibby and Brinkerhoff (1983) found that the same patterns of recruitment still existed.

Another important factor in relative growth rates is switching. How do the patterns of switching from one denomination or religion to another affect church growth and decline?

Switching

According to surveys (NORC, 1992), approximately 40 percent of American Protestants switch to another denomination during their lifetime. Switching has increased in the past thirty years, and the patterns of changes have been transformed. People no longer switch upward for status; they either switch out of religion altogether or move to more conservative groups. More significantly, the mainline denominations have been less stable in attracting and keeping their switchers and the switchers' children.

In terms of net gains, according to Hadaway (1978), the conservative churches per se do not show the greatest advantage, but rather groups at the extremes of both conservative and liberal orientations. Hadaway suggests, however, that the groups at either end of the continuum display quite different modes of gaining new membership. The sects exhibit considerable net gain through switching, but their greatest gain seems to come from mobilizing those who are not members of any church. Lutherans and Baptists make only modest gains through switching, but since they hold onto the members they have they do not fare badly. The moderate churches, on the other hand, make only moderate gains from switching and are unable to hold onto the members they already have. The liberal denominations also lack a good hold on their existing members.

While the numbers have not been as startling as for such groups as, say, the Southern Baptists, some Orthodox churches have been gaining an impressive number of new members or converts. While some Orthodox groups, e.g., the Albanian Orthodox and Greek Orthodox churches, continue to stress ethnicity, others, particularly the Orthodox Church of America (basically the Russian Orthodox branch), welcome and have received a number of converts, some of whom attend a seminary and enter orders of the clergy (Chalfant, 1992). Those who convert (or switch) to the Orthodox faith generally report that they are attracted by a liturgy based on an ancient historical tradition as well as by a church which is serious about religion. An interesting feature is the high proportion of highly educated individuals who convert (Loft, 1991) and who find in Eastern thought patterns a way to maintain both conservative religious beliefs and a commitment to scientific facts.

Roof and Hadaway (1977) point out that denominational switching is very common for both liberal *and* conservative Protestants, while those in the theological middle tend to hold onto their members better. For example, Baptists and Lutherans tend to have the most success in keeping their members, while sectarians as well as such staunch mainline groups as the Presbyterians and the Methodists lose as many as 35 percent of their adherents to other faiths—as well as to unbelief. The Roman Catholic Church shows a higher proportion of defectors to no religion at all than do the Protestant churches.

But the patterns are not consistent. Net gains and losses vary considerably for different groups. For Roof and Hadaway, one point is clear: The switching process does not follow theological lines. Liberal Episcopalians and Congregationalists gain adherents; so, too, do the ultraconservative sectarian groups. At the same time, the liberal Methodist and Presbyterian churches lose in the switching process, as do conservative Baptists and Lutherans. Newport (1979) has confirmed these findings, but has also noted that the most likely switch is out of traditional religion altogether.

Two basic demographic characteristics dominate the switching scene (Roof and McKinney, 1987:151ff.): age structure and family patterns. The age of those who switch is of crucial importance. The population is aging and religious groups closer to the mainstream are more likely to find their switchers among the aging population. The percentage of members over fifty years of age within the mainstream churches has grown significantly over the past twenty-five years. The population of Catholics and Jews has also aged. For these groups, large numbers of young people dropped out during the 1960s as being nonaffiliated became more acceptable. As a result, liberal Protestants became older, on the average, than their conservative counterparts. Obviously, older members do not replenish the group's pool with children and the departure of the young left the groups without replenishments.

Also, family life had a differential impact on mainline and evangelical groups. Families in the mainline adjusted to the dominant values of individualism, freedom, and equality. Accommodating to the social and cultural changes of the 1960s, the mainline churches adjusted to new lifesyles, the changing roles for women, and the acceptance of new family forms. Such changes presented problems for the denominations, however. The new social forms and new attitudes contrasted with a "Norman Rockwell" portrait of the church accepted by the more conservative groups. While conservative families conformed to this conservative model of family life, those within the mainline did not. Such liberal attitudes did not promote large families or children coerced into the family religion.

STABILITY IN RELIGIOUS LIFE

The second possibility is that the outward signs we identify as marking dramatic changes in our religious life just do not reflect the lack of stability some claim to see. The fluctuations in church membership, for example, are more apparent than real. The history of the United States has been one of ups and downs in the vigor of religion. Although some groups are currently having difficulties, overall religious life is more or less stable.

Greeley (1970b, 1972) presents a quite different view of religion in the late twentieth century. According to him, traditional religious expression remains strong. Summing up his vision of the state of religion in the year 2000, he feels that, except in the event of some severe disaster, the traditional religious organizations will not lose members, and that church attendance will remain at about the same level as it has been for some time. Further, he believes that the majority of the population will continue to rely on religious interpretatins of Ultimate Reality. In this way, religion will still have at least an indirect impact on society, providing the foundation for a general social consensus. Greeley does not view secularizing forces as a serious threat to traditional religion, which will remain healthy.

While Greeley's predictions are based more on theoretical speculation than well-analyzed empirical data, research has borne them out to some extent. In researchers' replication of the study of "Middletown" (Muncie, Indiana)—you will recall that it was first investigated by the Lynds just before the Great Depression—the researchers found little evidence of a strong impact of secularization (Caplow, Bahr, and Chadwick 1983; Caplow, 1985; Tamney and Johnson, 1985). Only one of eleven proposed measures of secularization (the tendency to marry outside of one's religious faith) had increased significantly since the early study of Middletown. In addition, Himmelfarb (1967:22) has perceived a return to belief on the part of Jewish young people, a group not traditionally religious in the usual sense. In particular, he sees young, intellectual Jews as less antipathetic toward Judaism and anticipates an actual return to traditional Jewish practices.

In addition, national opinion polls (NORC, 1992) have continually shown an amazing strength in religious belief and practice in the United States. Over these years there have been some peaks and valleys, but overall indicators of religious involvement have remained high. Generally, less than 5 percent of the respondents reported *no* religious preference (although preference does not necessarily mean membership in a religious group). The tendency to attend religious services is high, certainly relative to other countries, with more than one-third of Americans reporting they attend religious services on a regular basis. And nearly four-fifths indicate they attend services at least some of the time. Attendance, of course, varies by the particular group; more than half of those who give sectarian groups as their religious preference attend regularly and just under one-half of Catholics report regular attendance. On the other hand, those who give the Presbyterian or Episcopal churches as their preference fall below the general attendance average.

Even the asserted return of Baby Boomers to religion only underlines a sort of stability in church life. The departure of young adults and their return during "parenting" has been a constant in our religious life. Although the return of the Baby Boomers is not as real as many people claim, those returning would underline, for some, the normal ebb and flow of religious participation.

In summary, according to this view, religion is no less but no more religious than at other times in an up-and-down history. The institutional church remains central to community and national life.

RENEWAL: REVIVING CONSERVATIVE BELIEFS

A third possibility for religion in the future is that the apparent revival and resurgence of evangelical religion, including fundamentalism, will continue, and that such faith will form the religious core of the nation's faith. In a number of ways, as we have pointed out (Chapter 7), there has been an upsurge in belief in conservative religion, including Pentecostal, charismatic expressions of religious experience. The success of such groups, in the face of mainline decline, could be seen as the future of religion—the victory of a fundamentalist or, at least, conservative interpretation of religion that will have an influence on national life and politics once held by the mainline.

The new evangelicalism, as discussed in Chapter 7, does not encompass the entire Christian population, but its growth makes pronouncing religion "sick unto death" difficult. This movement is one of numerous indicators of the vitality of religious belief, practice, and experience and what appears to some to be a renewal of faith. Further, beliefs of groups that are growing tend to be traditional and conservative. Indeed, as we have observed, many New Christian rightist groups are building a base of support on this conservative theology. One sign of this renewal may be found in the founding and rapid growth of independent fundamentalist and Pentecostal churches, some growing and expanding both in membership and the formation of new congregations.

While we have detailed the shrinking membership in mainline churches, such a decline has not characterized all religious bodies in recent decades. As we noted in Chapter 6, Kelley (1977) reported in the 1970s that although mainline liberal congregations were dwindling in actual size, the more conservative groups (like the Seventh-day Adventists and Jehovah's Witnesses) were experiencing rapid growth. In a later article, Kelley (1978) contended that the membership trends had remained the same since his original study, except that three somewhat conservative churches (the Presbyterian Church [U.S.A.], the Lutheran Church–Missouri Synod, and the Christian Reformed Church) had suffered membership losses for the first time. However, no such decline was experienced by fast-growing ultraconservative groups such as the Southern Baptists, Seventh-day Adventists, and the Church of the Nazarene. To the extent that this type of statistic indicates the health of denominations, Stark and Glock's predictions about the growth of an increasingly liberal version of Christianity appear to be totally wrong.

Another sign of renewal is found in responses to national opinion polls. The number of persons claiming that religion is increasing in influence has more than doubled since the early 1970s and, according to one survey (NORC, 1992), one out of every three persons claims to have been born again. About the same proportion, in the same survey, report feeling very close to God.

The charismatic renewal movement, which has appeared in various Protestant denominations and in some Roman Catholic parishes, provides further evidence of a type of renewal. As Poloma (1982) notes, this neo-Pentecostal movement in more or less mainline denominations has greatly expanded the influence of charismatic expression. The term *charismatic* can no longer be used only for the older Pentecostal sectarian groups, but can also apply to mainline congregations and to particular groups within some parishes.

Vitality is also to be seen in the changing style of the conservative churches with regard to the secular world (see Chapter 10). Once content to withdraw from the "evil" world, conservatives are now facing directly those things in society they consider evil and seeking, through law, to change them. Family and sexual issues, in particular, are political targets for the conservatives.

In assessing the growth of the conservative churches, Kelley (1977) has suggested that institutional factors are more important than contextual ones in the growth of conservative churches and in the decline of liberal ones. For Kelley, the real bottom line is that the more liberal churches do not appear to be taking religion as seriously as the conservative churches are, and thus the conservative churches have an apparent advantage over the liberal churches in that they do a better job of dealing with the problems of Ultimate Reality. What is particularly interesting to Kelley is that these conservative groups do not even *attempt* to be reasonable in terms of modern thought. They are neither ecumenical nor relevant, and in fact such groups stubbornly refuse to give in to acceptability. Attempts to be more reasonable and relevant do not appear to strengthen churches; rather, groups that stick to older, more traditional formulations seem to be doing best today. In light of this, Kelley suggests that strictness in both dogma and discipline leads to greater social strength for the churches that maintain it.

Supporting the contention that it is *serious* churches that are keeping their members and winning new converts are the experiences of conservative and orthodox Judaism and those of some churches related to the Eastern Orthodox tradition. Among young adult Jews, there has been a significant return to orthodox and conservative traditions. Davidman (1991) has detailed this return, especially as it relates to women. She discusses the large number of young Jewish women who are taking up the older, orthodox ways, despite the restrictions concerning the role of women.

Similarly, Chalfant (1992), in a study of one congregation of the Orthodox Church of America (with roots in the Russian Orthodox Church), interviewed one-half of those who had converted to this faith (about 50 percent of the congregation). He found the converts, in the main, to be young adults with considerably more than average educational attainment. Among other things, what appealed to them about the Orthodox Church was that through its liturgy it appeared to be taking the Gospel and religion very seriously.

But while some rejoice in what they see as a renewal, there are reminders that there have been numerous "renewals" but in the end religion—at least Protestantism—has simply taken a step backward. As

Bruce (1990) explains in *A House Divided: Protestantism, Schism, and Secularization,* the voluntarism underlying Protestant belief (and to an increasing extent the belief of U.S. Catholicism) produces a multiple religious marketplace that can give no pretense of legitimating the culture. Bruce sees the periodic revivals or renewals as part of the cycle of "increasing and decreasing religiosity" (13). According to him, while there are "tides" in religiosity, the ocean is gradually receding, falling further back with the end of each new renewal. Religion in Protestant countries, and one suspects also in Catholic and Orthodox strongholds, is becoming too fragmented to claim to be the primary source of values, beliefs, and public norms.

ALTERNATIVES TO TRADITIONAL CHRISTIANITY

Finally, there is the possibility that life in later modern or postmodern society (Giddens, 1990; Harvey, 1989) is so radically different that we should not expect religion (or the sacred) to appear in any of its former shapes (Shibley, 1990). Rather, while not expecting religion to wither away, we might expect its older forms to be replaced by new and in part unheard-of forms.

It has been suggested that people in modern society are actually as religious as those who lived in the eighteenth, thirteenth, or even first centuries. However, many are not religious in the same ways that have characterized Western civilization for two millenia. The beliefs and rituals through which belief in a sacred realm is expressed by many has been radically altered. Yinger (1969) suggested that when we inquire about religious belief, we need to ask in what particular ways a person is religious rather than whether a person is or is not religious. In this vein Yinger proposes a nondoctrinal religion as the basic faith of many late-twentieth century people, one in which strictures of dogma and creed do not bind and in which all that matters is a concern with certain essential problems of existence. As we have noted, Bellah et al. (1985) have found a wide variation of beliefs, ranging from the utterly individualistic to exotic communalities, to be part of the lives of many people in the United States who must be said to be religious in the sense that they believe in the sacred.

An interesting approach to the phenomenon of privatized religions is that suggested by Bailey (1983, 1990). He has introduced the concept of *implicit religion.* By this he intends to recognize that "what people stand for" (1990:3) may be outside the doctrinal creeds of established denominations. Their commitment is to less than formal concepts of the sacred which, nonetheless, are important in their construction of what makes sense out of their lives.

Further support is given to these comments by the increasing interest in New Religious Movements as evidenced not only by the number of such groups but also by the fact that the actual number of persons involved in them has increased considerably in recent years (Robbins, Anthony, and Richardson, 1978; Robbins, 1990). An important aspect of this phenomenon is that the participants are not drawn predominantly from the economically underprivileged but from the children of that bulwark of tradition—the middle class. As we pointed out in Chapter 6, religious experience of a direct kind is really frequent for what is supposed to be a secular age.

One factor which must be introduced in consideration of the future of religious life in the United States is the vitality of religions from non-Western origins. By this we do not refer to those New Religious Movements which have often had Eastern origins. Rather we refer to the increased strength of religions from the Near and Far East. The globalization of society evident in all aspects of late modern society also affects American religious life. For example, as we have seen, Muslims now form the third-largest single religious group in the United States. This faith, along with Buddhism and Hinduism, will certainly play a more significant role in American life as immigrants from parts of the world where these faiths are the rule bring their beliefs with them.

Even as we note these trends, we must also consider another alternative to the traditional scene. That is one in which liberal and conservative religious traditions become further separated from one another, leaving in the middle a large vacuum to be filled with those who profess no particular faith. This is sometimes referred to as the *polarization thesis*.

Polarization

It seems that two distinct processes are going on in the religious world of today. One is that, for various reasons, some conservative churches are growing. The other is that many liberal church members are drifting away from religion in its traditional or churchly sense. What hypothesis can we make to explain both processes? One suggestion is that religious belief has become polarized. At one pole are the mainline "liberal" groups, at the other the evangelicals. And... in between are the majority of the population who are not so much irreligious as picking and choosing, as noted above.

Our culture has always faced two conflicting worldviews: the traditional Christian one and a secular-humanistic approach. Some institutions, such as church-related universities, have traditionally attempted to assert a unity for the two; however, the tension between these two perspectives is slowly pulling them apart and polarizing them in our time (Hoge and Roozen, 1979).

Since the late nineteenth century, the secular-humanistic culture has been gaining strength in the United States, and mainline or liberal Protestantism has served as a bridge and a synthesis for the two worldviews. At certain times in history, this bridge has been strong and vital, providing an accommodation between the perspectives. This was especially true in the years immediately following the Second World War, in particular the cold war years. But from about 1965 that bridge has begun to weaken and crumble. In a time of increased dominance for the secular-humanistic culture among the educated circles, it is not surprising that widespread defection from traditional religion is taking place. For this educated group the need for the church and traditional religion has ceased to be vital, and many have left the mainline churches or have remained only as nominal members. At the same time other individuals in society have rejected the traditions of the mainline churches as too involved with secular-humanistic culture and too secularized.

Conservative churches are growing. But they are, as we have indicated, growing very much in their own sphere, attracting and retaining friends, relatives, and their children, as well as some who seek the more conservative approach of such groups. In their worldview, the traditional beliefs and moral values associated with Christianity are to be retained and a vigorous effort made to diminish the effects of the secular-humanistic point of view. In short, such groups reject the attempt to accept both worldviews, and thus they form one polarized and large portion of society. On the other hand, many of those who have clung to the mainline churches as a means of bridging the gap between the two belief systems no longer find this necessary or meaningful. They form the other polarized, but smaller, portion of the scene with regard to religion today. Many obviously still seek, with considerable vigor in some cases, to maintain the bridge between the two poles, but they appear to be fighting a losing cause, at least at this point in our history.

In summary, we believe that three groups are actually involved in the contemporary religious scene in our country. Those who continue to hold to the mainline tradition of attempting to accommodate will not disappear from our society, although they may continue in a weakened condition. The two polarized groups will probably become even more polarized, at least in the foreseeable future.

Members of the polarized group that has drifted away from the mainline churches have not necessarily all become secularized or lost all meaning systems for their lives. While this may be true of some, evidence indicates that new or alternative forms of religious meaning systems guide the lives of many in our society who have either left churchly religion or never been associated with it.

Our discussion of the relative strength of religion generally has been concerned with churchly religion. Yet, accepting only the narrowest substantive definition of religion and limiting discussion to such a narrow range of traditional religious expression cuts us off from consideration of much that can be seen as an expression of a religious meaning system, as well as much that may shape religion in the future. Indeed, Luckmann (1967), in his concept of the invisible religion, has pointed out the limitations of a sociology of religion that restricts itself to the official or traditional structures of religions.

Some scholars, notably Luckmann (1967), Berger (1967), and Yinger (1969), have pointed out that the functions served by religion will always need to be performed in some way. The problems of the human condition will always be with us and will need an answer. In this sense, a need will always exist for that which is basic to the idea of religion. As Geertz (1966:4) has noted, "at the limits of his analytic capacities, at the limits of his power of endurance, and at the limits of his moral insights" the individual cries out in need for something beyond the self.

Bibby (1987) found in a study of religion in Canada that while traditional religion continued to provide a meaning system for a large proportion of individuals, a significant pocket of people were finding answers to the permanent questions of meaning from the kind of nonconventional meaning systems suggested by Yinger's conception of invisible religion. Bibby suggests, though, that meaning for many contemporary Canadians may not come from either visible or invisible religion, but rather may be the result of a more privatized system related to family, other intimate relationships, and personal goals. Hadden and Swann (1981) have similarly suggested that religious belief and practice are still strong, but that religion has become more private and more focused on personal rather than communal meanings. And Hammond (1985) has contended that even movements such as the new Christian right are strongly influenced by the need to increase the power and significance of the individual in a mass society.

What is common to these arguments is that they do not see secularization and pluralism has having destroyed religion; rather they see these forces as having pushed religion into a more individual, private sphere. We remain religious, but our religion is more internal and takes the form of seeking identification or knowledge of the sacred within a secularized society (see Hammond 1985). Campbell (1978), in an essay on "the secret religion of the educated classes," continues this same argument. For him, secularization and the new expressions of religiosity are not contradictory developments but aspects of the same general trend. He reminds us of Troeltsch's (1931) third, much neglected category of spiritual and mystic religion. This type of religion may be more evident than other forms in our time—not simply as a renewed emphasis on the spiritual and mystical within traditional religious systems but rather as a totally new system, one whose cardinal doctrine centers around the presence of the seed or spark of God in the individual.

Chapters 8 and 9 discuss some of the new religious approaches that have appealed to many Americans. New Age beliefs have affected many while others have adjusted their religious beliefs to fit their personal beliefs—they have created the bricolage of faith forecast by Dobbelaere. The sacred is very much alive in the last years of the twentieth century. But for many its shape is outside the traditional.

Secularization, then, may be a process applicable to only one sort of religiosity, that related to the church as we have known it. Religiosity is applied to the solution of permanent, persistent questions (even when the range of solutions is limited to the transcendental) may well persist as long as such problems do; but in persisting, it may take new and unfamiliar shapes. Secularization may well be sweeping away the collected religious wisdom of two or more millennia, but it will not leave the void and emptiness some have predicted.

SUMMARY

As we come to the end of our exploration of religion and society in the late twentieth century, we must speculate on what concepts of the sacred will be like in the future. The predictions of such classical theorists as Durkheim have been partially fulfilled, but also partially negated. We have looked at four possibilities for the future of religion:

1. Religion will be so totally transformed that, as it continues, it will bear little resemblance to the religious dogmas of the past;
2. Religious beliefs will remain constant with little divergence from the patterns of the past;
3. Conservative, evangelical groups will become dominant, although they will continue to be in tension with the small group of mainline liberals; and

4. Religious belief will really represent totally new forms unrelated to the past experience of religion in Western society.

At one time many, if not most, sociologists would have opted for the first of these suggestions. As we have said, inevitable secularization was the accepted orthodox conclusion with regard to religion in modern times. Now it appears that for significant segments of the population each of these options is a possible reaction with regard to religion. The most significant change in sociological thought is the recognition, by many, that a need for something sacred or unconditional is needed to undergird life.

In his recent book, *A Generation of Seekers: The Spiritual Journeys of the Baby Boom Generation*, Wade Clark Roof (1993) points up what he refers to as a "widespread ferment" (4) among members of this generation that "reaches deep within their lives." As he puts it:

> This is a generation of seekers. Diverse as they are—from Christian fundamentalists to radical feminists, from New Age explorers to get-rich-quick MBAs—baby boomers have found that they have to discover for themselves what gives their lives meaning, what values to live by (Roof, 1993:8).

There is sound reason to believe that this ferment is not confined to the Baby Boom generation, but permeates all of late or postmodern society (see Giddens, 1990). There is an unease in our individual and communal lives which calls for something upon which we can anchor life. As Mestrovic (1992) suggests, we are at a *fin de siècle* or "phase change" in social history. It is a time not unlike that in which Durkheim wrote. The anomie found in that society without clear moral markers is repeated today. As in that time, our age is one in which tradition is open to question as we face a fragmentation and atomization of society which diminishes or destroys our basic cues to behavior.

This situation can threaten our sense of reality and plunge us into disorientation (ter Borg, 1992), leading to extreme anxiety—the dreadfulness of not knowing what causes our dis-ease while nevertheless feeling it quite intently. The ambiguity of our age has deeply affected our religious beliefs—precisely that set of norms and values that should provide us with a confirming, guiding myth. To the extent that this is an accurate description of contemporary life, individuals are thrown on their own to seek out that myth which will become their *unconditional*—that which is true for us without any conditions. Lacking any single myth or meaning structure to guide us, we are forced to turn to our own imagination to define what it is of which we are afraid. When we have found this unconditional, we will find relief from our fundamental uncertainties.

As we relate the story of religion in contemporary society, it seems clear that there is a continuing need for the unconditional or sacred in individual lives. The seeking for the sacred will continue in the most modern or postmodern of times, but it will probably infrequently be found in the traditional forms known to us in the twentieth century.

References

Ableman, Robert, and Stewart W. Hoover. 1990. *Religious Television: Controversies and Conclusions.* Norwood, N.J.: Ablex Publishing.

Ahlstrom, Sydney E. 1975. *A Religious History of the American People.* Garden City, N.Y.: Image Books.

Ainley, Stephen C., Royce Singelton, Jr., and Victoria L. Swigert. 1992. "Aging and Religious Participation: Reconsidering the Effects of Health." *Journal for the Scientific Study of Religion* 31 (2):175–88.

Albrecht, S. L., B. A. Chadwick, and D. S. Alcorn. 1977. "Religiosity and Deviance: Application of an Attitude-Behavior Contingent Consistency Model." *Journal for the Scientific Study of Religion* 16:263–74.

Alcock, James A. 1989. "Channeling: Brief History and Contemporary Context." *Skeptical Inquirer* 13:380–84.

Aleshire, Dan O. 1980. "Eleven Major Issues of Ministry." Pp. 27–53 in *Ministry in America,* edited by D. Schuller, M. Strommen, and M. Brekke. New York: Harper & Row.

Alexander, Jeffrey C. 1991. "Neofunctionalism and Modern Sociology." Pp. 267–75 in *The Renascence of Sociological Theory,* edited by H. Etzkowitz and R. Glassman. Itasca, Ill.: F. E. Peacock Publishers.

Ambert, Anne Marie, and Jean Francois Saucier. 1986. "Adolescents' Overt Religiosity and Parents' Marital Status." *International Journal of Comparative Sociology* 27:87–95.

Ammerman, Nancy T. 1987. *Bible Believers: Fundamentalists in the Modern World.* New Brunswick, N.J.: Rutgers University Press.

————. 1990. *Baptist Battles: Social Change and Religious Conflict in the Southern Baptist Convention.* New Brunswick, N.J.: Rutgers University Press.

_____. 1991. "North American Protestant Fundamentalism." Pp. 1–65 in *Fundamentalisms Observed,* edited by M. Marty and R. Appleby. Chicago: University of Chicago Press.

Amoetang, A.Y., and S. J. Bahr. 1986. "Religion, Family, and Adolescent Drug Use." *Sociological Perspectives* 29:53–76.

Amos, William E., Jr. 1988. *When AIDS Comes to Church.* Philadelphia: Westminster Press.

Anderson, Charles H. 1970. *White Protestant Americans: From National Origins to Religious Group.* Englewood Cliffs, N.J.: Prentice-Hall.

Anderson, Margaret L. 1988. *Thinking about Women: Sociological Perspectives on Sex and Gender.* New York: Macmillan.

Ang, A. L. 1989. *The Relationship between Moral Reasoning and Religious Orientation of Bible College Students in Singapore.* Ed.D. thesis, Biola University, Talbot School of Theology.

Anonymous. 1982. "Bishops Reviewing Question of Ordaining Women." *New York Times,* November 28:33.

Appel, Willa. 1983. *Cults in America: Programmed for Paradise.* New York: Holt, Rinehart & Winston.

Atchley, Robert. 1991. *Social Forces and Aging.* Belmont, Calif.: Wadsworth.

Babbie, Earl. 1990. "Channels to Elsewhere." Pp. 255–68 in *In Gods We Trust: New Patterns of Religious Pluralism in America,* edited by T. Robbins and D. Anthony. New Brunswick, N.J.: Transaction Books.

Baer, Hans A. 1993. "The Limited Empowerment of Women in Black Spiritual Churches: An Alternative Vehicle to Religious Leadership." *Sociology of Religion* 54 (1): 65–82.

Baer, Hans A., and Merrill Singer. 1992. *African-American Religion in the Twentieth Century.* Knoxville, Tenn.: University of Tennessee Press.

Bahr, Howard M., and Bruce A. Chadwick. 1985. "Religion and Family in Middletown, USA." *Journal of Marriage and the Family* 47:407–14.

Bailey, Edward I. 1983. "The Implicit Religion of Contemporary Society: An Orientation and Plea for its Study." *Religion* 13:69–83.

_____. 1990. "The 'Implicit Religion' Concept as a Tool for Ministry." *Sociological Focus* 23:203–17.

Bainbridge, William Sims, and Rodney Stark. 1979. "Cult Formation: Three Compatible Models." *Sociological Analysis* 40:283–95.

_____. 1980. "Sectarian Tension." *Review of Religious Research* 22:105–24.

Balswick, Jack. 1977. "The Jesus People Movement: A Generational Interpretation." Pp. 167–76 in *Sociological Stuff,* edited by H. P. Chalfant, E. W. Curry, and C. E. Palmer. Dubuque, Ia.: Kendall/Hunt.

Barker, Eileen, ed. 1982a. *New Religious Movements: A Perspective for Understanding Society.* New York: Edwin Mellin Press.

_____. 1982b. "From Sects to Society: A Methodological Programme." Pp. 3–15 in *New Religious Movements,* edited by E. Barker. New York: Edwin Mellin Press.

_____. 1984. *The Making of a Moonie.* London: Basil Blackwell.

_____. 1986. "Religious Movements: Cult and Anticult since Jonestown." *Annual Review of Sociology* 12:396–446.

_____. 1989. *New Religious Movements: A Practical Introduction.* London: Her Majesty's Stationery Office.

Bates, Vernon L. 1991. "Lobbying for the Lord: The New Christian Right Home-schooling Movement and Grassroots Lobbying." *Review of Religious Research* 33 (1): 3–17.

Baumann, Zygmunt. 1991. "Neofunctionalism and Modern Sociology." Pp. 267–75 in *The Renascence of Sociological Theory*, edited by H. Etzkowitz and R. Glassman. Itasca, Ill.: F. E. Peacock Publishers.

Beck, Scott H., Bettie S. Cole, and Judith A. Hammond. 1991. "Religious Heritage and Premarital Sex: Evidence from a National Sample of Young Adults." *Journal for the Scientific Study of Religion* 30:173–80.

Becker, Ernst. 1973. *The Denial of Death*. New York: Free Press.

————. 1975. *Escape from Evil*. New York: John Wiley & Sons.

Becker, Howard. 1932 *Systematic Sociology*. New York: John Wiley & Sons.

Becker, Lee B. 1977. "Predictors of Change in Religious Belief and Behaviors during College." *Sociological Analysis* 38:65–74.

Beckford, James. 1985. "Religious Organizations." Pp. 125–38 in *The Sacred in a Secular Age*, edited by P. Hammond. Berkeley, Calif.: University of California Press.

————. 1989. *Religion and Advanced Industrial Society*. London: Unwin Hyman.

————. 1990. "The Sociology of Religion and Social Problems." *Sociological Analysis* 51:1–14.

————. 1993. "The Media and New Religious Movements." Paper presented at the INFORM conference. London, March 28.

Beckley, Robert E. 1985. "The Other Side of Church and State: Social Issues of the Christian Political Left." Paper presented at the Society for the Scientific Study of Religion annual meeting. Savannah, Georgia, November.

————. 1990. Personal observations and notes from the annual meetings of the Baptist General Convention of Texas. Houston.

————. 1991. Personal observations and notes from the annual meetings of the Baptist General Convention of Texas, Waco, Texas.

Beckley, Robert E., and Baldwin J. Stribling. 1981. "Mainline Protestant Clergy View the Issues of the Moral Majority." Paper presented at the Mid-South Sociological Association. Shreveport, Louisiana, October.

Beckley, Robert E., H. Paul Chalfant, and Baldwin J. Stribling. 1987. "AIDS Comes to the Churches: Clergy Responses to the New Plague." Paper presented at the Society for the Scientific Study of Religion and the Religious Research Association. Louisville, Kentucky, November.

Beckley, Robert E., and H. Paul Chalfant. 1988a. "AIDS Comes to the Churches: Clergy Responses to Patients and Their Families." Paper presented at the Southwestern Social Science Association. Houston, March.

————. 1988b. "AIDS and Pastoral Counseling." Paper presented at the Society for the Scientific Study of Religion and the Religious Research Association. Chicago, November.

————. 1989. AIDS and the Reaction of the Clergy." Paper presented at the International Society for the Sociology of Religion. Helsinki, Finland, August.

————. 1990. "Dealing with Stigmatized Deviance: Pastors' Reaction to AIDS." Paper presented at the Association for the Sociology of Religion. Washington, D.C., August.

————. 1991. "A Comparison of the Roles of the Black Church in the American Civil Rights Movement and the Evangelical Protestant Church in the Democracy Movement in the German Democratic Republic." Paper presented at the 21st Conference of the International Society for the Sociology of Religion. Maynooth, Ireland, August.

_____. 1992a. "AIDS: A Texas Update." Paper presented at the Southwestern Social Science Association annual meeting. Austin, Texas, March.

_____. 1992b. "AIDS and the Clergy: The Continuation of a New Pastoral Role." Paper presented at the Association for the Sociology of Religion annual meeting. Pittsburgh, Pennsylvania, August.

Beckley, Robert, H. Paul Chalfant, and D. Paul Johnson. 1992a. "Germany's Reconstruction: The Role of the Eastern German Church before and after Unification." Paper presented at the Association for the Sociology of Religion annual meeting. Pittsburgh, August.

_____. 1992b. "Pastors' Narratives Concerning the Democracy Movement and the Reconstruction of Eastern German Society: A Contrast of World Views." Paper presented at the Religious Research Association and the Society for the Scientific Study of Religion annual meeting. Washington, D.C., November.

Bedell, Kenneth B., and Alice M. Jones, eds. 1992. _Yearbook of American and Canadian Churches_. Nashville, Tenn.: Abingdon Press.

Behar, Richard. 1991. "The Thriving Cult of Greed and Power." _Time_ 137 (May 6): 50–57.

Bell, Daniel. 1971. "Religion in the Sixties." _Social Research_ 38:447–97.

Bellah, Robert. 1964. "Religious Evolution." _American Sociological Review_ 29:358–74.

_____. 1967. "Civil Religion in America." _Daedalus_ 9:1–21.

_____. 1974. "American Civil Religion in the 1970s." Pp. 21–44 in _American Civil Religion_, edited by R. E. Richey and D. G. Jones. New York: Harper & Row.

_____. 1975. _The Broken Covenant: American Civil Religion in Time of Trial_. New York: Seabury Press.

Bellah, Robert, and Philip E. Hammond. 1980. _Varieties of American Civil Religion_. New York: Harper & Row.

Bellah, Robert, Richard Marsden, William Sullivan, Ann Swidler, and Steven Tipton. 1985. _Habits of the Heart: Individualism and Commitment in American Life_. Berkeley, Calif.: University of California Press.

Benson, P.L., M. J. Donahue, and J. A. Erickson. 1989. "Adolescence and Religion: A Review of the Empirical Literature 1970–1986." _Annual Review of Religious Research_ 1:153–81.

Berger, Peter. 1967. _The Sacred Canopy: Elements of a Sociological Theory of Religion_. Garden City, N.Y.: Doubleday.

Berger, Peter, and Thomas Luckmann. 1967. _The Social Construction of Reality_. Garden City, N.Y.: Doubleday.

Berkley, James. 1991. "The Marketing of a Boomer Church." _Christianity Today_ 35 (2):34–36.

Bernholz, Adolph. 1960. "The Family and Its Aged Members." _Franciscan Educational Conference_ 41:159–68.

Best, Joel. 1991. "Endangered Children and the Antisatanist Rhetoric." Pp. 95–106 in _The Satanism Scare_, edited by J. Richardson, J. Best, and D. Bromley. Hawthorne, N.Y.: Aldine Publishing.

Bibby, Reginald W. 1978. "Why Conservative Churches Really Are Growing: Kelley Revisited." _Journal for the Scientific Study of Religion_ 17:129–37.

_____. 1987. _Fragmented Gods: The Poverty and Potential of Religion in Canada_. Toronto: Suddeth.

Bibby, Reginald, and Merlin B. Brinkerhoff. 1974. "When Proselytizing Fails: An Organizational Analysis." *Sociological Analysis* 35:189–200.

————. 1983. "Circulation of the Saints Revisted: A Longitudinal Look at Conservative Church Growth." *Journal for the Scientific Study of Religion* 22: 253–62.

Billingsley, K. L. 1990. *From Mainline to Sideline.* Washington, D.C.: Ethics and Public Policy Center.

Blazer, Don G., and Erdman Palmore. 1975. "Religion and Aging: An Analysis of a Longitudinal Panel." *Gerontologist* 15:68–76.

————. 1975. "Religion and Aging in a Longitudinal Panel." *Gerontologist* 15:68–76.

Blizzard, Samuel W. 1956. "The Minister's Dilemma." *Christian Century* 73:508–509.

————. 1958. "The Protestant Parish Minister's Integrating Roles." *Religious Education* 53:374–80.

————. (with the help of H. B. Blizzard). 1985. *The Protestant Parish Ministry: A Behavioral Science Interpretation.* Washington, D.C.: Society for the Scientific Study of Religion.

Blumer, Herbert. 1969. *Symbolic Interactionism.* Englewood Cliffs, N.J.: Prentice-Hall.

Bollar, Melinda. 1990. *God's Schools: Choice and Compromise in American Society.* New Brunswick, N.J.: Rutgers University Press.

Bonfante, Joseph, Helen Gibson, and Ratu Kamlani. 1992. "The Second Reformation." *Time* 140 (November 23): 53–58.

Bonn, Robert L., and Sheila M. Kelley. 1973. *Clergy Support 1973: Salary, Income, and Attitudes.* New York: National Council of Churches in Christ.

Bord, Robert J., and Joseph E. Faulkner. 1983. *The Catholic Charismatics.* University Park, Pa.: Pennsylvania State University Press.

Boughey, Howard. 1978. *The Insights of Sociology: An Introduction.* Boston: Allyn & Bacon.

Bouhmama, D. 1990. "A Study of the Relationship between Moral Judgement and Religious Attitude of Algerian University Students." *British Journal of Religious Education* 12:81–85.

Bouma, Gary. 1973. "Beyond Lenski: A Critical Review of Recent Protestant Ethic Studies." *Journal for the Scientific Study of Religion* 12:141–55.

Brereton, Virginia Lieson. 1989. "United and Slighted: Women as Subordinated Insiders." Pp. 143–67 in *Between the Times: The Travail of the Protestant Establishment in America, 1900–1960*, edited by W. R. Hutchinson. Cambridge, England, and New York: Cambridge University Press.

Brewster, Lawrence G. 1984. *The Public Agenda.* New York: St. Martin's Press.

Brinkerhoff, Merlin B., and Marlene Mackie. 1985. "Religion and Gender: A Comparison of Canadian and American Student Attitudes." *Journal of Marriage and the Family* 47: 415–29.

Bromley, David G. 1991. "Satanism: The New Cult Scare." Pp. 49–72 in *The Satanism Scare*, edited by J. Richardson, J. Best, and D. Bromley. Hawthorne, N.Y.: Aldine Publishing.

Bromley, David. 1985. *Journal for the Scientific Study of Religion* 24:253–74.

Brownfield, David and Ann Marie Sorenson. 1991. "Religion and Drug Use among Adolescents: A Social Support Conceptualization and Interpretation." *Deviant Behavior* 12:259–76.

Bruce, Steven. 1990a. *A House Divided: Protestantism, Schism and Secularization*. New York: Unwin.

_____. 1990b. *Pray TV: Televangelism in America*. London and New York: Routledge & Kegan Paul.

Budd, Susan. 1973. *Sociologists and Religion*. London: Collier-Macmillan.

Burchard, Waldo. 1954. "Role Conflicts in Military Chaplains." *American Sociological Review* 19:528–35.

Burkett, S. R., and M. White. 1974. "Hellfire and Delinquency: Another Look." *Journal for the Scientific Study of Religion* 13:455–62.

Bynum, Carolyn Walker, Steven Harrell, and Paula Richman. 1986. *Gender and Religion: The Complexity of Symbols*. Boston: Beacon Press.

Campbell, Colin. 1978. "The Secret Religion of the Educated Classes." *Sociological Analysis* 39:46–56.

Caplow, Theodore. 1985. "Contrasting Trends in European and American Religion." *Sociological Analysis* 46: 101–108.

Caplow, Theodore, Howard M. Bahr, and Bruce A. Chadwick. 1983. *All Faithful People: Changes and Continuity in Middletown's Religion*. Minneapolis: University of Minnesota Press.

Capps, Donald. 1992. "Religion and Child Abuse: Perfect Together." *Journal for the Scientific Study of Religion* 31 (1): 1–14.

Carmody, Denise. 1979. *Women and World Religions*. Nashville, Tenn.: Abingdon Press.

Carroll, Jackson W. 1991. *As One with Authority: Reflective Leadership in Ministry*. Louisville, Ky.: Westminster/John Knox Press.

_____. 1992. "Toward 2000: Some Futures for Religious Leadership." *Review of Religious Research* 33:289–304.

Carroll, Jackson W., D. W. Johnson, and Martin E. Marty. 1979. *Religion in America: 1950 to the Present*. New York: Harper & Row.

Carroll, Jackson W., and Robert Wilson. 1978. *The Clergy Job Market: Over-supply and/or Opportunity?* Hartford, Conn.: Hartford Seminary Foundation.

Carroll, Jackson W., Barbara Hargrove, and Adair Loomis. 1983. *Women of the Cloth*. San Francisco: Harper & Row.

Casto, R. Michael. 1987. *AIDS and the Ministry of the Church*. Nashville, Tenn.: General Board of Discipleship of the United Methodist Church.

Catholic Bishops of America. 1983. *The Challenge of Peace: God's Promise and Our Response*. Washington, D.C.: United States Catholic Conference of Bishops.

Chalfant, H. Paul. 1967. "Classification of the Variables of Socioeconomic Class, Ecological Place, and Leadership Style in Urban Church Congregations." Unpublished master's thesis, Oklahoma State University.

_____. 1984. "Bellah's Broken Covenant: Religion as a Social Problem." *Proceedings of the Association for the Scientific Study of Religion/Southwest*. Dallas: ASSR/SW.

_____. 1986. "Religion in Lubbock." Pp. 298–323 in *Lubbock: From Town to City*, edited by L. L. Graves. Lubbock, Tex.: West Texas Museum Association.

_____. 1992. "Stepping to Redemption: Twelve Step Groups as Implicit Religion." *Free Inquiry in Creative Sociology* 20 (November): 115–20.

_____. 1993. "The Journey of Faith: Return to the Ancient Tradition of Orthodoxy." Paper presented at the Western Social Science Association annual meeting. Corpus Christi, Texas, April.

Chalfant, H. Paul, and Peter L. Heller. 1985. "A Cross-sectional Perspective on Religiosity and Social Justice." *Review of Religious Research* 26:261–68.
_____. 1991. "Rural-Urban versus Regional Differences in Religiosity." *Review of Religious Research* 33 (September): 76–86.
Chalfant, H. Paul, and Emily LaBeff. 1991. *Understanding People and Social Life*. St. Paul: West Publishing.
Chambers, Patricia Price, and H. Paul Chalfant. 1978. "A Changing Role or the Same Old Handmaidens: Women's Role in the Church Today." *Review of Religious Research* 19: 192–97.
Cherry, Conrad. 1970. "American Civil Ceremonies." Pp. 303–16 in *American Mosaic: Social Patterns of Religion in the United States*, edited by P. E. Hammond and B. Johnson. New York: Random House.
Chesen, Eli. 1972. *Religion May Be Hazardous to Your Health*. New York: Peter Wynden.
Childerston, J. K. 1985. "Understanding Religious 'Fundamentalists': A Study of Typology and Moral Judgement." Ph.D. thesis, Fuller Theological Seminary.
Chinnici, Rosemary. 1991. "Angry yet Faithful: How Women Cope with Their Non-Responsive Church." *Catholic World* 234: 244–47.
Christ, Carol P. 1987. *The Laughter of Aphrodite*. San Francisco: Harper & Row.
Christ, Carol P., and Judith Plaskow. 1979. *Womanspirit Rising: A Feminist Reader in Religion*. New York: Harper & Row.
Christiano, Kevin. 1991. "The Church and New Immigrants." Pp. 169–86 in *Vatican II and U. S. Catholicism*, edited by H. R. Ebaugh. Los Angeles: JAI Press.
Christiansen, Drew. 1978. "Dignity in Aging: Notes on Geriatric Ethics." *Journal of Humanistic Psychology* 18:41–54.
Chworowsky, Karl M., and C. G. Raible. 1975. "What Is a Unitarian Universalist?" Pp. 263–76 in *Religions of America: Ferment and Faith in an Age of Crisis*, edited by Leo Rosten. New York: Simon & Schuster.
Clausen, John A. 1968. "Perspectives on Childhood Socialization. Pp. 130–81 in *Socialization and Society*, edited by J. Clausen. Boston: Little, Brown.
Cleage, Albert B., Jr. 1974. "The Gospel of Black Liberation." Pp. 298–301 in *Religion American Style*, edited by P. McNamara. New York: Harper & Row.
Coalter, Milton J., John M. Mulder, and Louis B. Weeks, eds. 1990. *The Presbyterian Predicament: Six Perspectives*. Louisville, Ky.: Westminster/ John Knox Press.
Cochran, J. K. 1987. "The Variable Effects of Religiosity on Deviant Behavior." Ph.D. thesis, University of Florida.
Cochran, John K., Leonard Beeghley, Glenna Van Metre, and Carolyn S. Morgan. 1991. "Religion, Feminism, and Attitudes toward Legalized Abortion: A Note on the Competing Effects of Rival Referents." Paper presented at the Southwestern Social Science Association annual meeting. San Antonio, Texas, March.
Cochran, John K., and Leonard Beeghley. 1991. "The Influence of Religion on Attitudes toward Nonmarital Sexuality: A Preliminary Assessment of Reference Group Theory." *Journal for the Scientific Study of Religion* 30:45–62.
Cone, James H. 1969. *Black Theology and Black Power*. New York: Seabury Press.
Conger, J. J., and A. C. Petersen. 1984. *Adolescence and Youth: Psychological Development in a Changing World*, 3rd ed. New York: Harper & Row.

Conover, Pamela Johnston, and Virginia Gray. 1983. *Feminism and the New Right*. New York: Praeger Publishers.

Conrad, Peter. 1986. "The Social Meaning of AIDS." *Social Policy* (Summer 1986):51–56.

Conway, Flo, and Jim Siegelman. 1982. *Snapping: America's Epidemic of Sudden Personality Change*. Philadelphia: J. B. Lippincott.

Cooley, Charles Horton. 1902. *Human Nature and Social Order*. New York: Charles Scribner's Sons.

Cooper, Lee R. 1974. "Publish or Perish: Negro Jehovah's Witness Adaptation in the Ghetto." Pp. 700–21 in *Religious Movements in Contemporary America*, edited by I. Zaretsky and M. Leone. New York: Simon & Schuster.

Cornwall, M. 1987. "The Social Bases of Religion: A Study of Factors Influencing Religious Belief and Commitment." *Review of Religious Research* 29:44–56.

Cox, Harold, and André Hammond. 1988. "Religiosity, Aging, and Life Satisfaction." *Journal of Religion and Aging* 5:1–21.

Crabtree, Deidre F. 1970. "Women's Liberation and the Church." Pp. 115–45 in *Women's Liberation and the Church*, edited by S. B. Doely. New York: Association Press.

Crandall, Rebecca. 1992. "The Motorcycle Ministers." *Newsweek* 119 (June 22): 60.

Crawford, Alan. 1980. *Thunder on the Right*. New York: Pantheon Books.

Crook, Stephen, Jan Pakulski, and Malcolm Waters. 1992. *Postmodernization: Change in Advanced Society*. London: Sage.

Crouch, Ben, and Kelly Damphouse. 1991. "Law Enforcement and the Satanic Crime Connection: A Survey of 'Cult Cops.'" Pp. 191–204 in *The Satanism Scare*, edited by J. Richardson, J. Best, and D. Bromley. Hawthorne, N.Y.: Aldine Publishing.

Cummings, Judith. 1985. "Diverse Crowd Hears Farrakhan in Los Angeles." *New York Times*, 16, September 10.

Curry, Evans W., and H. Paul Chalfant. 1991. "Religious Justice or Economic Justice." Paper presented at the Religious Research Association annual meeting. Pittsburgh, November.

Daly, Mary. 1972. "The Woman's Movement: An Exodus Community." *Religious Education* 67:332–41.

_____. 1973. *Beyond God the Father*. Boston: Beacon Press.

_____. 1975. *The Church and the Second Sex*, 2nd ed. New York: Harper & Row.

_____. 1979. "Theology after the Demise of God the Father." Pp. 126–37 in *Women and the Church*, edited by A. Hageman. New York: Association Press.

Daner, Francine Jeanne. 1976. *The American Children of Krsna: A Study of the Hare Krsna Movement*. New York: Holt, Rinehart & Winston.

D'Antonio, William V. 1983. "Family Life, Religion, and Societal Values and Structures." Pp. 81–108 in *Families and Religions: Conflict and Change in Modern Society*, edited by William V. D'Antonio and J. Aldous. Beverly Hills, Calif.: Sage Publications.

_____. 1985. "The American Catholic Family: Signs of Cohesion and Polarization." *Journal of Marriage and the Family* 47: 395–405.

D'Antonio, William V., W. Newman, and S. Wright. 1982. "Religion and Family Life: How Social Scientists View the Relationship." *Journal for the Scientific Study of Religion* 21:218–25.

D'Antonio, William V., James D. Davidson, Dean R. Hoge, and Ruth A. Wallace. 1989. *American Catholic Laity in a Changing Church.* Kansas City, Mo.: Sheed & Ward.

Danzger, M. Herbert. 1989. *Returning to Tradition: The Contemporary Revival of Orthodox Judaism.* New Haven, Conn.: Yale University Press.

Davidman, Lynn. 1990. "Accommodation and Resistance to Modernity: A Comparison of Two Contemporary Orthodox Jewish Groups." *Sociological Analysis* 51 (1): 35–51.

_____. 1991. *Tradition in a Rootless World: Women Turn to Orthodox Judaism.* Berkeley, Calif.: University of California Press.

Davidson, James D. 1975. "Glock's Model of Religious Commitment: Assessing Some Different Approaches and Results." *Review of Religious Research* 16:83–93.

Davis, Rex, and James T. Richardson. 1976. "The Organization and Functioning of the Children of God." *Sociological Analysis* 37:321–29.

Deck, Alan Figuero. 1990. "The Crisis of a Hispanic Ministry: Multiculturalism as an Ideology." *America* (July 14): 34–36.

Deiros, Pablo A. 1991. "Protestant Fundamentalism in Latin America." Pp. 142–96 in *Fundamentalisms Observed,* edited by M. Marty and S. Appleby. Chicago: University of Chicago Press.

DeJong, Gordon, Joseph E. Faulkner, and Rex H. Warland. 1976. "Dimensions of Religiosity Reconsidered: Evidence from Cross-cultural Study." *Social Forces* (June):866–90.

Demerath, Nicholas J., III. 1961. "Religious Orientation and Social Class." Master's thesis, University of California at Berkeley.

_____. 1965. *Social Class in American Protestantism.* Skokie, Ill.: Rand McNally.

_____. 1974. *The Tottering Transcendence.* Indianapolis: Bobbs-Merrill.

_____. 1983. "The Separation of Church and State? Mythical Past and an Uncertain Future." Paper presented at the Society for the Scientific Study of Religion annual meeting. Knoxville, Tennessee.

Demerath, Nicholas J., III, and Phillip S. Hammond. 1969. *Religion in Social Context: Tradition and Transition.* New York: Random House.

Denton, John. 1978. *Medical Sociology.* Boston: Houghton Mifflin.

Derber, Charles. 1979. *The Pursuit of Attention: Power and Individualism in Everyday Life.* New York: Oxford University Press.

Dinges, William D. 1991. "Roman Catholic-traditionalism." Pp. 66–101 in *Fundamentalisms Observed,* edited by M. Marty and S. Appleby. Chicago: University of Chicago Press.

Dirks, D. H. 1988. "Moral Development in Christian Higher Education." *Journal of Psychology and Theology* 16:322–38.

Dobbelaere, Karel. 1981. "Secularization: A Multi-dimensional Concept." *Current Sociology* 29:3–213.

_____. 1984. "Secularization Theories and Sociological Paradigms: Convergences and Divergences." *Social Compass* 31:199–219.

_____. 1990. "From Pillar to Postmodernity: The Changing Situation of Religion in Belgium." *Sociological Analysis* 51:S1–S13.

Dolan, Jay P., R. Scott Appleby, Patricia Byrne, and Debra Campbell. 1990. *Transforming Parish Ministry: The Changing Roles of Catholic Clergy, Laity and Women Religious.* New York: Crossroad Publishing.

Dollard, John. 1937. *Caste and Class in a Southern Town.* Garden City, N.Y.: Doubleday.

Draper, Robert. 1992. "Beware the Grace of God." *Texas Monthly* 20 (January):100–103, 120 passim.

Driver, Ann Barstow. 1976. "Religion." *Signs* 2:434–42.

DuBois, W. E. B. [1899] 1971. "The Functions of the Negro Church." Pp. 77–81 in *The Black Church in America,* edited by H. Nelsen, R. Yokely, and A. Nelsen. New York: Basic Books.

Dukes, James T., and Barry L. Johnson. 1984. "Spiritual Well-being and the Consequential Dimensions of Religiosity." *Review of Religious Research* 26:59–72.

Durkheim, Emile. 1947. *The Elementary Forms of Religious Life.* New York: Free Press.

_____. 1951 (1897). *Suicide: A Study in Sociology.* Translated by John A. Spaulding and George Simpson. New York: Free Press.

Earle, John, Dean Knudsen, and Donald Shriver. 1976. *Spindles and Spires.* Atlanta: John Knox Press.

Ebaugh, Helen Rose. 1991. "The Revitalization Movement in the Catholic Church: The Institutional Dilemma of Power." *Sociological Analysis* 52 (1): 1–12.

Eckhart, K. W. 1970. "Religiosity and Civil Rights Militancy." *Review of Religious Research* 11:197–203.

Eister, Allen W. 1967. "Toward a Radical Critique of Church-Sect Typology." *Journal for the Scientific Study of Religion* 6:85–90.

_____. 1973. "H. Richard Niebuhr and the Paradox of Religious Organization." Pp. 355–408 in *Beyond the Classics? Essays in the Scientific Study of Religion,* edited by C. Glock and P. Hammond. New York: Harper & Row.

Elinson, Kirk W., David M. Peterson, and Kirk Hadaway. 1983. "Religion and Delinquency: A Contextual Analysis." *Criminology* 21:505–27.

Ellis, L., and R. Thompson. 1989. "Relating Crime, Arousal, and Boredom." *Sociology and Social Research* 73:132–39.

Enroth, Ronald M., Edward E. Ericson, Jr., and C. B. Peters. 1972. *The Jesus People: Old-time Religion in the Age of Aquarius.* Grand Rapids, Mich.: Wm. B. Eerdmans Publishing.

Erickson, Joseph A. "Adolescent Religious Development and Commitment: A Structural Equation Model of the Role of Family, Peer Group, and Educational Influences." *Journal for the Scientific Study of Religion* 31: 131–52.

Etzkowitz, Henry, and Ronald M. Glassman. 1991. "Introduction." Pp. 1–64 in *The Renascence of Sociological Theory,* edited by H. Etzkowitz and R. Glassman. Itasca, Ill.: F. E. Peacock Publishers.

Evans, Richard L. 1989. "What Is a Mormon?" Pp. 186–99 in *Religions of America: Ferment and Faith in an Age of Crisis,* edited by L. Rosten. New York: Simon & Schuster.

Evans-Pritchard, E. E. 1972. *Witchcraft, Oracles, and Magic among the Azande.* Oxford: Clarendon Press.

Eve, Raymond, and Francis B. Harrold. 1991. *The Creationist Movement in Modern America.* Boston: Twayne Publishers.

Family, The. 1993. "An Overview of Our Beliefs and Practices as Expressed in Our Statements." *The Family.* Whittier, Calif: The Family Press Release.

Farley, Edward W. 1990. "The Presbyterian Heritage as Modernism: Reaffirming a Forgotten Past in Hard Times." Pp. 49–66 in *The Presbyterian Predicament,* edited by M. J. Coulter, J. M. Mulder, and L. B. Weeks. Louisville, Ky.: Westminster/John Knox Press.

Feagin, Joe R. 1978. *Racial and Ethnic Relations.* Englewood Cliffs, N.J.: Prentice-Hall.

Fee, Joan M., Andrew M. Greeley, William McReady, and Teresa Sullivan. 1981. *Young Catholics in the United States and Canada.* New York: William H. Sadlier.

Felty, Kathryn M., and Margaret M. Poloma. 1990. "From Sex Differences to Gender Role Beliefs: Exploring Effects on Six Dimensions of Religiosity." Paper presented at the Association for the Sociology of Religion annual meeting. Washington, D.C., August.

Fichter, Joseph. 1951. *Southern Parish.* Chicago: University of Chicago Press.

_____. 1954. *Social Relations in the Urban Parish.* Chicago: University of Chicago Press.

_____. 1961. *Religion as an Occupation: A Study in the Sociology of Professions.* Notre Dame, Ind.: University of Notre Dame Press.

_____. 1968. *America's Forgotten Priests.* New York: Harper & Row.

_____. 1975. *The Catholic Cult of the Paraclete.* New York: Sheed & Ward.

Filippi, Linda. 1991. "Place, Feminism and Healing: An Ecology of Pastoral Counseling. *Journal of Pastoral Care* 45(3): 231–42.

Finke, Roger. 1989. "Demographics of Religious Participation: An Ecological Approach, 1850–1980." *Journal for the Scientific Study of Religion* 28:27–44.

_____. 1990. "An Unsecular America: Defiance or Delay?" Paper presented at the Society for the Scientific Study of Religion annual meeting. Virginia Beach, Virginia, November.

Finke, Roger, and Rodney Stark. 1989. "How the Upstart Sects Won America: 1776–1850." *Journal for the Scientific Study of Religion* 28 (March): 27–44.

_____. 1992. *The Churching of America: Winners and Losers in the Economic Struggle, 1776–1990.* New Brunswick, N.J.: Rutgers University Press.

Finney, Henry C. 1991. "American Zen's 'Japan Connection': A Critical Case of Zen Bhuddism's Diffusion to the West." *Sociological Analysis* 52 (Winter):379–98.

Finney, J. M. 1978. "A Theory of Religious Commitment." *Sociological Analysis* 39:19–35.

Finney, John M., and Gary R. Lee. 1977. "Age Differences on Five Dimensions of Religious Involvement." *Review of Religious Research* 18:173–219.

Fitts, Leroy. 1985. A *History of Black Baptists.* Nashville, Tenn.: Broadman Press.

Flora, Cornelia Bretler. 1973. "Social Dislocation and Pentecostalism: A Multivariate Analysis." *Sociological Analysis* 34:296–304.

Flynn, Eileen P. 1985. *AIDS: A Catholic Call for Compassion.* Kansas City, Mo.: Sheed & Ward.

Forsyth, Craig J., and Marion D. Olivier. 1990. "The Theoretical Framing of a Social Problem: Some Conceptual Notes on Satanic Cults." *Deviant Behavior* 11:281–92.

Fortunato, James. 1983. *Embracing the Exile.* New York: Seabury Press.

Fowlkes, Mary Anne. 1988. "Religion and Socialization." Pp. 125–51 in *Handbook of Preschool Religious Education,* edited by D. Ratcliff. Birmingham, Ala: Religious Education Press.

Frankl, Razelle. 1987. *Televangelism: The Marketing of Popular Religion.* Carbondale, Ill.: Southern Illinois University Press.

Frazier, E. Franklin. 1974. *The Negro Church in America*. New York: Schocken Books.

Freud, Sigmund. 1930. *Civilization and Its Discontents*. New York: W. W. Norton.

_____. 1950. *Totem and Taboo*. Translated by James Strachey. New York: W. W. Norton.

Fukuyama, Yoshio. 1961. "The Major Dimensions of Church Membership." *Review of Religious Research* 2:154–61.

Fulton, John. 1991. *The Tragedy of Belief: Division, Politics, and Religion in Ireland*. Oxford: Clarendon Press.

Furnham, A. F. 1895. "Why Do People Save? Attitudes to, and Habits of, Saving Money in Britain." *Journal of Applied Social Psychology* 15:354–73.

Gaede, Stan. 1977. "Religious Affiliation, Social Mobility and the Problem of Causation: A Methodological Critique of Catholic-Protestant Socioeconomic Achievement Studies." *Review of Religious Research* 19:54–62.

Galanter, Marc. 1989. *Cults: Faith, Healing and Coercion*. New York: Oxford University Press.

Gallup, George, Jr., and Jim Castelli. 1989. *The People's Religion: American Faith in the 90s*. New York: Macmillan.

Gardner, Martin. 1992. "Marianne Williamson and 'A Course in Miracles.'" *Skeptical Inquirer* 17:17–23.

Gargan, Edward A. 1991. "Indian Myth Sharpens Reality of Religious Strife." *New York Times* 141 (December 22): 6.

Geertz, Clifford. 1966. "Religion as a Cultural System." Pp. 1–46 in *Anthropological Approaches to the Study of Religion,* edited by M. Banton. New York: Praeger Publishers.

Gehrig, L. 1981. *American Civil Religion: An Assessment*. Monograph Series, no. 3, Storrs, Conn.: Society for the Scientific Study of Religion.

General Assembly Special Committee on Human Sexuality. 1991. "Keeping Body and Soul Together: Sexuality, Spirituality, and Social Justice." Reports to the 203rd General Assembly of the Presbyterian Church (U.S.A.). Louisville, Ky.: Presbyterian Church (U.S.A.).

General Assembly of the Presbyterian Church (U.S.A.). 1990. *The Presbyterian Hymnal*. Louisville Ky.: Westminster/John Knox Press.

General Assembly of the United Presbyterian Church in the U.S.A. 1972. *The Worshipbook*. Philadelphia: Westminster Press.

Gerrard, Nathan L. 1968. "The Serpent-Handlers of West Virginia." *Transaction* 5:22–28.

Giddens, Anthony. 1979. *Central Problems in Social Theory: Action, Structure and Contradiction in Social Analysis*. Berkeley, Calif.: University of California Press.

_____. 1984. *The Constitution of Society: Outline of the Theory of Structuration*. Berkeley, Calif.: University of California Press.

_____. 1990. *The Consequences of Modernity*. Cambridge, England: Polity Press.

_____. 1991. *Modernity and Self-Identity*. Cambridge: Polity Press.

Gilbert, Dennis, and Joseph A. Kahl. 1993. *The American Class Structure*, 4th ed. Belmont, Calif: Wadsworth.

Gilkes, Cheryl. 1988. "Together and in Harness." Pp. 223–44 in *Black Women in American Society: Social Science Perspectives,* edited by M. R. Malson, E.

Mudimbe-Boy, J. Barr, and M. Wyer. Chicago: University of Chicago Press.

Gillquist, Peter E. 1989. *Becoming Orthodox: A Journey to the Ancient Christian Faith*. Brentwood, Tenn.: Wolgemuth and Hyatt, Publishers.

Glassman, Ronald M. 1991. "Max Weber, the Modern World, and Modern Sociology." Pp. 125–47 in *The Renascence of Sociological Theory*, edited by H. Etzkowitz and R. Glassman. Itasca, Ill.: F. E. Peacock Publishers.

Glazer, Nathan. 1972. *American Judaism*. Chicago: University of Chicago Press.

Glenn, Norval. 1964. "Negro Religion and Negro Status in the United States." Pp. 623–39 in *Religion, Culture, and Society*, edited by L. Schneider. New York: John Wiley & Sons.

Glock, Charles. 1959. "The Religious Revival in America." Pp. 25–42 in *Religion and the Face of America*, edited by J. Zohn. Berkeley, Calif.: University of California Press.

_____. 1962. "On the Study of Religious Commitment." *Religious Education* 42:98–110.

_____. 1973. *Religion in Sociological Perspective*. Belmont, Calif.: Wadsworth.

Glock, Charles, and P. Roos. 1961. "Parishioner's Views of How Ministers Spend Their Time." *Review of Religious Research* 2:170–75.

Glock, Charles, and Rodney Stark. 1965. *Religion and Society in Tension*. Skokie, Ill.: Rand McNally.

_____. 1966. *Christian Beliefs and Anti-Semitism*. New York: Harper & Row.

Goen, C. C. 1959. "Fundamentalism in America." Pp. 85–93 in *American Mosaic: Social Patterns of Religion in America*, edited by P. E. Hammond and B. Johnson. New York: Random House.

Goldscheider, Calvin. 1986. *Jewish Continuity and Change: Emerging Patterns in America*. Bloomington, Ind.: Indiana University Press.

Goldscheider, Calvin, and Jacob Neusner. 1990. *Social Foundations of Judaism*. Englewood Cliffs, N.J.: Prentice-Hall.

Goode, Erich. 1967. "Some Critical Reflections on the Church-Sect Dimension." *Journal for the Scientific Study of Religion* 6:69–77.

Gordon, Henry. 1989. "The Shirley MacLaine Phenomenon." *Skeptical Inquirer* 13:405–7.

Gordon, Steven L. 1990. "Social Structural Effects on Emotions." Pp. 125–47 in *Research Agendas in the Sociology of Emotions*, edited by T. D. Kemper. New York: State University of New York Press.

Goss, Elizabeth. 1989. "Living and Dying with AIDS." *Journal of Pastoral Care* 43 (Winter): 297–308.

Grasmick, Harold, Linda Patterson, and Sharon R. Bird. 1990. "The Effects of Religious Fundamentalism and Religiosity on Preference for Traditional Family Norms." *Sociological Inquiry* 60:352–69.

Gray, Helen. 1992. "Women's Leadership Roles Challenge Tradition." *Progressions* 4 (1): 14–15.

Greeley, Andrew. 1963. *Religion and Career: A Study of College Graduates*. New York: Sheed & Ward.

_____. 1970. *Religion in the Year 2000*. New York: Sheed and Ward.

_____. 1972. *The Denominational Society*. Glenview, Ill.: ScottForesman.

_____. 1977. *The American Catholic: A Social Portrait*. New York: Basic Books.

_____. 1979. "Ethnic Variations in Religious Commitment." Pp. 113–34 in *The Religious Dimension: New Directions in Quantitative Research,* edited by Robert Wuthnow. New York: Academic Press.

_____. 1988. "Defection among Hispanics." *America* (July 30): 61–62.

_____. 1989. *Religious Change in America.* Cambridge, Mass.: Harvard University Press.

_____. 1990a. "Why Catholics Stay in the Church." Pp. 177–83 in *In Gods We Trust: New Patterns of Religious Pluralism in America,* 2nd ed., edited by T. Robbins and D. Anthony. New Brunswick, N.J.: Transaction Books.

_____. 1990b. *The Catholic Myth: The Behavior and Beliefs of American Catholics.* New York: Charles Scribner's Sons.

Greeley, Andrew, and Peter Rossi. 1966. *The Education of Catholic Americans.* Hawthorne, N.Y.: Aldine Publishing.

Greely, A. M., and G. L. Gockel. 1971. "The Religious Effects of Parochial Education." Pp. 265–301 in *Research on Religious Development,* edited by M. Strommen. New York: Hawthorne Books.

Green, John C., and Margaret Poloma. 1990. "The Issue Agenda of American Protestant Clergy: An Analysis of Ministers Across Six Denominations." Paper presented at the Society for the Scientific Study of Religion annual meeting. Virginia Beach, Virginia.

Greil, Arthur L., and David R. Rudy. 1984a. "Social Cocoons: Encapsulation and Identity Transformation Organizations." *Sociological Inquiry* 54:260–78.

_____. 1984b. "What Have We Learned from Process Models of Conversion? An Examination of Ten Studies." *Sociological Focus* 17:306–23.

Groothuis, Douglas. 1991. "The Shamanized." *Christianity Today* 35:20–23, April 29.

Gustafson, Paul M., and William H. Swatos, Jr. 1990. "Max Weber and Comparative Religions." Pp. 1–11 in *Time, Place, and Circumstance,* edited by W. Swatos. Westport, Conn.: Greenwood Press.

Guth, James. 1992. "Evangelical Voters in 1992." Paper presented at the Society for the Scientific Study of Religion and the Religious Research Association. Washington, D.C., November.

Guth, James L., and John C. Green. 1991. *The Bible and the Ballot Box: Religion and Politics in the 1988 Election.* Boulder, Colo.: Westview Press.

Hadaway, Kirk. 1978. "Denominational Switching and Membesrhip Growth." *Sociological Analysis* 39:321–37.

_____. 1981. "The Demographic Environment and Church Membership Change." *Journal for the Scientific Study of Religion* 20:77–89.

_____. 1989. "Identifying American Apostates: A Cluster Analysis." *Journal for the Scientific Study of Religion* 28:201–205.

Hadaway, C. Kirk, and Wade Clark Roof. 1979. "Those Who Stay Religious Nones and Those Who Don't." *Journal for the Scientific Study of Religion* 18: 194–200.

Hadaway, Kirk, Daniel Hackett, and James Fogle Miller. 1984. "The Most Segregated Institution: Correlates of Interracial Church Participation." *Review of Religious Research* 25:204–19.

Haddad, Yvonne Yazbeck, and Adair Lummis. 1987. *Islamic Values in the United States.* New York: Oxford University Press.

Hadden, Jeffrey K. 1969. *The Gathering Storm in the Churches: The Widening Gap between Clergy and Laymen.* Garden City, N.Y.: Doubleday.

_____. 1983. "Televangelism and the Mobilization of a New Christian Right Policy." Pp. 247–66 in *Families and Religions: Conflict and Change in*

Modern Society, edited by W. V. D'Antonio and J. Aldous. Newbury Park, Calif.: Sage Publications.

_____. 1986. "Toward Desacralizing Secularization Theory." *Social Forces* 65:587–611.

_____. 1987. "Religious Broadcasting and the New Christian Right." *Journal for the Scientific Study of Religion* 26 (1): 1–24.

_____. 1990. "Conservative Christians, Televangelism, and Politics: Taking Stock a Decade after the Founding of the Moral Majority." Pp. 463–72 in *In Gods We Trust: New Patterns of Religious Pluralism in America,* 2nd ed., edited by T. Robbins and D. Anthony. New Brunswick, N.J.: Transaction Books.

Hadden, Jeffrey K., and Charles E. Swann. 1981. *Prime Time Preachers: The Rising Power of Televangelism.* Reading, Mass.: Addison-Wesley Publishing.

Hadden, Jeffrey K., and Anson Shupe. 1986. *Prophetic Religions and Politics: Religion and the Political Order.* New York: Paragon Publishing House.

_____. 1989. *Secularization and Fundamentalism Reconsidered: Religion and the Political Order.* Vol. 3. New York: Paragon House.

Hall, Douglas, and Benjamin Schneider. 1973. *Organization Climates and Careers: The Work Lives of Priests.* New York: Seminar Press.

Hall, John R. 1988. "Collective Welfare as Resource Mobilization in the People's Temple; A Case Study of a Poor People's Religious Social Movement." *Sociological Analysis* 49:64s–77s.

_____. 1990. "The Apocalypse at Jonestown (with Afterword)." Pp. 269–78 in *In Gods We Trust: New Patterns of Religious Pluralism in America,* edited by T. Robbins and D. Anthony. New Brunswick, N.J.: Transaction Books.

Hall, Tom T. 1971. *Me and Jesus.* Nashville, Tenn.: Hallnote Music.

Hammond, Phillip E. 1976. "The Sociology of American Civil Religion: A Bibliographic Essay." *Sociological Analysis* 37:169–82.

_____, ed. 1985. *The Sacred in a Secular Age.* Berkeley, Calif.: University of California Press.

_____. 1992. *Religion and Personal Autonomy: The Third Disestablishment in America.* Columbia, S.C.: University of South Carolina Press.

Hammond, Philip, and N. J. Demerath III. *Religion in Social Context.* New York: Random House.

Hargrove, Barbara. 1979a. "Informing the Public: Social Scientists and Reactions to Jonestown." Paper presented at the Society for the Scientific Study of Religion annual meeting. San Antonio, Texas.

_____. 1979b. *Sociology of Religion.* Arlington Heights, Ill.: AHM Publishing.

_____. 1983. "The Church, the Family, and the Modernization Process." Pp. 21–49 in *Families and Religions: Conflict and Change in Modern Society,* edited by William V. D'Antonio and J. Aldous. Beverly Hills, Calif.: Sage Publications.

_____. 1989. *The Sociology of Religion: Classical and Contemporary Approaches,* 2nd ed. Arlington Heights, Ill.: Harlan Davidson.

Hargrove, Barbara, Jean Miller Schmidt, and Sheila Greve Devaney. 1985. "Religion and the Changing Role of Women." *Annals* 480: 117–31.

Haritos, Rosa, and Ronald M. Glassman. 1991. "Emile Durkheim and the Sociological Enterprise." Pp. 69–98 in *The Renascence of Sociological Theory,* edited by H. Etzkowitz and R. Glassman. Itasca, Ill.: F. E. Peacock Publishers.

Harrell, David Edwin, Jr. 1975. *All Things Are Possible: The Healing and Charismatic Revivals in Modern America*. Bloomington, Ind.: Indiana University Press.

Harrison, Michael I. 1974. "Sources of Recruitment to Catholic Pentacostalism." *Journal for the Scientific Study of Religion* 13:49–63.

Harrison, Paul M. 1959. *Authority and Power in the Free Church Tradition*. Princeton, N.J.: Princeton University Press.

Hart, Stephen. 1986. "Religion and Changes in Family Patterns." *Review of Religious Research* 28:51–70.

Hartland, E. Sidney. 1951. "Totemism." Pp. 383–407 in *Encyclopedia of Religion and Ethics*, Vol. 2, edited by J. Hastings. New York: Charles Scribner's Sons.

Harvey, David. 1989. *The Condition of Postmodernity*. Cambridge, Mass.: Basil Blackwell.

Haywood, Carol Lois. 1983. "Women's Authority in Spiritualist Groups." *Journal for the Scientific Study of Religion* 22:157–66.

Heap, James L., and Phillip A. Roth. 1978. "On Phenomenological Society." Pp. 279–93 in *Contemporary Sociological Theories*, edited by Alan Wells. Santa Monica, Calif.: Goodyear.

Heilman, Samuel. 1990. "The Jews: Schism or Division." Pp. 185–198 in *In Gods We Trust: New Patterns of Religious Pluralism in America*, 2nd ed., edited by T. Robbins and D. Anthony. New Brunswick, N.J.: Transaction Books.

Heilman, Samuel C., and Steven M. Cohen. 1989. *Cosmopolitans and Parochials: Modern Orthodox Jews in America*. Chicago: University of Chicago Press.

Heinerman, John, and Anson Shupe. 1985. *The Mormon Corporate Empire*. Boston: Beacon Press.

Henschel, Milton G. 1975. "Who Are Jehovah Witnesses?" Pp. 132–41 in *Religions in America: Ferment and Faith in an Age of Crisis*, edited by L. Rosten. New York: Simon & Schuster.

Herberg, Will. 1955. *Protestant—Catholic—Jew: An Essay in American Religious Sociology*. Garden City, N.Y.: Doubleday.

Hernandez, Edwin I., and Roger L. Dudley. 1990. "Persistence of Religion through Primary Group Ties among Hispanic Seventh-Day Adventist Young People." *Review of Religious Research* 32:157–72.

Hertel, Brad, and Michael Hughes. 1987. "Religious Affiliation, Attendance and Support for 'Pro-family' Issues in the United States." *Social Forces* 65 (March):858–82.

Hertzke, Allen D. 1988. *Representing God in Washington: The Role of Religious Lobbies in the American Polity*. Knoxville, Tenn.: University of Tennessee Press.

Heyword, William C., and James W. Curran. 1988. "Epidemiology of AIDS in the U.S." *Scientific American* 259 (October 4):72–81.

Hicks, Robert D. 1990. "Police Pursuit of Santanic Crime." *Skeptical Inquirer* 14:276–86.

_____. 1991. "The Police Model of Satanism Crime." Pp. 175–90 in *The Satanism Scare*, edited by J. Richardson, J. Best, and D. Bromley. Hawthorne, N.Y.: Aldine Publishing.

Higgins, Paul C., and Gary L. Albrecht. 1977. "Hellfire and Delinquency Revisited." *Social Forces* 55:952–58.

Hill, Samuel S., and Dennis E. Owen. 1982. *The New Religious Right in*

America. Nashville. Tenn.: Abingdon Press.

Himmelfarb, Milton. 1967. "Secular Society? A Jewish Perspective." *Daedalus* 96:220–36.

Himmelstein, Jerome. 1986. "The Social Basis of Antifeminism: Religious Networks and Culture." *Journal for the Scientific Study of Religion* 25:1–15.

Hirschi, Travis, and Rodney Stark. 1969. "Hellfire and Delinquency." *Social Problems* 17:202–13.

Hitchcock, James. 1991. "Catholic Activist Conservatism in the United States." Pp. 101–41 in *Fundamentalisms Observed*, edited by M. Marty and S. Appleby. Chicago: University of Chicago Press.

Hochschild, Arlie R. 1979. "Emotion Work, Feeling Rules, and Social Structure." *American Sociological Review* 85:551–75.

_____. 1990. "Ideology and Emotion Management: A Perspective and Path for Future Research." Pp. 117–42 in *Research Agendas in the Sociology of Emotions*, edited by Theodore Kemper. New York: State University of New York Press.

Hoge, Dean. 1976. *Division in the Protestant House: The Basic Reasons behind Intra-church Conflict*. Philadelphia: Westminster Press.

_____. 1979. "A Test of Theories of Denominational Growth and Decline." Pp. 179–97 in *Understanding Church Growth and Decline*, edited by D. Hoge and D. Roozen. New York: Pilgrim Press.

Hoge, Dean, and Jackson Carroll. 1978. "Determinants of Church Commitment and Participant." *Journal for the Scientific Study of Religion* 17:107–27.

Hoge, Dean, John Dyble, and David Polk. 1973. "Religiosity and Prejudice in Northern and Southern Cities." *Journal for the Scientific Study of Religion* 12: 181–197.

_____. 1981. "Influence of Role Clarity on Vocational Commitment of Protestant Ministers." *Sociological Analysis* 42:1–16.

Hoge, Dean, and David Roozen. 1979. "Some Sociological Conclusions about Church Trends." Pp. 315–33 in *Understanding Church Growth and Decline*, edited by D. Hoge and D. Roozen. New York: Pilgrim Press.

Hollingshead, A. B. 1948. *Elmtown's Youth*. New Haven, Conn.: Yale University Press.

Holt, J. B. 1940. "Holiness Religion: Cultural Shock and Social Reorganization." *American Sociological Review* 5:740–47.

Hoover, Stewart M. 1988. *Mass Media Religion: The Social Sources of the Electronic Church*. Nutley Park, Calif.: Sage Publications.

Hornsby-Smith, Michael. 1991. *Roman Catholics in England*. Oxford: Clarendon Press.

Hougland, James G., and James R. Wood. 1979. "Determinants of Organizational Control in Local Churches." *Journal for the Scientific Study of Religion* 18:132–45.

Huber, Joan, and Glenna Spitze. 1983. *Sex Stratification: Children, Housework and Jobs*. San Diego, Calif.: Academic Press.

Hudson, Winthrop S. 1981. *Religion in America*, 2nd ed. New York: Charles Scribner's Sons.

Hughes, Cornelius G. 1992. "Views from the Pews: Hispanic and Anglo Catholics in a Changing Church." *Review of Religious Research* 33 (4): 364–75.

Hunsberger, B. E. 1985. "Parent–University Student Agreement on Religious and Nonreligious Issues." *Journal for the Scientific Study of Religion* 24:314–20.

Hunsberger, B., and L. B. Brown. 1984. "Religious Socialization, Apostasy and the Impact of Family Background." *Journal for the Scientific Study of Religion* 23:239–51.

Hunter, James Davidson. 1983. *American Evangelicism: Conservative Religion and the Quandry of Modernity*. New Brunswick, N.J.: Rutgers University Press.

———. 1987. *Evangelicism: The Coming Generation*. Chicago: University of Chicago Press.

———. 1991. *Culture Wars: The Struggle to Define America*. New York: Basic Books.

Husserl, Edmund. 1931. *Ideas: General Introduction to a Pure Phenomenology*. Translated by W. R. Boyce. New York: Humanities Press.

Hutchison, William R., ed. 1989. *Between the Times: The Travail of the Protestant Establishment in America, 1900–1960*. Cambridge, England, and New York: Cambridge University Press.

Hyde, Kenneth E. 1990. *Religion in Childhood and Adolescence: A Comprehensive Review of the Research*. Birmingham, Ala.: Religious Education Press.

Ice, Martha Long. 1987. *Clergy Women and Their World Views: Calling for a New Age*. Westport, Conn.: Praeger Publishers.

Ingram, Larry. 1980. "Notes on Pastoral Power in the Congregational Tradition." *Journal for the Scientific Study of Religion* 19:40–47.

Jacobs, Jerry. 1971. "From Sacred to Secular: The Rationalization of Christian Ideology." *Journal for the Scientific Study of Religion* 10:1–9.

Jameson, Frederic. 1991. *Postmodernism: Or, the Cultural Logic of Late Capitalism*. Durham, N.C.: Duke University Press.

Javits, Jacob. 1970. "Jews as a Class." Pp. 140–45 in *Cracks in the Melting Pot: Racism and Discrimination in American History*, edited by M. Steinfield. Beverly Hills, Calif.: Glencoe Press.

Jelen, Ted. 1986. "Fundamentalism, Feminism, and Attitudes toward Pornography." *Review of Religious Research* 28 (December):97–103.

———. 1988. "Changes in the Additudinal Correlates of Opposition to Abortion, 1977–1985." *Journal for the Scientific Study of Religion* 27 (2): 211–28.

———. 1989. *Religion and Political Behavior in the United States*. New York: Praeger Publishers.

———. 1991. *The Political Mobilization of Religious Beliefs*. New York: Praeger Publishers.

Jenkins, Philip, and Daniel Maier-Katkin. 1991. "Occult Survivors: The Making of a Myth." Pp. 175–90 in *The Satanism Scare*, edited by J. Richardson, J. Best, and D. Bromley. Hawthorne, N.Y.: Aldine Publishing.

Jennings, Diane, and John Yearwood. 1993. "Myriad Groups Rallies for Koresh Rights." *Dallas Morning News*, 31a, Sunday, April 4.

Jensen, Gary F., and Maynard L. Erickson. 1979. "The Religious Factor and Delinquency: Another Look at the Hellfire Hypothesis." Pp. 157–77 in *The Religious Dimension: New Directions in Quantitative Research*, edited by R. Wuthnow. San Diego, Calif.: Academic Press.

Johnson, Benton. 1971. "Church-Sect Revisited." *Journal for the Scientific Study of Religion* 10:124–37.

_____. 1985. "Liberal Protestantism: End of the Road?" *Annals* 480:39–52.
Johnson, Doyle Paul. 1979. "Dilemmas of Charismatic Leadership: The Case of the People's Temple." *Sociological Analysis* 40:315–23.
_____. 1986. *Sociological Theory: Classical Founders and Contemporary Perspectives.* New York: Macmillan.
Johnson, Doyle Paul, and Larry C. Mullins. 1989. "Religiosity and Loneliness among the Elderly." *Journal of Applied Gerontology* 110–31.
Johnson, Doyle Paul, and H. Paul Chalfant. 1993. "Contingency Theory and Church Organization." *Social Compass* 44 (April):75–82.
Johnson, Stephen D., and Joseph B. Tamney. 1988. "Factors Related to Inconsistent Life-views." *Review of Religious Research* 30 (1): 40–46.
Johnson, Stephen D., Joseph B. Tamney, and Ronald Burton. 1992. "Pat Robertson: Who Supported His Candidacy for President? *Journal for the Scientific Study of Religion* 284:387–99.
Johnstone, Ronald L. 1966. *The Effectiveness of Lutheran Elementary and Secondary Schools as Agencies of Christian Education.* St. Louis: Concordia Seminary.
_____. 1975. *Religion and Society in Interaction.* Englewood Cliffs, N.J.: Prentice-Hall.
_____. 1992. *Religion in Society,* 4th ed. Englewood Cliffs, N.J.: Prentice-Hall.
Jones, Arthur. 1992. "Small Christian Communities Thrive in America." *National Catholic Reporter* 28 (May 15): 4–5.
Jorstad, Erling. 1990. *Holding Fast/Pressing on: Religion in America in the 1980s.* New York: Praeger Publishers.
Judah, J. Stillson. 1974. "The Hare Krishna Movement." Pp. 463–78 in *Religious Movements in Contemporary America,* edited by I. Zaretzky and M. Leone. Princeton, N.J.: Princeton University Press.
Kane, A. L. 1988. *Religious Orientation, Moral Development and Ego Identity Status.* Ph.D. thesis, Yeshiva University.
Karp, David A., and William C. Yoels. 1993. *Sociology and Everyday Life,* 2nd ed. Itasca, Ill.: F. E. Peacock Publishers.
Kaufman, Debra Renee. 1991. *Rachel's Daughters: Newly Orthodox Jewish Women.* New Brunswick, N. J.: Rutgers University Press.
Kayal, Phillip M. 1985. "Morals, Medicine, and the AIDS Epidemic." *Journal of Religion and Health* 24:218–38.
_____. 1992. "Healing Homophobia: Volunteerism and 'Sacredness' in AIDS." *Journal of Religion and Health* 31:113–28.
Kelley, Dean M. 1977. *Why Conservative Churches Are Growing.* New York: Harper & Row.
_____. 1978. "Why Conservative Churches Are Still Growing." *Journal for the Scientific Study of Religion* 17:165–72.
Kelly, James R. 1972. "Attitudes toward Ecumenism: An Empirical Investigation." *Journal of Ecumenical Studies* 9:34–51.
Kemper, Theodore D. 1987. "How Many Emotions Are There? Wedding and the Social and Autonomic Components." *American Journal of Sociology* 93:263–89.
Kemper, Theodore D., ed. 1990. *Research Agendas in the Sociology of Emotions.* New York: State University of New York Press.
Kent, R. R. 1987. *The Religiosity and Parent/Child Socialization Connection with Adolescent Substance Abuse.* Ph.D. thesis, Brigham Young University.
Kephart, William, and William W. Zellner. 1991. *Extraordinary Groups: An*

Examination of Unconventional Life-styles, 4th ed. New York: St. Martin's Press.

Kertzer, Morris N. 1975. "What Is a Jew?" Pp. 142–55 in *Religions in America: Ferment and Faith in an Age of Crisis,* edited by L. Rosten. New York: Simon & Schuster.

Kieren, Dianne K., and Brenda Munro. 1987. "Following the Leaders: Parents' Influence on Adolescent Religious Activity." *Journal for the Scientific Study of Religion* 26:249–55.

Kilbourne, Brock B. 1983. "Conway-Siegelman Data on Religious Cults." *Journal for the Scientific Study of Religion* 22:380–85.

Kilduff, Marshall, and Ron Javers. 1978. *Suicide Cult.* New York: Bantam Books.

King, Morton, and James Hunt. 1967. "Measuring the Religious Variable: Nine Proposed Dimensions." *Journal for the Scientific Study of Religion* 6:173–90.

_____. 1969. "Measuring the Religious Variable: National Replication." *Journal for the Scientific Study of Religion* 14:13–22.

_____. 1975. "Religious Dimensions: Entities or Constructs?" *Sociological Focus* 8:57–63.

Kohlberg, Lawrence. 1973. "Stages and Aging in Moral Development: Some Speculations." *Gerontologist* 13:487–502.

Koplin, M.D. 1987. "Family, Religiousness, and Peer Influence on Adolescent Drug-Use." Ph.D. thesis, Brigham Young University.

Koval, John. 1970. "Priesthood as Career: Yesterday and Today." Pp. 85–100 in *Evolving Religious Careers,* edited by W. Bartlett. Washington, D.C.: Center for Applied Research in the Apostolate.

Kowalewski, Mark R. 1990. "Religious Constructions of the AIDS Crisis." *Sociological Analysis* 51 (1): 90–96.

Krajick, Kevin. 1992. "Vision Quest." *Newsweek* 119 (June 15): 62–63.

Kurtz, Paul. 1989. "The New Age in Perspective." *Skeptical Inquirer* 13:365–67.

Kurtz, Richard A., and H. Paul Chalfant. 1991. *The Sociology of Medicine and Illness,* 2nd ed. Boston: Allyn & Bacon.

LaBarre, Weston. 1971. "Materials for a History of Studies of Crisis Cults: A Bibliographic Essay." *Current Anthropology: A Bibliography for Cultural Anthropology* 12:3–27.

Lane, Richard. 1984. "Catholic Attitudes toward Abortion: Are They Softening?" Paper presented at the Association for the Sociology of Religion annual meeting. San Antonio, Texas, November.

Lasker, Arnold A. 1971. "Motivations for Attending High Holy Day Services." *Journal for the Scientific Study of Religion* 10:241–48.

Latkin, Carl A. 1990. "The Self-Concept of Rajneeshpuram Commune Members." *Journal for the Scientific Study of Religion* 29:91–98.

_____. 1991. "From Device to Vice: Social Control and Intergroup Conflict at Rajneeshpuram." *Sociological Analysis* 52 (Winter): 363–78.

Lauer, Robert H. 1975. "Occupational and Religious Mobility in a Small City." *Sociological Quarterly* 16:380–92.

Lee, Marc. 1984. *Profiles in American Judaism: The Reform, Conservative, Orthodox, and Reconstructionist Traditions in Historical Perspective.* San Francisco: Harper & Row.

Lefevere, Patricia. 1991. "Russian Orthodox Church Sees Burst of Energy." *National Catholic Reporter* 27 (October 4): 11.

Lehman, Edward. 1980. "Placement of Men and Women in the Ministry." *Review of Religious Research* 22:18–40.

———. 1981. "Organizational Resistance to Women in the Ministry."*Sociological Analysis* 42:101–18.

———. 1985. *Women Clergy: Breaking through Gender Barriers*. New Brunswick, N.J.: Transaction Books.

———. 1993a. "Gender and Ministry Style: Things Not What They Seem." *Sociology of Religion* 54 (1): 1–11.

———. 1993b. *Gender and Work: The Case of the Clergy*. Albany, N.Y.: State University of New York Press.

Lemert, Edwin. 1951. *Social Pathology*. New York: McGraw-Hill.

Lenski, Gerhard F. 1961. *The Religious Factor*. Garden City, N.Y.: Doubleday.

Levine, Art. 1988. "On the Trail of High Weirdness." *U.S. News and World Report* 105 (November 14): 67.

Levine, Betty. 1986. "Religious Commitment and Integration into a Jewish Community in the United States." *Review of Religious Research* 27:328–43.

Lincoln, C. Eric. 1973. *The Black Muslims in America*, rev. ed. Boston: Beacon Press.

———. 1974. *The Black Church Since Frazier*. New York: Schocken Books.

Lincoln, C. Eric, and Lawrence H. Mamiya. 1990. *The Black Church in the African American Experience*. Durham, N.C.: Duke University Press.

Lipset, Seymour M., and Earl Raab. 1970. *The Politics of Unreason: Right-Wing Extremism in America 1790–1970*. New York: Harper & Row.

Littell, Franklin. 1962. *From State to Church Pluralism: A Protestant Interpretation of Religion in American History*. Hawthorne, N.Y.: Aldine Publishing.

Lofland, John. 1977. *Doomsday Cult*, enlarged ed. New York: Irvington Publishers.

———. 1978. "Becoming a World-Saver-Revisited." Pp. 10–23 in *Conversion Careers: In and Out of New Religions*, edited by J. Richardson. Newbury Park, Calif.: Sage Publications.

———. 1985. *Protest: Studies of Collective Behavior and Social Movements*. New Brunswick, N.J.: Transaction Books.

Lofland, John, and L. N. Skonovd. 1981. "Conversion Motifs." *Journal for the Scientific Study of Religion* 20:373–85.

———. 1983. "Patterns of Conversion." Pp. 1–24 in *Of Gods and Men: New Religious Movements in the West*, edited by E. Barker. Macon, Ga.: Mercer University Press.

Lofland, John, and Rodney Stark. 1981. "Becoming a World Saver: A Theory of Conversion to a Deviant Perspective." *American Sociological Review* 30:862–74.

Loft, Sarah. 1991. Personal conversation concerning research on converts to Orthodoxy. Boston.

Long, Theodore, and Jeffrey Hadden. 1983. "Religious Conversion and the Concept of Socialization: Integrating the Brainwashing and Drift Models." *Journal for the Scientific Study of Religion* 22:1–14.

Luckmann, Thomas. 1967. *The Invisible Religion: The Problem of Religion in Modern Society*. New York: Macmillan.

———. 1990. "Shrinking Transcendence, Expanding on Religion." *Sociological Analysis* 51:127–38.

Luft, G., and G. T. Sorrell. 1987. "Parenting Style and Parent-Adolescent Religious Value Consensus." *Journal of Adolescent Research* 2:53–68.

Lummis, Adair. 1991. "Life after Seminary for Clergywomen: Fulfillment of Expectations and Attributions of Blame." Paper presented at the Society for the Scientific Study of Religion and the Religious Research Association annual meeting. Pittsburgh, Pennsylvania, November.

Lumpkins, Barbranda. 1992. "Expanded Duties Nudge Pastors Back to School." *Progressions* 4 (1): 10–13.

Lustgarden, Steve. 1992. "Transcendentally Speaking, It's Amusing." *Vegetarian Times* 181 (September): 12.

Lynd, Robert S., and Helen Merrell Lynd. 1929. *Middletown*. New York: Harcourt, Brace and World.

MacCannell, Dean. 1973. "Staged Authenticity: Arrangements of Social Space in Tourist Settings." *American Journal of American Journal of Sociology* 79:589–603.

Machalek, Richard. 1977. "Definitional Strategies in the Study of Religion." *Journal for the Scientific Study of Religion* 16:395–402.

Machalek, Richard, and Michael Martin. 1976. "Invisible Religions." *Journal for the Scientific Study of Religion* 15:395–402.

Mariani, John. 1979. "Television Evangelism: Milking the Flock." *Saturday Review* 3 (February 3): 22–25.

Martin, David. 1978. *A General Theory of Secularization*. Oxford: Basil Blackwell.

Martin, William. 1979. "A Joyful Noise." *Texas Monthly* (July): 184–86.

———. 1991. *A Prophet with Honor: The Billy Graham Story*. New York: William Morrow.

Marty, Martin. 1970. *Righteous Empire: The Protestant Experience in America*. New York: Dial Press.

———. 1984. *Pilgrims in Their Own Land: 500 Years of Religion in America*. Boston: Little, Brown.

———. 1991a. "Never the Same Again: Post-Vatican II Catholic-Protestant Interactions." *Sociological Analysis* 52 (1): 13–26.

———. 1991b. *The Noise of Conflict, 1919–1941*. Chicago: University of Chicago Press.

Marty, Martin E., and R. Scott Appleby, eds. 1991. *Fundamentalisms Observed*. Chicago: University of Chicago Press.

Marx, Gary T. 1967. "Religion: Opiate or Inspiration of Civil Rights Militancy among Negroes?" *American Sociological Review* 32:64–73.

Marx, Karl. 1964. *The Economic and Philosophic Manuscripts of 1844*. New York: International Publishers.

Marx, Karl, and Friederich Engels. 1957. *On Religion*. New York: Schocken Books.

Maxwell, Joe. 1992. "New Kingdoms for the Cults: Aberrant and Unorthodox Groups Join Christians in Filling Eastern Europe's Spiritual Vacuum." *Christianity Today* 36 (January 13): 37–40.

Mayer, Tom. 1991. "On Marxism." Pp. 99–123 in *The Renascence of Sociological Theory*, edited by H. Etzkowitz and R. Glassman. Itasca, Ill.: F. E. Peacock Publishers.

McCarthy, James. 1979. "Religious Commitment, Affiliation, and Marriage Dissolution." Pp. 179–97 in *The Religious Dimension: New Directions in Quantitative Research*, edited by Robert Wuthnow. San Diego, Calif.: Academic Press.

McGuire, Meredith. 1992. *Religion in Social Context,* 3rd ed. Belmont, Calif.: Wadsworth.

McKinney, William, and Dean R. Hoge. 1983. "Community and Congregational Factors in the Growth and Decline of Protestant Churches." *Journal for the Scientific Study of Religion* 22:55–61.

McLaughlin, William C. 1967. "Is There a Third Force in Christendom." *Daedalus* 96:43–68.

McNamara, Patrick H. 1984. *Religion American Style.* New York: Harper & Row.

_____. 1985. "The New Christian Right's View of the Family and Its Social Science Critics: A Study in Differing Propositions." *Journal of Marriage and the Family.* 47:449–58.

McRae, J. A. 1977. "Patterns of Marriage Dissolution in the United States." Ph.D. dissertation, Princeton University.

Mead, George Herbert. 1934. *Mind, Self and Society.* Chicago: University of Chicago Press.

Mellenkott, V. R. 1983. *The Divine Feminine: The Biblical Imagery of God as Female.* New York: Crossroads Publishers.

Melton, J. Gordon. 1978. *The Encyclopedia of American Religion.* Wilmington, N.C.: McGrath Publishing.

_____. 1986. *Encyclopaedic Handbook of Cults in America.* New York: Garland Publishing.

_____, ed. 1991. *The Encyclopedia of American Religions: A Comprehensive Study of the Major Religious Groups in the United States and Canada.* Vols. 1, 2, 3. Tarrytown, N.Y.: Triumph Books.

_____. 1992. *Encylopedic Handbook of Cults in America,* revised and updated version. New York: Garland Publishing.

Menendez, A. J. 1977. *Religion at the Polls.* Philadelphia: Westminster Press.

_____. 1988. "Evangelicals Helped Win It for Bush." *National and International Religious Report* 23: (November 21): 2.

Mestrovic, Stjepan. 1992. *Durkheim and Postmodern Culture.* Hawthorne, N.Y.: Aldine Publishing.

Michalet, Guy. 1990. "The Catholic Identity of French People. II. Membership and Socialization." *Revue Française de Sociologie* 31: 609–33.

Middleton, Russell. 1973. "Do Christian Beliefs Cause Anti-Semitism? *American Sociological Review.* 38: 33–61.

Mills, Edgar. 1985. "The Sacred and the Ministry." Pp. 167–83 in *The Sacred in a Secular Age,* edited by P. Hammond. Berkeley, Calif.: University of California Press.

Mindel, Charles H., and C. Edwin Vaughan. 1978. "A Multidimensional Approach to Religiosity and Disengagement." *Journal of Gerontology* 33:103–8.

Minder, W. E. 1985. *A Study of the Relationship between Church Sponsored K–12 Education and Church Membership in the Seventh-Day Adventist Church.* Ed.D. thesis, Western Michigan University.

Minutes of the General Assembly of the Presbyterian Church (U.S.A.). 1991. Louisville, Ky.: Presbyterian Church (U.S.A.).

Moberg, David. 1985. *The Church as a Social Institution.* Grand Rapids, Mich.: Baker Book House.

Mollenkott, V. R. 1983. *The Divine Feminine: The Biblical Imagery of God as Female.* New York: Crossroad Publishers.

Moore, R. Laurence. 1986. *Religious Outsiders and the Making of America*. New York: Oxford University Press.

Morrow, Lance. 1978. "The Lure of Doomsday." *Time* (December 4):30.

Morton, Nell. 1974. "Preaching the Word." Pp. 12–20 in *Sexist Religion and Women in the Church*, edited by A. L. Hageman. New York: Association Press.

Mosely, R. J., and K. Brockenbrough. 1988. "Faith Development in the Preschool Years." In *Handbook of Preschool Religious Education*, edited by D. Ratcliff. Birmingham, Ala.: Religious Education Press.

Mosher, W. D., and C. Goldscheider. 1984. "Contraceptive Patterns of Religious and Racial Groups in the United States, 1955–1976: Convergence and Distinctiveness." *Studies in Family Planning* 15:101–11.

Mueller, G. H. 1980. "The Dimensions of Religiosity." *Sociological Analysis* 41:1–24.

Myers, Gustavus. 1960. *The History of Bigotry in the United States*.

Myrdal, Gunnar. 1944. *The American Dilemma*. New York: Harper & Row.

Nathan, Debbie. 1991. "Satanism and Child Molestation: Constructing the Ritual Abuse Scare." Pp. 75–94 in *The Satanism Scare*, edited by J. Richardson, J. Best, and D. Bromley. Hawthorne, N.Y.: Aldine Publishing.

National Opinion Research Center (NORC). 1992. *General Social Survey*. Chicago: National Opinion Research Center.

Neal, Sister Marie Augusta. 1984. "Social Justice and the Right to Use Power." *Journal for the Scientific Study of Religion* 23:329–40.

Needleman, Jacob. 1970. *The New Religions*. Garden City, N.Y.: Doubleday.

Neitz, Mary Jo. 1987. *Charisma and Community: A Study of Religious Commitment within the Charismatic Renewal*. New Brunswick, N.J.: Transaction Books.

_____. 1990. "In Goddess We Trust." Pp. 353–72 in *In Gods We Trust: New Patterns of Religious Pluralism in America*, 2nd ed., edited by T. Robbins and D. Anthony. New Brunswick, N.J.: Transaction Books.

Nelsen, Hart M. 1980. "Religious Transmission versus Religious Formation: Preadolescent-Parent Interaction." *Sociological Quarterly* 21:207–18.

_____. 1985. "Ministers and Their Milieu: Socialization, Clergy Role, and Community." Pp. 1–18 in *The Protestant Parish Ministry: A Behavioral Science Interpretation*, edited by S. Blizzard. Washington, D.C.: Society for the Scientific Study of Religion.

Nelsen, Hart, and William E. Snizek. 1976. "Musical Pews: Rural and Urban Models of Occupational and Religious Mobility." *Sociology and Social Research* 660:279–89.

Nelsen, Hart, Raytha Yokeley, and Thomas Madron. 1971. "Rural-Urban Differences in Religiosity." *Rural Sociology* 36:389–96.

Neville, Gwen K. 1974. "Religious Socialization of Women within U.S. Subcultures." *In Sexist Religion and Women in the Church*, edited by A. L. Hagemen. New York: Association Press.

Newman, William M., and Peter L. Halvorsen. 1984. "Religion and Regional Culture." *Journal for the Scientific Study of Religion* 23:304–15.

Newport, Anthony. 1979. "The Religious Switcher in the United States." *American Sociological Review* 44:528–52.

Niebuhr, Gustav. 1993. "The Family of Love and the Final Harvest." *Washington Post* 116 (June 2): A7, A16.

Niebuhr, H. Richard. 1932. *The Social Sources of Denominationalism*. New York: Henry Holt.

Nielsen, Donald A. 1989. "Sects, Churches and Economic Transformations in Russia and Western Europe." *International Journal of Politics, Culture, and Society* 2:493–522.

Nock, David A. 1989. "Differential Ecological Receptivity of Conversionist and Revolutionist Sects: A Reconsideration of Stark and Bainbridge." *Sociological Analysis* 50:229–46.

Nottingham, Elizabeth. 1971. *Religion: A Sociological View.* New York: Random House.

Novak, Michael. 1967. "Christianity: Renewed or Slowly Abandoned?" *Daedalus* 96:237–66.

O'Dea, Thomas, and Janet O'Dea Aviada. 1983. *Sociology of Religion*, 2nd ed. Englewood Cliffs, N.J.: Prentice-Hall.

O'Hara, Maureen. 1989. "A New Age Reflection in the Magic Mirror of Science." *Skeptical Inquirer* 13:368–74.

Oliver, Mary Eunice. 1983. "The Last Woman Not to Be Seated." *Witness* 66: 10–12.

Olmstead, Clifton E. 1961. "Special Religion in Urban America." Pp. 139–48 in *American Mosaic: Social Patterns of Religion in the United States*, edited by P. Hammond and B. Johnson. New York: Random House.

Olson, D. V. 1989. "Church Friendships: Boon or Barrier to Church Growth?" *Journal for the Scientific Study of Religion* 28:432–47.

Orleans, Myron. 1991. "Phenomenological Sociology." Pp. 167–85 in *The Renascence of Sociological Theory*, edited by H. Etzkowitz and R. Glassman. Itasca, Ill.: F. E. Peacock Publishers.

Osborne, Thomas M. 1977. "A Sociological Approach to Religion: Another Consideration." Paper presented at the Society for the Scientific Study of Religion annual meeting. Storrs, Connecticut, October.

Oser, F., and K. H. Reich. 1990. "Moral Judgement, Religious Judgement, Worldview, and Logical Thought: A Review of Their Relationship." *British Journal of Religious Education* 12:94–101.

Oser, F., and P. Gmunder. 1988. *Der Mensch–Stufen seiner religösen Entwicklung: Eine structurgenitscher Ansatz.* Gutersloh: Gutersloher Verlagshaus Gerd Mohn.

Ostling, Richard N. 1992. "The Second Reformation." *Time* 140 (November 23): 53–58.

Ozorak, E. W. 1989. "Social and Cognitive Influences on the Development of Religious Beliefs in Adolescence." *Journal for the Scientific Study of Religion* 28:448–63.

Pagels, Elaine H. 1970. "What Became of God the Mother? Conflicting Images of God in Early Christianity." *Signs* 2:293–303.

Palmer, C. Eddie. 1991. "Human Emotions: An Expanding Sociological Frontier." *Sociological Spectrum* 11:213–19.

Palmer, C. Eddie, and Dorinda N. Noble. 1986. "Premature Death: Dilemmas of Infant Mortality." *Social Casework: The Journal of Contemporary Social Work* 67:332–39.

Parsons, Arthur S. 1989. "The Secular Contribution to Religious Innovation: A Case Study of the Unification Church." *Sociological Analysis* 50:209–27.

Passas, Niko, and Manuel Escamilla Castillo. 1992. "Litigation and Scientology." *Behavioral Science and the Law* 10:1–14.

Payne, Barbara Pittard. 1980. "Religious Life of the Elderly: Myth or Reality?" Pp. 218–29 in *Spiritual Well-Being of the Elderly*, edited by J. Thorson and T. Cook. Springfield, Ill.: C. C. Thomas.

Pazhayapurakal, E. J. 1989. "The Influence of Parents, Peers, and Schools on the Religious Attitudes and Practices of Catholic School Students." Ph.D. thesis, Fordham University.

Peek, Charles W., H. Paul Chalfant, and Edgar V. Milton. 1979. "Sinners in the Hands of an Angry God: Fundamentalist Fears about Drunk Driving." *Journal for the Scientific Study of Religion* 18:29–39.

Peek, Charles W., Evans W. Curry, and H. Paul Chalfant. 1985. "Religiosity and Delinquency over Time." *Social Science Quarterly* 66:120–31.

Perrin, Robin D., and Armand L. Mauss. 1991. "Saints and Seekers: Sources of Recruitment to the Vineyard Christian Fellowship." *Review of Religious Research* 33 (December):97–111.

_____. 1993. "Strictly speaking…: Kelley's Quandry and the Vineyard Christian Fellowship." *Journal for the Scientific Study of Religion* 32:125–35.

Pettigrew, J., and Ernest Q. Campbell. 1958–59. "Racial and Moral Crisis: The Role of the Little Rock Ministers." *American Journal of Sociology* 64:599–616.

Pfeffer, Leo. 1953. *Church, State and Freedom*. Boston: Beacon Press.

_____. 1974. "The Legitimation of Marginal Religions in the United States." Pp. 9–26 in *Religious Movements in Contemporary America*, edited by I. Zaretscy and M. Leone. Princeton, N.J.: Princeton University Press.

Photiadis, John, and John Schnabel. 1977. "Religion: A Persistent Institution in Changing Appalachia." *Review of Religious Research* 19:32–42.

Poloma, Margaret. 1982. *The Charismatic Movement: Is There a New Pentecost?* Boston: Twayne Publishers.

_____. 1989. *The Assemblies of God at the Crossroads: Charisma and Institutional Dilemmas*. Knoxville, Tenn.: University of Tennessee Press.

Poloma, Margaret, and Brian F. Pendleton. 1989. "Religious Experiences, Evangelicism, and Institutional Growth within the Assemblies of God." *Journal for the Scientific Study of Religion* 28:415–31.

Pope, Liston. 1942. *Millhands and Preachers*. New Haven, Conn.: Yale University Press.

Potvin, Raymond. 1976. "Role Uncertainty and Commitment among Seminary Faculty." *Sociological Analysis* 37:45–52.

Press, Aric. 1993. "Priests and Abuse." *Newsweek* (August 16): 42–44.

Proctor, Priscilla, and William Proctor. 1976. *Women in the Pulpit*. Garden City, N.Y.: Doubleday.

Quinley, Harold. 1974. *The Prophetic Clergy: Social Activism among Protestant Ministers*. New York: John Wiley & Sons.

Rabateau, Albert J. 1978. *Slave Religion: "The Invisible Institution" in the Antebellum South*. New York. Oxford University Press.

Raff, G. Elson, and Albert P. Standerman. 1975. "What Is a Lutheran?" Pp. 156–69 in *Religions in America: Ferment and Faith in an Age of Crisis*, edited by L. Rosten. New York: Simon & Schuster.

Raffkind, Myrna, and Jean M. Low. 1992. "Jewish Identification: A Survey of the Jewish Community in Amarillo, Texas." *Journal of Jewish Communal Service* 69:63–74.

Ramet, Sabrina Petra, ed. *Protestantism and Politics in Eastern Europe and Russia: The Communist and Post-Communist Eras*. Durham, N.C.: Duke University Press.

Ramsden, William E. 1985. "A Public Sanctuary Church: History and Development." Paper presented at the Religious Research Association annual meeting. Savannah, Georgia.

Raulin, Anne. 1991. "The Aesthetic and Sacred Dimension of Urban Ecology: Paris' Little Asia." *Archives de Sciences Sociales des Religions* 73:35–49.

Redekop, Calvin. 1969. *The Old Colony Mennonites: Dilemmas of Ethnic Minority Life*. Baltimore, Md.: John Hopkins University Press.

———. 1974. "A New Look at Sect Development." *Journal for the Scientific Study of Religion* 13:345–53.

Reed, Graham. 1989. "The Psychology of Channeling." *Skeptical Inquirer* 13 (4):385–90.

Reese, Thomas J. 1989. *Archbishop: Inside the Power Structure of the American Catholic Church*. San Francisco: Harper & Row.

Reilly, Mary Ellen. 1975. "Perceptions of the Priest Role." *Sociological Analysis* 36:347–56.

Renzetti, Claire M., and Daniel J. Curran. 1989. *Women, Men, and Society: The Sociology of Gender*. Boston: Allyn & Bacon.

Rhodes, Lynn. 1987. *Co-creating: A Feminist Vision of Ministry*. Philadelphia: Westminster Press.

Riccio, James A. 1979. "Religious Affiliation and Socioeconomic Achievement." Pp. 179–228 in *The Religious Dimension: New Directions in Qualitative Research*. San Diego, Calif: Academic Press.

Richards, David E. 1980. "Anglican-Episcopal Churches." Pp. 227–44 in *Ministry in America*, edited by D. Schuller, M. Strommen, and M. Brekke. New York: Harper & Row.

Richardson, James T., ed. 1978. *Conversion Careers: In and Out of the New Religions*. Newbury Park, Calif.: Sage Publications.

———. 1979. "People's Temple and Jonestown: A Corrective Comparison and Critique." Plenary address at the Society for the Scientific Study of Religion annual meeting. San Antonio, Texas.

———. 1984. "Studies of Conversion: Secularization or Re-enchantment? Pp. 104–21 in *Conversion Careers: In and Out of the New Religions*, edited by J. Richardson. Newbury Park, Calif.: Sage Publications.

Richardson, James T., and Mary Stewart. 1978. "Conversion Process Models and the Jesus Movements." Pp. 24–42 in *Conversion Careers: In and Out of New Religions*, edited by J. Richardson. Newbury Park, Calif.: Sage Publications.

Richardson, James T., Mary Stewart, and Roberta B. Simmonds. 1979. *Organized Miracles*. New Brunswick, N.J.: Transaction Publishers.

Richardson, James T., Joel Best, and David G. Bromley. 1991. "Satanism as a Social Problem." Pp. 3–20 in *The Satanism Scare*, edited by J. Richardson, J. Best, and D. Bromley. Hawthorne, N.Y.: Aldine Publishing.

Richardson, Laurel. 1988. *The Dynamics of Sex and Gender: A Sociological Perspective*. New York: Harper & Row.

Richardson, Miles. 1975. "Anthropologist—The Myth Teller." *American Ethnologist* 2:517–33.

Ridder, N. F. 1985. *The Religious Beliefs and Pratices of Catholic Graduates of Catholic and Public High Schools in the State of Nebraska, 1972–1981*. Dr. Ed. thesis, University of Nebraska—Lincoln.

Robbins, Thomas. 1984. "Constructing Cultist 'Mind Control.'" *Sociological Analysis* 45:241–56.

———. 1990. *Cults, Converts, and Charisma*. Newbury Park, Calif.: Sage Publications.

Robbins, Thomas, and Dick Anthony, eds. 1990. *In Gods We Trust: New Patterns of Religious Pluralism in America,* 2nd ed. New Brunswick, N.J.: Transaction Books.

Robbins, Thomas, Dick Anthony, Madeline Douglas, and Thomas Curtis. 1976. "The Last Civil Religion: Reverend Moon and the Unification Church." *Sociological Analysis* 37:111–25.

Robbins, Thomas, Dick Anthony, and James Richardson. 1978. "Theory and Research on Today's 'New Religions.'" *Sociological Analysis* 37:95–122.

Roberts, Keith A. 1990. *Religion in Sociological Perspective,* 2nd ed. Belmont, Calif.: Wadsworth Publishing.

Robertson, Roland. 1970. *The Sociological Interpretation of Religion.* New York: Schocken Books.

Rochford, E. Burke, Jr. 1989. "Factionalism, Group Defection, and Schism in the Hare Krishna Movement." *Journal for the Scientific Study of Religion* 28:162–79.

Rokeach, Milton. 1979. "Paradoxes of Religious Beliefs." Pp. 172–77 in *Sociological Footprints,* edited by L. Cargan and J. Ballantine. Boston: Houghton Mifflin.

Roof, Wade Clark. 1974. "Religious Orthodoxy and Minority Prejudice: Causal Relationship or Reflection of Localistic World View?" *American Journal of Sociology.* 80: 643–64.

_____. 1978. *Community and Commitment.* New York: Elsevier-Nelson Books.

_____. 1979. "Socioeconomic Differentials among White Sociological Groups in the United States." *Social Forces* 58:280–89.

_____. 1993. *A Generation of Seekers: The Spiritual Journeys of the Baby Boom Generation.* San Francisco: Harper San Francisco.

Roof, Wade Clark, and William McKinney. 1987. *American Mainline Religion: Its Changing Shape and Future.* New Brunswick, N.J.: Rutgers University Press.

Roof, Wade Clark, and Kirk Hadaway. 1977. "Shifts in Religious Preference—The Mid-seventies." *Journal for the Scientific Study of Religion* 16:309–12.

Roozen, D. A., and Jackson W. Carroll. 1979. "Recent Trends in Church Membership and Participation: An Introduction." Pp. 21–41 in *Understanding Church Growth and Decline: 1950–1978,* edited by D. Hoge and D. Roozen. New York: Pilgrim Press.

Rose, Susan D. 1988. *Keeping Them Out of the Hands of Satan: Evangelical Schooling In America.* New York: Routledge, Chapman, and Hall.

Rosenberg, Florence. 1979. "Catholic Women in Ministry: Ideological and Functional Origins." Paper presented at the Association for the Sociology of Religion annual meeting. Boston.

_____. 1989. *The Southern Baptists: A Subculture in Transition.* Knoxville, Tenn.: University of Tennessee Press.

Rosner, Fred. 1987. "AIDS: A Jewish View." *Journal of Halacha* 13:21–41.

Ross, Michael W. 1988. "Effects of Membership in Scientology on Personality: An Exploratory Study." *Journal for the Scientific Study of Religion* 27:630–36.

Rosten, Leo. 1975. *Religions of America: Ferment and Faith in An Age of Crisis.* New York: Simon & Schuster.

Rothman, Barbara Katz. 1991. "Symbolic Interactionism." Pp. 151–65 in *The Renascence of Sociological Theory,* edited by H. Etzowitz and R. Glassman. Itasca, Ill.: F. E. Peacock Publishers.

Rouche, Douglas. 1968. *The Catholic Revolution*. New York: David McKay.

Royle, Majorie H. 1982. "Women Pastors: What Happens after Placement." *Review of Religious Research* 24:116–26.

Rudy, David R., and Arthur L. Greil. 1987. "Taking the Pledge: The Commitment Process in Alcoholics Anonymous." *Sociological Focus* 20:45–59.

Ruether, Rosemary R. 1975. *New Women/New Earth*. New York: Seabury Press.

Russell, Letty, ed. 1976. *The Liberating Word*. Philadelphia: Westminster Press.

_____. 1987. *Household of Freedom*. Philadelphia: Westminster Press.

Safran, Claire. 1990. "Today's Cults Want *You*." *Woman's Day* 46:52–55, July 10.

St. George, Arthur, and Patrick McNamara. 1984. "Religion, Race and Psychological Well-being." *Journal for the Scientific Study of Religion* 23: 351–63.

Saliba, John A. 1990. *Social Science and the Cults: An Annotated Bibliography*. New York: Garland Publishing.

Sandberg, Neil C. 1986. *Jewish Life in Los Angeles: A Window to Tomorrow*. New York: University Press of America.

Sandeen, Ernest R. 1970. *The Roots of Fundamentalism*. Chicago: University of Chicago Press.

Sawyer, Mary R. 1983–84. "A Moral Minority: Religion and Congressional Black Politics." *Journal for Religious Thought* 40:55–66.

Schaller, Warren E., and Charles R. Carroll. 1976. *Health, Quackery and the Consumer*. Philadelphia: W. B. Saunders.

Scharf, Betty. 1970. *The Sociological Study of Religion*. New York: Harper & Row.

Schneider, Herbert W. 1952. *Religion in Twentieth Century America*. Cambridge, Mass.: Harvard University Press.

Schoenfeld, Eugen, and Stjepan G. Mestrovic. 1991. "With Justice and Mercy: Instrumental-Masculine and Expressive-Feminine Elements in Religion." *Journal for the Scientific Study of Religion* 30:363–80.

Schoenherr, Richard A. 1987. "Power and Authority in Organized Religion: Desegregating the Phenomenological Core." *Sociological Analysis* 47:52–71.

Schoenherr, Richard A., and Andrew M. Greeley. 1974. "Role Commitment Processes and the American Catholic Priesthood." *American Sociological Review* 39:407–26.

Schoenherr, Richard A., and Annette Sorenson. 1982. "Social Change in Religious Organizations: Consequences of Clergy Decline in the U.S. Catholic Church." *Sociological Analysis* 43:25–52.

Schuller, David. 1980. "Basic Issues in Defining Ministry." Pp. 3–11 in *Ministry in America*, edited by D. Schuller, M. Strommen, and M. Brekke. New York: Harper & Row.

Schuller, David S., Merton P. Strommen, and Milo L. Brekke, eds. 1980. *Ministry in America*. New York: Harper & Row.

Schultz, Ted. 1989. "The New Age: The Need for Myth in an Age of Science." *Skeptical Inquirer* 13:375–79.

Scimecca, Joseph A. 1979. "Cultural Hero Systems and Religious Beliefs: The Ideal-Real Social Science of Ernest Becker." *Review of Religious Research* 21: 62–70.

Seidler, John, and Katherine Meyer. 1989. *Conflict and Change In the Catholic Church*. New Brunswick, N.J.: Rutgers University Press.

Shaver, D. G. 1987. "Moral Development of Students Attending a Christian Liberal Arts College and a Bible College." *Journal of College Student Personnel* 28:211–18.

Shelp, Earl E., and Ronald H. Sunderland. 1985. "AIDS and the Church." *Christian Century* (September 11–18): 797–800.

————. 1987. *AIDS and the Church.* Philadelphia: Westminster Press.

————. 1991. *AIDS and the Church,* 2nd ed. Louisville, Ky.: Westminster/John Knox Press.

Shibley, Mark. 1990. "Fragmented Gods: Postmodernism, Structuration Theory, and the Sociology of Religion." Paper presented at the Society for the Scientific Study of Religion annual meeting. Virginia Beach, Virginia, November.

Shulick, Richard N. 1979. "Faith Development, Moral Development, and Old Age: An Assessment of Fowler's Faith Development Paradigm." *Dissertation Abstracts International* 40:2097.

Shupe, Anson D., Roger Spielmann, and Sam Stigall, n.d. *Deprogramming and the Emerging American Anti-cult Movement.* Unpublished report.

————. 1978. "The New Exorcism." Pp. 145–60 in *Conversion Careers: In and Out of the New Religions,* edited by J. Richardson. Newbury Park, Calif.: Sage Publications.

Shupe, Anson, and William A. Stacey. 1982. *Born Again Politics and the Moral Majority: What Social Surveys Show.* New York: Edwin Mellin.

Sidey, Ken. 1991. "Church Growth Fine-tunes Its Formula." *Christianity Today* 35:44–47.

Simmel, Georg. 1905. "A Contribution to the Sociology of Religion." *Sociological Review* 11:336–67.

Sklare, Marshall. 1971. *America's Jews.* New York: Random House.

Slade, Margot. 1979. "New Religious Groups." *Psychology Today* (January).

Sloane, D.M., and R. H. Potvin. 1986. "Religion and Delinquency: Cutting through the Maze." *Social Forces* 65:87–105.

Smidt, Corwin, and James Penning. 1990. "A House Divided: A Comparison of Robertson and Bush Delegates to the Michigan Republican State Convention." *Polity* 23:127–38.

Smidt, Corwin, and Paul Kellstedt. 1992. "Evangelicals in the Post-Reagan Era: "An Analysis of Evangelical Voters in the 1988 Presidential Election." *Journal for the Scientific Study of Religion* 31:330–38.

Smilgis, Martha. 1991. "Marianne Williamson Is Hollywood's New Age Attraction, Blending Star-studded Charity Work with Mind Awareness." *Time* 138 (July 29): 60.

Smith, Tom W. 1992. "Are Conservative Churches Growing?" *Review of Religious Research* 33 (4): 305–29.

Snook, John B. 1975. "An Alternative to Church-Sect." *Journal for the Scientific Study of Religion* 13:191–204.

Snow, David, and Cynthia Phillips. 1980. "The Lofland-Stark Conversion Model: A Critical Reassessment." *Social Problems* 27:430–47.

Snow, David A., and Richard Machalek. 1983. "The Convert as Social Type." Pp. 259–89 in *Sociological Theory 1983,* edited by R. Collins. San Francisco: Jossey-Bass.

————. 1984. "The Sociology of Conversion." *Annual Review of Sociology* 10:167–90.

Songer, Harold S. 1980. "Southern Baptists." Pp. 265–306 in *Ministry in America,* edited by D. Schuller, M. Strommen, and M. Brekke. New York: Harper & Row.

South, Kenneth. 1993. Personal interview concerning AIDS National Interfaith Network.

Spector, Michael. 1993. "Hot Tombs." Pp. 194–96 in *Dying, Death and Bereavement,* edited by G. Dickinson, M. Leming, and A. C. Hermann. Guilford, Conn.: Dushkin Publishing Group.

Stafford, Tim. 1991. "The Kingdom of the Cult Watchers." *Christianity Today* 35 (October 7): 18–22.

Stamp, K. M. 1956. *The Peculiar Institution.* New York: Knopf.

Stark, Rodney. 1968. "Age and Faith: A Changing Outlook on an Old Process." *Sociological Analysis* 29:1–10.

_____. 1972. "The Economics of Piety: Religious Commitment." Pp. 483–503 in *Issues in Social Inequality.* Boston: Little, Brown.

_____. 1984. "Religion and Conformity: Reaffirming a Sociology of Religion." *Sociological Analysis* 45:273–82.

_____. 1985. "Church and Sect." Pp. 139–49 in *The Sacred in a Secular Age,* edited by P. Hammond. Berkeley, Calif.: University of California Press.

_____. 1992. *Sociology,* 4th ed. Belmont, Calif.: Wadsworth.

Stark, Rodney, William Sims Bainbridge, and Daniel P. Doyle. 1979. "Cults of America: A Reconnaissance in Space and Time." *Sociological Analysis* 40:347–59.

_____. 1985. *The Future of Religion: Secularization, Revival and Cult Formation.* Berkeley, Calif.: University of California Press.

Stark, Rodney, and Charles Y. Glock. 1968. *American Piety: The Nature of Religious Commitment.* Berkeley, Calif.: University of California Press.

_____. 1973. "Prejudice and the Churches." Pp. 70–95 in *Prejudice USA,* edited by C. Glock and E. Siegelman. New York: Praeger Publishers.

Steinfeld, Melvin, ed. 1970. *Cracks in the Melting Pot: Racism and Discrimination in American History.* Beverly Hills, Calif.: Glencoe Press.

Stewart, Thomas A. 1989. "Turning around the Lord's Business." *Fortune* 7:117–17, 120, 124, 128.

Stokes, J. Burroughs. 1975. "What Is a Christian Scientist?" Pp. 69–82 in *Religions of America: Ferment and Faith in an Age of Crisis,* edited by L. Rosten. New York: Simon & Schuster.

Strader, M., and A. Thornton. 1987. "Adolescent Religiosity and Contraceptive Use." *Journal of Marriage and the Family* 49:117–28.

Straus, Roger. 1976. "Changing Oneself: Seeker and the Creative Transformation of Life Experience." Pp. 252–72 in *Doing Social Life,* edited by J. Lofland. New York: John Wiley & Sons.

Strober, Gerald S. 1974. *American Jews.* Garden City, N.Y.: Doubleday.

Strommen, Merton P. 1972. *A Study of Generation.* Minneapolis, Minn.: Augsburg Publishing House.

Stryker, Sheldon. 1980. *Symbolic Interactionism: A Social Structural Version.* Menlo Park, Calif.: Benjamin/Cummins.

Stump, Roger. 1984a. "Varieties of American Religious Experiences: Regional Divergences in the United States." *Sociological Analysis* 45:283–303.

_____. 1984b. "Regional Migration and Religious Commitment." *Journal for the Scientific Study of Religion* 23:292–303.

Swatos, William H. 1981. "Church-Sect and Cult: Bringing Mysticism Back In." *Sociological Analysis* 42:17–26.

_____. 1988. "Picketing Satan Enfleshed at 7-Eleven: A Research Note." *Review of Religious Research* 30:73–82.

_____. 1990. "Renewing 'Religion' for Sociology: Specifying the Situational Approach." *Sociological Focus* 23:141–53.

Tamney, Joseph B., and Stephen D. Johnson. 1985. "Consequential Religiosity in Modern Society." *Review of Religious Research* 15:339–50.

Tamney, Joseph B., Stephen D. Johnson, and Ronald Burton. 1992. "The Abortion Controversy: Conflicting Beliefs and Values in American Society." *Journal for the Scientific Study of Religion* 31: 32–46.

ter Borg, Meerten B. 1992. "Mythology in Modern Society: Richard Wagner and Bob Dylan." Paper presented at the Religious Research Association annual meeting. Washington, D.C.

Thevenaz, Pierre. 1962. *What Is Phenomenology?* Translated by James W. Edie. New York: Quadrangle Books.

Thomas, Darwin L., and Gwendolyn C. Henry. 1985. "The Religion and Family Connection: Increasing Dialogue in the Social Sciences." *Journal of Marriage and the Family* 47:369–79.

Thomas, William I. 1937. *Primitive Behavior.* New York: McGraw-Hill.

Thomas, William I., and Dorothy S. Thomas. 1928. *The Child in America.* New York: Alfred A. Knopf.

Thornton, Arlan. 1985. "Reciprocal Influences of Family and Religion in a Changing World." *Journal of Marriage and the Family* 47:381–94.

Thornton, Arland, and Donald Camburn. 1989. "Religious Participation and Adolescent Sexual Behavior and Attitudes." *Journal of Marriage and the Family* 51: 641–53.

Tipton, Steven M. 1984. *Getting Saved from the Sixties.* Berkeley, Calif.: University of California Press.

Tittle, Charles R., and Michael Welch. 1983. "Religiosity and Deviance: Toward a Contingency Theory of Constraining Effects." *Social Forces* 63:658–82.

Traviasano, Richard. 1969. "Alternation and Conversion as Qualitatively Different Transformations." Pp. 594–606 in *Social Psychology through Symbolic Interaction,* edited by G. Stone and H. Faberman. Waltham, Mass.: Ginn-Blaisdell.

Trebbi, Diana. 1990. "Women-Church: Catholic Women Produce an Alternative Spirituality." Pp. 347–351 in *In Gods We Trust: New Patterns of Religious Pluralism in America,* 2nd ed., edited by T. Robbins and D. Anthony. New Brunswick, N.J.: Transaction Books.

Troeltsch, Ernst. 1931. *The Social Teachings of the Christian Churches.* New York: Macmillan.

Turner, James. 1985. *Without God, Without Creed: The Origins of Unbelief in America.* Baltimore, Md.: Johns Hopkins University Press.

United States Department of Public Health. 1992. *Sexually Transmitted Diseases: Surveillance.* Alanta: U.S. Department of Health and Human Services, Center for Disease Control/Division of Sexually Transmitted Diseases—HIV Prevention.

Time Staff. "Oh My God, They're Killing Themselves." *Time* 131 (May 3, 1993): 36–37.

United States Supreme Court. 1964. *United States Supreme Court Reports: Lawyer's Edition.* New York: Lawyer's Cooperative.

U.S. Department of Public Health. 1992. *Epidemiology of AIDS.* Atlanta: Center for Disease Control.

van Driel, Barry, and James T. Richardson. 1988. "The Categorization of

New Religious Movements in American Print Media." *Sociological Analysis* 49:173–74.

van Driel, Barry, and Jacob van Belzen. 1990. "The Downfall of Rajneeshpuram in the Print Media: A Cross-national Study." *Journal for the Scientific Study of Religion* 29:76–90.

Van Zandt, David. 1991. *Living in the Children of God.* Princeton, N.J.: Princeton University Press.

Verdesi, Elizabeth Howell. 1976. *In But Still Out.* Philadelphia: Westminster Press.

Vernon, Glenn. 1962. *Sociology and Religion.* New York: McGraw-Hill.

Victor, Jeffrey S. 1990. "The Spread of Satanic-Cult Rumors." *Skeptical Inquirer* 14:287–91.

———. 1991. "The Dynamics of Rumor-panics about Satanic Cults." Pp. 221–36 in *The Satanism Scare,* edited by J. Richardson, J. Best, and D. Bromley. Hawthorne, N.Y.: Aldine Publishing.

Voskuil, Dennis. 1989. "Reaching Out: Mainline Protestantism and the Media." Pp. 72–92 in *Between the Times: The Travail of the Protestant Establishment in America,* edited by William R. Hutchinson. New York: Cambridge University Press.

Wach, Jacob. 1944. *Sociology of Religion.* Chicago: University of Chicago Press.

Wald, Kenneth, Dennis E. Owen, and Samuel S. Hill. 1989. "Evangelical Politics and Status Issues." *Journal for the Scientific Study of Religion* 28: 1–16.

Wallace, Ruth A. 1993. "The Social Construction of a New Leadership Role: Catholic Women Pastors." *Sociology of Religion* 54 (1): 31–42.

Wallis, Roy. 1975. "Scientology: Therapeutic Cult to Religious Sect." *Sociology* 9:89–100.

Walls, Dwayne. 1979. "The Jesus Mania: Bigotry in the Name of the Lord." Pp. 177–82 in *Sociological Footprints,* edited by L. Cargan and J. Ballantine. Boston: Houghton Mifflin.

Washington, Joseph R., Jr. 1964. *Black Religion.* Boston: Beacon Press.

Weaver, Mary Jo. 1985. *New Catholic Women.* San Francisco: Harper & Row.

Weber, Max. 1958. *The Protestant Ethic and the Spirit of Capitalism.* New York: Charles Scribner's Sons.

Weigel, George. 1989. *Catholicism and the Renewal of American Democracy.* Rahway, N.J.: Paulist Press.

Weiss, Arnold S., and Richard H. Mendoza. 1990. "Effects of Acculturation into the Hare Krishna Movement on Mental Health and Personality." *Journal for the Scientific Study of Religion* 29:173–84.

Welch, Michael R., and John Baltzell. 1984. "Geographical Mobility, Social Integration and Church Attendance." *Journal for the Scientific Study of Religion* 23:75–91.

Werblowsky, R. J. 1982. "Religion New and Not-So-New: Fragments of an Old Agenda." Pp. 39–56 in *New Religious Movements: A Perspective for Understanding Society,* edited by Eileen Barker. New York: Edward Mellin Press.

Westley, Frances. 1978. "The Cult of Man: Durkheim's Predictions and New Religious Movements." *Sociological Analysis* 39:135–45.

White, Leslie. 1959. *The Evolution of Culture.* New York: McGraw-Hill.

White, R. E. 1985. *Christian Schooling and Spiritual Growth and Development.* Ed.D. thesis, Northern Arizona University.

Whitehead, Harriet. 1974. "Reasonably Fantastic: Some Perspectives on Scientology, Science Fiction, and Occultism." Pp. 547–90 in *Religious Movements in Contemporary America*, edited by I. Zaretsky and M. Leone. Princeton, N.J.: Princeton University Press.

Whitley, Oliver R. 1964. *Religious Behavior: When Sociology and Religion Meet*. Englewood Cliffs, N.J.: Prentice-Hall.

Wilcox, Clyde. 1988. "Political Action Committees of the New Christian Right." *Journal for the Scientific Study of Religion* 27:60–71.

———. 1989a. "Evangelicals and the Moral Majority." *Journal for the Scientific Study of Religion* 28:400–14.

———. 1989b. "The New Christian Right and the Mobilization of Evangelicals." In *Religion and Political Behavior in the United States*, edited by T. Jelen. New York: Praeger Publishers.

Wilcox, Clyde, Sharon Linzey, and Ted Jelen. 1991. "Reluctant Warriors: Premillenialism and Politics in the Moral Majority." *Journal for the Scientific Study of Religion* 30:245–59.

Wilke, Richard B. 1986. *And Are We Yet Alive? The Future of the United Methodist Church*. Nashville, Tenn.: Abingdon Press.

Williams, J. Paul. 1962. "The Nature of Religion." *Journal for the Scientific Study of Religion* 2:3–14.

Williams, Preston N. 1971. "Toward a Sociological Understanding of Black Religious Community." *Soundings* 54:260–70.

Willits, F. K., and D. M. Crider. 1989. "Church Attendance and Traditional Beliefs in Adolescence and Young Adulthood: A Panel Study. *Review of Religious Research* 31:68–81.

Wilmore, Gayraud S. 1990. "Identity and Integration: Black Presbyterians and Their Allies in the Twentieth Century." Pp. 109–33 in *The Presbyterian Predicament: Six Perspectives*, edited by Milton J. Coalter, John Mulder and Louis Weeks. Louisville, Ky.: Westminster/John Knox Press.

Wilson, Bryan. 1958–59. "The Pentecostalist Minister: Role Conflicts and Status Contradictions." *American Journal of Sociology* 64:497.

———. 1963. "A Typology of Sects in a Dynamic and Comparative Perspective." *Archives de Sociolgie de Religion* 16:49–63.

———. 1966. *Religion in Secular Society*. Baltimore, Md.: Penguin Books.

———. 1975. The Secularization Debate. *Encounter* 45:77–83.

———. 1982. *Religion in Sociological Perspective*. Oxford: Blackwell.

———. 1990. *The Social Dimensions of Sectarianism: Sects and New Religious Movements in Contemporary Society*. Oxford: Clarendon Press.

Wilson, John. 1978. *Religion in American Society: The Effective Presence*. Englewood Cliffs, N.J.: Prentice-Hall.

Wilson, Martha. 1973. "Women, the Bible, and Religion." Pp. 15–27 in *Women and Religion: 1972*, edited by Judith Goldenberg. Bozeman, Mont.: University of Montana Press.

Wimberly, Ronald C. 1979. "Continuity in the Measurement of Civil Religion." *Sociological Analysis* 40:59–62.

———. 1980. "Civil Religion and the Choice for President: Nixon in '72." *Social Forces* 44–61.

Wimberly, Ronald C., and James E. Christenson. 1980. "Civil Religion and Church and State." *Sociological Quarterly* 21:35–40.

———. 1981. "Civil Religion and Other Religious Identities." *Sociological Analysis* 42:91–100.

Winston, Diane. 1992. "Churches Endure as Havens of Hope." *Progressions* 4 (1): 1–4.

Winter, J. Alan. 1977. *Continuities in the Sociology of Religion: Creed, Congregation, and Community.* New York: Harper & Row.

———. 1992a. "Religious Commitment, Zionism and Integration in a Jewish Community: Replication and Refinement of Levine's Hypothesis." *Review of Religious Research* 33:47–59.

———. 1992b. "The Transformation of Community Integration among American Jewry: Religion or Ethnoreligion? A National Replication." *Review of Religious Research* 33 (4): 349–63.

Winter, Miriam Therese. 1989. "The Women-Church Movement." *Christian Century* 106 (8):258–60.

Woocher, Jonathan S. 1986. *Sacred Survival: The Civil Religion of American Jews.* Bloomington, Ind.: Indiana University Press.

Wood, James R. 1981. *Leadership in Voluntary Organizations: The Controversy over Social Action in Protestant Churches.* New Brunswick, N.J.: Rutgers University Press.

Wooden, Kenneth. 1981. *The Children of Jonestown.* New York: McGraw-Hill.

Woodruff, J. T. 1984. "Premarital Sexual Behavior and Religion in Adolescence." *Journal for the Scientific Study of Religion* 24:436–60.

Woodrum, Eric. 1992. "Pornography and Moral Attitudes." *Sociological Spectrum* 12 (October–December):329–48.

Woodrum, Eric, and Beth L. Davison. 1992. "Reexamination of Religious Influences on Abortion Attitudes." *Review of Religious Research* 33:229–43.

Woodrum, Eric, and Thomas Hoban. 1992. "Support for Prayer in School and Creationism." *Sociological Analysis* 53 (3):309–21.

Wright, Stuart, A. 1983. "Dyadic Intimacy and Social Control in Three Cult Movements." *Sociological Analysis* 44:137–50.

———. 1984. "Post-involvement Attitudes of Voluntary Defectors from Controversial New Religion." *Journal for the Scientific Study of Religion* 23:172–82.

Wuthnow, Robert. 1988. *The Restructuring of American Religion: Society and Faith since World War II.* Princeton, N.J.: Princeton University Press.

———. 1990. "The Restructuring of American Presbyterianism: Turmoil in One Denomination." Pp. 27–48 in *The Presbyterian Predicament: Six Perspectives,* edited by M. Coalter, J. Mulder, and L. Weeks. Louisville, Ky.: Westminster/John Knox Press.

Yazbeck, Haddad, and Adair T. Loomis. 1987. *Islamic Values in the United States: A Comparative Study.* New York: Oxford University Press.

Yinger, J. Milton. 1946. *Religion and the Struggle for Power.* Durham, N.C.: Duke University Press.

———. 1969. "A Structural Examination of Religion." *Journal for the Scientific Study of Religion* 8:88–100.

———. 1970. *The Scientific Study of Religion.* New York: Macmillan.

Ziegenhals, Gretchen E. 1989. "Meeting the Women of Women-Church." *Christian Century* 106 (16): 492–94.

Zikmund, Barbara Brown. 1990. "Ministry of Word and Sacrament: Women and Changing Understandings of Ordination." Pp. 134–58 in *The Presbyterian Predicament: Six Perspectives,* edited by M. Coalter, J. Mulder, and L. Weeks. Louisville, Ky.: Westminster/John Knox Press.

Zinnser, C. F. 1985. *Teaching Children in a Fundamentalist Church: An Ethnographic Study*. Ph.D. thesis, University of Pennsylvania.

Zygmunt, Joseph F. 1970. "Prophetic Failure and Chiliastic Identity: The Case of Jehovah's Witnesses." *American Journal of Sociology* 75:926–48.

Index

Religion in Contemporary Society
Edited by Robert Cunningham
Production supervision by Kim Vander Steen
Designed by Lesiak/Crampton Design, Inc., Chicago, Illinois
Composition by Point West, Inc., Carol Stream, Illinois
Paper, Finch Opaque
Printed and bound by Arcata Graphics, Kingsport, Tennessee